Handbook of Int

The *Handbook of Intelligence Studies* examines the central topics in the study of intelligence organizations and activities. This volume opens with a look at how scholars approach this particularly difficult field of study. It then defines and analyses the three major missions of intelligence: collection-and-analysis; covert action; and counterintelligence. Within each of these missions, some of the most prominent authors in the field dissect the so-called intelligence cycle to reveal the challenges of gathering and assessing information from around the world. Covert action, the most controversial intelligence activity, is explored in detail, with special attention to the issue of military organizations moving into what was once primarily a civilian responsibility. The contributions also cover the problems associated with protecting secrets from foreign spies and terrorist organizations: the arcane but important mission of counterintelligence. The book pays close attention to the question of intelligence accountability, that is, how a nation can protect its citizens against the possible abuse of power by its own secret agencies – known as "oversight" in the English-speaking world.

The volume provides a comprehensive and up-to-date examination of the state of the field and will constitute an invaluable source of information to professionals working in intelligence and professors teaching intelligence courses, as well as to students and citizens who want to know more about the hidden side of government and their nation's secret foreign policies.

Loch K. Johnson is Regents Professor of Public and International Affairs at the University of Georgia. His books include *Secret Agencies* (1996); *Bombs, Bugs, Drugs, and Thugs* (2000); *Strategic Intelligence* (2004, co-edited with James J. Wirtz); *Who's Watching the Spies?* (2005, co-authored with Hans Born and Ian Leigh); *American Foreign Policy* (2005, co-authored with Daniel Papp and John Endicott); and *Seven Sins of American Foreign Policy* (2007).

Handbook of Intelligence Studies

Edited by
Loch K. Johnson

Routledge
Taylor & Francis Group

LONDON AND NEW YORK

This edition first published in 2009
by Routledge
2 Park Square, Milton Park, Abingdon, Oxon, OX14 4RN

Simultaneously published in the USA and Canada
by Routledge
270 Madison Avenue, New York NY 10016

Routledge is an imprint of the Taylor and Francis Group, an informa business

© Loch K Johnson, selection and editorial matter; individual chapters, the contributors

Typeset in Bembo by RefineCatch Ltd, Bungay, Suffolk
Printed and bound in Great Britain by
CPI Antony Rowe, Chippenham, Wiltshire

British Library Cataloguing in Publication Data
A catalogue record for this book is available from the British Library

Library of Congress Cataloging in Publication Data
Handbook of intelligence studies / edited by Loch K. Johnson.—1st ed.
 p. cm.
 Includes bibliographical references and index.
 1. Intelligence—Handbooks, manuals, etc.   I. Johnson, Loch K., 1942–
UB250.H35 2007
327.12—dc22

                                                      2006021368

ISBN10: 0–415–77050–5 (hbk)
ISBN13: 978–0–415–77050–7 (hbk)
ISBN10: 0–415–77783–6 (pbk)
ISBN13: 978–0–415–77783–4 (pbk)

Contents

Part 1: The study of intelligence

Part 2: The evolution of modern intelligence

Figures and Tables

Figures

Tables

Notes on Contributors

Michael Andregg is a professor at the University of St Thomas in St Paul, Minnesota.

Hans Born is a Senior Fellow in Democratic Governance of the Security Sector at the Geneva Centre for Democratic Control of the Armed Forces (DCAF). He holds a Ph.D. and is a guest lecturer on civil–military relations at the Federal Institute of Technology (ETH) in Zurich and on governing nuclear weapons at the United Nations Disarmament Fellowship Programme.

William J. Daugherty holds a Ph.D. in government from the Claremont Graduate School and is Associate Professor of Government at Armstrong Atlantic State University in Savannah, Georgia. A retired senior officer in the CIA, he is the author of *In the Shadow of the Ayatollah: A CIA Hostage in Iran* (Annapolis, 2001) and *Executive Secrets: Covert Action & the Presidency* (Kentucky, 2004).

Jack Davis served in the CIA from 1956 to 1990, as analyst and manager and teacher of analysts. He now is an Independent Contractor with the Agency, specializing in analytic methodology. He is a frequent contributor to the journal *Studies in Intelligence*.

Peter Gill is Professor of Politics and Security, Liverpool John Moores University, Liverpool, United Kingdom. He is co-author of *Introduction to Politics* (1988, 2nd ed.) and *Intelligence in an Insecure World* (2006). He is currently researching into the control and oversight of domestic security in intelligence agencies.

John Hollister Hedley, during more than thirty years at CIA, edited the *President's Daily Brief*, briefed the PDB at the White House, served as Managing Editor of the *National Intelligence Daily*, and was Chairman of CIA's Publications Review Board. Now retired, Dr Hedley has taught intelligence at Georgetown University and serves as a consultant to the National Intelligence Council and the Center for the Study of Intelligence.

Frederick P. Hitz is a Lecturer (Diplomat in Residence) in Public and International Affairs, Woodrow Wilson School, Princeton University.

Rhodri Jeffreys-Jones is Professor of American History at the University of Edinburgh. The author of several books on intelligence history, he is currently completing a study of the FBI.

Loch K. Johnson is Regents Professor of Public and International Affairs at the University of Georgia and author of several books and over 100 articles on US intelligence and national security. His books include *The Making of International Agreements* (1984); *A Season of Inquiry* (1985); *Through the Straits of Armageddon* (1987, co-edited with Paul Diehl), *Decisions of the Highest Order* (1988, co-edited with Karl F. Inderfurth); *America's Secret Power* (1989); *Runoff Elections in the United States* (1993, co-authored with Charles S. Bullock, III); *America As a World Power* (1995); *Secret Agencies* (1996); *Bombs, Bugs, Drugs, and Thugs* (2000); *Fateful Decisions* (2004, co-edited with Karl F. Inderfurth); *Strategic Intelligence* (2004, co-edited with James J. Wirtz); *Who's Watching the Spies?* (2005, co-authored with Hans Born and Ian Leigh); *American Foreign Policy* (2005, co-authored with Daniel Papp and John Endicott); and *Seven Sins of American Foreign Policy* (2007). He has served as Special Assistant to the chair of the Senate Select Committee on Intelligence (1975–76), Staff Director of the House Subcommittee on Intelligence Oversight (1977–79), and Special Assistant to the chair of the Aspin-Brown Commission on Intelligence (1995–1996). He is the Senior Editor of the international journal *Intelligence and National Security*.

Wolfgang Krieger is Professor of History at Philipps University in Marburg, Germany, and a frequent contributor to the international journal *Intelligence and National Security*.

Ian Leigh is Professor of Law and the co-director of the Human Rights Centre at the University of Durham. His books include *In From the Cold: National Security and Parliamentary Democracy* (1994, with Laurence Lustgarten); *Making Intelligence Accountable* (2005, with Hans Born); and *Who's Watching the Spies* (2005, with Loch K. Johnson and Hans Born).

Minh A. Luong is Assistant Director of International Security Studies at Yale University where he teaches in the Department of History. He also serves as an adjunct Assistant Professor of Public Policy at the Taubman Center at Brown University.

Fred Manget is a member of the Senior Intelligence Service and a former Deputy General Counsel of the CIA.

Stephen Marrin is an Assistant Professor of Intelligence Studies at Mercyhurst College. He previously served as an analyst in the CIA and the Government Accountability Office.

Kathryn S. Olmsted is Professor of History at the University of California, Davis. She holds a B.A. degree with Honors and Distinction in History from Stanford University, and a M.A. and Ph.D. in History from the University of California, Davis. She is author of *Challenging the Secret Government: The Post-Watergate Investigations of the CIA and FBI* (University of North Carolina Press, 1996) and *Red Spy Queen: A Biography of Elizabeth Bentley* (University of North Carolina Press, 2002).

Mark Phythian is Professor of International Security and Director of the History and Governance Research Institute at the University of Wolverhampton, United Kingdom. He is the author of *Intelligence in an Insecure World* (2006, with Peter Gill), *The Politics of British Arms Sales Since 1964* (2000), and *Arming Iraq* (1997), as well as numerous journal articles on intelligence and security issues.

Paul R. Pillar is on the faculty of the Security Studies Program at Georgetown University. Concluding a long career in the CIA, he served as National Intelligence Officer for the Near East and South Asia from 2000 to 2005.

John Prados is an analyst of national security based in Washington, DC. He holds a Ph.D. from Columbia University and focuses on presidential power, international relations, intelligence and military affairs. He is a project director with the National Security Archive. Prados is author of a dozen books, and editor of others, among them titles on World War II, the Vietnam War, intelligence matters, and military affairs, including *Hoodwinked: The Documents That Reveal How Bush Sold Us a War, Inside the Pentagon Papers* (edited with Margaret Pratt-Porter), *Combined Fleet Decoded: The Secret History of U.S. Intelligence and the Japanese Navy in World War II, Lost Crusader: The Secret Wars of CIA Director William Colby, White House Tapes: Eavesdropping on the President* (edited), *America Responds to Terrorism* (edited), *The Hidden History of the Vietnam War, Operation Vulture, The Blood Road: The Ho Chi Minh Trail and the Vietnam War, Presidents' Secret Wars: CIA and Pentagon Covert Operations from World War II Through the Persian Gulf, Keepers of the Keys: A History of the National Security Council from Truman to Bush*, and *The Soviet Estimate: U.S. Intelligence and Soviet Strategic Forces*, among others. His current book is *Safe for Democracy: The Secret Wars of the CIA*.

Jeffrey T. Richelson is a Senior Fellow with the National Security Archive in Washington, DC, and author of *The Wizards of Langley, The US Intelligence Community, A Century of Spies*, and *America's Eyes in Space*, as well as numerous articles on intelligence activities. He received his Ph.D. in political science from the University of Rochester and has taught at the University of Texas, Austin, and the American University, Washington, DC.

Richard L. Russell is Professor of National Security Studies at the National Defense University. He is also an adjunct Associate Professor in the Security Studies Program and Research Associate in the Institute for the Study of Diplomacy at Georgetown University. He previously served as a CIA political–military analyst. Russell is the author of *Weapons Proliferation and War in the Greater Middle East: Strategic Contest* (2005).

Robert David Steele (Vivas) is CEO of OSS.Net, Inc., an international open source intelligence provider. As the son of an oilman, a Marine Corps infantry officer, and a clandestine intelligence case officer for the Central Intelligence Agency, he has spent over twenty years abroad, in Asia and Central and South America. As a civilian intelligence officer he spent three back-to-back tours overseas, including one tour as one of the first officers assigned full time to terrorism, and three headquarters tours in offensive counterintelligence, advanced information technology, and satellite program management. He resigned from the CIA in 1988 to be the senior civilian founder of the Marine Corps Intelligence Command. He resigned from the Marines in 1993. He is the author of four works on intelligence, as well as the editor of a book on peacekeeping intelligence. He has earned graduate degrees in International Relations and Public Administration, is a graduate of the Naval War College, and has a certificate in Intelligence Policy. He is also a graduate of the Marine Corps Command and Staff Course, and of the CIA's Mid-Career Course 101.

Mark Stout is a defense analyst at a think-tank in the Washington DC area. Previously, he has served in a variety of positions in the Defense Department, the State Department, and the CIA. He has a bachelor's degree from Stanford University (1986) in Political Science and

Mathematical and Computational Science, and a master's degree in Public Policy from the John F. Kennedy School of Government at Harvard University (1988). He is presently pursuing a Ph.D. in military history with the University of Leeds.

Stan A. Taylor is an Emeritus Professor of Political Science at Brigham Young University in Provo, Utah. He has taught in England, Wales, and New Zealand and in 2006 was a visiting professor at the University of Otago in Dunedin, New Zealand. He is founder of the David M. Kennedy Center for International Studies at Brigham Young University. He writes frequently on intelligence, national security, and US foreign policy.

Michael Warner serves as the Historian for the Office of the Director of National Intelligence.

Nigel West is a military historian specializing in security and intelligence topics. He is the European Editor of *The World Intelligence Review* and is on the faculty at the Center for Counterintelligence and Security Studies in Washington, DC. He is the author of more than two dozen works of non-fiction and most recently edited *The Guy Liddell Diaries*.

Thorsten Wetzling is a doctoral candidate at the Geneva Graduate Institute of International Studies (IUHEI) and is writing his dissertation on international intelligence cooperation and democratic accountability. He teaches seminars in political science and international organization at the IUHEI.

James J. Wirtz is a Professor in the Department of National Security Affairs at the Naval Postgraduate School, Monterey, California. He is the Section Chair of the Intelligence Studies Section of the International Studies Association, and President of the International Security and Arms Control Section of the American Political Science Association. Professor Wirtz is the series editor for *Initiatives in Strategic Studies: Issues and Policies*, which is published by Palgrave Macmillan.

Glossary

AFIO	Association of Former Intelligence Officers
AG	Attorney general
Aman	Agaf ha–Modi'in (Israeli military intelligence)
AVB	Hungarian intelligence service
AVH	Hungarian security service
BDA	Battle damage assessment
BfV	German equivalent of the FBI
BMD	Ballistic missile defense
BND	Bundesnachrichtendienst (German intelligence service)
BW	Biological weapons
CA	Covert action
CAS	Covert Action Staff (CIA)
CBW	Chemical/biological warfare
CCP	Consolidated Cryptographic Program
CDA	Congressionally directed action
CE	Counterespionage
CHAOS	Codename for CIA illegal domestic spying
CI	Counterintelligence
CIA	Central Intelligence Agency
CIC	Counterintelligence Corps (US Army)
CIG	Central Intelligence Group, precursor of CIA
CMS	Community Management Staff
CNC	Crime and Narcotics Center (CIA)
COINTELPRO	FBI Counterintelligence Program
COMINT	Communications Intelligence
CORONA	Codename for first US spy satellite system
COS	Chief of Station (CIA)
COSPO	Community Open Source Program Office
CT	Counterterrorism
CTC	Counterterrorism Center (CIA)

CW	Chemical weapons
D & D	Denial and deception
DARP	Defense Airborne Reconnaissance Program
DAS	Deputy assistant secretary
DBA	Dominant battlefield awareness
DC	Deputies Committee (NSC)
DCD	Domestic Contact Division (CIA)
DCI	Director of Central Intelligence
D/CIA	Director of Central Intelligence Agency
DDA	Deputy Director of Administration (CIA)
DDCI	Deputy Director for Intelligence (CIA)
DDO	Deputy Director for Operations (CIA)
DDP	Deputy Director for Plans (CIA, the earlier name for the DDO)
DDS & T	Deputy Director for Science and Technology (CIA)
DEA	Drug Enforcement Administration
DGI	Cuban intelligence service
DGSE	Direction Générale de la Sécurité Extérieure (French intelligence service)
DHS	Department of Homeland Security
DI	Directorate of Intelligence (CIA)
DIA	Defense Intelligence Agency
DIA/Humint	Defense Humint Service
DIE	Romanian intelligence service
DINSUM	*Defense Intelligence Summary*
DNI	Director of National Intelligence
DO	Directorate of Operations (the CIA's organization for espionage and covert action)
DoD	Department of Defense
DOD	Domestic Operations Division (CIA)
DOE	Department of Energy
DOJ	Department of Justice
DOS	Department of State
DOT	Department of Treasury
DP	Directorate of Plans (from 1973, the CIA's DO)
DS	Bulgarian intelligence service
DST	Direction de la Surveillance du Territoire (France)
ELINT	Electronic intelligence
EO	Executive order
EOP	Executive Office of the President
ETF	Environmental Task Force (CIA)
FBI	Federal Bureau of Investigation
FBIS	Foreign Broadcast Information Service
FISA	Foreign Intelligence Surveillance Act (1978)
FOIA	Freedom of Information Act
FRD	Foreign Resources Division (FRD)
FSB	Federal'naya Sluzba Besnopasnoti (Federal Security Service, Russia)
GAO	General Accountability Office (Congress)
GCHQ	Government Communications Headquarters (the British NSA)
GEO	Geosynchronous orbit

GEOINT	Geospatial intelligence
GRU	Soviet military intelligence
GSG	German counterterrorism service
HEO	High elliptical orbit
HPSCI	House Permanent Select Committee on Intelligence
HUMINT	Human intelligence (assets)
HVA	East German foreign intelligence service
I & W	Indicators and Warning
IC	Intelligence Community
IG	Inspector general
IMINT	Imagery intelligence (photographs)
INR	Bureau of Intelligence and Research, Department of State
INTELINK	An intelligence community computer information system
INTs	Collection disciplines (IMINT, SIGINT, OSINT, HUMINT, MASINT)
IOB	Intelligence Oversight Board (White House)
IRBM	Intermediate Range Ballistic Missile
ISC	Intelligence and Security Committee (UK)
ISI	Inter-Services Intelligence (Pakistani intelligence agency)
IT	Information technology
JCS	Joint Chiefs of Staff
JIC	Joint Intelligence Committee (UK)
Jstars	Joint Surveillance Target Attack Radar Systems
KGB	Soviet secret police
KH	Keyhole (satellite)
MASINT	Measurement and signature intelligence
MFA	Soviet Ministry of Foreign Affairs
MHBK	Magyar Harcosok Bajtársi Közössége or Association of Hungarian Veterans
MI5	Security Service (UK)
MI6	Secret Intelligence Service (UK)
MONGOOSE	Codename for CIA covert actions against Fidel Castro of Cuba (1961–62)
MOSSAD	Israeli intelligence service
MRBM	Medium Range Ballistic Missile
NBC	Nuclear, biological, and chemical (weapons)
NCTC	National Counterterrorism Center
NFIP	National Foreign Intelligence Program
NGA	National Geospatial-Intelligence Agency
NGO	Non-governmental organization
NIA	National Intelligence Authority
NIC	National Intelligence Council
NID	*National Intelligence Daily*
NIE	National Intelligence Estimate
NIO	National Intelligence Officer
NKVD	National Commissariat for Internal Affairs, the Soviet secret police under Stalin
NOC	Non-Official Cover
NPIC	National Photographic Interpretation Center
NRO	National Reconnaissance Office
NSA	National Security Agency

NSC	National Security Council (White House)
NSCID	National Security Council Intelligence Directive
NTM	National Technical Means
OB	Order of battle
OC	Official Cover
ODNI	Office of the Director of National Intelligence
OMB	Office of Management and Budget
ONI	Office of Naval Intelligence
OSD	Office of the Secretary of Defense
OSINT	Open-source intelligence
OSS	Office of Strategic Services
P & E	Processing and exploitation
PDB	*President's Daily Brief*
PFIAB	President's Foreign Intelligence Advisory Board (White House)
PM	Paramilitary
RADINT	Radar intelligence
RCMP	Royal Canadian Mounted Police
SA	Special Activities Division (DO/CIA)
SAS	Special Air Service (UK)
SBS	Special Boat Service (UK)
SDO	Support to diplomatic operations
SHAMROCK	Codename for illegal NSA interception of cables
SIG	Senior Interagency Group
SIGINT	Signals intelligence
SIS	Secret Intelligence Service (UK, also known as MI6)
SISDE	Italian intelligence service
SMO	Support to military operations
SMS	Secretary's *Morning Summary* (Department of State)
SNIE	Special National Intelligence Estimate
SO	Special Operations (CIA)
SOCOM	Special Operations Command (DoD)
SOE	Special Operations Executive (UK)
SOG	Special Operations Group (CIA)
SOVA	Office of Soviet Analysis (CIA)
SSCI	Senate Select Committee on Intelligence
StB	Czech intelligence service
SVR	Russian foreign intelligence service
TECHINT	Technical intelligence
TELINT	Telemetry intelligence
TIARA	Tactical Intelligence and Related Activities
TISC	Trade and Industry Select Committee (UK)
TPEDs	Tasking, processing, exploitation, and dissemination
UAV	Unmanned aerial vehicle (drone)
UB	Polish Intelligence Service
UN	United Nations
UNSCOM	United Nations Special Commission
USFA	US Forces in Austria
USIB	United States Intelligence Board

USSOC	United States Special Operations Command
USTR	United States Trade Representative
VENONA	Codename for NSA SIGINT intercepts against Soviet spying in America
VX	A deadly nerve agent used in chemical weapons
WMD	Weapons of mass destruction

Introduction

Loch K. Johnson

The meanings of intelligence

In a "handbook" for intelligence studies, the place to begin is with a definition of what intelligence means. Formally, professional officers define the term in both a strategic and a tactical sense. Broadly, a standard definition of strategic intelligence is the "knowledge and foreknowledge of the world around us – the prelude to Presidential decision and action." At the more narrow or tactical level, intelligence refers to events and conditions on specific battlefields or theaters of war, what military commanders refer to as "situational awareness." In this volume, the focus is chiefly on strategic intelligence, that is, the attempts by leaders to understand potential risks and gains on a national or international level.

The phrase may refer to concerns about threats at home – subversion by domestic radicals or the infiltration of hostile intelligence agents or terrorists inside a nation's borders; or it may focus on dangers and opportunities overseas. In the first instance in the United States, the Federal Bureau of Investigation (FBI) is the lead agency; in the second instance, the Central Intelligence Agency (CIA) and a host of military intelligence organizations take the lead. (See Appendix A for an organizational diagram depicting America's sixteen major intelligence agencies, and Appendix B for the names of the leaders of the "intelligence community").

In addition to the two geographic dimensions (global versus local), "strategic intelligence" has a number of other possible meanings. Most frequently, the phrase refers to *information*, a tangible product collected and analyzed (assessed or interpreted) in hopes of achieving a deeper comprehension of subversive activities at home or political, economic, social, and military situations around the world. An example of an intelligence question at the international, strategic level would be: to what extent are Al Qaeda cells located in and operating from the nation of Pakistan? A related question: do these cells enjoy allies in that nation's official intelligence and military bureaucracy? In contrast, at the tactical level overseas, one can imagine a US military commander in Iraq demanding to know the location of the most well-armed strongholds of the insurgency in the suburbs of Baghdad. Or how much additional armor is necessary on the side paneling of Humvees to defend against rocket-propelled grenades (RPGs) fired by insurgents in Iraq?

On the home front, a strategic intelligence question for American intelligence officers might be: how many Chinese espionage agents are inside the United States and what are their objectives? Or: are there any more home-grown terrorists like Timothy McVeigh, the man convicted of bombing a federal building in Oklahoma City in 1995, and are they planning the use of violence against other government institutions inside the nation?

Intelligence as information is different from the kind of everyday information one can find in the local library, because intelligence usually has a secret component. Those in the business of gathering intelligence blend together the open-source information gleaned from the public domain (newspapers, magazine, blogs, public speeches) with information that other nations try to keep hidden. The hidden information must be ferreted out of encoded communications or stolen from safes and vaults, locked offices, guarded military and intelligence installations, and other denied areas – a potentially dangerous task involving the penetration of an enemy's camp and its concentric circles of defense, from barbed-wire barriers patrolled by armed security forces and sentry dogs to sophisticated electronic alarms, surveillance cameras, and motion detectors. As intelligence scholar Abram N. Shulsky has written, intelligence often entails access to "information some other party is trying to deny."[2]

While the overwhelming percentage – sometimes upwards of 95 percent[3] – of the information mix provided to America's decision-makers in the form of intelligence reports is based on open sources, the small portion derived from clandestine operations can be vital, providing just the right secret "nugget" necessary to understand the likely plans of a foreign adversary. After all, the *New York Times* provides good information about world affairs for the most part, but it has no reporters inside North Korea, Al Qaeda cells, or several places around the globe that might be of interest to the United States (say, Angola or Darfur in Sudan). So the government must send its own intelligence officers to such places. Even in locations from which the *Times* reports on a regular basis, such as France and Germany, its correspondents may not be asking the questions that an American secretary of state, treasury, or defense may wish to have answered. That is why the United States has a CIA and other secret services: to go where journalists may not be allowed to go, or where they are not assigned to go by their managing editors, and to seek the answers to questions that a nation's leaders may need to know beyond what may interest the average newspaper reader.

In short, the world has secrets that the United States and other nations may want to know about, especially if they threaten the safety and prosperity of their citizens or their foreign allies. Sometimes stealing this kind of information is the only way to acquire it. Beyond secrets that may be obtained through theft or surveillance by satellite cameras and listening devices (such as the number, location and capabilities of Chinese nuclear submarines and intercontinental missiles), the world also has mysteries, that is, information that may well be impossible to know about regardless of how many newspaper reporters and spies one may have. Who knows, for instance, how long Kim Jong il will survive as the leader of North Korea, or what kind of regime will follow in his wake? Who knows who will succeed President Vladimir Putin in Russia? The best one can hope for, from an intelligence point of view, is an educated guess by experts who have carefully studied such questions. These hunches are called "estimates" by intelligence professionals in the United States, or "assessments" by their British counterparts.

A useful metaphor for thinking about strategic intelligence is the jigsaw puzzle. The aspiration in both cases is to gather as many pieces as possible to provide a thorough picture. In the case of intelligence, the "picture" one seeks is full information about subversive activities at home or the capabilities and intentions of existing and potential adversaries on the world stage. Most of the intelligence pieces of the puzzle will be from publicly available documents; some will be derived from spying, whether with human agents or machines (such as satellites and U-2 reconnaissance aircraft). Almost always there will be missing pieces: the mysteries of the world or, in some instances, secrets that are so well hidden or guarded that they remain out of sight or out of reach. The great frustration of strategic intelligence is that rarely does one operate in an environment of full transparency. Rather, the world is replete with uncertainties and, as a result, intelligence gaps are inevitable and sometimes result in the failure of intelligence officials to provide robust and timely warning of dangers. In the words of Secretary of State Dean Rusk, "Providence has not given mankind the capacity to pierce the fog of the future."[4] No one has a crystal ball.

At times, intelligence failures are the result of missing pieces of the puzzle. Sometime, though, mistakes stem from the inability of individuals to accurately analyze the meaning of the pieces that are available, improperly judging their meaning and significance. Usually failures are a product of both problems: an incomplete jigsaw puzzle and an inability to decipher the complete picture from the few pieces one does have. Thus, both an exhaustive collection of information and a sagacious analysis of its meaning are indispensable for skillfully estimating or predicting what events may mean for a nation's future. Above all, every nation seeks information that will provide an adequate alert about impending attacks – "indicators and warnings" or I & W, in the vernacular of professional intelligence officers. The surprise attacks against the United States at Pearl Harbor in 1941 and, more recently, against the Twin Towers and the Pentagon in 2001 illustrate the importance of accurately, timely, and specific I & W intelligence.

A nation seeks to know much more, though, than warnings about potential attacks. For example, leaders want to understand the weapons capabilities of potential adversaries, such as Iraq in 2002. In that instance, US and British intelligence agencies estimated that the Saddam Hussein regime probably had weapons of mass destruction (WMDs). America and the United Kingdom went to war against Iraq, in part, to eliminate these weapons – only to discover that the intelligence estimates had been incorrect. There were no WMDs to be found in Iraq in 2003, when the British and the United States invaded. The 9/11 and WMD cases vividly underscore the importance of having reliable intelligence, what President George H.W. Bush often referred to as the nation's "first line of defense."

process + info.

Intelligence has a second meaning beyond that of an information product, such as the number of tanks in Iran and their firepower. Intelligence is also thought of as *a process*: a series of interactive steps, formally referred to as an "intelligence cycle." (See Appendix C for a diagram of the cycle.) The process begins with intelligence managers and policy officials planning what information to gather related to threats and opportunities at home and abroad. They must also determine what methods to use in the gathering of this information – the right mix of human agents and surveillance machines, for instance. Then the information is collected, to the extent one can succeed in this regard against adversaries who are skillful at concealing their activities. This information must be processed into readable text, say, from an intercepted telephone conversation in Farsi; and the contents must be analyzed for its meaning to American interests – all as quickly as possible. Finally, the "finished" information – that is, intelligence that has been studied and interpreted – must be disseminated to those officials in high public office or troops in the field who rely on these insights as they plan their next policy initiatives or military moves.

process, Info., + missions

From a third perspective, intelligence may also be thought of as a set of *missions* carried out by secret agencies. The premier mission is that of collecting and analyzing information. Important, too, though, is the mission of counterintelligence and, its subsidiary concern, counterterrorism. These terms refer to the methods by which nations try to thwart secret operations directed against them by hostile foreign intelligence services or terrorist organizations. Yet another

3

mission is <u>covert action</u> — the secret intervention in the affairs of other nations or organizations in hopes of improving America's security and other interests, such as economic prosperity. Covert action goes by a number of euphemisms, including "the quiet option" (that is, less noisy than sending in the Marines), the "third option" (between diplomacy and open war), or "special activities."

Before turning to an examination of these missions, a fourth and final definition of intelligence is offered: intelligence may be considered *a cluster of people and organizations* established to carry out the three missions — the sixteen entities and staff of Appendix A. "Make sure you check with intelligence before completing your invasion plans," the prime minister might advise his minister of defense. "Get intelligence on the line and find out the exact coordinates of the insurgents in Kirkuk," a US artillery commander in Iraq might order.

The US intelligence "community," as the cluster is called, is led by the president and the National Security Council (NSC), who in turn rely on a Director of National Intelligence (DNI, before 2005 known as the Director of Central Intelligence or DCI) to manage the sixteen agencies. (Appendix B provides a list of the twenty men — no women yet — who have served as either DCI or DNI.) According to various newspaper accounts, the intelligence community or IC employs over 150,000 people and has a budget of some $44 billion a year, making it the largest and most costly collection of intelligence organizations ever assembled by any nation in history.

The CIA and the FBI are the most well-known of these agencies. The CIA is located in a campus-like setting along the Potomac River in the Washington, DC, suburb of Langley, Virginia, fourteen miles north of the White House. The CIA is mainly responsible for managing the collection of intelligence abroad by human agents, and for analyzing the information gathered by agents and machines. The FBI has a primarily domestic focus, with responsibilities for tracking the activities of suspected subversives, terrorists, and foreign intelligence officers inside the United States. Several of the remaining intelligence agencies are embedded within the organizational framework of the Defense Department, including the National Geospatial-Intelligence Agency (NGA), which handles the photographic side of foreign surveillance; the National Security Agency (NSA), responsible for codebreaking and electronic eavesdropping; the National Reconnaissance Office (NRO), chartered to coordinate the development, launching, and management of surveillance satellites; the Defense Intelligence Agency (DIA), in charge of military intelligence analysis; Coast Guard Intelligence, a part of the new Department of Homeland Security; and the four military intelligence services, Army, Navy, Air Force, and Marines, each gathering tactical intelligence related to their missions.

Joining the CIA and the FBI on the civilian side of intelligence (in the sense that they are located in civilian departments, rather than within the Department of Defense) are the Bureau of Intelligence and Research (INR) in the Department of State; an intelligence unit in the Department of the Treasury; the Drug Enforcement Administration (DEA) in the Department of Justice; an intelligence unit in the Department of Homeland Security; and an intelligence unit in the Department of Energy, responsible for tracking the world's supply of uranium and other nuclear materials, as well as guarding the nation's weapons laboratories.

Among all of these organizations, the CIA is unique in that it stands outside any Cabinet department; it is an independent agency. It is unique as well in being the centerpiece of the National Security Act of 1947, the founding legislation for America's modern intelligence establishment. Originally, President Harry S. Truman envisioned the CIA as the central coordinating structure for American intelligence, designed to draw together the work of all the other agencies into a package that a president could deal with more readily than hearing separately from an array of agencies. The DCI was the individual Truman chose to manage this important coordinating role.

The plan never worked, though, because Truman – buckling under pressure from the Pentagon, which opposed a strong civilian leader for intelligence – failed to provide the DCI with adequate budget and appointment power over all of the agencies. Instead, the DCI became the leader of the CIA, but only the titular head of the full intelligence community.

[handwritten margin note: no $ power + no app. power]

After the 9/11 attacks, reformers vowed to correct this flaw, but again the Pentagon was able to dilute efforts to establish a strong DNI with funding and appointment powers over all of America's intelligence agencies. The DNI, like the DCI before, became the nation's chief spymaster largely in name only, with each of the sixteen agencies having a large degree of autonomy, enclosed or "stovepiped" within their own walls and enjoying considerable leeway to resist the orders of a DNI. This resistance was especially notable from the defense intelligence agencies – NGA, NSA, NRO, DIA, and the military services – who enjoyed the bureaucratic protection of the powerful secretary of defense, a member of the NSC.

The Office of the DCI had been located on the CIA's seventh floor. Since 2005, soon after a law was passed that replaced the DCI with a DNI, the nation's intelligence chief has moved from the CIA into temporary quarters at the DIA, also along the Potomac, only this time south of the White House by seven miles. A search is underway for a building inside the District of Columbia where the DNI can set up shop closer to the White House.

The DNI move out of the CIA Headquarters Building cast into doubt that agency's role as the central coordinating entity in the government for intelligence, as did its mistakes related to 9/11 and the Iraqi WMD fiasco. Consequently, in the quest for a more effective intelligence community after the 9/11 attacks, the United States ended up – ironically – with a weakened CIA and an even more emasculated intelligence chief, now removed from the one major resource that had given the nation's spy chief some clout in Washington circles: the analytic resources of the CIA.

The methods of intelligence

Regardless of which aspect of intelligence one has in mind – product, process, mission, or organization – the bottom line is that good governmental decisions rely on accurate, complete, unbiased, and timely information about the capabilities and intentions of other nations, terrorist organizations, and subversive groups. "Every morning I start my day with an intelligence report," President Bill Clinton once remarked. "The intelligence I receive informs just about every foreign policy decision we make."[5]

The intelligence agencies face quite a challenge in meeting the government's needs for insightful information about threats and opportunities. The world has some 191 countries and an untold number of organizations and groups, many that are hostile toward the United States and its allies. Further, these adversaries have become skillful in hiding their plans and operations from the prying eyes of espionage agents and spy machines. North Korea, for example, has constructed deep underground bunkers, where its scientists work on nuclear weaponry out of the sight of foreign surveillance satellites. A former US secretary of state has commented on the fear of intelligence failure: "The ghost that haunts the policy officer or haunts the man who makes the final decision is the question as to whether, in fact, he has in his mind all of the important elements that ought to bear upon his decision, or whether there is a missing piece that he is not aware of that could have a decisive effect if it became known."[6]

In their search for as perfect information about risks and opportunities as they can find, nations turn to a wide array of spying methods. Foremost among them, for nations with large enough budgets, are the expensive instruments of technical intelligence (or "techint"). By definition, techint refers chiefly to imagery intelligence ("imint") and signals intelligence ("sigint"). Imint employs photography, such as snapshots of enemy installations by surveillance satellites, for example; sigint encompasses the interception and analysis of communications intelligence, whether telephone conversations or e-mail transmissions.

In a time of accelerated technological advances around the world, the United States faces serious challenges in trying to maintain an information advantage over other nations. Its current edge in satellite photography is rapidly eroding. In 1999, the private US company Space Imaging launched a surveillance satellite named *Ikonos II* that yields photographs almost as detailed as the American government's most secret satellite photography, pictures of almost any part of the planet for sale to anyone with cash or a credit card. Within a few years, Iran and other nations at odds with the United States will be able to manufacture home-grown spy satellites or acquire commercially available substitutes (the Rent-a-Satellite option) which will provide them with their own capacity for battlefield transparency – a huge advantage for the United States during its wars against Iraq in 1991 and 2003.

America's advantages in signals intelligence are in decline as well. The listening satellites of the NSA are designed to capture analog communications from out of the air. The world, though, is rapidly switching to digital cell phones, along with underground and undersea fiber-optic modes of transmission – glass conduits ("pipe lights") that rely on light waves instead of electrons to carry information. These new forms of communication are much harder to tap, leaving the NSA with a sky full of increasingly irrelevant satellites. Furthermore, the NSA has traditionally depended on its skills at decoding to gain access to foreign diplomatic communications; but nations and terrorist groups are growing more clever at encrypting their messages with complex, computer-based technologies that can stymie even the most experienced NSA cryptologists. Under pressure from the US software industry and the Department of Commerce, the Clinton administration decided in 1999 to allow the export of advanced American software that encrypts electronic communications, making it more difficult for the NSA and the FBI to decipher the communications of foreign powers that might intend harm to the United States. Responding to market pressures of its own, the European Union is considering the removal of its restrictions on the sale of encryption software by European companies.

America's intelligence community suffers as well from an excessive redundancy built into its collection systems, with satellites, airplanes, and unmanned aerial vehicles (UAVs) often staring down at the same targets. Moreover, many of the satellites are gold-plated Cadillac de Ville models, with all the latest accessories. For certain missions, as in the broad coverage of a battlefield, they are valuable; but for many others, they could be replaced with less expensive, smaller satellites: serviceable Chevies. (The smaller the satellite, the less expense involved in positioning it in space, since launch costs are linear with weight.) The U–2 *Dragon Lady* piloted aircraft and the RQ-4A *Global Hawk* UAV are also far less expensive than the large, fancy satellites and much more effective in locating foes in places like Iraq and Afghanistan.

One of the most important responsibilities of the intelligence agencies is to warn the United States about terrorist efforts to acquire weapons of mass destruction, an extraordinarily difficult mission. The case of a suspected chemical weapons plant in Sudan is illustrative. In 1998 at a pharmaceutical factory near Khartoum, CIA sensing devices sniffed out what seemed to be the chemical Empta, a precursor for the production of the deadly nerve agent VX. The intelligence community had already collected signals intelligence and agent reports that linked the factory in the past with the terrorist Bin Laden and his Al Qaeda organization. Putting two and two

6

together, analysts estimated with a high degree of confidence that the factory was manufacturing chemical weapons. This intelligence led the Clinton administration to attack the
facility with cruise missiles. In response, the Sudanese government denounced the United
States and claimed that it had gone to war against an aspirin factory. The CIA stuck with its
original assessment, but did acknowledge that detective work of this kind is difficult and
imprecise. "The turning of a few valves can mean the difference between a pharmaceutical
company and a chemical or biological plant," said the agency's leading proliferation specialist.[7]

The failure of the CIA to anticipate the Indian nuclear test in 1998 is also instructive.
America's intelligence agencies were well aware that the Indians intended to accelerate their
nuclear program. After all, this is what top-level party officials had been saying publicly
throughout the Indian election season. Even the average tourist wandering around India in the
spring of that year, listening to the local media, would have concluded that a resumption of
the program was likely. What surprised the intelligence agencies was how fast the test had
taken place. It was "a good kick in the ass for us," admits a senior CIA official.[8] In part the
miscalculation was a result of what a CIA inquiry into the matter, led by retired Admiral David
Jeremiah, referred to as "mirror imaging." Agency analysts assumed that Indian politicians were
just like their American counterparts: both made a good many campaign promises, few of
which were ever kept. To win votes for boldness, Indian politicians in the victorious party (the
BJP) had promised a nuclear test; now that the election hoopla was over, surely they would back
away from this rash position. Such was the thinking at the CIA.

Further clouding accurate analysis by CIA analysts were successful efforts by officials in India
to evade America's spy satellites. The Indians knew exactly when the satellite cameras would
be passing over the nuclear testing facility near Pokharan in the Rajasthan Desert and, in
synchrony with these flights (every three days), scientists camouflaged their preparations.
Ironically, US officials had explicitly informed the Indian government about the timing of
US satellite coverage for South Asia, in hopes of impressing upon them the futility of trying to
conceal test activity. Even without this unintended assistance, though, the Indians could have
figured out the cycles for themselves, for even amateur astronomers can track the orbits of spy
satellites.

Moreover, the Indians had become adroit at deception, both technical and political. On the
technical side, the ground cables normally moved into place for a nuclear test were nowhere to
be seen in US satellite photographs of the site. The Indians had devised less visible ignition
techniques. The Indians also stepped up activities at their far-removed missile testing site in an
attempt to draw the attention of spy cameras away from the nuclear testing site. On the political
side, Indian officials expanded their coordinated deception operation by misleading American
and other international diplomats about the impending nuclear test, offering assurances that it
was simply not going to happen.

Finally, a dearth of reliable intelligence agents ("assets") contributed to the CIA's blindness.
During the Cold War, spending on techint far outdistanced spending on old-fashioned
espionage, known as human intelligence or "humint." A strong tendency exists among those
who make budget decisions for national security to focus on warheads, throw weights, missile
velocities, and the specifications of fancy spy satellites – things that can be measured. Humint, in
contrast, relies on the subtle recruitment of foreign agents, whose names and locations must be
kept highly secret and are not the subject of budget hearings. Yet, Ephraim Kam has emphasized
the importance of humint. An adversary's most important secrets, he notes, "often exist in the
mind of one man alone.. . or else they are shared by only a few top officials."[9] This kind of
information may be accessible only to an intelligence officer who has recruited someone inside
the enemy camp.

During the Cold War, South Asia received limited attention from the US intelligence agencies, compared to their concentration on the Soviet Union and its surrogates; therefore, building up an espionage ring in this region after the fall of communism still had a long ways to go at the time of the Indian nuclear tests. These excuses notwithstanding, American citizens may have wondered with a reasonable sense of indignation — not to say outrage — why their well-funded intelligence community proved ignorant of what was going on inside the largest democracy and one of the most open countries in the world.

Far more difficult than keeping an eye on India is the challenge of gaining access to intelligence on reclusive terrorist organizations and renegade states like Iran and North Korea — dangerous, isolated, and unpredictable adversaries known to leave footprints of fire. It is difficult as well to keep track of companies engaged in commercial transactions that aid and abet the spread of weaponry, like the German corporations that secretly assisted the Iraqi weapons buildup and the construction of the large chemical weapons plant at Rabta in Libya.

During the Carter administration, the nation was reminded of the importance of humint when Iranian student militants took American diplomats hostage inside the US embassy in Tehran. America's satellites had good photographs of Tehran and the embassy compound; but to plan a rescue operations, the White House and the CIA needed information about the whereabouts of the hostages inside the embassy. Recalls one of the planners:

> We had a zillion shots of the roof of the embassy and they were magnified a hundred times. We could tell you about the tiles; we could tell you about the grass and how many cars were parked there. Anything you wanted to know about the external aspects of the embassy we could tell you in infinite detail. We couldn't tell you shit about what was going on inside that building.[10]

The methods of intelligence collection became skewed as well during the Cold War. Awed by the technological capabilities of satellites and reconnaissance airplanes (U-2s, SR-21s, UAVs), officials channeled most of the intelligence budget into surveillance machines capable of photographing Soviet tanks and missiles silos and eavesdropping on telephone conversations in communist capitals. Human spy networks became the neglected stepchild of intelligence.

Machines certainly have their place in America's spy defenses and they played an important role in Afghanistan after the 9/11 attacks, as US satellite cameras stared down at Kabul and Kandahar, and UAVs swooped into mountain valleys in search of Al Qaeda terrorists and their Taliban accomplices. But these cameras cannot peer inside caves or see through tents where terrorists gather. A secret agent in the enemy's camp — humint — is necessary to provide advance warning of future terrorist attacks. Humint networks take time to develop, though, and only recently have the last DCI (Porter Goss) and the new DNI (John Negroponte) launched major recruitments drive to hire into the intelligence community Americans with language skills and an understanding of Afghanistan, Iraq, Iran, and other parts of the world largely ignored by the United States until now. American intelligence officers with these skills are needed to recruit local agents overseas who carry out the actual espionage for the CIA. The 9/11 attacks and the Iraqi WMD controversy accelerated these recruitment efforts, but it has proven difficult to find Arabic, Farsi, and Pushto speakers who are citizens of the United States and who want to work for the CIA abroad at a modest government salary and in conditions that are less than luxurious — and sometimes downright dangerous.

The intelligence missions

Collection-and-analysis. The foremost intelligence mission is to gather intelligence, whether by techmint or humint, then analyze its meaning, bringing human insight to bear on the mountain of data that has been collected. At the beginning of every administration, senior officials work with the DNI to prepare a "threat assessment" – a priority listing of the most dangerous circumstances facing the United States. These officials then decide how much money from the annual intelligence budget will be spent on the collection of information against each target nation or group.

Throughout the Cold War, the United States concentrated mainly on gathering intelligence against the Soviet Union and other communist powers, giving far less attention to the rest of the world. Terrorism has been on the list of intelligence priorities for decades, but until September 11, 2001, it was treated by the intelligence agencies as only one of several assignments. Now it has jumped to a position of preeminence on America's threat list, resulting in a greater focus of US intelligence resources on Osama bin Laden and his associates.

When a recent director of the NSA was asked what his major problems were, he replied, "I have three: processing, processing, and processing."[11] In this phase of the intelligence cycle, information is converted from "raw" intelligence – whether in Arabic or a secret code – into plain English (see Appendix C). Beyond needing more language translators, the chief difficulty faced by intelligence officers is the sheer volume of information that pours into their agencies. Each day millions of telephone intercepts and hundreds of photographs from satellites stream back to the United States. A former intelligence manager recalls feeling as though he had a fire hose held to his mouth.

The task of sorting through this flood of information to isolate the important facts from the routine can hinder quick access to key information. Before the September attacks, for example, FBI agents dismissed as routine a CIA report concerning two individuals headed for the United States and suspected of associating with terrorists. The men turned out to be among the nineteen suicide hijackers of 9/11.

Once information is processed, it must be studied by experts for insights into the intentions of our adversaries – the step known as analysis. If the CIA is unable to provide meaning to the information gathered by the intelligence community, all the earlier collecting and processing efforts are for nought. Good analysis depends on assembling the best brains possible to evaluate global events, drawing upon a blend of public knowledge and stolen secrets. Once again a major liability is the CIA's shortage of well-educated Americans who have deep knowledge of places like Afghanistan and Sudan. While all of the intelligence agencies have been scrambling to redirect their resources from the communist world to the forgotten world of the Middle East and Southwest Asia, hiring and training outstanding analysts takes time, just like the establishment of new humint spy rings.

Finally, the analyzed intelligence is disseminated to policymakers. It must be relevant, timely, accurate, comprehensive, and unbiased. Relevance is essential. Intelligence reports on drug-trafficking in Colombia are good to have, but what the White House and Whitehall want right now is knowledge about Bin Laden's operations. Analysts can become so wedded to their own research interests (say, the efficiencies of Russian rocket fuel) that they fail to produce what policymakers really want and need to know.

Timeliness is equally vital. The worst acronym an analyst can see scrawled across an intelligence report is OBE – "overtaken by events." Assessments on the whereabouts of terrorists are especially perishable, as the United States discovered in 1999 when the Clinton administration fired cruise missiles at Bin Laden's supposed encampment in the Zhawar Kili region of

9

Afghanistan's Paktia Province, only to learn that he had departed hours earlier. Similarly, the accuracy of information is critical. One of America's worst intelligence embarrassments came in 1999 when the National Geospatial-Intelligence Agency (NGA) misidentified the Chinese embassy in Belgrade as a weapons depot, leading to a NATO bombing of the building and the death of Chinese diplomats.

Intelligence must be comprehensive as well, drawn from all sixteen intelligence agencies and coordinated into a meaningful whole – what intelligence officers refer to as "all-source fusion" or "jointness." Here one runs into the vexing problem of fragmentation within the so-called intelligence "community" – a misnomer if there ever was one. The US secret agencies often act more like separate medieval fiefdoms than a cluster of agencies working together to provide the president with the best possible information from around the world.

Intelligence must also be free of political spin. An analyst is expected to assess the facts in a dispassionate manner. Usually intelligence officers maintain this ethos, but occasionally they have succumbed to the wiles of White House pressure for "intelligence to please" – data that supports the president's political agenda rather than reflecting the often unpleasant reality that an administration's policy has failed.

Much can go wrong, and has gone wrong, with intelligence collection-and-analysis. For it to function properly in America's three ongoing wars – against insurgents in Iraq, remanent Taliban fighters in Afghanistan, and the global struggle against terrorism – collection must employ an effective combination of machines and human spies. Moreover, data processing must be made more swift and more discerning in the discrimination of wheat from chaff. Analysts must have a deeper understanding of the foreign countries that harbor terrorist cells, as well as a better comprehension of what makes the terrorists tick. Further, at the end of this intelligence pipeline, the information provided to the policymaker must be pertinent, on time, reliable, comprehensive, and unbiased. Finally, the policymakers must have the courage to hear the truth rather than brush it aside, as President Lyndon B. Johnson sometimes did with intelligence reports on Vietnam that concluded America's involvement in the war was leading to failure.[12]

Counterintelligence. The term counterintelligence (CI) encompasses a range of methods used to protect the United States against aggressive operations perpetrated by foreign intelligence agencies and terrorist groups. These operations include attempts to infiltrate the CIA, FBI, and other US intelligence agencies through the use of double agents, penetration agents (moles), and false defectors. Counterintelligence employs two approaches: security and counter-espionage. Security is the defensive side of CI: physically guarding US personnel, installations, and operations against hostile forces. Among the defenses employed by America's secret agencies are codes, alarms, watchdogs, fences, document classifications, polygraphs, and restricted areas. Counterespionage represents the more aggressive side of CI, with the goal, above all, of penetrating with a US agent the inner councils of a foreign intelligence service or terrorist cell.

Aldrich Ames (CIA) and Robert Hannsen (FBI), the premier spies in the United States run by the Soviet Union and then Russia, caused the most grievous harm to America's intelligence operations and stand as the greatest counterintelligence failures in US history. As a result of their handiwork in stealing top-secret ("blue-border") documents – for which the KGB, and later, the Russian SVR paid Ames alone over $4 million – the espionage efforts of the CIA and the FBI against the Soviet Union lay in tatters at the end of the Cold War. The Kremlin executed at least nine of the CIA's assets in Russia and rolled up hundreds of operations. Ames and Hannsen also disclosed some of America's most sensitive technical intelligence capabilities to their Moscow handlers, including (from Hannsen) details about US listening devices in the new Russian embassy in Washington, DC.

Covert action. Here is the most controversial mission of the three, as exemplified by the Bay of

10

Pigs fiasco in 1961 – a failed paramilitary covert action against the Castro regime in Cuba. Covert action consists of aiming secret propaganda at foreign nations, as well as using political, economic, and paramilitary operations in an effort to influence, disrupt, or even overthrow their governments (as in Iran in 1953, Guatemala in 1954, and – without success – Iraq in the 1990s). The objective of covert action is to secretly shape events overseas, in so far as history can be shaped by mere mortals, in support of US foreign policy goals. ⟶ *objective*

The most extensively used form of covert action has been propaganda. As a supplement to the overt information released to the world by the United States under the rubric of "public diplomacy," the CIA over the years has pumped through its wide network of secret media agents a torrent of covert propaganda that resonates with the overt themes. These foreign agents have included reporters, magazine and newspaper editors, television producers, talk show hosts, and anyone else in a position to disseminate without attribution the perspectives of the US government as if they were their own. One of the major examples of a CIA propaganda operation was the financing of Radio Free Europe and Radio Liberty during the Cold War. These radio stations broadcast into the Soviet Union and Eastern Europe with programming geared to break the communist government's totalitarian control over news, entertainment, and culture, as well as to advance America's views of the world. These programs are credited with having helped sustain dissident movements behind the Iron Curtain, and to have contributed to the eventual fall of Soviet communism and Moscow's control over Eastern Europe.

Of greater controversy were the CIA's propaganda efforts in Chile during the 1960s and 1970s. In 1964, the CIA spent $3 million – a staggering sum at the time – to blacken the name of Salvador Allende, the socialist presidential candidate with suspected ties to the Soviet Union. Allende was elected, nonetheless, in a free and open democratic electoral process. The CIA continued its propaganda operations, now designed to undermine the Allende regime, spending an additional $3 million between 1970 and 1973. According to US Senate investigators, the forms of propaganda included press releases, radio commentary, films, pamphlets, posters, leaflets, direct mailings, paper streamers, and wall paintings. The CIA relied heavily on images of communist tanks and firing squads, and paid for the distribution of hundreds of thousands of copies, in this very Catholic country, of an anti-communist pastoral letter written many years earlier by Pope Pius XI.

Covert action sometimes takes the form of financial aid to pro-Western politicians and bureaucrats in other nations, money used to assist groups in their electoral campaigns or for party recruitment. Anti-communist labor unions in Europe received extensive CIA funding throughout the Cold War, as did many anti-communist political parties around the world. One well-known case involved the Christian Democratic Party in Italy during the 1960s, when it struggled against the Italian Communist Party in elections. The CIA has also resorted to the disruption of foreign economies. In one instance, during the Kennedy administration (although without the knowledge of the president), the CIA hoped to spoil Cuban–Soviet relations by lacing sugar bound from Havana to Moscow with an unpalatable, though harmless, chemical substance. A White House aide discovered the scheme and had the 14,125 bags of sugar confiscated before they were shipped to the Soviet Union. Other methods have reportedly included the incitement of labor unrest, the counterfeiting of foreign currencies, attempts to depress the world price of agriculture products grown by adversaries, the contamination of oil supplies, and even dynamiting electrical power lines and oil-storage facilities, as well as mining harbors to discourage the adversary's commercial shipping ventures.[13]

The paramilitary, or war-like, forms of covert action have stirred the most controversy. This category includes small- and large-scale "covert" wars, which do not remain covert for long; training activities for foreign military and police officers; the supply of military advisers, weapons, and battlefield transportation; and the planning and implementation of assassination plots. This last endeavor has been the subject of considerable criticism and debate, and was finally prohibited by executive order in 1976 – although with a waiver in time of war. That year congressional investigators uncovered CIA files on assassination plots against several foreign leaders, referred to euphemistically in secret CIA documents as "termination with extreme prejudice" or simply "neutralization." At one time the CIA established a special group, called the "Health Alteration Committee," to screen assassination proposals. The CIA's numerous attempts to murder Fidel Castro all failed; and its plot against Congolese leader Patrice Lumumba, requiring a lethal injection of poison into his food or tooth paste, became a moot point on the eve of its implementation when Lumumba was murdered by a rival faction in Congo.

After the end of the Cold War, spending for covert action went into sharp decline. It has been revived, though, with the wars in Iraq, Afghanistan, and against global terrorists. The most lethal new form of paramilitary covert action is the Hellfire missile, fired from UAVs like the Predator.

Intelligence and accountability

The existence of secret agencies in an open society presents a contradiction and a dilemma for liberal democracies. In the 1970s, investigators discovered that, in addition to carrying out assassination plots, the CIA had spied against American citizens protesting the war in Vietnam (Operation Chaos and Operation HQLINGUAL), the FBI had spied upon and harassed citizens involved in the civil rights and anti-Vietnam War protests (Operation Cointelpro), and the NSA had intercepted and read the cables of citizens to and from abroad (Operation Shamrock). In response to these abuses of power, America's lawmakers created an exceptional approach to the problem of restraining intelligence agencies, including the establishment of Senate and House intelligence oversight committees. Since 1975, both branches of government in the United States have struggled to find the proper balance between legislative supervision of intelligence, on the one hand, and executive discretion for its effective conduct, on the other hand. Although the quality of congressional supervision of intelligence has been infinitely better since 1975, accountability in this domain has suffered from inattention by members of Congress and a rising level of partisan debates when intelligence does come into focus for the members.

The *Handbook of Intelligence Studies*

Here, then, are the main topics addressed in this *Handbook*, in essays written by many of the top intelligence authorities in the United States and abroad. Michael Warner, an historian with the CIA's Director of National Intelligence, begins Part 1 of the volume with a broad look at sources and methods for studying intelligence, which is a relatively new field of intellectual inquiry. Before 1975, the number of reliable books and articles on this subject was few. In the past three decades, however, the scholarly literature on intelligence has mushroomed, thanks in large part to a series of congressional and executive-branch inquiries into espionage failures that unearthed and placed in the public domain a rich lode of new data on the workings of America's secret agencies. In the second chapter, James Wirtz of the Naval Postgraduate School writes about the approach to intelligence studies that he observes in the writings of American researchers. Next Professor Rhodri Jeffreys-Jones at the University of Edinburgh examines research specifically related to the FBI. Almost every government activity has an ethical dimension and Michael Andregg of the University of St Thomas explores the moral implications of secret intelligence operations in the fourth chapter.

Part 2 turns to the evolution of intelligence in the modern era. British scholar Ian Leigh provides a legal analysis of how the subject of accountability has come to play an important role in intelligence research; and Peter Gill, another British scholar, offers a comparative perspective on intelligence studies. Professor Wolfgang Krieger of Germany discusses the development of modern intelligence in his nation, which was heavily influenced by the United States.

The *Handbook* moves in Parts 3 and 4 to an exploration of key issues related to the core mission of intelligence: collection-and-analysis. In Part 3 Jeffrey Richelson, a leading researcher on techint, lays out the central debates over this approach to intelligence collection. He is followed by a former inspector general of the CIA, Frederick P. Hitz, who makes the case for the importance of humint. Next, Robert David Steele argues in favor of a more effective use of open-source materials in the preparation of intelligence reports; and Paul R. Pillar presents a case for the improved adaptation of intelligence to the changing policy issues that confront government officials. Minh A. Luong takes on the increasingly vital topic of economic espionage – how nations use intelligence to seek an advantage in a highly competitive global marketplace.

Shifting in Part 4 from collection questions to the subjects of intelligence analysis, production, and dissemination, another group of experts offer decades of experience and research about how these final phases of the intelligence cycle work – or fail to work. Jack Davis, a long-time CIA analyst, dissects the critical topic of early warning intelligence; Richard L. Russell explores the goal of all-source intelligence fusion, the goal envisioned by President Truman in 1947 before "stovepiping" got in the way of interagency cooperation; Stephen Marrin ponders how to add value to intelligence products, bringing to top policy officials insights beyond what they can acquire in the pages of the *Wall Street Journal* or the *New York Times*; and John Hollister Hedley, too, probes the possibilities for improved analysis.

Part 5 of the *Handbook* takes up the missions of counterintelligence/counterterrorism and covert action. Another British scholar, Nigel West, scrutinizes the value of defectors – often considered a major source of intelligence about the machinations of anti-democratic nations and factions in the world. Professor Stan Taylor of Brigham Young University reviews the CI record in the United States, shedding light on the failures that have occurred and why. Mark Stout focuses on a major difficulty for counterintelligence officers: how to tell when an émigré with intelligence knowledge is telling the truth to US interrogators. In the next piece on counterintelligence, Kathryn S. Olmsted provides by way of a case study a sense of how overzealous CI officers can damage the reputation of a law-abiding American citizen.

Turning to covert action, William Daugherty, who has had hands-on experience in this controversial compartment of intelligence activities while serving in the CIA, makes a case for this approach to foreign policy, but is quick to point out its hazards, too. John Prados, an independent scholar, examines what is currently the hottest topic within the rubric of covert action: the uses and misuses of paramilitary operations.

Finally, in Part 6, the *Handbook* offers a series of essays on the challenges of maintaining accountability in the secret domain of intelligence. British scholar Mark Phythian begins the section with a close look at the experience with intelligence supervision on his side of the Atlantic, while Hans Born (Netherlands) and Thorsten Wetzling (Germany) provide a comparative examination of how a variety of nations have approached the challenge of intelligence accountability. The judiciary plays a part in the supervision of intelligence, too, and CIA attorney and former Rhodes Scholar Fred F. Manget sheds light on the workings of the Foreign Intelligence Surveillance Act court. Finally, the editor presents a "shock theory" of intelligence accountability on Capitol Hill, underscoring the reactive nature of Congress in fulfilling its oversight responsibilities.

I am pleased to acknowledge my gratitude to Andrew Humphrys, Editor for Routledge, who encouraged the writing of this *Handbook* and helped shepherd it through the various gates to completion, and Colin Morgan and Richard Willis of Swales & Willis, who oversaw its production with great skill and patience; Julie Maynard at the University of Georgia for her administrative assistance; Larry Lamanna for his untiring research assistance; Leena Johnson for her encouragement and counsel; and the contributors for their thoughtful research and willingness to meet deadlines.

Finally, the *Handbook* is enthusiastically dedicated to all the young scholars who are entering the field of intelligence studies. Welcome! I hope these essays will suggest future research directions for you, and that they will also provide insights to the general reader interested in intelligence and national security affairs.

Notes

1 *Factbook on Intelligence*, Office of Public Affairs, Central Intelligence Agency (September 1991), p. 13.
2 Abram N. Shulsky, *Silent Warfare: Understanding the World of Intelligence*, 2nd ed., revised by Gary J. Schmitt (New York: Brassey's US, 1993), p. 193.
3 Aspin-Brown Commission on the Roles and Capabilities of the US Intelligence Community, *Preparing for the 21ˢᵗ Century: An Appraisal of US Intelligence* (Washington, DC: US Government Printing Office, March 1, 1996), p. 88.
4 Comment to the editor, Athens, Georgia (July 4, 1983).
5 Remarks to the CIA (July 14, 1995, editor's notes).
6 Dean Rusk, testimony, *Hearings*, US Senate Committee on Foreign Relations (December 11, 1963), p. 390.
7 Loch K. Johnson, *Bombs, Bugs, Drugs, and Thugs: Intelligence and America's Quest for Security* (New York: New York University Press, 2000), p. 24.
8 Loch K. Johnson, "The CIA's Weakest Link," *Washington Monthly* 33 (July/August 2001), p. 11.
9 Ephraim Kam, *Surprise Attack* (Cambridge, MA: Harvard University Press, 1988), p. 62.
10 Quoted in Steve Emerson, *Secret Warriors: Inside the Covert Military Operations of the Reagan Era* (New York: Putnam's, 1988), p. 20.
11 Editor's interview with senior NSA official (July 15, 1994); see Loch K. Johnson, *Secret Agencies: US Intelligence in a Hostile World* (New Haven, CT: Yale University Press, 1996), p. 21.
12 See Thomas L. Hughes, "The Power to Speak and the Power to Listen: Reflections in Bureaucratic Politics and a Recommendation on Information Flows," in Thomas Franck and Edward Weisband, *Secrecy and Foreign Policy* (New York: Oxford University Press, 1974), pp. 28–37.
13 See Loch K. Johnson, *America's Secret Power: The CIA in a Democratic Society* (New York: Oxford University Press, 1989); and Johnson, *Secret Agencies*, see n. 11.

Part 1

The study of intelligence

1

Sources and methods for the study of intelligence

Michael Warner

Intelligence can be thought of as that which states do in secret to support their efforts to mitigate, influence, or merely understand other nations (or various enemies) that could harm them. By its nature as an activity that could involve the loss of fragile sources or means of understanding and influence – not to mention the lives of troops, subjects, and even leaders – intelligence is treated by its practitioners as sensitive and confidential. Even the accidental disclosure of some analytical, informational, or operational advantage over a rival or an enemy is presumed to be tantamount to the loss of that advantage while it is still potentially useful. Thus the penalties for disclosure have always been severe – and those for espionage even harsher. Nations have sought thereby to terrify disloyalty and also to protect the advantages that secret means seem to bring to decisionmaking. Wherever such life-and-death stakes obtain, intelligence is conducted with some full or partial cloak of secrecy, and the evidence of it is typically unavailable to onlookers.

Intelligence thus by definition resists scholarship. As a result, the study of intelligence is not one field but two. Intelligence studies have been conducted one way on the "outside," with no official access to original records, and another way on the "inside," where a few scholars have intermittently enjoyed sanctioned (if not always complete) access to the extant documentation. The differing natures of the source materials available to scholars on the inside and the outside, naturally, have caused academic researchers and students of intelligence to work differently from official historians and investigators in the employ of the state.

The sources and methods of both the "outside" and the "inside" scholars, interestingly enough, can bring their practitioners quite close to genuine historical understanding. Over the last 60 years, a handful of governments have episodically sought to understand the experiences of their various intelligence services. The results have been uneven, across and within governments, but they have been real, and in places they have laid a solid foundation for historical and even theoretical work on intelligence on the outside. Intelligence studies in academia, on the other hand, have quickened over the last two decades in the fields of history and political science as more scholars of the diplomatic and military arts grasp the importance of intelligence for their own disciplines, and gain familiarity with the relevant documentation. In so doing, they have begun to create a community of intelligence scholars and have helped to reclaim

17

the study of intelligence from those who would have us believe in the omniscience or the omnipotence of the discipline's practitioners.

Both inside and outside scholars, however, labor under differing strains imposed by the nature of intelligence as a secret enterprise. These strains need not be debilitating, but they impose significant impacts on the quality of the final products. What follows is not a bibliographical or archival guide to records-holdings in any particular country. It is not possible in one article to survey the literature and collections around the world that hold documents of possible interest to researchers in the intelligence field. Even for researchers of intelligence in the United States, such a survey would have the ironic disadvantages of being both lengthy and vague. It would also be quickly out of date as new files are released. This chapter is rather a set of field notes for using the sources that are available and are likely to emerge over the foreseeable future. It is also a reflection on the burdens that must be shouldered by researchers on both sides of the wall of secrecy that surrounds intelligence.

What are the sources?

In describing the sources used in the historical study of intelligence, it is easier to start on the inside and work outward. That is, by examining first the way in which intelligence activities appear to those holding access to the official records, and then how they appear to the much larger set of scholars who do not enjoy such access. Historians in the employ of their governments work primarily from the office and operational files, from cable traffic and budget data, and from interviews, artifacts, and other sources, to identify and assemble the clues to what happened and what it meant.

The first place for the official historian to look is always "the file." Like virtually all governmental organizations from the late nineteenth century onward, intelligence agencies are hierarchies, and their officers at multiple levels have created and preserved files on their activities. The growing professionalism and rationalism of the various agencies gradually supplanted the work of the amateurs, the friends of royalty, and the charlatans who had dominated espionage since ancient times. Efficient paperwork and good filing systems were keys to this evolutionary triumph. The sort of files that got saved – and eventually made their way to official historians – have tended to be archived by office first, by subject next, and then sometimes by operation or activity, according to the records protocols governing the larger department or organization in which they are embedded. Even the independent intelligence agencies of the United States adapted this classification scheme from the filing systems of the State and War Departments, without much change. Indeed, filing systems in their fundamental outlines seem so similar across organizations and eras that they would seem to be following almost a law of nature.

A mature organization will follow protocols governing how and when files are opened, maintained, archived, or purged. The extent to which such protocols are set and followed is an indicator of the quality of the organization's leadership – or at least of its administrative acumen. The researcher typically checks all the extant and relevant files he or she can locate, which means reading those from all the organization's levels of approval and review. Activities or subjects enduring over several years will have multiple files, some of them running for multiple volumes. Smaller and simpler activities or operations (which is not to say less successful or important ones) will obviously have thinner files. Files kept overseas are typically abbreviated; those at headquarters in the capital are longer, because there is more time to keep them, more clerical staff to do so, and usually more storage space.

One rule of thumb for the official researcher is that the more expensive the activity or topic, the more places one finds files on it. Costly activities and projects ordinarily require more personnel and logistical expenses, hence more accounting and security controls, and therefore more legal counsel, and thus more files. The agency's legal, financial, logistical, and security offices can be expected to keep their own files on larger activities. The director of the agency may have a file on it, if it demands his attention or a briefing for higher authorities. Something really important will merit files in other agencies, and in the executive branch's archives as well. These can be quite valuable for the researcher because they provide a different (if not always more objective) perspective on the activity.

Not all important incidents, projects, issues, or events are well documented. The converse is also true: events or topics with scanty documentation are not always insignificant. Here is a quandary in intelligence research: what to infer from a situation in which there are few or no files? That can happen in at least two circumstances. First is when events are happening too quickly for everything to be documented by the people on the spot. In such cases the documentation will typically come in the form of summary cables and after-action reports, which are good to have, but not always as accurate and complete as a researcher might wish. The second case is when the head of the agency or one of its units was specifically ordered to keep the "paper trail" as short as possible – possibly by destroying it. Such instances would seem to be rare, even in secret services, but there are exceptions that prove the rule (like the CIA's "Track II" in Chile in 1970), for reasons that should be obvious.[1] It is difficult to do anything in a bureaucracy without authorizations and funds, and difficult to show such authorization if it is not written down somewhere. More typical is that some extraordinary aspect will be added to an operation already under way, as with the abortive assassination plotting in the CIA's Guatemala coup operation in 1954.[2] Such operational annexes will most likely have been authorized orally.

Various officials for reasons of their own will sometimes keep "private" files. As these files are by definition maintained outside of the office's records management protocols, they are naturally structured in whatever way that keeps them useful and convenient for the individuals who created them. The saintly and conscientious intelligence officer who deliberately seeks to keep future historians well informed, however, is another rarity. Indeed, a savvy official historian immediately (if silently) questions the motives of anyone who keeps such a file, and wonders what axe he or she is grinding. The first such collection this author ever encountered was surely started because the compiler of it thought he should have been kept on as head of an office that had been assigned to the care of a younger rival. Simply put, he saved the items that made him look prescient, and hoped someone would notice someday. The more common private files to be saved, however, are compiled willy-nilly over the course of a career, as the official runs across something he thinks is interesting or amusing or otherwise worth squirreling away. Eventually he leaves or retires, and either "wills" his collection of miscellany to some colleague, or leaves it behind in a desk or safe to be found months or even years later by successors who might or might not take the trouble to save its contents.

The next place to look for records, especially if the activity took place overseas, is in the cable traffic. Intelligence agencies (even domestic ones) live by their official communications channels, and the messages sent along them are meticulously preserved and organized. Cable files are rigidly chronological, and cables themselves are supposed to be drafted so as to be economical and clear in their prose. They have to be, for the safety and success of the operation and the people involved, not to mention the expense of sending them.

Cables can be a wonderful source for historians, even when misleading, trivial, or turgid – or sometimes all at once. Indeed, when compared with staff memoranda produced at a leisurely pace in the home offices, cables generally seem terse, articulate, and definitive. Cables are the residue of a dying technology, however, and thus in reading them it is vital for the contemporary researcher to understand how cable traffic differs from modern messaging over computerized, global networks. Cables could take many hours to reach their recipients, especially if there were significant time-zone differences between the end points of the messages. In the days of hand encoding and decoding, moreover, a long cable usually meant late hours in the coderoom for some poor junior officer. Not a few cabled instructions had been overtaken by events by the time their addressee finally read them.

It almost goes without saying that telephone conversations are usually lost. Senior officials have always had their aides or secretaries keep office diaries and phone logs, and perhaps to paraphrase important calls as well. Prime ministers or presidents may even have had their conversations taped. The era is long past, however, and it did not last long to begin with, when senior *intelligence* officials would tape phone calls. By the 1960s important intelligence telephone calls were supposed to be placed on secure phones, the use of which has increased steadily over time as the secure phone networks expanded. Sometimes phone calls have presumably been recorded by foreign adversaries, but such third parties are rarely so kind as to release the transcripts to scholars.

A third key source for insider researchers is budget data. Budgets are sure indicators of the priorities of an organization, and to that organization's priority in the larger scheme of policy implementation. They are also an index for comparison in looking at operations themselves; they indicate the relative size of the operation, giving a rough indication of whether the project in question represents a barn, a table, or a thimble.

Agency-wide budgets serve another purpose – that of giving the researcher a benchmark for the quality of and challenges facing the organization's leadership. Declining budgets are a severe test of a leader's ability. Indeed, sometimes it can be high praise indeed to say that a agency head was only able to hold his ground; that he preserved the organization's core mission and staff and even maintained its operational tempo while his budgetary base eroded. Tough decisions are forced on a leader in such times; he or she has to trim somewhere to preserve other priorities, and such choices generally result in disagreements and even bitterness among the managers whose projects and offices lose out. On the other hand, growing budgets force a different set of challenges on a leader. Budget hikes allow him to throw money at problems, and many directors are tempted to do just that, often with meager and short-lived results. In a situation of sharply increasing resources, merely maintaining previous levels of staff and activities is a sign of poor or challenged leadership.

Another help on the inside, sometimes, is the personnel file of someone involved in an activity. This is helpful especially when living memory is deficient. If it contains performance evaluations for the time in question, or names of other people involved, such a file gives a researcher important reference points. It also provides clues to the orientation of the officer in question – his professional training and background – that may have had a bearing on the decisions or operation in question. A roster of the personnel involved also helps in surmounting the difficulties posed for intelligence scholarship that are caused by secrecy and compartmentation. One cannot assume that an event that was prior in time helped to cause a later one, or a prior report caused a subsequent decision, since the personnel involved may have had no access to such information. Sometimes it is possible to show that someone involved in an earlier operation was – or could not have been – in a position of responsibility to have had a role in a later one. The converse is true as well – sometimes two things that looked similar were really independent, with no common personnel.

Lastly, for intelligence agencies after the mid-1980s, internal electronic mail records can be important, or even vital. American governmental agencies began putting crude computers on the desktops of their officials in the 1980s; the employees using these early hub-and-spoke systems could sometimes communicate with one another via simple messaging programs. It took another decade, and the decisive victory of the IBM-clone personal computer, for such technology to become ubiquitous in the government and its intelligence bureaus. After about 1995, the internal e-mail becomes an indispensable source.

These various forms of e-mail present several problems to the researcher. They might not exist for certain offices or periods, given the archiving requirements and habits of the agencies and the officials manning them. They may not reflect the views of all the important officers involved in a decision or an operation. The most important officials in any organization typically have the least time to write them, and thus an agency head will typically leave behind a thin collection of e-mails. E-mails collectively carry a huge amount of information – and more importantly, circumstance – but it is often highly fragmented and elliptical. They cannot substitute for traditional sources, both oral and documentary, because even in the age of e-mail, many decisions still get made face-to-face, or over the telephone.

Inside scholars use published secondary materials as much as they can get them, but generally for establishing context for narratives that are based primarily on still-classified files. It can be tough to square the outside histories with the inside information, and the insiders always worry that something produced on the outside is incomplete. Official researchers can rarely call a colleague on the outside to ask if she checked collections X and Y in preparing her latest book – in part because security considerations can preclude such contacts. This is the signature weakness of inside scholarship – it can never be placed fully in the context of the literature written on the outside and reviewed by all the people in the various scholarly disciplines who might be able to explain or expand upon its findings.

This lengthy discussion of sources for official research in intelligence must seem quite elementary to any historian working in the documentary record of twentieth-century military or diplomatic history. That is no coincidence, for military and diplomatic history is precisely what historical research in intelligence is. Intelligence is not some privileged realm where the usual dynamics of organizational and group behavior do not apply; intelligence agencies are bureaucracies, and thus no exception to the rules of historical scholarship. In studying them, the scholar gathers the records and facts and arranges them according to the time-honored ways of archival practice and scholarship. An intelligence service will possess more secrets, and sometimes more colorful characters, but its job is to assist the making and the implementing of a nation's strategic decisions. Its records therefore exist in the same milieu and the same patterns as the diplomatic and military ministries that intelligence serves.

Sources on the outside

Scholarly work on the inside is often dedicated to the production of uncomplicated organizational or operational narratives. In contrast, writing intelligence history from academia or private life – that is, without access to the official, classified documentation – is in some ways more interesting because it is more difficult, depending on the availability of declassified documentation. Where there are files to work from, the outside researcher will use them in ways quite similar to that of his or her counterparts on the inside who have access to the complete official record. On the other hand, where few records have been released, the researcher has to appraise his or her sources in the knowledge that they are surely fragmentary. He has to word his judgments accordingly, erring always on the side of caution, and building to generalizations only on stable bases of fact.

Such a labor has traditionally resembled the writing of ancient history, with the advantage (sometimes) of having living participants to interview. Like ancient history, much of the best work is heavily literary in character, rather than historical in the Rankean sense of depicting events *wie es eigentlich gewesen war* ("as they actually happened"). This is not meant as a criticism or a pejorative. Livy, Tacitus, and Thucydides, to name but three ancient historians, sought by the portrayal of fascinating but flawed characters against the backdrop of grand narratives to illustrate the larger themes of nature, society, and Man himself.[3] Where histories of intelligence aspire to be more Rankean than literary, they tend to resemble in some ways the works of modern historians writing about ancient times. They have to rely on fragments, not files. Their chronologies are sometimes hazy. Physical evidence is sparse, and mostly monumental (i.e. on the scale of ruined public works). There are few surviving pictures to consult. Rumor and myth are everywhere, often so intertwined with fact that, in some cases just beyond the reach of living memory, truth and fiction can no longer be separated. The one obvious advantage that intelligence historians have over ancient historians is in the opportunity to interview their subjects – if they will talk.

A careful researcher first tracks down any and all official documents, studies, reports, and histories that might be available on his or her topic. In Western countries these documents are usually well-intended attempts at explaining their subjects. Such official releases have their distinct limitations: they are restricted by the scope of their charters (sometimes lamentably narrow), by the rigors of the declassification process (sometimes exhaustive), and by the objectivity, aptitude, and curiosity of their authors (sometimes curiously lacking). Nonetheless, they provide an important touchstone of accepted fact that the researcher can use as a platform for further inquiry, or at least a landmark along the way.

Such official products can be crucial. Indeed, the quality of the work done on the inside can eventually determine the prospects that outside scholars have for getting a story right (that should be a sobering thought for official historians). The multi-volume history of British intelligence in World War II produced under the supervision of Sir F.H. Hinsley in the 1980s remains a seminal work and a guide to scholarship not only in British but in Allied and Axis activities as well. The big break for scholars of the US Intelligence Community was the publication of the *Final Report* of the US Senate's special committee that met under the leadership of Sen. Frank Church in 1975–76. The so-called Church Committee's seven volumes mark the watershed in forming public knowledge of American intelligence. The Committee's survey of the history of the Central Intelligence Agency from its founding to the mid-1970s is not comprehensive but it is still particularly valuable, in being balanced, insightful, and reliable (in large part because it was based on the still-classified histories produced or held in the CIA's History Staff) The Church Committee volumes laid the bedrock for academic work on the Intelligence Community.

The researcher next looks for the declassified documents themselves, beginning with the most authoritative. The availability of such records depends on the country and the time period in question. For the years before World War II, many Western nations have made military and diplomatic files related to intelligence available to scholars, although often not the files of the actual intelligence bureaus. Many researchers in intelligence are interested in the period of the Cold War and its aftermath, however, and declassifications for them are typically piecemeal and incomplete. In some countries few if any records have been declassified. The bulk of those released in the United States represent finished intelligence products.[4] Few policy or administrative documents, and even fewer operational records, are available. Complete files are rarer still.

Church Committee

Integrating the inside and the outside is another parallel with ancient history. When real documents begin turning up in public archives, it can be tricky to match them up with the accreted legends that both informed and were themselves formed by an earlier body of literature written without any access to the sources. Ancient historians have to do a similar thing in trying to square the tangible discoveries of modern archeology with the epics of Homer, for instance, or the writings of Herodotus. Indeed, here is the capital shortcoming of intelligence scholarship on the outside: the lack of reliable data, and the consequent inability to determine when all the important records have been consulted.

News reports that are roughly contemporaneous with the activity under scrutiny are useful for both inside and outside research. They are fragmentary and often wrong, but they have a certain vitality and immediacy, and they not infrequently touch on ground truth (sometimes better than reporters know). Some intelligence operations show up in garbled form in the newspapers not long after they take place. The trouble for any outside observer is that of determining which of the myriad press reports accurately reflect real activities. This can be all but impossible to do, even for friendly intelligence officers reading in the newspapers about contemporary operations that security compartmentation gives them no formal access to. For adversaries it can be even tougher.

Memoirs of intelligence professionals, and of decisionmakers who relied on them, are often useful, especially if one bears in mind the adage that no memoirist loses an argument in his own memorandum-for-the-record. There are few "inside" memoirs, produced by an officer given access to the classified files and written as part of his official duties. Occasionally, a senior official will be given limited access to selected files some years after her retirement, and her manuscript will be sanitized to remove any classified information before it is published. More typical is the memoir produced with no access at all. A handful of memoirs are themselves small-scale intelligence operations – witness Kim Philby's *My Silent War*, produced while Philby was a pet of the KGB in Moscow.[5] His subtle mockery of CIA counterintelligence chief James Angleton – to name but one example – must be viewed according to how it may have served the KGB's interests to embarrass a pillar of its Main Enemy's defenses.

Oral histories should be viewed in a similar light. There are a surprising number of former intelligence officers at large who can be (but usually have not been) interviewed. Indeed, at the time of this writing, there are still several hundred living intelligence veterans of World War II, a handful of them actually working with US intelligence organizations today, six decades removed from the end of the war. This (sometimes) allows researchers to have their drafts commented on by participants in the historical events, or at least by people who knew "how it felt" to do intelligence work in 1944, or 1964, or 1984. Oral history, however, falls in the same historiographical genre as the memoir literature and has to be judged by basically the same rules (indeed, when the subject of an oral history has died, the transcript of his or her interview is for all intents and purposes an informal memoir). The advantages and pitfalls of oral history are well known, and need not be reviewed here. Researchers on the outside probably make better use of oral history than their counterparts on the inside, in part because for the former, memories may be their only sources.

Research methods

Intelligence emerged as a professional discipline before and during World War I, first in Britain, and soon afterward in the other belligerents. It developed from three prior disciplines: diplomacy, reconnaissance, and internal security, and the dividing lines between it and these fields have remained ambiguous, and porous. The scholar of it must know something of each of these fields – particularly how states defend themselves and employ their "levers of national power" – to understand intelligence. Just as the sources for intelligence history are often the same as those used by military and diplomatic historians, the methods are similar as well.

The sources largely determine the methods, in the sense that one must work with what one has. Over the last three decades we have seen rapid progress in the methods of historical inquiry in intelligence. The key to this development has been scholarly access to (and use of) declassified intelligence files from several of the combatants in World War II. That war was a conflict so vast and revolutionary (for some aspects of intelligence) that a familiarity with its details affords insights into the functioning of all twentieth-century intelligence disciplines and many of the organizations that undertook them. The benefits of this heightened understanding have particularly enriched scholarship among academic and private researchers in intelligence, but its independent impact on official historians in the intelligence agencies should not be overlooked. It affords them detailed knowledge of the personnel and precedents of Cold War agencies, and provides bases for comparison across agencies, disciplines, and even national intelligence systems. The resulting progress in methodology, both inside and outside the intelligence agencies, has at last raised intelligence scholarship in many instances to the level of quality achieved by diplomatic and military historians a generation or more earlier.

The key method for inside researchers – and their chief methodological advantage – is the drafting of a reliable chronology for the activity or organization under scrutiny. It is easier to write a coherent narrative when one can say what happened first, next, and last. Where chronology is not, or cannot be, established, the conclusions drawn from the evidence must be regarded as tentative or even as suspect. Chronology is a vital clue in sorting causes and effects, and more than one "urban legend" circulated among intelligence officials (and even among scholars) has been debunked by the simple method of carefully charting events along a reliable time sequence.

Chronology is vital in another way as well. Knowing not only the sequence of activities and events but also the timing of the production and subsequent release of (both internal and public) information about them helps one judge the value of secondary reference materials (and even of some primary sources). It is crucial to understand how much material was and was not available to the author of a history or the drafter of a memo. This is an obvious factor to consider in reading the work of historians on the outside. Anything written about strategic intelligence and military campaigns against Germany in World War II, for instance, must be read with particular care if it was published before the revelation of the ULTRA secret in 1974. Similarly with works on certain Cold War espionage cases in the United States, if published before the public release in 1995 of the "Venona" cables (the decryptions of Soviet intelligence telegrams sent to and from foreign posts, mostly during World War II). It is a factor to consider when reading histories written by government historians as well. Several early official histories of US intelligence, for example, were written without access to the mysteries of signals intelligence or "humint" operations. This reality does not falsify the arguments or discredit the facts cited in works published before these key releases, but it does make them incomplete in important ways.

Inside researchers also have an advantage in being able to establish reliable organizational charts. They can determine the degrees and channels of command and control. It is crucial to chart the hierarchy of organizations, sub-units, and personnel; accurate knowledge can hardly be overstated in its importance to understanding activities that take place in secret for the benefit of a handful of decisionmakers. This can also be done by outside researchers, when enough files are available; witness the labors of Philip H.J. Davies in charting the early history of Britain's MI6.[6] Determining subordination can be tricky for an observer of intelligence agencies, however, even when the individual under scrutiny held military rank. Not a few intelligence officers in the past have held deceptively insignificant ranks or titles, yet wielded considerable influence in their own agencies, and even over rival or allied organizations working in the same locale (Sir William Wiseman of MI6 during World War I comes to mind in this context).[7]

Another avenue into what intelligence was doing in a particular capital or operation is to undertake a careful reading of the political, diplomatic, and military events that provided the backdrop for the intelligence activities in question. Understanding what a president, premier, or commander had in mind (and what was far from his mind) provides a vital clue to a researcher. It allows later observers to speculate as to what those decisionmakers might have asked their intelligence operatives to obtain, to do, or to prevent. Whether one finds documentation of such "requirements" that way will obviously depend on whether the requirements were levied or not – on whether the leader actually asked for such results from his intelligence services, and whether the operatives in those agencies had the will and the capability to meet his needs.

The researcher should also read what the target of the intelligence activities has to say about the subject operation (or the agency that mounted it). That is, if a target says anything at all – in some instances an adversary never notices his pocket was picked. But ordinarily the adversary discovers the operation or activity at some point, and reacts. The scope and sharpness of that reaction can reveal how effective the operation might have been. Indeed, this gets close to another "method" for understanding intelligence activities: that of gauging the impact of an operation on the enemy. What if anything did it make him do, or what options did it deny him? If it seemingly did nothing, why not? These are vital questions to ask, and to answer, although they entail a significant risk. More than one researcher (and practitioner) has become captivated by the action-reaction-deception nature of the clandestine world and consequently been lost in the "wilderness of mirrors" that some critics take all intelligence work to be.   *risky*

Conclusion

Guarding against such wandering among the mirrors of spy legends can be a difficult task, given the paucity of sources, but it is ultimately a worthwhile one. The researcher has three principal defenses, or rather three standards that transcend the seemingly closed world of secret activities. These are comparison, objectivity, and impact. All are tough to achieve, but consistently aspiring to achieve them has the beneficial effect of keeping intelligence scholarship from wandering into partisanship or irrelevance.

Both inside and outside scholars have sought to compare and contrast intelligence disciplines and organizations across multiple national experiences and time periods. Unfortunately, this is not yet possible to do in a systematic manner. Among large nations, only the United States has declassified almost all of its intelligence files from before 1941, and US intelligence before World War II still lacked certain operational components that several other countries had already developed. Undeterred, several scholars – Glenn Hastedt, Kevin O'Connell, and the late Adda Bozeman, among them – have done promising work in this field, drawing what seem to be valid generalizations from the secondary literature.[8] But even these pioneers of comparative intelligence systems would readily concede that their judgments must be tentative ones for the time being.

Objectivity is vital in intelligence scholarship. Partisan or bureaucratic biases have always afflicted writings about recent and contemporary events, of course, but they are easy to spot and probably do not do permanent harm. Many authors, of many persuasions, have managed to set such biases aside and write valuable works on intelligence. What is more debilitating in the long run is the subtler (and less conscious) bias that seeps in from the researcher's basic approach to writing intelligence history. One should remember that a bias can be for something or someone as well as against it. In the present case, one may be forgiven for concluding that academic historians will tend to favor "complexity" in their explanations; that journalists like to tell a good story, and that official historians will give their own agency the benefit of the doubt when narrating disputes with other agencies. All researchers, moreover, can tend to privilege the views of the people who talked to them or were thoughtful enough to write things down and save their files. The historian must bear in mind the adage that "the man who saves his files tells the story" − but that man's piece of the story may not always be the most interesting or important part. Bias is admittedly a hazard for scholars working in the records of any organization, and not just for intelligence historians. It probably is a more serious one for intelligence scholars, however, given the paucity of reliable source material. Therefore the obligation to adhere to objective standards and judgments is all the heavier.

What these methods collectively point to is a constant need to search for the impact that intelligence made on events. The researcher, both inside and outside the organization, must constantly ask what it was that an intelligence agency actually accomplished with the mission, resources, and authorities allotted to it. How well did it serve decisionmakers in their deliberations and the conduct of their offices? These are tricky questions to answer even with full access. Determining how well an agency worked with what it had to work with is the intelligence scholars' contribution to achieving the ultimate goal of all intelligence scholarship: learning how intelligence made a difference. Did it make policy more effective, or less, and why? That in turn is a question that ultimately has to be answered by a community of intelligence scholars, both those on the inside and those on the outside, who can compare their respective sources and methods and reach consensus on the best ones to apply to various historical issues and questions. It is also a question that must be addressed by scholars of national and international affairs writ large, who must bring their techniques to bear alongside the findings of the intelligence scholars in crafting a fuller understanding of the past.

Patient and sometimes brilliant scholarship, both inside and outside the spy agencies, has taught us much about the history and the nature of intelligence. Such progress has been accomplished despite the problems faced by both "inside" and "outside" researchers. Those on the outside lack access to the full official record, while those on inside have a subtler but still serious impairment: their inability to have their findings reviewed by the optimum range of scholarly peers, and thus to consider the fullest possible context for their conclusions. Nonetheless, one can be encouraged by the growing tendency of official, academic, and private researchers alike to conclude from their studies that intelligence is, in the most charitable sense of the term, subordinate. By definition, it does not make decisions, negotiate treaties, win wars, or settle disputes; those functions are performed by policymakers, diplomats, judges, commanders, and their staffs. It is neither an omniscient conspiracy, nor an omnipotent panacea. Intelligence is a support function, sometimes usefully informing and implementing decisions. Its contribution assists (or hampers) national leaders in the conduct of their duties, but it cannot perform said duties for them. Beware any piece of scholarship that says it has.

Michael Warner serves as the Historian for the Office of the Director of National Intelligence. The opinions voiced in this article are his own, and do not represent those of the Office of the Director of National Intelligence or any other US Government entity.

Notes

1 The Chilean campaign is discussed in detail by Kristian C. Gustafson in "CIA Machinations in Chile in 1970," *Studies in Intelligence* 47 (2003).
2 See Gerald Haines' addendum on this plot in Nicholas Cullather, *Secret History: The CIA's Classified Account of its Operations in Guatemala, 1952–1954* (Palo Alto, CA: Stanford University Press, 1999).
3 "My purpose is not to relate at length every motion, but only such as were conspicuous for excellence or notorious for infamy. This I regard as history's highest function, to let no worthy action be uncommemorated, and to hold out the reprobation of posterity as a terror to evil words and deeds." Tacitus, *Annals*, III:65.
4 James Van Hook of the Department of State observes that the most authoritative varieties of finished intelligence – such as the American "National Intelligence Estimates" – are truly committee products produced under tightly controlled conditions. In that way, and others, they may represent prime specimens for the application of textual "deconstruction" and other critical methods.
5 Kim Philby, *My Silent War* (New York: Grove, 1968).
6 Philip H.J. Davies, *MI6 and the Machinery of Spying: Structure and Process in Britain's Secret Intelligence* (London: Frank Cass, 2004).
7 Richard B. Spence, "Englishmen in New York: The SIS American Station, 1915–21," *Intelligence and National Security* 19/3 (2005).
8 Glenn P. Hastedt, "Towards the Comparative Study of Intelligence," *Conflict Quarterly*, 11/3 (Summer 1991). Kevin O'Connell, "Thinking About Intelligence Comparatively," *Brown Journal of World Affairs*, Vol. 11/1 (Summer/Fall 2004). Adda Bozeman, "Political Intelligence in Non-Western Societies: Suggestions for Comparative Research," in Roy Godson, ed., *Comparing Foreign Intelligence: The US, the USSR, the UK, and the Third World* (Washington, DC: Pergamon-Brassey's, 1988).

2

The American approach to intelligence studies

James J. Wirtz

Introduction

Is there an American approach to the study of intelligence? The question calls to mind Russell Weigley's *The American Way of War*, which suggested that Americans did in fact have a national "style" when it came to warfare. According to Weigley, Americans preferred to obliterate their opponents through attrition, not to use limited means for limited objectives.[1] Although many have disputed Weigley's characterization of the American way of warfare,[2] his work renewed interest in the idea that the way officers and officials wage war is influenced by strategic culture, and this idea has been championed and contested by succeeding generations of strategic theorists. Yet, this debate about strategic military culture has not been mirrored by a similar discussion about the existence of a specific American approach to intelligence or intelligence studies.

Some might argue that it makes little sense to describe a national approach to intelligence or intelligence studies because any such characterization would have to reflect either unflattering stereotypes or overly generous depictions of a nation's intelligence attributes or weaknesses. Moreover, it would be easy to think of an exception that disproves every observation about national style. For example, Americans are not particularly accomplished practitioners of denial and deception because they prefer to flaunt their superior military capabilities before potential opponents in the hope of getting them to comply with US demands without a fight.[3] British officers and officials deserve the bulk of the credit for Allied deception operations during World War II. Analysts repeatedly warned about the effectiveness of Soviet *maskarova* (deception) during the Cold War, while noting that the United States lacked a similar capability. Yet, Barton Whaley, one of the greatest students of deception, is an American.[4] Consequently, Whaley's body of work could easily be used as a prima facie refutation of the idea that "Americans don't do deception." National intelligence style also is a relative term. Americans' apparent lack of interest in human intelligence (HUMINT) only becomes clear when one contemplates how Russian or Chinese intelligence agencies strive to cultivate networks of active agents and sleeper cells across the globe to seek out information of interest. Without a complete and consistent comparative framework for assessing intelligence culture, it will always be a simple matter to point out inconsistent, partial or biased characterizations of national intelligence efforts and scholarship. Additionally, by highlighting some scholarly efforts at the expense of others, any attempt to identify a national approach to intelligence or intelligence studies will further downplay the part played by scholars, practitioners or literatures that are already in short supply in a given state.

With these caveats in mind, however, one may venture to characterize the American study of intelligence, which to some extent is also reflected in the actual conduct of foreign and domestic intelligence in the United States. Four factors shape the American approach to intelligence studies. First, Americans are relatively open even about their most secret intelligence organizations and practices. As a result of deliberate and inadvertent revelations about finished intelligence and the sources and methods employed in intelligence analysis, Americans periodically obtain accurate and important insights about the actual capabilities and state of affairs within the US intelligence community. Second, American intelligence professionals and scholars have embraced an intelligence paradigm that uses a combination of the scientific method and history to understand both intelligence pathologies and best practices. While some foreign intelligence agencies and scholars treat intelligence as a subject worthy of organized inquiry – here Israeli scholars and intelligence practitioners come to mind – most countries lack a scholarly community that addresses the subject of intelligence. Third, Americans focus on intelligence oversight and the issues raised by the presence of secret organizations within democracy. Indeed, concerns about the abuse of secrecy and surveillance have recently been exacerbated by intelligence activities undertaken on the domestic front in the Global War on Terror. Fourth, Americans have a strong bias towards technical intelligence. This emphasis on technical collection systems comes at the expense of HUMINT and better tradecraft, and creates an expectation that no area of the earth is beyond technical surveillance. Yet technical collection systems are not equally capable against all targets, and some opponents have become quite sophisticated in defeating "overhead surveillance" systems.

The chapter will unfold by discussing each of these traits that contribute to the American approach to intelligence. It will conclude by offering some observations about the ability of this style of intelligence study and practice to cope with today's security challenges.

A culture of openness

The US intelligence community is made up of bureaucracies that work in secrecy and deal in secrets. Its personnel are screened through rigorous procedures to help prevent leaks of classified information and penetration by foreign intelligence agencies. Counterintelligence programs and hiring procedures also attempt to stop unstable people, who might have habits or weaknesses that make them vulnerable to blackmail, from ever getting on the intelligence payroll. Information also is restricted in terms of levels of secrecy and compartmentalization, i.e. regardless of one's security clearance, access to information is granted on a "need to know" basis. In terms of day-to-day operations, the US intelligence community is set up to maintain the secrecy of its operations. Its output, finished intelligence, is intended for senior officials and officers. Most countries have intelligence organizations that would more or less match this description of the US intelligence community.

Compared to other nations, however, Americans appear to be remarkably open about discussing policies, procedures, failures and even the tradecraft employed by their intelligence organizations. There are several traditions that create this culture of openness. First, in the aftermath of strategic surprise, official intelligence post-mortems, often conducted by blue-ribbon commissions or Congressional committees, collect the facts about the disaster that has recently transpired. These committees attempt to determine exactly what intelligence shortfalls contributed to the calamity, and to suggest fixes to prevent future instances of strategic surprise. The most famous, or at least the longest-lived, intelligence inquiry involved the surprise attack suffered by the United States at Pearl Harbor, Oahu on December 7, 1941. To date, there have been *ten* official investigations of this incident. In fact, the last, official word on the attack was issued December 15, 1995 when Undersecretary of Defense Edwin Dorn rejected a plea to restore posthumously Rear Admiral Husband E. Kimmel, USN (who was the commander of the US Pacific Fleet in December 1941) and Major General Walter Short, USA (who was responsible for the defense of Hawaii in December 1941) to their highest wartime rank. Similarly, the Congressional Joint Inquiry into the September 11, 2001 terrorist attacks on the United States, chaired by Senator Bob Graham and Congressman Porter Goss, and the subsequent 9/11 Commission (the National Commission on Terror Attacks) issued significant reports on the events leading up to the al-Qaeda strikes against the World Trade Center and the Pentagon. Influenced by the Pearl Harbor inquiries, especially the way Roberta Wholstetter used the findings of the penultimate investigation of Pearl Harbor, the Joint Congressional Committee on the Investigation of the Pearl Harbor attack, to write her famous treatise on surprise, *Pearl Harbor Warning and Decision*, the 9/11 commissioners attempted to capture the context of the September 11, 2001 disaster. The Commissioners wanted to create an historical record that would be a launching point for future scholarship on the tragedy.[5] In the aftermath of intelligence failure, the American intelligence community has been subjected to intense public and official scrutiny, which creates a treasure trove of information for scholars interested in intelligence.

Second, accusations of scandal or abuse of intelligence power often push aside the veil of secrecy surrounding intelligence organizations, providing scholars with additional insights into relationships between officials and intelligence professionals. These investigations not only reveal much about the sources and methods used to produce finished intelligence, but also information about covert intelligence operations. Investigations by the Pike and Church Committees in the 1970s, for example, produced a laundry list of questionable Central Intelligence Agency (CIA) operations, everything from experiments with LSD to various assassination attempts against Fidel Castro. In a political atmosphere dominated by the US defeat in Vietnam and revelations about the Watergate scandal, many Americans believed that the CIA was a "rogue elephant" that was beyond the control of elected officials and standard government regulation. More recently, Congressional scrutiny of the Iran-Contra scandal during the Reagan administration provided insights into the shadowy world of covert operations and diplomacy.[6] The Commission on the Intelligence Capabilities of the United States Regarding Weapons of Mass Destruction also offered insights into US collection and analytic capabilities following the failure to assess accurately the status of Iraq's ability to manufacture and stockpile chemical, biological or nuclear weapons.[7]

Third, elected officials sometimes deliberately reveal classified information in support of US foreign policy and diplomacy. These revelations not only divulge classified information, but they also disclose much about the sources and methods that go into intelligence production. Probably the most famous and dramatic use of intelligence to bolster US diplomacy was undertaken by the John F. Kennedy administration during the Cuban Missile Crisis. On October 25, 1962, Ambassador Adlai Stevenson's use of photo reconnaissance pictures taken by U-2 spy planes and low-level surveillance aircraft in a presentation at a UN Security Council meeting convinced the world that the Soviets were deploying ballistic missiles in Cuba, while simultaneously highlighting US photoreconnaissance capabilities. In a speech delivered to the nation on September 5, 1983, President Ronald Reagan also provided insights into US Signals Intelligence (SIGINT) capabilities by playing a tape of conversations between Soviet ground controllers and the pilots of Soviet interceptor aircraft as they zeroed in on Korean Airlines Flight 007. The decision to release intercepts of Soviet military communication helped gain international support for the idea that the Soviet government and military acted in a reckless fashion by shooting down a civilian airliner on September 1, 1983, but it also revealed much about US SIGINT capabilities. In fact, Secretary of State Colin Powell's speech to the UN General Assembly on February 13, 2003 incorporated misleading SIGINT and photographic intelligence of Iraq's alleged WMD capabilities. Powell, who described the speech as "the lowest point" in his life, provided a convincing demonstration of the limits of technical intelligence and the weaknesses of US analytical capabilities.[8]

Fourth, in the United States, intelligence commissions and blue ribbon panels often attempt to identify problems and make recommendations to improve intelligence procedures or organizations.[9] Several of these studies provided recommendations that would have improved coordination between the Federal Bureau of Investigation (FBI) and the intelligence community, possibly eliminating the "seams" between US domestic and international intelligence and law enforcement activities and institutions that were exploited by al-Qaeda on September 11, 2001. A report issued in 2000 by the National Commission on Terrorism, which was headed by Ambassador Paul Bremmer, for example, called for a series of reforms that would have improved the ability of the US intelligence community to meet the terrorist threat. The Commission called for measures clarifying the FBI's authority to investigate terrorist groups, eliminating CIA regulations that hindered the use of informants linked to terrorist organizations, placing terrorism high on the agendas of officials at the CIA, FBI and National Security Agency, and establishing new reporting procedures to deliver quickly information related to terrorism to all interested officials.[10]

Fifth, deliberate or inadvertent leaks of classified information are commonplace. Much to the chagrin of intelligence professionals, elected officials can and do reveal classified information when they believe that such information should be in the public realm or if disclosure becomes a convenient means to achieve a political end. Sometimes the disclosure of classified information is inadvertent. Sometimes it is undertaken because it is sensational or helps to undermine existing policies. Classified information that the intelligence community had monitored overseas calls made by US citizens, maintained prison facilities for terrorist suspects in foreign countries, or even monitored mosques in the United States for evidence of radioactive substances became public, despite the fact that these programs were considered important national security secrets. This unauthorized and illegal disclosure of classified information gives intelligence professionals fits,[11] but as long as officials have an interest in providing this information to the press, "leaks" will remain commonplace. ouch.

When combined, intended and unintended disclosures of finished intelligence reports, information about intelligence operations, and insights into intelligence sources and methods provide scholars with large amounts of what was recently classified information from secret organizations. This information provides a sufficient historical record to support serious scholarship on intelligence matters in the United States. Few states generate as much documentary evidence about their intelligence activities as the US government, and this relative openness is a necessary condition for the American approach to intelligence.

The intelligence paradigm

The intelligence paradigm developed by the American scholarly community is an effort to apply analytic methodologies and insights drawn from the social sciences, to understand the fundamental nature of intelligence, to explain the history of intelligence successes and failures, to understand intelligence organizations and processes, and to assess and improve upon the craft of analysis itself.[12] While Israeli[13] and British[14] scholars have contributed greatly to this paradigm, other states and scholarly communities often fail to apply any sort of social science methodology to their study or production of intelligence. For instance, Soviet intelligence services, the KGB (Komityet Gosudarstvennoii Bezopasnosti) and the GRU (Glavnoe Rasvedyvatel'noe Upravlenie) relied on espionage or the open press for information and largely functioned as a clipping service for the Kremlin. During the Cuban Missile Crisis, Soviet Premier Nikita Khrushchev also served as his own intelligence analyst.[15] Because many dictatorships have used intelligence agencies as instruments of domestic surveillance and terror, the "counterintelligence state," in its many varieties, was never a safe subject for study by those subjected to its abuses.[16]

Political scientists, historians, psychologists and practitioners have all played an important part in creating the intelligence paradigm. Those who work within this paradigm, unlike most other endeavors in the social sciences, share a general agreement about methodology, data, the issues to be addressed, and the problems that remain to be resolved. Most are concerned with exploring the intelligence cycle: setting intelligence requirements, collecting data, analyzing data, and disseminating finished intelligence. Alexander George, for example, has suggested that intelligence failure can occur at any point in the intelligence cycle, if intelligence professionals and policymakers fail to answer any one of six questions: (1) identifying the adversary (who?); (2) estimating the probability of attack (whether?); (3) determining the type of action involved (what?); (4) determining the location of the attack (where?); (5) estimating the timing of the action (when?); (6) determining the motivation behind the initiative (why?).[17] This scholarship strives to understand why failures of intelligence occur and to devise best practices when it comes to analyzing and disseminating intelligence.

In their search for answers to the questions that frame the intelligence paradigm, scholars and practitioners focus on four levels of analysis: factors that are idiosyncratic to the production of finished intelligence; human cognition; organizational behavior; and the relationship between the intelligence community and policymakers. In terms of idiosyncratic factors, analysts often explore problems that complicate the intelligence cycle. The "Cry Wolf," syndrome, for example, occurs when analysts repeatedly sound false alarms that causes recipients to dismiss what eventually turns out to be a legitimate alert. The "Ultra" syndrome, named after the codeword given to Allied signals intelligence intercepts during World War II, occurs when analysts become overly reliant on an accurate and timely source of information.[18] Although the information revolution has created many benefits and challenges for society, it also has introduced new intelligence pathologies. Observers ritualistically point out that analysts are constantly at risk of being overwhelmed by a deluge of information from both open and classified sources. Yet, the real danger may be the fact that, within this data stream, there is little *valuable* information about the highest priority targets and issues facing analysts. Additionally, the demand for current, original and even entertaining intelligence products is so great that the drumbeat of constant intelligence warning and analysis output may take on a life of its own, creating an impression of certainty, threat, and immediacy that is not justified by the contents and data used in the production of finished intelligence.[19]

Scholars have turned to human cognition and psychology to understand both intelligence successes and failures. Scholars have identified several common cognitive biases that can impede analysis. Mirror imaging, the tendency to interpret another actor's behavior using one's beliefs, experiences, values, or standard operating procedures, can impede the creation of accurate estimates. Individuals also tend to see the behavior of other actors to be highly rational in the sense that all policy and action is directed toward achieving specific objectives, even though similar behavior is beyond their own personal or even bureaucratic capacity.[20] A host of these biases can bedevil analysts; practitioners have even devised methodologies to help analysts avoid common cognitive errors.[21]

Today, many observers criticize analysts for a lack of imagination or a failure to "connect the dots" when it comes to anticipating the nefarious activities of terrorist syndicates or the next move made by the megalomaniacal leaders of kleptocracies. There is, in fact, a little recognized "rationality bias" inherent in official analysis, making it difficult to acknowledge truly irrational or maniacal behavior on the part of states, criminal syndicates or terrorist networks. Yet, what generally inhibits "imaginative" analysis is "the concept": shared assumptions among analysts and policymakers of what constitutes rational behavior on the part of a potential opponent.[22] Prior to the 1973 Yom Kippur War, for example, Israeli officials based their defense policy on three assumptions: Egypt would be at the center of any Arab coalition against Israel, Egypt would not undertake a significant attack without a strong prospect of victory, and, unless Egypt destroyed the Israeli Air Force, an Arab victory was not possible. Israeli officials also believed that their intelligence agencies would provide a "war warning" in time for them to mobilize their reserves or even launch a pre-emptive attack, actions that would produce an Arab rout. The effects of "the concept" on policymakers and analysts alike was staggering. Even though they were equipped with actual Syrian and Egyptian war plans, reconnaissance photographs showing unprecedented force deployments along the Suez Canal and Golan Heights, a warning from a credible and trusted spy within the inner circle of the Egyptian government, information that Soviet personnel and dependents were high-tailing it out of Cairo and Damascus, and signals intelligence suggesting that their opponents were about to strike, the Israelis never managed to act as if they were about to be hit by an all-out Arab assault. As a result, the outbreak of the 1973 Yom Kippur War was marked by one of the greatest intelligence-command failures in military history.[23] The "concept" held sway, despite some unusually compelling contradictory evidence. Similarly, the idea that Saddam Hussein had used chemical weapons, had gone to great lengths to procure WMD, and appeared willing to bear enormous costs to hide his WMD infrastructure from the prying eyes of UNSCOM, was seen by US analysts as prima facie evidence that Iraq retained a WMD capability. Their concept of Iraqi behavior and intentions, not hard evidence, shaped analysts estimates of Iraq's WMD capability.

Scholars also have turned to organizational behavior for insights into the production of finished intelligence. Compartmentalizaton, for example, is endemic in intelligence production because the "need to know" principle governs individual analysts' access to information. But organizations are jealous guardians of information and bureaucratic rivalry or differences in standard operating procedures can slow the flow of information within organizations or across the intelligence community to a trickle. Bureaucratic rivalry also can take on a life of its own; the quest to trump analysts from other organizations can take precedence over the effort to serve the needs of policymakers.[24] Small-group dynamics can also shape intelligence estimates: the well-known phenomenon of "group think" can emerge among small teams of analysts and intelligence managers. Institutional affiliation also tends to color one's perceptions and prescriptions, and it is a rare analyst or manager who will advance a position that is at odds with the interests of his or her home organization or career interests. Bureaucracy itself – hierarchy, specialization, centralization, routine, and secrecy – and the need to continuously justify budgets and priorities, which creates an endless reporting requirements and innovative "metrics," all work to impede creative thinking and effective analysis.

The fourth level of analysis, the intelligence–policy nexus, focuses on how relations between intelligence professionals and policymakers shape the dissemination and response to finished intelligence and warning. A variety of problems can emerge to bedevil relations between the intelligence and policymaking communities. The best-known pathology, politicization, emerges when policymakers place overt or subtle pressure on intelligence analysts and managers to produce intelligence estimates that support current political preferences or policies. Although there is no consensus about what constitutes best practices when it comes to intelligence–policy interaction, two schools compete as a guide to relations between policymakers and the intelligence community. One school of thought, most closely associated with the work of Sherman Kent, focuses on ensuring the independence of intelligence analysts.[25] Kent's thinking, which shaped the evolution of the US intelligence community, identifies the importance of political and policy detachment in producing finished intelligence. The other school, most closely associated with the reforms instituted in the mid-1980s by then Director of Central Intelligence Robert M. Gates, focuses on producing "actionable" intelligence, information of immediate and direct use to policymakers.[26] To produce actionable intelligence, analysts have to maintain close working relationships with policymakers, literally looking into the policymakers' inboxes to make sure finished intelligence addresses important policy issues of the day.

Scholars also are beginning to explore new developments in the intelligence–policy nexus. The information revolution is creating new points of friction as intelligence analysts and policymakers interact using less formal channels of communication, producing new challenges for those charged with monitoring the contents of finished intelligence – formal written reports that reflect a deliberate judgment made by analysts and backed by the intelligence community. Other scholars are focusing on the political costs of responding to surprise. In contrast to the tentative estimates often offered by the intelligence community, the costs of responding to possible threats are clear, which makes elected officials leery of responding to warnings that might turn out to be false alarms. To overcome this reluctance to act on all but the most compelling warning, new ways to undertake limited alerts of military and police forces have to be devised, eliminating the need to place an entire city on a "war footing" in response to uncertain threat assessments.

Intelligence oversight

Students of public policy and government also have contributed to the American approach to intelligence studies by undertaking an open and evolving project dealing with the oversight of secret organizations within a democracy. The United States is based upon the idea of limited government: intelligence operations and intelligence agencies are subjected to uneven government oversight. During the Cold War, many elected officials believed that the intelligence community needed to be given free rein, at least overseas, in fighting the militarily powerful Soviet Union and the ideological menace posed by communism. In the aftermath of the Vietnam War, however, this attitude changed and during a series of hearings in 1975, Congressional committees heard about a variety of misdeeds perpetrated by the intelligence community: plots to assassinate foreign leaders, wiretaps, drug experiments and plans to conduct surveillance against US citizens who chose to express their right to protest government policies. In response to these revelations of misconduct, improved Congressional and executive branch oversight was launched: the Senate Select Committee on Intelligence, the White House Intelligence Oversight Board, and a House Permanent Select Committee on Intelligence were all created during the 1970s.[27]

The academic question at the heart of intelligence oversight has been stated succinctly by

Marvin Ott: "Can a democracy maintain an effective, capable intelligence service without doing violence to the norms, processes and institutions of democracy itself?"[28] Thus, the debate about intelligence oversight is generally between those who want more Congressional effort to monitor intelligence activities and to protect civil liberties, and those who believe that too much oversight can hamper the intelligence community, especially in its conduct of covert operations overseas and domestic intelligence-gathering. In the American context, democracy usually trumps the needs of secret organizations: Congress, an institution based on the open, public debate of policy issues, has responsibility for oversight of the intelligence community. But the proper balance between secrecy and openness, between the needs of national security and civil liberties, at least from a political perspective, reflects threat perceptions. When threats are high, most observers seem willing to give the intelligence community more leeway. When threats are reduced – a time when past "intelligence abuses" often become public – most observers clamor for greater intelligence oversight.

The September 11, 2001 attacks revealed that terrorist cells had indeed penetrated the United States and that al-Qaeda was committed to killing Americans. Events overseas – the bombings in 2004 of Madrid trains, of Bali tourists in 2002 and 2005, of the Marriott Hotel in Jakarta in 2003, and in 2005 of the London Underground and Amman hotel – continue to highlight the fact that al-Qaeda and its sympathizers are hell bent on creating death and destruction. To many observers, this ongoing threat is evidence of a need to strengthen US foreign and domestic intelligence and police efforts. Debate about these efforts, and the renewal by Congress of the USA Patriot Act of 2001, are just the latest chapters of the ongoing debate about the role of secret organizations and surveillance in democracy. This dialogue is likely to continue indefinitely because scholars, and the American public, want both civil liberties and a shield against foreign threats. As Loch Johnson has recently noted, both scholars and intelligence practitioners alike will continue to "search . . . to find the right formula for power sharing in this most difficult of government domains – knowing full well that no formula exists, only the hope that in the spirit of comity, the Congress, the executive, and the courts will carry on the quest for a modus vivendi that takes into account liberty and security."[29]

The American technological bias

Americans have an obsession with technology, which is reflected in their approach to intelligence. US HUMINT efforts are relatively undeveloped. Intelligence managers are limited in their ability to traffic with the kinds of unsavory characters who are able to penetrate terrorist or criminal networks. Gaining access to agents in "denied areas," a significant problem during the Cold War, still hamstrings HUMINT operations today. Targets of greatest interest – North Korea comes to mind – are probably the most closed and tightly policed societies in the world. Intelligence managers and analysts increasingly turn to open-source intelligence (OSINT) to make up shortfalls in HUMINT, but they apparently have a bias against over-reliance on sources readily available to the public. If the Internet is all that is required to stay informed, then who would need special organizations with access to secret information?

Since the early 1960s, analysts have come to rely increasingly on technical collection methods to access denied areas of interest or for general surveillance. Some of these systems are ground-based or rely on aerial reconnaissance, but most of them are deployed in space and are dependent on satellite access to low-earth or geo-synchronous orbit. The best-known technical collection systems rely on satellite photography (imagery) or IMINT. Originally based on technology requiring the physical retrieval of exposed film, which parachuted to earth in a capsule, today's IMINT satellites can provide digital high-resolution images in real time. SIGINT, or signals intelligence, is eavesdropping on all sorts of communication and often provides insights by listening into unencrypted conversations. Over time, even encrypted transmissions can be made to reveal important information By undertaking analysis of encrypted communications, command relationships as well as patterns and levels of activity can be discerned. The movements of specific individuals can be tracked, especially if they use cellular or satellite telephones to communicate. Measurement and Signatures Intelligence (MASINT) is the collection of information about the capabilities and location of an opponent's electronic systems or even industrial processes. For instance, waste plumes emanating from smokestacks can be monitored to detect the presence of trace elements associated with the manufacture of chemical weapons.

Although the American fascination with and reliance on technical collection systems has yielded enormous benefits, these systems also create costs. There is a tendency, for example, to believe that they have increased international transparency and that virtually nothing is beyond their reach. In reality, technical collection systems are best at monitoring significant industrial processes and manufacturing operations, large military units, and crew-served weapons. Small manufacturing operations and micro-scale industry are difficult to identify. Individuals or small units can blend into the background of everyday activities, making them difficult to detect or monitor. Some opponents also are aware of US surveillance capabilities and can take rudimentary measures that significantly degrade the ability of US systems to monitor their activities.[30] The emphasis on technical collection systems also draws interest and attention away from HUMINT and efforts to improve tradecraft. Technical collection is important, but it must be incorporated into an effective analytical process to yield real benefits.

Humint also impt.

In lieu of conclusions

Is there an American approach to intelligence studies that differs from other national styles? This chapter suggests that the American approach to intelligence and intelligence studies shares several characteristics that support this idea. Americans live in an open society and are kept relatively well informed through a variety of inadvertent and deliberate revelations about the intelligence community. American scholars also combine history and an approximation of the scientific method to study intelligence pathologies and best practices. Indeed, the intelligence paradigm emerged nearly twenty years ago and continues to produce a coherent research agenda. American scholars and practitioners also devote much attention to understanding the role of secret organizations within democracy and devising the proper balance between effectiveness and restraint when it comes to intelligence organizations. The American fascination with technology also influences the US approach to intelligence collection: practitioners and scholars alike are preoccupied with technical collection systems at the expense of other methods for collecting information.

American and non-American participants in the intelligence paradigm exhibit a vitality not present among other scholarly communities. Unlike other countries, where the study of intelligence might be underdeveloped or even taboo outside of official circles, intelligence studies are considered to be a legitimate academic field within the United States. Scholars continue to address new problems uncovered by the latest intelligence fiasco or to devise better methods of intelligence oversight. In a negative sense, a preoccupation with technology threatens the American analytic tradition as both scholars and practitioners mistakenly seek technical solutions for problems rooted in the limits of human cognition or bureaucracy. Yet, as long as a spirit of inquiry animates the American study of intelligence, scholars will continue to search for best practices and to understand how new security threats create unique intelligence challenges. The American approach to intelligence studies has no ready response to these challenges, but it does have a community of scholars who are willing to address the issues confronting not only the intelligence communities, but the societies in which they are embedded.

Notes

1 Russell F. Weigley, *The American Way of War: A History of US Military Strategy and Policy* (Bloomington, IN: Indiana University Press, 1973).

2 For example, Max Boot, *Savage War of Peace: Small Wars and the Rise of American Power* (New York: Basic Books, 2002).

3 Walter Jajko makes the point well: "The United States armed forces, despite the revolutionary rhetoric of the National Military Strategy concerning the information dominance of the battle-space, are predisposed to attack an enemy's capabilities, not an enemy's strategy. Systematic shaping of an enemy's strategy and attacking an enemy's intentions through deception in peacetime are unusual undertakings." See "Commentary," in Roy Godson and James J. Wirtz (eds.), *Strategic Denial and Deception: The Twenty-First Century Challenge* (New Brunswick, NJ: Transaction Publishers, 2002), pp. 115–122.

4 Barton Whaley, "Stratagem: Deception and Surprise in War," Rand Corporation, 1969; Barton Whaley, *Codeword BARBAROSSA* (Cambridge, MA: MIT Press, 1971); and J. Bowyer Bell and Barton Whaley, *Cheating and Deception* (New Brunswick, NJ: Transaction Publishers, 1991).

5 James J. Wirtz, "Responding to Surprise," *Annual Review of Political Science*, Vol. 9 (2006), pp. 45–65.

6 United States Congress, *Report of the congressional committees investigating the Iran-Contra Affair: with supplemental, minority, and additional views.* H. rept., no. 100–433. S. rept., no. 100–216. Washington, DC: For sale by the Supt. of Docs., US GPO, 1987.

7 The Commission on the Intelligence Capabilities of the United States Regarding Weapons of Mass Destruction, *Report to the President of the United States*, March 31, 2005.

8 "Former aide: Powell WMD Speech 'Lowest point in my life'." http://www.afterdowningstreet.org/?q=node/1907

9 Commission on the Roles and Capabilities of the United States Intelligence Community. *Preparing for the 21st Century: An Appraisal of US Intelligence : Report of the Commission on the Roles and Capabilities of the United States Intelligence Community* (Washington, DC: The Commission, 1996).

10 Amy B. Zegart, "September 11 and the Adaptation Failure of US Intelligence Agencies," *International Security* Vol. 29, No. 4 (Spring 2005), pp. 78–111.

11 James B. Bruce, "How Leaks of Classified Intelligence Help US Adversaries: Implications for Laws and Secrecy," *Studies in Intelligence* Vol. 47, No. 1 (March 2003), pp. 39–49.

12 James J. Wirtz, "The Intelligence Paradigm," *Intelligence and National Security* Vol. 4, No. 4 (October 1989), pp. 829–837.

13 For example, see Ephraim Kam, *Surprise Attack: The Victim's Perspective* (Cambridge, MA: Harvard University Press, 1988); and Ariel Levite, *Intelligence and Strategic Surprises* (New York: Columbia University Press, 1987).

14 Michael Herman, *Intelligence Power* (Cambridge: Cambridge University Press, 1996); Nigel West, *Venona: The Greatest Secret of the Cold War* (London: Harper Collins, 2000); and Christopher M. Andrew, *Her Majesty's Secret Service: The Making of the British Intelligence Community* (New York: Penguin Books, 1987).

15 Aleksandr Fursenko and Timothy Naftali, "Soviet Intelligence and the Cuban Missile Crisis," in James G. Blight and David A. Welch (eds.) *Intelligence and the Cuban Missile Crisis* (London: Frank Cass, 1998), pp. 64–87.

16 Thomas C. Bruneau, "Controlling Intelligence in New Democracies," *International Journal of Intelligence and Counterintelligence* Vol. 14 (Fall 2001), pp. 323–341. The term "counterintelligence state" was coined by John Dziak to describe the Soviet Union, a state where the domestic police/intelligence function was synonymous with the dominant governing body of the state. See John

Dziak, forward by Robert Conquest, *Chekisty: A History of the KGB* (New York: Ballantine Books, 1988).

17 Alexander George, "Warning and Response: Theory and Practice," in Yair Evon (ed.) *International Violence: Terrorism, Surprise, and Control* (Jerusalem: Leonard Davis Institute, 1979).

18 Kam, *Surprise Attack*, pp. 42, 64, 186.

19 *Report to the President of the United States*, pp. 12–14.

20 Robert Jervis, *Perception and Misperception in International Politics* (Princeton, NJ: Princeton University Press, 1976).

21 Richards J. Heuer, Jr., *Psychology of Intelligence Analysis* (CIA: Center for the Study of Intelligence, 1999).

22 "The concept" was the term originally coined by the Agranat Commission Investigation into the failure of Israeli intelligence prior to the Yom Kippur War; see Ephraim Kahana, "Early Warning Versus the Concept: The Case of the Yom Kippur War 1973," *Intelligence and National Security* Vol. 17 (Summer 2002), pp. 81–104.

23 Uri Bar-Joseph, *The Watchman Fell Asleep: The Surprise of Yom Kippur and its Sources* (Albany, NY: State University of New York Press, 2005).

24 William E. Odom, *Fixing Intelligence: For a More Secure America* (New Haven, CT: Yale University Press, 2003).

25 Sherman Kent, *Strategic Intelligence for American World Policy* (Princeton, NJ: Princeton University Press, 1946).

26 H. Bradford Westerfield, "Inside Ivory Bunkers: CIA Analysts Resist Mangers' 'Pandering' – Part II," *International Journal of Intelligence and Counterintelligence* 10 (Spring 1997), pp. 19–54; Richard K. Betts, "Politicization of Intelligence: Costs and Benefits," in Richard K. Betts and Thomas Mahnken (eds.) *Paradoxes of Strategic Intelligence* (London: Frank Cass, 2003), pp. 59–79.

27 Loch Johnson, *Bombs, Bugs, Drugs and Thugs, Intelligence and America's Quest for Security* (New York: New York University Press, 2000), pp. 188–195.

28 Marvin C. Ott, "Partisanship and the Decline of Intelligence Oversight," *International Journal of Intelligence and Counterintelligence* Vol. 16, No. 1 (Spring 2003).

29 Johnson, *Bombs, Bugs, Drugs and Thugs*, p. 222.

30 Stephen Biddle, "Afghanistan and the Future of Warfare," *Foreign Affairs* Vol. 82, No. 2 (March/April 2003).

3

The historiography of the FBI

Rhodri Jeffreys-Jones

By studying what historians in different eras and of various persuasions have written about the Federal Bureau of Investigation (FBI), scholars in this field can place their own work in a more meaningful context. But there is an immediate problem here. Can an institution, as distinct from great events or political tendencies, have an *independent* historiography, or must there be *dependency*, with institutional historiography drawing on the historiographies of contextual problems and events?[1]

In the case of some *commanding* institutions, for example the Presidency or the Supreme Court, independent historiographies have developed. But the argument in this chapter is that the FBI, a *commanded* institution, has no autonomous historiography, and that the prospects for its emergence are slim. However, dependency historiography has produced and continues to yield some promising lines of investigation into the FBI's history.

While crediting other dependency strategies, the essay argues that the link to African American historiography produces the most promising results. This seems the likeliest hypothesis after an assessment of possible typologies, a chronological review of works, and a consideration of the strengths and weaknesses of pertinent parent historiographies.

The need for this explanatory approach arises because of the scarcity, hitherto, of general historiographical analysis. To be sure, those writing about the FBI have been influenced by what has been written before. But, perhaps partly because the FBI itself has been until recently a practical rather than an intellectual organization, they have stopped short of introspection. They have rarely analyzed the existing literature in the manner of historians who, in other fields, consciously place their work in an intellectual context.

Exceptions can be found in specialized aspects of FBI history. For example, David J. Garrow wrote an article on "FBI Political Harassment and FBI Historiography." Here, he took issue with Gary Marx's view that FBI surveillance of the Socialist Workers Party and the Communist Party had little impact on the development of those organizations. But Garrow's essay was not only specialist in scope, but also more a *methodological* than a historiographical plea – he made the case for wider use of oral history and for closer attention to the role of FBI informants.[2]

The Danish scholar Regin Schmidt also offered, in the year 2000, an explicitly historiographical analysis. His book on the FBI and the early development of American anti-communism contained a review of the literature in the field. He took issue with civil liberties historians like Frank Donner and Kenneth O'Reilly, arguing that they had accepted un-critically Richard Hofstadter's thesis that social paranoia lay at the root of anti-communism. Schmidt argued that historians such as Athan Theoharis had paid too little attention to the FBI's political role prior to 1936, that the field was overly dominated by biographies of J. Edgar Hoover and under-populated by "comprehensive" histories, and that the study of the FBI was marred by a heavily bureaucratic focus and by assumptions that "the Bureau was out of political control." Though Schmidt by definition had a narrow focus of the type he seemed to deplore in others, he at least offered, perhaps assisted by a certain European detachment from the American scene, a perspective on the literature concerning his particular branch of FBI studies. Such attempts have been rare.[3]

A list of general typologies of use in classifying works on the FBI might well begin with the bureaucratic approach that so upset Schmidt. Here, a leaf may be taken from the historiography of labor history. This is generally understood to begin with the Progressive-era institutional school associated with the University of Wisconsin scholar, John R. Commons. In a useful manner, and drawing on conveniently preserved records, journals and other publications, the institutionalists recorded the histories of individual labor unions and employers' associations. Subsequently, the historiography marched on, with the institutional approach giving way to other schools of thought: Old Left, New Left, New Social, Corporatist, Neoconservative.[4]

There are certainly institutionalist traits in the historiography of the FBI. Some weaknesses are shared: just as the Commons school neglected workers who were not organized into unions, and thus the entire pre-history of the modern wage-earner, so historians like Don Whitehead ignored federal law enforcement before the creation of the Bureau of Investigation in 1908/9.[5] However, the shortcomings of FBI historiography would appear to be more deep-seated than those of labor. Possibly because the institutional records are less accessible on account of secrecy requirements, and because this presents a mesmerizing challenge, historians are still striving to tell the story of the FBI as an institution. The temptation is to use the Bureau's own records insofar as they are available, neglecting a broader evidential approach. Compared with labor historiography, the progression of viewpoints has been relatively stunted.

As Schmidt observed, biographies have loomed large in the historiography of the FBI. It might be argued that, as history is about people, biography is the most helpful way of explaining the FBI's past. The case might be considered stronger on account of the striking personality of Hoover, who was director from 1924 until his death in 1972. Hoover did have a major impact, but there are nevertheless dangers, even in his case, in reliance on biography. With the passage of time, his role is beginning to sink into a proper perspective. Significant leaders like John Wilkie preceded him, and subsequent directors like Louis Freeh have been just as controversial. It is becoming evident not only that other personalities need to be considered, but also that personality is not the only factor of importance. Historians who look at particular problems closely tend to see more complex factors at work. For example, in his book on the FBI's investigations of the New Left and the Ku Klux Klan in the 1960s, David Cunningham remarked that this kind of intelligence work "clearly transcends Hoover" and noted that it had continued since his death.[6]

A third type of approach to FBI history is that of the civil libertarian. If one sets aside popular works such as adventure stories, and focuses on books and articles written by scholars, the civil libertarian approach has probably been the most frequent type of endeavor. In a nation dedicated to justice and liberty, such scholarship serves a deeper purpose than that found in most historical writing. Yet, for precisely that reason, civil libertarian historians tend to plow their own furrow, disregarding the field beyond. To treat the history of the FBI as the story of a conspiracy against civil liberty is to ignore the facts that its origins lay in an effort to protect civil liberty, that causes and effects of important events are not always connected with civil liberties, and that most of the work of the FBI is not intrinsically political in nature. In one of his books, Athan Theoharis implicitly defended civil libertarians against the charge that they were indifferent to the need for an effective FBI. The Bureau's obsession with political work, he argued, undermined its effectiveness against spies and terrorists. But such arguments are not characteristic of the main thrust of civil libertarian history.[7]

A fourth way of looking at FBI history might be through the prism of police history, especially when broadly defined to include urban and crime history. The work of the historian Eric H. Monkkonen, for example, contains lessons for any student of the FBI – about the need for caution in treating some of the more lurid claims about murder rates, about the limits to what police forces can achieve, and about the plurality and variety of the American police system. Nor can historians afford to ignore the work of sociologists like Gary Marx, who pointed out that when J. Edgar Hoover died and special agents were allowed discard their suits and to venture in disguise into the gutters of the American drug trade, corruption and contamination set in, the inevitable price of the long overdue victory against the Mob. The public puritanism of the old cross-dresser had at least some uses after all, it seems. However, while Monkkonen, Marx and their like provide ample inspiration for FBI historians, there has thus far been little inclination to take up the challenge that their work represents.[8]

Rounding out our list of possible typologies are two approaches that will receive further attention later in this essay, but can be mentioned here to serve the needs of symmetry. The first is national security and intelligence studies. The historian Richard Aldrich noted the emergence of a "division between institutionalist and contextualist writings" in this field, arguing that while the insitutionalist approach had advanced beyond the "airport bookstall" school of history, contextualists like Robin Winks and W. Scott Lucas were still effectively challenging it. Although Aldrich referred chiefly to *foreign* intelligence, subject to qualifications made later in this essay that field shares at least some methodologies with the study of the domestically orientated (if increasingly international) FBI.[9]

The last typology is the study of race relations. Here, as in labor history and intelligence history, there has been an institutionalist tendency. Established in 1909, the National Association for the Advancement of Colored People (NAACP) is virtually the same age as the Bureau. As in the case of the FBI, the identification of an independent historiography for that institution is problematic. But the NAACP does have a vibrant context in which it may be intelligently considered, namely the historiography of black America. Given the deep and tragic intertwining of FBI and African American history, is black-history historiography the most promising context in which to place the Bureau's past, as well?

The need to impose some kind of shape on FBI historiography is confirmed by its sheer quantity. For while the literature on the Bureau does not match in scale that on topics like the American Revolution, Civil War, or Vietnam War, each of which prompts more than 10,000 book hits when entered as a keyword in the Library of Congress electronic catalog, keying in "FBI" still calls up 986 books. If popular interest is the bedrock of historical inquiry and if Google hits are an index of popular interest, the need for imposing some kind of order on a chaotic mass becomes even more apparent: 48 million hits for the FBI, compared with 47 million for the Vietnam War (the American Revolution and Civil War generate 70 and 121 million hits respectively, and the CIA 53 million).[10]

What follows is not a review of all or even a fraction of the books written on the FBI, but a chronological survey of a selection of works. However, the coverage does extend beyond scholarly items. All those shelves groaning under the weight of junk history should not be allowed to obscure the real insights into the Bureau's past offered by non-academic writers such as memoirists, journalists, and practicing lawyers. The focus here will be on those authors who aimed, or purported to aim, substantively to comment on and to interpret FBI history and prehistory as a whole. It reveals, as one might expect in any field, a progression of period concerns, confirming the existence of at least the raw materials for FBI historiography. It also signals the absence of referentialism. Writers on the FBI may have been influenced by what previous writers said, but they tended not to critique, refer to, or even admit those influences. Finally, the following literature review offers clues to what might be useful historiographical contexts within which the history of the FBI can be considered.

The acronym "FBI" entered the English language in July 1935 when, after a number of name changes, Washington settled on the enduring title, "Federal Bureau of Investigation." But the FBI's continuous institutional history stretches back further, to the formation of a Special Agent Force in 1908, renamed the Bureau of Investigation one year later. And its prehistory started even earlier, with the formation of the Department of Justice in 1870 and its borrowing, in the following year, of a group of US Secret Service detectives. President Lincoln had established the Secret Service in 1865, and in the 1860s its detectives operated against moonshiners and counterfeiters, bringing it under the supervision of the Treasury Department. On loan to Justice and known as "special agents" (a commonly used contemporary term), these detectives had the task of penetrating and destroying the Ku Klux Klan. The search for commentaries on the FBI's history must, then, begin with works published not just before 1935, but also before 1908.

Memoirists supply some of the earliest commentary. Hiram C. Whitley was chief of the Secret Service from 1869 to 1874. His autobiography, *In It*, contained both self-promotional tales of detection and some insights into the development of an embryonic federal police force. But he glossed over his post-1871 period of service to the Justice Department. In his book, Whitley referred to one of his *earlier* investigations of the Klan, to President Ulysses S. Grant's "hearty indorsement" of that work, and to the "bitterness of the rebels" whom he brought to trial. But, he wrote, "I will not go into any particulars in regard to the case." His reluctance to go into detail reflected changing times. For, by the year of publication of the book, 1894, the Jim Crow reaction to Reconstruction was in full swing. In white southern society and indeed beyond, the Klansmen were being reconstituted as heroic figures who had resisted federal oppression. Truth in its customary manner had become a casualty of racism, and proto-FBI historiography had offered itself as a candidate for dependency.[11]

William J. Burns served as director of the Bureau of Investigation from 1921 to 1924. But, by this time, he had already published a memoir – in 1913, it appeared under the not very unassuming title, *The Masked War: The Story of a Peril that Threatened the United States by the Man Who Uncovered the Dynamite Conspirators and Sent them to Jail*. Potentially, Burns had an interesting tale to tell and perspective on events. He was a brilliant detective who as a Secret Service agent had helped to crack Spain's Montreal-based spy ring in the War of 1898, and to put timber robbers behind bars in a case that had led directly to the formation of the Bureau of Investigation. Moreover, he would soon win fame for working for the accused in the notorious anti-semitic trial in the state of Georgia that culminated with the lynching of Leo Frank.

His book, however, appeared at a time when Burns was promoting his recently formed private detective agency, which would soon rival the Pinkertons as a successful business enterprise. In an era when Americans worried that European-style class conflict might arrive on their shores, Burns advanced a hypothesis that was, we can see with the wisdom of hindsight, absurd – that a pair of Irish-American Catholic labor leaders, the Bridgeworkers' Union's McNamara brothers, were spearheading a proletarian revolution in the United States. Instead of commenting in his memoir on the development of a federal police system, he drummed up *Burns* business for his private agency by inventing a revolutionary threat and posing as America's savior.[12]

It is popularly perceived that William J. Donovan, head of the Office of Strategic Services in World War II, was a seminal force in the creation (in 1947) of the Central Intelligence Agency. Just so, in 1908 John E. Wilkie was a prominent mover in the creation of what came to be known as the FBI. Wilkie was the dominant federal investigative and counterintelligence officer of the William McKinley and Theodore Roosevelt presidencies. However, like Donovan, the Secret Service chief was too controversial a figure to head the new agency he had advocated. Given this turbulence, the biography of him by his son Don is of interest. It appeared in 1934 at a time of heightened interest in law and order and in federal policing, and in the wake of legislation that dramatically increased the powers of the FBI.

Like his father, Don Wilkie worked for the Secret Service, so he was doubly partisan. Written at a time when the burgeoning Bureau of Investigation was eclipsing the Secret Service, his book was an implicit corrective to the idea that the FBI was the only show in town. Indeed, the book is eloquent in its omissions. Don Wilkie enlivened his pages with an account of his father's fight with the corrupt Congress of 1908, but contrives not to mention that the Bureau of Investigation was formed in that year. In fact, neither the Bureau nor J. Edgar Hoover appears in the book at all. It would be an understatement to say that Don Wilkie eschewed the prerequisites of historical balance.[13]

If the 1930s revitalization of federal policing inspired Don Wilkie to write as he did, it also prompted the birth of official FBI history. It might be objected that this is a more recent development, as the Bureau's first official historian was not appointed until 1984.[14] But the propagation of an official version of history does not depend on the engagement of in-house professionals, and, in the case of the FBI, started well before that happened. In the 1930s, it was New Deal policy to remake the image of the FBI to portray it as a valiant corps of men who could take on the mobsters and put them in jail or the morgue. Hoover encouraged Hollywood to cease depicting the gangster as a romantic, Robin Hood type of hero, and to replace him, in the role of the hero, with the G-Man, the Fed who could shoot straight. He began what became a lifelong publicity habit, and started to sponsor a particular image of the FBI, an image that contributed to an official view of its history. *Interesting...*

In 1938, Hoover published his book *Persons in Hiding*. This was a collection of stories indicating the ingenuity and valor of the FBI's special agents. The main text was probably shadow-written like most of the director's publications, and the historical introduction was authored by Courtney Ryley Cooper. This journalist had published an earlier work on a similar theme, with the same American publishers, Little, Brown, and with an introduction by Hoover. Cooper had also developed what one cultural historian called "the official FBI formula" for radio broadcasts based on the Bureau's crime records. But it should be remembered that Hoover worked hand in hand with Cooper and other sympathetic writers, and that the point of view in all resultant publications was that of "The Boss."[15]

Though brief, Cooper's introduction outlined the lineaments of what became an official approach to FBI history. It lionized Hoover. In Cooper's version, the business of seriously coordinating the American fight against crime "really began in 1921," when Hoover became assistant director. In the 1920s, the Bureau chief remained at the mercy of difficulties stemming from the federal nature of the American political system. Major criminals were adept at "jumping the fence," moving, when things got too hot where they were, to another state. That put them beyond the jurisdiction of local policemen, and, because of the scarcity of enabling legislation, immune to federal agencies.

According to Cooper's account, Hoover knew that he had to play catch-up and win increased FBI powers that would override states' rights objections and the vanities of local policemen. But he had to bide his time until the political climate was right. The propitious moment arrived in 1933, with the conjunction of a sympathetic attorney general, Homer Cummings, and the Kansas City massacre in which "Pretty Boy" Floyd and his confederates cold-bloodedly shot dead a Bureau agent and two local law officers, shocking the nation. Now, Hoover started a campaign to disabuse "the average honest citizen" who "secretly admired the gangster." New laws swept through Congress. Henceforth, the Feds could make arrests, carry guns, and enforce a wider range of laws.[16]

With the coming of the Cold War, debate on security arrangements intensified. Possibly with a view to curtailing Hoover's influence, President Harry Truman encouraged his friend Max Lowenthal to write a book on the agency. A graduate of Harvard Law School, Lowenthal had run his own firm and had served as a consultant to the Senate Committee on Interstate Commerce. After prodigious research, the veteran lawyer in 1950 published his tome, *The Federal Bureau of Investigation.* His account started in 1908 not the 1930s, and offered the first informed narrative of FBI history, running through to 1950.

Instead of focusing on Hoover, Lowenthal detailed concerns, especially as expressed in Congress, that the FBI was propelling America toward becoming a police state. He showed how President Theodore Roosevelt and his attorney general Charles Bonaparte had sneakily set up the new agency during a congressional adjournment, and how outraged legislators attacked this high-handed action by the great-nephew of Napoleon Bonaparte, the emperor who (as critics gleefully pointed out) had employed the notorious internal security chief, Joseph Fouché. Lowenthal gave full vent to the Gestapo anxieties expressed in America in the wake of the war against Hitler, and to suspicions that the FBI was backing the new Red Scare of the early Cold War. These critical civil libertarian concerns caused him to overlook the Bureau's pre-1908 antecedents, and to ignore the point that, as Attorney General Bonaparte's agents had been investigating corrupt practices in the "millionaire senate," criticism from the Hill might best be taken with a pinch of salt.

Hearing of the imminent publication of the book, Hoover tried to stop it. Failing in that endeavor, he took steps to limit its circulation, to intimidate Lowenthal's publisher, and to smear Lowenthal as a Pinko. This might be taken to indicate that Lowenthal's book was, manna to the historiographer, "revisionist." In one sense, it was, as it marked a significant and persuasive departure from the official version of FBI history – even the FBI now traces its origins to 1908, rather than the 1930s. On the other hand, it was not referential, avoiding discussion of previous literature, and today it reads more like a single-minded defense of civil liberties than a serious historical investigation.[17]

Lowenthal's book marked an intensification in the ping-pong debate between defenders of civil liberties who excoriated the FBI, and Bureau supporters who justified its actions. Hoover's next book, *Masters of Deceit*, dealt with the history of the Communist menace, not the FBI, and testified to the way in which the Bureau changed its targets over time. But he had no need to address the Bureau's history directly, as he had already rolled out his heavy artillery in the shape of a court historian.[18]

In his preface to Don Whitehead's book *The FBI Story*, Hoover expressed his "complete confidence" in the author, who was the winner of two Pulitzer Prizes for journalism and had already done some reporting on the Bureau. For his part, Whitehead was indebted to the director for allowing him "a look behind the scenes" and for making available to him "a tremendous amount of unpublished material." Whitehead essentially added flesh and bones to the outline of FBI history supplied in Courtney Ryley Cooper's 1938 mini-oeuvre. While there was still no mention of the Bureau's antecedents, there were additional details about the menace of organized crime in the 1930s and how Hoover and his men had triumphed. Appearing in 1956, the book gave a boost to the Bureau at a time when McCarthyism and FBI anti-Red activities were losing their appeal, and when the Bureau's inefficacy against the Mafia was an embarrassing talking point. In 1959, a movie based on Whitehead's book starred James Stewart and was a box-office hit.[19]

To borrow from Newton, to every ping in FBI historiography there was an equal and opposite pong. Fred Cook's *The FBI Nobody Knows* (1964) was incipiently referential. Like Lowenthal, Cook operated within a tradition of liberal journalism that was critical of the FBI – he had contributed on the subject to the journal *Nation* – and he both drew on Lowenthal's book and specifically defended him as a non-partisan writer who had been smeared as "pink." Cook repeated the claim that the Bureau had been "created in secrecy, by executive order, in defiance of the will of Congress." But he added his individual gloss. *critical of FBI*

Cook highlighted, in a manner that reflected the civil rights crusade of his day, the FBI's pervasive racism. Here, he was assisted by the testimony of an apostate, Jack Levine, who had trained with the FBI before leaving it in disgust on account of its agents' overt racial prejudice. Cook also anticipated a concern that would fuel congressional discontent in the 1970s, the notion that the FBI was too "autonomous." His book reflected the emerging intellectual disorientation of the liberal left in America, for he attributed to the "liberal" presidents Theodore Roosevelt and Franklin D. Roosevelt (FDR) the creation of an "all-powerful" FBI, and acknowledged that the Bureau, with Assistant Director Hoover masterminding operations, had smashed the Klan in Louisiana in 1922. In the absence of historiographical guidelines, it was becoming difficult for "liberal" writers to make sense of the FBI.[20]

In 1971, John T. Elliff published a historical monograph on the FBI. Elliff had recently received a doctorate in political science from Harvard University, and was now a professor at Brandeis University. His contribution was entitled "Aspects of Civil Rights Enforcement: The Justice Department and the FBI, 1939–1964." It attracted no publicity or controversy, appearing initially in Harvard's *Perspectives in American History*, a serial publication dedicated to the publication of items that would normally be considered to be too long for publication in a journal, and then, in 1987, as part of a learned, 814-page tome.

This background helps to explain why Elliff broke out of the ping-pong mold, supplying a perspective that was both civil libertarian and broadly supportive of the FBI. Though Attorney General Cummings had been aware that Justice Department agents had operated against the Klan in the 1870s, most people had forgotten that Justice meant justice, and remembered only that Hoover was a racist. But Elliff detailed the work of the Justice Department's Civil Rights Section (CRS), first established by Attorney General Frank Murphy, in the area of investigations into lynching and other terrorist actions against black citizens.

Elliff's quiet, scholarly contribution took second place, in the 1970s, to sensational media revelations about the FBI's dirty tricks campaign against Martin Luther King, Jr. But, in more recent times, historians Kevin J. McMahon and Christopher Waldrep have developed the theme that the FBI's civil rights work in support of the CRS diminished the climate of terror in the South, thus contributing to the rise and triumph of the civil rights campaign of the 1950s and 1960s.[21]

In spite of Elliff's 1971 disquisition, David Garrow complained in 1981 about the "poor quality" of public discourse on the FBI, a deficiency stemming from the fact that "academic curiosity about the FBI appears almost nil." His complaint appeared in the afterword to a book he published on the FBI and Martin Luther King, Jr. Here, he also challenged prevailing assumptions that most FBI ills could be traced to J. Edgar Hoover, and that the Bureau enjoyed "autonomy" from political control.[22]

As things turned out, though, academic work on the FBI was on a boom trajectory. The post-Watergate investigations of the intelligence community by journalists and by congressional investigators, especially the Church inquiry of 1975–6, stimulated the "curiosity" that Garrow craved. Loch Johnson, a Church inquiry staff worker who became a prolific writer on intelligence affairs (and is the editor of the volume in which this essay appears) noted that the Church investigation unearthed "a huge amount of new information for scholars to study" and got him "completely hooked" on the field in which he was to make his name. Others labored in the same vineyard, and there was an upsurge in scholarship on the FBI. This was already under way when Garrow made his observation, and gathered pace thereafter.[23]

John Elliff headed the Church Committee's Domestic Task Force. He engaged Athan Theoharis, already an established historian, to scour the presidential libraries. In trying to uncover FBI records, Theoharis encountered serious obstruction. However, the obstruction was counter-productive, as it spurred him to ever-greater efforts. He devoted much of the remainder of his career to publishing prolifically on the FBI. He also advised graduate students at Marquette University who went on to write about the Bureau, assisted by an FBI archive that Theoharis built up at that institution.[24]

Theoharis himself made an early imprint on FBI studies. In the course of the Church investigation, the Republican administration had resorted to the tactic of releasing information on how *Democrats* had used the FBI to undermine civil liberties, with the iconic FDR and John F. Kennedy receiving special attention. In an article for the *Political Science Quarterly* in 1976, Theoharis implicitly challenged the Republican premise when he argued that Hoover's interpretation of FDR's directions did "not capture the more limited nature of the president's objective."[25] He also spread the blame, claiming "no president after Franklin Roosevelt spurned the opportunity to obtain valuable political intelligence."[26]

However, the Republicans were joined by incongruous bedfellows in taking a harsher view of the architect of the New Deal. Adherents of the New Left thought Roosevelt had not gone far enough in pursuit of social and racial reforms. Expanding their attack, Stanford University's Barton J. Bernstein drew on congressional hearings and on Theoharis's scholarship but also on the Official File in the FDR Library in expounding his view that FDR had personally directed the FBI to overstep the mark in keeping tabs on his political opponents, and in authorizing wiretapping.[27]

With the old Democratic coalition crumbling away and with "liberal" presidents under scrutiny, civil libertarians began to adjust their perspectives. One such was Frank Donner, a lawyer who had argued cases before the Supreme Court and directed an American Civil Liberties Union project on political surveillance. His well-researched 1980 book on the latter subject noted how FDR had given the FBI greater powers and jurisdiction, but, while noting the Bureau's "Southern mentality," Donner drew attention also to its COINTELPRO "White Hate" operation against race supremacists. The old game of unconscious historiographical ping-pong was getting increasingly blurred around the edges.[28]

In a nation dedicated to free speech and based on pluralism, the evolution of new attitudes rarely proceeds in a uniform manner, and this was the case with writings on the FBI. In 1989, Princeton University Press issued a book in which political scientist William Keller argued that the FBI placed "liberals" in a quandary. They were dedicated to the principle of statism, and the Bureau was a prime example of that, but they just could not warm to the institution. To extrapolate from Keller, this opened the door for conservatives to re-embrace the Bureau. By the twenty-first century, "neoconservatives" had re-indorsed both the FBI and statism in the interest of national security.[29]

But did that mean the restoration of J. Edgar Hoover's reputation? This was by no means necessarily the case. William C. Sullivan had already published a memoir that was critical of the formerly powerful but now deceased director – and Sullivan wrote from a staunchly pro-FBI perspective, having at one time been its third most senior official. On the other hand, in a 1995 memoir Cartha DeLoach, who in the course of his 28-year career with the Bureau had headed its Crime Records Division, staunchly supported Hoover. DeLoach denied the long-serving director had been gay, described a critical biographer as "disingenuous," and claimed that Hoover's war on organized crime had been more effective than his critics allowed.[30]

But, to borrow a phrase from the British political lexicon, there was by now a tradition of "loyal opposition." Ronald Kessler was a prominent case in point. Kessler, who as a *Washington Post* journalist in the Watergate era had gained the confidence of FBI officials, received from Bureau director Williams S. Sessions (1987–1993) the kind of access to inner sanctums that Don Whitehead had once enjoyed. In his books and columns, Kessler shed light on FBI history as well as on current practices. But when he found out that Sessions was taking advantage of the US taxpayer through various financial scams, he reported adversely and helped to bring him down. Later, he was critical of Director Louis J. Freeh (1993–2001) out of a similar motive, the desire to see an important agency headed only by the best people. For Kessler was a staunch supporter of the Bureau – even before the new imperatives of 9/11, he was pressing for an expanded FBI budget.[31]

FBI loyalism lived on not just in modified mode, but also in original format on the lines of the Hoover-friendly perspective of Courtney Ryley Cooper and Don Whitehead. Bryan Burrough's book *Public Enemies* (2004) may have sniped at the legendary director's vanity, but its subtitle indicates how firmly Burrough was wedded to the Cooperite view that a positive revolution took place under Hoover's leadership early in the New Deal: *America's Greatest Crime Wave and the Birth of the FBI, 1933–34.*[32]

In his dissection of schools of intelligence history, Richard Aldrich mentions what he terms the cost-benefit approach.[33] This was much in evidence in America after 9/11. The FBI came in for more criticism than any other agency in connection with the alleged negligence that lay behind US lack of preparedness in the face of imminent terrorist attack. The main concern now was not how to protect America against the Gestapo-like activities of the FBI, but how to equip the Bureau more effectively to confront future threats to American security. Scholars, journalists and legislators began to reconsider the FBI's past in this functionalist light.

The tendency did not grow out of a vacuum. For some time, historians like John E. Haynes and Harvey Klehr had been attacking the evidential basis of the work of civil libertarian historians like Athan Theoharis who, they claimed, "made a career out of deploring in extravagantly sinister terms FBI monitoring of domestic radicals and others suspected of being involved in espionage and political subversion." The Communist Party of the United States, they pointed out on the authority of newly declassified evidence, was not an innocent if misguided victim of Bureau harassment. Its instructions and money had always come from Moscow, and its leaders wittingly engaged in or allowed systematic espionage against the United States.[34]

With the Cold War over, such revelations might seem to have been archaic. But they did prepare the way for the post-9/11 challenge: look not at what the FBI does wrong, but at how it might become more effective, and how it might be freed from arcane criticisms and from regulation based on unfounded police state fears.

From this background sprang the utilitarian tendency in the assessment of FBI history. One of its notable practitioners, Richard Gid Powers, was already known as a biographer of J. Edgar Hoover and as a slightly waspish authority on the FBI's publicity efforts. After 9/11, Powers formed the view that the problem lay more with the FBI's critics than with the Bureau itself. He now argued in a general history of the FBI that the Bureau was shackled by excessive restrictions that had been placed on it by 1970s reformers. Because of the critics' strictures, it had become "risk averse." This functionalism began to affect other historians, too, even those excoriated by Harvey and Klehr. In response to 9/11, Theoharis turned his critique of the FBI's political work into a critique of its effectiveness, arguing in a concise overview of FBI history that if you concentrate on surveillance against your own citizens, you will be unable to spot the threat from strangers.[35]

The foregoing chronological review of historical literature on the FBI indicates that writing in this field is no exception to the rule that interpretations of the past often reflect current concerns. But it also reveals a continuing lack of historiographical awareness. That absence of self-awareness breeds an approach whose aridity threatens to be self-perpetuating, as, by definition, it fails to irrigate the parched ground of FBI historiography.

It seems that an institution, even one with a long history and with changing goals, does not always lend itself to *sui generis* historiography. However, that does not absolve the FBI historian from the duty to be historiographically self-aware, for it is possible to borrow from kindred or parent disciplines. One of these might be intelligence history, for the FBI has ever since World War I been engaged in counter-intelligence. In recent times, there has been urgent attention to that and to its cousin, counter-terrorism.

One could treat FBI historiography as an intellectual client of CIA historiography, a field that has both embraced institutionalism and moved beyond it.[36] The FBI, like the CIA, has been subject to the vigorous debates associated with the Cold War. The surprise attack on Pearl Harbor, with which 9/11 has understandably been compared, generated a whole school of interpretation and debate. The Pearl Harbor debate for that reason serves as contextual historiography for both the CIA and the FBI.[37] To give another example, there are parallels between the founding of the FBI in 1908 and the CIA in 1947: both were the products of reform impulses; snoopery fears and police state fears (Fouché/Gestapo) were prominent on each occasion; in both cases, the prime architects of intelligence reform (Wilkie/Donovan) were jettisoned as part of the acceptance compromise. The riches of 1940s historiography have been visited in the debate on the founding of the CIA, and there is every reason why FBI historiographers should learn from that.

On the other hand, there are differences. One of the features of CIA historiography is the asynchronicity of official and revisionist history. The CIA supported in-house official history from the very start. Because in-house official histories were classified documents, they were sometimes not released to the public until revisionist interpretations were already in print. As the FBI has not had in-house histories, this issue simply does not arise.

It can further be noted that CIA historiography, or even foreign intelligence historiography more broadly defined, is no more a *sui generis* field than FBI historiography. Intelligence history is now regarded as the missing dimension of diplomatic history, but it is still only a dimension, or, as one pair of scholars phrased it, a "sub-field." Should FBI historiography be allowed to become a sub-field of a sub-field?[38]

More important than all this, though, is the fact that, for all the Bureau's overseas expansion in recent years, FBI history has been, primarily, domestic. For this reason especially, a closer match, given the Bureau's Justice background, is with the historiography of African American history. The prehistory of the FBI, the struggle of federal special agents against the Klan in the

1870s, has been forgotten for precisely the same reasons that gave rise to amnesia about Black Reconstruction and the later scourge of lynching. The emergence of the Dunning school of Reconstruction historiography coincided with the founding of the Bureau of Investigation, and, as historian Eric Foner puts it, exercised a long-lasting, "powerful hold on the popular imagination."[39] The lessons of its obliteration of significant memories are as applicable to the historiography of the FBI as they are to the understanding of black historiography. The later work of the Bureau in crushing white terrorism and upholding civil rights can be considered in tandem with the decline of the Dunning school and the rise of its competitors.

The black history framework of discussion has been a good fit for FBI history in a number of different circumstances, and right down to the present day. After 9/11, there was a debate between twenty-first-century cosmopolitans who believed it would be good for FBI analysts to be able to read Arabic, and nationalists who saw political correctness as the enemy of security. The debate took place not in a vacuum, but in the context of a living tradition with its roots in the debate on black history.

As in the case of other institutional historiographies, the historiography of the FBI raises questions of frameworks and of interpretive dependency. The historian of the FBI is not only a child of his age, but also a child with a borrowed compass. But he is also free to choose his own map, be it that of labor, urban, intelligence or race historiography. With the proviso that he shows cartographic awareness, that may one day free him (or her) to stumble on the truth with a little less ideological and cultural impediment.

Notes

1 An earlier version of this chapter was presented as a paper to the American History Research Workshop at the University of Edinburgh. On that occasion, Alex Goodall, Susan-Mary Grant, and Vassiliki Karali offered helpful comments. Further learned instruction came from Athan Theoharis. Douglas Charles, Frank Cogliano, and Christopher Wardrep read a draft of the essay and supplied informed critiques. The essay is a product of the "History of the FBI Project" funded by the Leverhulme Trust and the Arts and Humanities Research Council. The author is most grateful to all of these individuals and institutions.

2 David J. Garrow, "FBI Political Harassment and FBI Historiography: Analyzing Informants and Measuring the Effects," *The Public Historian*, 10 (Fall 1988), 5–18 at 16.

3 Regin Schmidt, *Red Scare: FBI and the Origins of Anticommunism in the United States* (Copenhagen: Museum Tusculanum Press, 2000), pp. 12, 15, 18.

4 Reviews of American labor historiography have appeared with regularity. See, for example, Ronald Ziegler, "Workers and Scholars: Recent Trends in American Labor Historiography," *Labor History*, 13 (Spring 1972) and David Brody, "Reconciling the Old Labor History and the New," *Pacific Historical Review*, 62:1 (1993). For yet another challenge to preconceptions about labor history, see Joseph A. McCartin, "Bringing the State's Workers in: Time to Rectify an Imbalanced US Labor Historiography," *Labor History*, 47/1 (February 2006), 75, 87.

5 Don Whitehead, *The FBI Story* (London: Frederick Muller, 1957).

6 David Cunningham, *There's Something Happening Here: The New Left, the Klan, and FBI Counterintelligence* (Berkeley, CA: University of California Press, 2004), p. 8.

7 Athan Theoharis, *The FBI and American Democracy: A Brief Critical History* (Lawrence, KS: University Press of Kansas, 2004), pp. 2, 3, 13.

8 Eric H. Monkkonen, *Police in Urban America, 1860–1920* (Cambridge: Cambridge University Press, 1981), p. 7; Monkkonen, "Policing in the United States since 1945" in *The State, Police and Society* (Brussels, 1997), pp. 285–306; Monkkonen, *Murder in New York City* (Berkeley: University of California Press, 2001), p. 8; Gary T. Marx, *Undercover; Police Surveillance in America* (Berkeley, CA: University of California Press, 1988), pp. 4–5, 169–171. Rather more spectacular indications of local FBI corruption appeared in connection with the James J. "Whitey" Bulger case: see Dick Lehr and Gerard O'Neill,

Black Mass: The True Story of an Unholy Alliance between the FBI and the Irish Mob (New York: Perennial/ HarperCollins, 2004).

9 Richard J. Aldrich, *Espionage, Security and Intelligence in Britain, 1945–1970* (Manchester: Manchester University Press, 1998), p. 6.

10 The Library of Congress catalog was accessed for these data on 30 November 2005, and Google on 6 February 2006. For an annotated bibliography of a selection of books, articles, congressional hearings and microfilm reprints concerning the history of the FBI, see Athan G. Theoharis, ed., *The FBI: A Comprehensive Reference Guide* (New York: Checkmark/Facts on File, 2000), pp. 385–396.

11 Hiram C. Whitley, *In It* (Cambridge, MA: The Riverside Press, 1894), p. 91.

12 William J. Burns, *The Masked War* (New York: Doran, 1913). For a more sober account of the events that Burns describes, see Sidney Fine, *"Without Blare of Trumpets": Walter Drew, the National Erectors' Association, and the Open Shop Movement, 1903–1957* (Ann Arbor, MI: University of Michigan Press, 1995). Steve Oney portrays Burns and his men as "bullying dissemblers" in his book *And the Dead Shall Rise: The Murder of Mary Phagan and the Lynching of Leo Frank* (New York: Pantheon, 2003), p. 416.

13 Donald W. Wilkie, *American Secret Agent* (New York: Frederick A. Stokes, 1934), pp. 67–70.

14 Susan Rosenfeld Falb served in that capacity from then until 1992, and issued a number of guides to facts and sources on the FBI. More recently, John F. Fox, Jr., has served in the post. He unearthed some documents on early FBI history which, for a while, the Bureau mounted on its website. Fox also published articles on counterintelligence in World War I in the journal *Studies in Intelligence*, a publication run by the CIA, but nevertheless having a semi-official imprimatur as far as the Bureau was concerned. See Susan Rosenfeld (prior to 1992, Susan Rosenfeld Falb), "Organization and Day-to Day Activities" and "Buildings and Physical Plant" in Theoharis, ed., *FBI*, pp. 205–259; Fox, "Bureaucratic Wrangling over Counterintelligence, 1917–18," *Studies in Intelligence*, 49/1 (2005), accessed on the web: http://www.cia.gov/csi/studies/vol49no1/html_files/bureaucratic_wragling_2.html.

15 Richard Gid Powers, "The FBI in Popular Culture," in Theoharis, ed., *FBI*, pp. 261–307 at 276.

16 Cooper, *Ten Thousand Public Enemies* (Boston, MA: Little, Brown, 1935); Cooper introduction to Hoover, *Persons in Hiding* (London: J.M. Dent, 1938), pp. viii–xvii.

17 Max Lowenthal, *The Federal Bureau of Investigation* (New York: William Sloane, 1950), chapters 1, 38.

18 Hoover, *Masters of Deceit: The Story of Communism in America and How to Fight It* (New York: Henry Holt, 1958).

19 Whitehead, *The FBI Story* (London: Frederick Muller, 1957 [1956]), pp. 7, 16, 96–98, 103.

20 Fred J. Cook, *The FBI Nobody Knows* (London: Jonathan Cape, 1965 [1964]), pp. 1, 22, 49, 70n3, 123–125, 363, 405–411.

21 Homer Cummings and Carl McFarland, *Federal Justice: Chapters in the History of Justice and the Federal Executive* (New York: Macmillan, 1937), p. 230; John T. Elliff, "Aspects of Federal Civil Rights Enforcement: The Justice Department and the FBI, 1939–1964," *Perspectives in American History*, 5 (1971), 605–673 and *The United States Department of Justice and Individual Rights, 1937–1962* (New York: Garland, 1987); Kevin J. McMahon, *Reconsidering Roosevelt on Race: How the Presidency Paved the Road to Brown* (Chicago, IL: University of Chicago Press, 2004), pp. 144–150; Christopher Waldrep, "American Lynching, Civil Rights, and the Changing Meaning of Community, 1865–1965" (paper delivered on January 11, 2006 to the School of History and Classics staff seminar at the University of Edinburgh, supplied by kind courtesy of its author, and forming the basis of an anticipated book).

22 David J. Garrow, *The FBI and Martin Luther King, Jr.* (Harmondsworth: Penguin, 1983 [1981]), pp. 221, 223.

23 Email, Johnson to author, February 10, 2006. Johnson mentioned Richard K. Betts, Fritz Schwarz, and L. Britt Snider as examples of other Church staff who wrote or are writing in the intelligence field. On the workings of the Church inquiry staff, see Loch K. Johnson, *A Season of Inquiry: The Senate Intelligence Investigation* (Lexington, KY: University Press of Kentucky, 1985), pp. 15, 25–26, 33.

24 Letter, Theoharis to author, January 19, 2006. Douglas Charles, one of Theoharis's MA students, identified the following historians of the FBI as having come from the same stable: Susan Dion, Christopher Gerard, Patrick Jung, Francis MacDonnell, Kenneth O'Reilly and David Williams: email, Charles to author, 15 January 2006.

25 Athan G. Theoharis, "The FBI's Stretching of Presidential Directives, 1936–1953," *Political Science Quarterly*, 91 (Winter 1976–77), 654.

26 Theoharis, *Spying on Americans: Political Surveillance from Hoover to the Huston Plan* (Philadelphia, PA: Temple University Press, 1978), p. 156.

27 Barton J. Bernstein, "The Road to Watergate and Beyond: The Growth and Abuse of Executive Authority since 1940," *Law and Contemporary Problems*, 40 (Spring 1976), page 58n3, page 62nn11, 12, page 63n16.

28 Frank J. Donner, *The Age of Surveillance: The Aims and Methods of America's Political Intelligence System* (New York: Knopf, 1980), pp. 204–211, 289.

29 William W. Keller, *The Liberals and J. Edgar Hoover: Rise and Fall of a Domestic Intelligence State* (Princeton, NJ: Princeton University Press, 1989), pp. 6, 190; Anne Norton, *Leo Strauss and the Politics of American Empire* (New Haven, CT: Yale University Press, 2004), pp. 171–172.

30 William Sullivan, *The Bureau: My Thirty Years in Hoover's FBI* (New York: Norton, 1979), pp. 203–204; DeLoach, *Hoover's FBI: The Inside Story by Hoover's Trusted Lieutenant* (Washington, DC: Regnery, 1995), pp. 61, 299ff.

31 Ronald Kessler, *The FBI: Inside the World's Most Powerful Law Enforcement Agency* (New York: Pocket Books, 1993), pp. 484–485; Kessler, *The Bureau: The Secret History of the FBI* (New York: St Martin's Press, 2002), pp. 400–411; Kessler quoted in *The Christian Science Monitor*, June 25, 2001; FBI veteran William W. Turner's review of Kessler's *The Bureau* in the *Los Angeles Times Book Review*, May 19, 2002.

32 Burrough, *Public Enemies: America's Greatest Crime Wave and the Birth of the FBI, 1933–34* (New York: Penguin, 2004), p. 248n.

33 Aldrich, *Espionage*, p. 5.

34 John E. Haynes and Harvey Klehr, *In Denial: Historians, Communism, and Espionage* (San Francisco, CA: Encounter Books, 2003), p. 197 and passim. The earlier evidential challenge posed by Haynes and Klehr is encapsulated in their *Venona: Decoding Soviet Espionage in America* (New Haven, CT: Yale University Press, 1999).

35 Richard Gid Powers, *Broken: The Troubled Past and Uncertain Future of the FBI* (New York: The Free Press, 2004), pp. 24–25; Theoharis, *FBI and American Democracy*, p. 3.

36 For some examples of writing on CIA and foreign intelligence historiography, see Rhodri Jeffreys-Jones, "Introduction: The Stirrings of a New Revisionism?" in Jeffreys-Jones and Andrew Lownie, eds., *North American Spies: New Revisionist Essays* (Edinburgh: Edinburgh University Press, 1991), pp. 1–30; John Ferris, "Coming In from the Cold War: The Historiography of American Intelligence, 1945–1990," *Diplomatic History*, 19 (Winter 1995), 87–115; Gerald Haines, "The CIA's Own Effort to Understand and Document its Past: A Brief History of the CIA History Program, 1950–1995," in Jeffreys-Jones and Christopher Andrew, eds., *Eternal Vigilance? 50 Years of the CIA* (London: Frank Cass, 1997), pp. 201–223.

37 David Ray Griffin, *The New Pearl Harbor: Disturbing Questions about the Bush Administration and 9/11* (Northampton, MA: Olive Branch Press, 2004).

38 Len Scott and Peter Jackson, "The Study of Intelligence in Theory and Practice," *Intelligence and National Security*, 19 (Summer 2004), 139.

39 Eric Foner, *Reconstruction: America's Unfinished Revolution, 1863–1877* (New York: Harper & Row, 1988), p. xxi. William A. Dunning's influential work appeared in 1907: *Reconstruction, Political and Economic, 1865–1877* (New York: Harper). For a concise history of the Dunning School, see Foner, *Reconstruction*, pp. xix–xxi.

4

Intelligence ethics

Laying a foundation for the second oldest profession

Michael Andregg

Introduction

The first reaction to the idea of ethics for spies is often a big laugh or comments with "oxymoron" in them. Spies lie, cheat, steal, deceive, manipulate and sometimes do much worse in the course of their work, so this reaction is understandable. That masks a more important point. The world needs a professional code of ethics for spies and other "intelligence professionals." So some are working hard to create one now.[1] A former operator asked, why have intelligence agencies at all if you want to encumber them with rules? Because the nation is in danger, and our world is at war with "terrorists" who don't obey any rules at all. To win, spies must be better than mere terrorists.

Before discussing that developing code of ethics, a brief review of the varieties of spy is in order, since different types of intelligence professional often have different ideas of virtue and vice. For example, those who monitor phone calls or read other people's mail every day often take great offense when lumped into the same category as the "spies" who betray their countries for us, or betray us to serve some other country. I will reduce the many different kinds of intelligence professionals into five broad types.

- *Collectors* gather information, data or both, usually by technical means like satellites or from human agents, and feed it up a chain of command. Protecting "methods," "sources" and especially their own anonymity are cardinal virtues to them.
- *Analysts* process that information, and combine it with "open sources" information to generate higher order papers or other "products" that provide their policy masters with more *useful* information. Usefulness means timely, relevant and "actionable" as well as accurate information. Avoiding "politicization" of their information products is an important virtue to analysts. Politicization means altering one's formal opinion to suit the prejudices of policy makers, and this is a special but common sin among analysts.
- *Operators* go places and do things, sometimes very dramatic things like starting wars and such, more often they are doing quiet things they would prefer we not observe or talk about. Of all the types of intelligence professional, operators are the most likely to kill, blackmail, extort or torture in their work, and they often "handle" spies who are at

risk from their own governments. So guarding "operational security" is a core value to operators in order to protect their operations, the people they employ, and themselves.

- *Managers* organize the work of all of these people and the budgets that support them. Managers must contend with many bureaucratic forces, so their morality or lack thereof is more familiar to us all. And finally,
- *Policy makers*, in theory, make the decisions that have the greatest impact. In theory, all the others are working to support good decisions by policy makers in governments. The most obvious policy makers are politicians, who also must contend with odd forces in their work. Most have security clearances, but some do not. All lie; it is required by the job. So in contrast to analysts, "truth" is far less important to most policy people than expedience, or practical utility in their political struggles, 80 percent of which are domestic.

These types of real intelligence professional are all different from the James Bond-like image of a spy who sails into town in a cool car, steals secrets from rich bad men, grabs a beautiful woman or two and leaves just in time to avoid the building blowing up. They are also different from the Mata-Hari image of a beautiful woman who trades sex for secrets and then kills the foolish king or bureaucrat. The real spies also need a real professional ethic more sophisticated than that found in James Bond movies.

Ethics is the study of moral logic and paradigms, but it is not just lists of rules or laws. If ethics were that simple, attorneys would have a different reputation than they do. In ordinary life we can more easily observe the ancient moral virtues: be honest, don't steal, kill or assault, respect your neighbors, honor your debts and so forth. But the world of official intelligence involves activities in many grey areas of moral thought, and generates perplexing dilemmas where agents must balance the national interest in security, which they are bound to protect, against some other virtue like the ancient rules against lying, stealing, killing and so forth.

Classical Western philosophy as written by Plato, Aristotle and others concentrated on identifying moral "virtues" and asked how these could be cultivated in civilized men. Later Europeans generated doctrines that are now called "deontological" (or rule-based) as in Kant, or "consequentialist" (based on the consequences of an act) of which a good representative is the philosopher John Stuart Mill. To put these broad theories of moral reasoning into a small frame, any serious decision involves three things: an actor, an act and consequences of the act. Virtue theory concentrates on the actor, deontological theories concentrate on the morality of acts, and consequentialist theories focus on what happens after.

These Western theories of ethics often ignore parallel but not identical thinking from Asia, Africa and indigenous peoples world-wide. Buddha had many things to say about this, for example, as did Confucius and Lao Tzu. There are also more elaborate theories from Western tradition that are especially appropriate models for the spy world, like "Just War Theory" developed by Catholic priests and theologians searching for their own guides to moral clarity in difficult circumstances. There are many connections and similarities between "national intelligence" and war, so Just War Theory is sometimes used in training spies too. At least, it is referred to occasionally! Such complex ideas are what philosophy courses are for. With this sparse introduction, we will now turn to the major ways that spies or intelligence professionals of any kind must struggle with the moral dilemmas most peculiar to their unusual, but ancient profession.

Covert action

The most serious ethical dilemmas occur in the realm of covert, or secret, action. A career covert operator once told a colleague that "we use less than 10 percent of the budget, but we generate over 90 percent of the bad publicity." This is true because covert operations may employ all of the dark arts, and are responsible directly or indirectly for millions of deaths during the twentieth century. On the other hand, covert operations can also prevent wars from starting and there is no accurate way to number the lives saved by such methods. This captures the core dilemma of spies and spying quite sharply. Spies are extremely important to the question of whether wars start or do not start, as well as to who wins and who loses. Consequences for life and death can be vast. But measuring those effects is almost impossible, even after the events in question.

This is a problem for consequentialist theories of what constitutes moral behavior. If you cannot really know consequences, how can you judge if an act is moral? If you could save a city from a nuclear terrorist, for example, a consequentialist would usually conclude that it is perfectly OK to torture that terrorist if one might obtain information enabling you to recover and neutralize the bomb before it goes off. But who can know for sure, especially during crisis moments? These situations, called "ticking time bomb" scenarios, are discussed in law schools when they are considering the laws that (most say) strictly forbid torture under any circumstances. The deontological group would generally conclude that if the law forbids torture under any circumstances, well, that is the rule and it should be obeyed regardless of consequences. Others conclude that it would be cruel to let a silly rule keep one from saving thousands of innocent children. I leave the reader to determine what course of action the virtuous person would pursue.

Let us consider a more complex case based on real events. During the early and mid-1980s the US President Ronald Reagan decided that a political party in Nicaragua called the Sandinistas who had deposed a previous dictator was too closely aligned with the Soviet Union and should be removed. Simpler measures failed, but energized some in the US Congress, who wrote amendments to national legislation prohibiting any US intelligence agency from trying to overthrow the Sandinista government. Frustrated by these "Boland Amendments," the then-Director of Central Intelligence, William Casey, authorized an "off the books" project in 1983 run out of the National Security Council which raised tens of millions of dollars by various clever and illegal means like selling American weapons to a country that was an official enemy at that time, Iran. This affair became known as the "Iran–Contra" scandal.

That operation broke a great many national and international laws, but it is important to recognize that it also accomplished its political goals. A "secret" army was created, armed, and funded which came to be known as the "Contras." They created such chaos in Nicaragua that, combined with clandestine economic warfare and psychological operations from abroad, they managed to push the Sandinistas from power.

Regardless of whether one approves or disapproves of that political goal, this case vividly illustrates the dilemmas and the powers of secret operations. They won, by cheating. One document that was written by a CIA contract officer (on loan from the US Army) and published in tens of thousands of copies distributed to Contra troops, for example, called for selected assassinations of mayors and attacks on humanitarian groups, schools and medical clinics to demoralize Sandinista supporters. It was titled "Psychological Operations in Guerrilla Warfare"[2] and it is well worth study by professionals interested in insurgencies or in developing an ethic for spies that is higher than the gutter. To win the secret war, America was disgraced, with powerful long-term consequences that continue to this day. No longer would the USA be seen as a genuine moral leader in the international effort to establish and strengthen human rights.

It has been a canon of diplomacy for centuries that morality has no place in international affairs, and putting ethical boundaries on projects like the Iran-Contra operation seems near impossible. This is the reasoning of cynical men. In a world with weapons of mass destruction (WMDs) and millions of people angry enough to use them, we must do better than that. So I want to share the simple guidance of an operator I know well. His rules, based on experience rather than books, are:

- First, do no harm, especially to innocents. (Innocents have a very high place in his moral framework – this is not true for all operators or all "intelligence professionals.") When colleagues laugh, he tells them "Be an artist, not an oaf, and if you absolutely must; be a sniper, not a bomb. *Most* missions *can* be accomplished without undue harm, and even wetwork can be quite precise – stop excusing incompetence."
- Second, and only if techniques under rule 1 cannot protect the people, chose the lesser evil when moral dilemmas cannot be avoided. Thus if you must lie, cheat and steal to protect the people, this is permissible with reservations. Torture, murder, extortion and so forth should not be used except under the most extreme, compelling circumstances.
- Third, remember that the law of unintended consequences is real, and that perfection is not possible. So, he urges us to remember that the means chosen to do a thing usually determine the actual results achieved. Intentions matter little, consequences much, and millions of people have tried to do good by doing a little evil first. This almost never works in the long run. Rather, one wins tactical battles while losing the strategic war.
- Thus he urges spies to go back to the gold standard rule of solving one's problems without doing harm, especially to innocents. Avoid harsher measures unless absolutely compelled by extreme circumstances. The argument that good ends justify any practical means to achieve them is a treacherous, slippery ethical slope. Down that slope lie the rationalizations that excuse murdering doctors in clinics or teachers in schools or children in a village as a method of war to accomplish political objectives.

Handling agents

America's CIA has a category of career employee called a case officer whose primary job is to recruit and to manage (or "handle") spies from foreign countries (called assets or agents). Avoiding more jargon, the core point of this section is to point out that these agents often have families at risk, and a spy always risks his freedom or her life when s/he agrees to betray their country to benefit ours. This risk may be assumed for money, or it may be assumed for ideological reasons or for other reasons, although money and politics are by far the most common. Sometimes agents are blackmailed or may become victims of extortion and, in this manner, pressed into serving their handlers, so coercion may be involved. But always the agent has put his or her life in the hands of the officer who handles them. This puts enormous responsibility on the case officer, and presents some extraordinary moral dilemmas.

For example, what do you do if your superiors order you to send your agent into a trap to serve the larger interests of the nation? There is a reason some agents are called "expendable" but that will not help you sleep better at night if you betray someone you have spent years building trust with. On the other side of moral dilemmas, what do you do if your trusted agent begins blackmailing you, by threatening to reveal your entire espionage operation to their counterintelligence people, for example? This could endanger many other agents in the field, maybe even you if you are in the country in question right now.

It is for reasons like this that "protecting sources and methods" is such a core value to so many intelligence professionals. First, the effectiveness of the operation is usually destroyed if it is discovered. But also they recruit each other to take mortal risks sharing secrets when the penalty for detection can include at best prison and disgrace, and at worst, torture and death. They tend to recruit each other after long periods of earning trust slowly. But spying is a business of deception and betrayal, so sometimes these arrangements go awry. This is painful enough if it involves only individuals. If it involves war plans or national secrets, thousands of people may die because of bad decisions made in the darkness of false, incomplete or compromised information.

Analysis

Analysts are more like college professors who don't talk openly about their work than like the action commandos and sneaky divas called covert operators. Thus one might think their moral dilemmas are small, and they certainly would prefer to think so too.

But this is not true. Rather, this is an illusion encouraged by the "compartmentation of information" within official intelligence agencies. Analysts send their papers into a kind of black hole from which they seldom receive feedback whether anyone cared or took action on their recommendations. But the opinions of intelligence analysts can have profound consequences far from the desks where they were written. For example, one colleague spent three years of his life researching ways to destroy the economy of a small and already poor country. Economic warfare can have very profound effects. While many papers are ignored in official intelligence as in life, it is escapism to pretend that such analyses are never used, especially when covert wars are involved.

One cardinal sin among analysts has already been mentioned, politicization. Analysts are never, ever supposed to color their analyses to suit the prejudices of policy makers, even though policy people are often making very clear what they want to hear. Analysts are supposed to "speak truth to power" "without fear or favor," telling things like they are, no matter what. Of course, reality differs from theory here, since the easiest thing a policy maker can do (rather than changing their own mind) is to stop listening to one analyst and start listening to another who says what the politician wants to hear.

A reciprocal issue of especial importance to analysts is to avoid making policy oneself by what one writes. This is easy to say, but hard to do. Analysts are supposed to remain as objective as possible and to let the policy people do the policy. But being human beings, analysts inevitably develop opinions and even political values of their own.

This can become a significant moral dilemma when analysts warn about grave dangers, but are ignored by policy makers intent on other objectives. Those who warn loudest may be dismissed or just ignored by politicians who don't want to hear contrary views or who have simply already made up their minds on a course of action. Losing the ear of leaders is a serious issue to analysts; it is a grave issue to others when life and death is involved. Whether Iraq had active weapons of mass destruction (WMD) programs before the Gulf war of 2002 or not, for example, generated great controversy when such weapons were not found. A closely related question was whether this was a failure of intelligence or of policy, since the policy makers had made their preferences very well known before hand. Thus many analysts in the CIA and elsewhere had to ponder what they should do when the leaders were clearly determined to pursue a course of action with great peril, and on false evidence, no matter what analysts wrote or said.

Whistle blowers vs. leakers; treason vs. saving the nation from mad leaders

To "leak" secret information to the press is considered a cardinal sin among those for whom protecting sources and methods and also operational security are prime values. Yet to reveal criminal activity among governments is considered a virtue among the media and many citizens of democracies. When is a person bravely "blowing the whistle" on wrong doing, and when are they merely "leaking" secret information for bad purposes? These two inter-pretations involve exactly the same act, telling a reporter something that he or she wants to write about, but that someone else wants to keep secret. Finally, leaking information is as common as dirt among politicians. Who prosecutes them?

This dilemma is of the same kind, but much less severe than another which many intelligence professionals have had to face. What should one do if the supreme commander becomes insane, and orders things that put the nation itself at risk? Closely related to this is the issue of hubris. Derived from a Greek word, hubris means "overweening pride" or "dangerous arrogance" and it is an occupational hazard for kings, spies and professors. Any of these may come to believe that they are so special or so smart that rules which apply to lesser people need not be obeyed by them. Such overweening pride can lead to serious disasters if combined with power. Hubris is also extremely corrosive to wisdom, which is quite a different thing from intelligence.

Most intelligence professionals work for governments, or if not for governments for kings and other supreme commanders. They are pledged, and paid, to serve those institutions and individuals with great loyalty on some of their most difficult tasks. What does one do if the commander threatens the lives of all the innocents in his domain? Issues of nuclear war and other WMDs make this not a theoretical question.

Here there may be (should be) a significant difference between dictatorships, police states, and constitutional democracies. In constitutional democracies all power is ultimately derived from and vested in the people, and states are empowered in order to protect the people primarily. In kingdoms and police states power is held by a single man, or by one political party or government, not by the people *per se*. To legalists this is a very significant difference, because the relevant laws are certainly different. But intelligence professionals are distinguished by a degree of indifference to laws. At a deeper level, even democracies are ruled by men and women with mixed motives, and even tyrannies require a substantial degree of active support by the people they organize and oppress. What does one do if the sovereign goes nuts, and threatens the very life of the state, and the lives of its people?

Do not expect an answer here, because this is the most delicate question intelligence pro-fessionals must face, and its answer depends on many nuances one cannot truly address in an academic exercise. But have no doubt there are reasons why sovereigns both value, respect, and fear their intelligence communities.

Just be advised that people who deal in the life or death of millions actually have to ask questions like that, and answer them. Like a commander in the field who must decide whether to blow up a building full of armed men who are killing his troops (plus a few dozen utterly innocent children held as hostages) these are questions that tear hearts apart. What to do when one must choose between evil alternatives? What to do when sacred values conflict? It appears that the hardest questions are often those where two "good" values come into conflict. These are the same kind of questions whistle blowers ask. They have been taught from the beginning that revealing secrets can harm many people far away. But they also see something criminal, or dangerously wrong, which cries out to be revealed to the public that, in theory, the state is created to protect. What should spies or junior commanders do if their leaders become insane or grossly corrupt?

What is the responsibility of democratic citizens under the same circumstances? What about the ordinary soldier, pledged to support his leaders and his team? What about ordinary people, who also have great stakes in the life or death of their communities? These are difficult questions for anyone, but they are questions life presents from time to time. Citizens may chose to answer or ignore them, but sometimes intelligence professionals must decide concretely because the lives at risk are in their eyes.

Propaganda and psychological operations

The previous section may have left an impression that intelligence agencies rarely leak information to the press. On the contrary, this is a primary operational method for influencing political opinions. Amateurs call this propaganda, which is common as dirt in political discourse. Professionals use a near-science called psychological operations, which is more devastating precisely because such "PsyOps" are professionally designed, managed and deployed with the resources only governments possess. The evolution from propaganda as practiced by the Germans and many others during World War II to modern psychological operations is one of the darker chapters of spy history.

Space does not allow even an outline of techniques involved, except to note that they employ all the methods of advertising and public relations that are taught in business schools, as well as darker arts employed to destroy individual people's minds or to hoodwink whole populations. Some of those darker arts were discovered during a period of great fear in America, when apparently "brainwashed" prisoners of war prompted a massive effort to find drugs or other methods by which individual beliefs and behaviors could be manipulated. That program, called MKULTRA among other names, remains one of the least discussed chapters of the hidden history of American intelligence. Of course, the Russians had their version too, and the British, the Israelis, the Chinese and the Koreans who started this ball rolling. It appears that most large intelligence agencies have some psychological operations capability in their inventory.

The primary ethical problem with psychological operations is that its foundation is calculated lying. In theory, the ultimate goal of intelligence agencies is pursuit of "truth" uncontaminated by the prejudices of top leaders, biases of the analysts, or by the propaganda of other nations that are ever intent to conceal their dark secrets. In theory, bumblebees can't fly. In reality, even simple propaganda often works, so it is routinely employed in statecraft. The problem is that lies sent to alter behavior in other nations often "blow back" to contaminate thinking among domestic populations too.

This violates a bedrock principle of democracies, which is that the people need to know what is going on so that they can wisely select leaders based on realistic consideration of the policies they propose. For this reason the CIA was expressly forbidden from conducting propaganda operations within America when it was created. Unfortunately, even when the letter of this law is followed, modern technology makes a story planted in an obscure paper half way around the world instantly accessible to anyone who seeks it. Thus lies sown to bamboozle others far away may quickly blow back to contaminate domestic thinking. There is a reason many spies snort at public news.

Despite these grave complications of propaganda and psychological operations, it is important to recognize that there are some very good uses to which they may be put. For example, if one is about to destroy an enemy army, what is wrong with bombarding them with surrender leaflets first? This is now a standard practice, and when thousands do surrender, their lives are spared along with allied troops who would also die if compelled to destroy their enemy in close combat. And is it not better for professional interrogators to use sophisticated and less brutal means of persuasion to get tactical information from their prisoners of war, than to try torture, which is ever a temptation?

Technology and the surveillance society

Not long ago, to bug a telephone required a human being to put a physical device on the phone or physical phone line, and to do that legally required an actual warrant signed by a live judge attesting to probable cause to believe that the owner was a danger to someone. Now the NSA (National Security Agency) can tap almost any ordinary telephone just by pushing a button thousands of miles away, and they do so every day. Controversy over the laws involved is being overrun by technical developments which make it ever easier to monitor anyone, and as importantly, everyone.

In fact, it is much easier to monitor anyone if you are routinely but secretly recording everyone, which is the darkest secret of modern eavesdroppers. When the "Echelon" system was adopted by the signals intelligence agencies of the United States, Great Britain, Canada, Australia and New Zealand, they relied on trapdoors built into almost every communications satellite deployed in space, or major relay station on the earth's surface. These trapdoors split the signals, sending a copy to massive arrays of supercomputers whose job was to scan everything looking for keywords or codewords or simply picking off all communications to any designated number for review by human analysts. That was 20 years ago; we have come a terribly long way since then.

Today, the more electronically connected you are, the more accessible you are to automated systems looking for "terrorists" or whatever they are told to look for. And it is not just phone or computer data. The average person in London, for example, is photographed or videotaped at least 50 times per day, by cameras installed to watch the streets and deter crime. Such systems are incredibly useful for looking back when a serious crime has been committed, because real culprits may then be observed, their faces analyzed by specialty software and coded like a fingerprint. Your cell phone can be used to track you, and a phone in a home can be turned into a microphone for others to listen with, even when the phone is not being used for its normal purpose. Technical enthusiasts drool at what modern digital devices can do, especially when employed by the secret services of major nation states. Civil libertarians despair, and they don't know half of what is out there.

For just one more obvious example, your computer keeps the most detailed records on what you look for, write or do, and the same kind of trapdoors that were built into satellites were built into many mass market computer systems by agreement with the governments that could say yes or no to many aspects of business important to large corporations. So if they want to, they can peek from very far away and you will never know unless they knock on your door. The surveillance society is here. The question for professionals and for ordinary citizens is what to do about that?

One concept offered by some signals intelligence people is that of "minimum trespass" which roughly corresponds to the police ethic of "minimal force." In other words, they urge their colleagues to pry as little as possible into the private lives of their citizens while doing the business of looking for "terrorists" or other criminals out to do harm. This standard is notoriously weak because "minimal" is a very subjective concept and there is no real guarantee that the powers of surveillance won't be used for private gain, or for those currently in power to cripple those who aspire to power. The latter is fundamentally undemocratic, but ever a temptation to governments anywhere. In police states, this is actually the main job of the security services rather than protecting the people *per se*. That presents ethical dilemmas to some, who quickly become not employed by the secret political police . . . or suffer much worse fates.

A different conundrum presents itself. When one can look at what nearly everyone is saying or writing, one is immediately paralyzed by the vast volume involved. So most of the snooping is done by automated software instead of by human beings, and even those humans who must read the sifted gleanings are routinely overwhelmed by the volume of "potentially interesting" but ultimately irrelevant stuff that hits their screens. Second, to the consternation of professional intelligence agencies, the best media and the best academics are now getting more accurate answers to many questions faster than the professional spies. This is very disconcerting to intelligence professionals.

The reason why this is so provides a clue to resolving the inevitable ethical tensions that come when people spy on everyone. The best media and academics must *collaborate* with others every day. So accuracy, honesty, and open information sharing are core values to them. When reporters or professors make mistakes, these are quickly exposed by others in the business, which is embarrassing. So when working on collaborative projects, these "open source" professionals routinely ask each other to expose their mistakes while material is in draft form, so that errors will be corrected before public release. This concept of openly sharing information instead of keeping secrets and of collaborative searching for truth rather than solitary, aggressive attempts to penetrate information barriers, is absolutely central to the ethics and to the performance of top-quality media and academic people and institutions. Betraying people you share with ends the sharing; this is the misery of many spies today.

Restoring a more healthy relationship between spy agencies more sharply focused on con-sensus endeavors (like protecting the people) with the academic and media communities is the key to a revolution in intelligence affairs more fundamental than mere computer power. As I write, Google is trying to create a global brain accessible to all. Wish them well, because you can be sure that dark forces will also try to build the brain, but they would like to keep its power entirely to themselves. This is the fundamental ethical dilemma for those in the electronic intelligence domain today.

Codes of ethics for government agencies and commercial spies

There is a Society of Competitive Intelligence Professionals (SCIP) that concentrates on those who work for businesses, full-time or often as contractors. Their code of ethics is among the simplest and has been reproduced in hundreds of places, so we shall begin this section there. The University of Illinois has a collection of ethical codes from many sources at its Institute of Technology Code of Ethics website, http://ethics.iit.edu/codes. This site was gleaned from Jan Goldman's excellent book on the "Ethics of Spying," which has the unclassified versions of ethical codes from most of the main American intelligence agencies, and of a few international groups like SCIP, in its Appendix A. He also provides cases in Appendix B, which are especially useful for realistic training.

The SCIP Code of Ethics is:

- To continually strive to increase the recognition and respect of the profession.
- To comply with all applicable laws, domestic and international.
- To accurately disclose all relevant information, including one's identity and organization, prior to all interviews.
- To fully respect all requests for confidentiality of information.
- To avoid conflicts of interest in fulfilling one's duties.
- To provide honest and realistic recommendations and conclusions in the execution of one's duties.
- To promote this code of ethics within one's company, with third-party contractors, and within the entire profession.
- To faithfully adhere to and abide by one's company policies, objectives and guidelines.

As you can see, there is nothing here about industrial espionage much less blackmail, theft, assassination or the many other dark arts, except the injunction to "obey all laws." If theory and reality were more closely related, we would have little to write about!

Government ethics codes face a more difficult problem, because many governments have special laws for their spies that grant them immunity from laws that apply to ordinary citizens. Some of those special laws can be found in the public domain, but many are secret. In America, the annual Intelligence Appropriations Acts often contain classified codicils related to current operations of political importance. Another source of special laws are "Executive Orders" by the President, most of which are published, and a range of other orders that are more or less secret. During Reagan's time, these were called National Security Decision Directives or NSDDs. The First President Bush called his NSDs, Clinton called them PDDs, and George W. Bush issues NSPDs and HSDDs (the latter are Homeland Security Decision Directives). The acronyms chosen do not matter: the fact that special and often secret rules are created for spies does.

Furthermore, every national governmental spy agency expects its agents to obey most domestic laws, but specifically empowers many to go break the laws of other countries. And finally, agencies of police states may or may not have any legal boundaries at all on their activities, but if any exist, these are widely seen as window-dressing only. So the gap between written codes and actual practice is, as one might expect, quite wide!

A brief look at assassination is in order here. In 1976 US President Gerald Ford issued Executive Order 11905 to specifically forbid assassinating foreign leaders, partly because CIA plots to assassinate Fidel Castro had become publicly embarrassing, and partly due to the historic memory of the murders of President John F. Kennedy and of Martin Luther King by dark forces. To this day, despite vast international skepticism, the CIA denies any involvement in the murders of Patrice Lumumba of the Congo, Rafael Trujillo of the Dominican Republic, Salvador Allende of Chile and a long, long list of other political leaders and ordinary people. And who doubts that America wants to kill Osama bin Laden today (2006) whatever domestic or international law says about that?

But let us be fair. "Targeted killing" is employed by many, many nations. The Russians certainly killed Bulgarian dissident Georgi Markov by inserting a platinum pellet loaded with ricin (a specialty poison) into his thigh, and when they killed Chechen Rebel General Dzokhar Dudayev, the US actually helped them home in on his cell phone which provided the target data for the missile they used. The Israelis certainly killed most of the Palestinians who had been involved in the murders of athletes at the Munich Olympics (along with an utterly innocent man in Lillehammer, Norway); and even the gentle French killed an innocent man who was sleeping on a Greenpeace boat they decided to bomb in New Zealand. When innocents die, it is always an "accident" in spooky-luky land. Back to American sins, we wanted to kill an Al Qaeda leader in Yemen, so we blew up his car with a high-tech missile fired from a pilot-less airplane. Four other people were in the car including an American citizen, but guilt by association is often assumed when intelligence agencies wage war. Death squads empowered by intelligence entities murdered six priests, their cook and her daughter at the University of Central America in El Salvador in 1989, and another assassin killed the Archbishop Romero while preaching at his church in 1980. The list of people murdered in Latin America, Africa and Asia alone by agencies of various governments would be too long for this book if it could be written accurately. And when politicians desire a fig leaf, some hire mercenary killers from the contract world. So do not be deceived when governments say they have "outlawed" assassinations. This is what propagandists call a "partial truth," that is, technically true but quite misleading.

Most of these assassins thought that they were obeying the laws of their governments and whatever ethical codes their agencies employed for training. But deception and betrayal are the business of spies, and the principal tools called tradecraft have always been extortion, blackmail and murder or threats of murder whatever they say on paper or in public. So the presence of secret laws and special codes for secret agents is a central problem for those who would attempt to create a professional ethic for spies.

The official codes of the CIA, the FBI, the NSA, the DIA and the US government in general are full of excellent words like "integrity" and "honesty" and avoiding conflicts of interest and such. This is not to denigrate excellent words and noble goals, but rather to highlight the difference between legalistic codes and the core of moral thought.

In the nature of their work spies must deal with issues that challenge the best moral thinking, and while most people who enter this strange business are not moral morons, they are also not Snow White Bambi-kissers either. Many were military officers first, so many are accustomed to accomplishing missions as a primary value, some of which risk death of someone. So while codes, and rules of engagement, or lists of do's and don't can help, they cannot ever deal well with wrenching dilemmas like what do you do if terrorists threaten an entire city, but shield themselves with babies? Or what do you do if the leadership is insane, or just so blinded by lust for power or hubris that they would destroy society in their quest for some objective? What does one do, when the ancient laws of God and the modern codes of men are inadequate to the challenges before you? This is a question for you, dear citizen reader, as much as it is for spies.

Conclusion

Every era has pivotal forces or events that define that generation. The pivotal forces of today are Peak Oil, Globalization and the technical information revolution that has so empowered police states and the wealthy everywhere. As we come down from the peak of global oil production, energy will become more expensive faster because the easiest, cheapest and best has already been used. Globalization and the information revolution cause problems anywhere to metastasize much faster than before, from emerging diseases to the latest device for spying on your neighbor.

Rather than engage in the global struggle between those who have and those who don't, it is the sacred duty of intelligence professionals during this generation to rise above the habits of the past. Your policy masters will give you many missions, some wise, others not. It is imperative for you to distinguish between the two, and to help your leaders to comprehend that the only way to beat this crisis is to save almost everyone. The nation is in danger and the children are in peril . . . from ignorance and hubris, as much as from any other forces at work on this earth. Be professional, and protect them.

Notes

1 *Ethics of Spying: A Reader for the Intelligence Professional.* Edited by Jan Goldman, 26 contributors, published by Scarecrow Press of Lanham, Maryland, 2006.
2 "Psychological Operations in Guerrilla Warfare." By "Tayacan," a pseudonym for a U.S. Army psychological operations professional who wrote this for the CIA for use during the Contra war in Nicaragua. Original text can be accessed at a Federation of American Scientists website, http://www.fas.org/irp/cia/guerilla.htm. A paper edition was published in 1985 by Random House, under the title *Psychological Operations in Guerilla Warfare: The CIA's Nicaragua Manual*, with essays by Joanne Omang and Aryeh Neier (human rights advocates who put the text in contextual perspective). Like the CIA's earlier torture manual (called "KUBARK" and still used during the 1980s) they would prefer you not read it at all, but especially not with "context" unauthorized by their publications review board.

Part 2

The evolution of modern intelligence

5

The accountability of security and intelligence agencies

Ian Leigh

Intelligence is an inescapable necessity for modern governments. Few states take the view that they can dispense with an intelligence service and none is sufficiently immune from terrorism or the inquisitiveness of its neighbours to forgo a security service. It is true that a variety of patterns for organising security and intelligence exists. Some states (for example, Bosnia and Herzegovina, the Netherlands, Spain and Turkey) have a single agency for security and intelligence (both domestic and external). Others have distinct agencies for domestic and external intelligence and security, with either separate or overlapping territorial competences, as in the United Kingdom, Poland, Hungary and Germany. More rarely, a state may have a domestic security agency but no acknowledged or actual foreign intelligence agency; Canada is the exemplar of this approach. A further variable is that either intelligence or security services may have either a more pro-active mandate or be restricted to the gathering and analysis of information. However, whatever the precise organisational structure or governmental setting, security and intelligence pose a common set of challenges for accountability the world over.

The basic problem is easily stated: how to provide for democratic control of a governmental function and institutions which are essential to the survival and flourishing of the state but which must operate to a certain extent in justifiable secrecy. Sir Humphrey Appleby, the civil servant anti-hero of the classic BBC television series "Yes Minister", was parodying a bureaucratic maxim when he advised his political master Sir James Hacker that "Open Government" was a contradiction in terms. Nevertheless, in contrast to many other areas of governmental activity, in the case of security and intelligence it is widely accepted that official advice cannot be transparent, otherwise operations, sources and assets will be compromised. This implies corresponding restraint in the oversight and accountability of the secret world. Restraint is perhaps the wrong word, for, due to the secrecy involved, the need for rigorous control is greater not less than with more mundane government functions, such as education or transport.

The necessary secrecy surrounding security and intelligence runs the risk of encouraging illegal and ethically dubious practices on the part of the agencies involved. The democratic process itself may be subverted by infiltration of political parties, trade unions or civil society groups. The privacy of countless individuals may be interfered with by the collection, storage, and dissemination of personal data, whether accurate or flawed. Inefficiency and corruption may go unchecked. In the increasingly multi-lateral spirit of intelligence co-operation after 9/11 the risk has grown also of sharing information with discreditable regimes.

The discussion that follows first considers the place of administrative and executive accountability, then the role of parliamentary accountability, followed by legal accountability. Finally attention turns to the procedures for handling complaints and forms of independent review. In all these fields we shall see that the challenge is to balance justifiable secrecy with accountability, democratic governance and the rule of law.

Administrative and executive controls

In modern states the security and intelligence agencies have a vital role to play serving and supporting government in its domestic, defence and foreign policy by supplying and analyzing relevant intelligence and countering specified threats. This is equally true of domestic security (especially counter-terrorism, counter-espionage and countering threats to the democracy nature of the state) and in the realm of international relations, diplomacy and defence. It is essential, however, that the agencies and officials who carry out these roles are under democratic control through elected politicians, rather than accountable only to themselves: it is elected politicians who are the visible custodians of public office in a democracy. The risk of a state within the state, accountable to no one, is a real one, unless there are mechanisms in place for firm control by elected politicians.

Yet there is an opposite and just as real danger: the temptation for politicians to use these exceptional agencies to serve a domestic party political agenda. The possibility of gathering information to discredit or influence domestic politics must be guarded against.

There is an inherent tension between these two concerns. Sensitive accountability structures therefore attempt to insulate security and intelligence agencies from political abuse without isolating them from executive governance. On the whole the solutions adopted by democratic states deal with this paradox in two ways. Firstly, by balancing rights and responsibilities between the agencies and their political masters and, secondly, by creating checking mechanisms outside the executive branch.

Balancing rights and responsibilities

Effective democratic control and policy support depends on a two-way process of access between politicians and officials. Ministers need access to relevant information in the hands of the agency or to assessments based upon it through intelligence assessments and, they must also be able to give a public account where necessary about the actions of the security sector. Conversely, officials need to be able to brief government ministers on matters of extreme sensitivity.

Commonly on the ministerial side, intelligence legislation deals with the allocation of responsibility for formulating policy on security and intelligence matters (within, of course, the legislative mandate of the agencies); it also covers a right to receive reports from the agencies and a reservation of the right to approve matters of political sensitivity (for example, co-operation with agencies from other countries) or activities that affect fundamental rights (such as the approval of the use of special powers, whether or not additional external approval is required, for instance, from a judge). In contrast, the agency may be under a duty to implement government policy, to report to ministers and to seek approval of specified sensitive matters, such as covert action. Ministers may set written policies or targets to guide agency priorities, and be involved in processes of budgetary approval, reporting and audit.

Approval of covert action is a special case deserving of mention. Covert action raises issues of accountability for at least two reasons. Firstly, since this type of action is secretive it will be difficult for the legislature to control (even if legislators are aware of it). Nevertheless, there is a legitimate parliamentary interest in action taken by the state's employees and using public money. Secondly, there is an ethical dimension. Historically, a number of covert action programmes have involved controversial strategies and techniques. The fact that these are covert and usually illegal according to the law of the state in whose territory they take place makes the temptation to abuse perhaps all the greater. It is therefore all the more important that elected politicians set ground-rules for what is acceptable (for instance, compliance with international human rights law) and are responsible for authorising covert action. For example, the US Executive Order asserts a measure of *Presidential* control: "No agency except the CIA (or the Armed Forces of the United States in time of war declared by Congress or during any period covered by a report from the President to the Congress under the War Powers Resolution (87 Stat. 855)) may conduct any special activity unless the President determines that another agency is more likely to achieve a particular objective."

In some countries, the executive is aided in the task of control by an Inspector-General, an institution most often established by law and endowed with various rights and responsibilities *vis-à-vis* both the executive and the parliament. In this context, the Inspector-General monitors whether the government's intelligence policies are appropriately implemented by the services (Intelligence and Security Committee, 2002, Appendix 3 for a comparison of Inspectors-General). These offices exist to provide assurance for the government that it has all the relevant information and that secret agencies are acting according to its policies. In other instances (discussed below) they report to parliament rather than to the government.

A variety of safeguards on the agency side against political manipulation and abuse can be used. One method is to give legal safeguards for the agency heads through security of tenure, to set legal limits to what the agencies can be asked to do, and to establish independent mechanisms for raising concerns about abuses. These provisions help safeguard against both improper pressure being applied on the director and abuse of the office. Hence, it is common to find provisions for security of tenure, subject to removal for wrongdoing, as in the case of a legislation example from Poland (Article 16, Internal Security Agency and Foreign Intelligence Act 2002, Poland). Where staff from security agencies fear improper political manipulation it is vital also that they have available procedures with which to raise these concerns outside the organisation. These include the right for officials to refuse unreasonable governmental instructions (for example, to supply information on domestic political opponents) and whistle-blowing or grievance procedures.

There are also commonsense reasons for a formal separation between executive oversight and managerial control of the agencies and their operations. It will be impossible for political leaders to act as a source of external control if they are too closely involved in day-to-day matters, and the whole oversight scheme will be weakened. There is the danger also (seen during the build-up to the second Gulf war) of politicising the intelligence cycle, with the consequence that the analysis stage and the end-product will be less useful (Gill 2005). This suggests that there should be a clear delineation of distinct but complementary roles for the executive and agency heads. Canadian legislation embodies the principle in the Canadian Security Intelligence Service Act 1984, referring to the director of the service having "the *control and management* of the Service" that is "*under the direction*" of the Minister. Similarly, Polish intelligence legislation clearly distinguishes between the respective competences of the Prime Minister and the heads of the agencies (Art. 7 Internal Security Agency and Foreign Intelligence Agency Act 2002).

Checking mechanisms

The purpose of embodying checks and balances on executive governance of the agencies is to enlist either a cross-section of political opinion or to involve politically neutral institutions. These checks may take the form of external approval or confirmation of certain decisions or – somewhat weaker – a duty to inform external actors of sensitive or controversial matters. The mere existence of such duties may serve as a deterrent and act as safeguard for the agency.

One safeguard is for external involvement or scrutiny of the appointment of the director of the intelligence and security agencies. The head of agency will inevitably be a senior official position and it is important that the process of appointment reinforces and guarantees the status of the position and ensures the necessary qualities of leadership, integrity and independence. In some countries (for instance, the United Kingdom) the safeguards against abuse in official appointments such as this rest on conventions which, if broken, lead to political criticism and possible censure by independent officials. Other countries employ formal confirmation or consultation procedures, to allow the legislature to either veto or express their opinion on an appointment. There may be a constitutional requirement either that official appointments must be approved by parliament or, at least allowing them to be blocked by a parliamentary vote (e.g. the practice in the US). In Belgium, the director-general is obliged to take the oath before the chairman of the Permanent Committee for Supervision of the Intelligence and Security Services before taking office (Act Governing the Supervision of the Police and Intelligence Services, 1991, Art. 17). In Australia, the Prime Minister must consult with the Leader of the Opposition in the House of Representatives concerning the proposed appointment (Part 3, Section 17 (3), Intelligence Service Act, Australia, 2001 (Cth)). The aim of such provisions is to achieve a broad political backing for the director's appointment.

Another area for safeguards concerns political instructions. A legal requirement that certain ministerial instructions be put in writing (for example, Canadian Security Intelligence Service Act 1984, Sections 7(1) and (2); Act on the National Security Services 1995, Hungary, Section 11) can act as aid to accountability by preventing "plausible deniability" and even some questionable instructions from being given in the first place because to do so would involve a paper trail. An example combining protection of human rights is the Australian legislation requiring the ministers responsible for the Australian Secret Intelligence Service, and the responsible minister in relation to the Defence Signals Directorate, to issue written instructions to the agency heads dealing with situations in which the agencies produce intelligence on Australians: the Intelligence Services Act 2001, s. 8(1). In addition, a requirement that ministerial instructions must be disclosed outside the agency may act a checking device. Examples can be found in Canadian law, which requires them to be given to the Review body, and Australian legislation, requiring them to be given to the Inspector-General of Intelligence and Security as soon as practicable after the direction is given (Canadian Security Intelligence Service Act 1984, s. 6(2), and Australian Inspector-General of Intelligence and Security Act, 1986, Section 32B, respectively).

One important consideration in maintaining a bipartisan approach to security and intelligence is to include prominent opposition politicians within the "ring of secrecy". In the United States and the United Kingdom intelligence briefing of senior politicians (for example in the run-up to the invasion of Iraq) is a relatively informal practice, but with obvious political benefits. In Australian law there is a formal duty on the Director-General of the intelligence service to brief the Leader of the Opposition (Intelligence Services Act, Australia 2001, Section 19).

Scrutiny of the security sector cannot, however, remain the exclusive preserve of the government alone without inviting potential abuse. It is commonplace, aside from their role in setting the legal framework, for parliaments to take on the task of scrutinising governmental activity. There is no inherent conflict between effective executive control and parliamentary oversight. Quite the contrary: effective parliamentary oversight *depends* on effective control of the agencies by ministers. Parliaments can only reliably call politicians to account for the actions of the intelligence agencies if ministers have real powers of control and adequate information about the actions taken in their name. Where this is lacking, the only democratic alternative is for a parliamentary body or official to attempt to fill the vacuum. This, however, is a poor substitute because legislative bodies can effectively review the use of powers and expenditure ex post facto, but they are not inherently well equipped to direct and manage these matters, whereas governmental structures are.

Oversight by parliament

The case for the involvement of legislators in oversight rests on several factors. The ultimate authority and legitimacy of intelligence agencies rest upon legislative approval of their powers, operations and expenditure. The security and intelligence sector should not be a *zone sanitaire* for democratic scrutiny, otherwise there is a risk that the agencies may serve narrow political or sectional interests, rather than the state as a whole and protecting the constitutional order. Proper control ensures a stable, politically bipartisan approach to security which is good for the state and the agencies themselves. Since the agencies have large budgets (the more so since 9/11), the involvement of parliamentarians can also help ensure that the use of public money in security and intelligence is properly authorised and accounted for.

Although the case for parliamentary oversight is compelling, there are some risks. The security sector may be drawn into party and political controversy; an immature approach by parliamentarians may lead to sensationalism in public debate, and to wild accusations and conspiracy theories being made in the chamber with all the attendant publicity. Away from the public gaze effective scrutiny of security is painstaking and unglamorous work that may be unattractive to politicians who seek immediate public credit for their contribution.

Mandate of the parliamentary oversight body

From a comparative international perspective the most frequent arrangement is for parliament to establish a single oversight body for all the major security and intelligence agencies, rather than having multiple oversight bodies for specific agencies. Where there is one single oversight body this facilitates seamless oversight. Since different parts of the intelligence machinery work closely with each other, an effective oversight body needs to be able to cross agency boundaries. Correspondingly, oversight arrangements designed to track separate agencies can be hampered if they lead in the direction of information supplied by or to an agency outside the legal range of operation.

There are some significant divergences from the single all-agency parliamentary oversight body model, however. In the US there are separate congressional intelligence committees in the House of Representatives and the Senate, each with legal oversight of the agencies (Johnson 2005). In the United Kingdom the Intelligence and Security Committee's legal remit covers only part of the intelligence establishment (Defence Intelligence Staff, the Joint Intelligence Committee and National Criminal Intelligence Service are not included in the legal remit of the committee). In practice, however, and with the cooperation of the government, the Intelligence and Security Committee has examined their work as well (Leigh 2005).

The remit of these parliamentary oversight bodies varies considerably. Some have the power to scrutinize the *operations* of intelligence agencies. Thus, both the US congressional oversight committees as well as the Control Panel of the German Bundestag have the right to be briefed about the operations of the agencies (Bundestag 2001). Where a parliamentary oversight body is able to examine intelligence operations clearly, its reports may have greater credibility. It may also be given greater powers (for example, to compel the production of evidence). However, inevitably some operational detail will have to be excluded from its reports to parliament and the public. Operating within the ring of secrecy in this way runs the risk of creating a barrier between the oversight body and the remainder of parliament. There is also the danger of a too close relationship between the oversight body and the agencies it is responsible for overseeing. For example, although a legal requirement that it be notified in advance of certain actions by the agency may appear to strengthen oversight, it could also inhibit the oversight body from later criticism of these operational matters.

A parliamentary oversight body whose remit is limited to scrutiny of matters of policy, administration and finance (as is the case in the United Kingdom) is able to work more readily in the public arena and can operate under fewer restrictions on what is disclosed. This second approach, however, detracts from one of key tasks of parliamentary scrutiny of the *effectiveness* of the agencies in carrying out government policy. To assess that effectiveness, access to *some* operational detail is necessary so that an oversight body can provide public assurance about the efficiency of the security and intelligence agency in implementing published policies. This applies also to auditing issues of legality or the agencies' respect for human rights (as is the case with the Norwegian Committee: The Act relating to the Monitoring of Intelligence, Surveillance and Security Services, Act No. 7 of 3 February 1995; Sejersted 2005). Exercises in parliamentary oversight such as these will appear hollow unless based on clear evidence about the behaviour of the agency concerned.

The difference between oversight bodies designed to review policy and those concerned with operational matters is inevitably reflected in the powers that such bodies have. This explains why the approach in the United Kingdom and Australia has been to give a wide remit and then to detail specific matters which may *not* be investigated (respectively, Intelligence Services Act 1994, s. 10; Intelligence Services Act 2001 No. 152, 2001, ss 28 and 29). In the US, however, the law provides a comprehensive list of oversight functions of the parliamentary oversight body (Section 13, United States Rules of the US Senate Select Committee on Intelligence).

Access to classified information

The extent to which a parliamentary oversight body requires access to security and intelligence information and the type of information concerned depends on the specific role that it is asked to play. An oversight body whose functions include reviewing questions of legality, effectiveness and respect for human rights will require access to more specific information than one whose remit is solely policy (for examples of powers to obtain documents see the [Australian] Intelligence Services Act 2001, s. 30.2(4)). Similarly, it will have a stronger case for a right of access to documents (rather than information or testimony from identified witnesses).

These differences in role explain some of the variations in the extent to which oversight bodies are given access to operational detail in different constitutional systems. Some countries, e.g. the US, provide that the executive has the legal responsibility to keep the Congressional intelligence committees fully and currently informed of the intelligence activities of the Unitₑ States. Moreover, the US Congressional Oversight Provisions demand that the President keeps the Congressional intelligence committees informed about all covert actions operations, including significant failures, before initiation of the covert action authorised by the Presidential finding (United States Code, Title 50, Section 413). In the Intelligence Authorization Act of 1991 the President promised to continue to inform the Congress in advance in most instances, but he insisted on flexibility in times of crises – as defined by the White House (Johnson 2005: 64–65).

Systems vary also in how they handle reporting of sensitive material. In the US, the onus of *being informed* not only rests with the oversight body, but with the executive as well. In Australia, in contrast, the Parliamentary Committee is forbidden from requiring "operationally sensitive information" from being disclosed (Intelligence Services Act 2001, s. 30); requests for documents cannot be made be made by the committee to agency heads or staff members or to the Inspector-General, and ministers may veto evidence from being given (Intelligence Services Act 2001, s. 32). A power of veto of this kind effectively returns disputes over access to information to the political arena.

Adequate support is important to the success of parliamentary oversight. Some countries have stipulated therefore that the oversight body is also entitled to obtain information and documents from experts, for example in think tanks or universities. For example, in Luxembourg the Parliamentary Control Committee can decide, with two-thirds majority and after having consulted the Director of the Intelligence Services, to be assisted by an expert (Art. 14(4), Loi du 15 Juin portant organisation du Service de Renseignement de l'Etat, Memorial-Journal Officiel du Grand-Duché de Luxembourg, 2004, A-No. 113). This allows for alternative viewpoints to those of the government and the services to be considered.

Naturally, however, oversight bodies of various countries have made great efforts to protect information and documents related to sensitive issues (about persons) and/or about national security from unauthorised disclosure. Unauthorised disclosure of information may not only harm national security interests, but may also harm the trust which is necessary for an effective relationship between the oversight body and the services. This may be governed by legislation; see for example, United States Code Section 413, General Congressional Oversight Provisions, (d) and the Act Relating to the Monitoring of Intelligence, Surveillance and Security Services, 1995, Section 9, (Norway). It is also, however, partly a matter of proper behaviour of the members of the oversight body in dealing with classified information with care and attention. Leaks of sensitive material will almost certainly undermine the relationship of trust with the agencies themselves and, therefore, adversely affect oversight.

Membership of the parliamentary oversight body

The appointment of the membership of oversight bodies is inevitably a key factor affecting public confidence in and the success of new oversight arrangements. Two factors in particular enhance legitimacy. First is the question of "ownership" of the oversight arrangements, for example reflected in the power of the parliament to make appointments and cross-party representation. Second, there is the need for a clear demarcation between the oversight body and the agencies overseen; this is often part of a more general "civilianisation" of transitional societies. A particular difficulty arises in transition states: the presence of former members of the security agencies on the oversight body. Where the services were implicated in maintaining a repressive former regime this is bound to undermine confidence in the oversight process and is best avoided, if necessary by a legal prohibition.

r distinction between those states where legislators themselves take on the
ough a parliamentary committee (for example, Argentina, Australia, South
gdom and the USA) and those where a committee has been set up outside
ose members are not parliamentarians, but reporting to parliament (e.g. the
im, Norway). The former may seem more democratically legitimate.
, the latter allows for greater expertise and time in the oversight of security and
intelligence services and avoids the risks of political division and grand-standing to which
parliamentary committees can be prone. A third possibility should be mentioned also: in the
case of Canada there are proposals to supplement the long-standing (non-parliamentary)
Security Intelligence Review Committee with a committee of parliamentarians (Farson
2005).

There are various options for appointing the membership of parliamentary oversight bodies.
The head of government may appoint (after consultation with the leader of the opposition, in
the case of the United Kingdom; see Intelligence Services Act 1994, s. 10). The executive may
nominate members but parliament itself appoints (as in Australia; after consultation of other
party leaders by the Prime Minister: Intelligence Services Act 2001, s. 14). Finally, there are
countries in which the legal responsibility for appointment rests solely with the legislature, as in
Argentina, Germany and Norway (see respectively: Estevez, 2005; Law on the Parliamentary
Control of Activities of the Federal Intelligence Services [PKGrG] [1978; 1992, 1999 and 2001
amended version]; Instructions for Monitoring of Intelligence, Surveillance and Security
Services [EOS], 1995, Section 1). Although traditions vary within parliamentary systems
concerning the chairmanship of parliamentary committees, it can be safely stated that the
legitimacy of a parliamentary oversight body is enhanced if it is chaired by a member of the
opposition (as in Hungary, Section 14, 1, Act nr. CXXV of 1995 on the National Security
Services), or if the chairmanship rotates between the opposition and the government party, or
if the chair is chosen by the committee itself (as in Argentina), rather than being appointed by
the government (as in the United Kingdom).

Legal accountability

The previous sections have described the importance of the executive and of parliament in
relation to accountability of intelligence agencies. However, the third organ of the state – the
judiciary – also has a role to play, both as the ultimate guardian of the constitution and the law,
and, outside of court, in various review functions. This section begins with an explanation of
the need for legal standards, followed by a discussion of the role of the judiciary.

The need for legislation

The rule of law is a fundamental and indispensable element of democracy. Only if security and
intelligence agencies are established by law and derive their powers from the legal regime can
they be said to enjoy legitimacy. Without such a framework there is no basis for distinguishing
between actions taken on behalf of the state and those of law-breakers, including terrorists.
It is therefore appropriate that in democracies where the rule of law prevails, intelligence and
security agencies derive their existence and powers from legislation, rather than exceptional
powers such as the prerogative. This enhances the agencies' legitimacy and enables parliamentarians to address the principles that should govern this important area of state activity
and to lay down limits to the work of such agencies. Moreover, in order to claim the benefit

of legal exceptions, for the sake of national security, to human rights standards it is necessary that the security sector derive its authority from legislation.

Within Europe the European Convention on Human Rights ("ECHR") – a regional human rights treaty ratified by 46 states and interpreted by the European Court of Human Rights at Strasbourg – has been an important influence in promoting reform. The European Convention allows restrictions to the rights of public trial, respect for private life, freedom of expression and of association "in accordance with law" where "necessary in a democratic society" in the interests of national security (see Cameron 2000 and 2005). Additionally, if the services possess the legal power to interfere with private property and communications, citizens should have a legal procedure available for making complaints if any wrongdoing occurs. This is one way in which states that are signatories to the ECHR can meet their obligation to provide an effective remedy for arguable human rights violations under Article 13 of that Convention.

As a result the European Convention has been influential in requiring signatory states to introduce legislation giving a clear legal basis for the actions of the services in these fields and to provide domestic means for challenging the actions of the services affecting human rights. Several states have been found by the European Court of Human Rights to have breached the Convention where these laws were defective or where individual practices, such as telephone-tapping or bugging, lacked clear legal authority (*Harman and Hewitt* v. *UK* [1992] 14 EHRR 657; *Rotaru* v. *Romania*, No. 28341/95, 4 May 2000, European Court of Human Rights; *V and Others* v. *Netherlands*, Commission Report of 3 Dec. 1991). The Convention requires more than a simple veneer of legality, however. The Court refers additionally to the "Quality of Law" test. This requires the legal regime to be clear, foreseeable and accessible. For example, where a Royal Decree in the Netherlands set out the functions of military intelligence but omitted any reference to its powers of surveillance over civilians, this was held to be inadequate. Similarly, in *Rotaru* v. *Romania* the Strasbourg Court held that the law on security files was insufficiently clear as regards grounds and procedures since it did not lay down procedures with regard to the age of files and the uses to which they could be put, or establish any mechanism for monitoring them.

It is no surprise then to find that over the last three decades many states have reformed or introduced laws governing the security and intelligence agencies. Some recent European examples include legislation in Bosnia and Herzegovina (2005), Slovenia (1994), Lithuania (1996) and Estonia (2000).

The role of the judiciary

There are two main strengths to judicial scrutiny. Judges are perceived to be independent of the government and, therefore, have the appearance of giving an external view which lends credibility to the system of oversight in the eyes of the public. A traditional role of the courts is the protection of the rights of the individual, and judges are well suited to oversight tasks where the interests of individuals are involved, for example, surveillance.

However, there are a number of problems also. Some are in-built tensions in judicial review of any governmental function, others are specific to the field of security (Lustgarten and Leigh 1994: ch. 12). Judicial involvement inevitably means that sensitive data has to be shared outside of the controlled environment of the security sector itself. Even if public proceedings in open court are avoided, the judge, court staff and lawyers may be required to handle the information. The seniority and reputation of the judges involved may be sufficient guarantee that they can be trusted with secret information (although some in countries judges are vetted; in others this would be constitutionally unacceptable).

Too intrusive control by the judges carries them into the executive sphere, i.e. it blurs the separation of powers between the two branches of the state. The use of judges to conduct inquiries with a security dimension in particular runs the risk of the politicisation of judiciary. This suggests that judicial involvement may only be suitable for some functions, and not, perhaps, where policy is a substantial element.

Legal control by the courts proper only operates within the limited sphere where a person's rights are affected. Since much security work is below this horizon of visibility (e.g. gathering information on individuals from public sources/surveillance in public places), the courts are ineffective as sources of control in these areas. Moreover, by their nature the operations of the security sector are often not apparent to the individuals most affected (for example, the targets of surveillance). Unless legal procedures, such as prosecution or deportation, are invoked these people will therefore be unlikely to challenge the legality of the activities, and those activities will remain immune from review. However, most security work is not directed towards legal procedures and it is therefore likely to remain unchecked by these processes. In other countries legal barriers effectively prevent review; for example, in the United Kingdom evidence obtained from telephone tapping is generally not admissible in court under the Regulation of Investigatory Powers Act 2000, consequently the propriety of warrants for phone tapping cannot be challenged by that route.

Several states employ specially adapted judicial procedures in a security context: in Canada designated Federal Court judges hear surveillance applications from the Canadian Security Intelligence Service and deal with immigration and freedom of information cases with a security dimension (Leigh 1996). In the US the Foreign Intelligence Surveillance Act has cast judges in the guise of approving intelligence-related surveillance for nearly two decades. In the United Kingdom designated judicial commissioners deal with some forms of authorisation of surveillance under the Regulation of Investigatory Powers Act 2000 while others are responsible for reviewing the system and the grant of ministerial warrants and authorisations to the security and intelligence services.

Even where judges are used for tasks affecting the rights of individuals there is a danger that they will in effect lose the qualities of independence and external insight through a process of acclimatisation. For example, as judges hearing warrant applications based on security information become familiar with the types of techniques, information and assessments used they may become, in effect, "case hardened". This suggests a pattern of declining effectiveness in protecting individuals' rights in practice. Evidence from countries which require prior judicial approval of surveillance warrants such as Canada and the USA does not suggest high rates of refusal. There may be little difference in the end result to approval within the agency itself or by a government minister.

Some of these processes have produced innovations designed to balance "open justice" with the state's security interests. One idea, adapted from Canadian procedure, is the use of special, security-cleared counsel, in deportation and employment cases, and (increasingly) in criminal cases (Treasury Solicitor 2005). This gives protection for state secrets without totally excluding any opportunity of challenge to the evidence on the applicant's behalf (in the United Kingdom, see especially the Special Immigration Appeals Commission). It allows a vetted lawyer to test the strength of the government's case even where the complainant and his lawyer are excluded from parts of the legal process on security grounds. Such procedures have been commended by the European Court of Human Rights as a means of satisfying Article 6 (the right to a fair and public trial), even in security cases (*Chahal* v. *UK* (1997) 23 EHRR 413). They have, however, received more critical responses from some of those involved in the role of special counsel and from a parliamentary select committee (Constitutional Affairs Select Committee 2005).

These innovations apart, for the reasons discussed regular courts are not well suited as instruments of accountability for or redress against security and intelligence agencies. This leads naturally to a discussion of other processes for handling complaints.

Complaints processes

There is a clear need for some avenue of redress for individuals who claim to have been adversely affected by the exceptional powers, such as surveillance or security clearance, often wielded by security and intelligence agencies. In addition, as an aspect of accountability, complaints may have a broader role to play also in highlighting administrative failings and lessons to be learned, leading to improved performance. Clearly, however, any system for redress needs to be designed to prevent legitimate targets of a security or intelligence agency from finding out about the agency's work. Achieving this balance in a complaints system between independence, robustness and fairness, on the one hand, and sensitivity to security needs on the other is challenging but not impossible. The requirements of human rights treaties, and especially for European states, the European Convention on Human Rights, with its attendant protection of fair trial, respect for private life and the requirement of an effective remedy also have a considerable bearing on these matters (see further Cameron 2000 and 2005).

Different oversight systems handle complaints in a variety of ways. An independent official, such as an ombudsman, may have power to investigate and report on a complaint against an agency; this is the case in the Netherlands (Intelligence and Security Services Act 2002, Art. 83). In some countries an independent Inspector-General of security and intelligence deals with complaints against the services as part of the office's overall oversight remit in a rather similar way. This is the case, for example, in New Zealand (Office of Inspector-General of Intelligence and Security, established in 1996) and South Africa (Office of Inspector General of Intelligence, appointed pursuant to section 12 of the Constitution). In addition, specific offices established under freedom of information or data protection legislation may have a role in investigating complaints against the agencies.

Ombudsman-type systems place reliance on an independent official investigating on behalf of the complainant. They usually exist to deal with an administrative failure rather than a legal error as such. They give less emphasis to the complainant's own participation in the process and to transparency. They typically conclude with a report and (if the complaint is upheld) a recommendation for putting matters right and future action, rather than a judgment and formal remedies.

Less commonly some countries deal with complaints and grievances of citizens through use of a parliamentary intelligence oversight committee, as is the case in, for example, Germany and Norway (Sejersted 2005). There may be a benefit for a parliamentary oversight body in handling complaints brought against security and intelligence agencies since this will give an insight into potential failures – of policy, legality and efficiency. Yet, if the oversight body is too closely identified with the agencies it oversees, or operates within the ring of secrecy, the complainant may feel that the complaints process is insufficiently independent. In cases where a single body handles complaints and oversight it is best if there are quite distinct legal procedures for these different roles. On the whole it is preferable that the two functions be given to different bodies but that processes are in place so that the oversight body is made aware of the broader implications of individual complaints.

In some countries not only citizens but also members of the services are permitted to bring service-related issues to the attention of an ombudsman or parliamentary oversight body.

For example, in Germany officials may raise issues with the Parliamentary Control Panel (Bundestag 2001: 19–20) and in South Africa members of the service may complain to the Inspector General.

Another method of handling complaints is through a specialist tribunal. This may be established to deal with complaints either against a particular agency or in relation to the use of specific powers, as in the United Kingdom (the Intelligence Services Commissioner and the Commissioner for the Interception of Communications). Or complaints may be handled in a tribunal-type procedure but by a specialist oversight body, as with the Security Intelligence Review Committee in Canada. A tribunal of this kind has some advantages over a regular court in dealing with security- and intelligence-related complaints: it can develop a distinct expertise in the field of security and intelligence, and follow procedures devised for handling sensitive information. In view of the nature of the subject matter these are unlikely to involve a full public legal hearing. In contrast, while some tribunals may give the complainant a hearing, he or she is likely to face severe practical difficulties in proving a case, in obtaining access to relevant evidence, or in challenging the agency's version of events. To combat some of these problems special security-cleared counsel have been introduced in Canada and in the United Kingdom. These counsel have the task of challenging security-related arguments, especially those aspects not disclosed to the complainant. This can help the tribunal reach a more object-ive assessment of the evidence and the arguments.

Inspectors-general and audit

The final area of accountability to be examined is the role of independent officials. Apart from redress of complaints another reason for the creation of independent offices is to pro-vide impartial verification and assurance for the government that secret agencies are acting according to its policies, effectively and with propriety. For this reason a number of countries have devised offices such as inspectors-general, judicial commissioners or auditors to check on the activities of the security sector and with statutory powers of access to information and staff (Intelligence and Security Committee 2001: Appendix 3).

This notion derives from the US intelligence community, which now has around a dozen inspectors-general. All are independent of the agencies concerned. There are, however, signifi-cant variations among them: some are established by legislation (for example, the Inspectors-General for the Central Intelligence Agency and the Department of Defense), others are the creatures of administrative arrangements established by the relevant Secretary (for example, with regard to the Defense Intelligence Agency and the National Reconnaissance Office). Irrespective of this distinction some report to Congress as well as to the executive branch. A number of these offices have a remit that extends to efficiency, avoiding waste and audit, as well monitoring legality and policy compliance.

Inspectors-general (I-G) commonly operate within the ring of secrecy: their primary func-tion is not to provide public assurance about accountability, but rather to strengthen account-ability to the executive. The Canadian Inspector-General is a clear illustration of this type of office and the I-G is entrusted with unrestricted access to information in the hands of the service in order to fulfill these functions (Canadian Security Intelligence Service Act 1984, ss 33.2 and 33.3). Likewise in Bosnia and Herzegovina the Inspector-General exercises "an internal control function" (Law of the Intelligence and Security Agency of Bosnia Herze-govina, Art. 32). To this end, the Inspector-General may review the agency's activities, investi-gate complaints, initiate inspections, audits and investigations on his or her own initiative, and issue recommendations. The Inspector-General has a duty to report at least every six months to the Security Intelligence Committee and to keep the main executive actors informed of developments in a regular and timely fashion. The Inspector-General's powers include questioning agency employees and obtaining access to agency premises and data.

In other countries – notably South Africa – the role is different, i.e. to report to Parliament. In this respect the office bridges the ring of secrecy: the purpose is to provide public assurance in a report to Parliament that an independent person with access to the relevant material has examined the activities of the security or intelligence agency. However, inevitably most of the material on which an assessment of the agency's work is made has to remain within the ring of secrecy, although it may be shared with other oversight bodies.

Even some inspectors-general whose statutory brief is to report to the executive may maintain an informal working relationship with parliamentary bodies; this is so in Australia for instance and, as noted above, a number of the US inspectors-general report periodically to Congress.

Whether an office of this kind reports to the government or to Parliament, in either case careful legal delineation of its jurisdiction, independence and powers are vital. Independent officials may be asked to review an agency's performance against one or more of several standards: efficiency, compliance with government policies or targets, propriety or legality. In any instance, however, the office will need unrestricted access to files and personnel in order to be able to come to a reliable assessment. In practice an independent official is unlikely to be able to scrutinize more than a fraction of the work of an agency. Some of these offices work by "sampling" the work and files of the agencies overseen – this gives an incentive for the agency to establish more widespread procedures and produces a ripple effect. Some also have jurisdiction to deal with individual complaints (as in Australia, Inspector-General of Security and Intelligence Act 1986, ss 10–12).

A second independent review function concerns financial propriety (Born and Leigh 2005: ch. 23). Both the executive and the legislature have a legitimate interest in ensuring that budgets voted for intelligence are spent lawfully and effectively. However, as with the handling of complaints, it requires some ingenuity to devise systems for protecting secrecy while nevertheless ensuring that auditors have the wide access to classified information necessary to certify whether the services have used government funds within the law. Understandably limited restrictions to protect the identities of certain sources of information and the details of particularly sensitive operations may be imposed on the access granted to an auditor-general.

Primarily what distinguishes the auditing of security and intelligence services from regular audits of other public bodies, however, are the reporting mechanisms. In order to protect the continuity of operations, methods and sources of the services, in many countries special reporting mechanisms are in place. For example, in the United Kingdom only the Chairmen of the Public Accounts Committee and the Intelligence and Security Committee are fully briefed about the outcome of the financial audit. These briefings may include reports on the legality and efficiency of expenditure, occurrence of possible irregularities, and whether the services have operated within or have exceeded the budget. In many countries, the public annual reports of the security and intelligence service (e.g. in the Netherlands) or of the parliamentary oversight body (e.g. in the United Kingdom) include statements about the outcome of the financial audits.

Conclusion

As we have seen there are some recurring issues in the design of oversight procedures. First is the need to establish mechanisms to prevent political abuse while providing for effective governance of the agencies. Overall, the objective is that security and intelligence agencies should be *insulated* from political abuse without being *isolated* from executive governance. Second is the upholding of the rule of law in the sense of subjecting the agencies to legal control. As in other areas, one key task of the legislature is to delegate authority to the administration but also to structure and confine discretionary powers in law.

The challenge for oversight and accountability is to adapt or devise processes that simultaneously command democratic respect while protecting national security. This is a theme that runs through all of the approaches to accountability discussed in this chapter, whether by the executive, to parliament, in the courts, or during complaints processes or independent audit procedures.

A useful, if overly simplistic, distinction is between issues of policy, operations, and review. Policy matters include the issues of: what constitutes a security threat; which actions should be criminal; which powers should be available; which agencies should be established and on what terms? On the other hand, the case for secrecy here is weak and that for public disclosure as an aid to accountability very strong. Operations, on the other hand, covers issues such as: should this group/country be targeted and with what priority; should this form of surveillance be conducted on X? Operational detail affecting the methods, sources and specific activities of the agencies has a much more convincing case for secrecy. Operational matters are primarily for the executive and controls would reside at the administrative level. Review takes place ex post facto and considers, for example, whether the operational action was in accordance with policy, proportionate, legal, economical, and effective. Review, however, is more problematic, as parliament, the executive and the judiciary all have legitimate interests in aspects of it.

These distinctions should not be taken too rigidly. The development of policy must be informed by intelligence and operations which in some cases it may be necessary to keep secret. However, where governments perceive it to be necessary, ways can be found around this: witness the recent release of intelligence assessments in the United Kingdom in order to win over public support for potential military action against Iraq. Another borderline issue concerns the development of surveillance methods or technologies; these may raise controversial policy issues which are difficult to discuss publicly without rendering them ineffective by effectively giving notice to potential targets. There are difficulties too in fully differentiating operations and review. The continuing nature of some intelligence operations makes it difficult to draw a line between authorisation and review, or to engage in review without compromising secrecy.

Nevertheless, and with those provisos, the distinctions between policy operations and review can help to sharpen our understanding of accountability. They make clear that in policy issues there is a strong democratic interest in favour of public discussion and accountability. Secrecy in this field requires compelling argument to tip the scales.

Although the case of operational secrecy is much stronger, that does not mean that this is a road-block to accountability. It is right for the executive to set the parameters for security and intelligence operations, and to be involved in the approval of controversial operations even if, quite properly, the services are insulated from political pressure. Moreover, at the level of review, independent offices such as inspector-general can bridge the barrier of secrecy and provide assurance for the executive, legislators and the public that operations are being carried out effectively, lawfully and in accordance with policy. Some countries have gone further and allow parliamentary committees to review operational detail.

No one level of accountability stands alone. They are interlinked, complementary and interdependent. What is clear, however, is that with so many innovative models for oversight on display, it is no longer open to any state to argue that the secret world and accountability are mutually incompatible.

References

Born, H. and Leigh, I., *Making Intelligence Accountable: Legal Standards and Best Practice for Oversight of Intelligence Agencies* (Oslo: Norwegian Parliament Printing House, 2005).

Born, H., Johnson, L. and Leigh, I. (eds), *Who's Watching the Spies? Establishing Intelligence Accountability* (Dulles, VA: Potomac Publishers, 2005).

Bundestag, Secretariat of the Parliamentary Control Commission, *Parliamentary Control of the Intelligence Services in Germany* (Berlin: Bundespresseamt, 2001).

Cameron, I., *National Security and the European Convention on Human Rights* (Uppsala: Iustus Forlag, 2000).

Cameron, I., "Beyond the Nation State: The Influence of the European Court of Human Rights on Intelligence Accountability", in Born, H., Johnson, L. and Leigh, I. (eds), *Who's Watching the Spies? Establishing Intelligence Accountability* (Dulles, VA: Potomac Publishers, 2005).

Constitutional Affairs Select Committee, *Seventh Report for 2004–5, The Operation of the Special Immigration Appeals Commission (SIAC) and the Use of Special Advocates*, HC 323-I.

Estevez, E. "Argentina's New Century Challenge: Overseeing the Intelligence System", in Born, H., Johnson, L. and Leigh, I. (eds), *Who's Watching the Spies? Establishing Intelligence Service Accountability* (Dulles, VA: Potomac Publishers, 2005).

Farson, S., "Canada's Long Road from Model Law to Effective Oversight of Security and Intelligence", in Born, H., Johnson, L. and Leigh, I. (eds), *Who's Watching the Spies? Establishing Intelligence Accountability* (Dulles, VA: Potomac Publishers, 2005).

Gill, P., "The Politicization of Intelligence: Lessons from the Invasion of Iraq", in Born, H., Johnson, L. and Leigh, I. (eds), *Who's Watching the Spies? Establishing Intelligence Accountability* (Dulles, VA: Potomac Publishers, 2005).

Intelligence and Security Committee, *Annual Report for 2001–2*, Cm 5542.

Johnson, L., "Governing in the Absence of Angels: On the Practice of Intelligence Accountability in the United States", in Born, H., Johnson, L. and Leigh, I. (eds), *Who's Watching the Spies? Establishing Intelligence Accountability* (Dulles, VA: Potomac Publishers, 2005).

Leigh, I. "Secret Proceedings in Canada" (1996) 34 *Osgoode Hall Law Journal* 113–173.

Leigh, I. 2005, "Accountability of Security and Intelligence in the United Kingdom", in Born, H., Johnson, L. and Leigh, I. (eds), *Who's Watching the Spies? Establishing Intelligence Accountability* (Dulles, VA: Potomac Publishers, 2005).

Lustgarten, L. and Leigh, I., *In From the Cold: National Security and Parliamentary Democracy* (Oxford: Oxford University Press, 1994).

Sejersted, Fredrik, "Intelligence and Accountability in a State without Enemies", Born, H., Johnson, L. and Leigh, I. (eds), *Who's Watching the Spies? Establishing Intelligence Accountability* (Dulles, VA: Potomac Publishers, 2005).

Treasury Solicitor, *Special Advocates: A Guide to the Role of Special Advocates* (London: HMSO, 2005).

6

"Knowing the self, knowing the other"

The comparative analysis of security intelligence

Peter Gill

Introduction

By comparison with other social sciences the academic study of intelligence[1] is young. It has been dominated to date by Anglo-American work with primarily an historical focus, especially in the UK, and more work examining issues of organisational structure and process in the US. In the last fifteen years this has been supplemented by an increasing body of writing about other countries, especially those in Eastern Europe, Latin America and South Africa where regime change has been accompanied by some process of democratisation. Therefore what we have is an increasingly rich array of accounts of national intelligence systems including fascinating insights into processes of transition. Analyses of single agencies, companies, countries and even non-governmental organisations involved in intelligence will always provide the bedrock for intelligence studies but even where these accounts are collected together they may amount to no more than juxtaposition. Although Glenn Hastedt pointed out fifteen years ago that the comparative study of intelligence was but a fledgling,[2] it is still the case that too much writing is structured with too little thought given as to how it might facilitate comparison. This chapter does not attempt a comprehensive review of the intelligence literature but draws on social science literature more generally in order to identify major issues and suggest a way forward.

Why do comparative analysis?

We need to note, first, the argument that we have no choice:

> All science is comparative in the sense of depending upon analysis of multiple cases. Science is the systematic observation of many instances of a phenomenon . . .[3]

When people talk about comparative work, they often assume that this refers to cross-national studies; this is not necessarily the case, as we shall see below, but it is true that particular issues and problems arise in the case of cross-national work. Here, the first reason for doing comparative analysis (as with indulging in any science) is curiosity about how the world works. But the point of comparison is not just to find out about how other people do things but also to find out about one's own country through the study of others, as Adda Bozeman put it: "Knowing the self, knowing the other, and knowing how to measure the distance between the two . . ."[4] Therefore comparative analysis is the first antidote to ethnocentrism; to argue against international study "elevates parochialism to the level of scientific principle".[5]

Second, classification is the first step of any science and clearly we are interested in the classification of intelligence systems. This requires the study of multiple systems in order to generate the empirical material on which comparison can be based; some of these may be intranational, some cross-national. Classificatory schemes in turn depend on our use of models and theory, as discussed below.

Third, any classification will throw up similarities and differences that we need to understand. But these cannot be understood simply by close examination of intelligence for

> . . . intelligence is not an isolated activity. It is an integral part of government. It reflects the character of national constitutions and the societies in which it is set.[6]

Yet intelligence is just not any government activity – along with other security functions it has a "peculiarly intimate relationship to political power".[7] Therefore we need to examine how national systems are related to the social, political, economic and cultural conditions within which they have developed.

Fourth, this will help us to develop theory via our reformulation of problems in the light of moving beyond our own country and culture, including understanding "the other" without resorting to stereotypes or denying "difference".[8] In our writings, many of us have identified the problem of "mirror-imaging" as it afflicts analysts and prevents them from understanding other countries – we must try to avoid a similar fault.

Fifth, while the blurring of national borders that has resulted from globalisation might seem to have *reduced* national differences and thus the need for comparative analysis, the perceived need for greater cross-national co-operation with many more countries than was the case during the Cold War has dramatically *increased* the need for awareness of different intelligence traditions and practices. For example, this is required if intelligence-sharing agreements are to be negotiated and even more so if joint operations such as peacekeeping are contemplated.

Sixth, it is not just national boundaries that are blurring, so too are the traditional distinctions between the "INTS" and the sectors within which intelligence is organised. Therefore, it is no longer possible, if ever it was, to account for a national intelligence system simply in terms of, say, its state sector foreign intelligence agencies. National systems need to be examined in terms of security intelligence networks including foreign, domestic and police systems across public and private sectors.[9] This is given added weight by the fact that in many areas, especially the Middle East and Africa, the state is not the "decisive working unit" for intelligence studies[10] – it may be a clan, tribe, warlord or gang.

Seventh, Security Sector Reform (SSR) and within that intelligence reform, requires a sophisticated understanding of the extent to which laws, institutions and practices may be transferable from one country to another.[11] Great care must be taken that inappropriate structures are not foisted on countries in transition by international organisations, even if they have good intentions, or adopted by reformers simply in the hope that the ambition of early entry to EU and/or NATO will thereby be enhanced. Governing processes are complex systems and the outcome of transferring institutions will be subject to various interactions, most of them unpredictable. In the worst case, the adoption of democratic *forms* may actually be regressive if they simply provide a cloak of legality for unreconstructed authoritarian practices.

How to do comparative analysis?

Comparative work in social science reflects the general tension between more positivist or behavioural approaches, on the one hand and interpretive or constructivist approaches on the other. The former seek to generate general law-like propositions that can be subjected to empirical research and validated or modified accordingly and has preferred to work quantitatively. The latter reject the possibility of generating useful generalisations and emphasise instead the importance of understanding cultural specificity by means of qualitative methods, sometimes described as "thick description".[12] Within intelligence studies, a similar debate has existed between those emphasising the shared features of different intelligence systems and those stressing the enormous differences between them. The most significant differences facing us are those between Western and non-Western societies.[13]

As far as the study of intelligence systems and processes are concerned, we have to recognise the significance of these differences and acknowledge the fundamental trade-off between the respective virtues of complexity and generalisation.[14] For now, we are left with little choice but to conduct relatively small-scale qualitative analyses since the large data sets used in, for example, comparative voting and crime studies, simply do not exist. Even where statistics are available, they must be used with due regard for the purposes for which they were prepared.

Peters notes five types of study that are considered to be comparative within political science:

(a) Single country descriptions
(b) Analyses of different processes and institutions in a limited number of countries
(c) Studies involving typologies or other forms of classification for countries or sub-national units
(d) Statistical or descriptive analyses of data from a sub-set of the countries selected in order to test a hypothesis
(e) Statistical analyses of all countries attempting to develop patterns and/or test relationships across the entire range.[15]

Intelligence studies has a significant volume of (a) but their utility increases to the extent that they deploy some common framework of analysis. Certainly, the value of collections of country studies is much greater if the editors provide contributors with a brief rather than simply requesting an account of the country in question. There is also a growing number of (b) and (c). For example, we have had for some time comparative work that focuses on "surprise",[16] on the legal basis for intelligence[17] and, more recently, on the democratisation of intelligence.[18] We are some way off developing (d) and I cannot imagine (e) in the foreseeable future.

Whatever our approach, however, our comparison must be adequately theorised if we are to avoid merely describing differences. Theory and empirical work are inextricably linked:

> . . . theory is a guide to empirical exploration, a means of reflecting more or less abstractly upon complex processes of institutional evolution and transformation in order to highlight key periods or phases of change which warrant closer empirical scrutiny. Theory sensitises the analyst to the causal processes being elucidated, selecting from the rich complexity of events the underlying mechanisms and processes of change.[19]

Even if we are contemplating a single agency or country case study, our work should be theorised so that it will be of most use to other scholars embarking on comparative work.

While we may be a long way off generating the quantitative law-like propositions sought by behaviouralists, we can make use of some core concepts that appear to have applicability well beyond Anglo-American intelligence studies. I would suggest the following: surveillance, power, knowledge, secrecy and resistance.[20] Surveillance is constituted by two components: first, the gathering and storing of information and, second, the supervision of people's behaviour. In other words, it is concerned with knowledge and power: "Much of the study of intelligence concerns the relationship between power and knowledge, or rather the relationship between certain kinds of power and certain kinds of knowledge."[21] Arguably, all the non-trivial study of intelligence is concerned with this relationship. It is not a linear relationship: sometimes "knowledge is power" while at others knowledge may inform the exercise of power. Yet, as we have seen in the case of Iraq, at other times power may determine what is "knowledge".

Suggesting concepts have universal application is to invite accusations of cultural imperialism but we need to start somewhere. Indeed, establishing the different national understandings of core terms is itself an important study in order to avoid "careless conceptualisation".[22] If interviewer and interviewee use the same words but understand quite different things by them we have a serious problem. This can occur even within one's own culture but the danger increases in line with the cultural distance between those involved – concepts do not always travel well. Yet "surveillance" travels better than most.

In contemporary Western social theory surveillance is seen both as the central aspect of the establishment of modern "sovereign" state forms[23] and of the more recent decline of sovereignty as it is replaced by "governance" including the concomitant recognition of the significance of private forms of governance. Furthermore, studies of non-Western societies show that surveillance is similarly central there: its philosophical basis may be crucially different, for example, rooted in the rejection of individualism, but its core goals – understanding and control – are constants.[24] So, not surprisingly, global surveillance is argued to be an intrinsic part of the general economic restructuring of capitalism that is referred to as globalisation, and post-9/11 developments have served only to accelerate this already existing trend.

Secrecy is not just a defining element of intelligence because it distinguishes intelligence structures and processes from many other aspects of governance but also because its targets – individual, organisational and state – seek to keep their affairs secret. Secrecy may also apply to power: some actions make no sense unless carried out with an element of "surprise" such as arrests. But there are other, more controversial examples where actions are taken secretly in the hope that responsibility can be disguised or "plausibly denied".

Attempts to maintain personal privacy or business confidentiality are forms of resistance to the efforts of others to collect information. But if privacy fails then lying and deception are other forms of resistance. Evaluation or analysis is, in turn, an attempt to resist the attempt of others to mislead. Resistance to other forms of power such as coercion may well take on a more physical aspect but often these will be intertwined with the use of information. The central point here is that the relation between surveillance and its subjects is dialectical: efforts at gathering information and wielding power (in whatever form) will provoke greater or lesser attempts to resist. If resistance succeeds then fresh approaches to surveillance may be deployed and so on.[25]

Pathways for comparative research

Surveillance is the core governing process that incorporates the central knowledge–power relationship. Within intelligence studies our more specific *research focus* is a sub-set of surveillance: the *intelligence process*. This is a commonly deployed tool already and is normally characterised in terms of targeting, gathering, analysis and dissemination. Of course, this is an analytical device; in practice intelligence is far from linear. Just how "process" is understood in different national systems is a fundamental research question. (Phrases in *italic* indicate headings in Table 6.1 that appears below)

In social sciences the device of "levels" is used in order to simplify what is a highly complex reality. The *research elements* correspond to the "levels" of analysis usually identified: individual, small-group, organisational, societal and trans-societal. Each provides the context for, and is influenced by, the actions and dispositions of those "below". But phenomena or actions at any one level cannot be explained simply in terms of processes or properties at lower "levels": new causal factors and mechanisms emerge at each level – the whole is greater than the sum of the parts.[26]

At each of these levels we can identify *theoretical approaches* that already exist within social science and that can be deployed by scholars and researchers. Our choice of theoretical approach will depend largely on the "level" of our analysis but, in order to develop our discipline, analysts must test out alternative approaches with a view to identifying those that are most fruitful. For example, if, at the macro level, we are seeking to explain the different capacities of national intelligence systems then an approach drawn from political economy relating governmental structures and ideologies to national wealth would seem to be appropriate.[27] If we were interested in examining the conditions under which international intelligence-sharing is most likely to take place, then relevant theories from international relations would be appropriate.

Comparisons may be made along a *historical dimension*: it was noted at the outset of the chapter that historical work constitutes the bulk of UK research and this has been much invigorated by the continuing flow of file releases that commenced in the post-Thatcher era. Studies of single agencies, operations and countries at particular times are important both in their own right and as potential building blocks for broader, comparative work but there are significant methodological differences between, for example, comparing different historical "snapshots" and examining the process of change itself, as in the work of historical institutionalists.[28]

Also, in the form of comparative analysis with which we are most familiar, studies may be conducted on a *spatial dimension*. In order to build on the now extensive array of country studies, the time is now ripe for more detailed comparative work, for example, at the meso level, comparing who are recruited as intelligence officers to agencies in the same country or to equivalent agencies in different countries. Similarly, the impact of organisational cultures and the phenomenon of "groupthink" might be studied intra- or inter-nationally. Phil Davies provides an interesting comparison of intelligence cultures in UK and US with their relative tendencies to collegiality or conflict and how these account for failures up to and including Iraq.[29] But are "groupthink", "turf wars" and other "pathologies" of the intelligence process confined to Anglo-American liberal democracies or are they also a problem in *Rechtstaat* countries of Europe, or Asian countries with a more communitarian approach to matters of security?[30]

Analysts will use various *research techniques* as they focus on different levels of intelligence processes in order to produce the detailed empirical work we need but individual case-studies

Table 6.1 A map for theorising and researching intelligence

Historical dimension	Research element	Research focus: intelligence process			Theoretical approaches	Spatial dimension
	context (a) (trans-societal)	international relations; transnational corporations; international co-operation			*macro (a):* realism, international political economy, constructivism	
	context (b) (societal)	macro social organisation: values, traditions, forms of organisation and power relations, e.g., types of regime,			*macro (b):* hierarchies, markets, networks; realism, idealism, constructivism; social divisions	(i) study of intelligence at different "levels": transnational national local/ regional
nature of regime through history and of transition between regimes	setting (organisational)	*sectors of intermediate social organisation:*			*meso:* incrementalism; rational action; bureaucratic politics; cybernetic systems; profit-maximisation; risk-minimisa-tion; organisational cultures	(ii) comparative studies
		state: departments, agencies	*corporate:* profit-making corporations	*community:* neighbour-hood, community associations, non-gov-ernmental organisa-tions (NGOs)		
	situated activity (small group)	face-to-face activity in small work			*micro (a)* social psychology; "groupthink"	
	self (individual)	self-identity and individual's social			*micro (b)* cognitive psychology	
Research techniques	Taking "slices" across levels and sectors, applying theoretical approaches to case studies, for example, comparisons between states, regime transitions, intelligence "successes" and "failures", modifying those approaches in the light of research findings and so on . . .					

Source: Peter Gill and Mark Phythian, *Intelligence in an Insecure World*, Cambridge: Polity, 2006, p. 37.

must be conducted with an awareness of the larger picture. We know already how important are the mutual interactions between these "levels": for example, how the organisation of intelligence agencies reflects broader issues of political culture and regime type or how the formal bureaucratic organisation of agencies clashes with the working preferences of officers working in specialised groups. At the organisational level a particularly important issue for research is the relationships between state agencies and those "beyond the state" in the corporate and community sectors. If cases are to be compared, there are two main ways in which this can be done: taking those agencies or countries that are apparently similar and examining their differences or taking those that are ostensibly very different and looking for similarities.[31] Another approach might be problem-oriented, for example, how do different agencies or national systems deal with the problem of politicisation? Hypothetical questions might be posed: if a minister or political appointee orders an intelligence official to carry out an intelligence operation that the official believes to be illegal, what happens? If a group of analysts believe that their product is being ignored or distorted, what can they do about it?

The pitfalls of comparative analysis

Comparative work as between countries is, to put it mildly, challenging. First and foremost is that our own location in a particular country, culture and language combine to give us a worldview that will always struggle to comprehend "the other". However, languages can be learnt and countries visited so perhaps all is not lost. Nelken has distinguished between being "virtually there", "researching there" and "living there" as different ways in which we might try to surmount this problem.[32] Whichever approach is taken, language is a major problem and this fact, apart from the relative size of both the intelligence and interested academic communities, may well account for the fact that the overwhelming majority of intelligence literature studies the Anglo-American countries and is in English. If the time and money for extended visits to other countries are not available, then Nelken's first option is left. This may rely on the study of documents – not always plentiful or enlightening in the intelligence area – or on country experts. Given the paucity of comparative work in intelligence this is worth doing but we must remember that local experts may have "interested as well as interesting views"[33] or may miss factors just because they are so familiar.[34] Whether our sources are written – official, media and so on – or oral, issues of validity always arise.

"Researching there" has the advantage of giving the analyst first-hand experience of the country, and interpreters can be hired. Perhaps paradoxically, my experience (and of others with whom I have discussed this) is that it can be easier to get access to intelligence officials in countries not one's own, but one must be beware the danger of being fed an official view that is highly contestable. The exoticism of "the other" may reduce us to the equivalent of intellectual tourists. But, in any case, it is more difficult than "at home" to understand the nuances in what one is being told, especially if working in another language. "Living there" is simply not an option open to many but clearly provides the best opportunity for an individual to carry out a systematic and culturally sensitive analysis between countries. Yet analysts must retain some intellectual distance – "going native" is no more helpful to the comparative project than ethnocentrism.

Whatever the source of our information, there are procedures that need to be adopted in order to reduce the dangers of misinterpretation: triangulation is required so that different sources are examined in order to provide confirmation or disconfirmation.[35] When data can be so hard to come by in studying intelligence, this can be seriously frustrating and, being pragmatic, often one has to take chances with information that is not triangulated. Prior to publication in these cases, the sensible course is to submit drafts to all interviewees and other "experts" in the hope that someone will point out any serious errors of fact or interpretation.

Conclusion

We really have no choice: if "intelligence studies" is to build on its growing store of historical accounts and institutional-legal descriptions, we need to get serious about theoretically informed comparative work both within and between nations and sectors. This is potentially a very rich field for development but cannot be undertaken purely for intellectual pleasure. The issues at stake for intelligence reform (and regression) within nations and for intelligence co-operation (and conflict) between nations are just too important.

Peter Gill is Professor of Politics and Security at Liverpool John Moores University, UK. An earlier version of this chapter was presented to an Intelligence Studies Panel at the International Studies Conference, San Diego, March 2006 and grateful acknowledgement is made to the participants for their helpful comments.

Notes

1 To the extent that definitions of intelligence vary, comparative analysis is hindered. At a minimum, those carrying out comparative analysis need to make clear how they are defining the term. Here, intelligence is defined as "the umbrella term referring to the range of activities – from planning and information collection to analysis and dissemination – conducted in secret, and aimed at maintaining or enhancing relative security by providing forewarning of threats or potential threats in a manner that allows for the timely implementation of a preventive policy or strategy, including, where deemed desirable, covert activities." Gill, P. and Phythian M., *Intelligence in an Insecure World*, Cambridge: Polity, 2006. Of course, comparative analysis will examine also the other two senses of the term identified by Sherman Kent: the *agencies* conducting the activities and their *product*.

2 Hastedt, G.P., "Towards the Comparative Study of Intelligence," *Conflict Quarterly* XI:3, 1991, 55–72.

3 Bayley, D., Policing: The World Stage," in R.I. Mawby (ed.) *Policing Across the World: Issues for the Twenty First Century*, London: UCL Press, 1999, 3–12 at 3–4.

4 Bozeman, A., "Knowledge and Method in Comparative Intelligence Studies," in Bozeman, A., *Strategic Intelligence and Statecraft*, Washington, DC: Brassey's Inc., 1992, 180–212 at 182; cf. also Bayley, ibid., 10–11; Nelken, D., "Whom Can You Trust? The Future of Comparative Criminology," in D. Nelken (ed.) *The Futures of Criminology*, London: Sage, 1994, pp. 220–243 at 221.

5 Bayley, ibid., 5.

6 Herman, M., *Intelligence Services in the Information Age*, London: Frank Cass, 2001, 138.

7 Cawthra, G. and Luckham, R., "Democratic Control and the Security Sector," in Cawthra and Luckham (eds.) *Governing Insecurity: Democratic Control of Military and Security Establishments in Transitional Democracies*, London: Zed Books, 2003, 305.

8 Barnett, J.W., *Insight into Foreign Thoughtworlds for National Security Decision Makers*, Alexandria, VA: Institute for Defence Analysis, 2004; Nelken, 1994, op. cit., 223.

9 This is clearly the case in, say, Canada, USA and UK. It is less true of, for example, France.

10 Bozeman, op. cit., 196.

11 Cf. Bayley, op. cit., 10; Born, H. and Leigh, I., *Making Intelligence Accountable: Legal Standards and Best Practice for Oversight of Intelligence Agencies*, Oslo: Parliament of Norway, 2005.

12 For example, Nelken, 1994, op. cit., 225–226; also Pakes, F., *Comparative Criminal Justice*, Cullompton: Willan, 2004, 14–16.

13 Bonthous, J.-M., "Understanding Intelligence Across Cultures," *International Journal of Intelligence and Counterintelligence*, 7:3, 1994, 275–311, especially regarding Japan; Bozeman, op. cit., 198–205; Hastedt, op. cit., 65–66.

14 Peters, B.G., *Comparative Politics: Theory and Methods*, Basingstoke: Macmillan, 1998, 5.

15 Ibid., 10.

16 For example, Betts, R., *Surprise Attack: Lessons for Defense Planning*, Washington, DC: Brookings, 1982; Kam, E., *Surprise Attack: The Victim's Perspective*, Cambridge, MA: Harvard University Press, 1988.

17 Lustgarten, L. and Leigh, I., *In From the Cold: National Security and Parliamentary Democracy*, Oxford: Clarendon Press, 1994.

18 Born, H., Johnson, L. and Leigh, I. (eds.), *Who's Watching the Spies? Establishing Intelligence Service Accountability*, Washington, DC: Potomac Books Inc., 2005; Brodeur, J.-P., Gill P. and Töllborg, D. (eds.), *Democracy, Law and Security: Internal Security Services in Contemporary Europe*, Aldershot: Ashgate, 2003; Bruneau, T., (ed.) *Reforming Intelligence Across the World: Institutions and Cultures*, Austin, TX: University of Texas Press, forthcoming, 2007.

19 Hay, C., *Political Analysis: A Critical Introduction*, Basingstoke: Palgrave, 2002.

20 Gill and Phythian, op. cit., ch.2.

21 Scott, L. and Jackson, P., "The Study of Intelligence in Theory and Practice," *Intelligence and National Security*, 19:2, 2004, 139–169 at 150.

22 Hopkin, J., "Comparative Methods," in D. Marsh and G. Stoker (eds.) *Theory and Methods in Political Science*, 2nd edn., Basingstoke: Palgrave Macmillan, 2002, 249–267 at 259–260.

23 Dandeker, C., *Surveillance, Power and Modernity*, Cambridge: Polity, 1990; Giddens, A., *The Nation State and Violence*, Berkeley, CA: University of California Press, 1985, 181–192.

24 Bozeman, op. cit., 198–205; Der Derian, J., "Anti-Diplomacy, Intelligence Theory and Surveillance Practice," *Intelligence and National Security*, 8:3, 1993, 29–51 at 34–35.

25 Cf. Herman's spiral of threat perceptions, *Intelligence Power in Peace and War*, Cambridge: Cambridge University Press, 1996, 371.

26 Danermark, B. et al., *Explaining Society: Critical Realism in the Social Sciences*, London: Routledge, 2002, 60–61; cf. also Hastedt, op. cit., 62–64; Peters, op. cit., 43–46.

27 Cf. Johnson, L., "Bricks and Mortar for a Theory of Intelligence," *Comparative Strategy*, 22, 2003, 1–28.

28 Hay, op. cit., 135–167; Hopkin, op. cit., 260–263.

29 Davies, P.H.J., "Intelligence Culture and Intelligence Failure in Britain and the United States," *Cambridge Review of International Affairs*, 17:3, 2004, 495–520.

30 For example, Bonthous, op. cit.; Bozeman, op. cit.; Leishman, F., "Policing in Japan: East Asian Archetype?" in R. Mawby (ed.) *Policing Across the World*, London: UCL Press, 1999, 109–125.

31 For example, Hastedt, op. cit., 68; Peters, op. cit., 37–41.

32 Nelken, D., *Contrasting Criminal Justice: Getting from Here to There*, Aldershot: Ashgate, 2000.

33 Roberts, P., "On Method: The Ascent of Comparative Criminal Justice," *Oxford Journal of Legal Studies*, 22:3, 2002, 539–561.

34 Bayley, op. cit., 6.

35 Peters, op. cit., 97–102; cf. also Hastedt, op. cit., 60.

7

US patronage of German postwar intelligence

Wolfgang Krieger

The American involvement in setting up what eventually became the Bundesnachricht-endienst (BND), today's German foreign intelligence service, has long been common knowledge. From the summer of 1945 until March 1956 the US engaged, developed, and financed a German intelligence organization which was led by former Wehrmacht officers and intelligence professionals and which essentially provided Washington with information and studies on the Soviet Union and its satellites. The first detailed account was published by the key figure on the German side, Reinhard Gehlen, in his 1971 memoirs. Later publications elaborated somewhat on that story but failed to add much because archival sources were tightly closed on both the American and the German sides. No original documents from that period were available until 2002 when the CIA released a "documentary history" prepared by Kevin C. Ruffner of the CIA history staff. A year later, and obviously in tandem with those CIA releases, James H. Critchfield published his book *Partners in the Creation*. Critchfield had been an important figure on the US side of that peculiar intelligence relationship, acting as an on-site CIA supervisor of the Gehlen group.[1]

Quite possibly those two efforts to release original testimony would not have happened without the 1998 Nazi War Crimes Disclosure Act which demanded the disclosure of all US government contacts with Nazi criminals. This initiative touched on the sensitive issue of how to label the Gehlen group. While Gehlen and his senior associates were never charged with Nazi war crimes there was no way to overlook the fact that German military intelligence – leaving aside SS-intelligence – was deeply involved in the brutal ways in which Nazi Germany conducted the war. What is more, Gehlen's organization harbored a number of individuals of highly questionable background in the SS or the Gestapo or elsewhere in Heinrich Himmler's vast "security" empire.

On the basis of the source material released so far it is quite clear that the worst Nazis to be employed or used by US intelligence were handled outside the Gehlen group, as several American specialists have shown in their book *US Intelligence and the Nazis* published in 2005.[2] Nevertheless the disclosures demanded by the 1998 law could not leave the Gehlen group unblemished and therefore it appears reasonable to assume that the work of Ruffner and Critchfield was an effort to protect the German–American intelligence relationship as much as possible. After all, Gehlen was at the head of the BND until 1968; his close associate and successor Gerhard Wessel retired in 1978; Eberhard Blum, another former Wehrmacht officer, who had joined the Gehlen group as early as 1947, headed the BND from 1982 to 1985. Beyond any doubt, therefore, German–American intelligence relations were profoundly shaped by people who had directly worked for or with US intelligence for 40 years.

Although the German side has so far released no original documents on this most peculiar intelligence relationship, the new American documentation fills many gaps in what is publicly known about that remarkable history. It is now possible to strip away much of the layered ex-post justifications which Gehlen and his faithful associates had publicized in order to glorify their own role in the success story of West German history. Now we also see more clearly what was done on the part of US military officers and intelligence officials. But we should not deceive ourselves into thinking that everything has now been disclosed. The new material leaves many of the essential issues hidden behind a foggy screen of archival denial. A careful reading shows that the relased material does not only protect "sources and methods" but also institutional reputations.

Here is how the Gehlen memoirs capture the origins of that intelligence relationship. During the last weeks of the Third Reich a handful of officers from the Wehrmacht's military intelligence organization on the eastern front ("Fremde Heere Ost" or FHO) made preparations to put their knowledge of the Soviet military at the disposal of the Americans. They packed copies of their most valuable files into metal boxes, hid them in the Bavarian Alps, surrendered to the American forces and eventually convinced some key figures in US military intelligence to reassemble the former FHO ex-Wehrmacht officers in order to build up an intelligence outfit, led by Gehlen, which would produce raw intelligence and some analyses of Soviet activities in central and east-central Europe. Gehlen's ultimate purpose was to be at the helm of Germany's future intelligence service.

No source material is publicly available which allows us to reconstruct what was on Gehlen's mind in early 1945. We can only speculate on the basis of his acts and of his later explanations. If, indeed, he thought the Americans would urgently need to be told "the truth" about Soviet communism he would only have subscribed to a myth widely shared at the time by conservative minds in postwar Germany and indeed throughout western Europe. Given its wide acceptance among American critics of Roosevelt's Soviet policies it may well have been a transatlantic myth, which, in turn, is of interest here because it may shed some light on the communalities which eventually evolved between the Germans and the Americans as they faced the Soviet threat.

It also serves to remind us that the author of the Gehlen 1971 memoirs was no longer the same person, mentally and perhaps even politically, as the ex-chief of FHO in 1945–1946 when the German–American intelligence relationship began. In 1968, when Gehlen retired from the BND and sat down to write his book, he was a highly unpopular figure in Germany, laden with all sorts of BND "scandals and failures". Since then various efforts have been made to come to grips with his biography and his record in intelligence, none of them entirely satisfactory to the critical historian. In turn, this difficulty poses numerous problems in assessing the source material released recently. But even with this caveat it is impossible to accept Gehlen's own claim, and the claim of his many admirers within the BND, that it was essentially his own expertise and forceful personality which convinced the Americans to place him at the head of German intelligence. As the new source materials overwhelmingly document, it was a much more complicated story in which Gehlen's role is significantly less prominent than earlier accounts have made it out to be. Among the most important yet so far unresolved issues remains the question of the actual intelligence value of what Gehlen's group did. By hiding "sources and methods" from the public the present-day US intelligence establishment is in fact making it impossible to answer that most obvious of questions.

This chapter explores what new information has now come out, how it fits into the larger picture of early cold war politics, and what its limitations are in explaining the peculiarities of the German–American intelligence relationship. For the reasons indicated some of this will have to be speculative, more focussed on phrasing questions than on providing confident answers.

Different from what Gehlen may have assumed, the US military had no particular agenda in how it dealt with the remains of German military intelligence. It certainly did not pursue any phantasies of continuing the war against the Soviet Union. Few American officials believed that a confrontation with the Soviet Union was "inevitable". Their interest in FHO derived from that simple but powerful idea that military history was the essential resource of military professionalism. Therefore one would harvest all the military experience which had been accumulated on the Germans side. Whatever the Germans had developed in terms of weaponry, tactical experience, intelligence and so on would be assembled and exploited because it might ultimately be useful to the American military – somehow, somewhere.[3] Banal as this conclusion may be, there is little or no indication to the contrary for the years 1945 to 1946, when Gehlen's group was put to work for Washington.

The extent to which the US exploited German military hardware and expertise has long been obscured by a rigorous policy of denying archival access. The same, incidentally, is true of the other three victor powers who occupied Germany.[4] While it has long been known that senior Wehrmacht officers were thoroughly debriefed and were asked to write numerous military studies on their wartime experience, we have only begun to realize the depth of intelligence exploitation and especially of intelligence relating to advanced German technology.[5] Therefore we are only beginning to understand what part the Gehlen group played (or did not play!) in this wider context.

There has been the cliché that during and right after the war the Americans in particular, but also the other western powers, had very little intelligence on the Soviet Union and greatly benefitted from what the Germans could tell them. Since the Gehlen group was the only example of German–American intelligence cooperation "known" publicly, all the benefit somehow accrued to that project. Recent work by Richard Aldrich has reconstructed in considerable detail the multi-year British–American intelligence effort to secure Luftwaffe overhead photography, which was taken to England and exploited by a very large staff.[6] Quite possibly, that project, with the help of dozens of Luftwaffe specialists, yielded much more useful intelligence material than what could be gathered from Gehlen's secret FHO boxes. While the Luftwaffe photography and mapping covered a huge number of permanent installations such as bridges, airfields, power stations, military depots and so on, Gehlen's order of battle tables and situation reports essentially addressed tactical situations which had long passed. His order of battle information contained numerous Red Army units which no longer existed. Other American or British–American intelligence projects which targetted the Soviet Union must have yielded considerable amounts of information. How much, we still do not know for sure. But it seems clear that the German–American intelligence exchange took place in a much wider context of exploiting German resources. It also gave the Americans many points of reference from which to judge and to verify the Gehlen output.

From a considerable number of reports on the circumstances under which Gehlen's group came to work for the Americans one thing becomes quite clear. Gehlen's initiative to surrender himself and his documentary materials could be interpreted in various ways and did not necessarily indicate that he had left behind all thinking which had hitherto guided his work. As the CIA's documentary history shows, the American officials who took charge of him and of his associates checked and rechecked the genesis of this offer very carefully. Even as late as late as 1953 they had Heinz Herre, one of Gehlen's closest associates, write down his recollections of what had happened in 1945/1946.[7] On several occasions Gehlen was asked to describe, in fact to justify, his relations with Walter Schellenberg, the SS officer and overall German intelligence chief since mid-1944. At issue was an understanding he had reached with Schellenberg in March 1945 to transfer both FHO staff members and working files to southern Germany for the purpose of organizing a German guerilla effort along the lines of the Polish armed resistance against Germany. While Gehlen claimed that this was a ploy directed at Hitler and his entourage to cover the transfer of his assets, thus saving both his staff and his files from falling into the hands of the Soviets, several German officers interrogated by the Americans confirmed that a Gehlen plan for post-defeat resistance against the western forces had actually existed.[8]

This issue could not be resolved at the time and even today, six decades later, it is hard to know what was on Gehlen's mind in early 1945. Surely he needed an excuse to move his staff far away from the Red Army frontline. But what did he intend to do with it? Did he hope to continue "the war against bolshevism" under US leadership? The benefits to the Wehrmacht leadership would have been obvious. Such a new military alliance would have amounted to justifying the German war against the Soviets and would have made the German war crimes into somewhat "exaggerated" efforts to overcome Polish and Soviet resistance. In that way the Nazi and Wehrmacht leadership might have been forgiven rather forced to stand trial on war crimes charges as had repeatedly been announced by the Allied powers.

This logic points to the debate raised by the late Andreas Hillgruber in 1986 when he asserted that German soldiers on the eastern front were genuinely motivated by their fear of bolshevism rather than by Nazi propaganda and were ready to fight the Red Army to the bitter end.[9] Might Gehlen have hoped (rather than feared) that the war against the Soviets would be continued? Was he thinking primarily in terms of the obvious benefit which such a constellation would have had for all but the worst of the Nazi and Wehrmacht leaders?

No documentation appears to exist which allows us to answer those questions. But they are useful in as much as they call to our attention the mind-set of Germans who offered their services to the western powers. Their motives may have been quite far from noble. They may have been unrelated to freedom and democracy as understood by the west – and later on by the political leadership around German Chancellor Konrad Adenauer. In other words, to make Reinhard Gehlen the logical protector of the Adenauer government, as he later saw himself, is to stretch one's imagination unduly.

While the Americans were well aware of those potentially questionable motives they focussed on the immediate benefits of their new intelligence client. In fact they were, at least initially, less interested in Gehlen's grand strategy or even in his Red Army analysis. Among the first studies to be undertaken was a history of German counter-intelligence methods in dealing with the Soviets. Among their cherished exploits were the manufacturing of a printing press with Russian type, the theft of several hundred original pay books and the forging of several Soviet army documents and stamps.[10] Next came the intelligence-gathering units which Germany had employed on its front with the Red Army to collect information from enemy civilians, from POWs and from radio intelligence. Of those groups the one headed by Oberst Hermann Baun was the most discussed in 1945/46 though Baun's proposal to make available his agent network was exaggerated, given the tight control the Red Army established quickly east of the Elbe river and the general turmoil in that area. His specialists on Soviet radio traffic, however, were assembled on the outskirts of Frankfurt am Main and put to work for the US Army's G-2 as early as January 1946.

Getting control of Baun was Gehlen's third leadership challenge after redeploying to southern Germany and after convincing the Americans to "reactivate" parts of the FHO. During the war Baun's organization (Stab-Walli) had been independent of Gehlen's FHO. In early April 1945, Gehlen and his FHO-deputy Gerhard Wessel visited Baun at Bad Elster to make a deal with him with respect to the planned transfer to the Americans. Baun went along but resented Gehlen's claim to overall leadership. And many others more or less agreed with him on that point, for Gehlen was neither a recognized Soviet expert – he spoke no Russian (and indeed no foreign languages at all) – nor an expert in intelligence-gathering. FHO never handled any agents or any radio intelligence or code-breaking. What is more, Gehlen had no experience in counter-intelligence and indeed developed little understanding of that specialty even later on – which was to get him into all sorts of troubles!

It was mostly Baun's difficult personality which convinced Army G-2 to favor Gehlen for the leadership of RUSTY, a task which became increasingly difficult as its operations were expanded from handling an agent network in the Soviet zone of Germany to operations in Austria and in other parts of eastern Europe.

Since RUSTY's American patrons badly lacked the staff needed to supervise and coordinate its activities various problems developed which time and again put the whole idea of a German intelligence outfit into question. By expanding so quickly in various directions RUSTY became a heavy financial burden on the Army. Poor management led to the hiring of numerous useless, even dangerous people often engaging in black market activities. The Army feared for its budget as well as for its reputation.

By the fall of 1946 a stormy debate evolved at the upper levels of US intelligence. When Maj.-Gen. Withers A. Burress took over as intelligence chief of US Army in Europe, he suggested that the newly created Central Intelligence Group (CIG) take charge of RUSTY. But CIG was not prepared to have "any large scale US-sponsored intelligence unit" operate "under even semi-autonomous conditions".[11] Too difficult to control, too expensive, too much exposed to Soviet penetration, and too potentially damaging to America's international reputation – those were the main charges.

To end the experiment would have amounted to an indictment of senior army leaders like General Edwin Sibert, Burress's predecessor, who had made the initial deal with the Gehlen group. And it would have come at a bad time when the Soviets had already shown a great deal of unwillingness to come to a European peace settlement and when war-torn Europe faced its worst winter of hunger and deprivation. On December 19, 1946, the CIG leadership in Washington commissioned a more extensive study of RUSTY's "value . . . to a peace time intelligence organization".[12] Samuel B. Bossard from CIG was given two months to prepare a comprehensive report. In parallel, certain "German" files, particularly counter-intelligence material concerning communists and refugees in Germany, would be cross-checked with US-only material to assess their reliability and intelligence value.

Before Bossard arrived in Germany, US military intelligence tried to control RUSTY more tightly. They issued an itemized "Assignment of Responsibilities" to Gehlen.[13] But too few qualified US personnel was available for the task. The situation only began to improve somewhat when a large part of the Gehlen group was brought together, in December 1947, in a big, fairly isolated compound south of Munich – which in 1956 became the headquarters of the German Bundesnachrichtendienst in Pullach. When Bossard undertook his field trip he found an American lieutenant-colonel "enlisting the various skills of some 2500–3000 bodies", that is people undertaking intelligence work in "an area roughly embracing Stockholm, Prague,

Sofia, Rome, Paris".[14] He may have exaggerated somewhat, since most of the work was done in Germany. But he could not possible exaggerate the lack of US supervision, since the afore-mentioned senior US military officer was only assisted by a Captain Eric Waldman, who turned out to be an important figure in that story, three non-commissioned officers plus a civilian secretary. Apart from processing about 200 reports per month those people had to manage the supplies, finances, quarters, transport, and much else for hundreds of German staffers and their numerous people in the field. The cost to the US tax-payer was estimated at some US$47,367.29 a month or about $15 dollars per capita.[15]

Was this a good bargain? Was the glass half full or half empty? Mr Bossard came to the optimist's conclusion. He assured his bosses in Washington that responsible accounting and file-keeping was in place and that there were considerable intelligence assets all around eastern Europe which made RUSTY much more than an operation for observing Soviet forces and policies in Germany. After discussing the various American concerns with America's most unsusual intelligence arm, Bossard refered to its potential "as a German postwar underground movement. Since [the] organization leaders have it within their power to resurrect former German collaborators throughout Central Europe and [since] longterm agents have already been planted in Soviet occupied territory, the organization could turn into a partisan band."[16] By the same token, however, that German outfit could become a danger if cut loose from the American purse, as Bossard added in his report.

Eventually, Bossard proposed a thorough reform but not a liquidation of RUSTY. Personnel and projects should be reviewed. Those to be kept on should be more tightly controlled. SIGINT components should be transferred to American SIGINT services (in the Army and the Navy). In the battle between Gehlen and Baun a clear preference is expressed for the former. ("[E]very effort should be made on the part of the American authorities to allow G to dominate the organization at the expense of B."[17]) American military government as well as British and French services should be officially informed of RUSTY's existence, presumably to ease political tensions.

When judging those recommendations it must be kept in mind that four-power policy in German was still in limbo. While Soviet aggressive and subversive policies in eastern Europe and the failure to implement key provisions of the 1945 Potsdam agreement were already defining US security policy a European settlement had not been completely ruled out by the west. General Lucius D. Clay, the American military governor in Germany, forcefully respresented that position.[18] If therefore Bossard stated: US intelligence "will have at its disposal the nucleus of a future German Intelligence Service",[19] he was not necessarily thinking of the kind of western Germany which emerged in 1948/1949 from the fusion of the three western zones of occupation. A united Germany, based on some sort of compromise with Moscow, was still considered a possibility. Even less could one foresee in 1947 that a western Germany founded in 1949 would have to wait until 1955/1956 before it could reestablish its own armed forces and foreign intelligence service.

Another point deriving from those 1947 debates on US and German intelligence needs to be placed in its context: the issue of employing SS/SD personnel. The origins are to be found in the years 1944 to 1945 when US intelligence feared that Allied forces might encounter fanatical Nazi resistance and that measures would have to be taken against the possibility of clandestine Nazi stay-behind networks running violent operations against Allied forces as well as against newly-installed post-Nazi German administrations established by the four victor powers. To guard against this potential threat it seemed appropriate to build up an early warning system consisting of mid-level and junior figures who were likely to have access to such underground networks. Some of them had come to the attention of the Americans during the chaotic final weeks of the war when local commanders, and even some senior SS–leaders, negotiated local cease-fires and surrenders. (Operation SUNRISE in northern Italy, which involved SS-General Karl Wolff among others, is perhaps the best-known example.) Both assumptions were reasonable under the circumstances: (1) precautions were required against clandestine Nazi networks; and (2) cooperative people could be found and employed from among the ranks of former SS and SD members.[20] It was therefore only logical that such people would be engaged both in CIG, which had prime responsibility for anti-Nazi and anti-terror intelligence, and in RUSTY, particularly in its counter-intelligence side. The latter point remained relevant for some time since Soviet behavior toward former SD/SS people was unknown. (As it turned out they also employed a considerable number of them for intelligence as well as for scientific research.)

When, however, such clandestine Nazi operations did not materialize US intelligence was burdened with those unpleasant people. Clearly, one did not wish to discharge them summarily since many had useful contacts to ex-Nazis employed by the Soviets and to anti-communist groups around Europe. As Bossard wrote: "[E]very instant of employment of a former member of the Nazi party or the SS should be made a separate case for consideration and the employment of individuals in this category should be restricted to the agent level as far as possible."[21] Keep them away from the center but leave at least some of them in the field! – that was his recommendation.

In Washington the Bossard report met with considerable scepticism, particularly among civilians. But US military intelligence did not wish to lose RUSTY, particularly the tactical intelligence on Soviet forces. Its chief, General Stephen Chamberlin, insisted "that, if necessary, he thought G-2, EUCOM, could run the operation."[22] On 26 June 1947, at a meeting of military and civilian intelligence chiefs in Washington, it was decided to do just that as an interim measure. More study would be needed to consider a large-scale restructuring. In December 1947 a military unit named the "7821st Composite Group" was founded in Pullach, near Munich, where RUSTY would now be centered.

During 1948 the problems associated with RUSTY remained but the importance of its tactical intelligence became a critical element in American policy during the Berlin crisis. In fact, it may well have been a precondition for initiating and sustaining the Berlin airlift. By observing each and every Soviet unit deployed around Berlin Gehlen's agents could be relied on to provide sufficient advance warning in case of a planned Soviet attack. In addition they had access to the top echelon German communists who were in constant touch with local Soviet military commanders. Across the open borders of the four Berlin sectors intelligence reports could be received frequently and in person from many of the agents.

Without such frequent and timely reporting the airlift might have been considered too risky. After all, the US committed a vast number of modern US transport aircraft, putting them almost undefended within easy reach of Soviet tactical air units. Thus the Berlin airlift is a classical example where intelligence made it possible for decision-makers to take considerable military risks for the benefit of a non-military political strategy. In this case the focus was on demonstrating to Stalin that he could not grab West Berlin or West Germany by political means – that is without risking major war.

In November 1948, right in the middle of the Berlin crisis, a new effort was made to evaluate the entire RUSTY operation. James Critchfield, an Army colonel with extensive experience in post-1945 intelligence work around Europe, was put in charge of supervising RUSTY.[23] Critchfield had recently joined the CIA and began to work hard to overcome anti-Gehlen feelings in Washington. His support for Gehlen and his ex-Wehrmacht entourage is evident from his first cable reports. He strongly emphasizes the tactical value of RUSTY's intelligence work: "Airforce [ha]s greatest interest in RUSTY and in results of RUSTY monitoring, DF-ing [direction finding] and cryptoanalyzing Soviet air force radio traffic which is only source of timely info[rmation] on Soviet tactical air activity in central Europe. . . . Airforce has further suggested that RUSTY look into possibilities of developing air crew evacuation and escape routes out of [the] USSR.[24] . . . In the strategic field RUSTY is doing valuable work in the preparation of target folders for [the] Air Force."[25]

From his reporting we also learn that RUSTY had "completed [its] detailed emergency plan to be implemented in [the] event of war [with the Soviet Union]." It provided for relocating its headquarters from Pullach to Switzerland and on to Spain. This had been coordinated "on [an] official level with [the] Swiss, Spanish and French . . ." – particularly with a view toward continuing "collection effort and radio communications from eastern and western Germany." Moreover, that plan had been integrated with EUCOM's emergency plan.[26]

Apart from violating Swiss neutrality this plan appears to indicate that France, or at least some leading figures in the military as well as in foreign intelligence, was much more closely associated with Anglo-Saxon planning and thinking than is usually assumed by historians.[27] This included secret preparations for German rearmament, complete with a revived German intelligence system. As Critchfield emphasized in his cable, the 4,000 people involved in RUSTY were an important political factor with respect to Germany's future. "Another factor is that RUSTY has closests ties with German general staff officers throughout Germany. If Germany will, in any eventuality, play a role in a western European military alliance this factor [is] important."[28] This means that Critchfield viewed the hiring of senior German Wehrmacht officers no longer as a convenient way of acquiring intelligence expertise but as a hidden effort to recruit the nucleus of a future German military establishment and – most importantly – of bringing it under the direct influence of the Americans. He saw in RUSTY a far-reaching agenda related to the future of Germany and western European defense – far beyond the original interest in German military expertise resulting from her war against the Soviet Union and quite apart from the intelligence value the Gehlen group may or may not have had for US forces in Germany.

It is this message which finally gets the CIA leadership interested in taking RUSTY under its wings. Here was a way for the CIA to get involved in foreign policy-making. And here was also a way in which it could acquire a piece of military intelligence work, a domain which the Pentagon did not happily share with anyone. Of course there were serious risks attached to this new relationship. RUSTY had grown much too fast and in too chaotic a fashion to allow for the kind of careful screening and vetting which intelligence services like to see in their recruiting and promotions. As Donald Galloway, the CIA's assistant director of special operations, wrote to his DCI on December 21, 1948: "[T]he security and basic orientation of RUSTY is most dubious . . . we do not know very much about the inner workings of the RUSTY organization, and it is probable that the [US] Army does not either . . . we might well lay CIA open to wholesale penetration . . . [and] . . . we have no idea whether or not the Russians are feeding deception into the RUSTY pipeline."[29]

In the first half of 1949 the transfer to CIA was delayed because General Clay did not wish for the CIA to operate in Germany on such a large scale, in potential rivalry with US military government run by the US Army, and with such a politically questionable organization as RUSTY.[30] But with Clay's departure from Germany and the establishment of a German government the Army's administrative and political role was largely reduced anyhow. Reinhard Gehlen used this transition to request a thorough review of his relationship with the Americans. He did not wish to continue being subordinate to US military intelligence, given its narrow interests and its lack of coordination, aggravated at times by incompetent US supervisory officers. But there was also a more fundamental political issue to be resolved. If Germany, or at least western Germany, was about to have a freely elected government based on a German constitution and on German laws, though still supervised by an Allied High Commission, German nationals could not serve – on their own territory – a foreign intelligence organization without some sort of consent by the German government.

For these reasons Gehlen and the CIA concluded a written agreement, based on a draft on June 13, 1949 and followed by an exchange of letters.[31] Such a contractual basis is common in intelligence cooperation between nations. For example, the most extensive known example involving the United States, that is their cooperation with the British since the 1940s, was based on separate agreements for each and every project. In the case of the German–American cooperation before 1955/1956, however, the west German government could not formally be a party because it was not fully sovereign in matters of foreign and security policy. Thus the the Gehlen–CIA agreements were of a special nature both in legal and in political terms. From the available documents it is very clear that 1949 marked a turning point. And it did so not simply because CIA took over from the US Army but because there was now a west German government, headed since September 15, 1949 by Konrad Adenauer.

The prestige and credibility of that government was a huge stake for Washington and for its British and French allies. To support and to preserve it was infinitely more important than any potential gains from the CIA–Gehlen relationship. And since Adenauer obviously had much more to gain from getting on well with those three powers than from dealing with the "Gehlen Organization", as RUSTY now came to be called, Gehlen's political leverage was very limited.[32] Indeed, it is hard to see how his organization could have lasted until 1956 had it not been for the aggressive communist policies in Asia, as exemplified by Mao's victory in the Chinese civil war and in the Korean war soon thereafter, and for the new threat which Soviet nuclear weapons posed to western Europe in particular.

Though many of the CIA–Gehlen agreements are of a technical and book-keeping nature, a few points from them deserve to be highlighted because they characterize the scope of this changed intelligence relationship.

Gehlen undertook to direct his organization "solely against communist Russia and her satellite governments . . ., [to work] in the interest of the German people in combatting communism . . . [and] to ensure that the acceptance and support of this project by the German government is obtained." In other words, he did not wish to engage in intelligence work of interest only to the US and unrelated to Germany. In return, the Americans insisted on controlling Gehlen's relations with any other foreign power and on having access to the "complete details of operational activities."[33]

The financial picture had already changed after June 1948, with the introduction of the Deutschmark, ending an era of uncontrolled inflation under the "cigarette economy" when RUSTY had in part been financed through its black market dealings. The remainder was to a large extent charged via US Army accounting to the German economy as "occupation costs". In terms of per capita expenditure RUSTY was cheap intelligence but now in mid-1949 none of those factors survived. Real US taxpayer funds would have to be expended. The CIA tried to get the US Air Force to pay for activities it was particularly eager to have. Those parts of RUSTY were estimated at 25 per cent of its total budget.[34]

All of a sudden, however, the cost issue lost its importance. In September 1949, a few weeks after the first Soviet nuclear test, Gehlen was assured that the funding of operations against the Soviet Union would no longer be a problem.[35] The Organization Gehlen was only one of many cold war institutions which were ultimately prolonged as a result of outrageous Soviet policies.

After the Gehlen Organizations came under direct CIA control, its code name was changed to ZIPPER. Gehlen was referred to as UTILITY, though his old cover as "Dr. Schneider" remained in use within the organization until Gehlen's retirement in 1968. Alas, there is as yet little original source material on ZIPPER's history. Gehlen's "name file" at the National Archives contains a few documents describing various personality conflicts. The old game of "who is he really?" and "what is he up to" apparently went on right up to the spring of 1956 when ZIPPER became the Bundesnachrichtendienst under the Bonn government. Gehlen spent a lot of time involving himself in the Bonn politics of rearmament. His key aim was not only to become merely the chief of German military intelligence but to create a single foreign intelligence organization which included military affairs and was headed by himself.

The odds of reaching that goal were clearly stacked against him. Gehlen's Pullach head-quarters was 400 miles away from Bonn. He had to depend on all sorts of middle men to keep track of what was discussed in political party circles and among the key figures around Adenauer. The chancellor was not only deeply suspicious of Hitler's former military officers. He also deeply resented the old Protestant, Prussian, and military elites who had been instrumental in bringing Hitler to power and who once again sought to influence foreign and military policy by hammering his rearmament policy and his search for a defense alliance with western Europe and the United States. But Gehlen managed to make himself useful in two ways. Firstly, he fed the chancellor's close collaborator, Hans Globke, with all sorts of unsavory personal information about various political figures from around Germany. Gehlen ran a domestic spying service which went far beyond ZIPPER's counter-intelligence mission. The second way in which he made himself useful was to provide intelligence briefings not only to the chancellor's office but also to various members of the Bonn parliament. In the German tradition key political decisions are made (or prevented) by the political party leaderships rather than by the executive. Thus Gehlen's briefings provided key parliamentarians with an information advantage.

To this Gehlen added a third political effort. He rudely fought any potential German intelligence entrepreneurs who were not directly controlled by him. Within the emerging Bundeswehr he could count on the support of ex-Wehrmacht officers who had been employed by RUSTY during the darkest postwar days. One of his closest collaborators from FHO times, Gerhard Wessel, pursued a career in the Bundeswehr. Many others were part of this "early warning system" which Gehlen controlled thoughout the Bonn bureaucracy and the Bundeswehr.

Absent the classified German files, it is still impossible to study ZIPPER or the early BND in any depth. It is not even possible to track the exact decision-making process by which the German government decided to create the Bundesnachrichtendienst on April 1, 1956. Gehlen's net-working skills must have contributed much to its outcome. So did the promotion efforts on the part of the CIA. Gehlen was taken on several official tours to the USA and, in September 1955, on a naval exercise of the 6th US Fleet in the Mediterranean. Such visits were arranged for the purpose of "strengthening our position in general with the German Intelligence Service" and in view of concluding "a secret Bilateral Intelligence Agreement with ZIPPER" for the post-transition era.[36] Whether or nor the CIA–Gehlen relationship had been fruitful for the US side, the opportunity to have intimate relations with west Germany's new intelligence service was of considerable value. Nothing the British or the French had built up since 1945 was of comparable importance.

On the German side, the balance was perhaps a mixed one. By its peculiar history and due to its weaknesses in personnel recruiting before 1956 the BND was wide open to Soviet and East German subversion. Some of it was used to sabotage their intelligence work. But perhaps the propaganda value which the East German communist regime got out of the BND was the heaviest burden it put on the Bonn republic. If the Bundeswehr was suspicious to many Germans the BND was outright hated and despised even more widely. Today, given the archival access to the files of the BND's East German rival, the "Stasi" (or Ministerium für Staatssicherheit, MfS), it is possible discover why that propaganda was frequently so well targetted. Both Stasi and Soviet intelligence had ample sources embedded in the BND. As happens so often in intelligence history a proper historical balance sheet of failures and successes would require more knowledge about the successes of the US–German intelligence relationship. At the political level, things are much clearer. While the American side was able to have a controlling influence on an important element of Bonn's foreign and security policy-making the Germans got at least some access to the power corridors of Washington. Intelligence relations between states may be about exchanging secret information. But they can be important far beyond. By controlling the Gehlen organization and, to a large extent, the later BND the Americans could be sure that no secret preparations were made by the Bonn republic which might have been hostile toward Washington. It was an insurance policy which turned out to be unnecessary – like most insurance. But during the darkest days of the cold war that particular insurance seemed worth its premium.

Notes

1 Reinhard Gehlen, *The Service*, transl. by David Irving (New York: World Publishing 1972, German ed. 1971); Kevin C. Ruffner (ed.), *Forging an Intelligence Partnership: CIA and the Origins of the BND, 1945–49* (Washington, DC: Center for the Study of Intelligence 1999) 2 vols, declassified in 2002 [below quoted as CIA vol 1 or 2]; James H. Critchfield, *Partners at the Creation: The Men behind Postwar Germany's Defense and Intelligence Establishments* (Annapolis, MD: Naval Institute Press 2003).
2 Richard Breitman et al., *US Intelligence and the Nazis* (New York: Cambridge University Press 2005).
3 Cf. Kevin Soutour, "To Stem the Tide: The German Report Series and Its Effect on American Defense Doctrine, 1948–1954", in *Journal of Military History* 57 (1993) 653–688.
4 Very little is known about German intelligence members who fell into the hands of the two other western powers. As to the Soviets, there is the sad story of Walter Nicolai, Germany's military intelligence chief in World War I, whom the Soviets mistreated and killed in 1947 – apparently because they refused to believe that the long-retired ex-colonel had ended his career in 1918! (The Russians rehabilitated him in 1999.) See Z. Taratuta/A. Zdanovic: *Tainstvennyj sef Mata Chari* (Moskau: Neisvestnaja vojna 2001).
5 A recent example would be a book on Hitler's atomic weapons projects, based on amazing new German as well as Russian sources. Rainer Karlsch, *Hitlers Bombe: Die geheime Geschichte der deutschen Kernwaffenversuche* (München: DVA 2005).
6 Richard J. Aldrich, *The Hidden Hand: Britain, America and Cold War Secret Intelligence* (Woodstock, NY: Overlook Press 2002).
7 CIA vol 1 pp. 11–15.
8 CIA vol 1, pp. 17–18.
9 Andreas Hillgruber, *Zweierlei Untergang: Die Zerschlagung des Deutschen Reiches und das Ende des europäischen Judentums* (Berlin: Siedler 1986).
10 CIA vol 1 pp. 25–26.
11 CIA vol 1 p. 160; the overall evaluation by CIG is documented on pp. 159ff.
12 CIA vol 1 p. 195.
13 CIA vol 1 p. 201 (dated 25 February 1947).
14 CIA vol 1 p. 333 and 341.
15 CIA vol 1 p. 344.
16 CIA vol 1 p. 353.
17 CIA vol 1 p. 357.

18 Wolfgang Krieger, *General Lucius D. Clay und die amerikanische Deutschlandpolitik 1945–1949* (Stuttgart: Klett-Cotta 1987); Jean E. Smith, *Lucius D. Clay: An American Life* (New York: Henry Holt 1990).

19 CIA vol 1 p. 368.

20 This aspect is, alas, not given a fair hearing in the otherwise valuable studies found in Breitman et al. (2005) discussed above.

21 CIA vol 1 p. 355. Later, in 1950, Gehlen employed a small number of former SD officers for counter-intelligence operations inside West Germany. It was "Gehlen's most costly mistake" as Critchfield wrote (Critchfield, *Partners*, p. 164) because it allowed the KGB to insert at least two highly productive spies, Heinz Felfe and Hans Clemens.

22 CIA vol 1 p. 392 record of Bossard's discussion with Chamberlin and others on June 11, 1947.

23 Crichfield, *Partners*, pp. 77ff.

24 Cable dated December 17, 1948, see CIA vol 2 pp. 38–39. A more detailed account is on pp. 105–109.

25 This point concerns targetting and flight route information needed for long-range bombers in atomic warfare against the Soviet Union and is quoted from Critchfield's 17 December, 1948, report. See CIA vol 2 p. 54.

26 CIA vol 2 p. 39; further information on emergency planning is found on pp. 71–72.

27 Wolfgang Krieger, "American Security Policy in Europe before NATO", in Francis H. Heller/John R. Gillingham (eds.), *NATO: The Founding of the Atlantic Alliance and the Integration of Europe* (London: Macmillan 1992), pp. 99–128; George-Henri Soutou, "La sécurité de la France dans l'aprè-guerre", in Maurice Vaïsse/Pierre Mélandri/Frédéric Bozo (eds.), *La France et l'OTAN 1949–1996* (Bruxelles: Complexe 1996) pp. 21–52.

28 CIA vol 2 p. 40.

29 CIA vol 2 p. 126. This suspicion never subsided and turned out to be well-founded. Indeed, between 1950 and 1955 the CIC (US Army Counterintelligence Corps) ran operation CAMPUS which was targetted on the Gehlen organization. The CIA was never informed and apparently never found out (Critchfield, *Partners*, pp. 167–171).

30 CIA vol 2 pp. 137ff.

31 CIA vol 2 pp. 231–309 contains these agreements and letters, however, with major deletions.

32 For a more detailed discussion, see Critchfield, *Partners at the Creation*, pp. 122ff.

33 CIA vol 2 pp. 233–234.

34 CIA vol 2 p. 263.

35 CIA vol 2 pp. 282–286.

36 Memorandum for DCI, dated March 29, 1955 (based on suggestions from Col. Critchfield).

Part 3

The intelligence cycle and the search for information

Planning, collecting, and processing

8

The technical collection of intelligence

Jeffrey T. Richelson

Introduction

For much of mankind's history, the collection of intelligence was conducted largely through the efforts of spies – who observed enemy activities and purloined documents. Intelligence was occasionally acquired when coded messages were stolen and decoded. Only in the last hundred years have technological advances allowed intelligence to be collected by a vast array of mechanical systems, often operated a considerable at a considerable distance from the target, an activity referred to as "technical collection."[1]

There are six key aspects to technical collection activities. One is the sensors – such as photographic equipment – used to gather data. A second is the platforms that carry the sensors, which with the sensors constitute a technical collection system. The targets of the collection effort – including missile fields, nuclear reactors, and terrorist training camps – constitute a third component. Fourth is the product of the collection effort – such as the images of the missile fields, reactors, and training camps, or intercepted communications between the chief of a weapons of mass destruction production facility and a senior government official. In addition, there is question of the value of technical collection operations – which is determined by the uses to which the intelligence obtained can be put – such as supporting diplomacy, guiding weapons acquisition, planning and carrying out military operations, treaty verification, and warning of upcoming attacks or other events that a nation might wish to forestall.

A final, but important, consideration is the limitations of technical collection. While such systems may produce a wealth of data, they do not guarantee that all key intelligence desired will be obtained. The plans of a foreign government or terrorist group, for example, may be unobtainable by technical means if the target government or group are sufficiently vigilant in the safeguarding their plans.

Imagery sensors, platforms, and targets

The value of observing foreign activities, particularly military-related activities, from overhead has been apparent to military and intelligence officials for at least as long as there have been the

105

means for obtaining an overhead vantage point. According to Chinese and Japanese folklore, spotters ascended in baskets suspended from giant kites or were strapped directly onto to them. In April 1794, French forces were reported to have kept a balloon aloft for nine hours, with its passenger, Colonel Jean-Marie Joseph Coutelle, making continuous observations during the battle at Fleurus, Belgium. Balloons were used to carry observers and, less frequently, cameras, during the American Civil War.[2]

As a result of the Wright Brothers' invention of the airplane in 1903, a key intelligence resource in World War I were reconnaissance aircraft – planes equipped with cameras that could photograph enemy fortifications, troop deployments, and the battlefield. During, and in the years leading up to, World War II photographic reconnaissance aircraft played an even greater role. Britain managed to conduct covert flights over Germany, while German aircraft brought back photographs of Soviet territory prior to the German invasion of the Soviet Union in June 1941. During the war, British and American planes photographed German military and industrial installations and areas on a regular basis – to aid in targeting and damage assessment.[3]

The advent of the Cold War ensured that overhead reconnaissance retained its importance, particularly for the United States, as it sought to pierce the veil of secrecy established about almost every aspect of Soviet life – especially its military capabilities. The possibility that a satellite could be outfitted with a camera to take pictures of any place on earth that it passed over was noted by the RAND Corporation as early as 1946. In August 1960 that vision was realized when the United States orbited a camera-carrying satellite codenamed Corona.

A satellite such as Corona, in a polar orbit that took it over all of the earth from pole to pole, could photograph Soviet military activities in the northern reaches of the Soviet Union, airfields in the Middle East, and battles in sub-Saharan Africa. In the decades since the first Corona orbited the earth, the capabilities of such satellites have increased dramatically – as has the number of nations that operate such satellites.

The photographic reconnaissance satellite has become the imagery satellite – for capturing the visible light reflected by an object is not the sole means of obtaining an image of a target. The infrared radiation (heat) reflected by an object can also be used to produce an image during daylight, and in the absence of cloud cover (which blocks the reflected radiation). The heat independently generated by an object can also be used to form an image, even in darkness. That second type of infrared imagery can provide data on developments taking place at night that ordinary visible light sensors cannot.

A third means of obtaining imagery from a satellite is through the use of radar (radio detection and ranging). Radar imagery is produced by bouncing radio waves off an area or an object and using the reflected returns to produce an image of the target. Since radio waves are not blocked by clouds, radar imagery can be obtained not only day or night but even when clouds block the view of a satellite's visible-light and infrared imagery sensors.

Imagery satellite capabilities have also advanced in a number of other ways. The most important is the development of real-time capabilities. The Corona satellites and several other US and Soviet spy satellite systems operated in the 1960s, 70s, 80s were "film-return" satellites. An image was formed on film, just as an image would be formed on a conventional camera. When the film supply carried by the satellite was exhausted, part of the satellite (in the case of the United States, a capsule) carrying the film would be returned to earth and recovered.

Today, almost all imagery satellites are digital and operate in near real-time – the optical systems rely on charged couple devices which translate the varying visible-light levels of the object viewed into numbers, which are immediately relayed back to earth (via a relay satellite) and reconstructed into an image. Infrared and radar imagery are also transmitted in real-time.

Even before the advent of real-time satellites, whose lifetimes are not limited by film supply, the lifetimes of film-return satellites grew from the single day of early Corona missions to weeks, and, for some satellites, many months. But real-time imagery satellites can operate for between five and ten years. Satellites today also have far greater resolution than the first photographic reconnaissance satellites – that is they can detect far smaller objects than the first satellites. While it is incorrect to claim that a satellite can read a license plate, they can certainly detect a white object of similar dimensions laid on a dark surface.

As noted, there has also been a growth in the number of nations operating high-resolution imagery satellites. For the first decade of space reconnaissance the United States and Soviet Union were duopolists. In 1975, China launched its first photographic reconnaissance satellite. It would not be until 1995 that another nation would join the space reconnaissance club – when France launched a spacecraft designated Helios into orbit from a site at Kourou in French Guiana. Israel and Japan followed. Israel has launched several Ofeq (Horizon) satellites into orbits that focus primarily on the Middle East. Japan has launched a pair of reconnaissance satellites, one radar imagery satellite (Radar-1) and one visible-light satellite (Optical-1). And there is the prospect that a number of other nations, including Germany and Italy, will deploy imagery satellites for military intelligence purposes.

Today, the United States operates a constellation of about six imagery satellites, all of which provide real-time imagery. The constellation includes three advanced versions of the first real-time imagery satellites, the KH-11, which can produce both visible-light and infrared imagery. It also includes two radar imagery satellites (codenamed Onyx) and one stealth satellite (originally designated Misty) which was intended to be difficult for target nations to detect.

Russia, faced with resource constraints, operates a less extensive military space program than did the Soviet Union but still operates real-time imagery satellites. France has continued to launch Helios satellites, the latest being Helios 2A, which was launched in December 2004 and is reported to carry both visible-light and infrared sensors. Meanwhile, Japan has plans to add radar and optical satellites to its present constellation.[4]

The targets for those satellites are determined by the national security concerns of each nation, as well as by their intelligence alliances. United States satellites, reflecting their owners' global interests, have been targeted on nuclear facilities in North Korea, Iran, Pakistan and other nations; construction of underground weapons of mass destruction production or command and control facilities in Libya and Russia, refugee movements in Africa, and terrorist training camps in Afghanistan and elsewhere.

Other nations' targets will often be a subset of those of the United States. Russian satellites undoubtedly photograph terrorist facilities in Chechnya, nuclear facilities in Iran, and missile sites in China. Israeli satellites are focused on the Middle East – particularly terrorist and weapons of mass destruction facilities, as well as airbases and other military facilities in the region. Japan's spy satellite program owes it existence to North Korea's 1998 launch of a ballistic missile that passed over its territory. North Korean missile and nuclear facilities and activities are among the primary targets of Japan's imagery satellites, along with Chinese missile sites and airfields. French military, diplomatic, and commercial interests in the Middle East, Asia, Europe, and Africa provide its satellites with a large array of potential targets – including military developments in the Balkans, Iran's construction of nuclear facilities at Arak and Natanz, and the territory surrounding France's space launch facility at Kourou.

The initial development and improving capabilities of imagery satellites has not made other forms of overhead imagery collection obsolete. During the early days of the Cold War, United States Air Force pilots flew modified bombers, equipped with cameras, along the periphery of the Soviet Union and China to obtain imagery of airfields, ports, and other facilities that could be photographed from outside those nations' borders. Occasionally, those modified bombers were sent into Soviet airspace to obtain imagery of targets farther inland.

Then in 1956, the CIA pilots began flying deep into the Soviet territory employing a specially designed plane, the U–2, which flew at over 65,000 feet and which the CIA believed, incorrectly, would not be detected by Soviet radar. It carried a special long–focal–length camera capable of photographing objects as small as a man, and bringing back images of roads, railroads, industrial plants, nuclear facilities, aircraft, and missile sites within a strip 200 miles wide by 2,500 miles long.[5]

Overflights of the Soviet Union ceased after Francis Gary Powers and his U–2 were shot down on May 1, 1960. But the US still continues to operate U–2s, and has employed a variety of additional spy planes, particularly the Mach 3 SR–71, in the decades after the US mastered the art of conducting reconnaissance from space – even after the quality of satellite photos equaled or surpassed that of the lower–flying aircraft.

Some countries were restricted to employing aerial reconnaissance until they developed satellite imagery capabilities – for example, Israel and France. The United States continued their use because, while satellites could provide far more extensive coverage and were immune to being shot down like aircraft, planes still could play an important role.

They can supplement satellite coverage – a single plane costs far less than an additional satellite. They can provide a quick reaction capability since an aircraft can head directly for a target, while a satellite cannot photograph a target until its orbit and the rotation of the earth place the target in view – a process which can take several days. Those same constraints mean that a satellite cannot arbitrarily cover any stretch of territory desired – but aircraft can cover the territory between any two points, for example, the movement of an invading army toward its objective or the movement of refugees toward a border.

Another type of overhead imagery system has some of the virtues of satellites and aircraft, and some of its own advantages. Unmanned aerial vehicles (UAVs) equipped with electro–optical systems or infrared sensors are operated without a pilot by remote control – thus the political risks and risk to life involved in manned reconnaissance operations are eliminated. And unlike satellites or aircraft, UAVs can remain over a target, at high altitudes, for extended periods of time (e.g. 20 hours) keep watching on a particular target or area – such as a terrorist training camp or nuclear test site.

While the US began operating drones (pilotless aircraft that could not be maneuvered) and UAVs during the Cold War, it is in the post–Cold War that UAVs have become a more significant component of US reconnaissance activities. The CIA began flying Predator UAVs over Bosnia in 1994. After the initiation of military operations in Afghanistan the US began equipping Predators with Hellfire missiles so that immediate action could be taken if imagery indicated the presence of a terrorist target. Even more recently, the US has been deploying the Global Hawk UAV – capable of operating at over 60,000 feet for 20 hours and carrying electro–optical, infrared, or radar–imaging sensors.

Signals intelligence sensors, platforms, and targets

Traditionally, signals intelligence (SIGINT) is treated as one of the most important and sensitive forms of intelligence. The interception of foreign signals can provide data on diplomatic, military, scientific, and economic plans or events as well as on the characteristics of radars, spacecraft, and weapons systems.

SIGINT can be broken down into two basic subcategories: communications (COMINT) and electronics intelligence (ELINT). As its name indicates, COMIN gence obtained through the interception, processing, and analysis of the electronic cc tions of foreign governments, organizations, or individuals, excluding radio and broadcasts. The communications intercepted may be transmitted in a variety of ways – conventional telephones, walkie-talkies, cell phones, the Internet, and computer networks.

ELINT encompasses electronic non-communications signals, including the electronic emanations of radar systems and foreign instrumentation signals – the signals transmitted during the operation of space, aerial, terrestrial, and sea-based systems. The signals from radar systems can be used to identify their existence as well as determine their characteristics, such as pulse repetition frequency and pulse duration. Intelligence about pulse repetition and pulse duration can be used in designing electronic countermeasures to neutralize the radars in the event of combat.

One category of foreign instrumentation signals intelligence (FISINT) is telemetry intelligence (TELINT) – obtained from intercepting the signals transmitted during missile tests to those conducting the tests, permitting them to evaluate the missile's performance. Interception of those signals by a foreign intelligence organization makes it possible for analysts to determine many of the capabilities of foreign missile systems – including the number of warheads carried, payload and range, warhead accuracy, and warhead size (which can be used to estimate yield).

Collection of signals intelligence is accomplished by a multitude of systems, from satellites in outer space to submarines under the seas. The proliferation of satellite reconnaissance systems with imaging missions to a variety of different nations has not yet been matched by an equivalent proliferation of SIGINT satellite systems, and the US remains, by a large margin, the foremost user of such systems.

Several types of satellites are used to collect signals intelligence – including geosynchronous and low-earth orbiting satellites. Geosynchronous satellites operate about 22,000 miles above the earth's equator, with their rotation around the earth matching the rotation of the earth below, so they, in effect, hover over the same point on the equator. In that orbit the same portion of the earth (about 1/3) remains in their electronic view constantly – which is important in being able to continuously monitor a communications link or insuring that a satellite is in the right place when infrequent missile tests take place. The United States pioneered the use of such satellites for communications intelligence purposes in 1968 with the launch of a satellite designated CANYON. Presently, the US operates two separate constellations of geosynchronous signals intelligence satellites, which can intercept communications transmitted on UHF and VHF frequencies, as well telemetry from missile tests.[6] The Soviet Union has been the only other nation to operate geosynchronous signals intelligence satellites.

ELINT satellites operate in lower orbits. Both the US and Soviet Union/Russia have operated ocean surveillance satellites, orbiting the earth at about 600 miles altitude, which intercept the electronic signals from ships at sea as a means of detecting the presence of the ships and tracking their movements. The US, Russia, and China have also operated satellites in about 500-mile orbits which targeted the electronic emissions from radar systems – including ballistic missile warning radars as well as aircraft-detection radars. France has placed experimental SIGINT packages on satellites with other primary missions, possibly as a prelude to developing its own signals intelligence satellite. In the US, in the 1990s, the two systems were combined into one system that targeted both ships at sea and radars on land.

Britain aborted plans in the 1980s to build its own geosynchronous SIGINT satellite, codenamed ZIRCON, for budgetary reasons. A willingness to devote considerable financial resources to a SIGINT satellite program is only one challenge facing a nation with such ambitions. There is also the technological challenge involved in developing and operating the satellites as well as the requirement for ground stations, often on foreign territory, to operate the satellites as well as receive their data in a timely fashion.

One of the advantages satellites have over signals intelligence aircraft is that they can intercept signals from across a much wider territory than aircraft. Thus, the first US ELINT satellite, GRAB, first launched in 1960, could intercept signals from territory 3,790 miles in diameter, while the P2V Neptune, an ELINT aircraft that operated in the same era could only target signals within a 460 mile diameter.[7]

In addition, such aircraft, and their crews, may be targets for hostile forces. Over one hundred US airmen were lost in the early days of the Cold War on ELINT missions that flew into or near Soviet territory. In 1968, North Korea shot down a US EC-121 on a signals intelligence mission, while in 2001 a Chinese aircraft forced a US Navy EP-3 to land on Hainan Island.

But given the economics involved, many more nations are involved in other forms of signals intelligence collection. The US conducted the first aerial missions during World War II, which were targeted on Japanese radars in the Pacific. Today, not only the United States, but China, Israel, Britain, France, Italy, Germany, Russia are among the nations that use aircraft to intercept signals – both communication signals as well as radar emanations. And such aircraft, in addition to being far more financially viable than satellite systems for many nations, can get much closer to the source of the targeted communications or electronic signals than a satellite – thereby improving the ability to capture the signals of interest, some of which satellites may not be able to intercept.

Ground-based signals intelligence systems are also deployed extensively throughout the world. During the Cold War the United States operated a series of circular antenna arrays in Europe and Asia targeted on the high-frequency communications of the Soviet Union, China, and other communist countries. Unlike the VHF and UHF signals that leaked out into space, making them vulnerable to space collection, high-frequency signals bounce off the atmosphere and return to earth where they can be intercepted – often thousands of miles away. Not surprisingly, the Soviet Union also operated an extensive network of ground stations, with stations in widely dispered locations – including Soviet Union, Vietnam, and Cuba.

While the collapse of the Soviet Union led to the closure of many of sites where such arrays were operated – in Augsburg, Germany and San Vito, Italy for example – another type of ground-based SIGINT collection is flourishing due to the growth of communications satellites.

In the 1960s, the United States military and private corporations began placing satellites into geosynchronous orbit to relay communications between widely distant spots on earth. The Soviet Union followed with its own constellations of military and civilian communications satellites. The signals sent to and/or from those satellites can be intercepted by satellite dishes stationed in any areas that either receives the signals from the satellite or can access the signals sent to the satellite.

The US first targeted Soviet military communications satellites, such as the Molniya satellites which operated in highly elliptical orbits, using intercept equipment located in Great Britain, Japan, and elsewhere. In the 1970s it began improving its ability to intercept civilian satellite communications. One outshoot of that effort was the ECHELON program – an ability to do keyword searches of the communications traffic (particularly written communications such as faxes) intercepted at ground stations operated by the US and key SIGINT allies (including the United Kingdom and Australia). But the United States and those allies are not alone in this practice. The signals intelligence organizations of a number of nations – including China,

110

Switzerland, Germany, and France – also maintain one or more satellite dishes allowing them to intercept the traffic being relayed through communications satellites.

Another often-used platform for intercepting foreign signals are embassy or consular rooftops. The United States and Soviet Union made extensive use of their embassies and consulates to intercept communications in foreign capitals and other key cities during the Cold War. That practice continues today, with internal military, police, political, and economic communications all being targets.

Using ships outfitted with intercept equipment to monitor communications or intercept other electronic signals was not uncommon during the Cold War. The Soviet Union maintained a large fleet of antenna-laden ships, know in US terminology as AGIs (for Auxilliary General – Intelligence), that operated near US submarine facilities in the United States and abroad, as well as near US space launch facilities such as Vandenberg Air Force Base in California. For a time the United States maintained a set of ships dedicated to the SIGINT collection. The risks involved in such activities were illustrated when Israel bombed a US ship collecting SIGINT during the June 1967 Six-Day War and the following year North Korea seized a similar ship. While the US stopped using such unarmed ships, it did outfit others with intercept equipment and continues to conduct such operations today.

While most other nations are not able to, and have no need to, deploy fleets of SIGINT collection ships, they do operate some. Britain, France, Germany, and Italy are European nations with such ships. Thus, in May 2000, the French newspaper *Le Monde* reported that the French ship, the *Bougainville*, was headed for a secret destination on a signals intelligence mission. Five years earlier, it had been reported that China was operating eight SIGINT ships – including the *Xiangyang Hong 09*, which was used to monitor US–South Korean Team Spirit exercises in the Sea of Japan and Yellow Sea.[8]

Submarines have also been used for signals intelligence collection. During the Cold War a US attack submarine might be instructed to locate itself in the White Sea, close enough to the Soviet coast to allow it to intercept the telemetry signals associated with the test of a submarine-launched ballistic missile. Other submarine missions involved transporting frogmen to locations in the Barents Sea and Sea of Okhotsk so they could place taps on Soviet cables carrying military communications. Many such SIGINT missions were conducted under a joint program involving both US and British submarines. In 2006, a new US attack submarine was sent to operate off the coast of Latin America, with a signals intelligence mission.

Collectively, signals intelligence systems can be used to gather intelligence about a wide variety of foreign activities – the negotiating strategies of foreign nations; diplomatic exchanges between a foreign ministry and its embassies or between countries; the details of military exercises; the capabilities and performance characteristics of missile, space, aerial, and other military systems; the intentions of foreign governments and terrorist groups, and the plans and technical secrets of foreign corporations.

Measurement and signature intelligence, sensors, and targets

Photographic and communications intelligence can trace their identities as major collection disciplines back to the early twentieth century. The broader imagery intelligence (IMINT) and signals intelligence disciplines were clearly established between 1940 and 1965. In contrast the concept of "measurement and signature intelligence" (MASINT) as a discipline encompassing a number of distinct collection and analysis activities is far more recent, first being coined by the Defense Intelligence Agency in the 1970s. As will become clear, in many ways, MASINT is, essentially, "all other technical collection." MASINT categories include radar, geophysical, infrared and optical, nuclear radiation, materials, and multi- and hyper-spectral imagery.

As noted above, radar can be used to obtain images of targets. But the use of non-imaging radar for intelligence collection is the more traditional use. The US has used ground-based and sea-based radars – such as COBRA DANE on Shemya Island and COBRA JUDY aboard the USNS *Observation Island* – to detect and track missile launches and to gather data on missile characteristics. In the 1970s, an official historian of the COBRA DANE program described it as providing the "primary source" of data on the Soviet missile tests that terminated on Kamchatka.[9] Smaller radars, in aircraft, may be used to produce instantaneous intelligence on whether an approaching aircraft is hostile. A radar on the F-15E aircraft, when focused head-on another aircraft can determine the number of blades in the opposing aircraft's engine fan or compressor. The blade count helps determine the type of engine, and assess if the plane is hostile. The shooting down of two Iraqi EXOCET-equipped Mirage F-1s during the first Persian Gulf War has been attributed to such collection and analysis.

Three sensors fall into the geophysical category: acoustic, seismic and magnetic. Acoustic sensors detect sound waves. In the 1960s the US employed ground stations with acoustic sensors to detect the sound waves generated by atmospheric nuclear tests. Since the 1950s, the United States has operated the Sound Surveillance System (SOSUS) – an network of undersea hydrophones that can detect the acoustic signals produced by submarines. The data collected by SOSUS allows far more than simple detection of submarines. The distinct noises made by a submarines engine, cooling system, and movement of its propellers can be translated into a recognition signal. And in 1995 and 1996, SOSUS hydrophones off California picked up the sound of French nuclear weapons being exploded under the atolls in the South Pacific.[10]

Seismic sensors have been used by the United States and a multitude of other nations to detect the signals generated by nuclear tests. Such detection relies on the fact that nuclear detonations, as do earthquakes, generate waves that travel long distances either by passing deep through the earth (body waves) or by traveling along the earth's surface (surface waves). Body and surface waves can be recorded by seismometers or seismic arrays at significant distances (over 1,200 miles) from the point of detonation. Exploitation of the data involves distinguishing between earthquakes (which originate from two bodies of rock slipping past each other) and detonations (a point source), filtering out background and instrument noise, and converting the seismic signal into an estimate of explosive yield when appropriate.

Magnetic sensors are often used on anti-submarine aircraft such as the P-3C Orion, which the US employs and has sold to a variety of other nations in Europe and Asia. The plane's Magnetic Anomaly Detector (MAD) is used in concert with its Submarine Anomaly Detector to determine whether known submarine magnetic profiles are present. To get a good MAD reading, the plane must fly as low as 200 to 300 feet above the water.

Infrared and optical sensors that are considered MASINT sensors are ones which produce data without imagery. Both the United States and the Soviet Union/Russia have operated satellite systems – the Defense Support Program (DSP) in the case of the United States – which detect missile launches by the infrared (heat) signature generated by their missile plumes. Beyond providing warning or notification of missile launches DSP's non-imaging infrared sensor has proven capable of providing several types of intelligence information. In addition to being able to identify specific missile types by the uniqueness of their plume's infrared signature, DSP satellites have proven useful, due to their ability to detect a variety of heat sources, in monitoring the movement of aircraft flying on afterburner, the movements of spacecraft, large detonations (including exploding ammunition dumps and plane crashes), and certain industrial processes.

112

Optical sensors, known as bhangmeters, have been placed on a variety of US (and probably Soviet/Russian) satellites to detect the bright flashes of light associated with the fireball from an atmospheric nuclear explosion. In September 1979, a US VELA satellite appeared to detect a double flash of light somewhere in the South Atlantic, which had uniformly been associated with nuclear tests. That apparent detection set off a controversy, that persists to this day, as to whether some nation had attempted to covertly set off a low-yield nuclear device.[11]

Nuclear radiation sensors, largely placed on satellites, including the DSP, VELA, and Global Positioning System (GPS) satellites, detect such phenomenon as the X-rays and gamma rays associated with a nuclear explosion. Such information, along with other nuclear detonation signatures, can help estimate the yield, location, and altitude of the detonation.

Materials sampling – the gathering and analysis of effluents, debris, and particulates – associated with weapons of mass destruction programs has been a significant element of the intelligence activities of the United States, the Soviet Union/Russia, the United Kingdom, and other nations for many decades. In World War II the United States obtained samples of water from the River Rhine, in order to search for any signs that the Germans were operating a plutonium-producing nuclear reactor in the vicinity.

Another aspect of these activities has been the use of aircraft and ground stations to gather the debris from nuclear detonations – either atmospheric detonations, or underground detonations that have vented debris into the atmosphere. Such debris can be crucial for determining, among other things, whether the device employed plutonium or enriched uranium, and whether it was a nuclear or thermonuclear device. The US first determined that the Soviet Union had detonated an atomic bomb by the analysis of debris obtained by a US weather reconnaissance aircraft. After the examination of the debris collected after China's first test, in October 1964, US analysts concluded, to their great surprise, that China's first atomic bomb had relied on highly enriched uranium rather than the expected plutonium.

More recently, during William J. Clinton's presidency, the US analysis of soil collected from the vicinity of a Sudanese pharmaceutical factory led to the identification of EMPTA – a precursor chemical in the production of chemical weapons. That identification led to the targeting of the factory in retaliation for the 1998 al-Qaeda attacks on two US embassies in Africa.[12]

Conventional visible–light, infrared, and radar systems produce imagery whose content can be mined for intelligence by looking at its size and shape – e.g. does the image show a missile, and if so, what are its dimensions? Or, does the image show a nuclear testing ground, a nuclear reactor, or an airfield? In contrast, intelligence is extracted from multi-spectral and hyper-spectral imagery, which can be obtained from satellites (such as LANDSAT) or aircraft, on the basis of detecting and understanding the spectral signatures of the targets, available from the image.

Multi-spectral imagery is produced from the collection of multiple, discrete bands of electro-optical imagery collected simultaneously. Hyper-spectral imagery employs at least sixty narrow contiguous spectral bands, including the visible light, infrared, thermal infrared, ultraviolet, and radio wave segments of the electromagnetic spectrum. The data produced by examining those bands allows analysts to detect an object's shape, density, temperature, movement, and chemical composition.

The primary missions to which such imagery is expected to contribute are: support to military operations; non-proliferation; counternarcotics; mapping, charting, geodesy; technical intelligence; and civil applications (for example, urban planning). Specific applications may include the determination of beach composition; the location of amphibious obstacles; battle

uses.

damage assessment; support of special operations; countering camouflage, concealment, and deception; analysis of the terrain; and vegetative cover and stress determination.

Identification and classification of targets such as operational nuclear facilities can be achieved by the exploitation of multi-spectral data – since such data yields "false color" images in which hot water discharges from a reactor would appear in red and orange in the image. Likewise, the reflectivity of healthy vegetation differs from that of dead vegetation (as well as vegetation which overgrows an earth-covered object such as a bunker) for wavelengths beyond visible light. Thus, examination of multi-spectral photography can lead to visual identification of such camouflaged sites by their distinct colors.

The utility of multi-spectral imagery (MSI) was demonstrated during Operation Desert Storm in 1991. Ground forces found the multi-spectral data useful in identifying disturbances in the terrain (indicating possible passage of Iraqi forces), as well as detecting wet areas that could slow down an advance. In addition, the "planning and execution of ground maneuvers, including the 'Left Hook,' were highly dependent on multispectral imagery." Naval forces employed it to identify shallow areas near coastlines for operational planning, to determine water depths, and to plan amphibious operations. Air Force planners used MSI data in conjunction with terrain elevation data to display attack routes and targets as they would appear. Subsequently, MSI data was used in support of operations in Haiti, Bosnia, and elsewhere.[13]

The value and limitations of technical collection

That technical collection operations can produce intelligence of significant value was demonstrated throughout the twentieth century. During World War I, photographic reconnaissance provided intelligence on enemy troop movements. Communications intelligence allowed the British, as a result of their interception and decoding of a telegram from the German foreign minister to his envoy in Mexico, to accelerate US entry into World War I – for the telegram offered Mexico the chance to regain lost territory in the American southwest if it entered the war on Germany's side and attacked the United States.

In World War II, all sides conducted extensive photographic reconnaissance operations to identify targets and assess the impact of bombing runs – particularly important in an era where precision bombing was only a dream. The ability of British codebreakers to penetrate the Germany Enigma machine proved of enormous value – both in fighting the land war and in the Battle of the Atlantic. America's ability to break Japanese codes was crucial in winning the Battle of Midway, the battle which turned the war in America's favor.

World War II also saw the birth of two other forms of technical collection. As noted earlier, the US conducted the first ELINT mission – to gather the emissions from Japanese radar systems – during that war. The collection of water from the River Rhine to determine if any nuclear reactors were in operation represented one form of what would come to be known as measurement and signature intelligence. Another US operation, the flights of bombers equipped to detect a gas associated with the production of plutonium was yet of another early example of MASINT.

During the Cold War satellite imagery and the telemetry intelligence branch of ELINT were of primary importance for the United States in assessing the capabilities of Soviet strategic forces. Imagery was vital in determining the numbers of intercontinental ballistic missiles (ICBM) and submarine-launched ballistic missiles and the locations of ICBMs fields. Telemetry intelligence, whether obtained through space or other systems, allowed the US to determine the specific characteristics of Soviet missiles, including the number of warheads each carried.

Soviet photographic reconnaissance satellites allowed the Kremlin's rulers to be confident that they had a good understanding of US strategic capabilities. Collectively, the existence of overhead reconnaissance and other technical collection capabilities allowed the negotiation of arms control agreements, since each side had an independent means of monitoring compliance, and providing reassurance that the other side was not in the process of preparing for a surprise attack.

Today the international environment is significantly different from what it was two decades ago – with the collapse of the Soviet Union, the concern over rogue state acquisition of nuclear weapons, the threat from fundamentalist Islamic forces, and the global reach of international terrorist organizations such as al-Qaeda.

Despite those developments technical collection capabilities remain a significant factor in the ability to gather intelligence. Imagery can still identify the dispersal of strategic and conventional military forces, from missile silos to airbases, the presence of above-ground nuclear facilities, and suspicious construction activities. It remains important to treaty verification, and can provide warning of events that a nation's senior officials and diplomats would seek to forestall with advance knowledge – as when, in 1995, the US was able to persuade India to forego conducting a planned nuclear test after imagery indicated that preparations were underway.

It also remains vital in providing support to military planners and combat commanders when diplomacy fails. Imagery continues to help identify potential targets, particular points in such targets to attack, and in assessing the damage done from such attacks. And with real-time capabilities, properly equipped commanders in the field have the ability to look over the horizon and see the enemy – his numbers, deployments, and movements – without delay.

SIGINT as well as MASINT continues to be of relevance. Intelligence about the radar systems of nations that might be the subject of air attacks is of great value to the potential attacker. Intelligence about Iraqi radar systems was of importance to US and British air forces during both wars with Iraq – allowing aircraft whose mission was to jam Iraqi radars to do their job before attack aircraft arrived.

Telemetry intelligence also remains important to a number of nations – especially the United States, whose senior officials are concerned with the development of new missile systems not only in traditional countries of interest – Russia and China – but in Iran, North Korea, India, and Pakistan.

Communications intelligence, in the form of intercepted and deciphered diplomatic communications, ordinary telephone communications, cell phone traffic, e-mails, and Internet traffic, continues to be a significant activity of large and medium powers, as well as smaller nations. Collectively the world's signals intelligence organizations are looking for diplomatic secrets, plans for military or terrorist actions, violations of arms and commercial agreements, and industrial secrets.

The increased concern with the development of weapons of mass destruction by rogue states, and the possible acquisition of such weapons by terrorist groups has only heightened the pre-existing concern about the proliferation of weapons of mass destruction. The potential ability of a variety of MASINT systems and techniques – such as material sampling of soil and water and collection of gases emitted by plutonium production – to provide warning that the production of weapons of mass destruction is underway provides an incentive for nations to develop and operate such systems.

Of course, the fact that technical collection systems can produce significant intelligence does not necessarily imply that they are not without their limitations or that they are, in relative terms, as valuable as they were in an earlier era. Thus, key documents that may shed light on

115

diplomatic or military intentions or capabilities – unless foolishly transmitted by fax in an insecure manner – are immune from technical collection systems. At times, such documents can be obtained via a human source.

Technical collection systems can be subject to denial and deception. A nation which knows or suspects that some activity – for example, preparations for a nuclear test or WMD production – would be of interest to another nation's reconnaissance satellites may take care to eliminate or minimize the chance that those satellites will detect the preparations. Measures that might be taken include operating at night, not operating when a foreign reconnaissance satellite is estimated to be in range, and conducting test preparations under cover of another, more innocuous activity. A significant factor in India's ability to surprise the US with its 1998 nuclear test was the precautions taken to avoid detection by US spy satellites – including operating at night.

As both terrorist groups and some nations have learned, one means of avoiding having one's plans or activities detected through foreign communications intercept operations is to either communicate by means that are either not subject to remote interception, sufficiently cryptic to provide no crucial information, or are transmitted in a manner unlikely to be detected. Use of a courier, a phone conversation in which one terrorist alerts another that "tomorrow is the day" without providing further information, and a covert message accessible only through an obscure Internet site are respective examples.

Nations interested in hiding their weapons of mass destruction activities can also take actions to prevent other nations' MASINT collection from revealing those activities. During the Cold War the US actively sought to suppress the emissions of the krypton-85 gas associated with plutonium production. Other nations closely guard their WMD facilities, which can prevent foreign intelligence assets from collecting soil or other samples that can be used to shed more light on what is going on inside those facilities.

The international environment may also conspire to reduce the value of technical collection. The Soviet Union was a nation that did not try to hide the fact that it had a nuclear weapons program, engaged in extensive testing of its missile systems, and built a variety of naval vessels in its well-known shipyards. In contrast, some nations have small nuclear programs, make an enormous effort to conduct such activities covertly, and may engage in minimal or no testing of any nuclear devices they develop. Further, terrorist groups do not have the infrastructure that allows accumulation of intelligence from monitoring a large number of facilities, and are adept at covert communications.

The response from those seeking to detect such activities may include more intensive use of resources. Wider satellite reconnaissance operations can reduce the ability of a target nation to conduct operations in secret. Further, the distribution among the types of reconnaissance might be altered – for example, relying more extensively on radar imagery. Attempts may also be made to emplace technical collection devices – such as video cameras and eavesdropping antennae – near a target to obtain continuous coverage, rather than relying on intermittent coverage from satellites and aircraft.

Technical collection may also be conducted in different ways. Different types of sensors might be used, which focus on different parts of the electro-magnetic spectrum or collect information in entirely new ways – just as the first ventures to collect debris from a nuclear explosion, or the gases emitted during plutonium production represent new ways to uncover other nations' nuclear secrets.

One can expect that the value of technical collection will continue to be significant, but to also rise and fall, reflecting the continued contest between hiders and finders – with the developers of technical collection systems seeking to overcome the tactics that their targets employ to evade their collection systems.

Notes

1 Technical collection is often incorrectly referred to as technical intelligence – this term, however, means the intelligence concerning technical details of objects such as weapons systems, space systems, and nuclear facilities.

2 William E. Burrows, *Deep Black: Space Espionage and National Security* (New York: Random House, 1986), pp. 28–29.

3 Jeffrey T. Richelson, *A Century of Spies: Intelligence in the Twentieth Century* (New York: Oxford, 1995), pp. 33–37; 157–172.

4 Jeffrey T. Richelson, "The Whole World is Watching," *Bulletin of the Atomic Scientists*, January–February 2006, pp. 26–35.

5 On the history of the U-2, see: Chris Pocock, *The U-2 Spyplane: Toward the Unknown* (Atglen, PA: Schiffer Military History, 2000).

6 There are two types of geosynchronous satellites. One type, of which CANYON is an example, trace figure-eights about the equator, rising to about 10 degrees above and below the equator. In doing so their altitude above the earth varies from 19,000 to 24,000 miles. A second type is a subclass of geosynchronous satellite – the geostationary satellite. Such satellites stay above the same point on the equator, at an altitude of 22,300 miles, without tracing significant figure-eights.

7 Dwayne A. Day, "Listening from Above: The First Signals Intelligence Satellite," *Spaceflight*, August 1999, pp. 339–347.

8 Desmond Ball, "Signals Intelligence in China," *Jane's Intelligence Review*, 7,8 (August 1995), pp. 365–370.

9 Dr Michael E. del Papa, *Meeting the Challenge: ESD and the Cobra Dane Construction Effort on Shemya Island* (Bedford, MA: Electronic Systems Division, Air Force Systems Command, 1979), pp. 2–3.

10 Science Applications International Corporation, *Fifty Year Commemorative History of Long Range Detection: The Creation, Development, and Operation of the United States Atomic Energy Detection System* (Patrick AFB, FL: Air Force Technical Application Center, 1997), p. 114; William J. Broad, "Anti-Sub Seabed Grid Thrown Open to Eavesdropping," *New York Times*, July 2, 1996, pp. C1, C7.

11 Jeffrey T. Richelson, *Spying on the Bomb: American Nuclear Intelligence from Nazi Germany to Iran and North Korea* (New York: W.W. Norton, 2006), pp. 283–316.

12 Daniel Benjamin and Steven Simon, *The Age of Sacred Terror* (New York: Random House, 2002), pp. 259, 355–356.

13 James R. Asker, "US Navy's Haiti Maps Merge Satellite Data," *Aviation Week & Space Technology*, October 17, 1994, p. 49; Ben Ianotta and Steve Weber, "Space-Based Data Found Useful in Haiti," *Space News* September 26–October 2, 1994, p. 6.

9

Human source intelligence

Frederick P. Hitz

When President Truman signed the National Security Act of 1947 into law, creating the Central Intelligence Agency (CIA), he scarcely believed he was creating a new espionage organization for the United States, but rather that he was greatly improving the manner in which important national intelligence would find its way to his desk. Earlier he had disestablished the Office of Strategic Services (OSS), the wartime foreign intelligence collection and analytical entity, declaring that he did not want an American Gestapo in peacetime. By 1947, he had changed his mind on the need for a civilian intelligence organization for three principal reasons. First, and most importantly, the lessons of the 1941 Pearl Harbor attack strongly suggested the need for greater early warning of a future surprise attack on the United States. Second, he needed a centralizing intelligence organization that would gather and analyze all the intelligence reports headed for the Oval Office and attempt to make something coherent out of them so he would not have to do it himself. It is not clear that he wanted the new organization to go out and collect intelligence information on its own, as this had been tasked primarily to the Armed Services and to the FBI. Third, he was convinced by Secretary of the Navy James Forrestal and others in his cabinet that the USSR would become a problem now that the Nazis were defeated, and that he needed a window into Stalin's thinking and imperial ambitions, especially in Western Europe. The Cold War was beginning.

CIA got off to a slow start. Its early directors were military men who had a limited idea of the coordinating role CIA was intended to play and were aware of the bureaucratic sharks circling them, representing the parochial interests of the military departments, the Federal Bureau of Investigation (FBI), and the State Department, all of which wanted to maintain their direct access to the President on intelligence matters. Two events conspired to change this modest approach. George F. Kennan penned his famous "Long Telegram" from Moscow, alerting Washington in 1946 to Stalin's imperialist designs on that part of Europe not already under Soviet control, and recommending a policy of "containment" by the United States. At the very least, this would require affirmative action by the US in funding democratic political parties, labor unions, student groups and cultural organizations in Italy, France and Western Germany to oppose the Communist elements seeking to dominate these entities. In addition, to be most effective, the hand of the US should remain hidden. The military were not the appropriate weapon to oppose clandestine Soviet infiltration, and the State Department rejected

118

the assignment, so the fledgling CIA got the job. Luckily, there was language in the 1947 Act creating CIA that directed it to perform, with the authorization of the President, Vice-President, and Secretaries of Defense and State acting as the National Security Council, "such other functions and duties related to intelligence affecting the national security as the National Security Council may from time to time direct." Thus was created the covert action responsibility of CIA that grew enormously from 1948 to 1952 under the leadership of Frank Wisner. Wisner's so-called Office of Policy Coordination (OPC) was lodged ostensibly in the Department of State, but in reality it was an operational element of CIA.

The second major development was the arrival on the scene of two savvy Directors of Central Intelligence (DCI). Air Force Lieutenant General Hoyt S. Vandenberg and retired Army General Walter Bedell Smith (who had been Eisenhower's wartime chief of staff) knew what the organization required to move up to the big leagues and were prepared to fight for it. Vandenberg was responsible for securing for future DCIs the requisites to do their job. The National Security Acts of 1947 and 1949 that he had lobbied for (and that had also shown the handiwork of an outside commission appointed by President Truman in 1949 that included Allen Dulles) gave the DCI unparalleled authority in Washington. They gave Vandenberg and his successors as DCI the power to hire and fire his subordinates; gave them the power to spend money on their own say-so without further justification; gave them the power to short-circuit the federal government's cumbersome procurement authorities in order to perform the intelligence mission; and gave them the power to act across the range of intelligence collection, analysis and dissemination responsibilities. The scope of authority was to include activities from classic espionage, to special operations (covert action), to all-source analysis, to briefing the President's National Security Council. In short, Vandenberg got CIA, and the DCI especially, off to a running start before he returned to the Air Force. Bedell Smith took the new organization the rest of the way. *Vandenberg —> Smith*

Bedell resuscitated CIA's estimative intelligence, a function that had earned its stripes during the wartime OSS period but had lain dormant upon OSS's demise. Estimative intelligence looks out to the future, attempting to foresee problems of concern to the President that may be coming down the line. With Truman's go-ahead, Bedell created a Board of National Estimate reporting to the DCI, led by the same Harvard history professor, William Langer, who had put it together for General Donovan during World War II. Professor Langer managed to convince a number of wise men from the nation's best universities to come to work for him and Bedell, tasking them with tracking the future course of the Cold War rivalry with the USSR.

DCI Smith also made it clear that covert action and special operations existed in a chain of command extending from the DCI, and in coordination with the other espionage capability that the DCI oversaw for the President, the Office of Special Operations (OSO). He thus contrived to bring Wisner's OPC into the CIA in fact. *OSO = espion.*

The OSO's responsibility was to gather foreign intelligence information by secret means (i.e. classic espionage). It was often stumbling over or wandering into operations conducted by OPC, because the foreign actors who stole the secrets were often the same ones who could manage the propaganda or organize the political meetings for OPC. This is an important historical point. If CIA did not take the field to secretly oppose Soviet propaganda, backdoor *esp. = very impt.* electioneering and subversion in Western Europe, several of the United States' most important allies might have been in jeopardy. Furthermore, intelligence activity that connoted "action" was very much in the American character. It drew many adherents in the early CIA both because there was a perceived need (as the constant stream of National Security Directives from the President and National Security Council attested) and because, if successful, you could see the results. At the same time, the slow, painstaking process of recruiting spies to report on

119

happenings behind the Iron Curtain and in the Soviet Union itself had to be undertaken. In the late 1940s and 1950s, this was difficult and dangerous work, new to Americans of whom very few spoke the relevant languages, Russian, Polish, Czech and Hungarian. It required a patience and professionalism in terms of tradecraft that the OPCers sometimes overlooked or made fun of. The spy recruiters and handlers (of whom DCI-to be, Richard Helms was a prominent representative) were dubbed "the prudent professionals" and were not as esteemed or promoted as quickly as the OPC "action" types. Bedell tried to end all that by making of OSO and OPC one clandestine service, directed by one chief, Allen Dulles, who reported to him. Over time it worked. The two skill sets became a little more interchangeable, although DCI Smith noted in his farewell remarks to President Truman that he thought CIA was expending far too little effort with too meager results in acquiring intelligence penetrations of the Soviet Union.

Bedell was, of course, succeeded by DCI Allen Dulles, who jumped on the Eisenhower Administration's desire to contain the Soviet Union by mounting covert action programs rather than confronting it with US military force. As Supreme Commander Allied Forces, Europe in World War II, General Eisenhower had been a consumer of Britain's Enigma German code-breaking successes and knew both the role and the limitations of intelligence. As President, he believed strongly that the Soviet world-wide advance had to be stopped, if not rolled back, and covert action operations seemed a cheap and relatively low-risk way to do it. Enamored of early successes in overthrowing regimes in Iran (1953) and Guatemala (1954), the President and his advisors at CIA grew accustomed to pushing the envelope in operations, overlooking close shaves and longer-term backlash. However, this extraordinary progress in spying on the USSR and containing its influence during the Eisenhower years encountered several highly public setbacks as well. The revelation in May 1960, initially denied by President Eisenhower, that the Soviets had shot down a U-2 surveillance aircraft flying over Soviet territory, disrupted the Paris Summit. The plan to secretly train Cuban exiles to land on Cuban soil to overthrow the Castro regime, later adopted by President Kennedy and put into practice half-heartedly, and in an indefensible location at the Bay of Pigs, abruptly ended a run of successes by CIA. Kennan's X article had alerted Washington to the bitter adversities ahead in confronting as politically hardened a foe as the Soviets; so it was naturally only a matter of time before a handful of poorly conceived or blighted operations gave CIA an enduring notoriety and taint abroad, and dispelled the aura of the agency's infallibility around Washington. The Bay of Pigs disaster triggered the replacement of Allen Dulles by John McCone, whose signal innovation as DCI was to put the analytical consensus within his own agency under intense personal scrutiny. The tattered doctrine of plausible deniability, however, still held an occasionally disproportionate allure for Kennedy and later presidents. After a national wake-up on the shores of Cuba's Bay of Pigs, JFK raised CIA's operational arm from the ashes, only to shoot for the moon all over again in *Operation Mongoose*, which saw the agency embark on a rash of sometimes frantic missions to overthrow a now-entrenched Fidel Castro.

Despite the evident hazards of the profession, presidents relied substantially on CIA spies in Berlin to counter Soviet pressure there. The Eisenhower-Kennedy years were the beginning of the era of America's greatest technical intelligence successes as well, with spies and electronics working hand-in-glove in Berlin and elsewhere; with the construction of the U-2 high-altitude photo-reconnaissance aircraft; and with the refinement beginning in the 1960s of overhead satellite surveillance, eventually able to communicate images and intercepted electronic signals to Washington in real time. Nonetheless, it was on Cuba, in the October missile crisis in 1962, that US intelligence showed that it had arrived at a position of sufficient maturity in its collection systems to be able to support President Kennedy with intelligence from all three principal collection branches: *sigint, photint* and *humint*. The U-2 flyovers were the first to supply photographs of Soviet medium- and intermediate-range ballistic missiles being transported to, unloaded and installed in Cuba. Signals intercepts pointed to a heavy buzz of communications around the part of the island where the missiles were being installed, and human sources witnessed the transfer of mysterious long tubes on highways too small to accommodate them. Although there were many details that human sources were unable to provide, our principal spy, Oleg Penkovsky, from his vantage point at the pinnacle of Soviet military intelligence, reported on the ranges and characteristics of the IRBMs and MRBMs which were being installed; and also revealed that General Secretary Khrushchev was way out in front of his Politburo in thus challenging the US so close to its home territory. The fact that President Kennedy had Penkovsky's insights into Khrushchev's over-exposure, confirming the observations of his own former ambassador to the USSR, Llewelyn Thompson, meant that JFK was prepared to give up the strategic advantage of a surprise attack on the installation and, in a masterstroke of statecraft, give General Secretary Khrushchev an opportunity to escape from the corner into which he had painted himself. In my view, this was the apex of US intelligence support to the President during the Cold War. ˃ Soviets give IRBM + MRBMs to Cuba

After October 1962, prosecution of the Vietnam War became the over-riding national security concern of Presidents Kennedy, Johnson, and Nixon. CIA built up its presence in South Vietnam and collected useful human intelligence, from captured Vietcong and North Vietnamese prisoners especially, that permitted it to report consistently that the Government of South Vietnam (GOSVN) was unlikely to prevail in the war unless it took a more active role in the fighting and was able to win over greater support in the Vietnamese countryside. CIA's rejection of the validity of high body counts, that were held by American military intelligence to signal attrition in the North Vietnamese capacity to wage the war, is reminiscent of today's intelligence controversy about the import of the non-existence of Weapons of Mass Destruction (WMD) in Iraq. In the case of Vietnam, CIA more or less stuck to its guns that North Vietnam was not being defeated in 1968 despite its loss of manpower, whereas it was "dead wrong" in its assessment of the existence of chemical and biological weapons stores in Iraq in 2003, according to the Silberman-Robb Presidential Commission Report. In both cases the requirement of good, on-the-ground, contemporaneous human source reporting was critical to CIA's intelligence judgments. In Vietnam we had it, while in Iraq we did not. ✳ Silberman-Robb found that the critical National Intelligence Estimate (NIE) of October 2002 on Iraqi WMD was based on unilateral spy reporting that dated from 1991, and UN Weapons Inspector reporting that dated to 1998. There was no direct, on-the-ground *humint* after that before the outbreak of the war. Over the decades, the NIE process had taken on its share of taxing intelligence puzzles, but it was clearly compromised and out of date in this one. Humint innpt. current.

It is ironic that, as today, the great blows to the quality and competence of CIA human source reporting in the 1970s were delivered during a Republican presidency, on the watch of a national security establishment that valued and to some extent depended on good intelligence for its activist foreign and defense policy. Although Richard Nixon privately disparaged the ivy leaguers at Langley whom he believed had favored his opponent in the 1960 presidential race against JFK, he needed good intelligence on Vietnam to support the Paris Peace talks his Secretary of State Henry Kissinger was conducting with the North Vietnamese, and also his overtures to China. Indeed, when it looked as if an unabashed Marxist, Salvador Allende, was poised to win the Chilean presidential election of 1970, it was to CIA that President Nixon turned, improperly bypassing the rest of his foreign policy establishment and the US Congress to mount a coup against a democratically elected Latin American leader. ˃ CIA

Watergate and the Nixon resignation turned the tide against this manifestation of executive imperialism, while the CIA caught a fair measure of popular and Congressional backlash.

Investigative reporter Seymour Hersh wrote a series of articles in the *New York Times* in December 1974 setting forth the ways in which CIA (and the FBI) had illegally spied on American anti-Vietnam War protesters; opened people's mail; tested hallucinogenic substances on unwitting subjects and otherwise acted outside the bounds of an already broadly demarcated charter without the knowledge of Congress or the American people.[1] Congressional reaction was swift and severe. The US Senate and House of Representatives each convened investigating committees to hold extensive public hearings on CIA abuses. Senator Frank Church, a Democrat from Idaho who was running for President, tried to lock then-DCI William Colby into admissions that the agency had attempted to assassinate several world leaders such as Fidel Castro, Patrice Lumumba of the Congo, Rafael Trujillo of the Dominican Republic, and Salvador Allende, without a president's authorization, and claimed that CIA was a "Rogue Elephant." In the end, the Church Committee was unable to substantiate these allegations. There was some assassination plotting at CIA, directed by presidents, but none was shown to have been carried out successfully.

However, the Senate's inquiry caused President Ford to create a blue ribbon panel headed by Vice-President Rockefeller to look into the matter and to pre-empt the Congress's certain desire to legislate restrictions on US intelligence activity. Thus was born the effort to establish greater executive and legislative branch oversight of the Intelligence Community. President Ford promulgated Executive Order 11905 in February 1976, which banned assassination of foreign political leaders by US intelligence operatives or their surrogates, among other restrictions. The order contained a number of additional dos and don'ts that were binding on the Intelligence Community, and it was re-issued by Ford's successors, Carter and Reagan, in substantially the same form. After several years of trying to pass legislation establishing more comprehensive and binding charters for Intelligence Community agencies such as the FBI, CIA, NSA, and NRO, real-world dangers posed to the United States by the Soviet Union caused the public and Congress to regain some equilibrium on the subject of further restraining US intelligence-gathering capabilities, and the effort was dropped. The Congress settled for one paragraph in the Intelligence Authorization Act of 1980. It required the DCI and the President to keep the Congress "fully and currently informed" of all intelligence activities, including covert action, consistent with the President's constitutional authorities and the DCI's duty to protect "sources and methods from unauthorized disclosure."

The Congress believed it could settle for this paragraph instead of the several-hundred-page charter bill, because it had established in 1975 and 1976 permanent oversight committees of the House and Senate to review Intelligence Community programs and operations, just as every other department and agency in the executive branch is reviewed.

Some argue that since the creation of the House Permanent Select Committee on Intelligence (HPSCI) and the Senate Select Committee on Intelligence (SSCI), with rotating memberships after seven years' service, CIA has never been the same aggressive collector of human intelligence that it was during the height of the Cold War. I disagree. The world had changed by 1975. Although the Soviets still maintained a nuclear arsenal pointed at America's heartland, the USSR was on the downhill side of the slope economically and politically. It had an aging leadership and an increasing inability to provide for the needs and wants of its people. The US was receiving more volunteers as spies from the Soviet Union, as its high-ranking cadres became increasingly gloomy about the country's future prospects. In the US, Vietnam had exploded the post-war consensus surrounding US foreign policy, and a stronger demand for oversight and accountability for all of America's overseas activities had emerged.

Within CIA, the chaos that followed the controversial CIA mail-opening program known as Operation CHAOS lasted well into the Carter presidency and the tenure of DCI Stansfield

Turner. President Carter put CIA back on the offensive in his changing attitude to the Sandinistas in Nicaragua, and the covert action he instigated to oppose the Soviet take-over of Afghanistan in 1979. Still it remained for Ronald Reagan to initiate an across-the-board revitalization of both US defense and intelligence resources that would reverse the post-Vietnam War drawdown and counter ongoing outbreaks of Soviet aggressiveness. President Reagan authorized a covert action to train and reinforce the Contra resistance to the Marxist Sandinista revolution of 1979 in Nicaragua, and a second covert program to build up the mujahideen factions opposing the Soviet-controlled government in Afghanistan. At the same time, he initiated a research program to intercept incoming missiles in space. The Kremlin began to believe the US was trying for a first-strike capability against the USSR and initiated a world-wide intelligence alert called Project Ryan to report on indicators confirming such an effort. At the same time, old age and sickness were removing Soviet premiers at a record rate. In March 1985, a completely new figure ascended to power in the Kremlin, Mikhail Gorbachev, who was focused on curtailing Soviet commitments to defend communism everywhere (the Brezhnev Doctrine) and reforming the economy to provide a better response to the needs of the Soviet peoples. Meanwhile the Reagan administration was having a difficult time keeping the US Congress on board for the operation to support the Contras. After the second amendment curtailing CIA support for the Contras passed Congress – and was signed into law by the President because it was attached to an omnibus year-end appropriations bill – some members of the administration on the National Security staff and in CIA concocted a scheme to sell embargoed weaponry to Iran in exchange for information about terrorists who had abducted Americans in the Middle East, using the proceeds from the sales to supply weapons illegally to the Contras. The Iran–Contra scheme finally blew up in the press in the fall of 1986, sending the Reagan White House and William Casey's CIA into a tailspin.

It took the appointment in 1987 of Judge William Webster as DCI, a former Director of the FBI and US Court of Appeals judge, to restore legitimacy and integrity to CIA operations after the Iran–Contra fiasco. Meanwhile CIA's covert operators got Congressional approval to supply Stinger missiles to the Afghan mujahideen, a policy that proved pivotal to driving the Soviets out of Afghanistan. As unintentionally transparent as the Nicaraguan covert action was to the world, so the cooperation by CIA with the Pakistani intelligence service to supply armaments to Afghani and Arab guerillas in Afghanistan was painted as a state secret within the boundaries of "plausible deniability." The Soviets knew where the weaponry, especially the Stingers, was coming from, but they were in no position to do much about it, despite the concerns of Pakistan's nervous chief of state, Mohammed Zia-ul-Haq. To date, the Afghan covert action has been the last big successful clandestine political operation mounted by CIA, where the US hand did not show to an impermissible degree. By and large, the CIA officers involved kept their promise to Pakistan's rulers that they would physically stay out of Afghanistan, and work through the Pakistani intelligence service, the ISI. Both the advent of round-the-clock cable news programming, and instant world-wide communications via the internet have successfully impinged upon the US's ability to maintain the necessary secrecy of a major covert political operation. This was made manifest in the administration of President George H.W. Bush, when the President, despite his tour of duty as DCI and his appreciation for the role of intelligence, turned instead to the American military to deal with both Manuel Noriega in Panama in 1989 and Saddam Hussein in the first Gulf War in 1991. When President Clinton sought to make use of covert action in overthrowing Saddam in the mid-1990s he found it was impossible. Congress had gained an appetite for micro-managing an operation that could have high domestic stakes, and CIA had too few covert assets to bring it off.

123

By the same token, viewed in retrospect, in the mid-1980s it would turn out that the US had suffered unprecedented high-level penetrations of its intelligence services, through the handiwork of Aldrich Ames in CIA and Robert Hanssen in the FBI. Ames began his espionage for Soviet handlers in March 1985 in order to get $50,000 to buy himself out of debt. He was a 30-year spy in CIA's operations directorate who had specialized in Soviet matters, arriving at a senior level even though he had a mediocre record – which included numerous episodes of alcohol abuse, security violations and a chronic inability to get his financial accountings and contact reports about meetings with Soviet officials in on time. In short, Ames probably should never have been permitted to be on the front line, meeting and assessing Soviet officials one-on-one. But he was. And he used his position and his knowledge of how both the Soviet and US intelligence systems operated to betray, over a period of nine years, every agent working for the US against the USSR; details of numerous US operations against the Soviets; and the names of his colleagues who were engaged in the effort. Ames's betrayal led to the certain execution of ten US spies and probably more, along with the compromise of *hundreds* of US intelligence operations. The arrest of Aldrich Ames in 1994 provoked a wave of disillusionment and dismay in the American public, and among the Congressional oversight committees, that such a sloppy and seemingly inept spy could betray so much over such a long period, not only without being caught, but without CIA having mounted a serious effort to track him. The damage to the agency's reputation was nothing short of devastating.

For the FBI, no less damaging was the tale of Robert Hanssen, a dour misfit who had used his superior information technology skills to eventually burrow into the deepest corners of the bureau's counterintelligence operations against the USSR. Hanssen managed to turn over vast amounts of operational detail and names of US agents to the Soviets in an on again–off again career of espionage which began in the late 1970s and continued until his arrest in February 2001. Hanssen's case was a tougher one to crack than Ames's because Hanssen had been careful never to meet with his Soviet handler, conducting all his business with the Soviets through dead drops in a park near his home in Northern Virginia. Furthermore, Hanssen had compromised many of the same spies named by Ames or by Edward Lee Howard, another CIA turncoat of the period; so it took an analysis of operations that had gone sour that could not have been compromised by Ames or Howard, and also the help of a Soviet source, before Hanssen's own activities could be distinguished, and an arrest finally made.

At the same time that these spy wars were taking place between the Soviet and US intelligence services, CIA was beginning to enjoy real success in running Soviet and Bloc volunteer spies who were supplying vast amounts of useful intelligence information about Soviet and Warsaw Pact war-fighting plans in Europe, and Soviet military R&D. In the former case, Ryszard Kuklinski, a high-ranking member of the Polish General Staff, passed CIA all of the Warsaw Pact plans that crossed his desk from 1972 until his defection in 1981; and in the second case, Adolph Tolkachev provided his US case officer with the latest Soviet military R&D on stealth technology and air defense missilery from the late 1970s until 1985, saving the US taxpayer millions of dollars in unnecessary defense expenditure. These successful Soviet spy volunteer recruitments at the end of the Cold War, and others like them, proved the value of a vigorous human source collection program at the time that the Soviet regime was under severe internal stress.

The need for espionage did not disappear with the dismantling of the Berlin Wall in 1989 and the dismemberment of the USSR in 1991. The successor Russian government kept its intelligence officers in the field and the West at bay on a number of important issues. Yet however slowly, over time, the threats targeted by American intelligence agencies began to shift. As authoritarian regimes calcified or collapsed over the decade of the 1990s – frequently ex-Cold War client governments – the new threats would become proliferating weapons of mass destruction and emerging non-state terrorist factions, exemplified by Osama bin Laden and al Qaeda.

Osama bin Laden mounted a series of bold and ever more sophisticated attacks, beginning with that on the Khobar Towers, a US Air Force billet in Saudi Arabia in 1997; followed by the bombings of US Embassies in Dar es Salaam and Nairobi in 1998; and the attack on the USS Cole in 2000. This affluent Saudi veteran of the mujahideen effort against the Soviets in Afghanistan showed he was capable and desirous of inflicting unacceptable damage on the United States in order to drive it out of the Muslim holy places of the Middle East. His organization, known as al Qaeda, or the Franchise, had in 1991 volunteered to lead the Islamic effort to force Saddam Hussein to leave Kuwait, but his offer was overlooked by the Saudi royals. Subsequently in exile in the Sudan, and after 1995 in Afghanistan as a guest of the Taliban regime, Osama preached Islamic unity and defiance in opposing the West's continued military basing in the region and the support it was giving to autocratic and selfish rulers in Saudi Arabia, Egypt and the Gulf who were doing nothing to provide for their populations. CIA, in particular in the US Intelligence Community, became alarmed at the growing strength, sophistication and appeal of Osama's rhetoric against the United States' role in the Middle East, which targeted it as the "far enemy." After President Clinton's weak and ineffective response to the African embassy bombings, CIA established a task force to track Osama and al Qaeda, but it was never able to deliver the knock-out punch on his compound in Afghanistan or stop his continuing deadly momentum during the Clinton years, even though then DCI George Tenet "declared war" on al Qaeda in an attempt to bring focus to American intelligence's counter-terrorist strategy.

In 2001, CIA began receiving heightened liaison reporting from US allies in Europe and the Middle East that al Qaeda was planning something big. But where – in the region or against a US installation overseas – was unknown. This was becoming Osama's trademark: long months of preparation and then a sudden strike. But just like the US Government's previous experience with a massive surprise attack on US territory at Pearl Harbor, we were not prepared nor really expecting an attack in the continental United States. September 11, 2001 was an unforeseen and life-shattering wake-up call on the capacity of non-state, religious-inspired terrorism to threaten stable societies like the United States and our European allies. It took President George W. Bush minutes to declare that the US was involved in a war against terror and that all the military and intelligence resources of the United States would be deployed to win it.

What were those intelligence resources? In late 2001, in what condition did the Intelligence Community find itself to take on Osama bin Laden, al Qaeda, and the challenge of religious-based international terror? With the passing of the Cold War, CIA had been down-sized and had in addition witnessed the dramatic departure of large numbers of expert spy handlers and analysts whose skills had been shaped by the challenge of the Soviet Union, and who did not have much interest in and familiarity with the milieu of terrorism, drugs, crime and weapons proliferation, issues which would be the meat and potatoes of Presidential Decision Directive 35 that set the blueprint for IC targeting after the Cold War ended. So they retired, and took with them their knowledge of spy tradecraft and of foreign languages. On top of that, as the 9/11 post-mortems would show, the intelligence agencies had grown into mature bureaucracies without much initiative, imagination or creativity. They faced a target that operated in the shadows of nation-states but wasn't one; that had low overheads and a tight network of collaborators that it deployed with iron-handed discipline; and that possessed one unassailable attribute: many of its adherents were willing to commit suicide for the cause, and would strap on a bomb just to take civilian bystanders with them.

125

Other problems beset the intelligence agencies in 2001 as well. A division between domestic and international spheres of terrorism no longer existed. A plot that could begin in a Hamburg mosque or a Madrid suburb could be planned for immediate execution in New York or Washington. The divided responsibilities between the FBI and CIA that historical accident and concern about domestic civil liberties had spawned in the aftermath of World War II were hindrances in the twenty-first century to the kind of instant information-sharing and team-work that cell phones and internet access in the hands of our terrorist attackers demanded. Compartmentation and "need to know" take on sinister meanings, when the effect is to deny intelligence to a sister agency equally charged with the responsibility to pre-empt a terrorist act.

Some of the more egregious barriers to intelligence-sharing and teamwork between the intelligence agencies were struck down in the USA PATRIOT Act passed in October 2002, and in the Intelligence Reform Bill, passed in December 2004. Now, wiretap permissions, when granted, run to the individual who is the target of the surveillance, not the instrument by which he intends to communicate. Grand jury testimony in terrorist cases can be shared among the law enforcement and intelligence entities having an interest in the matter. The Foreign Intelligence Surveillance Act (FISA) has been amended to include, among the parties against whom the US Government may seek authorization for electronic surveillance from the special Foreign Intelligence Surveillance Court, not just spies but terrorists as well; and the standard for authorizing surveillance has been broadened to encompass those as to whom terrorism is "a principal purpose" of their activity and not "the" purpose. There are additional sections in the 2001 Act that beef up the anti-money-laundering provisions of federal statute and enhance the "sneak and peek" possibilities open to law enforcement, as well as enable more internet intrusion of suspected terrorists. It is possible that some of the more aggressive portions of the PATRIOT Act may be modified somewhat to include a greater measure of accountability.

The intended changes included in the Intelligence Reform Act of 2004 date back to the Church Committee era, but trespassed on more turf, and would only see the light of day three years after September 11th, with some of the most intense bureaucratic lobbying of any intelligence bill. In the Act, there has been a concerted effort to remedy one of the principal perceived deficiencies in the performance of the intelligence agencies prior to 9/11, namely the absence of "an attending physician" who could treat the patient as a whole and be responsible for the work of all the specialists racing around performing tests on the patient on their own. That metaphor, used by the 9/11 Commission to sway the Congress and the President, was the premise behind creating the new position of Director of National Intelligence (DNI). The DNI was intended to be the intelligence czar, a cabinet officer holding both managerial and budgetary authority over the entire Intelligence Community. He would also be the President's principal intelligence adviser.

When the dust settled after passage of the Act, the DNI's lines of command were not as clear as the Commission hoped. The Defense Secretary and the Department of Defense (DOD) continue to share many of the DNI's management and budgetary authorities relating to the intelligence agencies under the command of DOD. The DOD intelligence agencies, NRO, NSA, DIA and NGA account for 80 percent of the intelligence budget. There is also the matter of information-sharing, which the Act seeks to encourage by requiring the DNI to have a subordinate who is responsible for creating an Information Sharing Environment in the Intelligence Community.

The 2004 Act also treats the Intelligence Community's self-inflicted wounds represented by the failures to warn of the 9/11 attacks and to accurately account for the weapons of mass destruction stockpiled by Saddam Hussein since 1991 – believed ready for dispersal to terrorists by Saddam at some point if the U.N. embargo of Iraq was not lifted. The existence of Iraqi

WMD was one of the principal reasons cited by the Bush Administration for preparing to go to war against Iraq. A seemingly authoritative National Intelligence Estimate (NIE) circulated by CIA in October 2002 detailed the supposed holdings of chemical and biological weapons by the Iraqi Ba'athist regime, and the efforts of the regime to make nuclear weaponry advances. Furthermore, United Nations testimony drawn from the NIE by Secretary of State Colin Powell in February 2003, on the eve of the Iraq War, was used to sweep aside Allied opposition to the invasion. It has become painfully clear since, that Saddam suspended his WMD programs after 1991 to get out from under the UN-sponsored embargo. There were no WMD stockpiled in Iraq prior to the war, as Saddam had destroyed them.

What made the US Intelligence Community's views on Iraqi WMD so objectionable was not that they held such preconceptions (most other knowledgeable intelligence services held identical views – the UK, Russia, Germany, France and Israel), but that the NIE sought to justify the weapons' existence on outdated and unconfirmed reporting. The proprietary data dated from 1991; reports from UN Inspectors stopped in 1998; and assessments rested heavily on unilateral sources like "Curveball" whose credibility was in question. The analytical tradecraft employed by the CIA on the critical NIE was fatally deficient.

Where does that now leave CIA and the Intelligence Community, who bear the preponderant responsibility to inform the President about terrorists and their targets *before* these attacks occur? Future performance alone will provide the answer. The Intelligence Community has weathered its share of crises in the past. Yet there are some systemic reasons to be concerned.

To start with, the intelligence agencies allowed their capabilities to attenuate markedly during that ten-year period between the disintegration of the Soviet Union and September 11, 2001. There are still too few intelligence officers who have studied and understand Arabic civilizations or who have lived in the Middle East at some point in their careers. Moreover, many of the collection techniques of the Cold War have been rendered obsolete by cell phones, the internet and other aspects of changing technology. CIA cannot continue to operate as it did in the pre-Iraq period, largely excluded from the hard targets that the United States is up against. Where it has no physical presence, the agency has historically relied for *humint* primarily on defectors, detainees, legal travelers, opposition groups and foreign government liaison services, but these sources divulge their secrets at some distance in time and space from the ongoing developments inside the target they are reporting on. Getting inside the adversary's organization is thus a higher priority than it was even in the Cold War. Yet even though the Directorate of Operations budget is now more than double its pre-September 11th levels, an estimated 80–90 percent of intelligence information about al Qaeda still comes in as *sigint*.[2] The whereabouts, goals and tactics of terrorists are thus available only imprecisely and intermittently.

In the *humint* area, American intelligence is still behind other services in having linguists who speak the hard languages of the Middle East, Central Asia or Southeast Asia. In addition, this assignment is becoming less appealing to spy runners from the standpoint of safety and quality of life. Increasingly, CIA's operatives will bring back key intelligence only by acting with the flexibility, the skills, and the cover it takes to run operations unlinked with an official installation – under non-official cover. Consequently, the problems spies face conducting espionage will be more dangerous. Families too will be divided, as many overseas tours in areas of prime concern to the intelligence agencies are not safe for young children.

An equally fundamental point is that Americans are not the "good guys" any more in many areas of the Middle East. This sounds simplistic, yet much of US intelligence success during the mature stages of the Cold War occurred because Soviet and Soviet Bloc officials volunteered to work for the American or British intelligence services as a way to oppose the corruption and

127

misery of their own lives behind the Iron Curtain. That motivation appears less prevalent in the Middle East today. The USA is perceived as a threatening, non-Islamic outside force, only interested in the region's petroleum resources. Perhaps President Bush's hard push for democratic governments in the region will alter this attitude. It will be a hard sell.

The upshot of pervasive suspicions in the region about American aims is that, to be successful, CIA and the other Intelligence Community *humint* collectors will have to work indirectly, and multilaterally, through the good offices of friendly intelligence services, the operational channels called intelligence liaison. Since September 11th, CIA has been doing that in a major way, trading superior resources and technology for on-the-ground intelligence information about terrorist threats. The difficulty liaison relationships present, however, is that we are no longer in complete control of the spy operation. Our liaison intermediaries will influence both whom we target and how we manage the take. The result is bound in many cases to be a dilution of the product and a diminished timeliness. But the most worrisome deficiency will be a lack of confidence that one is getting the full picture, with the ongoing potential to leave the US vulnerable and the region unstable: it is worth remembering the lessons of the Pakistani ISI's control over our access to the mujahideen during the 1980s and 1990s in Afghanistan.

The Intelligence Community's technical collection programs may not be in much better shape than its *humint*. Signals intelligence-gathering is hindered by inadequate translation capabilities, while a wary target will be more willing to communicate by word of mouth, cleft stick and carrier pigeon, than by telephone or more modern means. From an operational standpoint, the fallout from the brouhaha over warrantless surveillance by NSA of communications from potential terrorists abroad with individuals in the United States that arose in early 2006 may further limit the gathering of useful intelligence. Actually, it appears that most al Qaeda instructions are moving through Arabic websites on the internet, which intelligence services worldwide are not yet recovering or translating in a comprehensive or timely fashion.

When all is said and done, counter-terrorism and counter-proliferation intelligence-gathering follows a new paradigm. It is less about classic espionage than persistent tracking of terrorists and their potential weapons by good detective work and perceptive mining of reams of open sources. This is no longer back-alley skulking in a trench coat. It is down-and-dirty police investigative work, tracing radicals and their bomb-making materials, and recruiting informants to watch mosques and radical meeting sites. That is why in the US it is so important for the CIA to work well with the FBI, with Customs, with Immigration and Naturalization and with local police first responders. Intelligence gathering in the twenty-first century is now less about James Bond or George Smiley than it is a Frankenstein composite of law enforcement, spies and forensics.

Notes

1 Seymour Hersh, "Huge CIA Operation Reported in US against Antiwar Forces, Other Dissidents During Nixon Years," *New York Times*, December 22, 1974; Hersh, "President Tells Colby to Speed Report on CIA," *New York Times,* December 24, 1974; Hersh, "3 More Aides Quit in CIA Shake-Up," *New York Times*, December 30, 1974.
2 Dana Priest, "Foreign Network at Front of CIA's Terror Fight," *Washington Post*, November 18, 2005.

10

Open source intelligence

Robert David Steele

Executive summary[1]

Definition and scope

Open source intelligence, or OSINT, is unclassified information that has been deliberately discovered, discriminated, distilled and disseminated to a select audience in order to address a specific question. It provides a very robust foundation for other intelligence disciplines. When applied in a systematic fashion, OSINT products can reduce the demands on classified intelligence collection resources by limiting requests for information only to those questions that cannot be answered by open sources.

Open information sources are not the exclusive domain of intelligence staffs. Intelligence should never seek to limit access to open sources. Rather, intelligence should facilitate the use of open sources by all staff elements that require access to relevant, reliable information. Intelligence staffs should concentrate on the application of proven intelligence processes to the exploitation of open sources to improve its all–source intelligence products. Familiarity with available open sources will place intelligence staffs in the position of guiding and advising other staff elements in their own exploitation of open sources.

Open source intelligence and joint or coalition operations

OSINT is a vital component of NATO's future vision. Through its concentration upon unclassified open sources of information, OSINT provides the means with which to develop valid and reliable intelligence products that can be shared with non–NATO elements of international operations. Experience in the Balkans, and the increasing importance of the Partnership for Peace and Mediterranean Dialogue members in security dialogue, illustrates the need to develop information sources that enable broader engagement with these vital partners.

Private sector information offerings

The Internet is now the default Command and Control, Communications, Computing, and Intelligence (C4I) architecture for virtually the entire world. The principal exceptions are

C4I

most militaries and intelligence organizations. The Internet facilitates commerce, provides entertainment and supports ever increasing amounts of human interaction. To exclude the information flow carried by the Internet is to exclude the greatest emerging data source available. While the Internet is a source of much knowledge, all information gleaned from it must be assessed for its source, bias and reliability.

As a source of reliable information, the Internet must be approached with great caution. As a means with which to gain access to quality commercial sources of validated information, the Internet is unbeatable.

A vision of open source exploitation must not be limited exclusively to electronic sources. Traditional print, hardcopy images and other analog sources continue to provide a wealth of data of continuing relevance to NATO intelligence.

The open source intelligence cycle

As the range of NATO information needs varies depending upon mission requirements, it is virtually impossible to maintain a viable collection of open source materials that address all information needs instantly. The focus should be on the collection of sources, not information. With knowledge of relevant and reliable sources of open source information, an intelligence staff can quickly devote collection energy and analytical expertise to develop tailored OSINT products to the mission need.

OSINT and the emerging future intelligence architecture of NATO

OSINT is an essential building block for all intelligence disciplines. Open sources have always played a role in classified intelligence production. In the NATO context, a robust OSINT capability greatly increases the range of information sources available to intelligence staffs to address intelligence needs.

Nations are capable of tasking classified intelligence sources to address intelligence gaps. Lacking organic intelligence collection assets, NATO intelligence staffs are unable to task classified collection. Rather than immediately directing a Request For Information (RFI) to a national intelligence centre, a robust OSINT capability enables intelligence staffs to address many intelligence needs with internal resources.

While unable to replace classified intelligence production, OSINT is able to complement an all-source intelligence production process with essential support including tip-offs, context, validation and cover for information sanitation.[2]

Introduction to open source intelligence

OSINT is not a substitute for satellites, spies, or existing organic military and civilian intelligence capabilities. It is, however, a foundation – a very strong foundation – for planning and executing coalition operations across the spectrum from humanitarian assistance to total war. OSINT provides strategic historical and cultural insights; it provides operationally helpful information about infrastructure and current conditions; and it provides tactically vital commercial geospatial information that is not available from national capabilities. In coalition operations, OSINT is both the foundation for civil–military cooperation, and the framework for classified bilateral intelligence-sharing.

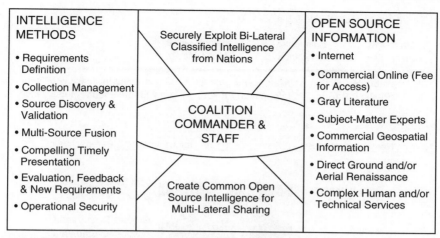

Figure 10.1 Relationship between open and classified information operations

OSINT is distinct from academic, business, or journalistic research in that it represents the application of the proven process of national intelligence to the diversity of sources, with the intent of producing *tailored* intelligence for the commander. OSINT is also unique, within a coalition operations context, in that it simultaneously provides a multi-lateral foundation for establishing a common view of the shared Area of Operations (AOR), while also providing a context within which a wide variety of bi-lateral classified intelligence sharing arrangements can be exploited. Figure 10.1 illustrates these relationships.

Since 2001, the Swedish government has advanced a concept for Multinational, Multi-agency, Multidisciplinary, Multidomain Information Sharing (M4IS), and the author has put forward the need for regional Multinational Information Operations Centers (MIOC). At the same time, in the private sector, organizations such as the Co–Intelligence Institute have brought forward robust concepts for Collective Intelligence, and books have been written about *Smart Mobs* and *Wisdom of the Crowds*. It is clear from these developments that OSINT is taking on a life of its own outside the government, in keeping with the author's original depiction of the seven tribes of intelligence (see Figure 10.2).[3]

OSINT is less about specific sources such as are listed ·in the column on the right of Figure 10.1, and more about "knowing who knows."[4]

Definitions

There are four distinct categories of open information and intelligence.

- *Open Source Data (OSD).* Data is the raw print, broadcast, oral debriefing or other form of information from a primary source. It can be a photograph, a tape recording, a commercial satellite image, or a personal letter from an individual.
- *Open Source Information (OSIF).* OSIF is comprised of data that can be put together, generally by an editorial process that provides some filtering and validation as well as presentation management. OSIF is generic information that is usually widely disseminated. Newspapers, books, broadcast, and general daily reports are part of the OSIF world.

Original 1993 Concept of Information Continuum

Schools & Universities	Business Intelligence	Mainstream & Niche Media
Libraries, Both Public & Private	Private Investigators & Information Brokers	Government Inclusive of Military, Law Enforcement, & Intelligence

Current New Concept of Seven Tribes, Each with Unique Access & Perspective

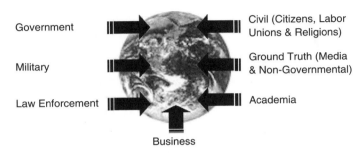

Government

Military

Law Enforcement

Business

Civil (Citizens, Labor Unions & Religions)

Ground Truth (Media & Non-Governmental)

Academia

Figure 10.2 Information continuum and the Seven Tribes

- *Open Source Intelligence (OSINT)*. OSINT is information that has been deliberately discovered, discriminated, distilled, and disseminated to a select audience, generally the commander and their immediate staff, in order to address a specific question. OSINT, in other words, applies the proven process of intelligence to the broad diversity of open sources of information, and creates intelligence.
- *Validated OSINT (OSINT-V)*. OSINT-V[5] is OSINT to which a very high degree of certainty can be attributed. It can be produced by an all-source intelligence professional, with access to classified intelligence sources, whether working for a nation or for a coalition staff. It can also come from an assured open source to which no question can be raised concerning its validity (images of an aircraft arriving at an airport that are broadcast over the media).

OSINT in context

In this summary chapter we will touch lightly on the context of OSINT, while distinguishing between OSINT as it supports government Intelligence & Information Operations (I2O) where secret sources and methods play a paramount role, and OSINT as the sole legal means of decision support for non-governmental organizations.

While OSINT is not "new" in that nations and organizations have always understood the value of legal travelers, direct observation, structured reading, and legal purchases of information services, what is new about OSINT is the confluence of three distinct trends: first, the proliferation of the Internet as a tool for disseminating and sharing overt information in all languages; second, the consequent and related "information explosion" in which published useful knowledge is growing exponentially; and third, the collapse of formerly denied areas accompanied by the explosion of non-traditional threats in the form of failed states and transnational non-state threats to public security and prosperity.

Below are four perspectives of how OSINT relates to the secret intelligence world, to the specific secret disciplines, to the wisdom of the crowds, and to the decision support process of any commander or Chief Executive Officer (CEO).

1   Open source information (OSIF) is the earth beneath the temple, while OSINT is the foundation, with each of the secret disciplines being a pillar, all holding up the temple's roof, all-source analysis. However, in recent years it has grown in importance, to the point that Dr John Gannon, former Deputy Director of Central Intelligence for Analysis & Production (ADDCI/A&P) is now on record as saying "Open-source information now dominates the universe of the intelligence analyst, a fact that is unlikely to change in the foreseeable future."[6]

2   If intelligence were a baseball game, then the clandestine service would try to recruit a player, the signals intelligence specialists would put a "bug" in the opposing team's dug-out, the imagery people would take a satellite picture of the game every three days. OSINT tells everyone in the audience that if they catch the ball, we will pay cash and it is an out. OSINT changes the rules of the game.

3   OSINT is both a subordinate discipline to each of the classified disciplines, and also uniquely an all-source discipline that can "stand alone" when necessary, combining overt humans, overt signals, commercial imagery, and public analysis.

4   OSINT is the only discipline that can simultaneously access all that can be known in all languages back in time, harness all available expertise and manpower without clearances, and produce intelligence that can be shared with anyone. This makes it especially valuable for law enforcement investigations, humanitarian assistance missions, and early warning for open discussion among members of the United Nations.[7]

OSINT and information operations

Information Operations (IO) is comprised of Information Peacekeeping (IP) and Information Warfare (IW). At the strategic level, IO is broadly related to influencing and messaging all parties (hostile, neutral, and friendly) for national advantage. IO must integrate OSINT (understanding their reality as well as our own), Joint Information Operations Centers or Commands (JIOC) as well as multinational and national variants (MIOC, NIOC) which comprise the tool-sets as well as the mind-sets; and Strategic Communication (the message).

At the operational and tactical levels, this translates into assuring one's own ability to see, hear, know, understand, decide, and act on "all information, all languages, all the time," while denying or distorting or altering adversarial information capabilities.[8]

This is an extraordinarily complex undertaking that has not been intellectually defined. The concepts, doctrines, tools, and mind-sets are a long way from being robust. What this means in practice is that nations and organizations must be able to devise unified campaign plans that fully integrate, on an interagency or inter-departmental basis, the activities of public diplomacy and public affairs or relations, strategic communication and influence (as well as strategic acquisition and force structure management), perception management, psychological operations (PSYOP), the propaganda and agent of influence aspects of covert operations (among governments), denial and deception, space control, network attack and defense, electronic warfare, information and communications and electronic security operations, information assurance operations, counter-intelligence and counter-deception operations, and so on.[9] Rarely emphasized except by the author, all of these demand that we understand reality, and not allow the United States to be driven into bankruptcy by ideological fantasies and consequent policy-level misjudgments.

OSINT and national security

It is a common misperception that most "intelligence" is classified and must come from secret sources and methods that are very expensive and relatively risky. The "cult of secrecy" has put us in a very disadvantageous position, where in the United States of America (USA) at least $50 billion a year is spent on collecting the 5 percent of the information that is secret and can or must be stolen, and virtually nothing is spent on the 95 percent of the information in all languages that is relevant to all but the most secretive threats.

The importance of this observation can be emphasized by listing the top threats to global security as documented in the Report of the High-level Panel on Threats, Challenges and Change, *A More Secure World: Our Shared Responsibility*:[10]

• **Economic and social threats including**	**95%**
– poverty	99%
– infectious disease and	95%
– environmental degradation	90%
• **Inter-state conflict**	**75%**
• **Internal conflict, including**	**90%**
– civil war,	80%
– genocide and	95%
– other large-scale atrocities	95%
• **Nuclear, radiological, chemical, and**	
biological weapons	**75%**
• **Terrorism**	**80%**
• **Transnational organized crime**	**80%**

Figure 10.3 OSINT relevance to global security threats

The average utility and relevant of OSINT to these global threats is – on the basis of my informed estimate – 82.5 percent, which comes very close to the generic "80–20" rule. We must conclude that any nation that persists in spending 99.9 percent of its intelligence funds on collecting secrets,[11] and less than one half of one percent of its intelligence funds on OSINT, is quite literally, clinically insane (or insanely corrupt) at the highest levels.

Naturally there are those who will quibble about whether the budgets of the National Aeronautics and Space Agency (NASA) or the Environmental Protection Agency (EPA) or the Department of Justice (DoJ) should be "counted." What matters here is that intelligence is nothing more or less than decision-support for the President and the top members of the Cabinet, as well as Congress in its oversight role. Most of the US Government budget, by way of example, is spent on weapons, manpower, and administration. Research & development (R&D) is focused on investigation, design, and the creation of capabilities, not on decision-support. Intelligence is *decision-support*.

It merits comment that those business enterprises and religions that choose to emphasize industrial espionage or the covert subversion of governments are making the same fundamental error of confusing "secret sources and methods" with "intelligence." Intelligence is information that has been collected, processed, analyzed, and presented in order to support a decision that increases security or profit, or reduces risk or cost. Nowhere is it written that "intelligence" must be secret or that intelligence is improved by a reliance on secret sources or methods.

Indeed, it has been demonstrated on more than one occasion, with Viet–Nam and Iraq as the extant examples,[12] that not only is secret intelligence easy to ignore and manipulate, but a reliance on secret intelligence can lead to a "shutting out" of overt common sense and open sources of information.[13]

Consider this, Daniel Ellsberg lecturing Henry Kissinger:[14]

> The danger is, you'll become like a moron. You'll become incapable of learning from most people in the world, no matter how much experience they have in their particular areas that may be much greater than yours [because of your blind faith in the value of your narrow and often incorrect secret information].

OSINT – intelligence that is publicly disseminated – is the single best antidote to the pathologies of secret executive power.

OSINT and the larger customer base for intelligence

Most citizens, and most legislators, assume that national intelligence or corporate intelligence is in the service of every part of the government, or every part of the corporation. This is not actually the case. In the USA, specifically, the focus continues to be on "secrets for the President," and on a few "hard targets" considered to be of the gravest possible concern – China, Cuba, Iran, North Korea. Within corporations, the emphasis is on serving the Chief Executive Officer (CEO). Consider the following questions as both a litmus test for intelligence managers, and as a broad definition of the possibilities for OSINT. To be explicit: every single customer ignored by the mandarins of secrecy or the sycophants to the CEO is a customer for OSINT.

- Do you believe that secrets are the ultimate form of knowledge, or do you believe that all sources including open sources should be brought to bear on decision–support?
- Do you believe that intelligence should focus only on the gravest of threats, what some call the "hard targets," or do you believe there is merit to "global coverage," seeking to monitor and understand all threats at some minimal mandatory level of detail?
- Is intelligence something that should be done only for the leadership, or should intelligence support – decision–support – be provided to agency heads, department heads, and even the individuals in the field, the front line that interacts with the real world?
- Is federal or corporate level intelligence only for the members of the federal government or the corporate headquarters, or should it support state and local jurisdictions, or subsidiaries?

OSINT and the levels of analysis

It is in the above context that we can conclude this overview by stating without equivocation that OSINT must be provided to all levels of any enterprise. This about empowering every individual, every segment of the enterprise, with decision–support (see Figure 10.4).

OSINT and coalitions

Although the concepts and doctrine that I have been developing for eighteen years recognize the seven tribes of intelligence as distinct historical, cultural, intellectual, and direct-access entities, it is the military and the concept of the military coalition that really serves as the spinal cord and nervous system for "harnessing the distributed intelligence of the Whole Earth."

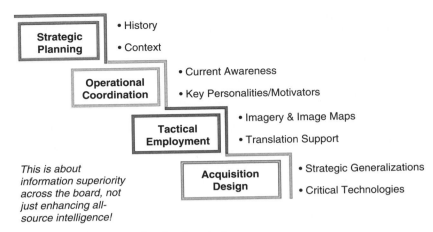

Strategic Planning
• History
• Context

Operational Coordination
• Current Awareness
• Key Personalities/Motivators

Tactical Employment
• Imagery & Image Maps
• Translation Support

This is about information superiority across the board, not just enhancing all-source intelligence!

Acquisition Design
• Strategic Generalizations
• Critical Technologies

Figure 10.4 OSINT and the four levels of analysis

Within the USA, as within most countries, the military is consistently the most professional, the most disciplined, the most structured, and the most reliable organization. It is also the only one that treats Command and Control, Communications, Computing, and Intelligence (C4I) as a distinct discipline with its own Military Occupational Specialty (MOS) for each aspect.

It is a fact that the USA is simply not capable of fielding sufficient citizens with sufficient language and foreign area qualifications. Given the rapid rate at which available information doubles (a rate that will accelerate as hand-held devices become the instrument of choice, and are used to register photographs, videos, voice recordings, and text inputs from tens of millions operating in all languages, all the time), there is only one possible solution for mastering "all information, all languages, all the time." We must provide our coalition partners, and particularly our military coalition partners, with the means to digitize, translate, and analyze (using both automated tools and their own unique human expertise) all information of mutual interest, and we must provide a global Information Arbitrage™ capability that enables all coalition partners, each responsible for harnessing and nurturing their respective seven tribes, to participate in what I call the Open Source Information System – External (OSIS-X). Bi-lateral intelligence-sharing may still predominate in the secret world, but in the open source world, it is M4IS – multi-lateral sharing – that will define the common approach.

OSINT and saving the world

C.K. Prahalad has taught us that our government and business focus to date, on the one billion richest people on the planet, who represent a one-trillion-a-year marketplace, is short-sighted. His brilliant book, *The Fortune at the Bottom of the Pyramid*, makes the important point that the five billion poorest people on the planet, because of their numbers and despite their low wages (an average of $1,000 a year, with half that number earning as little as $1 a day), actually represent a four-trillion-a-year marketplace – in short, a marketplace four times larger than the one that is active today.

It was not until I absorbed the wisdom of C.K. Prahalad that I understand that OSINT can help the poor cut costs, reduce disease, improve health, and increase revenue. It is now possible to show religions, labor unions, and civil societies how to leverage the Internet and low-cost hand-held devices (instead of the more expensive laptops or personal computers) to apply OSINT from the "bottom up," and consequently to double or triple revenue at the bottom of the pyramid. The creation of sustainable indigenous wealth is without question the single fastest way to save the world from itself.

OSINT as a transformative catalyst for reform

America has been adrift for some time. The "me" generation spawned the disengaged generation, and we suffer now from the twin curses of an uneducated public that is also inattentive to its civic responsibility. This affects the rest of the world. It prevents us from keeping our politicians and corporate leaders honest, and its spawns terrible mis-adventures undertaken on the basis of ideological fantasies, without due policy process, or any semblance of a coherent affordable sustainable grand strategy. There is hope. See Figure 10.5.

Electoral reform, which could be inspired by multiple compounding failures of any administration across the board, or alternatively by a more aggressive practice of collective intelligence among the public, could lead to governance reform. A coalition government could demand that intelligence reform be substantive and comprehensive. This would have the happy outcome of imposing national security reform, which would not only reduce America's risk around the world, but would reduce the cost of the heavy-metal military, and free up resources for waging peace. From peace will follow prosperity. The low-cost, high-return value proposition from OSINT cannot be exaggerated.

Alvin and Heidi Toffler have focused in the manner in which information is a substitute for violence, for capital, for labor, for time and space. Others followed, including Thomas Stewart in *The Wealth of Knowledge* and Barry Carter in *Infinite Wealth*.[15] This is *real*.

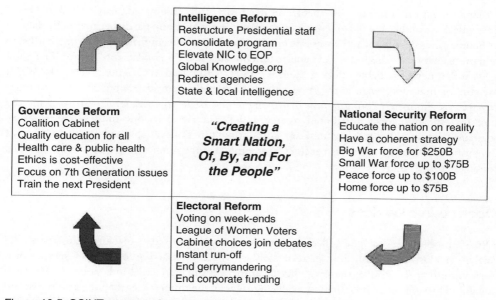

Figure 10.5 OSINT as a transformative catalyst for reform

Open sources of information[16]

Open sources of information consist of the following general categories:

- Traditional media sources
- Commercial online premium sources
- Other niche commercial online sources
- Gray literature (limited edition locally available information)
- Overt human experts
- Commercial imagery and geospatial information
- The Internet and the world wide web (including emails and voice calls)

Open source software and software for exploitation

As a general statement, open source software is one of the five "opens" that will converge to create the World Brain. The others are, apart from OSINT, open (electromagnetic) spectrum, open access copyright, and open hypertext document system (OHS). The following standards are emergent as enablers of M4IS while still compliant with copyright or other individual caveats desired by the originator or owner of the information:

- RDF   Resource Description Framework
- OWL   Web Ontology Language
- SOAP   Simple Object Access Protocol
- OHS   Open Hypertextdocument System[17]
- XML Geo   eXtended Markup Language Geospatial
- IEML   Information Economy Meta Language.

There is no one offering that meets the need for a fully integrated analyst toolkit. This is partly because of the lack of agreement on standards in the past, and partly because of the lack of coherence in government and corporate contracting, where the emphasis has been on hardware and proprietary software instead of generic functionality and ease of data integration. The good news is that newly available offerings such as CISCO's Application Oriented Network (AON) are eliminating middleware, at the same time that Google's innovative approach to commodity storage has eliminated configuration management and back-up costs, while also reducing the cost for efficient global distributed storage and fast retrieval to one-third of the industry standard. Below are listed the desktop computing functions established by the Office of Scientific and Weapons Research at the Central Intelligence Agency (CIA) in 1986 as essential for analysis (see Figure 10.6).[18]

Open source services

Open source services include collection, processing (inclusive of man-machine translation), and analysis (inclusive of statistical or pattern analysis). When contracting for OSINT services, it is very important to evaluate the capability from the bottom-up (actual indigenous or localized capabilities to collect all information in all languages all the time) rather than the traditional and unprofessional way, which throws money at large contractors who then "fake it" and keep the

- Revision tracking, RT review
- Desktop publishing
- Graphics/multimedia production
- Collaborative work
- Notetaking & organizing ideas
- Structured argument
- Interactive search & retrieval
- Graphic map-based visualization
- Modeling and simulation
- Clustering & linking of data
- Statistical analysis for anomalies
- Detection of changing trends
- Detection of alert situations
- Easy digitization of hard copy
- Automated language translation
- Processing of images, signals
- Automated data extraction
- Data standardization/conversion

Figure 10.6 Fundamental functions for online analysis

bulk of the money for themselves. Generally when contracting for professional OSINT services, a good rule of thumb is to earmark one-third of the money for raw information collection, one-third for small businesses providing world-class translation and machine analysis services, and one-third for in-house or on-site analysts and related facilities.

The open source intelligence cycle

The open source intelligence cycle consists of the following steps that can be summarized by remembering "the four D's" of Discovery (Know Who Knows); Discrimination (Know What's What); Distillation (Know What's Hot); and Dissemination (Know Who's Who).

- Requirements definition
- Practical triage
- Collection (FIND free, GET free, BUY cheap, TASK dear)
- Processing and exploitation
- Analysis and production
- Security
- Dissemination and evaluation (Feedback).

The OSINT intelligence cycle cannot make up for pathological mind-sets (including ideological fantasy and political corruption) or poor management.

OSINT has one advantage over the other sources: its exposure to millions of pairs of eyeballs. As it commonly understood in the open source software world, put enough eyeballs on it and no bug is invisible.[19] OSINT also offers analytic frames of reference that have stood the test of time.[20]

Another misconception relates to production. Too many people misconstrue reports and page counts as "production" when in fact production does not consist simply of reports and page counts, but also includes link tables, distance learning, and professional networking. Figure 10.7 illustrates how one activates OSINT using the Internet.

Figure 10.7 World Brain operational planning group virtual private network

The common mistake that most vendors of OSINT make is to confuse the weekly report or database-stuffing with "answering the mail." In fact, the weekly review is the foundation for a more complex process that requires each of eight distinct *iterative and interactive* capabilities to be present at all times.

OSINT is a continuous process of collection, processing, analysis, sharing, feedback, and expansion. Unlike secrets (for a spy, a secret shared is a secret lost), OSINT is enhanced, strengthened, validated, and monetarized by sharing.

At root, OSINT is about smart people creating smart organizations by sharing the burden of conceptualizing requirements, collecting all information in all languages all the time, doing multi-cultural inter-agency analysis, and then producing credible reliable intelligence that is actionable – it is useful and it leads to constructive outcomes. OSINT crosses all boundaries, and in so doing, brings us all closer together and helps us to both understand and to address common problems at every level of community and governance. OSINT saves lives, time, and money.

Applied open source intelligence

> Intelligence must be able to tell us, down to individual personalities and neighborhoods, "who," "where," and "how much" of "what" is needed, and whether what has been applied has been effective. If it doesn't know, it must have assets able to obtain and report the information within six hours of demand.
>
> (General Al Gray, Commandant, US Marine Corps)

When Dr Stephen Cambone, the Undersecretary of Defense for Intelligence, said in January 2004 that he needed universal coverage, 24/7, in all languages all the time, he was the first person at the highest levels of the US Government to formally adopt what General Al Gray recommended in 1988.[21] Sadly, despite various Commissions including the 9–11 Commission, as of this date the US Government is still not serious about open source intelligence.[22]

140

There is a simple reason for any leader to apply OSINT. It offers the best possible return on investment (ROI) for whatever resources – be they man-hours or dollars or Command interest – that can be earmarked for this emerging discipline. OSINT is the best possible way for any mission area specialist or professional to enhance their knowledge and increase their influence.

Open source intelligence tradecraft

This section simply itemizes key elements of tradecraft that are explained in more detail, with diagrams, in the *SOF OSINT Handbook*.

- *The Expeditionary Factors Analysis Model.* This model distinguishes between the four levels of conflict (strategic, operational, tactical, and technical) and the three interactive domains for conflict, military, civil, and geographic. The model also defines degrees of difficulty for the various mission areas as well as how the threat changes depending on the level of analysis.
- *The Revolutionary Analysis Model.* This model, for which a detailed analytic framework is available, distinguishes between political-legal, socio-economic, ideo-cultural, techno-demographic, and natural-geographic conditions, along a spectrum of psycho-social evaluation domains.
- *Analytic tradecraft.* Jack Davis is the *de facto* dean of the US national intelligence community's analytic cadre. The purpose of analysis is to help key individuals make intelligent decisions. The references should be read in their entirety.[23]
- *Social networking and expert networks.* The concept of "six degrees of separation,"[24] and the use of formal citation analysis,[25] will dramatically expand any analyst's effectiveness.

Mission relevance of open source intelligence

This section must of necessity be abbreviated. Twenty-five pages replete with search examples using only Google are available in the free *SOF OSINT Handbook*.

- *Strategic historical and cultural understanding* addresses the critical importance to any mission of going back in time to understand the history of the region, the history of foreign powers as well as the US in the region, and the history of anti-americanism in the region. If there is one thing we cannot afford when going in-country, it is to be delusional about just where we stand as we go about trying to win hearts and minds or as we capture single hostile individuals in a context where we do not realize the odds are stacked against us. *The greatest threat to any mission is not armed forces but rather hostile observers.* Understanding history and culture is fundamental.
- *Operational understanding for campaign planning* connects open sources of information to the theater level of warfare, and helps develop an understanding of open sources in relation to the current situation. Regional power sources, status discrepancies among tribal groups, change agents that are present or emergent, internal security and stability issues (water, food, energy, health, crime, for example) are all essential to understanding the weak links in a current social structure that we can either leverage for operational advantage, or must be aware of to avoid operational failure.
- *Tactical sub-state understanding for unit effectiveness* gets to the heart of the matter for units that will be working in-country. This chapter focuses on tribal orders of battle down to the village and elder level, on key leaders and value-based biographies, on understanding

the local media and how groups and individual communicate with one another, and finally, on content analysis – understanding *their* PSYOP themes.

- *Technical understanding for policy, acquisition, and operations* begins with an introduction to the *NATO Open Source Intelligence Handbook*, which is the technical reference and companion to this volume, and then provides a very brief overview that relates open sources of information to policy, acquisition, and operations in general. One of the great things about OSINT is that it can be used to study domestic US policy debates as well as allied debates. Understanding the players, both friendly and third party, and understanding how the players are perceived locally, is at the heart of any successful CA or PSYOP endeavor. OSINT can also enhance acquisition, and help decide what to leave on the pier and what to take along on the mission.

Mission area applications

Thirty-three pages with additional detail are in the *SOF OSINT Handbook*.

- *Civil affairs* can use OSINT in relation to human intelligence (understanding the demographics, the socio-economic environment, displaced persons, and crime, among other topics); to technical intelligence about the local command and control, communications, computing, and intelligence environment, the infrastructures of transportation, power, and finance; to welfare intelligence (water, food, medical); cultural intelligence about protected or restricted targets, and liaison intelligence.
- *Psychological operations* can use OSINT in relation to strategic, operational, and tactical campaign plans; revisits the mapping of themes in play, especially anti-US themes; the original collection and testing of themes for possible US play, and the litmus test for successful PSYOP: does the message produce actionable intelligence from indigenous volunteers?
- *Target analysis* discusses how OSINT might fulfill team needs in the absence of classified intelligence support, to create a detailed description and vulnerability assessment, evaluate the natural environment and the human environment, and carry out route-planning.
- *Terrain analysis* uses OSINT to establish key factors relevant to special aviation and covert ground movement, in part by leveraging commercial and Russian military combat charts, commercial imagery, and alternatives for terrain reconnaissance including unmanned aerial vehicles and indigenous scouts.
- *Weather analysis* uses OSINT as a means of rapidly getting to the basics of temperature, visibility and timing of sun and moon, wind, and inclement weather.

In addition to the *SOF OSINT Handbook*, see the Quick Links Guide for the Military Analysis, included in the one-page list of links at www.oss.net/BASIC.

Conclusion

Money matters

Funding trade-offs. As our larger world comes to grips with the end of cheap oil, the end of free clean water, the rise of pandemic disease, the twin deficits and rampant militarism of the USA under the Bush–Cheney Administration, the bottom line is clear: we have no slack left, we are at a tipping point, every mistake could be fatal. It is no longer adequate to muddle through, draw down on savings, or "make the best of it." Any manager, any person, that does not invest the time and as needed the money to make informed decisions using OSINT, is derelict in their duty to their employers and themselves. OSINT is now an established discipline required for "due diligence." Perhaps more importantly, information is a substitute for time, money, labor, and space. Practicing OSINT is a way of printing your own money! Practicing OSINT is also a means of restoring power to the people, allowing them to better hold accountable their policymakers and corporate executives all too inclined to manipulate or ignore secrets, or claim special knowledge that does not exist, as a means of justifying actions and expenditures that are not in the public interest.

Contracting mistakes. As a general comment, we have found that the biggest failure among both government and private sector clients is that of almost total ignorance with respect to the diversity and quality of open source services, and most especially of those offered by foreigners in their own localized environments. Even those organizations that have the wit to contract for a variety of open source services generally do not have a single focal point nor do they attempt to monitor best prices and best practices. The worst possible mistake is to attempt to procure OSINT from a major defense corporation that specializes in massive expensive projects to deliver technology that often does not work and "butts in seats," rather than niche expertise or direct access to all information in all languages all the time. It is also a mistake to contract for the delivery of OSINT without making provision for a working requirements process that will save time and money by getting the questions right in the first place, or to contract for the delivery of OSINT in hard-copy, without making provision for its delivery in a form that will allow its easy dissemination throughout the sponsoring organization's network. A more nuanced contracting mistake is to avoid seeing that information, once purchased, has a tangible value that can be used to barter for more information. Copyright issues notwithstanding, a coherent program for sharing information with varied members of the seven tribes in one's own home country, and with counterpart organizations from other countries, will generally produce a ten to one return on investment – ten new useful pieces of information for each single piece of information that is shared broadly.

Metrics for measuring return on investment. There are three valuation metrics that can be applied in evaluating the role of OSINT in any organization's Information Operations (IO).

- *Cost of secrecy.* Transaction costs are higher. Classification reduces competition from domestic and foreign providers of better information. Functional costs come from non-interoperability and operational disconnects. Clients tend not to access all that is offered because of the obstacles imposed by handling secret information (e.g. reading on a trip).
- *Relative value.* Is the OSINT "good enough" now? Does it provide, in context, "good enough" understanding to move forward? For the decision at hand, it is "good enough" to allow the decision to be made? Can the information be shared and thus engage other stake-holders?
- *Return on sharing.* Does this information, shared openly, attract other information that is equally useful? Does this information, shared openly, reach others who have a "need to know" and consequently include them and engage them in an expanded network for mutual benefit?

Commercial strategy. Dr Joseph Markowitz, the only truly competent manager of open source information endeavors within the US Intelligence Community, published a commercial strategy prior to resigning from government service. It has yet to be implemented.[26]

Budget and manning recommendations. Detailed proposed budgets are online[27] for a national Open Source Agency (OSA), a theater Multinational Information Operations Center (MIOC) and network, and a subordinate commercial imagery and geospatial procurement plan. It remains, then, to simply illustrate a standard OSINT "cell" such as could be added to any corporate or government library, with the observation that OSINT should be accomplished in three tiers:

- If it can be done online in less than 15 minutes, the analyst should do it.
- If it will take 15–60 minutes, or require specialized knowledge, the OSINT cell should receive the task (see Figure 10.8).
- If it will take more than 60 minute or require very specialized knowledge or direct access, it should be out-sourced to exactly the right source or service, by the OSINT cell, which should be expert at best prices and best practices for all sources in all languages all the time.

*Specializes in methods for finding and interviewing exactly the right individuals.

Figure 10.8 Standard OSINT cell

The value of sharing

We have, as J.F. Rischard puts it so well in *High Noon: 20 Global Problems, 20 Years to Solve Them*,[28] reached the point of no return. OSINT is relevant to individual security and prosperity; to organizational and national security and prosperity; and to global security and prosperity. He writes about sharing our planet, sharing our humanity, and sharing our rule book. Tom Atlee, founder of the Co-Intelligence Institute and author of *The Tao of Democracy: Using Co-Intelligence to Create a World that Works for All*[29] adds another group to these three groups: sharing our wisdom. Sharing our wisdom. That is what distinguishes OSINT from the secret collection disciplines, and that is what distinguishes the role of OSINT in the world of analysis: it can be shared without restriction. OSINT *is* democracy. OSINT *is* moral capitalism. OSINT *will* make our lives better and offer hope to future generations. *E Veritate Potens.*[30]

References

Visit http://www.oss.net and see especially http://www.oss.net/BASIC. See also the books by Robert Steele:

On Intelligence: Spies and Secrecy in an Open World (Foreword by Senator David Boren, D-KS), first published in 2000.

The New Craft of Intelligence: Personal, Public, & Political – Citizen's Action Handbook for Fighting Terrorism, Genocide, Disease, Toxic Bombs, & Corruption (Foreword by Senator Pat Roberts, R-KS), 2002.

Peacekeeping Intelligence: Emerging Concepts for the Future (contributing editor, Foreword by Dame Pauline Neville Jones), 2004.

Information Operations: All Information, All Languages, All the Time – The New Semantics of War & Peace, Wealth & Democracy (Foreword by Congressman Rob Simmons, R-CT-02), 2006.

The Smart Nation Act: Public Intelligence in the Private Interest (Foreword by Congressman Rob Simmons (R-CT-02), sponsor of The Smart Nation Act), 2006.

Acronyms

Acronyms are included in the Glossary to this *Handbook*.

Notes

1 The executive summary is a precise replication from the *NATO Open Source Intelligence Handbook* (November 2001), which remains the standard in the field. Drafted by the author, with important refinements from LCdr Andrew Chester, RN Canada, and under the leadership of Capt. David Swain, RN, United Kingdom, this volume was approved by General William Kernan, USA, then Supreme Allied Commander Atlantic. The NATO documents and other essential references on OSINT, including the original OSINT Executive Overview, are easily accessible by going to http://www.oss.net/BASIC. This chapter is of necessity a very summative rendition of the 20,000 pages of accumulated knowledge in the Archives at http://www.oss.net, most of which can be accessed in a structured manner via the above URL.

2 The most important new concepts to receive traction since the release of the NATO documents are those of the Seven Tribes, Collective Intelligence, and the World Brain. The seven tribes, each of which has unique access and perspectives, are those of government, military, law enforcement, business, academic, ground truth (media and non-governmental organizations), and civil (citizens, labor unions, and religions). Collective Intelligence and the World Brain are discussed in Note 3.

3 The Swedish concept was advanced at the third Peacekeeping Intelligence Conference sponsored by the Folke Bernadotte Academy and Swedish National Defence College under the direct leadership of the Supreme Commander, 4–6 December 2004. The Co-Intelligence Institute was founded by Tom Atlee, author of *The Tao of Democracy: Using Co-Intelligence to create a world that works for all* (The Writer's Collective, 2003). Howard Rheingold, former editor of *The Whole Earth Review*, is the author of *Smart Mobs: The Next Social Revolution* (Perseus, 2002) as well as seminal books on *Tools for Thinking, Virtual Reality*, and *Virtual Communities*. James Surowiecki is the author of *The Wisdom of the Crowds: Why the Many Are Smarter than the Few and How Collective Wisdom Shapes Business, Economies, Societies, and Nations* (Doubleday, 2004). Key works on the emerging World Brain include those of H.G. Wells, *World Brain* (Admantime, 1994 from 1938); Pierre Levy, *Collective Intelligence: Mankind's Emerging World in Cyberspace* (Plenum Trade, 1997); Willis Harman, *Global Mind Change: The Promise of the 21st Century* (Noetic Sciences, 1998); and Howard Bloom, *Global Brain: The Evolution of Mass Mind From the Big Bang to the 21st Century* (John Wiley, 2000).

4 This term was developed by Dr Stevan Dedijer, a Swede who was born and died in Croatia (former Yugoslavia), widely recognized as the father of modern business intelligence. He led fifteen Swedes to the first Open Source Intelligence Conference in 1992, where he made a passionate plea for government attention to this vital independent discipline.

5 Dr Joseph Markowitz, the first and only Director of the Community Open Source Program Office (COSPO) before it was destroyed by the Community Management Staff (CMS), devised this important distinction between OSINT such as can be done by private sector practitioners, and OSINT as validated by government analysts with full access to classified sources and methods.

6 In "The Strategic Use of Open-Source Information," *Studies in Intelligence* 45/3 (2001), pages 67–71.

Dr Gannon is, with Dr Markowitz and Dr Gordon Oehler, one of a tiny handful of all-source managers who understand the full range of OSINT. However, those who remain within CIA, well-intentioned as they may be, are so mired in legacy mind-sets, legalities, security encumbrances, and general malaise as to be pathologically ineffective at OSINT, even when trying to support only the small cadre of analysts within the CIA. A careful reading of all public references to OSINT by CIA managers shows a delusional focus on information technologies that have yet to be put on the analysts' desktops, while defining "sharing" as being limited to those with access to Top Secret "system-high" clearances and terminals.

7 Detective Steve Edwards of Scotland Yard, honored by the Queen for his accomplishments in applying OSINT to law enforcement, says this: "I now consider POLINT [Police Intelligence] to be a sub-category of OSINT as the collection and sourcing are largely the same. Anything else needed is largely supplied using other disciplines. OSINT is also the only real way for most interested parties to collect the information without recourse to methods that could be seen as over-intrusive; bearing in mind who the targets might be." Professor Hugo Smith, in his seminal article on "Intelligence and UN Peacekeeping" in *Survival* 26/3 (Autumn 1994), says: "The concept of 'UN intelligence' promises to turn traditional principles of intelligence on their heads. Intelligence will have to be based on information that is collected primarily by overt means, that is, by methods that do not threaten the target state or group and do not compromise the integrity or impartiality of the UN." Reprinted in Ben de Jong et al., *Peacekeeping Intelligence: Emerging Concepts for the Future* (OSS, 2003).

8 Dr Robert Garigue, formerly a top practitioner of Information Warfare as a Canadian naval officer, has articulated the new semantics of war and peace, wealth and democracy, in his Technical Preface to the author's book on *Information Operations: All Information, All Languages, All the Time* (OSS, 2006). His views are well in advance of existing doctrine.

9 The author is indebted to Admiral Bill Studeman, USN (Ret.), former Deputy Director of Central Intelligence (DDCI), former Director of the National Security Agency (NSA), and former Director of Naval Intelligence (DNI), who in his post-retirement years has become a master of IO and all that this implies. In the age of information, IO is the manifestation of "total war" and the need – not yet realized – to harness every source of national power including an educated citizenry and informed politicians to further national advantage.

10 (United Nations, 2004), The endeavor benefited from the participation of the Honorable LtGen Dr Brent Scowcroft, USAF (Ret.), former national security advisor to President George Bush. Terrorism is either fifth on this list or seventh if the first is counted as three. The report, 262 pages in length, can be seen at http://www.un.org/secureworld/report2.pdf.

11 While not the focus of this chapter, it merits comment that according to the Commission on the National Imagery and Mapping Agency, in a report published in December 1999, most of the intelligence money is spent on esoteric collection systems, and almost none at all is spent on actually making sense out of the collected information.

12 For Viet-Nam, the single best reference on cooking the books and spinning the truth is George Allen's *None So Blind: A Personal Account of the Intelligence Failure in Vietnam* (Ivan R. Dee, 2001). On the topic of Peak Oil, 9–11, and Iraq, there are numerous books, of which three stand out: James Bamford, *A Pretext for War: 9/11, Iraq and the Abuse of America's Intelligence Agencies* (Doubleday, 2004); James Risen, *State of War: The Secret History of the CIA and the Bush Administration* (Free Press, 2006); and Michael C. Ruppert, *Crossing the Rubicon: The Decline of American Empire at the End of the Age of Oil* (New Society, 2004). Many other books address various aspects of how 9/11 represented both a break-down of secret intelligence and a celebration of ideological fantasy unchecked by responsible oversight.

13 During the eighteen years of my campaign to secure added funding for and emphasis on OSINT, open source information has been derisively referred to as "Open Sores" by nominally intelligent but foolishly unprofessional managers and some analysts at the Central Intelligence Agency (CIA). Even the so-called open source professionals in the Foreign Broadcast Information Service (FBIS) have refused to be serious about anything other than mainstream broadcast media until allies of OSINT finally got an Open Source Agency into the 9/11 Commission Report (page 413). The mind-sets within CIA and its runt orphan FBIS (now nominally a DNI-level Open Source Center) have not yet matured on this topic.

14 Daniel Ellsberg, *Secrets: A Memoir of Vietnam and the Pentagon Papers* (Viking, 2002). The three pages on the pathological effects of falling prey to the cult of secrecy, on pages 237–239, should be forced rote memorization for all who receive clearances.

15 *PowerShift* (Bantam, 1990). Stewart (Currency, 2001). Carter (Butterworth Heineman, 1999).
16 The next four sections are superficial in relation to the *NATO Open Source Intelligence Handbook*. There is no substitute for downloading and studying that reference as well as the *NATO Open Source Intelligence Reader* and the NATO guide to *Intelligence Exploitation of the Internet*. These and other key references are freely available at http://www.oss.net/BASIC.
17 This is the only standard that may not be readily apparent when this chapter is published. Invited by Doug Englebart, inventor of the mouse and hypertext, this standard enables linkage of related content to take place at the paragraph level, which also allows copyright compliance to be executed at the paragraph level, for pennies instead of dollars.
18 Diane Webb, under the leadership of Dr Gordon Oehler, developed *CATALYST: A Concept for an Integrated Computing Environment for Analysis* (CIA/DI SW 89–10052, October 1989). To not have this now, close to eighteen years after precise requirements definition, tells us clearly of the sustained pathos of US Intelligence Community "leadership." Follow link at www.oss.net/HISTORY.
19 The actual quote is "given enough eyeballs, all bugs are shallow." This is generally attributed to Eric Raymond, is known as the Linus Law, and is associated with the Free/Open Source Software (F/OSS) movement.
20 See the analytic references at http://www.oss.net/BASIC.
21 General Al Gray, "Global Intelligence Challenges of the 1990's," *American Intelligence Journal* (Winter 1988–1989). At www.oss.net, Google for title.
22 The appointment of an Assistant Deputy Director of National Intelligence for Open Source (ADDNI/OS) on 5 December 2006 was a step in the right direction, but this individual has no program authority, no money, and no staff. Meanwhile, the Open Source Center at the Central Intelligence Agency, a cosmetic re-definition of the Foreign Broadcast Information Service (FBIS), has absolutely no likelihood of being relevant to anyone outside CIA in the next ten years. Fortunately, the Open Source Information System (OSIS) is a national-level system belonging to the Senate-confirmed Chief Information Officer for the Director of National Intelligence, an Air Force Major General who understands that the key to open source exploitation is sharing rather than secrecy, standards rather than security. Applied OSINT will flourish outside the secret intelligence world – to the extent that OSINT is ably developed by the US Intelligence Community, it will be through OSIS embracing the 90 nations forming the Coalition, rather than through the OSC/FBIS. We continue to lack a national Open Source Center under the auspices of the Department of State, a sister agency to the Broadcasting Board of Governors. In as much as 90% of the open source information we wish to gain access to is controlled by individuals who have no wish to be associated with the US Intelligence Community, US OSINT will not be effective until a national agency is established under diplomatic auspices – consequently, US IO will also be pedestrian absent that agency.
23 The compendium, the "New Rules" chapter from *The New Craft of Intelligence*, and a lecture on "Analysis: Making Magic" are all accessible via www.oss.net/BASIC.
24 Stanley Milgram, "The Small World Problem," *Psychology Today*, 1967. Google "small world problem."
25 Citation analysis is generally done for English-language information using the *Social Science Citation Index* and the *Science Citation Index*. Other countries, such as China, are now creating their citation analysis directories. Any analyst who does not know who the top 100 people in the world are for their respective area of interest should go to their library and ask them to do a DIALOG RANK Command for their topic. It will cost about $500. The superior analyst will then obtain biographies for each of those individuals, engage with all of them, and through them, identify the top 100 individuals that are not published (e.g. government and non-government officials).
26 See the link under Policy and Investment at www.oss.net/BASIC.
27 Ibid.
28 (Basic, 2002). The author is Vice President for Europe of the World Bank.
29 (The Writer's Collective, 2003). Observation made in a personal communication (electronic mail) of 18 March 2006. The Co-Intelligence Institute merits more attention and support.
30 This is the motto for OSS.Net, Inc., and before that for the Marine Corps Intelligence Command which the author helped create. It means "from truth, power" or literally, "one is made powerful by the truth." Thus does OSINT contribute to the power of every individual regardless of their race, nationality, religion, or station in life.

11

Adapting intelligence to changing issues

Paul R. Pillar

The shock of the new, and the not so new

The need to adjust US intelligence to address new, or newly salient, issues is one of the most commonly sounded themes in public commentary about intelligence in the United States. "The CIA" – or the entire US Intelligence Community – "needs to move away from a Cold War way of doing business!" has been voiced so often in the decade and a half since the end of the Cold War that it long ago became a cliché. The terrorist attack of September 11, 2001, which was one of the greatest attitude-changing events in American history, boosted the frequency and volume of this kind of call.

One reason for the strength and ubiquity of this theme since 9/11 is psychological. As Martha Crenshaw – who has been an expert student of terrorism as long as any American scholar – observes, the threat that manifested itself in the 9/11 attack is not nearly as new as it usually is made out to be.[1] Terrorism itself is very old, the current religious variety of terrorism that troubles us the most shares many characteristics with earlier varieties, and even the current variety was becoming all too apparent several years before 9/11. Because that one attack in 2001 was so traumatic, however, Americans have had difficulty coming to terms with the idea that their government could have allowed such a tragedy to come from a known and long-standing threat. It is less disturbing to believe that the threat was new and that an intelligence service stuck in old ways did not see it, implying that bringing that service up to date would prevent a recurrence.

Another reason is more political. Members of Congress and commissions of inquiry are in the business of identifying problems and making changes. Fish have to swim, birds have to fly, and politicians and commissions have to recommend legislative changes. The idea of new threats is one of the more persuasive bases for making a case for change. And so "adjusting to new issues" or something similar is a useful label to append to the rationale for changes to the Intelligence Community, regardless of the actual impetus for change.

Of course issues involving overseas events and threats really do change in important ways, and intelligence needs to change with them. But the use of this theme as a convenient label to pin onto changes motivated more by other considerations has left disparities between the concept of changing issues and what any particular change to intelligence can be expected to accomplish. A prime example is the most recent reorganization of the US Intelligence Community, enacted in December 2004 and implemented in the following year as a slightly modified version of a plan that the 9/11 Commission conceived and pushed. The centerpiece of that plan is separation of the jobs of director of the CIA and head of the Community, with the creation of a new layer of management in the form of the Office of the Director of National Intelligence. How exactly is this organizational scheme, compared with what it replaced, any less "Cold War" and any more suitable for today's issues than for the issues of 20, 30, or 50 years ago? How does the wiring diagram for the Intelligence Community relate to the nature of the issues it is charged with covering? Many other appeals to "move beyond the Cold War" similarly fail to explain what this idea means in terms of operational or organizational realities.

The distortions caused by manipulative use of the "new issues" theme obscure not only what new arrangements can be expected to accomplish in the future but also what old ones have done in the past. Judging by much of the public commentary about US intelligence, there is broad belief that the Intelligence Community in previous decades was much more narrowly focused on the USSR and on true Cold War issues than it ever really was. One indicator is the work of CIA's Directorate of Intelligence, which is the largest analytic component in the Community (and a better measure of relative attention to different issues than the agency's operational arm, which may recruit assets in one region to collect information about a country outside the region). The Cold War was still going strong when, for example, the directorate was also doing significant work in the 1970s on the "north–south" issues of trade, investment, and economics, not to mention energy. A reorganization of the directorate in 1981 moved from a functional arrangement to a regional one, which facilitated integrated political, economic, and military analysis on each of the world's regions, and in which the office covering the USSR was just one of several such components. As for terrorism, the big change came in 1986 with the creation of the DCI Counterterrorist Center, a bureaucratic revolution that put analysts to work alongside operators and other counterterrorist specialists. Led by this center, most of the counterterrorist techniques involving intelligence agencies (such as supporting the US Government's renditions of suspected terrorists) that have come to be familiar in recent years were being used long before 9/11. The common perception (again, psychologically and politically driven) that a "war on terrorism" only began in September 2001 has missed this.

To a large degree, the American public (abetted by some of the politicians and commissions looking for public support) has projected its own past inattention on to the Intelligence Community. Because most of the public was paying little attention to jihadist terrorism before 9/11, many believe the Intelligence Community was paying little attention as well. To some extent the same is true of attention to certain other issues such as the proliferation of nuclear weapons. The press, whose own attention tends to be heavily concentrated on hot topics of the moment and which suffers no penalty for lack of coverage of emerging long-term issues, has been part of this process. Pulitzer prizes, unlike Nobel prizes, reflect what seems important this year rather than what turns out to be important a decade or more later.

All of the foregoing is to say that – while there are important points and principles to elucidate, as will be done below, about keeping an intelligence service tuned to the challenges of an ever-changing world – this topic suffers from a lot of noise. Filtering out the noise is the first step to understanding the subject.

Mechanisms for prioritization

The US Government has a long history, filled with an alphabet soup of documents and directives, of different formal mechanisms for determining which topics warrant the Intelligence Community's attention. The procedures for prioritizing intelligence topics seem to have changed at least as often as the substantive issues that the procedures have been designed to track. To some extent this history reflects the political urges mentioned above and the desire to be seen as more responsive than the next person (or than the previous office-holder) to the national security challenges of the day. Changing the mechanisms for setting intelligence priorities has been part of larger changes to the apparatus for formulating foreign policy, including the structure of committees under the National Security Council. Each new administration feels a need to do things differently, or at least to be seen doing things differently, from the way its predecessor conducted business.

Underneath the political oscillations, however, has been a genuinely felt need to systematize decisions on where the Intelligence Community should apply its resources. That need in turn reflects the fact that those resources are limited. There always are important topics on which the community could usefully devote more of its money and manpower, despite possibly diminishing returns, if the supply of money and manpower were unlimited, which it is not. Responding to emerging issues and new needs means not only increasing effort on some topics but also necessarily reducing it on others.

Efforts to formalize an intelligence requirements process date from the earliest days of the CIA under the Truman administration. Some of the first few National Security Council directives charged the new Director of Central Intelligence (DCI) with outlining objectives and requirements for national intelligence. During the Eisenhower, Kennedy, and Johnson administrations, intelligence priorities were articulated in documents called Priority National Intelligence Objectives, but the White House often supplemented or overrode these with *ad hoc* directives. President Kennedy and his assistant for national security affairs, McGeorge Bundy, made liberal use of what were called National Security Action Memoranda for that purpose.

Dissatisfaction with the ineffectiveness of the prioritization system was voiced in a task force report during the Johnson administration and again in 1971 in the Nixon administration, in a report written by James Schlesinger (a future DCI, but then in the Office of Management and Budget). Schlesinger's study noted that producers of intelligence were setting priorities more than the consumers were, and that formal requirements lists the consumers submitted were accomplishing little. In response, President Nixon directed then-DCI Richard Helms to review the requirements process. This review led to creation of the Intelligence Community Staff (whose current incarnation constitutes part of the current Office of the Director of National Intelligence).

Helms's successor as DCI, William Colby, expressed his own frustration with the requirements process and tried to streamline it. As he later explained, "My object was to replace the enormous paper exercise called the 'requirements' process – which pretended to tell the community precisely what it should be reporting on – with a simple set of general questions about the key problems we should concentrate on."[2] Colby's questions were known as KIQs, or Key Intelligence Questions. Under President Carter's DCI, Stansfield Turner, the KIQs transformed into NITs (National Intelligence Topics). The overhaul of the national security apparatus at the start of the Carter administration also established a Policy Review Committee of the NSC, one of whose functions was to define and prioritize substantive intelligence requirements, although the DCI retained responsibility for translating these objectives into specific objectives and targets. In 1981 President Reagan signed Executive Order 12333, which addressed a wide range of intelligence policies (including a prohibition on assassination). This order stated that the DCI was responsible for establishing criteria for determining priorities for national intelligence, as well as for establishing mechanisms for translating objectives approved by the NSC into specific guidance to the Intelligence Community.

The advent of the Clinton administration brought yet another reconstruction of the national security apparatus, as well as a renewed effort to involve senior officials in consumer agencies more directly in the process of setting intelligence priorities. The most important step was the issuance in 1995 of Presidential Decision Directive 35, which set priorities for specific, named intelligence topics by assigning them to different "tiers." This directive, the contents of which are still classified, was welcomed by intelligence officers as the meatiest, most authoritative statement by senior policymakers of where the Intelligence Community should direct its attention, and of how certain issues were to be deemed more important than other issues. To get senior policymakers to agree on such a specific, substantive list − rather than leaving any such task to the DCI while retaining freedom to complicate the Intelligence Community's life by throwing *ad hoc* demands at it − was a significant achievement, which was partly why no comparable document had been produced any earlier. But for the same reasons, it was difficult to produce any successor document. The intent at the time was for PDD-35 to be a living directive, subject to periodic review and amendment by senior policymakers. But having already invested considerable high-level effort to produce this one PDD, the realities of limited time and attention of senior officials dictated otherwise, and no successor was produced. PDD-35 continued to be invoked as a reference point for decisions on deploying intelligence resources, but each passing year increased the unease of using a document that everyone knew was gradually becoming outdated.

Legislation in 1997 created new executive positions in the Intelligence Community that were important for the requirements process: Assistant Directors of Central Intelligence for Analysis and Production (ADCI/AP) and for Collection (ADCI/C). Subsequent DCI directives made it clear that the ADCI/AP would have primary responsibility for developing requirements and prioritizing those requirements to guide the allocation of resources and the selection of topics for intelligence production. With the assistance of a National Intelligence Production Board, he also would oversee the work of the Intelligence Community with an eye to ensuring that work actually reflected the requirements.

In an unclassified strategic plan for 2000–2001, the ADCI/AP stated that part of the challenge regarding intelligence priorities was that those priorities "shift frequently, complicating planning for both collection and analysis." Changes in the national security environment combined with a smaller analytic work force "have intensified the competition for analytic resources to meet both long-term priorities and near-term requirements." Responding to crises or other immediate needs often diverts analysts from their primary duties and areas of expertise. Thus "the analytic community must choose and limit which intelligence issues and targets receive priority coverage."[3] The plan listed as the leading characteristics of an effective requirements system that it provide an "agile, accessible, and automated framework" and a "rational, coherent structure to support analysis, collection, and systems acquisition," and that it balance resources "to deal with priority targets and global coverage requirements."[4]

The system that a task force under the ADCI/AP devised became known as the National Intelligence Priorities Framework (NIPF). It is the most comprehensive of any of the mechanisms for prioritizing intelligence work that have been tried. It involves a matrix that plots states (and nonstate groups) along one dimension against functional issues on the other dimension. Priorities are assigned to selected cells in the matrix bearing in mind the overall importance of the issue and the role that each state or group may play in it. The system is automated and easily accessed by intelligence officers, and the priorities are revised at regular intervals based on input both from intelligence officers and from representatives of policy departments. The NIPF is the prioritization system in effect today. Director of National Intelligence John Negroponte, a couple of months after taking office in 2005, affirmed his commitment to the system as the central basis for planning the use of resources across the Intelligence Community.

The NIPF probably is at least as well conceived and workable as any of the past formal mechanisms for keeping intelligence in tune with changing issues. But the half-century-long history of stumbling around for a better system, as well as the periodic expressions of dissatisfaction with whatever system was in effect at the moment, raises more fundamental questions about how much can be expected from any formal procedure. It remains to be seen how much impact the NIPF will have on decisions about reallocating resources. And the history of stumbling suggests that no system is perfect or even close to perfect, however carefully any particular mechanism has been conceived.

 Moreover, in the real world of managers making decisions about personnel and programs, any formal system tends to take second place to other practical exigencies and constraints. There are some instances in which a number on a priority chart can be useful ammunition for a manager seeking increased resources for a particular initiative. But the formal mechanisms play little part in the professional life of most intelligence officers. Some officers see the time required to support such mechanisms, by answering questionnaires or putting numbers into a matrix, as a distraction from their main job of performing collection or analysis on topics they already are convinced are important. Even most managers – those senior enough to have a significant say in allocating resources – probably do not bring up on their screens the current NIPF numbers as their first step in making programmatic decisions. Such a decision is as likely to be influenced by something the manager hears on the news as he is driving in to work that causes him to think "that's a potential crisis we need to look into more" or "the consumers are going to be asking more questions about that topic over the next few months."

Does a failure to conform to the dictates of a formal prioritization system indicate the kind of bureaucratic inertia that critics of bureaucracies love to criticize? To some extent, perhaps. And in the real world of Intelligence Community management such mundane matters as personnel slots, budgetary red tape, and even available office space often lay a heavy hand on decisions about expanding or contracting programs. There are more admirable reasons, however, for such decisions not to follow precisely the output of any formal system. Managers are paid to exercise leadership and good judgment, and to apply their own expertise and that of their subordinates to their decisions. So if a decision to move resources from issue X to issue Y reflects the sort of morning commute ruminations mentioned above, as well as subsequent discussions with subordinate managers about where they see those issues leading, isn't that a good thing, even if the decision cannot be matched with a number on a chart?

Moreover, maybe sound decisions about adapting intelligence to changing issues reflect so many variables and dimensions that they could not possibly be incorporated into any formal scheme, at least not without making the scheme so intractably complex as to be useless. It is to those variables and dimensions that we turn next.

Principles for allocating resources

Much of what the Intelligence Community does will not and should not change regardless of the issues it addresses. This includes the housekeeping and overhead, from paper clips to parking lots, which are a necessary part of any government bureaucracy, and to some extent of any large organization. It also includes many other things that are peculiar to, and an intrinsic part of, an intelligence service. A security structure, for example, which issues clearances to personnel, controls classified information, and performs internal counterintelligence investigations, is a necessary part of the intelligence business. Most of the recruitment, training, and management of officers who perform the core functions of collection and analysis of intelligence applies regardless of the topics on which those officers are working. Most of the same tradecraft skills are needed whether collecting intelligence on Russia or Rwanda. Even those skills that vary with the topic usually require a common infrastructure to develop and sustain them. Fluency in a foreign language, for example, obviously is one such skill; although different languages are needed to work on different issues, an agency is apt to have a common, fixed training apparatus for teaching all foreign languages. This unchanging core of functions means that even major shifts in the issues to be followed may imply relatively minor shifts in the structure of an intelligence service's program. As with the overall US Government budget, in which "entitlements," interest on debt, and other fixed obligations greatly limit what is subject to discretion, senior managers of the Intelligence Community have much less flexibility than the overall size of their budgets might suggest.

Insofar as the changing substance of issues does call for changes in intelligence programs and priorities, two basic criteria should govern which issues warrant attention. One is what the policymakers of the day say are their greatest interests and concerns. The other is whatever intelligence officers believe might affect important national interests, whether or not any current policymaker is asking about the topic.

The first category of issues is generally the easier to deal with — at least for intelligence officers, who can simply listen to the policymaker to determine what's important and what's not. In one sense this is a form of buck-passing, but in another sense it is an appropriate reflection of how a representative democracy like the United States works. What constitutes the national interest can be a matter of dispute and debate, and the winners of elections, at least for their terms of office, get to define it. Intelligence officers, who are not elected, need to follow the politicians' lead. (Following their lead in treating an entire subject as important is different from putting intelligence in the service of a specific policy or line of argument in favor of that policy, which would constitute politicization of intelligence.)

A legitimate reason for change and adaptation in US intelligence, therefore, is not just change in the world beyond America's borders but also political change within the United States. The Intelligence Community has in the past geared up to cover new and, for it, nontraditional issues for this reason. When Jimmy Carter entered office in 1977, for example, his administration's strong interest in human rights resulted in that becoming an expanded analytic account at the CIA.

Policymaker interests can be readily captured by a prioritization mechanism such as the Clinton administration's PDD-35. Most of those interests, however, are easily discernible anyway in the speeches and statements of administration leaders. Intelligence officers, eager to be relevant, usually learn much about administration priorities just from listening to those statements and often redirect their efforts accordingly, in addition to learning from the questions and tasks they receive directly from policymakers. The learning process sometimes begins even before a new president is elected. Some Intelligence Community components have tried in

153

election years to get a head start in gearing up for new issues by quietly seeking out foreign policy advisers to each of the candidates, to hear what subjects the Community is most likely to be asked about in the first months of a new administration.

The second category of issues – those that intelligence officers themselves think require attention – is at least as important as the first. Directing attention to subjects that policy currently neglects but that in the future may threaten the nation's interests is in some respects the most important intelligence function of all. The judgments of the Intelligence Community should guide the work and priorities of policy just as policy interests should guide the work and priorities of the Community.

Sometimes this process of cross-validation goes in both directions at once, with neither side having a monopoly on initiative. When the Intelligence Community was addressing in the mid-1990s – in the form of a National Intelligence Estimate it initiated – what it regarded as an increasing foreign terrorist threat to the US homeland, it focused partly on transportation infrastructure as an inviting target. The aviation security office in the Federal Aviation Administration requested that the Estimate pay special attention to its specific interest, which was civil aviation. The judgments in the Estimate, which highlighted aviation as particularly high-risk target, thus reflected both the Intelligence Community's sense of a growing threat and the FAA's strong interest in its mission of aviation security. It was intelligence–policy collaboration and good intelligence that – due mainly to economically motivated resistance by the aviation industry – unfortunately did not result in the hoped-for beefed-up security measures.

There is no set process for the Intelligence Community to make itself aware of issues that are not seizing attention now but may go bump in the night later, let alone to generate enough attention within the Community to make significant transfers of resources from other issues. There is, of course, a Catch-22 inherent in this challenge: if the Community is not already devoting considerable collection and analytic talent to a topic, how can it be expected to be expert enough to understand the dangers the issue poses to national interests? A systematic procedure like the NIPF can help, by forcing regular rethinking of topics that are not receiving priority treatment. Brainstorming with outside sources of expertise is also very useful. Ultimately the process depends on intelligence officers being sensitive to happenings on the fringes of their areas of responsibility that provide inklings of how those responsibilities might need to be expanded or realigned.

Beyond these basic categories, other dimensions complicate the problem of choosing issues worthy of intelligence attention. One dimension is time frame: short-term concerns versus long-term ones. This is partially related to the distinction between policymaker-driven issues and those issues the Intelligence Community itself has determined are worth watching. Policymakers' time frames tend to be short and often reflect the election cycle. Intelligence officers who are part of the permanent bureaucracy may worry just as much about very long-term problems as about short-term ones. How is one to decide which set of problems gets highest priority?

The short-term versus long-term distinction is hardly unique to intelligence issues, of course. Individual investors, for example, face similar choices in where to put their money. Investment advisory services may recommend some stocks as offering the best prospects for the next several months and different ones as better bets for performing well over the next several years. The investor makes choices based on his individual needs and circumstances, such as whether he has to finance a child's college education now or several years from now. The Intelligence Community, however, has no comparable benchmark for making similar choices. It needs to serve the policymakers of the moment, but it also needs to be prepared to serve the next batch of policymakers, as well as highlighting threats and problems that may in the future force attention from whoever is in office.

Investing too much in either short-term or long-term issues involves hazards. On one hand, major investment in something like training people in a difficult language to work on a current problem focusing on a particular country or region may turn out to be wasted effort as the problem is resolved or fades in importance. The Intelligence Community could find itself in the situation of the US Army as the Vietnam War wound down in the 1970s, when it had an excess of Vietnamese linguists who had been trained at considerable expense but had little opportunity to employ their language skills. On the other hand, investments in training or collection systems (either human or technical) aimed at an emerging or anticipated future problem may be just as wasteful if the problem simply does not materialize to the degree anticipated or is eclipsed by other concerns.

The short-term/long-term distinction is in turn related to another trade-off: between depth and quality of coverage of any one issue and the ability to change quickly and nimbly to coverage of different issues. Some of the attributes of an intelligence service that make for high-quality coverage of a particular country – such as a carefully cultivated network of human agents, a corps of analysts with deep expertise in the country, and fluency in the relevant language – are the least fungible when it comes to shifting coverage to other countries or issues.

To take CIA's Directorate of Intelligence again as an example, there has long been concern about the relative emphasis the directorate gives to generalists versus specialists. A common criticism has been that the former have been unduly rewarded in comparison with the latter. Recent years have seen increased opportunities for analysts to be promoted to higher grades while retaining their substantive specialties and not moving into management. The nimble generalist, however, probably still has better prospects for rising to the top than an analyst who makes his or her reputation as the Intelligence Community's foremost expert on, say, the Chinese economy. But what the directorate lacks in depth of expertise on selected issues is offset by its agility in very quickly responding to crises and bolts out of the blue by forming task forces and shifting resources to meet policymakers' current intelligence needs. In this respect, talented generalists have proven very useful.

A further criterion is how much intelligence can contribute in comparison with other sources of information and insight available to the policymaker. This distinction sometimes gets lost in using the formal mechanisms to establish priorities; the natural tendency is to assign numbers or tiers according to the overall importance of a topic rather than the particular niche that intelligence can best fill in addressing it. The Arab–Israeli conflict and Middle East peace process exemplify issues that are very important to US foreign and security policy but on which the intelligence contribution is relatively modest. The most important developments in that conflict are covered well in the press, and many of the developments that are not covered become known to policymakers through their own direct interactions with the protagonists. On an issue in which policymakers are heavily engaged and knowledgeable, the contribution of intelligence tends to be limited to more specific technical matters such as the monitoring of troop movements. By the same token, intelligence's contribution is broader on issues that have not yet seized the policymaker's attention. This points to the importance of staying ahead of, not just abreast of, future or developing issues. That in turn underscores the importance of the Intelligence Community – on its own initiative, not waiting to be pressured or told to do so – adapting itself to be able to cover those issues.

A final consideration in allocating resources is that what matters is not just the normative ranking of different topics but also the distribution of effort down through the entire ranking. What issue should be considered #1 in priority and what should be considered #2 often is widely discussed; much less discussed is how much intelligence effort issue #2 should nonetheless still receive. And yet this is where some of the more difficult management decisions about allocating resources arise. The decisions get even more difficult and more painful when looking at issues 3, 4, 5 and lower.

There tends to be a bias toward concentrating resources even more heavily toward the highest priority issues than would be the case in a rationally managed intelligence service that is well designed to respond to both current and emerging concerns. It always is easy to argue that issue X, if it is widely agreed to be of utmost importance, ought to receive more money and people and attention. It is more difficult to argue in favor of resources for issue Y when resources are limited and most people agree that X is more important.

This bias, by stripping coverage of many currently lower-ranking issues to bare bones, increases the difficulty in adaptation when events cause one of those issues suddenly to become a focus of attention. The procedural adroitness of an agency such as CIA in setting up task forces and the like can meet most of the policymaker's current intelligence needs but is not a substitute for standing expertise. Contractual arrangements for tapping the expertise of outside experts are used and can help, but only to a point.

Influence of outside pressure

The pressures exerted by consumers of intelligence in the executive and legislative branches, which invariably emphasize the issues of highest current concern, exacerbate the tension between focus on the most salient issues and coverage of the less salient ones. Former DCI George Tenet, during his last couple of years in office, frequently reminded these audiences that as long as he was expected to devote heavy attention to Iraq, terrorism, and weapons proliferation, he could not be expected to cover everything else particularly well. And yet, when a coup occurs in Chad, consumers expect to be able to pick up the phone and immediately talk to an analyst who can say something smart about it.

Congress, the public, and the Intelligence Community's executive branch masters not only tend to focus disproportionately on a few front-page issues; they also are prone to focus on the last crisis rather than future potential ones. This is a natural and unavoidable consequence of how politics and public opinion work in a representative democracy. It may inhibit adaptation to changing issues, however, by encouraging a "preparing to fight the last war" syndrome.

Even the response after 9/11 to coverage of terrorism – which almost everyone agrees should be a continued high-priority intelligence target – exhibited some of this syndrome. A huge and sudden transfer of resources to counterterrorism took place not because the nature or degree of the terrorist threat had suddenly changed – the threat of Islamist terrorism in particular had been developing for several years, and the Intelligence Community had been closely following it for years – but because a single event enormously altered the mood of the American public, which expected to see big changes in response. Community management had to respond the way they did, even though major questions can be raised about the effectiveness of some of the resource transfers that occurred. A surge in the number of analysts assigned to counterterrorist components meant analysts were almost stumbling over each other in turning out large numbers of papers, only a tiny proportion of which could be expected to be of real use in heading off the next major attack. Meanwhile, the stripping of some of these resources from other accounts with a country or regional focus may have decreased the chance of intelligence providing early word of emerging threats to US interests, including threats that might eventually materialize in terrorist attacks.

Congress in particular is prone to exerting a related kind of unhelpful pressure, which is to expect quantifiable measures – how many people, how many dollars – of the attention devoted to specific issues. The trouble is that the most effective way to cover a topic may not be to create or enlarge components that are dedicated to that topic and appear as such as a line item in a budget. To take another example from counterterrorism, the very heavy interest in the specter of chemical, biological, radiological, or nuclear (CBRN) terrorism has meant pressure to enlarge intelligence components devoted to that specific topic. But the best way to head off a CBRN terrorist attack is apt to be to develop the kind of human sources who could give warning of any kind of terrorist attack, CBRN or non-CBRN. A better use for resources – even accepting the avoidance of CBRN terrorism as a paramount objective – may thus be these recruitment efforts, as well as the general tracking of CBRN materials that the Intelligence Community does as part of its overall counterproliferation efforts.

All of these distortions in allocation of intelligence resources are in addition to those caused by the particular initiatives and preoccupations of whoever are the policymakers of the day. Intelligence must serve those needs, but there always are trade-offs. The biggest perturbation to the US Intelligence Community in recent years has been the war in Iraq. Meeting the intelligence requirements of that initiative has entailed an enormous drain on resources, at a time when many components were still reeling from having surrendered personnel to the post-9/11 expansion of counterterrorism – and Iraq-related requirements have been a drain on counterterrorism itself. One result is diminished surge capacity and a lessened ability to respond to any other crises or emerging issues. *9/11 = draining resources*

Reorganization as adaptation

Although, as noted earlier, the urge to reorganize is largely background noise rather an effective adaptation to changed circumstances, there are some respects in which reorganization – more at the level of offices than of entire agencies – can help to position an intelligence service to deal with new threats, concerns, or interests. Some such reorganizations are simply prudent measures to deal with management problems such as span of control. For example, the heavy demands related to the Iraq war led CIA to create a new Office of Iraq Analysis separate from the office that performs analysis on the rest of the Middle East. But an agency's organizational structure also can reflect – and promote – new and different ways of looking at an issue.

An example was CIA's handling of German matters in the late 1980s. Analysis of East Germany, along with the rest of Eastern Europe, had long been handled separately from coverage of West Germany. An Eastern Europe division had been part of the office that followed the USSR and later, still including the East German account, was moved to the Office of European Analysis. Then – well before the fall of the Berlin Wall, and before any negotiations on German reunification – the East and West German analytic accounts were merged into a single working group. It was a prescient move that enabled analysts to focus more sharply on inner German issues and later to support effectively the US diplomatic role in the reunification of Germany.

The placement of responsibility for whole regions or sub-regions may reflect an adaptation, or failure to adapt, to the changing nature or importance of issues associated with those regions. A reasonable argument could be made that South Asia – comprising a fifth of mankind – has been given insufficient attention because of the tendency to make it an organizational step-child of another region, most often the Middle East. Several South Asian issues would seem to call for increased intelligence attention, including heightened indications of Islamic extremism, the development of a strategic relationship between India and the United States, and the progression of the Indo-Pakistani confrontation to a new level since both countries tested nuclear weapons in 1998. The Intelligence Community may be moving in response, as suggested by the National Intelligence Council's creation in 2006 of the new position of National Intelligence Officer for South Asia.

The former Soviet republics of Central Asia raise similar issues. So far most parts of the Intelligence Community have continued to group Central Asia with Russia. Changing this organization could alter the framework within which intelligence officers think about Central Asia and could entail either a response to, or an anticipation of, the changing salience of issues there. Should the focus be on the Central Asian republics' role in oil and gas exports, their infiltration by transnational Islamist movements, their prospects for overcoming their authoritarian Soviet past, or their place in a new Asian geostrategic game played by the great powers? Each of these perspectives might imply a different organization for coverage of the region.

The most conspicuous organizational reflection of emphasis on a particular issue is the establishment of a component dedicated to covering the issue on a transnational, cross-regional basis. The creation of the DCI Counterterrorist Center, and subsequent centers modeled after it for intelligence coverage of narcotics and the proliferation of unconventional arms, are clear examples. To a lesser degree the same is true of analytic components that address other issues such as energy supplies or financial flows. For an issue to have its own component assures not just a certain way of looking at the issue but also a degree of clout in assuring continued focus on it. An offsetting hazard is that such components may acquire more permanence than the issues they originally were designed to address, possibly meaning that much more structure needs to be disassembled and reassembled as issues evolve further.

Collection disciplines

The primary structural divisions of the US Intelligence Community, and the basis for distinguishing entire agencies from each other, are the "ints" or different methods of collecting information. These include the collection of intelligence from human sources (HUMINT), electronic signals (SIGINT), overhead imaging (IMINT), and various other technical means (measurement and signatures intelligence, or MASINT), as well as open sources of information. Some of the easiest as well as the hardest aspects of adaptation to changing issues inhere in these methods of collection.

The easy part is that several of the biggest, most expensive components of these collection systems are quite versatile and can be redirected to a wide variety of targets. The codes that are broken as part of the National Security Agency's SIGINT operations may be peculiar to particular countries, for example, but the supercomputers and cryptologists who do the work can be applied to the messages of any foreign government. Similarly, to put an imaging satellite to work against a new target is usually as simple as aiming its camera in a different direction when it passes over that part of the earth. Both SIGINT and IMINT have well-established structures, including committees representing analysts from throughout the Intelligence Community, for quickly redirecting the collection systems. In fact, the responsiveness to short-fuse requirements is so good that the main difficulty with these tasking structures is a tendency for the short-fuse requirements to crowd out long-term ones. This is policed to some extent through periodic comprehensive reviews of collection requests, which are the occasion for updating all of the requirements and bringing them into conformity with changing policy needs and emerging threats.

Other elements of those collection systems, however, are more target-specific and not very versatile. Foreign language is one such element, as it relates both to linguists needed to process signals intelligence and operations officers who recruit human sources. In addition, long lead times are required for most major shifts in capabilities, whether it is the development of a new generation of satellites or the development of a network of human agents directed against a particular country of heightened interest.

A further complication is that although the division into collection disciplines dominates the structure of the overall intelligence effort – with budgetary overseers able to see at a glance how much money is spent on the National Security Agency (NSA), the National Reconnaissance Office, the National Geospatial-Intelligence Agency, or CIA's clandestine service – that division does not correspond to the substantive issues being covered. Only imperfectly and to a very limited degree can generalizations be ventured about how a particular "int" may be more, or less, important in covering new issues versus old ones. One could argue, for example, that overhead imagery was very important in monitoring Soviet strategic nuclear forces but is useless in uncovering terrorist plots being hatched behind closed doors, and for that reason imaging satellites should receive reduced priority. Valid or not, variations of that argument have in fact been made. But what about, say, the SIGINT activities of NSA, which have played major roles in monitoring Soviet military activity, terrorist operations, and much else besides? Staying abreast of changing issues is not a good guide for deciding how large a proportion NSA's operations should be of the overall US intelligence effort.

Issues of the present and future

So many words have been expended on the theme that the United States should "reform," "overhaul," "revamp," or "shake up" its intelligence programs to address new issues (again, the idea of "moving beyond the Cold War") that there is, at this level of generality, literally nothing left to say. Those parts of this rhetoric that are not noise have become a kind of mood music, constantly playing in the background of any discussion of US intelligence. And some of the motifs in that music are valid. There is indeed a need, more now than 30 or 40 years go, to pay as much attention to nonstate actors as to states and to pay heavy attention to developments within the Muslim world. And such specific issues as transnational terrorism and proliferation of nuclear weapons are not just trendy: they will require concentrated attention from the Intelligence Community for years to come, not only because of what is going on in the outside world but because of the policy attention those issues will continue to receive in Washington.

More valuable than simply singing along with the mood music is to add a countermelody or two. One such countermelody is the observation that once one drops below the level of generality at which so much is being said and looks for more specific ways to operationalize or implement the general themes, one discovers that almost nothing is being said. *Exactly how* should the Intelligence Community change to be more adept at covering new issues rather than old ones? *What specifically* about current intelligence activities is oriented toward old issues, *how* is it so oriented, *what* alternative arrangements would be better suited to handling new issues, and *how* and *why* would they be better suited? The absence of satisfactory answers to these questions, and for most of them the lack of any answers at all, forms a stark contrast to the ubiquity of the general rhetoric. The most plausible explanation for this absence is that there simply are no (or very few) good answers to the questions, that some of the expectations being placed on intelligence go beyond inherent limitations to what it can accomplish, and that most of the good ideas have already been tried and most of what the Intelligence Community does already is about as well suited to tackling new and emerging issues as any possible alternatives. That explanation is almost never voiced because it would inject a discordant note into the mood music. Meanwhile, the urge to reform can lead (and in the case of the most recent reorganization of the Intelligence Community, has led) to change for the sake of change, which more likely than not will be counterproductive.

A more detailed look at the most salient issues reveals the opportunities for mischief. On terrorism, what Americans most want from their intelligence services is the collection of tactical information that is specific enough to roll up individual terrorist plots before they can culminate in attacks. That objective has not changed; it always has been a major goal of counterterrorist operations. Also unchanged is the impossibility of ever achieving that goal completely, due mainly to the inherent difficulties of penetrating closely held terrorist plots in which a very few people – who are ruthless, security conscious, and extremely distrustful – ever have access to the information that matters.

One thing that did change after 9/11, of course, was the American people's insistence on expending more effort and resources in striving toward the goal. That is a legitimate reason – the suddenly heightened salience of an issue – for the Intelligence Community to consider changing how it addresses that issue. But the increased salience of terrorism did not point to any particular alterations in organization or operational technique, or to any better ideas on how to crack the very tough nut of terrorist plots.

Even the resource aspect of the issue does not have an obvious answer. Given the impossibility of ever warding off all terrorist plots, there is no level of effort that can be said to be "enough." Whether to undertake additional effort, however small the marginal return, involves trade-offs with other possible expenditures, either intelligence-related or not. Expanded counterterrorist efforts also may involve trade-offs with privacy, civil liberties, or other concerns, as demonstrated by controversies over interception of communications inside the United States. In short, at stake are broader policy questions rather than just an adaptation or "reform" of intelligence.

Besides seeking plot-specific information, the counterterrorist intelligence mission also includes the strategic appraisal of terrorist threats. This part of the mission also is unchanged. Moreover, it has been performed rather successfully: the Intelligence Community started devoting concentrated attention to the radical Islamist terrorist threat and more specifically Osama bin Laden's part of it years before the 9/11 disaster, and its imparting of the seriousness of the threat to policymakers was reflected in the latter's own considerable attention to that threat even before Al Qaeda attacked US embassies in Africa in 1998, more than three years before 9/11. Again, it is very difficult to see exactly what change in procedure, organization, or technique is implied, or whether and how any such changes could be expected to be an improvement.

The 9/11 Commission nonetheless successfully sold its own reorganization plan, partly through its political and public relations skills and partly by distorting the intelligence story alluded to above. In so doing, it promoted in the name of adaptation to changing issues a scheme that, to the extent it has any effect at all, makes the Intelligence Community less rather than more adaptable. This effect starts with the commission's defining of the problem not as terrorism but more narrowly as Islamist terrorism.[5] In one sense this is commendable precision in identifying actual adversaries rather than merely a technique those adversaries may use, and radical jihadism probably will indeed continue to be the variety of terrorism of most concern to the United States over the next several years. But this definition also is a statement of indifference to other varieties of terrorism – which a wide variety of groups, movements, and ideologies have employed through the years – that may emerge.

That indifference is reflected in the organizational structure that Congress enacted on the commission's recommendation, which includes a National Counterterrorism Center (NCTC) separate from CIA and other existing intelligence agencies. In addition to the jurisdictional confusion that creation of this additional body has caused, its separation from the country- and region-focused analytic elements in a component such as CIA's Directorate of Intelligence lessens the likelihood that it will tune early into the next emerging terrorist threat. Any such threat will not be detected by a group of counterterrorist specialists huddled in their own separate center. It will be detected through dialogue between those specialists and country or regional analysts who follow broader political and social trends and movements that could provide the breeding grounds for future terrorists.

Some of the same questions can be raised about intelligence coverage of proliferation of unconventional weapons. One also needs to ask what types of substantive information about this topic the Intelligence Community ought to be collecting and analyzing. The technical details of weapons programs surely are part, but only part. The intentions of regimes and the political context in which decisions about weapons programs are made also are important. And that implies intelligence efforts, such as to recruit human sources in senior levels of a regime, that may not bear the "nonproliferation" or "weapons of mass destruction" label and may not look much different from efforts aimed at other sorts of issues. One of the lessons of the Community's analytical shortcomings regarding Iraqi weapons programs is the need to integrate perspectives about a regime's political needs, and even the personality of the leader, into analysis of what invariably is ambiguous information about the weapons programs them-selves. And when nonproliferation efforts fail, the intentions of regimes regarding possible use of their newly acquired weapons becomes highly important.

The organizational arrangement hatched by the 9/11 Commission and established in 2005 includes a new nonproliferation center similar in nature and mission to NCTC. The center entails some of the same confusion as NCTC about division of responsibility with other components covering the same issue, and the same disadvantage of being separated from other analytic components following developments that may not be part of the same issue now but may prove to be pertinent to it. Moreover, creation of these additional boxes on the Intelligence Community's organization chart makes the Community that much more of a stratifying, pigeonholing bureaucracy. The new centers – unlike centers such as CTC that were created within existing agencies – are in many respects new agencies in their own right, with all of the additional turf and inertia that go with that. The Intelligence Community consequently has become less nimble in adapting itself to future changes in the nature and priority of the issues it must follow.

Perpetual adaptation

Against the backdrop of debate and confusion in recent years about intelligence "reform," how will one know when the Intelligence Community finally is well structured and well positioned to address the newest, most pressing issues of the day? Answer: one will never know that, and the Community will never achieve any such reformist nirvana. Because the issues keep changing, even perfection – if it were achievable, which it is not – in procedures and organization to tackle this year's issues will be outdated next year. A distinction that is important but often overlooked

consistently will be outdated

161

is between adapting intelligence to any one set of issues and making it more adaptable to any issues. Narrow pursuit of the first objective can hinder the second.

Would-be reformers of intelligence should keep in mind that however threatening and pressing any one issue seems today, there will come along some other issue that, when it comes, will seem even more threatening and pressing. We will expect our intelligence services to make us pay attention to any such danger, and we will blame them for an "intelligence failure" if they do not. And so the stakes involve not just Islamist terrorism and weapons of mass destruction and anything else that worries us at the moment, but all manner of coups, revolutions, wars, or other ogres or mayhem around the world that we may not even be thinking about now. The possibilities might include – just to pick one at random – political developments in Russia (still with its large nuclear arsenal) that make it a greater threat and more worrisome adversary than it is today. Maybe that Cold War expertise will come in useful again after all.

Notes

1 Martha Crenshaw, "Old and New Terrorism: Lessons Learned," Second Conference on Jihadi Terrorism, Royal Institute of International Relations, February 13, 2006, at http://www.irri-kiib.be/speechnotes/06/060213-jihad.terr/crenshaw.htm.
2 William E. Colby, *Honorable Men: My Life in the CIA* (New York: Simon and Shuster, 1978), p. 361.
3 Assistant Director of Central Intelligence for Analysis and Production, *Strategic Investment Plan for Intelligence Community Analysis, 2000–01*, p. 47.
4 Ibid., pp. 49–50.
5 *The 9/11 Commission Report* (Washington: Government Printing Office, 2004), p. 362.

12

The challenges of economic intelligence

Minh A. Luong

Introduction

Information regarding the state of critical industries, technologies, and future investments of other countries are among the most prized by intelligence services and their policymaking consumers. The term "economic intelligence" refers to policy or commercially relevant economic information, including technological data, financial, proprietary commercial, and government information, whose acquisition by foreign interests, either directly or indirectly, would assist the relative productivity or competitive position of the economy of the collecting organization's country. Economic intelligence can be an important element in obtaining economic security for a nation. The vast majority of economic intelligence is legally gathered from open sources, involving no clandestine, coercive, or deceptive methods.[1]

It is important to distinguish between the terms "economic intelligence" and "economic espionage." Economic espionage is the use or facilitation of illegal clandestine, coercive, or deceptive means by a foreign government or its surrogates to acquire economic intelligence. Economic espionage activities may include collection of information, or acquisition or theft of a manufactured item through clandestine means with the intent of using reverse engineering to gain proprietary or classified data.[2] In the twenty-first century, economic espionage has expanded to include theft of product plans and intellectual property such as software code that is easily captured on thumb-sized storage drives and sent electronically around the world via the Internet.

Virtually every national intelligence service gathers some form of economic intelligence, with the world's major economic powers having greatly expanded their economic intelligence capabilities since the 1990s. For example, the British Parliament passed the British Intelligence Services Act of 1994, which expanded the scope of its Secret Intelligence Service (SIS), also known as MI6, to include areas relevant to "the interests of the economic well-being of the United Kingdom."[3] In March 1994, the French government authorized its intelligence services to expand operations into collecting economic and industrial intelligence. Moreover, the following year, the French government established the Committee for Economic Competitiveness and Security which focused on protecting economic secrets and set up an economic intelligence office in the French Foreign Trade office.[4] France, which has been cited by

163

France

numerous sources as one of the largest collectors of economic intelligence and foremost practitioners of economic espionage, opened the École de Guerre Économique (EGE) or School of Economic Warfare in 1997.[5] The EGE's mission statement emphasizes "offensive strategy." It trains students in a wide range of intelligence disciplines and awards degrees in economic intelligence including the doctorate. The People's Republic of China (PRC), also frequently cited as a major collector of economic intelligence and a leading practitioner of economic espionage, operates mainly through the Ministry of State Security (MSS) and the People's Liberation Army, General Staff Department, Second Department (also known as the Military Intelligence Department), coordinating a vast and enhanced overseas collection effort.[6] In the United States, the Central Intelligence Agency (CIA) has maintained a large economic intelligence analysis capability since the end of World War II which was enhanced significantly during the Cold War[7] but that capability was further expanded as the National Security Agency (NSA) upgraded its signals intelligence collection capacity thorough its ECHELON system that reportedly is capable of intercepting millions of electronic messages per hour.[8] In 2001, US Presidential Decision Directive (PDD 75) on counterintelligence was released and the directive created a new office, the National Counterintelligence Executive (NCIX), responsible for protecting American economic and industrial interests.[9]

Countries use economic intelligence to assess the state of their own national industries, measure the competitiveness of industries in other countries, and inform policymakers and industry leaders about which domestic industries are in need of further investment or reorganization. Nations that engage in economic espionage do so to improve or maintain the competitiveness of their own national industries by lowering or eliminating associated research and development costs by illegally appropriating advanced technology and other proprietary information: this brings products and services to market at lower cost and frequently faster than if they were developed indigenously.

Economic intelligence: a key to national competitiveness

In an increasingly global marketplace, the competitiveness of domestic industries often means the difference between national prosperity and security versus poverty and instability. National governments, regardless of form or type, are under increasing pressure to satisfy the needs of their domestic populations and maintain economic stability and growth. Growing populations around the globe expect paying jobs in order to feed, house, and clothe their families and an educated elite, frequently educated in the best universities in Asia, Western Europe and the United States, have rising expectations for their own prosperity and well-being. For all countries, making intelligent investments in the right industries at the right time is a critical part of national economic policy. Economic intelligence gathered from competitor nations is an essential component in making the right investment decisions. These investment decisions affect different countries depending on their present stage of economic development. For developing countries, accurate economic intelligence helps direct scarce investment funds to industries that show the greatest promise for long-term growth. In the case of developed countries, economic intelligence is used to help support established but aging industries which need to improve its competitive standing against rival firms from other nations that frequently operate on a lower cost basis. For all nations, capital investment funds at competitive interest rates are a finite resource and managing those funds effectively requires access to accurate, complete, and timely economic intelligence.

164

Economic espionage: the acquisition of industrial technology and proprietary trade information

The National Counterintelligence Executive (NCIX), the US government agency charged with protecting American industry and trade information, noted that "[i]ndividuals from both the private and public sectors in almost 100 countries attempted to illegally acquire US technologies in FY2004."[10] The report also observed that the United States is not the only country that has experienced losses through economic espionage. The People's Republic of China, Russia, and South Korea all reported cases of foreign economic espionage occurring within their borders.[11] Economic espionage is a global phenomenon that occurs at three levels – national governments engage in economic espionage to benefit their national industries and military forces; companies steal intellectual property and trade secrets from competitors and even joint venture partners; and individual data collectors, also known as industrial spies, gain employment at target firms and steal proprietary information and trade secrets. This information is then sold to competitor firms or foreign governments.

Countries that collect economic intelligence frequently discover that their national industries require significant capital and technological investments in order to become or stay competitive in the global economy. The policy decisions that result from such findings frequently cross the dividing line between economic intelligence and economic espionage. For countries that can afford to raise capital funds to improve their industries, they certainly engage in economic intelligence but tend to avoid engaging in economic espionage in order to maintain positive relations with larger trading partners and to maintain access to overseas investment funds. But for countries which cannot afford to pay to improve their industries, they still face the same demographic, economic, and political pressures of other countries but choose to acquire stolen technology and proprietary information to bolster their uncompetitive industries. These countries maintain legitimate businesses and interact in the global economy but choose to supplement their economic growth with benefits from economic espionage.

The benefits of engaging in economic espionage are clear and straightforward. For example, by stealing completed or near-completed product plans, a competitor can produce and market a copy of the product without incurring the normal research and development costs of bringing that product to market. For industries with high research and development costs such as pharmaceutical, biotechnology, computer hardware and software, and military equipment, theft of even a single high-investment product can have enormous consequences. To make matters worse for the original developer, if products derived from stolen proprietary data are manufactured in a country with lower production costs, the original developers may find themselves in an uncompetitive position, even though they developed the product in the first place. Firms which manufacture products derived from stolen proprietary data frequently do not market them in the country or region where the product plans were acquired. This tactic reduces the likelihood of detection by the firms that originally developed the products.

Estimating the losses from global economic espionage is very difficult, if not impossible, due to the fact that some firms do not discover that their product plans or intellectual property have been compromised for months or even years after the initial loss. Many companies never learn of their losses and assume that their reduced market share or lack of success in the market is due to other business factors. Some firms who discover that they have been victims of industrial espionage make a business decision not to report the loss to the authorities for fear of negative publicity, loss of customer confidence, or even a drop in their stock prices.[12]

165

Types of industries targeted

While nearly every industry is at risk, economic espionage collectors have concentrated their efforts on a number of specific industries. In the commercial sector, these include agriculture, biotechnology, chemical, computer technology, fiber optics, medical devices, pharmaceuticals, robotics, and telecommunications.[13] Commercial sector industries all play a role in fostering economic growth. For example, in countries where domestic food production has leveled off or has dropped, purchasing agricultural technology and materials has proven to be a costly endeavor. Through industrial espionage, acquiring countries can obtain agricultural technology and the formulations to produce fertilizers and pesticides at a much lower cost, provided that they have the necessary domestic manufacturing capability and access to required raw materials. An important point to note here is that while copy-cat equipment and chemicals derived from economic espionage may not perform as well as products manufactured from its original makers, that issue is not the primary concern. The key factor is whether the copy-cat products are better than no products at all or are better than antiquated products currently in use. Given the low cost, high payoff of acquiring technology and products through economic espionage, the improvements are worth the expense.

With respect to military technologies, many countries use economic espionage to improve the capabilities of their military forces as well as to improve the competitiveness of their arms industries. Targeted military industries include aeronautics, armaments, energetic materials, chemical and biological systems, guidance and navigation systems, information systems, manufacturing and fabrication, marine systems, sensors and lasers, and space system technologies.[14] Countries that engage in economic espionage to collect military and dual-use technologies are frequently trading partners but are restricted from receiving military-grade technologies due to national security export restrictions. Countries with the most advanced military technology and greatest number of export restrictions include the NATO countries of Western Europe and the United States. The investments required to maintain military advantage of potential enemies are significant, running into the billions of dollars in research, development, and deployment costs. Compromised technology losses through economic espionage put these investments at significant risk. One example from the 1980s comes from a subsidiary of Toshiba Corporation, Toshiba Machine, which, in a violation of American and Japanese technology transfer restrictions designed and installed sophisticated milling machines in Soviet shipyards which enabled the Soviet submarines to run as quietly as any British or American nuclear submarine. This unauthorized transaction earned Toshiba Machine US$17 million but cost the American military US$30 billion to regain that lost advantage in submarine operation and detection.[15]

Collection methods

For collectors of economic intelligence, there is a significant difference in operating between open and closed economic systems.[16] In open economic systems, obtaining economic intelligence is relatively easy and utilizes tools not unfamiliar to a stock investor. Government economic reports and company quarterly and annual disclosures make up the foundation of any country analysis. This information can be supplemented and cross-verified by private data and analysis from research firms and investment companies. On-site visits of companies and manufacturing plants are possible if arranged in advance. Even open source analysis of media reports and academic and trade journals provide rich streams of economic data. In closed economic systems, the economic intelligence collection task becomes more challenging. Harassment from law enforcement officials and state security officers hampers collection activity. Government reports and company disclosures are frequently inaccurate, incomplete, misleading, or simply unavailable.[17] Travel restrictions within the country and the need for special permits encumber collection efforts. When contacted for interviews, company officials grow suspicious of any foreigners or persons asking for company data.

For countries with significant national technical means such as satellites and communications interception capabilities, a new dimension of economic data is available. Satellite imagery and analysis can help produce accurate agricultural yield estimates, projections of industrial output, even mortality rates. Interception of phone calls, Internet messages, fax transmissions and other communications can be used to verify or confirm intelligence findings. Finally, economic intelligence sources can include businesspeople, academics, and researchers who live in or visit targeted countries. Intelligence services around the world utilize these types of human sources and while some services prefer to debrief citizens who have returned from abroad, others provide a list of targets beforehand so citizens can exploit any opportunity that they encounter.

For economic espionage collectors, the method of operation can vary significantly. Because of their open economic systems, countries engaging in economic espionage frequently establish front companies in Europe and the United States from which to base their operations. These firms operate like domestic companies and their foreign ownership ties are either not disclosed or are hidden. For the past decade, acquisition of sensitive commercial, military, and dual-use technologies has been at the top of the target list for economic rivals of the European Union and the United States. These front companies attempt to purchase restricted technology and illegally transfer it out of the country. In other instances, these firms form joint venture partnerships with companies that have developed sensitive technologies and the foreign joint venture partner transfers the proprietary information to a third party in violation of the joint venture agreement. Another popular collection method is to arrange an on-site visit where the targeted technology or products are produced. While the information exchange is supposed to be bi-directional, there have been reported incidents of foreign experts entering restricted areas, photographing sensitive areas, and discussing topics and asking questions that are outside the agreed list of topics.[18] Some countries utilize their student and academic connections in targeted countries, recruiting them to serve as intermediaries or even collectors at academic conferences, university laboratories and libraries, industry meetings and trade shows. One potential area of concern for significant economic espionage losses is through compromised computer systems. An industrial espionage collector, working within a targeted firm with access to the company's computer system, can download and collect computer files containing critical proprietary data. With the advent of high-capacity, low-cost storage devices such as small hard drives and thumb-sized memory sticks, gigabytes of information can be stolen in minutes and detection is virtually impossible.

Economic espionage: a global challenge

Economic espionage can affect any country regardless of the state of development. In fact, there are countries that benefit from economic espionage and yet are victims of it at the same time. But the dangers to the international trade system from economic espionage are becoming increasingly clear and this phenomenon affects nearly every level of a nation's economy. Economic espionage greatly reduces or even destroys incentives to innovate. Inventors have been deterred from developing inventions and bringing them to market for fear of having their life's work and investment stolen. Bankers are increasingly leery of making business loans to firms whose products are at risk from industrial espionage. Investors may be discouraged from making investments in companies operating in foreign countries or whose bottom line may be negatively affected by losses from economic espionage. And joint ventures, hailed by many business scholars as a way of linking the developing and developed worlds, are fraught with dangers from one partner stealing from the other. Officials in countries that engage in economic espionage as national policy defend their practice by saying that their best minds study in highly industrialized nations but never return to help their native country, so stealing technologies and other industrial trade secrets is a way of equalizing for the potential loss of these educated citizens. The "brain drain" effect is difficult to quantify but it does provide a rationale for engaging in economic espionage.[19]

These types of risks lead to reduced business efficiencies. The risk from economic espionage has deterred companies from entering promising markets due to weak intellectual property protections and from risk of economic espionage. The additional expense for enhanced security increases overhead costs and reduces workplace efficiencies as more time is spent on maintaining security measures. Economic espionage has even led to discrimination in the workplace because certain nationalities and ethnicities are associated with industrial espionage.

stereotyping

Counterintelligence challenge

The counterintelligence challenge is to promote a robust international trading system while discouraging economic espionage activity that threatens the integrity and health of that system. Governments can work together to establish mutually acceptable intellectual property and patent conventions with the agreement to enforce them uniformly regardless whether the violator is from their country or another country. Companies need to be more aware of the dangers of economic espionage and take active measures to protect their proprietary information and inventions. Individuals should take responsibility if they encounter acts of industrial espionage in their firms by reporting incidents to their firm's security officer and law enforcement.[20] Some of the largest targets of economic espionage such as the United States have enacted laws punishing economic espionage collectors. For example, in 1996, the United States passed the Economic Espionage Act (EEA) which punishes firms and individuals who steals or transfers trade secrets with prison terms of up to 15 years and monetary fines up to US$10 million.[21] In 2002, the US Attorney General strengthened the EEA by giving federal prosecutors more latitude in interpreting violations of the Act. In 2005, the US adopted a new national counterintelligence strategy that signals a change in approach in addressing economic espionage. The new strategy shifts CI efforts from a reactive to a proactive approach with more emphasis on protecting sensitive technologies. Law enforcement agencies such as the Federal Bureau of Investigation will devote more resources to defeating foreign intelligence operations within US borders. The new strategy also promises to "ensure a level economic playing field for US businesses and industry." Whether that means that US intelligence agencies will be tasked to directly assist individual companies or industries is unclear but so far the official US government position is that the US intelligence community does not offer assistance to specific companies or firms.

Conclusion

There are relatively few objections to the collection of economic intelligence but there are many concerns over economic espionage. The challenge for the global economic community is three-fold: first, openness and transparency of all economic systems would allow other countries to make proper policy decisions with regard to investments in their own national industries. Second, promotion of fair and mutually beneficial trading rules and relationships is paramount, as is the need to continue to address the inequities that lead to the use of economic espionage. Third, private corporations and firms need to be proactive and take prudent measures to protect their own intellectual property and innovations. Governments can provide a strong counterintelligence function, investigate losses via law enforcement, and negotiate with other governments on behalf of firms, but governments are neither equipped nor able to protect individual firm or industries.

As long as global economic espionage continues, there will continue to be an atmosphere of distrust and unproductiveness that will permeate trade treaties, business negotiations, and even individual employment decisions. If countries and firms can be dissuaded from engaging in industrial espionage, then the global economic benefit from increased innovation and productivity would be significant and meaningful.

Notes

1 Interagency OPSEC Support Staff, "Economic Intelligence Collection Directed Against the United States," Operations Security Intelligence Threat Handbook, 1996. URL: <http://www.fas.org/irp/nsa/ioss/threat96/part05.htm>.

2 Ibid.

3 Controller of HMSO (being the Queen's Printer of Acts of Parliament), Intelligence Services Act of 1994. URL: <http://www.opsi.gov.uk/acts/acts1994/Ukpga_19940013_en_2.htm>.

4 B. Raman, "Economic Intelligence," South Asia Analysis Group Papers, February 1999. URL: <http://www.saag.org/papers/paper50.html>.

5 URL: <http://www.ege.fr/>.

6 Nicholas Eftimiades, author of *Chinese Intelligence Operations*, statement before the Joint Economic Committee, United States Congress, May 20, 1998.

7 By 1951, the National Security Council directed the CIA to determine the overall requirements for the collection and management of "foreign economic intelligence." See Philip Zelikow, "American Economic Intelligence," in *Eternal Vigilance?: 50 Years of the CIA*, ed. Rhodri Jeffreys-Jones and Christopher Andrew (London: Frank Cass, 1997), p. 166.

8 The actual capabilities of NSA's ECHELON system have been subject to intense debate. The Federation of American Scientists (FAS) maintains an ECHELON information website containing various reports on ECHELON including those of the European Parliament Temporary Committee on the ECHELON Interception System. URL: <http://www.fas.org/irp/program/process/echelon.htm>.

9 National Counterintelligence Executive, "History of Counterintelligence," undated. URL: <http://www.ncix.gov/history/CIReaderPlain/Vol4Chap4.pdf>.

10 "The Key Collectors," *National Counterintelligence Executive Annual Report, 2004*, p. 3. URL: <http://www.ncix.gov/publications/reports_speeches/reports/fecie_all/Index_fecie.html>.

11 Appendix A, *National Counterintelligence Executive Annual Report, 2004*, p. 15. URL: <http://www.ncix.gov/publications/reports_speeches/reports/fecie_all/Index_fecie.html>.

12 Ibid. at page x.

13 See Minh A. Luong, "Espionage: A Real Threat," Optimize, October 2003. URL: <http://www.optimizemag.com/issue/024/security.htm>.

14 Ibid.

15 Roderick Seeman, The Japan Law Letter, April 1987. URL: <http://www.japanlaw.info/lawletter/april87/fdf.htm>.

16 For the purposes of this discussion, an open economic system is defined as an economic system which promotes transparent and accurate financial and operations reporting. A closed economic system is defined as an economic system in which financial and operations reporting is restricted, secret, or distorted as to become inaccurate. Closed economic systems also tend to be heavily influenced or controlled by the government.

17 Field researchers have discovered that economic reporting in closed economies is heavily influenced by political concerns or to mask inefficiencies or corruption.

18 National Counterintelligence Executive Annual Report, 2004, p. 6. URL: <http://www.ncix.gov/publications/reports_speeches/reports/fecie_all/Index_fecie.html>.

19 This point is discussed briefly in John J. Fialka's War by Other Means: Economic Espionage in America, 1997.

20 Many acts of industrial espionage are caught by administrative assistants and support staff who stop and challenge individuals who are searching trash and recycling bins, attempting to access computer equipment outside their normal work area, and who access sensitive company files without authorization.

21 For the text of the EEA and other resources, visit the US Department of Justice EEA resource website at URL: <http://www.cybercrime.gov/ipmanual/08ipma.htm>.

Part 4

The intelligence cycle and the crafting of intelligence reports

Analysis and dissemination

13

Strategic warning

Intelligence support in a world of uncertainty and surprise

Jack Davis

This chapter is colored by the bold and devastating 11 September 2001 attack by al–Qa'ida terrorists on the symbols of American power. Fear of another "9/11" – a surprise terrorist attack within the United States – has focused the attention of government leaders and the population at large on the centrality of effective warning intelligence to the protection of the national interest. The need for improved warning intelligence underlies both the recent sharp increase in the national investment in intelligence collection and analysis and a congressionally mandated reorganization of the Intelligence Community, namely the establishment of a Director of National Intelligence. Fear and hope are joined in the title of the 2004 legislation: The Intelligence Reform and Prevention of Terrorism Act.

That said, this article is not about the daunting challenges of *tactical warning*, an aspect of intelligence covered at great length and impressive depth elsewhere. The focus, instead, is on a less well-illuminated aspect of intelligence and the national interest – *strategic warning*.

Warning analysis is the charge given to the Central Intelligence Agency and other governmental intelligence units to help policy officials prevent or limit damage from threats to US security interests. Tactical warning, as defined in this chapter, seeks to detect and deter terrorist attacks and other specific near-term threats to US interests; the objective is to avoid incident, surprise and thus block or blunt damage. Strategic warning addresses perceived dangers over a longer period and in broader terms, in order to inform policymaker decisions on general security preparedness – again to prevent or limit damage.

The analytic elements for tactical and strategic warning analysis are much the same: the processing of a vast volume of information from open sources as well as from specialized collection efforts that could signal either pending or over-the-horizon threats; insights from substantive expertise and practical experience regarding which of the many inconclusively defined threats deserve the most attention; and specialized tradecraft or analytic methodologies to determine how to reach judgments amidst substantive or issue uncertainty and when to press for policymakers' attention and action despite uncertainty.

The intelligence imperative for tactical warning is self-evident. If an adversary is judged to be about to launch an attack, develop a weapon, or effect a policy initiative that can harm US interests, intelligence analysts must set off an alarm bell, so to speak. US policymakers and action-takers need time for the appropriate response, whether to demarche, to detect, to deter, to destroy.

The rationale for strategic warning stems from the fact that, though robust, US national security resources are limited. Tactical warning cannot be counted on to support pinpoint deployment of defensive measures by providing timely notice of all specific attacks and menacing developments. In this context, the challenge of strategic warning is to help policy officials decide – in advance of specific indicators of danger – which of the many plausible general threats to US security interests deserve concerted preemptive and defensive preparations.

Strategic warning, to be effective, has to be credible in assessing contingent dangers and has to facilitate policymaker decision and action to protect against these dangers. If nothing else, the events of 9/11 illustrate the difficulties of getting policy officials, and through them Congress, affected special interests, and the public at large, to pay the costs and brook the inconveniences of a threat that, however serious intelligence analysts may see it to be, can only be depicted in general terms.

The complexity and uncertainty surrounding generalized threats to US interests cast a special challenge regarding strategic warning on both intelligence analysts and their policy-making and action-taking clients – the inherent vulnerability to error of estimative judgments regarding likelihood, character, and timing of threat.

Intelligence analysts must issue a strategic warning far enough in advance of a feared event for US officials to take protective action, yet with the credibility to motivate them to do so. No mean feat. Waiting for evidence that the enemy is at the gate usually fails the timeliness test; prediction of potential crises without hard evidence can fail the credibility test. When analysts are too cautious in making estimative judgments on threats, they risk incurring blame for failure to warn. When too aggressive in issuing warning, they risk being criticised for "crying wolf."

To address the consequence of this paradox and other obstacles that intelligence organizations must confront in order to produce effective strategic warning, this chapter will conclude by tabling a series of recommendations to advance two goals:

1 To reconstitute strategic warning as a collaborative governmental function by engaging policy officials responsible for advocating and effecting defensive measures in every step of the analysis process, including topic selection and trend monitoring.
2 To warrant a distinctive intelligence contribution to a collaborative warning effort by expanding dedicated analytic resources and sharpening requisite substantive expertise and specialized tradecraft.

Uncertainty, surprise, and warning

The central mission of intelligence analysis since the post-World War II reorganization of national security structures (the National Security Act of 1947) has been to warn US officials about foreign threats to US security interests. In large measure, determination to avoid another devastating setback to US defense such as that caused by the surprise Japanese attack on Pearl Harbor on 11 December 1941 convinced some reluctant members of Congress to support the creation of the Central Intelligence Agency (CIA). At the time, influential critics charged that the proposed agency would represent an "American Gestapo," with powers that could threaten US democracy.

Over the subsequent decades, and under the conceit that every CIA analyst was a warning officer, the bulk of analysts' written and oral deliverables pointed directly or indirectly to the existence, characteristics, and implications of threats to the broadly defined range of US national security interests. According to some policy officials and other critical observers, much of the output read more like quota-driven current reporting and research for the sake of research than like warnings that commanded serious attention and justified costly action.

As titular head of the community of intelligence agencies, the Director of Central Intelligence (DCI) would launch periodic reviews of what came to be known as the "National Warning System." The most recent review, in 1992 under then DCI Robert Gates, once again defined positions and mechanisms that had imposing titles and responsibilities. But their impact on analytic performance was limited, and thus the impact on improving policymaker respect for and reliance on warning analysis was limited.

As this chapter is written (April 2006), the National Warning System is supported by a National Intelligence Officer for Warning, a Strategic Warning Staff, and a Strategic Warning Committee. Each element has worked diligently to fulfill its mandate, but none has had much authority to affect the priorities of the line analytic units of the Intelligence Community. In recognition of this, the Director of National Intelligence has commissioned another effort to study and revamp the warning system, according to a recent unclassified memorandum of his National Intelligence Council.

Personalities count as well as organizational mechanisms. Over the decades individual analysts have had the will and talent to serve directly and well as warning officers for the policy officials who encouraged them to do so. In good measure, the following text reflects the this experience-based trail of "best practices."

What, in this author's view, are the characteristics and benefits of an effective warning regime? The central analytic task is to peel back substantive uncertainty about the meaning of past developments and the prospects for both pending and future developments that could endanger US interests. Prescient, timely, convincing analysis regarding imminent and potential dangers would then be an important force multiplier for US officials by reducing the likelihood, first, of incident surprise and, second, of inadequate defensive preparedness for dealing effectively with high-impact potential threats.

In order to identify and evaluate alternatives to current doctrine and practice of strategic warning, a clear, even if arbitrary, distinction from tactical warning can usefully be made. *Tactical warning* focuses on specific incidents that endanger US security interests, such as military attack, terrorism, developments regarding weapons of mass destruction (WMD), illicit transactions, and political crises abroad. Tactical warning analysis is usually characterized by a search for and evaluation of diagnostic information about incident, perpetrator, target, timing, and modalities. The goal is to deter and limit damage by identifying in advance *when, where,* and *how* an adversary will forcefully strike the United States directly, mount a challenge to US forces, personnel, or interests abroad, or make a menacing weapons breakthrough. Notably, counterterrorism, the most prominent and urgent target for tactical warning, has long been detached from the National Warning, System and housed in variously named independent "centers." → *comm. to policy makers*

Strategic warning aims for analytic perception and effective communication to policy officials of important changes in the character or level of security threats that therefore require re-evaluation of US readiness to deter, avert, or limit damage – well in advance of incident-specific indicators. Thus, strategic warning is characterized by inferential evidence and general depiction of the danger. The issues addressed here are *changes in the level of likelihood* that an enemy will strike, or that a development harmful to US interests (such as an oil embargo) will take place, and *changes in adversarial mechanisms for inflicting damage.* The goal is to assist policy

more general

175

decisions on defensive preparedness and contingency planning, including preemptive actions – ranging from diplomatic *démarches* to pre-positioning of military equipment and supplies – in order to manage the risks of potential threats.

How are the two aspects of warning analysis related? The ultimate goal of effective warning is to protect US interests. Incident surprise can amplify damage, at times tragically. Fore-knowledge can either avert or reduce damage. But not always, absent appropriate preparedness for dealing with a specific threat once it is identified. Effective strategic warning is often needed to ensure the subsequent availability of an appropriate level of resources for detecting and preventing specific attacks and harmful developments. That is, good strategic warning has the potential to enhance both the ability of intelligence analysis to provide tactical warning and the preparedness of government and society to avoid or blunt damage.

That said, a strong historical argument can be made that the occurrence of incident or tactical surprise can be reduced but not eliminated. Even the best and most focused of intelligence services cannot expect to penetrate every plot or otherwise anticipate every damaging incident. Witness the number of successful terrorist attacks against Israel.

Offensive forces – the perpetrators of military or terrorist attacks, for example – learn lessons from past attempts about how, and where, to achieve surprise, just as defensive forces – US intelligence, policymaking, war-fighting, and law enforcement professionals – learn lessons about prevention. Moreover, simple applications of denial and deception activities and innovations in means and modes of attack by adversarial forces (such as suicide missions) can increase the likelihood of incident surprise.

Some observers would argue that the absence of an attack on US territory since 9/11 is more a matter of the deliberated strategic decision of al-Qa'ida and related terrorist organizations not to attack, than of their inability to strike in, say, Washington, New York, or Los Angeles, as they have in Madrid and London.

Regarding the onset of dramatic developments abroad that could damage US interests – internal strife that threatens friendly governments, economic crises with global implications, outbreaks of regional wars – the substantive uncertainty that reflects the complexity and fluidity of relationships and rationales of foreign groups and leaders also can hinder timely specific warnings.

Finally, it is no easy matter for analysts who are convinced they have a sound tactical warning case to galvanize policy officials to defensive action. Distraction of other calls on policy officials' attention, their remembrance of unavoidable occurrence of warnings that proved to be false alarms or aborted positives, and their concern about high opportunity costs for what could prove to be "unnecessary" defensive measures can cause rejection or delay of preventive actions to ward off a specific threatening incident.

What role for analysis if incidents of tactical surprise are inevitable? A robust strategic warning effort can serve as the indispensable analytic supplement to tactical warning – by spurring, in advance of specific, harmful developments, preemptive and defensive measures that can mute the negative consequences of tactical surprise.

To paraphrase a Cold War observation by an academic specialist on warning about the danger of a surprise Soviet military attack on either Western Europe or the US homeland:

> If surprise can succeed despite robust tactical warning, then defense must utilize effective strategic warning to prepare to succeed despite surprise.

Think in terms of the analogy between homeland defense and household defense. A concerned and resourceful homeowner as a rule cannot know whether, when, and how a burglar or other predator will strike. Despite lack of incident foreknowledge, however, the homeowner (1) can deter many planned "attacks" by investing in ample outdoor and indoor lighting, (2) can abort attempted attacks with superior door and window locks, and (3) can reduce the damage should a break-in nonetheless occur through an alarm system, which will encourage the burglar to grab-and-run, rather than ransack. And if concern for security rises sharply – say, the neighborhood becomes a more accessible and attractive target – still more protection can be effected: neighborhood patrols, gated communities, coordination of police and resident intelligence.

That said, the challenges of effective strategic defense are formidable. The homeowner, like the national security policymaker, has got to be willing to pay the direct costs of heightened defense without being sure an attack will ever take place. Assuming a practical limit to expenditures to prepare for plausible but seemingly unlikely events, how much for flood insurance, for fire insurance, and so forth? *Insurance, ..*

Next, what of opportunity costs – inconvenience, reduced alternative consumption and reduced savings? And what of resistance to effort and expenditures (even ridicule) from inside and outside the household? Finally, as the responsible "policymaker," how best is the concerned homeowner to garner diagnostic information and expert judgment for informed decision making and action taking?

The imperative to seek more effective strategic warning

The terrorist attack of 11 September 2001 is fairly represented in open source commentary as a tactical surprise – if nothing else, a reminder of the inherent limitations of tactical warning. Judging whether there was a failure of strategic as well as tactical warning is a more difficult task, and depends largely on where one places the goal posts.

Evidence on the public record, especially *The 9/11 Commission Report* (2004), indicates that intelligence officials communicated clearly and often in the months before 11 September the judgment that the likelihood of a major al-Qa'ida terrorist attack *within* the United States was high and rising. The Commission Report cites George Tenet, then the Director of Central Intelligence, as saying that in the summer of 2001 "the system was blinking red."

The public record also indicates that a number of responsible policy officials had been convinced, from intelligence warnings and their other sources of information and analysis, that US vulnerability to such attack had grown markedly. Both governmental and non-governmental studies, in recognition of a mounting terrorist threat, had begun to recommend national investment in numerous protective measures – tougher air passenger scrutiny, greater cooperation between and among intelligence and law enforcement agencies, and stricter enforcement of immigration laws, to name three.

The bottom line? Even after taking account of inevitable hindsight bias that accompanies bureaucratic recollection of prescience of dramatic events, the public record indicates (1) strategic warning was given, (2) warning was received, (3) warning was believed, at least by some recipients. Yet commensurate protective measures were not taken. *sw ≠ action*

Whether in theory this represents a strategic warning success or failure by intelligence, the fact is that the national security components of the government, intelligence included, failed to convince the President and his top aides to generate appropriate, prudent, and affordable measures for increased preparedness.

Some observers have characterized the surprise attending the 11 September terrorist attack as an instance of *inconvenient warning*. The President's top policy officials, while convinced at one level of engagement with the warning process of the reality of the threat, did not commit

[handwritten margin note: policy / affects the / way intel. is / taken]

fully to the warning as perhaps they would have if the judgment reflected their own policy priorities. They apparently were unwilling to divert their attention from an agenda of domestic and other national security issues. And, if pressed, they were not ready to pay the political and economic costs of direct expenditures, public inconvenience, disapproving special interests, and the always difficult task of breaking bureaucratic rice bowls.

It took tragedy to effect what intelligence warning failed to do: move a concerned government and polity to act like the aforementioned concerned homeowner. That is, take inconvenient and expensive measures to deter or at least limit the damage to an attack that may never come: by no means not all the measures recommended by thoughtful observers such as the 9/11 Commission, but nonetheless defensive measures that, again, intelligence warning failed to launch. For one thing, the magnitude of intelligence resources and the skills of collectors and analysts devoted to monitoring and countering the operations of terrorist organizations now dwarfs pre-9/11 levels.

Whatever the ultimate judgment of the adequacy of measures taken to protect against the current and ongoing threat from international terrorism, a critical examination is needed to determine the adequacy of the doctrine, mechanisms, and practices for strategic warning against other potential dangers. This includes the challenge of timely policy action as well as effective intelligence warning.

The following recommendations address the two main aspects of the challenge:

[handwritten margin note: engage / pol. comm.]

1 How to reconstitute strategic warning analysis from essentially an intelligence function to a collaborative governmental responsibility – by engaging the policy community much more directly in every step of the strategic warning process.

[handwritten margin note: inc. analy. resources devoted to sw?]

How to expand and upgrade the analytic resources devoted to strategic warning, in order to ensure a distinctive intelligence contribution to policy decision-making and action-taking in response to warning.

Strengthening strategic warning

1 Clarify the warning mission

Any critical examination of the mission of warning analysis should give primacy of place to avoidance or limitation of damage – and not to the unrealistic standard of avoidance of surprise. In other words, as much as it may go against the grain of intelligence and national leaders and of the American public itself, the only realistic primary objective of an effective intelligence warning regime is to maximize damage limitation, not predictive accuracy.

Acquisition of foreknowledge to reduce incident surprise should be treated as an extremely important means to the larger goal of, when possible, avoiding damage, but when necessary, limiting damage to US interests. Security preparedness is also a means to the goal of avoidance or limitation of damage.

As indicated by the United States' relatively damage-free navigation of the Cold War, preparedness supports the goal of damage avoidance from surprise attacks mainly through the workings of deterrence. Preparedness advances damage limitation through erection of the means for appropriate preemptive offensive and post-attack defensive responses to all kinds of challenges to US interests.

Over the decades, the Intelligence Community has generated many worthy definitions of warning analysis. The one recommended here puts damage avoidance and limitation front and center. It also specifies *decision-enhancing assessments* as a requisite for a successful intelligence warning effort – that is, assessments with good potential to galvanize policy officials to take actions and invest in measures that help avoid or limit damage.

Warning analysis seeks to prevent or limit damage to US national security interests via communication of timely, convincing, and decision-enhancing intelligence assessments that assist policy officials to effect defensive and preemptive measures against future threats and to take action to defend against imminent threats.

Decisions on whether and how to take action and the effectiveness of actions taken remain the responsibility of policymakers and action-takers. The analysts' responsibility is to facilitate decisionmaking and action-taking processes by providing, for example, disciplined (that is, well-argued) depiction of perceived changes in the likelihood or means of the threat and identification and evaluation of US options for preempting, blunting, or otherwise limiting damage from the threat.

2 Increase resources for strategic warning

Which is the more important intelligence responsibility – tactical or strategic warning? A strong argument can be made that the vital role of technical and clandestine intelligence collection in executing tactical warning justifies its dominant command, over the decades and especially post-9/11 on analytic resources.

But intelligence scholars have argued that a government adequately prepared to respond to hostile action and other damaging events which receives no warning of a specific incident is better able to limit damage than a government that receives warning but is inadequately prepared to respond.

In 2004 testimony to the 9/11 Commission, then DCI George Tenet made a similar point by indicating that "good intelligence" (timely warning) would not by itself protect America. *both needed* "Good homeland defense" (preparedness to respond) was also needed.

Recognition of the need to prepare well in advance to meet threats to US interests calls into question the extent to which the current division of analytic resources favors tactical over strategic warning – in terms of *dedicated* personnel, perhaps in the order of 100 to 1.

When pressed, the leaders of CIA's Directorate of Intelligence and other Intelligence Community analytic units are likely to argue that every analyst is a warning officer. Probably so, if intent rather than effect is the standard. At the agency, at least through the 1980s, a rough balance prevailed between tactical and strategic warning, if all forms of event-reporting and crisis management support were generously defined as tactical warning, and all forms of research and estimative work were defined as strategic warning, with similar generosity.

The major post-Cold War downsizing of analytic resources in the 1990s seemed to cut much more sharply into strategic warning analysis and in-depth and long-term analysis generally than it did into tactical warning analysis and overall current policy support efforts. Understandably, the response of intelligence leaders to the 11 September 2001 terrorist attacks was to effect a sizeable additional shift of a substantially enhanced total work force into the tactical warning and current analysis efforts.

For the Intelligence Community to meet its professional responsibility to prevent and limit damage to national security in the uncertain years ahead, leaders now should expand substantially and quickly the community's capacity to execute a more robust strategic warning effort. This includes attention to (1) doctrinal development to clarify the essential characteristics of effective warning, (2) staffing levels for in-depth and over-the-horizon analysis generally and

179

thus potentially for strategic warning as well, (3) career incentives, (4) continuous leadership engagement, and (5) especially tradecraft training to ensure that policy officials receive warning analysis they see as *decision-enhancing*.

Even before 11 September 2001, Secretary of Defense Donald Rumsfeld, whose position affords considerable influence over the partitioning of intelligence resources, called for increased effort to avoid strategic surprise. Paul Wolfowitz, Deputy Secretary of Defense during 2001–2005, is long on record with charging intelligence analysts with "helping policymakers decide which seemingly unlikely threats to pay serious attention to." Since 11 September, other key policy officials have made statements that indicate they have joined this chorus.

Ironically, the war on terrorism and the Iraqi war have widened the gap between words and action. However, the reorganization of the Intelligence Community symbolized by the establishment of a Director of National Intelligence (DNI) supported by a large staff to effect, among other objectives, improvements in the quality and utility of analysis, has led recently to two promising initiatives.

First, CIA's Directorate of Intelligence, according to public statements by its leaders, and other Intelligence Community analytic units plan to increase substantially the resources dedicated to in-depth and long-term analysis. Second, as previously indicated, according to a publicly available pronouncement, the DNI is considering a major initiative in support of strategic warning, as this chapter is written (April 2006). Will the two initiatives be productively joined?

3 Strengthen strategic warning as sound estimative analysis

Intelligence analysts, as strategic warning officers, often have made a convincing case for a judgment that a danger overlooked or understated by policymakers is likely to occur. Analysts leverage the strengths of the warning process at its best – mastery of collection guidance, collaborative multidisciplinary substantive expertise, well-structured all-source information, sound tradecraft for dealing with uncertainty, awareness of but some distance from the daily policymaker pressures to "get things done." The analysts produce an assessment about a looming danger that is prescient, timely, and convincing, and thus provides a window for effective policy decision and action.

Many of the examples on the public record of strategic warning as sound estimative analysis – such as the successful US defusing of India–Pakistan war preparations in the early 1990s – depend on exploitation of all-source information that, while not conclusive, allows the accomplished analyst to make an estimative judgment about a looming danger with high confidence. As a rule, it takes both credible evidence and sound inference to galvanize responsible policy officials into action.

While the overall record on "making the call" is a respectable one, doctrinal emphasis on a straight-line estimative prediction – development of the seemingly most likely outcome – has been the root cause of high-profile warning failures. The analysts' expertise, in effect, is trumped by the hazards of estimating. Available data on a complex issue is inherently ambiguous, open to manipulation by denial and deception, and otherwise subject to misinterpretation. The analysts' understanding of how things usually work regarding the issue under scrutiny, what one academic observer calls "normal theory," does not adequately account for seemingly unprecedented or exceptional developments, often driven by foreign actors' distinctive – even unrealistic or self-defeating – risk-benefit calculations.

This was more or less the case with the September 1962 Intelligence Community estimate that judged the Soviet Union would not install nuclear weapons in Cuba – a warning failure that could have triggered nuclear warfare. The US analysts, for example, did not know the extent to which Nikita Khrushchev as dominant Soviet decision-maker was misinformed about the seriousness of US warnings against the introduction into Cuba of offensive nuclear weapons. Even more important, US analysts did not know that Khrushchev was more fearful of his own military, which could not tolerate the US advantage in deliverable nuclear weapons, than of the risks involved in his Caribbean gambit.

Increased numbers of better-trained analysts, greater leadership engagement, and more robust warning tradecraft (addressed in sections below) will improve the success record in terms of making the right call as well as galvanizing policy officials to timely action. But as with tactical warning, strategic warning as sound estimative analysis will inevitably produce what are perceived to be "intelligence failures" that serve in turn to reduce the willingness of policy officials to rely on intelligence warnings. = more

An admittedly apocryphal story has Sherman Kent, chief architect of the 1962 Cuban Missile Estimate, soon thereafter visiting the office of John McCone, Director of Central Intelligence. Kent looked out the Director's vast seventh-floor picture window, and said, "Boss, it looks like rain." McCone who had had serious doubts about the Estimate, replied, "How would *you* know?"

4 Strengthen strategic warning as alternative analysis

Almost by definition, an effective strategic warning effort should also be focused on threats to US security interests that are surrounded by considerable, even impenetrable, substantive uncertainty – potential threats that may or may not mature. Here, the analysts address a danger they judge to be plausible and potentially highly damaging, but about the details of which – timing, location, modalities, triggers, indicators, indeed, likelihood – they retain important doubts.

Analysts address some issues, such as the threat of a Soviet nuclear attack during the Cold War, because they judge that the danger, however unlikely, could prove to be so devastating that it has to be better understood. On other issues, analysts warn when they judge a danger was previously understated or has increased in magnitude or likelihood, and when policy officials seek help in refining contingency plans. But, again, for these strategic warning exercises, the danger addressed is either judged unlikely under prevailing conditions or is seen as too highly dependent on poorly understood factors and contingencies to assess with confidence the likelihood of its occurrence.

Strategic warning analysis, in these circumstances, should be treated as a branch of "alternative analysis," in that its tradecraft places emphasis on disciplined, if "alternative," tradecraft for assessment of developments that are seen as unlikely or indeterminate. Related forms of alternative or challenge analysis – including High Impact–Low Probability Analysis, What-If Analysis, Gaps in Information Analysis, and Devil's Advocacy – share the requirement with warning analysis to marshal all-source information, expert insight, and specialized tradecraft to illuminate developments that analysts judge to be plausible, potentially damaging or advantageous for US interests, but seemingly unlikely.

In recent years, CIA's Directorate of Intelligence and other Intelligence Community analytic units, in response to criticism of analytic performance, have increased tradecraft training in and production of alternative analysis. In fact, the requirement to establish alternative analysis units throughout the Intelligence Community is mandated in the Intelligence Reform Act of 2004. Unfortunately, the value of alternative analysis for strategic warning has not been fully realized.

The connection of alternative analysis to strategic warning would be to use the methodologies developed for challenge analysis to provide distinctive intelligence support to policy officials as they undertake the difficult task of deciding whether and how to prepare for threats to US strategic interests before the advent of specific indicators rings an alarm bell.

Perhaps High Impact–Low Probability Analysis (HILP) is the alternative analysis format best suited for adoption for strategic warning. With HILP, analysts put aside projections of developments they think likely to happen, and focus on developments their policy clients do not want to happen; in effect the potential developments they fear would be the most damaging to US interests. A military attack against a country the United States is treaty-bound to defend would be one such event; collapse of civil authority in a country in which the United States has major economic interests would be another example.

Under HILP, analysts develop one or more scenarios for the seemingly low-probability event, spelling out the constituent plausible assumptions and trigger events that could lead to or increase the likelihood of the high-impact development. As a strategic warning document, an HILP assessment would include a series of signposts that would help both analysts and policy officials monitor momentum either toward or away from the unwanted development. Additionally, analysts could use their expertise on the characteristics and predilections of foreign countries and players to provide, in cost-benefit terms, a list of measures the United States could take to deter the unwanted development and to limit damage if it occurred.

Here, too, there is reason to believe Intelligence Community programs that connect strategic warning to an enhanced alternative analysis effort will receive policymaker support. A key proposal of the 1998 *Report of the Commission to Assess the Ballistic Missile Threat to the United States*, which was chaired by Donald Rumsfeld, now Secretary of Defense, called for expanded efforts by analysts to address high-impact dangers they thought unlikely. More specifically the report called on the policymakers to probe analysts to ensure they were not too quick to dismiss dangers simply because of a lack of hard evidence or clear precedent.

5 Assign strategic warning efforts to regular analytic units

Most of an expanded strategic warning effort should be undertaken by analytic production units also responsible for tactical warning and other analytic deliverables. The goal should be to increase the number of analysts engaged in strategic warning and their skills in meeting its challenges – not the complexity of the table of organization. Closeness to colleagues engaged in assessment of the same countries, non-state entities, and global issues would provide benefits to the warning analyst in terms of policymaker contacts, databases, and collective substantive expertise.

Multi-function production units, admittedly, would face the age-old danger that crisis support analysis and feeding of the "daily pubs" will drive out strategic warning and other forms of in-depth analysis, either by management fiat or by implicit career-enhancing incentives. Intelligence leaders would have to get the word out to middle managers that Peter is not to be robbed to pay Paul.

Production unit analysts engaged in strategic warning at times will occupy the uncomfortable position of seeming to dispute and discredit not only their colleagues' established assumptions and conclusions about the issue at hand, but also their analytic acuity. This bureaucratic awkwardness would warrant an important role as well for specialized entities, including the National Intelligence Officer for Warning. One contribution here would be to help promote special formatting and a standardized explanation of the purposes and modalities for strategic warning assessments.

Another contribution would be to provide temporary work spaces for line analysts to engage in a strategic warning effort, that would both surround them with informed and supportive warning specialists and remove them from the event-driven production pressures of their home unit.

separate sw officers from pressures of home unit

6 Expand tradecraft training and research

A sizeable reduction in numbers of analysts was mandated by Congress in the 1990s, in search of a "peace bonus" to commemorate the end of the Cold War. Essentially, the process consisted of non-replacement of retiring veteran analysts.

A decade later, largely in response to the events of 9/11, Congress mandated a sizeable expansion in analyst numbers. One result of otherwise compensating workforce trends is the existence of a much less experienced analytic cadre today than, say, in the 1970s and 1980s. CIA's Directorate of Intelligence, to its credit, has responded to the challenge of its dependency on a youthful workforce by moving to become a "learning organization." *→ now very young unexper.*

Many of the training courses offered to new and journeymen analysts help prepare them for the challenges of strategic warning analysis by focusing on the elements of analytic tradecraft needed to assess substantive uncertainties and to ensure credibility with policy officials. Nonetheless, a special strategic warning training course is needed to help speed the readiness of analysts to meet these generalized challenges and to gain familiarity with specialized character of strategic warning assessments both as estimative analysis and alternative analysis.

The course content should probably include an exploration in depth of the character and analytic management of substantive uncertainty. This could include the implications for warning of recent academic studies that convert the concepts of complexity theory from mathematics and physics to political, economic, and societal systems. Especially over, say, a five-year time span, the course of, say, complex foreign political systems can be affected profoundly by players, relationships, and trends not yet on the analysts' scope. How, then, do warning analysts address these "unknown unknowns"?

The strategic warning training course should also contain a "lessons learned" segment; in effect, successes and failures in strategic warning. The course additionally should provide an opportunity for students to outline an approach to a strategic warning assessment in their areas of substantive responsibility.

The analysts' grasp of specialized skills for disciplined assessments of seemingly unlikely dangers would be key to distinguishing strategic warning analysis from exercises in worst-case speculation. As addressed in detail below, the analysts' strategic warning effort is most likely to generate timely action if policy professionals have an analytic stake in all steps of the process – from selection of priority warning issues to co-ownership of indicator or signpost lists that monitor changes in the likelihood of a threat. Policymakers would be more likely to engage in such close collaboration if intelligence analysts demonstrated specialized expertise that generates distinctive analytic insights for managing substantive uncertainty and for the other challenging tasks of strategic or over-the-horizon planning.

To strengthen policymaker reliance on strategic warning, research initiatives are much needed to expand the armory of warning analysis tradecraft. Whereas much has been written about the causes of warning failure, a search for a science or even a theory for strategic warning success is well beyond reach. What can be developed are doctrinal and skills refinements that give all participants in the strategic warning process – collectors, analysts, policy officials – increased confidence in identifying, weighing, and tracking threats. For the most part, tradecraft developments that serve to improve the quality and policy utility of warning as alternative analysis (for example, HILP) would also improve intelligence professionals' performance of warning as sound estimative analysis.

One promising area for more robust analytic tradecraft would be techniques for evaluating the authenticity and diagnosticity of information.

Regarding authenticity, use of denial and deception (D&D) is usually central to the planning of US adversaries, because of its effectiveness in compensating for other power weaknesses. From obsessive operational security to distractive reports about planned attacks overseas, D&D probably increased the odds for success for the 9/11 terrorists. The Intelligence Community has made important strides in understanding how a less powerful opponent can use D&D against the United States. The main frontier for improving warning analysis is conversion of this awareness into practical analytic tradecraft for identifying and countering an adversary's manipulation of specialized intelligence collection and open source information.

Regarding diagnosticity, the rapid expansion of both classified and open source information can be a burden as well as a benefit to the warning analyst. More than ever, powerful yet practical user-friendly tradecraft is needed to distill information that serves as reliable "signal" from the mass of collected information that is distracting "noise." Sharper analyst insight on what potentially collectable and accessible information holds the key to reducing substantive uncertainty about potential security threats must then be used to rationalize intelligence and open source collection efforts.

7 Encourage warning analysts to engage in action analysis

Also to ensure that policy clients take strategic warning seriously, analysts have to be better prepared to address with distinctive intelligence value-added the "so-what" of their assessments. This includes addressing not only the likely implications of a threat to US interests but also, in cost–benefit terms, measures the United States can take to reduce the likelihood and magnitude of potential damage.

Managers and senior analysts regularly join in policymaker efforts to identify and evaluate alternative measures the United States can take to avoid or limit damage from developments that would harm security interests. This form of support, variously called *action, implementation*, or *opportunities* analysis, is usually delivered in oral forums – including telephone exchanges, in-office briefings, teleconferences, and interagency working groups and other decision-oriented meetings. The analyst's professional role in action analysis is to identify and evaluate; policy-makers retain the professional responsibilities to recommend and choose.

All analysts, especially strategic warning analysts, have got to be well trained in the doctrines and skills associated with this professional division of labor – in effect, a replacement for the previously imbedded doctrine that sets a wall of separation between intelligence analysis and policy-support activities in any guise. Once analysts sense that policy clients have bought into the need to review defensive preparedness and contingency planning in response to a strategic warning effort, the analysts can best ensure continued contact and guidance by directing their substantive and tradecraft expertise to these "so-what-can-we do" issues.

The main intelligence asset that analysts bring to the table for action analysis is their expert knowledge of the history and culture, political and leadership dynamics, and back-stage agents of influence of the countries and organizations that could threaten US interests. While this substantive expertise is also central to the risk analysis phase of strategic warning, the goal in action analysis is to help US policy officials determine how best to demarche, divert, deter, disrupt, and generally leverage a threatening foreign entity.

One thing needed here is more extensive analyst training in the instrumentalities of US power and influence and in decisionmaking processes regarding their use. Agency analysts have come a long way from the point some 25 years ago, when a CIA Deputy Director for Intelligence observed that his analysts knew how every government in the world worked – except their own. But a continued shyness toward including action analysis in written assessments probably reflects analysts' insecurity about their understanding of the policymaking process as well as about the ethics of their selective engagement in the process.

analysts don't understand decision-making in govt.
ethical dilemma

8 Select strategic warning issues carefully

If the goal is to provide distinctive analytic values that policymakers incorporate into their national security decision-making and action-taking, the strategic warning effort will be resource intensive. In the CIA context, the analysis will usually require a multidisciplinary team of analysts, well connected to the collection community, analytic colleagues in other agencies and peer-level policy staffers. The National Intelligence Officer for Warning could serve to provide guidance on tradecraft and process, and to ensure access to and credibility with key policy officials and agency leaders.

The resource requirements for effective strategic warning efforts, thus, will dictate careful selection of topics – in a sense a triage approach. As a rule, topic selection should favor the national security threats deemed potentially most damaging rather than those viewed as most likely – that is, the plausible developments whose consequences well-informed policymakers fear most. Again, the main value of an expanded *strategic* warning effort should be damage limitation over the long haul and not short-term predictive accuracy. *long-term*

most damaging > most likely

This is not a call to avoid working on what was described earlier as strategic warning as sound estimative analysis. What is to be avoided are disguised "training exercises," where the warning mission is used for analysts to build their credentials on a subject with nothing much new to convey to well-informed policymakers who already have the dangers addressed well in mind.

Illustrative examples for selection of topics on developments that could do the most damage to US security interests include the prospects for a collapse of political stability in countries of concern (either those generally supportive or generally adversarial to US interests); and for the outbreak of regional warfare in potentially explosive regions such as the Middle East and South Asia. Catastrophic terrorism, environmental, or humanitarian disasters that have a global reach, and economic and societal breakdowns in world powers such as Russia or China might also be topics on which strategic warning analysis could play a major role in identifying, assessing, and monitoring major potential threats to US security interests.

thinking big or "picture"

Initially, while strategic warning resources are still scarce, policymakers should play a major role in topic selection, to ensure their active participation in the warning analysis process. That is, a production unit's main policy clients should be polled on what developments they fear most – the ones that keep them awake at night.

Once policymakers gain confidence in the utility of a strengthened strategic warning regime, and closer ties between the warning and policy planning process are thereby established, more of the initiative for topic selection can reside with intelligence producers. Even then, validation of topic selection should be obtained from the policy clients, whose active participation is required for an effective strategic warning effort.

The objective is not to forfeit the responsibility of the intelligence professional to call policymakers' attention to dangers they seem to be overlooking or understating. It is, rather, to increase the likelihood the busy policymaker's attention will be gained when the intelligence professional issues such warnings.

185

9 Expand policymaker role in warning analysis

Relations between the strategic warning and the policy-planning processes have demonstrated considerable variation over the decades, depending in good measure on the centrality and urgency of the threat addressed. At one extreme, during the Cold War, the intelligence analysis and policy-planning cycles regarding estimating and countering future threats from Soviet strategic and theater weapons development were closely tied and timed both to the Department of Defense yearly procurement planning schedules and to Congressional budgetary calendars.

Longstanding crises, such as the Vietnam War, produced more *ad hoc* relationships – but lines of communication that regularly put intelligence community assessment and policy community planning on the same page, even if not always harmoniously.

At times, strategic warning analysis and contingency policymaking develop useful lines of connection on certain issues through the efforts of individuals in both camps who actively seek it and institutions such as interagency working groups that are charged with effecting it.

That said, strategic warning on most issues, most of the time, has largely been an intelligence function, the practitioners of which hope will be taken seriously in policymaking. And contingency planning has essentially been a policy function, the practitioners of which hope to garner useful Intelligence Community support. While the record shows a mixture of successful and unsuccessful connections, policy community criticism of strategic warning comes across more vividly in the record than does praise.

Sherman Kent, arguably the most respected observer of analytic practice during CIA's first decades (1950s and 1960s), put his finger on the cause of disconnects between what he referred to as "Warner" and "Warnee."

- It is a lot easier for the Warner to warn than for the Warnee to get ready to take action.
- Realize that the Warnee has a full-time job and is not looking for extra work or needless interruption of his regular duties. His circuits are already overloaded.
- Realize when the Warnee receives a warning and elects to act upon it, the least that he must do is to begin some very speedy contingency planning. For a minor crisis in [an] . . . African or Latin American republic the waves of activity will hit 100 officers.
- Mark well that the Warner's record of fallibility is well known to the Warnee.

Kent's observations would explain the two common complaints by concerned policy officials about strategic warning efforts in the decades immediately before 11 September 2001: (1) inadequate influence over the timing and focus of National Intelligence Estimates and other over-the-horizon assessments, and (2) concern that periodic warning reports showed inadequate sensitivity to the wrenching shift in defensive resources that would be required if the warnings were taken seriously.

Regarding timing, one former intelligence analyst who had crossed over to serve as a policy official observed that her analyst colleagues seemed not to understand that policy decisions will be held up for many reasons – but not for lack of a well-timed intelligence input.

Regarding periodic warning lists, one senior policymaker expressed his indignation at what he saw as the bureaucratic imperative to warn to meet weekly deadlines and quotas.

To overcome producer–consumer disconnects, strategic warning should be reconfigured, as advocated throughout this chapter, as a *governmental responsibility* rather than an intelligence responsibility. The policy officials who will have to make the challenging decisions about resource commitments for defense against future threats should have a direct role at every

[handwritten annotation: ^policy-makers need to take a more "all in" intel.]

phase of the strategic warning process, including (1) intelligence resource allocations, (2) topic selection, (3) general analytic standards, (4) specific warning methodologies, and (5) selection and monitoring of indicators of change in likelihood, impact, timing, and character of dangers.

Under a collaborative system, when participants judge warning thresholds to have been breached and difficult policy decisions have to be made, policy officials would see the strands of their own analytic thinking in the warning process ideally amplified by the all-source information, expert insights, and distinctive tradecraft of intelligence analysts.

A rough (and perhaps romanticized) model for the relationship would be the workings of the United Kingdom's Joint Intelligence Committee (JIC). The main JIC deliverable is a "Government Assessment," in all phases of which serving policy officials participate alongside intelligence professionals. The policy officials are supposed to wear their "intelligence hat" when appropriate, and when appropriate their "policy hat." *[handwritten: 7 in UK JIC]*

Would such a system eliminate the phenomenon of "inconvenient warning" in the United States – where the numbers of bureaucratic entities and people involved are greater and the lines of intelligence–policy communication more stretched out than in the United Kingdom? Probably not. But it should reduce its frequency, and also set up feedback loops and other mechanisms for continual refinements of the processes of intelligence–policy cooperation needed to underwrite effective strategic warning.

What of the dangers of policymaker domination of the strategic warning process, to the derogation of analysts' integrity and specialized expertise? The US record on certain highly contentious issues – Vietnam in the 1960s, Central America in the 1980s – is a reminder that professionals do not always wear the "appropriate hat." ✰

What is needed here is commitment of top leaders of the intelligence and policy camps – perhaps with a push from Congress – to a regime of zero tolerance of abuses of established warning ethics down the line. On their own, analysts can warrant policymaker respect for their integrity by demonstrating command of distinctive warning expertise and tradecraft that help get the difficult contingency planning job done. In any case, in an era defined by surprise and uncertainty, walls that promote analysts' irrelevance in the name of protecting their integrity will not serve the National Interest. ✰

Note on sources

For a thorough examination of the 11 September terrorist attacks and recommendations for improving homeland security:

The 9/11 Commission Report: Final Report of the National Commission on Terrorist Attacks Upon the United States, Official Government Edition [2004].

For a description of CIA analytic reforms including increased emphasis on indepth or "strategic" analysis:

Kringen, John, "How We've Improved Itelligence: Minimizing the Risk of 'Group Think'," *Washington Post*, 3 April 2006.

For a series of views on warning, including those of three former National Intelligence Officers for Warning:
"Strategic Warning," *Defense Intelligence Journal* v. 7, no. 2 (Fall 1998).

For an explanation of High Impact–Low Probability analysis and alternative analysis generally:
George, Roger Z. "Fixing the Problem of Analytical Mind-Sets: Alternative Analysis," *International Journal of Intelligence and Counterintelligence* v. 17, no. 3 (Fall 2004).

The following publications by the author address the concept and practice of strategic warning:
Davis, Jack, *The Challenge of Managing "Uncertainty": Paul Wolfowitz on Intelligence–Policy Relations*, CIA, Product Evaluation Staff (March 1995).
Davis, Jack, *Improving CIA Analytic Performance: Strategic Warning*, CIA, Sherman Kent Center for Intelligence Analysis, Occasional Papers, v. 1, no. 1 (2002).
Davis, Jack, *Sherman Kent's Final Thoughts on Analyst–Policymaker Relations*, CIA, Sherman Kent Center for Intelligence Analysis, Occasional Papers, v. 2, no. 3 (2003).
Davis, Jack, *Strategic Waning: If Surprise is Inevitable, What Role for Analysis*, CIA, Sherman Kent Center for Intelligence Analysis, Occasional Papers, v. 2, no. 1 (2003).
Davis, Jack, *Uncertainty, Surprise, and Warning*. CIA, Product Evaluation Staff (February 1996).

14

Achieving all-source fusion in the Intelligence Community

Richard L. Russell

The surprise attack of 9/11 is seen by many as a failure of the multitude of American intelligence agencies – collectively and euphemistically called the Intelligence Community (IC) – to funnel their separate intelligence collection streams into a common pool. These observers argue that had the various intelligence collection agencies shared their information more widely and deeply with sister intelligence agencies, analysts might have been better able to put together or "fuse" raw intelligence reports into a finished strategic intelligence assessment which could have warned more concretely President Bush and his key national security lieutenants of al-Qaeda's plans and intentions. In post-9/11 parlance, this failure to fuse intelligence is commonly referred to as the failure to "connect the dots." *→ failure of all-source 9/11 & WWII*

The tragic irony is that the Intelligence Community's institutional foundations were laid in 1947 in large measure to ensure that US intelligence collection was fused by civilian analysts to form strategic intelligence for the commander-in-chief. A root cause of the Japanese surprise attack on Pearl Harbor in 1941 was the failure of the army and navy intelligence services as well as the State Department to share intelligence from their field collectors.[1] The United States also lacked an institutional "clearing house" to put intelligence puzzle pieces together to accurately assess Japan's strategic plans and intentions. The National Security Act of 1947 created the largely civilian Central Intelligence Agency (CIA) to be principally responsible for the all-source intelligence fusion for the president and his advisers. *meant to produce "fusion"*

Just as the intelligence failure of 1941 sparked intelligence reforms of 1947, the intelligence failure of 2001 spawned the intelligence reforms of 2005. The creation of the Director of National Intelligence (DNI) is the reform that has captured the most public and government attention.[2] The new DNI post represents the de facto demotion of the head of the CIA, who had been for nearly sixty years "dual-hatted" as the Director of Central Intelligence (DCI) responsible as the president's principal intelligence adviser, the director of the entire IC, as well as the head of the CIA. The DNI, Ambassador John Negroponte, has orchestrated numerous changes to the IC. The DNI is now in charge of the National Intelligence Council (NIC), which had been an advisory panel to the director of CIA. Negroponte also has created the National Collection Service (NCS), the Open Source Center (OSC), and the National Counterterrorism Center (NCTC), to name the largest changes.

Great public and government faith has been placed in the creation of the DNI, which many see as the cure to all that ailed the old IC and its failure to competently fuse all-source intelligence. A recent American public opinion poll, for example, found that "Some 65 percent of Americans polled believe that reforming the intelligence services is the best way to strengthen U.S. security significantly" and that "a significant minority of Americans (41 percent) give the government an A or a B for already 'making the changes need to improve U.S. intelligence and spying."[3]

But is this faith well grounded in reality? Has the creation of the DNI and the new organizations under his wing improved the abilities of the IC to fuse intelligence and "connect all the dots"? And if all the measures taken fall short, what must the DNI do to ensure that the fusion of our intelligence today and tomorrow is qualitatively better than it was pre-9/11?

The nature of intelligence

The business of intelligence is shrouded in myth, much of which is perpetuated by spy novels and movies. The reality of intelligence is much more mundane. Boiled down to its essence, intelligence is information, which, in turn, is power. Intelligence or information comes from a variety of clandestine sources such as human spies, defense attaché and diplomatic reporting, satellite imagery, and intercepted communications and signals. These clandestine means are used to "steal" information that potentially hostile nation-states or trans-national terrorist groups want to hide from the United States. But intelligence also comes from publicly available information from newspapers, radio, periodicals, trade, political, economic, and military journals, as well as internet sources.

American intelligence during the Cold War heavily relied on clandestine intelligence sources. And indeed, the American Intelligence Community had a comparative advantage over private scholars and observers in providing intelligence to the president and his key foreign and security policy advisers because the Intelligence Community's primary target was the Soviet Union. Penetration of the thick veil of secrecy regarding Soviet foreign and security policy demanded that the United States use clandestine means to "steal" Soviet secrets. The contribution of human intelligence in the Cold War struggle with the Soviet Union has been exaggerated in the public's mind, but there can be no gainsaying the substantial contribution that technical intelligence collection, especially satellite imagery, contributed to the United States' understanding of Soviet strategic forces during the Cold War.

The American Intelligence Community during the Cold War neglected the exploitation of publicly available information, in part because it was enamored with clandestinely acquired and classified information. But the keenest observers of the Soviet Union recognized that a great deal could be gleaned about Soviet behavior and activities from public sources. Most notably, diplomat and scholar George Kennan, who was more than anyone else the intellectual father of the American strategy of containment against the Soviet Union, argued that

> the need by our government for secret intelligence about affairs elsewhere in the world has been vastly overrated. I would say that something upward of 95 percent of what we need to know could be very well obtained by the careful and competent study of perfectly legitimate sources of information open and available to us in the rich library and archival holdings of this country.[4]

And if that were true of publicly available information during the Cold War, it is doubly true for today's era of the global technological-informational revolution. The amount of and quality of satellite imagery readily available today in the commercial marketplace is staggering and has shattered the IC's Cold War monopoly on imagery. The resolution of commercial imagery today is so good that it would have been classified as Top Secret during the days of the Cold War. The amount of information, moreover, available with several computer key strokes today is astounding. Major internet-accessible sources of information include major university research libraries, official government and unofficial websites, and news agencies operating seven days per week and 24 hours per day, to tick off just a few. These sources alone contain loads of information that readily overwhelm the analytic capabilities of individual scholars and observers of international affairs. *Vaccum of info.*

The blizzard of public information – as well as a parallel surge in the quantity, if not quality, of clandestinely acquired information – puts enormous strain on intelligence analysts tasked with reviewing as much information as humanly possibly. Analysts are tasked to separate the significant from a mass of insignificant information, making analytic sense of situations and crises, anticipating the likely evolutions and outcomes of situations, as well as examining the implications for American security policy. And all this has to be packaged in succinct analyses readily consumable by harried policy makers, most importantly the president and his National Security Council.

Challenges of all-source fusion in the Intelligence Community

The fusing together of these unclassified and classified data streams in the American Intelligence Community primarily takes place at the CIA. The CIA was formed in 1947 as a type of central clearing house for intelligence analysis for the president in response, in large measure, to the Japanese surprise attack on Pearl Harbor in 1941. American intelligence was splintered between the Army, Navy, and State Departments. Each of these services had significant snippets of information that pointed toward a Japanese surprise attack. But they failed to share them and the United States had no analytic intelligence entity charged with putting all the snippets together to form a strategic intelligence assessment, which might have warned policy makers of Pearl Harbor's vulnerability to Japanese surprise attack.

The CIA plays the central role in fusing intelligence today, although the IC continues to suffer from agencies that allow them selves to be splintered by their intelligence collection responsibilities. In contemporary parlance, this splintering is called "stove piping." To name just the largest intelligence agencies and their collection responsibilities to get a sense of the "stove piping" in today's IC: the National Security Agency (NSA) intercepts and decodes communications; the National Geospatial-Intelligence (NGA) analyzes satellite imagery; the Defense Intelligence Agency (DIA) runs military defense attaché collection abroad; and the Department of State collects information from its diplomats overseas. The CIA also has a collection mission and is charged with recruiting spies to provide the United States with the plans and intentions of actual and potential adversaries.[5]

There is a tendency among these IC components to hoard information from the rest of the community. Often the IC components have a legitimate reasons to severely restrict the dissemination of especially sensitive information, in order to reduce the chances of leaks and public exposures which would be damaging to the "sources and methods" of information collection. But at other times, the hoarding practice is nurtured by petty bureaucratic rivalries. The State Department's Bureau of Intelligence and Research for example, has access to "No Distribution" and Ambassador-to-Secretary of State cables that are jealously hoarded and not routinely shared with its IC counterparts. The NSA is notorious inside the IC for strictly limiting the distribution of highly sensitive intercepted communications, which are often

191

restricted to the most senior IC officials and policy makers. Working level analysts throughout the IC often are ignorant of these reports and not given the opportunity to provide an analytic context for these raw intelligence reports to better inform policy makers and senior military commanders. The CIA also hoards its human intelligence reports, or HUMINT, from other agencies and prefers to share the most sensitive – or perhaps sensational would be a more accurate depiction – with senior-most intelligence officials and policy makers.

The CIA's operational directorates' bad hoarding habit also extends to relationships with analytic counterparts in the CIA's Directorate of Intelligence (DI). The then Directorate of Operations' (DO) failure to share full and accurate source descriptions on its reports was found to be a key factor in the CIA's failure to accurately assess the fact that Iraq's weapons of mass destruction programs were defunct in the run-up to the 2003 war. An internal CIA review on the way it handled pre-Iraq war intelligence criticized the longstanding practice of the DO that

> shields information about the identity, motivations and even access to information of its sources from the directorate of intelligence. The reports produced by the operations directorate typically identify sources only by numbers or code words and assess their credibility only in bland, generic terms, often without sharing details about sources' motivation or their precise access to information.[6]

The then head of DI told a meeting of CIA employees that the CIA internal review found "cases in which a single source has different source descriptions, increasing the potential for an analyst to believe they have a corroborating source."[7]

The DO argues that vague HUMINT source descriptions are needed to protect the source's identity and "sources and methods" should HUMINT reports leak to the public. There is merit to this argument, but in light of the longstanding failure of the DO to consistently or reliably deliver high-quality HUMINT intelligence, more than a handful of well-seasoned and skeptical CIA analysts suspect that more often than not the DO does not adequately inform the DI about HUMINT sources, in order to hide their shoddy and suspect quality. Although the DO has pledged to make more source information available, the head of the DI has subsequently changed and the DO is prone to return to its old bad habits after the controversy surrounding intelligence failures, such as that surrounding Iraq, dies down.

A notable exception to this problem of fusing HUMINT intelligence with analysis in the CIA has been in its Counter Terrorism Center (CTC). The CTC was established in the 1980s and was bureaucratically innovative because it collocated DO and DI officers and harnessed a synergetic relationship between human intelligence collectors and analysts. Both formal and informal professional collaborative relationships were fostered between DO and DI officers with their co-location in the CTC. DO officers benefited from DI analysts evaluating the quality of human intelligence reports as well as identifying collection gaps and opportunities. DI analysts, in return, received greater access to operational reporting such as the context of agent meetings, debriefings, and access to intelligence targets that often provides invaluable background information for analysis.

Beyond the office spaces of the CTC, the fusion of agency intelligence had increasingly suffered over the years due to excessive "compartmentalization" of intelligence. Intelligence, especially from HUMINT sources, was increasing "compartmented" or restricted to limited numbers of people who had a strict "need to know" the information. The use of intelligence compartments, much as the use of water-tight compartments on ships limits the amount of damage or flooding in the event of hull breaches, is intended to limit the amount of damage in the event of a public leak of intelligence. The CIA's over-compartmentalization of HUMINT reports was in large measure an over-reaction to the treason and espionage committed by the CIA's Aldrich Ames and the Federal Bureau of Investigation's (FBI) Robert Hansen, who both spied for numerous years for Soviet intelligence and severely compromised American intelligence operations against the Soviet Union. = *compartmentalizing inc.*

The excessive use of compartmentalization of intelligence caused an appreciable drop in the ability of CIA analysts to adequately do their jobs. The Rumsfeld Commission charged with investigating the IC's poor performance in analyzing the proliferation of ballistic missiles found that compartmentalization caused IC and CIA analysts not to have full access to all the information available in the IC, which had a substantive negative impact on performing their analytic duties. Intelligence is so compartmentalized, Rumsfeld complained, that wrong information is sometimes given to policy makers because analysts do not have access to all the relevant classified intelligence.[8]

While the CIA, NSA, and the State Department are guilty of misdemeanors in hoarding some of their intelligence – in fairness, they do share most of their collection with their sister intelligence agencies – the FBI is guilty of serial felonies. Although the FBI is a component of the IC, it traditionally has not shared intelligence in the IC, which gravely undermined the IC's ability to fuse intelligence analysis of al-Qaeda. As an illustration of this point, former National Security Council counterterrorism officials Daniel Benjamin and Steven Simon lament that:

> Every day a hundred or more reports from the CIA, DIA, the National Security Agency, and the State Department would be waiting in their computer queues when they [policy makers] got to work. There was never anything from the FBI. The Bureau, despite its wealth of information, contributed nothing to the White House's understanding of al-Qaeda. Virtually none of the information uncovered in any of the Bureau's investigative work flowed to the NSC.[9]

The FBI's stubborn unwillingness to contribute information into the IC's intelligence pool contributed significantly to the 9/11 tragedy. In July 2001 an FBI agent in Phoenix, Arizona astutely warned FBI headquarters in Washington, DC about "an inordinate number of individuals of investigative interest taking flight lessons" and he urged the FBI to collect data on flight training for foreign students in the US. In mid-August 2001 the Minneapolis, Minnesota FBI field office similarly warned of another foreign student taking flight lessons, who authorities now suspect was the planned twentieth hijacker of the 9/11 attacks.[10] Tragically, the FBI headquarters had neither an analytic bureaucratic culture nor a critical mass of analysts to "connect the Phoenix and Minneapolis dots." Had the FBI shared its field appraisals with the IC pool of information, moreover, an analyst at the CIA's CTC might have been able to backstop the FBI's lack of analytic expertise and put two and two together and anticipate that al-Qaeda was planning to use commercial aircraft in a domestic attack. Notwithstanding the public criticisms of the CIA's intelligence failure on 9/11, the FBI shares a far greater burden of guilt for failing to "connect the dots" which led to the national catastrophe. *FBI more resp. for 9/11 than CIA*

The FBI had long and defensively argued that it needed to hoard information to protect it from potential contamination and invalidate it for use in criminal prosecutions against al-Qaeda operatives. The FBI's bureaucratic culture and operational procedures were geared toward preserving evidence for criminal prosecutions in a court of law and not to using intelligence to preemptively make arrests before terrorist attacks occurred. The institutional and intellectual barrier that separated the FBI's law and enforcement mission from the IC's intelligence mission had come to be known as the "invisible wall."

The "invisible wall" might well have been less a product of American law than a construct made by the managerial practices. As Judge Richard Posner points out:

[B]efore 9/11 the CIA and FBI exaggerated the degree to which they were forbidden to share information, and the FBI exaggerated the degree to which its intelligence officers and its criminal investigators were forbidden to share information with one another. The Bureau was mainly worried about transgressing legal limitations on the disclosure of testimony before grand juries, and the CIA was mainly concerned lest secret information be disclosed in court proceedings. The failure to clarify the limits on sharing was a managerial failure, however, rather than a structural fault.[11]

The dismantling of the "wall" to facilitate the fusion of IC intelligence and ensure greater FBI participation therefore could have been simply accomplished by the director of the FBI ordering his people to share intelligence and by the director of the CIA ordering his people to keep tabs on the process to ensure implementation. This would have been a readily achieved fix for intelligence fusion, in comparison to the now massive undertaking entailed in the creation of the DNI office.

Above and beyond the hoarding of FBI's intelligence and some of the intelligence collected by State, NSA, and the CIA among others, the globalization era has added other dimensions to the all-source fusion challenge, dimensions with which intelligence officials and analysts still have not yet come to grips. Since the Cold War CIA, defense attaché, and State diplomatic reporting has been transmitted between foreign official and diplomatic posts and Washington via classified cable traffic. Today in the globalized world, an increasing quantity and quality of government communications takes place by telephones – using encrypted lines called Stu-IIIs – and e-mail exchanges, which are much easier and faster to use than cable traffic. This increasing flow of information bypasses the eyes of CIA analysts and increasingly leaves them "out of the loop" in major international crises in which the United States plays a major role. The CIA is, of course, not tasked to analyze American foreign policy, but CIA analysts need to take US actions into account if they are to effectively gauge the policy options and calculations of foreign actors. And the increasing use of e-mail and Stu-III calls jeopardizes the CIA's ability to carry out its core analytic tasks.

The task for those responsible for fusing intelligence, especially CIA analysts, is to ensure connectivity with their DO colleagues, counterparts elsewhere in the IC, as well as policy makers. The potential pitfalls of close working relationships with policy makers will be discussed below, but these informal networks between working-level analysts are the means by which the savviest CIA analysts keep tabs on counterparts and stay ahead of the information power curve. And when analytic differences of opinion arise, these informal networks can play constructive roles in ironing out disputes as well as refining assessments. The task of forging webs of informal relationships is daunting when it is added to the already heavy time burden of mining the torrent of unclassified and classified data streams for nuggets of intelligence and then converting these nuggets into analyses for US policy makers and military commanders.

Whether or not to "fuse" with policy makers

The fusing of intelligence inside the Intelligence Community is the process by which finished intelligence is produced. But the production of finished intelligence analysis is not an end in of itself. That analysis has to be shared with American policy makers. The relationship between all-source intelligence analysts – especially those at the CIA – and American policy makers is complicated. How these relationships govern both the provision of intelligence to policy makers and the role that policy makers play in setting intelligence agency research agendas has been a perpetually running debate among intelligence professionals since the inception of the American Intelligence Community in 1947.

The debate on the nature of the relationship between intelligence officials and policy makers that has emerged in the post–9/11 environment has taken on a new intensity. Some observers charge that policy officials unduly influence intelligence assessments to reflect policy, especially on Iraq's WMD programs and links to al-Qaeda in the run-up to the 2003 war against Iraq. Others counter that policy makers did not tell intelligence communities what their assessments were to be as much as they completely ignored intelligence assessments in making the decision to wage war against Iraq. Most notably on this score, former National Intelligence Officer for the Middle East Paul Pillar assesses, "What is most remarkable about prewar U.S. intelligence on Iraq is not that it got things wrong and thereby misled policymakers; it is that it played so small a role in one of the most important U.S. policy decisions in recent decades."[12]

This debate is too complex to fully assess here, but it is illustrative of the tensions between the two major schools of thought on intelligence–policy relations. One school is characterized as the Sherman Kent approach. Kent was a founding father of the National Intelligence Estimates process in the CIA's formative years. He wanted intelligence analysts to keep at arm's length from policy makers lest their analyses became tainted by policy interests. The contrasting school is the Robert Gates approach. Gates – who rose up the CIA's analytic ranks to eventually become Director of Central Intelligence after a stint as Deputy National Security Adviser for President George H. W. Bush – argued that intelligence analysts had to nurture relationships with policy makers in order to intimately know what was on their policy plates. Gates judged that such an awareness of policy was essential for producing timely and relevant intelligence analyses to help inform policy decisions.[13]

[margin note: 2 schools of thought]

The largest downside of the Sherman Kent school approach is irrelevance, which may well be a greater pitfall than the risks of political subservience run by the Gates school advocates. At the risk of stating the obvious, the Intelligence Community does not exist as an end of itself, but as a collection of institutions purposefully designed to serve national interests as articulated by policy makers supported by the American public. A strict adherence to the Kent School runs too great a risk of sanctioning an Intelligence Community that justifies its existence in terms of its own internal processes rather than the intelligence products that are relevant to the interests of policy makers trying to advance national political interests. In the final analysis, the ideal intelligence–policy relationship is a pendulum swing towards the Gates school and away from the Kent school. *[handwritten note: ideal = more towards Gates.]*

The illusion of bureaucratic fixes for all-source fusion problems

The 9/11 Commission recommended major bureaucratic additions and changes which it assessed would fix the IC's problems and improve future capabilities to fuse all-source intelligence and to "connect the dots." President Bush accepted much of the 9/11 Commission's recommendations and the American public believes that the government has "solved" its pre–9/11 intelligence problems. Sadly, that assessment probably is mistaken. And to add insult to injury, the 9/11 Commission-inspired changes, in many respects, threaten to make all-source fusion even more difficult.

The 9/11 Commission recommended the creation of more vertical layers in the IC, which does nothing to promote the working-level lateral sharing or pooling of intelligence. The 9/11 argued that the creation of the DNI would in theory improve the unity and co-ordination of the IC's various components. In practice, however, the creation of the DNI post

195

added several layers of management to what was an already top-heavy and bloated IC management structure. But these additions to the IC wiring diagram are essentially irrelevant to getting the FBI to share intelligence generated by field investigations with the CIA.

There could have been a much easier fix to the all-source fusion that eluded the 9/11 Commission. The president could have simply ordered his attorney general and the FBI director to share intelligence on al-Qaeda as well as ordered the Director of Central Intelligence – the post has since been demoted to the director of the CIA with the creation of the DNI – to monitor the FBI's intelligence-sharing to ensure compliance with the president's order. In other words, all that was needed was a robust exercise in executive power, not more flabby and lethargic bureaucracy to further dilute IC management accountability.

The 9/11 commission also recommended the creation of the National Counterterrorism Center (NCTC) under direct authority of the DNI. The NCTC combines the former Terrorist Threat Integration Center with counterterrorism elements from the CIA, FBI, and the Departments of Defense and Homeland Security.[14] Unfortunately, the NCTC will undoubtedly siphon away personnel from the Counterterrorism Center before the CIA has had a chance to replenish the expertise needed to carry out the analysis performed by its counterterrorism unit. The joint House-Senate Investigation of the 9/11 attacks had assessed that the CIA's CTC was staffed by too many young and inexperienced analysts to be able to do sophisticated strategic analysis of the al-Qaeda and terrorism threat.[15] Even more damaging to all-source fusion is that the NCTC will not have direct access to CIA's operational officers. The divide will break the important synergizing effects of collocating collection officers with analysts that CIA's CTC had successfully nurtured for some twenty years. That divorce over the longer run might give CIA's operational officers too much flexibility to drift off and collect human intelligence that is easiest to collect and of little consequence to US national security. Analysts looking over operational officers' shoulders had a tendency in CTC to pressure CIA operational officers to go for harder human targets whose potential information would be of more interest to American policy makers.

In 2005 the director of the CIA Porter Goss announced the establishment of the National Clandestine Service (NCS) at the CIA, taking over what has been the called the DO for most of the agency's history. The NCS will coordinate but not direct the increasing spying and covert activities conducted by the Pentagon and FBI.[16] A critical observer, however, looks at this move as little more than a change of the DO's nameplate in the hallway in CIA's headquarters building in Langley, Virginia. The odds are that notwithstanding the name change, the CIA will simply go about doing business as usual just as it has in the wake of other reforms in the past.

The DNI recently announced the Open Source Center (OSC), which is intended to "gather and analyze information from the Web, broadcasts, newspapers and other unclassified sources around the world."[17] But, much as in the case of the creation of the NCS, the creation of the OSC may be less than meets the eye. It probably reflects a name change for the former Foreign Broadcast Information Service (FBIS), and not a revolution in past CIA business practices.

The FBIS's service throughout the Cold War and post-Cold War periods was the unsung hero of American intelligence. It performed yeoman service in translating countless articles from the foreign media for the IC and made much of its output of unclassified translations available to scholars. The former head of the CIA's bin Laden unit, Michael Scheuer, paid appropriate tribute to FBIS by writing that, "Though intelligence-community leaders have little regard for unclassified information – it cannot be important if it is not secret, after all – the FBIS should take comfort in knowing that it provided as much warning about bin Laden's lethal intentions as any other community component."[18] The CIA's institutional bias has always been tilted toward espionage and analysis. And FBIS operations were expensive undertakings that always fell between the bureaucratic cracks and never benefited from the personnel and budget support its mission deserved, especially not in the era of globalization in which the floodgates of information have opened up. The DNI will have to keep a watchful eye to protect the new OSC from the budgetary poaching of the CIA's human intelligence operations and analysis.

A significant omission in the DNI's reforms is the creation of an IC strategic studies center. The Presidential Commission on Weapons Proliferation recommended the creation of "at least one not-for-profit 'sponsored research institute' to serve as a critical window into outside expertise for the Intelligence Community" and that its "primary purpose would be to focus on strategic issues."[19] Such a center would be separated from the taxing burden of current intelligence production, have more expertise, and be better positioned than the CIA rank-and-file to fuse the information flows from public and clandestine sources to form strategic intelligence assessments.

The National Intelligence Council (NIC), which for much of the IC's history was an expert advisory board for the DCI, had traditionally been seen as the unit best situated to perform strategic analysis. In 2005, the NIC was moved out from underneath the authority of the CIA director to directly serve the DNI. The NIC might be able to perform this strategic intelligence fusion function, but its manpower and resources would have to be significantly expanded. The NIC has long been too sparsely manned and funded to perform more than a modest role by serving as a focal point for coordinating IC-wide intelligence assessments called National Intelligence Estimates (NIEs) written by IC components. The NIC has generally lacked the analytic depth to write its own NIEs or write strategic intelligence analyses to critically challenge the analyses bubbling up from the separate intelligence agencies, the most active of which are CIA, DIA, and the State Department's INR.

A large and unsettled question regarding the IC changes in 2005–06 is whether the DNI will have the stature and strength needed to deliver bad intelligence news to the White House. Some observers argue that the DNI will be too beholden to the president to "speak truth to power." At the end of the day, the ability of the DNI to give the president bad news ultimately will depend by the personal integrity and courage of the individual that occupies the DNI's chair, not the bureaucratic wiring diagram of the DNI's position. *more dep. on personal integrity*

And finally, aside from media depictions the DNI has yet to demonstrate real power and authority as a "unified commander" of the Intelligence Community. One potentially bold and constructive move to exert real DNI control as well as to facilitate all-source fusion would be to order a cut roughly by half in the number of hierarchical bureaucratic layers inside Intelligence Community agencies. There has been a steady bloating and ossifying of IC bureaucracies for decades and the creation of the DNI and his subordinates has significantly added to the problem. Major eliminations of bureaucratic rungs would make flatter organization and more nimble organizations across the IC. The working-level analysts responsible for "connecting the dots" and fusing intelligence would be able to spend more time sharing and exchanging information laterally in the IC in flatter and less bureaucratically top-heavy organizations. As it stands today, these overworked and underpaid working-level analysts spend too much of their time pushing intelligence ponderously up through excessive layers of bureaucrats who rarely add anything of qualitative substance to intelligence. These layers of bureaucrats routinely retard the timely all-source fusion of intelligence, something that the IC can ill afford with the quickened pace of international security and policy-making in the globalized and wired world.

bureaucracy = bad for timeliness

DNI needs 2 speak even truth even when bad

The views expressed are those of the author and do not represent the policy or position of the National Defense University, the Department of Defense, or the US government.

Notes

1 For the landmark study of the Pearl Harbor intelligence failure, see Roberta Wohlstetter, *Pearl Harbor: Warning and Decision* (Stanford, CA: Stanford University Press, 1962).

2 For the recommendation as to the creation of the Director of National Intelligence position, see *The 9/11 Commission Report*, 411–415.

3 Daniel Yankelovich, "Poll Positions: What Americans Really Think about U.S Foreign Policy," *Foreign Affairs* 84, no. 5 (September/October 2005), 13.

4 George F. Kennan, "Spy and Counterspy," *New York Times*, 18 May 1997.

5 For excellent introductions to the IC labyrinth, see Loch K. Johnson, *Secret Agencies: US Intelligence in a Hostile World* (New Haven, CT: Yale University Press, 1996) and Mark M. Lowenthal, *Intelligence: From Secrets to Policy*, Third Edition (Washington, DC: Congressional Quarterly Press, 2006).

6 Douglas Jehl, "Despite a Pledge to Speed Work, Fixing an Internal Problem Takes Time at the CIA," *New York Times*, 10 June 2004, A12.

7 Douglas Jehl, "Stung by Exiles' Role, CIA Orders a Shift in Procedures," *New York Times*, 13 February 2004, A14.

8 Walter Pincus, "Rumsfeld: Intelligence 'Need to Know' Smacks of Not to Know," *Washington Post*, 5 May 1999, A29.

9 Daniel Benjamin and Steven Simon, *The Age of Sacred Terror: Radical Islam's War against America* (New York: Random House, 2003), 304.

10 R. Jeffrey Smith, "A History of Missed Connections," *Washington Post*, 25 July 2003, A14.

11 Richard A. Posner, *Preventing Surprise Attacks: Intelligence Reform in the Wake of 9/11* (New York: Rowman & Littlefield Publishers, Inc., 2005), 31–32.

12 Paul R. Pillar, "Intelligence, Policy, and the War in Iraq," *Foreign Affairs* (March/April 2006), 16.

13 The author is indebted to Richard Betts for clearly articulating these schools of thought. See his "Politicization of Intelligence: Costs and Benefits," Chapter 2 in Richard K. Betts and Thomas Mahnken (eds.), *Paradoxes of Strategic Intelligence: Essays in Honor of Michael I. Handel* (London: Frank Cass, 2003), 60–61.

14 Walter Pincus, "Bush's Intelligence Panel Gains Stature," *Washington Post*, 7 February 2005, A19.

15 House Permanent Select Committee on Intelligence and Senate Select Committee on Intelligence, *Report of the Joint Inquiry into the Terrorist Attacks of September 11, 2001* (Washington, DC: December 2002), 59.

16 Walter Pincus, "CIA Spies Get a New Home Base," *Washington Post*, 14 October 2005, A6.

17 Scott Shane, "Intelligence Center is Created for Unclassified Information," *New York Times*, 9 November 2005.

18 Anonymous [Michael Scheuer], *Imperial Hubris: Why the West is Losing the War on Terror* (Washington, DC: Brassey's Inc., 2004), xiii.

19 The Commission on the Intelligence Capabilities of the United States Regarding Weapons of Mass Destruction, Report to the President of the United States, 31 March 2005, 399.

15

Adding value to the intelligence product

Stephen Marrin

value of intel + accuracy

The value of finished intelligence analysis is not measured solely by its accuracy, but rather by the value it has for decisionmakers. This value, however, can change depending on the information needs of the decisionmaker. Unfortunately, the intelligence community has – for the most part – failed to incorporate different perspectives and approaches into its standard operating procedures for the creation of intelligence analysis, limiting the potential contributions that intelligence analysis can make to decisionmaking. Improving both the art and the science of intelligence analysis would better meet decisionmaker needs for information and knowledge by providing them with analysis that is more rigorous, scenarios that are more imaginative, and improved insights of the adversary derived from empathy rather than intellect.

Defining the value of intelligence

The starting point for any assessment of intelligence analysis value should be the needs of the ultimate user; the decisionmaker. There are many different kinds of decisionmakers, depending on the kinds of power they wield, but all go through a similar decisionmaking process. In the 1960s, Sir Geoffrey Vickers – a well-respected systems analyst and conceptualizer – articulated a framework for understanding the steps in the decisionmaking process.[1] Vickers lays out a vision of the world in which each individual or organization is tied to many others through many different kinds of relationships. In this world, the process of decisionmaking entails monitoring both internal and external relations and comparing the current status with the norms and standards set for the relations. If the monitoring uncovers a disparity between the two, then actions to resolve the difference are considered. In this complex vision, any description of a set of relationships is only a snapshot of a dynamically shifting reality that constantly changes due to both internal and external forces.

In applying Vickers's framework to the role of intelligence in the foreign policymaking process, institutionalized intelligence monitors the external system for foreign policymakers, and alerts them to changes in the dynamic balance of relationships. Vickers described this kind of monitor as "a watchdog on a chain; he can bark and alert the householder, but he cannot bite."[2] In other words, while intelligence analysts can provide decisionmakers with warning

199

about the threats that might affect US interests, only decisionmakers can decide what to do about those threats. In addition, for decisionmaking to be effective, there must be close co-ordination between the intelligence analysts who interpret the meaning of the facts and the decisionmakers who decide their importance.[3]

Harvard University historian Ernest May has adapted Vickers's decisionmaking framework into a simple process that all decisionmakers – regardless of portfolio or discipline – go through, in which they ask three specific questions:

> "What is going on?", "So what?" (or "What difference does it make?"); and "What is to be done?" The better the process of executive judgment, the more it involves asking the questions again and again, not in set order, and testing the results until one finds a satisfactory answer to the third question – what to do.[4]

In May's three-step adaptation of Vickers's framework, intelligence organizations perform a delegated function, by first finding out what is going on (collection) and then determining what it means (analysis). Decisionmakers, on the other hand, engage in all three steps, focusing their attentions on what to do about the situation at hand. The decisionmaking process that May highlights is an iterative one entailing a process of continual learning.

As the process shifts from information-gathering to assessment to decisionmaking, both greater amounts and different kinds of information are needed. In order to tell decisionmakers about what is going on overseas and who is doing it, intelligence analysts spend much of their time linking disparate data together to either "connect the dots" or "create the mosaic," depending on the analogy used. For example, CIA's leadership analysts compile data into leadership profiles – or "biographic assessments of foreign leaders"[5] – so as to "help (senior US policymakers) understand and effectively interact with their foreign counterparts."[6]

To derive meaning from the aggregate data, however, requires linking the facts together into a broader framework that explains what the facts mean in terms of US interests. For example, practitioners of leadership analysis might look to a foreign leader's past decisions for insight into the decisions he or she might pursue in the future.

Unfortunately, because raw intelligence data of this kind is usually fragmentary – providing an incomplete picture of what is actually going on overseas or in the mind of the adversary – the gaps in the data must be filled in with assumptions drawn from various sources, running from the theoretical literature to the analysts' idiosyncratic judgment. In other words, intelligence analysis entails telling decisionmakers what may be going on overseas rather than what is going on overseas. But since intelligence is by definition fragmentary, this is an intrinsic part of what it means to produce intelligence analysis.

For decisionmakers, however, the most valuable information is that which focuses on the "why," or the reasons a foreign government pursues a particular policy or a foreign leader acts in a particular way. This knowledge of motivation or causation provides decisionmakers with some basis of information regarding "what to do" by developing policies that can – to use a medical analogy – focus on treating the disease itself rather than just the symptoms.

The different explanations regarding the causes or drivers of terrorism each provide insight into possible solutions. For example, if one accepts the argument that economic deprivation contributes to terrorist recruitment, then using policies to encourage economic development might alleviate the threat. Similarly, if one accepts the argument that the restrictive nature of an authoritarian government prevents a particular political faction's voice from being expressed and this increases the risk of terrorism, then fostering democracy could alleviate the threat. Alternatively, if a particular ideology espouses terrorism as a solution to political or social frustration, then fostering a counter-ideology could reduce the terrorist threat. The point is that – regardless of the issue at hand – the solution to a problem frequently depends on an assessment of its cause.

In the end, decisionmaking requires accurate knowledge of what is, what may be, and the intangibles that affect an adversary's decisionmaking process. Intelligence agencies exist to provide decisionmakers with some of this information.

Modeling intelligence analysis on the social sciences

In order to meet the decisionmaker's requirement for information, intelligence analysts use an approximation of the scientific method derived from the social sciences to determine meaning from the raw intelligence. The use of social science methodology to understand the reasons for the actions and policies pursued by adversaries and competitors is most explicit in the academic study of international relations. In order to simplify real-world complexity, international relations theorists have focused on causal forces that affect state behavior primarily at three levels: that of the individual, the state, and the international system. However, these categories are not complete in and of themselves. Other theories have isolated additional variables on the levels between the individual and the state including group decision-making, and the role of bureaucratic politics and organizational culture. Still more theories have located causal importance between the level of the state and that of the system including transnational actors, and global forces such as ideological and religious belief systems.

Debates over which level of analysis is best have occurred because the level chosen for analysis creates a specific kind of cognitive filter that determines which facts and implications are deemed relevant to study. In addition, the choice of a specific level of analysis determines the kinds of information needed. The theories that predominate in academia – systemic theories that assume states are rational unitary actors – are perhaps the most abstract and require the most general kinds of information, but the closer one gets to the foreign policymaking process the more important it is to provide information that a decisionmaker can use. Intelligence agencies have embraced this social science approach to area studies and international relations by breaking down the perspective of all-source intelligence analysts into "disciplines" based on the factors that shape the behavior of other countries: most frequently political, economic, military, and leadership. These causal factors are then interwoven into multi-disciplinary finished intelligence products through a process of coordination that integrates the various perspectives into a coherent whole, usually addressing a particular geographic area.

An intelligence analyst is someone who looks for patterns in the data, and tries to figure out what those patterns mean. The linkage between the pattern and the meaning should come from hypotheses drawn or derived from relevant academic theory such as economics, political science, or psychology. For example, in the case of leadership analysis, the political psychology literature provides the theoretical foundation for linking individuals' prior history and behavior to more fundamental issues such as personality or motivation, which can then be used to produce – at its best – accurate and insightful predictive assessments of future decisions.[7]

While intelligence analysts have used the scientific method for decades,[8] CIA institutionalized the explicit modeling of the analytic process on the scientific method in the 1990s by, as former CIA officer and senior methodologist Jack Davis observes, replacing the term "key variables" with "drivers" and "hypotheses" with "linchpins."[9] These methodologies have become, in essence, analytic doctrine. In 2001, the CIA Website noted:

201

Invariably, analysts work on the basis of incomplete and conflicting information. DI analysts are taught to clearly articulate what is known (the facts), how it is known (the sources), what drives the judgements (linchpin assumptions), the impact if these drivers change (alternative outcomes), and what remains unknown.[10]

An open question, however, is whether or not intelligence analysis methodology as modeled on the social sciences and the scientific method produces the kinds of analysis that would be useful for decisionmakers. Or – as Columbia University Professor Mark Lowenthal has observed – in terms of value-added, "what can the producer bring to the issue that is new, insightful, and useful?"[11]

Meeting decisionmaker needs?

The social science-based methodology applied by intelligence analysts is not without its critics. In 2003, *New York Times* columnist and policy commentator David Brooks argued that CIA's rigorous social science methodology is not the most effective way to meet the informational needs of the decisionmaker because it fails to take into account the intangible aspects of human behavior rooted less in rational decisionmaking than in cultural norms or idiosyncratic personalities.[12] In 2004, Brooks added to this critique by saying that the CIA's

> false scientism . . . is terrible now in the age of terror, because terror is largely nonrational. . . . How can corruption and madness be understood by analysts in Langley, who have a tendency to impose a false order on reality? . . . The methodology is the problem.[13]

Brooks makes a good point regarding the general problems of using social science methodology to understand international relations because thus far the social sciences have not done a good job in explaining or forecasting the kinds of specific international relations outcomes that intelligence analysts need to make.[14] No one fully understands causality in international relations. Practitioners have been engaged in the practice of international relations for millennia, and academics have been studying it as a subset of political science for decades. But no theoretical approach has been able to provide the same sort of explanatory power to international relations as exists in the natural sciences or even economics. Theorists have been unable to aggregate the many different kinds of international relations theory that focus on the various causal forces that impact the behavior of states, including our own, and as a result it can be very difficult to forecast how a particular country or state may respond in any particular situation. As Columbia University Professor and noted international relations theorist Robert Jervis has observed, "the impediments to understanding our world are so great that . . . intelligence will often reach incorrect conclusions [because] . . . the world is not very predictable."[15]

But Brooks's assessment of how the social scientific approach is misapplied in intelligence analysis is wrong on two counts. First, CIA has not ignored the effect of personality on state behavior. CIA's leadership analysts have taken into account the importance of a foreign leader – including the "passion" and "vision" that Brooks says is missing from CIA analysis – as well as they are able to determine it. But even if this kind of leadership analysis was not performed by CIA, Brooks would still be incorrect in arguing that that the CIA practices rigorous social science methodology because in only rare instances do CIA analysts use the kind of "sophisticated modeling" or "probability calculation" that he refers to.

Instead, for the most part intelligence analysis tends to be intuitive and entails the use of cognitive heuristics to simplify the process of generating hypotheses. Analysts tend to have a two-step analytic approach. They use intuitive "pattern and trend analysis" – consisting of the identification of repeated behavior over time and increases or decreases in that behavior – to uncover changes in some aspect of international behavior that could have national security implications. Once patterns are detected, they rely on *ad hoc* rules derived from study in relevant theory – for example, economics, political science, or psychology – to determine the significance of the pattern. However, most intelligence analysis is based more on informed intuition than structured or rigorous methods. For example, in the case of political analysis, frequently the hypotheses used to derive implications from the data are not drawn directly from the political science literature, but are instead derived from the analyst's idiosyncratic perception of politics and policies that he or she has built up over a lifetime. The use of this kind of personal intuition rather than structured methodologies frequently occurs in leadership analysis as well.

So in the end, while Brooks would argue that CIA has ignored the art of analysis for the science, others would counter that CIA has never actually implemented its social scientific approaches rigorously; in other words, CIA has ignored the science of analysis for the art.[16] Since both critiques may in fact be correct, improving the contributions that intelligence analysis makes to decisionmaking would require strengthening both the art and the science of intelligence analysis. The rest of the chapter outlines a research program designed to do this along three dimensions: by making intelligence analysis methodology more rigorous; by developing alternative methodologies modeled on history rather than the social sciences; and by examining the value of analytic empathy in understanding an adversary's behavior.

Increasing analytic rigor

Improving the science of intelligence analysis will require building up an improved base of knowledge regarding causation in international relations, evaluating analytic methods for accuracy and reliability, and modifying the personnel system so as to encourage the use of more structured and rigorous analytical techniques.

A first step in developing a more rigorous approach to intelligence analysis would be to improve the knowledge base that intelligence analysts have to work with regarding the causes of state behavior. Historically, intelligence analysis has been practiced more as an art than a science, reliant on each analyst's idiosyncratic mix of substantive, procedural and disciplinary expertise to derive meaning from the masses of raw intelligence. This occurs primarily because of the weaknesses in social science's ability to develop hypotheses that are both accurate and reliable in predicting the future behavior of states.[17] Since social scientists in academia do not have access to the kinds of specific data that intelligence analysts do, their models are usually general and at a high level of abstraction. The establishment of an internal intelligence community unit of social scientists devoted to the production of mid-level theory and hypotheses useful for intelligence analysts would provide intelligence agencies with an improved base of theory for finding meaning in the raw intelligence.[18] Additional work on the underlying "science" of intelligence analysis, such as the effort by Rob Johnston to develop a taxonomy of intelligence analysis variables,[19] the articulation of a framework by Timothy Smith to develop a "formal interdisciplinary science of intelligence,"[20] and the kinds of modeling and forecasting methodologies profiled by Stanley Feder,[21] should provide a greater foundation of knowledge that future intelligence analysts can use to create more accurate analysis.

A second way to increase analytic rigor would be to evaluate analytic methods against each other to determine their relative accuracy and reliability in different situations. According to Rob Johnston, there are over 200 analytic methods that intelligence analysts could choose from,[22] but because they have not been rigorously tested, intelligence analysts do not know if any particular method is better than any other. In 1999, Robert Folker – a military intelligence analyst – demonstrated how the use of one particular analytic method – structured hypothesis testing – produced better results than the use of an intuitive approach.[23] Additional research in this area is greatly needed in order to provide the foundation of knowledge necessary for intelligence analysts to apply the appropriate analytic method to each situation. In the CIA's journal *Studies in Intelligence*, Steven Rieber and Neil Thomason have recently recommended that the intelligence community create a National Institute for Analytic Methods – modeled on the National Institutes of Health – as a way to sponsor this kind of research on the effectiveness of analytic tools and techniques.[24] In this way it will be possible to gain knowledge – scientifically – about the effectiveness of different approaches, rather than rely primarily on anecdotal evidence as is currently the case.

A third way to increase analytic rigor would be to modify the personnel system so as to encourage the use of more structured and rigorous analytical techniques. The CIA's personnel model inhibits the use of structured analytic methodologies in favor of an environment where unstructured intuitive analysis dominates. The current structure is very flat, with each individual analyst considered to be an autonomous expert capable of producing the same kind of output with proficiency expectations linked to the appropriate pay scale. The analysts are responsible for their individual accounts and engage in teamwork only to the extent that they "coordinate" with other analysts in the production of finished intelligence to integrate their individual perspectives into a multi-disciplinary whole. However, since individuals possess different combinations of strengths and weaknesses, there is a legitimate question regarding whether the current approach – in essence a one-size-fits-all expectation – optimizes organizational performance.

An alternative model for analytic production is provided by the Government Accountability Office. Even though there are some differences in mission between the CIA and the GAO – for example, that GAO supports the legislative rather than executive branch – there are many similarities in process because both organizations require personnel with similar skill sets to produce written and verbal informational products for decisionmakers. Yet GAO is able to integrate the expertise of its specialists in a more effective manner than that used by CIA.

To produce each written report, GAO analysts work in teams of substantive and disciplinary experts under a single team leader. While all members of the team are evaluated according to the same set of competencies, the team-based approach provides the opportunity for the team leader to rely on the strongest member of the team at each stage in the process, running from conceptualization through data collection and analysis to drafting. Each analyst has less autonomy than CIA analysts do, but responsibility for the final analysis is more certain. GAO's substantive analysts are assisted by other experts including methodologists, accountants, economists, lawyers and even experienced writers who are assigned to their project on an as-needed basis. At its best this effectively integrates specialists and methodologists into analytic teams, providing the teams with their expertise on a daily basis during the information collection, analysis, and drafting process.

The analytic process at GAO is also much more rigorous and thorough than that performed by CIA. GAO has modeled its report production process on that used in academia to produce dissertations, including external peer review through an adaptation of a dissertation proposal defense, a research stage, a final defense of the report's reasoning and conclusions, and a drafting process requiring rigorous documentation of sources. Finally, the organizational structure and matrix management enables greater rigor in the analytic process through the integration of methodologists into teams of experts. Rob Johnston – a CIA officer in their Center for the Study of Intelligence – has argued that greater integration of methodologists into the analytic process was necessary because most intelligence analysts lacked the knowledge or training necessary to choose the most appropriate analytic method and then apply it effectively to the situation at hand.[25] He recommended that analytic methodologists "act as in-house consultants for analytic teams, generate new methods specific to intelligence analysis, [and] modify and improve existing methods of analysis," which is exactly what GAO's methodologists do.

While not all of GAO's specific processes may work if copied directly into a CIA context due to the differing timeframes in which reports are written, this more rigorous approach to analytic production could be used to foster additional ways to improving CIA's analytic processes in the future. In the end, greater rigor in both the substantive knowledgebase and the processes used to produce finished intelligence analysis should over time lead to more accurate and useful assessments regarding the capabilities and intentions of the adversary.

Greater imagination

A second way to improve intelligence analysis contributions to decisionmaking would to improve the art of analysis by incorporating imagination explicitly into the analytic process. The 9/11 Commission Report highlighted a "failure of imagination" on the part of intelligence organizations as one of the primary reasons for their inability to prevent the 2001 terrorist attacks.[26] The Report goes on to say that "imagination is not a gift usually associated with bureaucracies. . . . It is therefore crucial to find a way of routinizing, even bureaucratizing, the exercise of imagination."[27] The Report goes on to describe a methodology for using imagination as part of a strategic warning process, by imagining "how surprise attacks might be launched" and using these scenarios as starting points for intelligence collection purposes.[28] But it does not suggest a way to foster the kinds of imagination necessary to produce useful scenarios within an existing analytic process which – based on its approximation of social science methodology – does not rely very much on the imaginative abilities of analysts.

A model for increasing greater imagination in the production of intelligence analysis may be found in Yale University historian John Lewis Gaddis's *Landscape of History*. In this book, Gaddis compares historical methodology – in essence interweaving the various forces and influences that shaped events in the past into a compelling narrative – to the knowledge-building efforts of the social sciences, and concludes that standard social science methodology is inadequate. He argues that its structured methodology and emphasis on distinguishing causes from effects through articulation of independent and dependent variables fails to capture the inherent interdependency of those variables. In other words, the social scientist's strict differentiation of cause and effect fails to accurately capture the complexity of the real world, leading to artificially abstract models which – as Gaddis contends – means that "the social sciences are operating . . . at roughly the level of freshman physics experiments [and] that's why the forecasts they make only occasionally correspond with the reality we subsequently encounter."[29]

But Gaddis finds the comparison between historical methodology and that used by certain natural sciences – specifically astronomy, geology, and paleontology – to be more palatable. These sciences are those in which knowledge cannot be gained through direct experimentation, but instead must be inferred from the evidence left behind. Gaddis argues that these sciences require imagination to fill in gaps in the evidentiary record in a way that does not exist in most sciences, but is similar to that required for history. But because history deals with the actions of people, it is less of a natural science than a social science, or as Gaddis concludes, an "imaginative social science" because it relies primarily on imagination to understand how people have acted in the past.

The fragmentary nature of evidence that historians have to deal with is very similar to the fragmentary nature of evidence that intelligence analysts and national security decisionmakers have about the current and future actions and intentions of adversaries. A narrative that links the fragmentary information together into a story about what a foreign government may be doing would likely be more useful to a decisionmaker than the fragmentary data points themselves. Deriving implications from a fragmentary evidentiary record requires that the gaps be filled with something in order to create coherent stories of what a foreign government might be doing or might do in the future. These stories – or scenarios – can be considered hypotheses in a social science sense, but they also can be considered possible interpretations in a historical sense. In social science these gap-filling hypotheses are usually drawn from the theoretical literature, but for many intelligence issues the kinds of hypotheses necessary to link, for example, specific incidents of unrest in a foreign country to a theory of political instability, social change, or even revolution, do not exist. Rather, in the absence of useful hypotheses, intelligence analysts tend to rely on intuitive judgment and imagination in much the same way that historians do. In addition, just as disputes in historical interpretation frequently occur because of differences in their imaginative vision of the past, disputes in intelligence or decisionmaking frequently occur because of the interpretation of the meaning of gaps in the data. Just as historians have been able to distinguish good historians from the mediocre based on their ability to use imagination effectively – the art of history – so we should be able to distinguish good intelligence analysts and decisionmakers from the mediocre, based on their ability to imagine the adversary accurately; the art of intelligence analysis.

But this kind of imaginative effort is infrequently acknowledged or rewarded in the management and promotion of intelligence analysts, hindering an intelligence organization's ability to imagine the different possible avenues that an adversary is currently taking or may take in the future. As a result, improving the art of intelligence by enabling some analysts to shift their methodology from a social science base to one that is more like the "imaginative social science" Gaddis describes would be a step in the right direction. Improving the imaginative abilities of intelligence analysts should enable them to provide decisionmakers with more useful scenarios regarding what the competitor or adversary may be doing or may do in the future, thereby leading to a better base of knowledge from which to decide what to do.

Greater empathy

A final suggestion for improving the art of intelligence analysis to make it more useful for decisionmakers would be to examine the possible benefits arising from the use of empathy as a way to understand how cultural and individual idiosyncrasies contribute to the behavior of an adversary. In 1986, Ralph White – a former professor of psychology at George Washington University – argued that intelligence analysts' lack of empathy, which he defined as "understanding the thoughts and feelings of others," has led to "serious consequences" for decisionmakers and their respective countries because they misunderstood their adversaries and were surprised by their actions. Accordingly, he recommended that empathy be incorporated in a greater degree into intelligence assessments.[30,31]

A number of other scholars have highlighted the use of empathy as a specific device that intelligence analysts can use to understand the actions of others within cultures that have different social or religious mores. Gordon McCormick – a professor at the Naval Postgraduate School – has argued that intelligence analysts should "develop cultural empathy" for an adversary in order to "forecast enemy behavior with greater accuracy than has been the case historically."[32] In addition, Columbia University professor Robert Jervis has said that lack of empathy

> is perhaps (one of) the two most important kinds of intelligence errors [because] states are unable to put themselves in the other's shoes and instead assume that the other's behavior is driven by unusual – and frequently malign – internal characteristics. . . . Empathy requires entering into the other's perceived world, and this is rarely easy.[33]

Cultivating empathy is particularly difficult for intelligence analysts, who tend to be more scholarly than not, spending most of their day behind their computers reading and writing about what goes on overseas. Intelligence analysis is usually a highly intellectual exercise predicated on applying knowledge gained through area studies education – preferably including time spent immersed in that culture – and foreign language training to understand both the adversary and the situational context. Most of this kind of knowledge can be con- sciously acquired, aggregated, learned, and taught, but intellect alone will not be able to allow an analyst to put himself in the head of the other and understand the cultural and emotional context that contributes to his or her decisionmaking process. Part of the reason is because, as Robert Jervis has pointed out, intelligence analysts are not decisionmakers, and as a result "may not understand the pressures on those who have to act in the name of their states."[34]

It is the rare analyst that gets to experience first-hand the color and dynamism of foreign cultures or the drama and chaos of international crises. As many authors have observed, intelli- gence analysts tend to be intellectual and introverted. As a result, while the emphasis on the intellect may lead to greater knowledge, it does not provide a mechanism for understanding the mindset of a foreign leader, or the kinds of emotional decisionmaking process that can lead a person to risk his or her life in pursuit of an ideal like justice, or a group of people to risk their lives to oppose an occupying force. Their distance from the action provides them with greater objectivity but it is precisely this objectivity that also hinders understanding the emotional component of the decisionmaking process.

As William Burris has observed, intelligence "analysts and managers [tend] to play down or ignore the importance of affections – that fertile ground of humanness where the greed, irrationality, passion and lust of power that threaten our national security are often rooted."[35] Yet it is exactly those emotions that are crucial for the United States government to understand if it is to forecast a popular uprising or intractable guerilla conflict.

The kind of raw intelligence necessary to understand the motivations of an adversary is frequently fragmentary. In the absence of complete understanding, the analyst must still use some framework to interpret and forecast the actions of the adversary. Frequently this will entail some application of a rational-actor assumption or mirror-imaging, but assump- tions derived from stereotypes or prejudices about the adversary can also enter into the analysis. Empathy can provide a corrective to these kinds of analytic distortions by providing another way to understand the intangibles that can affect an adversary's decisionmaking process.

According to Ralph White:

207

empathy means understanding others from the inside looking out, not merely from the outside looking in . . . to imagine what the world would look like through their eyes, as they watch what we do, and through their ears, as they listen to what we say. . . . Empathy means "being" our actual or potential enemy.[36]

As such, White continues,

empathy permits intelligence analysts to make assessments and estimates that will enable consumers to understand more precisely the target nation's policy-makers, to influence them more effectively, and to predict their behavior more reliably. Such knowledge will also enable consumers to pin-point the target's most likely areas of compromise, concession, and tradeoff.

In order for an intelligence analyst to cultivate empathy, White suggests that he or she "continually ask oneself certain obviously relevant questions such as 'How would I feel if I were facing the situation they are facing now?', 'How would I feel if I had been through the experience I know they have been through?', and 'How should I correct my first answers to those questions on the basis of what I know about the differences between their political culture and mine?' "[37] The last question is particularly important, for as Gordon McCormick has observed, "failure to distinguish between differing styles of national behavior will result in culture-bound assessments of enemy activities" in which "our adversaries . . . will be conceived in our own image."[38]

As a result, use of empathy does not mean setting aside substantive expertise about the adversary, but rather layering on top of that substantive expertise a more intuitive or empathetic assessment of how that adversary might behave in different situations. In this way, it can provide a good corrective to "mirror-imaging or presumptions of rationality."[39] In 2000, Ernest May recommended that CIA "study why some analysts are better than others at empathizing – that is, at understanding how leaders and policymakers think and make decisions."[40] This kind of study could provide a starting point for identifying the role that empathy plays in understanding the adversary, and using that knowledge to hire and develop intelligence analysts who are able to incorporate empathy into their analysis. The end result should be greater insight for the decisionmaker regarding the intangibles that affect an adversary's decisionmaking process and likely courses of action.

Conclusion

The needs of decisionmakers should drive the kinds of intelligence analysis produced, but intelligence agencies have relied – perhaps too much – on a loose adaptation of the scientific method as the primary methodology for producing finished intelligence analysis. Improving both the art and the science of intelligence analysis should provide decisionmakers with analysis that better meets their need for knowledge regarding what is going on overseas, what may be going on today and in the future, and the various influences that impinge upon an adversary's decisionmaking process.

The next step in the process, after beginning to explore the value of improved rigor and greater empathy and imagination, would be to institutionalize these kinds of efforts.

The distinction between the art and the science of analysis roughly corresponds to the difference between a craft and a profession, or the unstructured and the structured. A craftsman is really an artist whose skill is developed through training and experience, while a professional is someone who has been educated in the "science" of his or her field, and then uses that knowledge in an applied way. Crafts rely primarily on the skill of the individual practitioner – which does not change very much from generation to generation – while professions build on the knowledge of past practitioners and relay it to new professionals through their educational process.

Further developing knowledge about both the art and the science of intelligence analysis should lead to improvements in both the craft and the profession. This kind of dual effort will enable the occupation as a whole to get past the unproductive debate over whether good intelligence analysts are born or made, to a future in which the performance of all analysts – regardless of their relative possession of scientific knowledge or artistic ability – can be improved. In the end, institutionalizing improvement in both the art and the science of analysis can only lead to an intelligence product that provides greater value to decisionmakers.

Notes

1 As Vickers observes, "facts are relevant only in relation to some judgment of value, and judgments of value are operative only in relation to some configuration of fact." Geoffrey Vickers, *The Art of Judgment: A Study of Policy Making*. Thousand Oaks, CA: Sage Publications, 1995: 50–51, 54.

2 Vickers, 225–226.

3 Vickers, 54.

4 Ernest R. May, *Strange Victory: Hitler's Conquest of France*. New York: Hill and Wang, 2000: 458–459.

5 According to a Congressional Research Service Memorandum, CIA's Leadership Profiles "are biographic assessments of foreign leaders, generally 1–2 pages in length. They often are tailored for a particular meeting or event. Whenever possible, LPs contain a photo of the leader being assessed." Alfred Cumming, "Congress as a Consumer of Intelligence Information." Congressional Research Service Memorandum. December 14, 2005. http://feinstein.senate.gov/crs-intel.htm For additional information on CIA's leadership analysis program, see Thomas Omestad, "Psychology and the CIA: Leaders on the Couch," *Foreign Policy* 95 (Summer 1994): 105–122.

6 Intelligence Community Website, Analysis: Occupations (Leadership Analyst). http://www.intelligence.gov/3-career_analysis_occupations.shtml#17

7 For an example of this kind of analysis, see Jerrold M. Post and Alexander George, *Leaders and Their Followers in a Dangerous World: The Psychology of Political Behavior*. Ithaca: Cornell University Press, 2004.

8 According to Klaus Knorr in 1964, "it is social science *methods* of gathering data, of deducing data from other data, and of establishing the validity of data that are of particular value – in principle at least – in producing appropriate kinds of information for intelligence." Klaus Knorr. "Foreign Intelligence and the Social Sciences." Research Monograph No. 17. Center of International Studies, Woodrow Wilson School of Public and International Affairs, Princeton University, June 1, 1964: 11.

9 Douglas J. MacEachin, "The Tradecraft of Analysis: Challenge and Change in the CIA," Consortium for the Study of Intelligence, Washington DC, 1994: 1; Jack Davis, "Improving Intelligence Analysis at CIA: Dick Heuer's Contribution to Intelligence Analysis," *Psychology of Intelligence Analysis*, Center for the Study of Intelligence, CIA, 1999: xvii–xix.

10 CIA Website, "Intelligence Analysis in the DI: Frequently Asked Questions." http://www.odci.gov/cia/di/work/analyst.html, as quoted in: Stephen Marrin, "CIA's Kent School: Improving Training for New Analysts." *International Journal of Intelligence and Counterintelligence*, Vol. 16. No. 4 (Winter 2003/2004): 627. This website has since been deleted from the CIA Website, but a mirror of the content can be found here: http://widit.slis.indiana.edu/TREC/showdocw.cgi?dname=-web&docID=G25–55–1777388

11 Mark M. Lowenthal, "Tribal Tongues: Intelligence Consumers, Intelligence Producers," *The Washington Quarterly*, Vol. 15. No. 1 (Winter 1992): 161.

12 David Brooks, "The Elephantiasis of Reason," *The Atlantic Monthly*, Vol. 29. No. 1 (Jan.–Feb. 2003): 34–35.

13 David Brooks, "The CIA: Method and Madness," *The New York Times*, February 3, 2004: A 23.

14 For an evaluation of the limited value of the social sciences in intelligence analysis as compared to the

value of the natural sciences in medicine, see Stephen Marrin and Jonathan D. Clemente, "Improving Intelligence Analysis by Looking to the Medical Profession," *International Journal of Intelligence and Counterintelligence*, Vol. 18. No. 4 (2005): 716–719.

15 Robert Jervis, "Improving the Intelligence Process: Informal Norms and Incentives," *Intelligence: Policy and Process*, eds. Alfred C. Maurer, Marion D. Tunstall and James M. Keagle. Boulder, CO and London Westview Press, 1985: 113.

16 For an excellent overview of the art versus science discussion as applied to intelligence analysis, see Robert D. Folker, Jr, "Intelligence Analysis in Theater Joint Intelligence Centers: An Experiment in Applying Structured Methods," Occasional Paper Number Seven. Joint Military Intelligence College, January 2000: 6–13.

17 For more on the few efforts to develop the underlying "scientific" foundation of intelligence analysis, see: R.A. Random. "Intelligence as a Science," *Studies in Intelligence*, Spring 1958; Richards J. Heuer, ed. *Quantitative Approaches to Political Intelligence: The CIA Experience*. Boulder, CO: Westview Press, 1978; Stanley A. Feder. "Factions and Policon: New Ways to Analyze Politics." *Studies in Intelligence* 31, No. 1 (Spring 1987): 41–57, reprinted in *Inside CIA's Private World: Declassified Articles from the Agency's Internal Journal, 1955–1992*, ed. H. Bradford Westerfield. New Haven, CT: Yale University Press, 1995: 274–292.

18 Marrin and Clemente, 724–725.

19 Rob Johnston, "Developing a Taxonomy of Intelligence Analysis Variables," *Studies in Intelligence*, Vol. 47. No. 3. http://www.cia.gov/csi/studies/vol47no3/article05.html

20 Timothy J. Smith, "Network-Centric Intelligence: Toward a Total-Systems Transformation of Analysis and Assessment," Unpublished Manuscript, September 2005: 14.

21 Stanley A. Feder, "Forecasting for Policy Making in the Post-Cold War Period," *Annual Reviews: Political Science*, 2002 5: 111–125.

22 Rob Johnston, "Integrating Methodologists into Teams of Substantive Experts," *Studies in Intelligence*, Vol. 47. No. 1. http://www.cia.gov/csi/studies/vol47no1/article06.html

23 Robert D. Folker, Jr., "Exploiting Structured Methodologies to Improve Qualitative Intelligence Analysis," Masters Thesis, Joint Military Intelligence College, July 1999: 2.

24 Steven Rieber and Neil Thomason, "Creation of a National Institute for Analytic Methods," *Studies in Intelligence*, Vol. 49. No. 4 (2005): 71–77.

25 Rob Johnston, "Integrating".

26 *The 9/11 Commission Report: Final Report of the National Commission on Terrorist Attacks Upon the United States*, Washington, DC: W.W. Norton & Co., 2004: 336.

27 *The 9/11 Commission Report*, 344.

28 *The 9/11 Commission Report*, 346.

29 John Lewis Gaddis, *The Landscape of History: How Historians Map the Past*, New York: Oxford University Press, 2002: 60.

30 Ralph K. White, "Empathy as an Intelligence Tool," *International Journal of Intelligence and Counterintelligence* Vol. 1. No. 1 (Spring 1986): 57–59.

31 White is careful to distinguish empathy as an instrumental tool for understanding the adversary from sympathy, which he defines as "sharing (or agreeing with) the thoughts and feelings of others." In fact, White says that those "intelligence analysts who find that emotionally their understanding leads to sharing should not be in the intelligence business." White, 60.

32 Gordon H. McCormick, "Surprise, Perceptions, and Military Style," *Orbis*, Winter 1983: 835; 838.

33 Robert Jervis, "Strategic Intelligence and Effective Policy," *Security and Intelligence in a Changing World: New Perspectives for the 1990s*, eds. A. Stuart Farson, David Stafford, and Wesley K. Wark, London: Frank Cass, 1991: 165–181 at 175.

34 Jervis, "Strategic Intelligence," 176.

35 William C. Burris, "The Uses of History in Intelligence Analysis," *International Journal of Intelligence and Counterintelligence*, Vol. 6, No. 3: 301.

36 White, 58–59.

37 White, 69–70.

38 McCormick, 836.

39 McCormick, 833.

40 "Symposium on the Psychology of Intelligence Analysis" sponsored by CIA's Center for the Study of Intelligence and the Sherman Kent School. June 20, 2000. http://www.cia.gov/csi/bulletin/csi11.html#toc2

16

Analysis for strategic intelligence

John Hollister Hedley

The cable news channel interrupts regular programming to switch to the capital of a Central Asian country. From the open window of a hotel in the city's center, a reporter excitedly reports that shots are ringing out. Tanks are blocking the boulevard leading toward the presidential palace. The reporter thrusts a microphone from the window and, yes, we hear the shots. A hand–held camera pointing from the window shows the tanks. Yes, we see them, now filling the intersection. We hear screams and shouts. People are running. Explosions reverberate.

In the offices of Washington policymakers, heads turn toward the television monitor. Simultaneously, heads turn toward monitors in the White House Situation Room and various operations centers. Any moment, the phone will ring in the office of an intelligence analyst who almost certainly has not been watching television. Through the phone will come urgent, insistent questions: What's going on? What does it mean? Who's behind this? How serious is it? The analyst understands that, lying behind the series of questions, is an implicit one: what should we do about it?

The analyst is on the spot. Modern technology reveals far–flung developments in real time. The caller, however, will not say, "I know no one was expecting this, so please take your time and try to get something to me in the next couple of days." More likely the caller wants the analyst's thinking now, orally, with maybe an hour or two before a written situation report must be on its way. There will be little if any time now for sharing views, testing alternative hypotheses, conducting peer reviews, and doing in–depth research before assessing what might be going on and making a judgment about what it means. This is when it pays for the analyst to have developed expertise, to be doing in–depth research and in–depth thinking already, to have been routinely consulting counterparts and exploring alternative hypotheses. This is when training and experience count.

The bottom line

Episodes such as this are among the many kinds of challenge that illustrate why intelligence analysis has been called "the most sophisticated and intellectually demanding activity in the

Intelligence Community."[1] It is why Richard Helms, who distinguished himself at espionage and served as a Director of Central Intelligence, called analysis "the bottom line of intelligence work ... where all the arcane techniques of intelligence come together."[2] And in every such instance – whether one that calls for a commentary on a fast-breaking development, or for a product of collaborative, in-depth research – the analyst must go beyond what appears to be happening and try to make sense out of often ambiguous, inconsistent, incomplete, and sometimes contradictory data.

Inconclusive data feature prominently in the daily diet of intelligence analysis. Indeed, the Intelligence Community owes its *raison d'être* to the "squishiness" of data. Policymakers need someone to assess data objectively and make judgments without direct, conclusive evidence.[3] It is unfortunate that the expression "connecting the dots" gained currency in discourse about whether analysts should reach certain conclusions quickly and confidently. It is not a good metaphor or analogy. Making analytic judgments is not akin to painting by the numbers. Ask any analyst how easy it is to connect the dots when you aren't sure you have two "dots," or verifiable dots, dots that correlate.

It should be clear from the outset that there is nothing nefarious about trying to know and understand as much as possible about what is going on in the world. And this is the purpose of analysis: to discern pertinent facts from a flood of information and apply judgments and insights that can inform those who must make decisions and direct actions to address developments on a global scale. The essence of analysis is information plus insight, derived from subject-matter knowledge. Intelligence analysis informs decisions and actions in ways that can make a positive difference. Timely intelligence warns of looming crises, identifies threats, monitors fast-breaking situations, illuminates issues, and detects trends. Intelligence helps US policymakers consider alternative options and outcomes.

Intelligence sources

The grist for the analyst's mill is a mix of all the kinds of information the US government is able to acquire. Much of the information is openly available in print or electronic form, including the Internet, newspapers, television, radio, journals, commercial databases, videos, graphics, maps, and drawings. A critical amount of intelligence information, however, is obtained from highly sensitive sources. These include:

- *Human-source intelligence*, acquired openly by civilian and military personnel assigned to US diplomatic posts, through official liaison contacts with other intelligence services, by debriefing foreign nationals and US citizens who travel abroad and have access to information of intelligence value; it is acquired clandestinely by recruiting foreign agents with unique access to the hardest targets of all, not just documents but the people who make policies and operational plans – and if possible, recruiting those people to be agents themselves.
- *Signals intelligence*, derived from intercepted communications, radar and telemetry.
- *Imagery intelligence*, whether obtained overhead from satellites or aircraft or from the ground.
- *Measurement and signature intelligence* involving a range of disciplines including nuclear, optical, radio frequency, acoustic, seismic, and materials sciences that can locate, identify, or describe distinctive characteristics of intelligence targets.

Complicating the mix of these sources of intelligence reporting is its sheer volume, its rapid-fire receipt, the ever-present "noise" of contradictory and inaccurate information, and deliberate deception designed to mislead.

The fact that analysts do "all-source analysis" reflects the reality that rarely is one source from a single one of these collection categories sufficient. Sources need to be supplemented and complemented to be as complete as possible and to be verified to the greatest extent possible. Research and analysis in open sources may turn up information, for example, on the strategic perspective of *jihadist* movements. But because these groups attach highest priority to the security of their communications and operations, it is difficult to identify leaders and uncover decision-making and attack-planning. It is likely to require the full range of intelligence collection capabilities to penetrate operations by cells of a few, isolated individuals whose fluid movements are "beneath the radar."

In making analytic judgments, the analyst facing a deadline typically yearns for additional sourcing. But actually *having* multiple sources to corroborate each other is the ideal; it is by no means the rule. And multiple sources can in some instances still lead you astray. Indeed, one of the differences between intelligence writing and academic writing is having to write before you feel ready to do so, before you have marshaled the supporting evidence you want to have at hand in order to craft your position. In this sense, writing current intelligence is very much like being a newspaper reporter or columnist; when it's time to go to press, you have to have your material ready to go.

From "raw" to "finished" intelligence

Intelligence analysis is the end product, the culmination of the intelligence process. Yet that process actually is a never-ending cycle. Analysis drives collection by identifying information needs and gaps, which in turn call for more collection which requires further analysis. What the key recipients of intelligence analysis – the President, the National Security Council, and senior officials in major departments and agencies – must be aware of, grapple with, or defend against in the world around us dictates collection requirements. They reflect the core concerns of national security policymakers and military commanders who need timely, reliable, and accurate foreign intelligence information – especially the kinds of information that are not readily available. As analysts address those needs from day to day, they identify and prompt the collection mission again and again.

Before the raw information that human or technical collectors acquire can be analyzed, however, some interim processing and exploitation may be needed to convert it into a usable form for analysis. It may be necessary, for example, to decrypt or translate intercepts, or to interpret images through highly refined photographic and electronic processes. After all, intelligence collection systems produce sensory data, not intelligence. Only the human mind can add the discernment and knowledge that makes sense of it. It is only after "raw" data are verified for accuracy and evaluated for their significance can they become the substance of intelligence.[4] Although personnel involved in this processing sometimes are referred to within their organizations as analysts, their specialized work – involving judgments about relevance and priority within a single collection category – is not the production of "finished" intelligence.

Although producing intelligence is a dynamic, continuous process, the term "finished intelligence" refers to any intelligence product – whether a one-paragraph bulletin or a lengthy study – which has completed the rigorous, all-source correlation, integration, evaluation, and assessment that enables it be disseminated. As we have noted, the intelligence analyst who is the author of such a product is expected to have checked it against intelligence information from all sources pertinent to his or her area of responsibility. The analyst will have assessed its validity and determined – with the substantive and editorial help of experienced managers and colleagues – that it can usefully advance its recipient's knowledge and understanding of a pertinent security policy issue. It will have been coordinated with counterparts elsewhere in the Intelligence Community, and officially reviewed before it is sent out.

Finished intelligence is made available in several forms, and analysts can expect to be called upon to produce in any or all of them:

- *Current intelligence* addresses day-to-day events – new developments and possible indicators of developments to come. Current intelligence not only reports intelligence information but assesses its significance, alerts readers to near-term consequences, and signals potentially dangerous situations. Current intelligence is disseminated daily. Sometimes it appears even more frequently, in the form of situation reports from a task force formed to deal with a crisis. Often it takes the form of *ad hoc* written memoranda and oral briefings. The *President's Daily Briefing* is the most elite example of current intelligence, but other highly sensitive publications for the most senior levels of government and the military appear daily, weekly or on request.
- *Estimative intelligence* takes stock of what is known and then delves into the unknown, even the unknowable. International issues rarely are conclusive, yet policymakers must address them with plans and decisions. Estimative intelligence provides strategic guidance for developing policies, usually looking three to five years ahead. It suggests alternative patterns that available facts might fit, and provides informed assessments of the range and likelihood of possible outcomes. The most formal and authoritative form of estimative intelligence is a National Intelligence Estimate, which the pertinent organizations of the Intelligence Community prepare collaboratively and issue collectively.
- *Basic intelligence* compiles reference data – biographic, geographic, military, economic, demographic, social, and political – presented in the form of monographs, in-depth studies, atlases, maps, order-of-battle summaries, and publications such as *Chiefs of State and Cabinet Members of Foreign Governments* and an annual *World Factbook* that is a comprehensive compilation of political, economic, and demographic data.[5]

Other types of finished intelligence include *warning intelligence* (which necessarily should be timely) designed to highlight threatening events that would require a potential policy response and which could cause the engagement of US military forces, and *intelligence for operational support* which, as the name indicates, is focused and tailored for the planning and conducting of a specific operation. *Scientific and technical intelligence* assesses technical developments and characteristics, and the capabilities and performance of foreign technologies including weapon systems. Technical analysis usually relates to defense planning, military operations, or arms-control negotiations.

None of these types of finished intelligence, however, brings the process to a conclusion. Whether a daily item or a national estimate, their production is part of a continuum involving dissemination, feedback, and more questions that fuel a truly dynamic effort.

What's more, whether current or longer-term, the analytic interpretation of intelligence reporting requires making judgments that go beyond the available information. Such a leap, from the information at hand into a meaningful analytic product, inevitably involves venturing from the known into the uncertain. Almost by definition, intelligence analysis involves confronting uncertainty and using one's judgment and subject-matter expertise in an effort to transcend its limits.

Information abundance

The intelligence analyst's work environment has changed dramatically from the early decades of the US Intelligence Community's existence. During the Cold War that dominated the second half of the twentieth century, the analytic challenge was often one of having too little data. The Soviet Union and its allies were closed societies going to great lengths to deny information. They denied travel, controlled the press, and jammed radio broadcasts. E-mail and cell phones did not exist. US intelligence agencies had a virtual monopoly on the information that was collected, essentially secret information obtained by agents, communication intercepts, or overhead photography, and there never seemed to be enough of it.

In the twenty-first century, a principal analytic challenge lies in the sheer volume of information available. Although especially hard targets such as terrorist cells are no less difficult to penetrate, the explosion of open-source information from news services and the Worldwide Web makes the speed and volume of reporting more difficult to sift through. Advances in information technology both help and hinder, as analysts strive to cope with the "noise," the chaff they must winnow away. Data multiply with dizzying speed. Whereas collecting solid intelligence information was the overriding problem of the past, selecting and validating it loom ever larger as problems for analysts today.

Still another challenge in the era of information abundance is that analysts must dig deeper to serve increasingly more knowledgeable policymakers who will be the recipients of their product. Modern communication technologies provide many more ways for policymakers to stay informed on current developments. Recipients of intelligence analysis who have newspapers and press summaries on their desk and CNN on the air have a high level of awareness. Many of them also read raw intelligence reports on a regular basis – sometimes before the reports reach the analyst. Today's policymakers are more sophisticated subscribers to intelligence products.

The deputy director of intelligence analysis at CIA, Carmen Medina, has observed that her directorate has probably always underestimated the extent to which policymakers serve as their own analysts. "Arguably," she has written, "policymakers have never needed [us] to tell them that riots undermine governments or that currency crises shake investor confidence."[6] What they do need is unique insights into relatively well-understood problems. So, in effect, the bar is set higher for the analysts. They must provide added value to policymakers who probably already have both a good sense of what is going on in their area of concern and a good feel for the significance and consequences of events that take place.

To a degree perhaps surprising to someone new to the inner sanctum of a Washington intelligence organization, the working climate that does *not* change is that which walls off the workplace from the bluster of partisan politics. Analysts must check their personal political views at the door. Objectivity is the analyst's byword, intellectual honesty the core value. The policymaking customers that analysts seek to inform – all the way to intelligence customer number one – need to get the straight scoop, unvarnished and politically neutral.

The author has been directly involved in producing intelligence for eight Presidents – five Republicans and three Democrats. Whatever the partisan rhetoric or the legislative agenda, without exception they all have been serious and conscientious about their role in foreign policy and as commander in chief, and they take seriously the intelligence that can inform their efforts. They have the best of intentions, and although they obviously differ in style, approach, and effectiveness, they want and need the best intelligence they can get. (So, for that matter, does the Congress. And the Congressional oversight committees – the Senate Select Committee on Intelligence, and the House Permanent Select Committee on Intelligence – by and large score well on bipartisanship, especially behind closed doors and apart from public rhetoric.)

Accordingly, an analyst is much the wiser and more effective by not taking sides on the job. No matter how much one might personally wish to see domestic policies that would expand healthcare on the one hand or cut taxes on the other (or both!), when it comes to helping the government better understand what is going on in the world beyond America's borders, the only rule to follow is to be scrupulously objective. As the umpire advised, "call 'em as you see 'em." There is no room in intelligence analysis for partisan advocacy or opposition when providing actionable intelligence and identifying options. In short, you don't craft assessments the way you'd like things to be. This will always come to light, and the cost will be in credibility.

The primacy of writing

The most basic skill required of the intelligence analyst is the ability to think and write clearly. Oral briefings are valued and often called for. But ultimately, writing is what the analyst's work is about – writing based on organizing material, conceptualizing, and thinking critically about it. Writing is always done with the audience, the reader, in mind. And the writing analysts do is different from that learned and practiced in the professorial ranks of graduate school, even though there are many similarities between the intelligence field and academia.

Like academicians, intelligence analysts attach the highest importance to knowledge and understanding, to objectivity in the search for truth, and to accuracy in the sources they use. Academics and analysts are interested in clear descriptions and explanations, though academics usually are describing past events and making sense of what had happened, while analysts are addressing what an event means and projecting what might happen next. They tend to differ when it comes to the material they work with, and their likely audience. Academic authors organize their data, make it as comprehensive as possible, reflect on it, develop a theoretical construct, and perhaps formulate methodologies. For the analyst – especially one writing current intelligence – this approach is likely to be an impossible luxury. As Douglas MacEachin, a former head of analysis at CIA, has put it, "one group gets to promote its reputations in journals, while the other works in a closed environment in which the main readers are members of the world's most challenging audience – the policymaking community."[7] The analyst may need to write for the next morning's publication, or contribute to this afternoon's situation report, on fast-breaking developments for which data is sorely lacking. There is not enough data to work into a meaningful methodology, and there is no waiting for more: the deadline must be met with whatever can be said.

Whereas academics usually write – particularly in the case of journal articles – for other scholars with a shared expertise, analysts usually write for non-experts who do not share their expertise and who do not have time for in-depth study or to follow an issue day in and day out to the degree the analyst does. Analysts therefore are called upon to bridge the gap between the specialist and the generalist. Getting the attention of senior officials – from the President to an Under Secretary – who, by the breadth of their responsibility, are forced to be generalists may mean the analyst has one page, or two or three minutes, in which to make sense of a development. No matter that, ideally, putting this development into historical perspective and into its international context should require considerable background reading and careful study and reflection. There is no such option. However much the generalist reader might benefit from a scholarly tutorial, he or she simply will not sit still for one. Even if you write the kind of paper you would like the policymaker to have in order to get a more comprehensive exposition of what is at issue, it probably will not be read at the highest level. So to reach the reader at that level, the analyst must take the opportunity that is available: one page or nothing, three minutes or none.

Different audiences dictate a different style. And the first rule of persuasive writing is to know your audience. For busy readers, shorter is usually better. The analyst's policymaker audience is unbelievably pressed for time, which may or may not be the case for the scholar reading the academic's work. The analyst's audience determines the writing style, and the one that is most effective for the generalist reader – whether the President, Chairman of the Joint Chiefs, or a cabinet officer – is simple, crisp, readable prose. Good journalistic writing is a good example. What is written must be easy to grasp in a quick reading. Editors, as a surrogate first reader, can provide indispensable help. No one could state the analyst's objective any better than the Scottish author Robert Louis Stevenson when he said, "Don't write merely to be understood. Write so you cannot possibly be misunderstood."[8] And although such writing should be concise, writing clearly and concisely does not necessarily require extreme brevity.

Here is an illustrative example from a declassified January 1964 memorandum entitled "Soviet Economic Problems Multiply," a research paper analyzing what is happening at the time:

In the past few years, Moscow's aggressive foreign policy has been accompanied by boasts of overtaking and surpassing US production by 1970, thus, in Khrushchev's words, defeating capitalism without war. However, an analytical review of recent Soviet economic performance compared with that of the US supports just the opposite conclusion – namely, that the Soviet Union is falling behind in the economic race.[9] . . . the Kremlin leadership for several years has been trying to do too much with too few resources. This living on borrowed capital, improvising cheap but temporary solutions to basic problems such as agriculture, and chronically neglecting balanced development to push ahead spectacularly on a narrow range of goals has finally caught up with the Soviet Union. A nearly disastrous crop failure in 1963 was not the root cause of Moscow's current economic difficulties; what it did was to bring to a head the many underlying problems of the Soviet economy . . . .[10]

Still another sample exemplifies estimative language – looking ahead. It is taken from a National Intelligence Estimate produced in 1978:

As the USSR begins its 11th Five-Year Plan, economic prospects are gloomier than at any time since Stalin's death, and there is a strong possibility the economic situation will get progressively worse in the second half of the decade. Annual increments to national output even in the early 1980s will be insufficient to avoid having to make choices among the competing demands for investment, consumption, the cost of empire, and continued growth in defense spending. As Soviet leaders survey what they regard as a hostile external environment, however, foreign policy and military requirements are likely to dominate their policy calculations. They will therefore try to maintain high defense spending, promote higher productivity and assure domestic control by appeals to a more extreme patriotism, and, if social instability arising from consumer dissatisfaction or ethnic tensions makes it necessary, by resorting to repressive measures.[11]

Sometimes, of course, finished intelligence must be done on the run and off the cuff. And it can work well that way. A friend who was an analyst in the State Department's Bureau of

217

Intelligence and Research remarked that the bureau's most effective analytic "product" often was a one- or two-sentence comment on a report in the Secretary of State's morning briefing, perhaps followed by one or two short paragraphs the next day. The *President's Daily Briefing* keeps items to a single page, sometimes less, with a lot of white space. Always, intelligence writing puts a premium on being able to state key points quickly, succinctly, and with clarity. Restrictions on time and space require an economy of words.

Rising expectations

Demands on the intelligence analyst – and the expectations – are increasing. Everyone is overwhelmed by information. Policymakers are looking to intelligence to help them know what they should be worrying about, what they should be addressing, what their options are, and the likely consequences. They value the ability of the intelligence analyst to integrate data with no axe to grind. Policymakers have insufficient time to read or to contemplate, so helping them cope with the flood of information has become a major service analysts provide.

All the while, the analyst's customers grow, in number and awareness. And no one ever wants less intelligence, in terms of products, briefings, or coverage – only more and better. Congress has an insatiable appetite for intelligence, as do the military services. Executive branch customers abound in the Departments of the Treasury, Energy, Justice, Homeland Security, Commerce, and Agriculture.

What the analyst writes must compete for attention with multiple sources of information including other intelligence producers. The trick is not to cheapen the currency by inundating the reader but to be timely, relevant, and – to emphasize it once again – to provide added value, even when addressing a much-reported issue of the day. Relevance requires contributing uniquely, going beyond what's in the news media. And of course it is worthless if it doesn't arrive when it can be used.

The neutrality question

The desire on the part of the users of intelligence is for analysis that is opportunity-oriented, or actionable – in other words, intelligence they can apply and actually use. Analysis has become an integral part of planning and implementing policy, and of intelligence operations. This is a far cry from what might be termed the traditional, or "old school," conception of analysis which held that to earn and maintain credibility, analysts must be more than policy neutral, they must literally keep their distance from those who were making the policy decisions. Traditional thinking also held that analysis should – again, to earn and maintain credibility – be done independently of those who collect it.

For a number of years, the trend has led away from this traditional view for a variety of practical reasons. Working in isolation only increased the guess-work involved in discerning what policymakers needed to know and thus what collectors needed to collect. In contrast, working collaboratively enables analysts to get an invaluable "feel" for what information the policymaker is missing. Learning at first hand the information needs and priorities of the day helps analysts guide what the collectors must target. Collectors can have a real-time sense of what to collect and analysts have a sharper awareness of what they have to work with and of the illumination and insights they must try to provide.

Today, intelligence analysts are at hand when the making and implementing of policy is on the table. The Director of National Intelligence or his deputy, usually with a substantive expert along, is there to provide an intelligence update and perspective – side by side with the National Security Adviser and representatives of State, Treasury, Defense, Justice, Energy, and the Joint Chiefs of Staff at the principal or deputy level, and involving the President at National Security Council meetings. Analysts and policymakers meet together frequently in deputies' committee and principals' committee meetings and in various gatherings at the working level. At CIA, analysts sit side by side with humint collectors in the operations directorate, now known as the National Clandestine Service. They do so as well at the various centers where analysts and collectors can better focus and share their combined efforts – such as the National Counterterrorism Center, the National Counterproliferation Center, and the International Crime and Narcotics Center.

How analysis informs policy might be answered with "very carefully." It has been said that for analysts to collaborate with policymakers in the interest of relevance while remaining absolutely policy-neutral is like trying to swim without getting wet. Analysts must walk a fine line if their analysis is not to be prescriptive. Somehow they must illuminate alternatives without suggesting which one to take. Clearly their collaboration with policymakers and collectors increases the risk of politicizing intelligence and, accordingly, raises the pressure on analysts to resist it. Tailoring intelligence by no means involves slanting its *content* to curry favor with its recipient; it means making it as relevant as possible by addressing as precisely as possible the policymaker's particular information needs. The analysts' highest calling is to speak truth to power. They must convey assessments that the policymakers surely will not want to hear.

Carmen Medina contends that this can and must be done, but that it does not require disengagement. Asserting that being completely neutral and independent may only gain irrelevance, she has argued that integrity and neutrality are not the same thing:

> Neutrality implies distance . . . and some near mystical ability to parse the truth completely free from bias or prejudice. Integrity, on the other hand, rests on professional standards . . . and if forced to choose between analytic detachment and impact on policymaking, the 21ˢᵗ century analyst must choose the latter.[12]

Fulton Armstrong, a former member of the National Intelligence Council – the Intelligence Community's center for strategic analysis and the production of national estimates – sees it as a matter of focusing on *national* interests rather than policy or political interests, while noting that this is not easily done. Defining and prioritizing national interests are at once more urgent and more difficult than ever, and analysts have to do a lot of the defining for themselves. Armstrong advocates steering clear of value judgments and value-laden labels that assume a certain interpretation of US national interests. The American people elected the policymaker (or his or her boss) to make the value judgments. For their part, analysts should provide a realistic assessment that reflects a range of legitimate interpretations of events and their implications. Then, using a reference to the medical profession, Armstrong recommends that the analyst be a radiologist: take the picture and read the spots on it to the best of your ability, but leave the diagnosis and cure to the doctors.[13]

A former long-time analyst and manager of analysts at CIA advises analysts to be aware that policymakers always have an agenda, and it is one in which domestic political equations are of primary importance. Analysts not only ought not try to tell policymakers what to do, they should recognize that analysis is not going to tell policymakers what to do. Policymakers know what they want to do. Intelligence may be the rationale, but not the reason. (There are never policy failures, only policy successes and intelligence failures![14]) Even though no one should be surprised that policymakers, for their part, "cherry pick" from the intelligence they receive, analysts must resist the temptation to "cherry pick" intelligence items to provide. Policymakers may point publicly to that which seems to support their policy and disregard that which does not. But woe unto the analyst who would cherry pick intelligence likely to please the policy recipient and suppress that which would not. Such a practice would cost the analyst's credibility, and credibility remains the currency of the analyst's realm.

Bias may happen, but nobody instructs you to change your interpretation. This author can honestly say that, as an analyst at CIA, as a manager of analysts, as managing editor of the *National Intelligence Daily*, and in editing the *President's Daily Brief*, he personally never experienced pressure from any higher-ranking officer to alter any analytic judgment to suit a policy line. He has, however, seen an instance or two in which analysts, convinced that their viewpoint was the embodiment of truth, became knee-jerk apologists or advocates for a position or outlook – to an extent that they were no longer seen as objective and open-minded – and whose analytic careers effectively ended as a result.

Walking the tightrope is trickier than ever. It is up to the analysts to negotiate it. Somehow they must maintain an invisible firewall separating the informing of policy from prescribing it, even as they work hand in glove both with policymakers and collectors in order to more effectively identify knowledge gaps and strive to fill them.

Reforms and realities

The shocking attacks of September 11, 2001 on the World Trade Center in New York and the Pentagon in Washington underscored the growing challenges to intelligence in an era of international terrorism in which small groups of individuals can inflict destruction once wielded only by nation-states. The bureaucratic dust still is settling following the hasty, election-year enactment of the Intelligence Reform and Terrorism Prevention Act of 2004, which was an outgrowth of those attacks. That legislation created the position of Director of National Intelligence as an institutional corrective for the failure of the vast US national intelligence apparatus to somehow prevent the terrible events of 9/11. The reorganization followed the completion of various inquiries and studies into what went wrong.[15] The general, overriding conclusion of these inquiries with respect to intelligence analysis (leaving aside the alleged operational and structural failings) was that there had been a failure of imagination. According to a professional staff member of the National Commission on Terrorist Attacks upon the United States, popularly known as the 9/11 Commission, there were several critical aspects to this, among them:

- "Relentless emphasis on current intelligence" had shifted the Intelligence Community's focus from the long term to the issue of the moment.
- The analytic community failed to recognize the attraction of politicized religion as the next big "ism."
- Bin Laden's proclamations were taken to be more of the same empty rhetoric typical of Middle East fondness for hyperbole unmatched by deeds.
- Hints of Sunni–Shia cooperation were dismissed as an alliance that would never occur, and Arab links with Malay and Indonesian extremists were unrecognized – in part because the Intelligence Community, organized regionally, had little ability to match events in one region with those in another.[16]

A consensus of criticism concluded that analysis had become risk averse, more concerned with avoiding mistakes than with imagining surprises, and that there was insufficient integration of analytic efforts across the US Intelligence Community. The Office of the National Director of Intelligence now is at pains to emphasize consultation and collaboration in intelligence analysis on the part of the now sixteen members of the Intelligence Community. The Office of the DNI is providing central direction aimed at rising above the bureaucratic fiefdoms that for years formed barriers to the sharing of sources and analytic perspectives.

Mental roadblocks to more imaginative analysis, however, are persistent challenges.

The post-9/11 studies also emphasized anew what analysts have grappled with for years: the fact that as human beings we all have cognitive bias or preconceived notions that we must acknowledge and beware of lest they color our perceptions and our judgment. We all are culture-bound in our outlook and must consciously strive to recognize this fact and rise above it.

Some of the particular pitfalls the analyst must constantly strive to avoid include:

- *"Clientitis,"* or the tendency to fall in love with your "client," the country you may be assigned to cover, is a sophomoric sin, but one that is not unknown. Developing expertise obviously means knowing a great deal about a country, usually involving extensive travel and often some time in residence. Analysis involves discerning and explaining the motives and point of view of its leaders. But admiration for its language, customs, and culture must not lead the analyst to become the advocate and defender of its leaders and their policies. Objectivity must reign supreme.

- *Mirror-imaging* is the assumption that others would think just the way you do – that, being confronted with the facts of a certain situation, they would calculate the pros and cons and decide their course of action with the same reasoning, and thus reach the same conclusion. (Anthropologist Rob Johnston points out that this term actually is a misnomer, inasmuch as a mirror image is a reverse image. He uses "ethnocentrism" to describe the concept that we tend to perceive foreigners – friends or adversaries alike – as thinking the same way as Americans. He also notes that "trying to think like them" often results in applying the logic of one's own culture and experience to try to understand the actions of others, without knowing that one is using the logic of one's own culture.[17])

- *Mindset* is the tendency to evaluate newly acquired information through an existing hypothesis, rather than using new information to reassess the premises of the hypothesis itself. Douglas MacEachin, former head of analysis at CIA, explains how this happened to analysts trying to determine if or when the Soviet Union would invade Afghanistan in early 1979. Once having judged what the Soviets would require for an invasion force, and thus what military indicators would presage an invasion, analysts disregarded indicators that did not fit that judgment.[18]

- *Groupthink* is the inclination to have one's interpretation reinforced by others coming to the same conclusion. As other analysts arrive independently at the same hypothesis, or simply accept and thereby endorse yours, the analyst is tempted to consider the assessment confirmed. Groupthink thus helps form or reinforces mindset. It also can lead to overconfidence.

- *Linear analysis* presumes a straight-line, sequential projection in which one development appears to flow logically from that which preceded it. An oversimplified illustration is that if we know, for example, that Saddam Hussein had weapons of mass destruction, we know that he tried in several ways to obtain more of them, and that he is successfully concealing what he has done subsequently, linear analysis would lead one to conclude that what he has done subsequently is acquire more weapons of mass destruction. Linear analysis does not allow for the unexpected outcome. As Princeton professor Robert L. Hutchings – former chairman of the National Intelligence Council – put it, "Linear analysis will get you a much-changed caterpillar, but it won't get you a butterfly. For that you need a leap of imagination."[19]

An old example is still one of the best examples of mirror-imaging. The most dangerous superpower confrontation of the Cold War posed the analytic question of whether or not the Soviet Union would send offensive missiles to Cuba. The judgment of analysts across the US Intelligence Community was that a rational actor would not do this, that Soviet leader Nikita Khrushchev would know better than to run such a risk. Yet he sent the missiles on their way. Ironically, the US analysts ultimately were right and Khrushchev was wrong. Sending the missiles was a major error. His humiliating withdrawal of them contributed to his ouster. But the analysts' misjudgment points up the need to be skeptical of a "rational actor" model. The Soviet leader did not see the risk equation in the same way. In the end, it was our insufficient understanding of his psychology and world view that led us to believe the act of sending the missiles would be an irrational option.

Analysts have on a number of occasions been surprised by what seemed from the US perspective to be irrational decisions by foreign leaders. Soviet tanks crushed the reformist government in Czechoslovakia in 1968 when it did not seem in Moscow's interest to do so. In 1973, US (and Israeli) intelligence analysts concluded that it made little sense for Egypt and Syria to attack Israel, given the military inferiority of the Arab side as demonstrated in the 1967 war. It seemed irrational for Saddam Hussein to invade Kuwait in 1990, and for India to explode a nuclear bomb in 1998. But the decision-maker who counted did not see these actions as irrational. (Who knows but what Saddam's analysts concluded in 2003 that the US was only bluffing and would not actually invade Iraq!) Getting out of one's "Western" mindset is always difficult, but it is critical if we are to assess correctly the motives and policies of foreign leaders.

The controversial analytic estimate in September 2002 concerning Saddam Hussein's weapons of mass destruction contained a "perfect storm" of analytic pitfalls. Virtually all of them – mindset, groupthink, and linear analysis – were in evidence to some degree, resulting in a warning for the ages to be wary and to question the conventional wisdom. As a British scholar describes it, the group-think consensus that Saddam was stockpiling weapons of mass destruction was formed

> [D]espite the intelligence community's own agreed assessments that the evidence didn't indicate that he was, or, for that matter, that he wasn't, since the information was too fragmentary to know with certainty and Saddam too mercurial to predict with confidence. The consensus at work had its roots not in raw intelligence or other substantive evidence but in unanswered questions and political assumptions . . . .[20]

Recognizing patterns

Analysis in the first instance is about recognizing patterns. There appears to be a pattern in the concern about how current intelligence analysis draws emphasis away from in-depth, long-term analysis. Although policymakers – especially when a new administration takes office – insist that they want long-term projections that will help them anticipate events and plan wise policies, their attention invariably becomes riveted on the here and now. This has happened time and again, and it should not come as a surprise. It is the here and now that must be addressed, which has to be dealt with. At the very least, the ever-present media will expect a reaction, which the media will spotlight and telecast, broadcast, and reproduce around the world for impact in the farthest corners of the globe. The fact that developments world wide are reported in real time contributes to an atmosphere of perpetual crisis, of needing to respond instantly to anything and everything – an atmosphere in which current intelligence carries the day.

The fact is, decision-makers want and need both long-range and current analysis. It is not an either-or proposition, but the balance probably had tipped away from the in-depth research that is critical to developing expertise. The chorus of conventional wisdom in which post-9/11 inquiries decried an over-emphasis on current intelligence is being heard and acted upon. The National Intelligence Council, for example, already a center of strategic analysis which produces national intelligence estimates and leads Intelligence Community projects, is placing increased emphasis on peer review and the use of outside experts. And the National Intelligence Council has created a new Long-Range Analysis Unit, walled off from any current intelligence demands, to help lead interagency analysis on long-term and under-examined strategic issues.[21]

Occupational hazard

It is easy, of course, to cite instances in which US intelligence assessments missed the mark. The news media do so rather gleefully. It is the nature of their business, just as missing the mark is in the nature of the intelligence business. It is the analyst's daily occupational hazard. More than twenty-five years ago, Columbia University scholar Richard Betts asserted that intelligence failures are not only inevitable, they are natural.[22] They still are, and will continue to be, because to do their job well, intelligence analysts must be willing to take risks. No matter how incomplete, inadequate, uncertain, or contradictory the information on which a judgment must be made, the judgment is nevertheless expected and must be made. And making it necessarily entails a recognition of the risk that the judgment can miss the mark.[23]

Sherman Kent, a former professor of European history who in a thirty-year career in intelligence earned a reputation as perhaps America's foremost practitioner of the analytic craft, was directly involved in the classic misjudgment at the outset of the Cuban missile crisis. Reflecting on it later, Kent asked rhetorically how it could have happened. "The short answer," he wrote, "is that, lacking direct evidence, we went to the next best thing, namely information which might indicate the true course of developments."[24] The reader should mentally underline "might." As Kent put it, if a national intelligence estimate "could be confined to statements of indisputable fact, the task would be safe and easy. Of course the result could not then be called an estimate."[25]

There is no bureaucratic reorganization that can solve once and for all the problem of preventing intelligence misjudgments, because uncertainty itself is the problem. The inevitability of intelligence failures – if this means not predicting exactly when and how something might catch the US by surprise – virtually has the certainty of a law of physics. No one can predict the future, and no one person or organization can be right on all subjects at all times. Allegations of intelligence failure therefore are inevitable, in large part because, in intelligence, failures are inevitable. And failures are trumpeted while successes often are publicly unknown. Analysts have to accept this as the cost of doing business. But rest assured that intelligence often is on target. Presidents would not insist upon it as a daily diet and Congress would not demand and fund it if it were not of value. Much of the value is incremental, and does not come in dramatic, bolt-from-the-blue revelations, but the value is there. And it is a safe bet that it is best produced by analysts who park their preconceptions at the door, constantly review indicators from all sources, question conventional wisdom and their own assumptions (especially if analytical consensus emerges quickly) and weigh alternative explanations.

Human nature being what it is, the various pitfalls discussed above will surely continue to challenge an objective perception and explanation of events. It seems a safe prediction that one or more of these pitfalls will derail an analyst, even if not in a cyclical pattern, in some future instance, notwithstanding any reorganization, training program, or degree of on-the-job emphasis. But new efforts are under way to improve the odds, and renewed efforts always are worth making. At CIA, for example, home of the Intelligence Community's largest analytic component, the creation by the year 2000 of the Sherman Kent School of Intelligence Analysis testified to an intensive effort to teach the tradecraft of intelligence analysis. It is unlikely that anyone will walk into any organization in the US Intelligence Community without having to learn and practice the tradecraft. So, at CIA, experienced intelligence officers with extensive analytic experience run a Career Analyst Program for new analysts, who now spend their first five months with the agency developing the specialized thinking, writing, and briefing skills of intelligence analysis. Interim assignments enable them to apply themselves in various jobs throughout the agency and elsewhere in the Intelligence Community.[26]

On-the-job training continues throughout an analyst's career. Supervisors provide mentoring. Editorial reviews help ensure that analysts communicate their message clearly. Peer review helps shape their research effort and critique their preliminary findings. The professionalizing of today's analysts emphasizes the use of multiple hypotheses and various alternative interpretations of trends and indications. The Office of the Director of National Intelligence promotes critical discussion among analysts throughout the Intelligence Community in addressing analytical challenges.

Personality and temperament also factor into what makes an effective analyst. Those who would work in current intelligence assignments, especially, must be able to work with short deadlines. Structure and predictability may be in short supply. What is guaranteed is a diet of long hours under pressure, and a need to be responsive and flexible. In-depth research requires sifting through mounds of data, and conceptualizing from that data calls for persistent, hard study, developing and bringing substantive knowledge to bear, and doing deep thinking for long stretches. But what also is guaranteed is an unparalleled opportunity to know more about what is happening around the globe. Excitement may not be constant, but a sense of satisfaction characteristically accompanies the work.

Intelligence analysis opens a unique window on world affairs. It offers the prospect that one person's contribution can make a difference in American foreign policy. It offers the thrill of the hunt, the adrenalin that pumps when deadline looms. Analysts who write an item that runs in the *President's Daily Briefing* know that their judgment is appearing in the publication with the smallest and most influential subscription list in the world. Joining forces throughout the US Intelligence Community, analysts illuminate complex issues, detect patterns, identify targets, and increase the US Government's understanding of far-flung developments. Together they contribute significantly to national security in a fascinating profession.

Notes

1 Ronald D. Garst and Max L. Gross, "On Becoming An Intelligence Analyst," in *Learning With Professionals: Selected Works from the Joint Military Intelligence College* (Washington, DC: Joint Military Intelligence College, 2005), p. 39.

2 Foreword to *The Unknown CIA*, by Russell Jack Smith (Washington, DC: Pergamon-Brassey's, 1989) pp. ix, x.

3 William F. Brei, "Getting Intelligence Right: The Power of Logical Procedure," in *Learning With Professionals* (Washington, DC: Joint Military Intelligence College, 2005), p. 55.

4 Ibid., p. 50.

5 *Chiefs of State and Cabinet Officers* and the *World Factbook* are published both in classified and unclassified versions, the latter for public use and available on CIA's Website.

6 Carmen A. Medina, "The Coming Revolution in Intelligence Analysis: What To Do When Traditional Models Fail," *Studies in Intelligence*, Vol. 46, No. 3, 2002, pp. 24–26.

7 Foreword to Richards J. Heuer, Jr., *Psychology of Intelligence Analysis* (Washington DC: Center for the Study of Intelligence, 1999) p. xi.

8 Quoted by James S. Major in "The Basic Tools of Writing With Intelligence," *Learning With Professionals*, p. 9.

9 Central Intelligence Agency, "Soviet Economic Problems Multiply," January 9, 1964, released by the CIA Historical-Review Program and quoted in *Fifty Years of Informing Policy* (Washington, DC: Directorate of Intelligence, 2002), p. 42.

10 Ibid., p 45.

11 NIE 11–4–78, "Soviet Goals and Expectations in the Global Power Arena," released by the CIA Historical-Review Program and quoted in Donald P. Steury (ed.), *Intentions and Capabilities: Estimates on Soviet Strategic Forces, 1950–1983* (Washington, DC: Center for the Study of Intelligence, 1996), p. 474.

12 Medina, op. cit., p. 28.

13 Fulton T. Armstrong, "Ways To Make Analysis Relevant but Not Prescriptive," *Studies in Intelligence*, Vol. 46, No. 3, 2002, pp. 37, 42–43.

14 Martin C. Petersen, Science Applications International Corporation, unpublished remarks at Conference on Intelligence Studies, University of Southern California, Los Angeles, CA, February 3, 2006.

15 See, for example, *9/11 Commission Report: Final Report of the National Commission on Terrorist Attacks upon the United States* (New York: Barnes and Noble, 2004), and *Report of the Commission on the Intelligence Capabilities of the United States Regarding Weapons of Mass Destruction* (Washington, DC: US Government Printing Office, 2005). Recommended as the best single assessment of the 9/11 Report and the consequent rapid congressional and White House response manifest in the Intelligence Reform Act is Richard Posner, *Preventing Surprise Attacks: Intelligence Reform in the Wake of 9/11* (Lanham, MD: Rowman and Littlefield Publishers, Inc., 2005).

16 Thomas Dowling, "Failures of Imagination: Thoughts on the 9/11 Commission Report," *Learning With Professionals*, pp. 133, 135.

17 Rob Johnston, *Analytic Culture in the U.S. Intelligence Community* (Washington, DC: Center for the Study of Intelligence, 2005), pp. 75–76.

18 Douglas J. MacEachin, *Predicting the Soviet Invasion of Afghanistan: The Intelligence Community's Record*, monograph published by the Center for the Study of Intelligence, 2002.

19 Robert F. Hutchings in the Preface to *Mapping the Global Future* (Washington, DC: National Intelligence Council, 2004), p. 1.

20 Philip H.J. Davies, "Intelligence Culture and Intelligence Failure in Britain and the United States," *Cambridge Review of International Affairs*, Vol. 17, No. 3, October 2004, p. 517.

21 Creation of the Long-Range Analysis Unit was announced publicly on March 23, 2006, at the annual meeting of the International Studies Association in San Diego, CA.

22 Richard K. Betts, "Analysis, War and Decision: Why Intelligence Failures Are Inevitable," *World Politics*, Vol. 31, No. 1, October 1978, reprinted with permission in *Studies in Intelligence*, Vol. 23, No. 3, Fall 1979, p. 54.

23 John Hollister Hedley, "Learning from Intelligence Failures," *International Journal of Intelligence and Counterintelligence*, Vol. 18, No. 3, Fall 2005, p. 437.

24 Sherman Kent, "A Crucial Estimate Relived," originally appearing in the classified Spring 1964 issue of CIA's internal journal, *Studies in Intelligence*, republished in *Studies in Intelligence*, Vol. 35, No. 4, Winter 1991, p. 67.

25 Ibid., p. 65

26 John Hollister Hedley, "The DI: A History of Service," in *Fifty Years of Informing Policy*, Washington, DC: Directorate of Intelligence, 2002, p. 17.

Part 5

Counterintelligence and covert action

17

Cold War intelligence defectors

Nigel West

The objective of every counter-intelligence organization is to identify, penetrate and then control or neutralize its adversary, and during the Cold War the opportunities afforded by intelligence defectors provided the principal protagonists with the most effective means of achieving their goals.

By way of definition, a defector is an individual who is either an intelligence officer, or has worked as a cooptee for an intelligence agency, or has sufficient knowledge of intelligence significance to be a valued asset and merit political asylum. Thus Arkadi Shevchenko, although a regular diplomat at the United Nations, should be counted as a defector, partly because he had acted as a spy for the CIA for several months prior to his defection, but also because his knowledge included information concerning the KGB's *rezidentura* in New York, and its operations. Equally, the Soviet pilot Viktor Belenko qualifies for inclusion as his MiG-25, which he flew to Japan, amounted to an impressive technical intelligence coup. Similarly, George Blake and Edward Lee Howard, who were not intelligence officers at the time of their defections, deserve the description, even if their settlement in Moscow was as a consequence of a fear of imminent arrest.

The physical act of seeking political asylum in an adversary's country is known as defection, and the perpetrators may have been motivated by self-preservation, ideology, resentment, a personal or professional crisis, or some other psychological factor. Defectors to Moscow were invariably driven by the need to escape the imminent consequences of their espionage, and this category includes Guy Burgess, Donald Maclean, Glen Souther and Ed Howard. Defectors to the United States were more numerous and most were prompted by a fear of recall to Moscow (Igor Gouzenko, Piotr Deriabin, Yuri Rastvorov, Vladimir Petrov, Anatoli Golitsyn, Vladimir Kuzichkin, Sergei Bokhan, Arkadi Shevchenko), or by the need to terminate a period of active espionage (Michael Goleniewski, Oleg Lyalin, Oleg Gordievsky). Although almost all subsequently espoused political or ideological motivations for the defections, their personal circumstances were invariably complicated by adverse personal, family or professional factors which could be remedied or improved by the lure of exchanging valuable information for resettlement.

Defectors have been proved to be an exceptionally important source of information and also act as good indicators of the integrity of a particular counter-intelligence agency. The statistics demonstrate that few spies are caught as a result of the "vigilance of colleagues" or routine security screening. Overwhelmingly, they are arrested because they have been identified to molehunters, either by an active source or, most likely, by a defector.

While the Czech, Romanian, Bulgarian, Cuban, East German and Polish services proved resilient to penetration by western agencies, they all suffered from very damaging defections. In contrast neither the FBI, CIA, MI5, DST, DGSE nor SIS ever endured the loss of a serving officer to physical defection, although the BND and BfV experienced long-term penetration and frequent defections throughout the Cold War.

Defectors have changed the course of history, and the way history has been interpreted. The defection of Igor Gouzenko in September 1945 may be taken as a useful starting-point for the Cold War, but his decision to switch sides predated similar choices taken by Louis Budenz, Whittaker Chambers and Elizabeth Bentley, all of whom supplied valuable information about Soviet espionage in the United States. Bentley, though widely disparaged in the media at the time, was responsible for initiating over a hundred investigations conducted by the FBI.

The defections of Guy Burgess and Donald Maclean in 1951 certainly changed British culture. Hitherto the concept of the mole, the agent farmed for a long-term return on investment, was almost completely unknown, although subsequent reexamination of the claims made by the prewar defector Walter Kritivsky suggested that when interviewed by MI5 in 1940 he had been the first to provide information about spies who would later turn out to be Donald Maclean, Kim Philby and John Cairncross. Similarly, the defection of Vladimir and Evdokia Petrov in Canberra in April 1954 was the first example of a *rezident* switching sides. For a variety of reasons 1954 was definitely the year of the defector, with Piotr Deriabin and Nikolai Khokhlov also line-crossing, all within two months of each other, and the drama played out in Australia.

The Cold War defectors earned their resettlement through a "meal-ticket", being the information they can trade for a new life, and were regarded highly by counter-intelligence agencies because they generally arrived well equipped, fully aware of the need to provide a meal-ticket of value. Very few, if any, made spontaneous decisions, and most took a long period agonizing over their choice and acquiring information that would guarantee them a good reception. This material falls into six distinct categories: knowledge of future plans; current operations; past events; order-of-battle data; canteen or corridor gossip; and the recommendations of other candidates for recruitment. All could prove to be of exceptional importance.

By the nature of their work defectors tended to be better informed than most of their contemporaries in their restricted societies, perhaps more politically aware, and generally well educated with experience of foreign travel and a grasp of other languages. However, their relative sophistication raised the specter of the despatched defector, as espoused by Anatoli Golitsyn, a phenomenon the existence of which has never been proved. The concept of sending a staff officer to an adversary is a high-stakes game, and there are few purported examples, although Yuri Nosenko received hostile treatment, including lengthy incarceration, because it was suspected he was just such an individual. The best-publicized example is that of Oleg Tumanov, but there is evidence to suggest that his version of events, as described in his autobiography, is a fabrication designed to conceal the truth, that he was a genuine defector who was found by the KGB and persuaded to spy after he had been resettled in Munich. His redefection occurred because he had been warned of his imminent betrayal by another defector, Viktor Gundarev, who knew the details of his cooperation with the KGB.

What makes the Tumanov case so *piquant* is that he gave evidence on the defection phenomenon to Senate Permanent Subcommittee on Investigations in October 1987, along with Stanislas Levchenko and Viktor Belenko.

In David Wise's *The Spy Who Got Away* Donald Jameson, a legendary CIA case officer (and later vice president of the Jamestown Foundation), recalled a false defector in Manila, a trade mission official who was debriefed in Munich in 1983, apparently for the purpose of testing the relationship between the CIA and the Philippine security apparatus. Precisely what happened thereafter is unknown.

There are three other examples. In Montreal Anatoli Maximov, codenamed GOLDMINE, appeared to succumb to a pitch from the Royal Canadian Mounted Police (RCMP) but seems to have declared at least a partial part of the recruitment to his *rezident* who authorized a continuing contact. This was a bold and dangerous strategy, but there were compelling reasons at the time to allow the relationship to continue. The KGB wanted to test its own mole already inside the RCMP, whose existence was unknown to Maximov, and believed it had control over the operational game. This was an extraordinarily exceptional case, requiring a sanction from the very top of the KGB, but it is an illustration of the very controlled environment in which such enterprises could be contemplated.

In one case, a contact was established with a high-value officer in Moscow (codenamed PROLOGUE) who expressed a desire to defect. The skeptics in the CIA were not surprised when, as the moment came for his exfiltration, PROLOGUE made a feeble excuse to break off the contact. Forensic analysis suggests the entire exercise had been undertaken to peddle certain disinformation designed to protect a mole inside the CIA, Aldrich Ames. The acid test had been PROLOGUE's willingness to take the crucial step and place himself entirely in the hands of the CIA, and when the moment came the KGB understandably backed away.

The overwhelming need to provide the CIA molehunters with alternative explanations for obvious leaks and to distract them from their quarry prompted the KGB to take some desperate measures, As well as PROLOGUE, a source in Germany supplied some authentic information about the case officer handling an agent with the codename GT/FITNESS. The source asserted that the leaks had come from the CIA communications center at Warrenton, Virginia. A lengthy investigation suggested the source was a KGB-controlled double agent, but not before the molehunters, then closing in on Aldrich Ames, were temporarily distracted.

The fear of the false defector essentially handicapped, if not paralysed, American counter-intelligence efforts to attract Soviet defectors between 1964, when Nosenko was denounced as a plant, and 1975 when the COURTSHIP project was initiated to reverse the policy. Another hazard was that of redefection, surely the ultimate rejection, and maybe a sign of failure on the part of the putative asylum host. Vitali Yurchenko, who returned to Moscow in 1985 is probably the best known, but is by no means a unique example. Others include: J.D. Tasoev and Oleg Bitov from London; Andrei Remenchuk from Montreal; Nikolai Petrov from Jakarta; Artush Hovanesian from Turkey; Evgenni Sorokin from Vientiane. Redefection may occur for a combination of reasons but it is an occupational hazard in all free countries where someone granted asylum is quite free to return home. Indeed, to prevent them would be a breach of the law in most circumstances. Nevertheless, redefection may offer the opportunity of a propaganda coup, and both Bitov and Yurchenko were paraded at press conferences despite the KGB's knowledge that neither had been the victim of an abduction, as alleged. Their separate stories, of being held against their will and being administered sedatives and other drugs, were never believed by the KGB, although political expediency ensured both men received a very sympathetic, if cosmetic, welcome. Yurchenko's change of heart, apparently spontaneous and unrehearsed, took place while he had been dining alone in Georgetown with an inexperienced young security officer, but it prompted an intense debate about the possibility that he was indeed a rare example of a despatched defector. On the one hand it appeared his information, about Ed Howard and Ronald Pelton, had been authentic, but might there have been an underlying subplot, perhaps an effort to discard unproductive agents so as to protect a more valuable spy? This interpretation would surface again when Aldrich Ames was arrested, and yet again when, following the exposure of Robert Hanssen, there was speculation about another, hitherto undetected supermole.

Ultimately, the counter-intelligence analysts concluded that Yurchenko had been a genuine defector, albeit one troubled by the belief that he was suffering from the terminal stomach cancer that had killed his mother. A series of disappointments followed during his resettlement, including rejection by his former lover, and an unsuccessful tour of the country, intended as a vacation, which sent him into a depression, apparently caused by the realization that he would find life on his own in the United States too great a challenge.

So what possesses an intelligence officer, presumably a member of his society's well-educated and urbane elite, to abandon the system he has grown up in and benefited from, for an alien culture? Can defectors be relied upon to tell the truth? Human nature suggests they may have sought to impress their hosts by pretending to have undergone a political conversion, in preference to revealing aspects of their own frailty which may not necessarily reflect well upon them. Under close examination, few defectors really seem to have really changed their political creed, but more likely have experienced professional, personal or family crises that have acted as a catalyst. Igor Gouzenko and Vladimir Kuzichkin, for example, feared the consequences of being disciplined for professional lapses. Oleg Gordievsky and Oleg Lyalin had experienced marital problems and found solutions that might have disadvantaged their careers.

A senior French intelligence officer, the Comte de Marenches, is credited with the observation that defector information is like wine: the first pressing is best, and subsequent growths are generally inferior. The implication is that some defectors are pathological attention-seekers who succumb to embroidery to retain contact with their new professional colleagues, and this accusation has been leveled at both Igor Gouzenko and Anatoli Golitsyn. Both proved exceptionally temperamental, and later complained that some of their initial information had been ignored, misinterpreted or deliberately overlooked, casting a pall over the standard of their resettlement handling.

Sensitive post-defection treatment is vital if others are to be encouraged to follow an individual's example, and litigation claiming breach of promise or other complaints are an anathema. Unfortunately, very few intelligence defectors can be found suitable work in their field, so retraining is invariably necessary, with mixed results. Occasionally a defector can be retained as a consultant, as happened with Anatoli Golitsyn, Yuri Nosenko and Nikolai Artamonov, but very few experience Piotr Deriabin's total absorption into the intelligence community, or find that their associated professional skills are as highly prized as those of the computer genius Viktor Sheymov. A large number become authors, intending to capitalize on their experiences, but very few go on to write more books, although Igor Gouzenko, Grigori Tokaev and Vladimir Rezun (alias Victor Suvorov) are notable exceptions.

Aside from the immediate and obvious value of a defector, whose meal-ticket can be exploited, defectors represent something of a yardstick by which the intelligence agencies of their host countries can be assessed. For example, Yuri Rastvorov originally intended to defect to the British, not the Americans, but changed his mind when he suspected the Secret Intelligence Service had been penetrated. Indeed, between the defections of Grigori Tokaty in 1946 and Oleg Lyalin in 1971, no British intelligence agency received *any* Soviet Bloc defector, whereas many opted for the CIA, a strong indication that potential candidates considered the security environment in England too dangerous because of high-level penetration. However, the safe receipt and resettlement of a defector can represent an opportunity to undertake a "dog-and-pony show," an international tour of allied intelligence agencies so other liaison services can meet and talk to an authentic defector. Such prestige events allow agencies to recover lost reputations and, in the case of Oleg Gordievsky's dramatic exfiltration from Moscow in August 1985, prove that a long-term source could be run successfully over a period of years, in his case eleven, and then be rescued from hostile territory should the need arise. Such achievements demonstrate eloquently that an agency's integrity remains intact.

Accordingly, defectors during the Cold War fulfilled many functions, far beyond their obvious utility as sources of reliable intelligence. Inevitably, of course, myths have been created around them, perhaps the most widely circulated being the danger of assassination. In fact, although the KGB is known to have traced Igor Gouzenko, Vladimir Petrov, Alexander Orlov and made considerable efforts to find Oleg Lyalin, the only intelligence defectors to have been the victims of a deliberate attempt on their lives were Nikolai Khokhlov and the Bulgarian defector Vladimir Kostov, and both survived the experience. Thus the phenomenon of Cold War defection can be viewed as having been not entirely risk-free, but was certainly an infinitely valuable source of counter-intelligence data.

Bibliography

Akhmedov, Ismail, *In and Out of Stalin's GRU*. London: Arms & Armour; 1984.
Andrew, Christopher and Gordievsky, Oleg, *KGB: The Inside Story*. London: Hodder; 1990.
Bailey, Geoffrey, *The Conspirators*. New York: Harper Bros; 1960.
———, *KGB: The Secret Work of Soviet Secret Agents*. Hodder; 1974.
Barron, John, *KGB Today: The Hidden Hand*. New York: Reader's Digest; 1983.
Bentley, Elizabeth, *Out of Bondage*. New York: Ivy Books; 1988.
Bernikow, Louise, *Abel*. New York: Trident; 1970.
Brook-Shepherd, Gordon, *The Storm Birds*. London: Weidenfeld & Nicolson; 1988.
Carr, Barbara, *Loginov: Spy in the Sun*. New York: Howard Timmins; 1969.
Chambers, Whittaker, *Witness*. London: Random House; 1952.
Corson, William and Crowley, Robert, *The New KGB*. New York: Morrow; 1985.
Corson, William, Trento, Susan, and Trento, Joseph, *Widows*. New York: Crown; 1989.
Dallin, David, *Soviet Espionage*. New Haven, CT: Yale University Press; 1955.
Deriabin, Peter, and Bagley, T.H., *The KGB: Masters of the Soviet Union*. New York: Hippocrene; 1990.
Deriabin, Peter and Gibney, Frank, *The Secret World*. New York: Doubleday; 1959.
Donovan, James, *Strangers on a Bridge*. New York: Atheneum; 1964.
Dzhirkvelov, Ilya, *Secret Servant*. London: Collins; 1987.
Dziak, John, *Chekisty*. New York: Lexington Books; 1988.
Epstein, Edward Jay, *Deception*. New York: Simon & Schuster; 1989.
Foote, Alexander, *Handbook for Spies*. London: Museum Press; 1964.
Golitsyn, Anatoli, *New Lies for Old*. London: Bodley Head; 1984.
Gouzenko, Igor, *The Iron Curtain*. New York: Dutton; 1948.
Hood, William, *Mole*. New York: W.W. Norton; 1982.
Hurt, Henry, *Shadrin: The Spy Who Never Came Back*. New York: McGraw Hill; 1981.
Kessler, Ronald, *Spy vs Spy*. New York: Scribner's; 1988.
Khokhlov, Nikolai, *In the Name of Conscience*. New York: McKay; 1959.
Krivitsky, Walter, *In Stalin's Secret Service*. New York: Harper Bros; 1939.
Kuzichkin, Vladimir, *Inside the KGB*. London: Andre Deutsch; 1990.
Levchenko, Stanislav, *On the Wrong Side*. Washington DC: Pergamon-Brassey; 1988.
Mangold, Tom, *Cold Warrior*. New York: Simon & Schuster; 1991.
Manne, Robert, *The Petrov Affair*. Sydney: Pergamon; 1987.

Martin, David C., *Wilderness of Mirrors*. New York: Harper & Row; 1980.

Massing, Hede, *This Deception*. New York: Duell, Sloan & Pearce; 1951.

Petrov, Vladimir and Evdokia, *Empire of Fear*. London: Frederick Praeger; 1956.

Philby, Kim, *My Silent War*. London: McGibbon & Kee; 1968.

Pincher, Chapman, *Their Trade is Treachery*. London: Sidgwick & Jackson; 1981.

——, *Too Secret Too Long*. London: Sidgwick & Jackson; 1984.

Richelson, Jeffrey T., *Sword and Shield*. New York: Ballinger; 1986.

Romerstein, Herbert and Levchenko, Stanislav, *The KGB against the "Main Enemy"*. New York: Lexington; 1989.

Rositske, Harry, *The KGB: The Eyes of Russia*. New York: Doubleday; 1981.

Sakharov, Vladimir, *High Treason*. New York: Putnam's; 1980.

Sigl, Rupert, *In the Claws of the KGB*. New York: Dorrance; 1978.

Suvurov, Viktor, *Inside Soviet Military Intelligence*. London: Hamish Hamilton; 1984.

Werner, Ruth, *Sonya's Report*. London: Chatto & Windus; 1991.

Wise, David, *Molehunt*. New York: Random House; 1992.

Appendix I. US defectors to the Soviet Union

Name	Agency	Date of defection	Conclusion
Barr, Joel	Contractor	1950	Died 1998
Carney, Jeffrey M.	Air Force	1985	38 years prison
Cohen, Lona		1950	Died 1993
Cohen, Morris	Army	1950	Died 1995
Field, Noel	State	1949	Died
Hamilton, Victor	NSA	1963	Found in Russia 1992
Howard, Edward Lee	CIA	1985	Accidental death 2000
Martin, William H.	NSA	1960	Now Sokolovsky
Mitchell, Bernon F.	NSA	1960	Return denied in 1979
Peri, Michael A.	Army	1989	30 years prison
Rohrer, Glen R.	Army	1965	
Sarant, Alfred	Contractor	1950	Died 1979
Souther, Glenn M.	Navy	1986	Suicide, June 1989

Appendix II. Soviet intelligence defectors

Name	Agency	Location	Conclusion
Gouzenko, Igor	GRU	Canada, September 1945	
Granovsky, Anatoli	NKVD	Stockholm, September 1946	
Bakhlanov, Boris	NKVD	Vienna, July 1947	
Borodin, Nikolai	GRU	London, August 1948	
Tasoev, J.D.	NKVD	Berlin, 1948	Redefected
Tokaev, Grigori	GRU	Berlin, 1948	
Rastvorov, Yuri	KGB	Tokyo, January 1954	
Burlutsky, Grigori	KGB	Berlin, June 1954	
Deriabin, Piotr	KGB	Vienna, February 1954	
Khokhlov, Nikolai	KGB	Frankfurt, February 1954	
Petrov, Vladimir	KGB	Canberra, April 1954	
Petrova, Evdokia	KGB	Darwin, April 1954	
Hayhanen, Reino	KGB	Paris, May 1957	
Tuomi, Kaarlo	KGB	Milwaukee, March 1959	

Name	Agency	Location	Conclusion
Kaznacheev, Alexander	KGB	Rangoon, June 1959	
Goleniewski, Michal	UB	Berlin, December 1960	
Stashinski, Bogdan	KGB	Berlin, December 1961	
Golitsyn, Anatoli	KGB	Helsinki, December 1961	
Krotkov, Yuri	KGB	London, September 1963	
Nosenko, Yuri	KGB	Geneva, February 1964	
Framakovsky, Olga	KGB	Beirut, October 1966	
Runge, Evgeni	KGB	Berlin, October 1967	
Sigl, Rupert	KGB	Berlin, April 1969	
Kiselnikova, Raya	KGB	Mexico City, February 1970	
Sakharov, Vladimir	KGB	Kuwait, July 1971	
Lyalin, Oleg	KGB	London, August 1971	
Chebotarev, Anatoli	GRU	Brussels, October 1971	Redefected
Sabotka, Anton	KGB	Montreal, March 1972	
Petrov, Nikolai	GRU	Jakarta, June 1972	Redefected
Hovanesian, Artush	KGB	Turkey, July 1972	Redefected
Sorokin, Evgeni	GRU	Vientiane, September 1972	Redefected
Myagkov, Aleksei	KGB	Berlin, February 1974	
Nadirashvili, Konstantin	KGB	Vienna, June 1975	
Belenko, Viktor	Red Air Force	Hakodake, September 1976	
Zemenek, Ludek	KGB	New York, May 1977	
Rezun, Vladimir	GRU	Geneva, June 1978	
Levchenko, Stanislav	KGB	Tokyo, October 1979	
Dzurkvelov, Ilya	GRU	Geneva, March 1978	
Bogaty, Anatoli	KGB	Morocco, September 1982	
Kuzichkin, Vladimir	KGB	Tehran, October 1982	
Unidentified		Manila, May 1983	
Fen, Chang	KGB	New York, December 1983	
Gezha, Igor	KGB	Delhi, March 1985	
Bokhan, Sergei	GRU	Athens, May 1985	
Yurchenko, Vitali	KGB	Rome, August 1985	
Gordievsky, Oleg	KGB	London, August 1985	
Gundarev, Viktor	KGB	Athens, February 1986	
Agranyants, Andrei	KGB	May, July 1986	
Remenchuk, Andrei	GRU	Montreal, December 1987	Redefected
Smurov, Yuri	GRU	Montreal, May 1988	
Ignaste, Vladimir	KGB		͵
Papushin, Sergei	KGB	1989	
Baranov, Vyacheslav	GRU	1991	Served 4 years
Gayduk, Anatoli	KGB	Canada, 1991	
Lunev, Stanislav	GRU	Washington, 1991	
Mitrokhin, Vasili	KGB	Riga, September 1992	
Dzheikya, Rollan	MFA	New York, 1996	
Tretyanov, Sergei	KGB	New York, 2001	
Zaphorovsky, Vladimir	KGB	New York, 2002	

Appendix III. Soviet Bloc intelligence defectors

Name	Service	Location	Conclusion
Shainberg, Maurice	Polish Army	Tel Aviv, March 1957	*Breaking from the KGB*
Tisler, Frantisek	StB	New York, 1958	
Monat, Pawel	UB	Vienna, June 1959	*Double Eagle*
Goleniewski, Michal	UB	Berlin, December 1960	
Szabo, Laszlo	AVB	London, 1965	
Lombard, Florentino	DGI	June 1967	
Bittman, Ladislav	StB	Vienna, 1968	
Sejna, Jan	Czech Army	Trieste, February 1968	*We Will Bury You*
August, Frantisek	StB	London, 1969	
Frolik, Jozef	StB	London, 1969	
Iacobescu, Ion	DIE	Paris, 1969	
Hidalgo, Orlando	DGI	March 1970	*A Spy for Fidel*
Svreddlev, Stefan	DS	1971	
Dumitrachescu, Constantin	DIE	Tel Aviv, 1972	
Rauta, Constantin	DIE	1973	
Tipanut, Virgil	DIE	Copenhagen, June 1975	
Kostov, Vladimir	DS	June 1977	
Marcu, Ion	DIE	Tehran, 1977	Canada
Pacepa, Ion	DIE	Bonn, July 1978	*Red Horizons*
Mantarov, Iordan	DS	Paris, 1981	
Svec, Milan	StB	Washington, 1985	
Winkler, Martin	HVA	Buenos Aires 1985	
Dombrovski, Siegfried	HVA	1985	
del Pino, Raphael	DGI	May 1987	

18

Counterintelligence failures in the United States

Stan A. Taylor

Introduction

As the name suggests, counterintelligence is the process of countering the hostile intelligence activities of other states or foreign entities. The Counterintelligence Enhancement Act of 2002 requires counterintelligence to identify, assess, prioritize, and counter intelligence threats to the United States. The US Intelligence Community (IC) is made up of sixteen somewhat independent intelligence agencies, many with semi-autonomous sub-agencies, each of which is responsible for its own counterintelligence.[1] A National Counterintelligence Executive (NCIX) exists within the IC, but its function, according to its official web site is to "improve the performance of the counterintelligence (CI) community in identifying, assessing, prioritizing and countering intelligence threats to the United States; to ensure CI community efficiency and effectiveness, and to provide for the integration of the CI activities of the US Government." Exactly how NCIX does this is not made clear, but it appears up to now that its primary power is hortatory.

Day-to-day actual counterintelligence work, however, is very fragmented and decentralized. The very nature of counterintelligence requires that it must be performed within each IC agency, within each of the IC sub-agencies and inter-IC offices, and by every private contractor or other entity that deals with sensitive information and activities. In other words, every entity that deals with classified information must keep its own house clean, neither the NCIX, the FBI, nor any other agency can do it for them. Proposals for a new super counterintelligence agency miss this point. Counterintelligence must be decentralized.

Measuring counterintelligence failures

Measuring counterintelligence failures is not easy. Counterintelligence failures, like morning cereal, come in many sizes, shapes, and varieties (and some are worse for you than others). Some failures are merely mischievous while others are malicious. The most significant may go undetected for long periods of time, some may be detected even before they occur, and some, though detected, may never be revealed. Nor is it possible to measure something that does not happen. Nevertheless, a failure occurs anytime some counterintelligence task or function is not carried out. Anytime a foreign nation or group gains access to US classified information, sensitive proprietary information, or technology, counterintelligence, to one degree or another, has failed. Anytime opportunities are missed to use the agents of hostile nations or groups to enhance your own security, counterintelligence has failed. In a general sense, anytime a hostile intelligence service has succeeded in diminishing US national security and placing American citizens at greater risk, some aspect of counterintelligence work has been inadequate.

No one really knows how much sensitive information ends up in the hands of those who wish to harm America. But estimates do exist of how many groups are seeking sensitive information. In a report to the House Judiciary Subcommittee on Immigration, Border Security and Claims in 2004, then National Counterintelligence Executive (NCIX) Michelle Van Cleve claimed that "[n]early 140 nations and some 35 known and suspected terrorist organizations currently target the United States for intelligence collection through human espionage and by other means." Many of these attempts involve sensitive economic or proprietary information and fall within the purview of economic espionage, but others may result in compromising American defenses. Often the information obtained is of little import, sometimes it is actually misleading, but occasionally it is very damaging to US national interests. Critical foreign policy or national security initiatives may be compromised, sensitive technology or information may be lost, and the economic advantage or gain that even seemingly insignificant proprietary information might bring to the nation may never be realized if counterintelligence fails.

The most glaring, often the most damaging, and always the ones that garner the most public and media attention are those failures in which US citizens who are in positions of trust and are charged to protect classified information reveal that information to others in violation of that trust. What follows is a list of the primary tasks or practices of counterintelligence followed by examples of failures to perform that particular task.[2] However, while this list focuses on individuals who have betrayed their country, it is important to keep in mind that many other kinds of failures occur that do not involve treason.

The analysis below draws from information about American traitors collected by either the Defense Personnel Security Research Center (PERSEREC) or the updated data base collected from open sources by Taylor and Snow.[3] According to the PERSEREC data base, 153 Americans have committed treason between 1947 and 2004. The Taylor and Snow data base consists of 186 traitors from 1941 to 2005.

Counterintelligence tasks and failures

Pre-employment background checks

All IC employees, as well as all people who handle classified information, are given background checks before they can gain access to that information. These background checks begin with biographical data but usually require interviews with people who have known the applicants. Ideally, questions will be asked that will reveal character flaws, divided loyalties, personality disorders, and other characteristics that might disqualify them from dealing with sensitive national security information. For many IC agencies, this background check may also involve polygraph or lie detector tests. While many scholars doubt the utility and validity of the polygraph, few doubt that the fear of being put on the box acts as a deterrent. While the CIA, the National Reconnaissance Office (NRO), the Defense Intelligence Agency (DIA) and the National Security Agency (NSA) have used the polygraph for many years, the Federal Bureau of Investigation (FBI) only began to polygraph employees after the disastrous Robert Hanssen case.

Inadequate background checking or vetting, as it is often called, can be a source of counter-intelligence failures. Failure to detect character flaws, indications of disloyalty, or other attributes that may reveal a reasonable possibility of treason at this stage of the employment process will result in dubious employees being placed throughout various intelligence agencies and in other positions of trust where classified or sensitive information is handled.

Unfortunately, pre-employment vetting does not work very well for two reasons; first, strictly speaking, it is not intended to detect treason but rather to check the suitability of new employees to handle classified information. According to Herbig and Wiskoff:

> The vetting procedures for security clearance focus on the applicant's background, past activities, and experiences, to generate information that serves as the basis of an educated judgment on the likelihood the person will be trustworthy and reliable. These procedures are not designed to identify spies, and when put to the test they have not done so. At least six individuals in the espionage database were screened and granted or retained security clearances while they were actively engaged in espionage.[4]

Second, not very many individuals enter intelligence professions in order to become traitors. Even those who later betray their country for ideological or other reasons may not have sought to gain access to classified material primarily to commit treason. Of the 186 traitors in the Taylor and Snow data base, possibly only five may have sought professions where they would deal with classified information for the primary purpose of providing that information to a foreign government. And even with these five, the open source information is not entirely clear.

Larry Wu-tai Chin may have been such a penetration agent. He joined the Communist Party in China while he was a college student in the 1940s. He was later recruited by the US Army to work in China during the war. After the war he became a naturalized US citizen and gained employment with the CIA in 1952. He delivered classified information to the Chinese People's Republic for 33 years before he was identified by a Chinese intelligence agent who defected to the United States.

Jonathan Pollard may also have entered work involving classified material primarily so he could provide information to Israel. An employee of the US Navy, Pollard supplied classified information to Israeli intelligence for nine years. His loyalty to Israel appears to have been greater than his loyalty to his own country long before he began working for the Navy. As Pollard and his wife grew accustomed to the monthly retainer the Israelis were paying them, their motivation for treason gradually changed from ideology to financial gain. At the time of their arrest, they even had a large collection of classified information they were apparently trying to sell to China. But it appears Pollard sought work with classified information so he could deliver it to Israel, a fact that should have been picked in his pre-employment vetting.

Ana Belen Montes may also fit into this category. She was a US citizen of Puerto Rican descent who worked in the Justice Department. Public sources suggest she may have sought employment with the Defense Intelligence Agency (DIA) under instructions from Cuban intelligence in order to have access to information desired by Cuba. She also refused advancement opportunities that might have reduced her access to classified information so she could continue to provide information to Cuba.

A more recent case involving a naturalized American of Chinese birth and his permanent resident alien brother, Chi Mak and Tai Wang Mak, may also illustrate a vetting failure.

Although this case has not yet been tried as of this writing, it appears they sought work with sensitive national security information primarily so they could provide that information to China.

These may be the only cases in which people sought employment with national security related agencies primarily to betray their country. If so, only five out of 153 traitors might have been detected during pre-employment vetting. It does not appear that many future traitors seek work with classified information so they can then commit treason. Nevertheless, Chin, the Pollards, Montes, and the Mak brothers were all vetted before they were given access to classified information and should have been stopped at that stage. Clearly, most traitors enter the path of treason once they are into their careers. This does not prevent pre-employment vetting from detecting character flaws, but it does make it much more difficult to do so.

No statistics have been made public by the government as to how many applicants for clearances are denied access because of something detected at this stage. Obviously, those who enter this work in order to betray their country can disguise their motives and avoid detection during pre-employment vetting.

In-service security monitoring

Each agency also monitors its own employees during their careers. Many require periodic polygraph tests during which the employees are asked questions about their lifestyles as well as questions about foreign contacts and about classified material they have handled. New and younger employees tend to be somewhat intimidated by these periodic lie detector tests. Older ones know that "most of the devices now available, like the polygraph, detect not the lie but anxiety about the lie."[5] Moreover, the results of polygraph tests are no better than the training, experience, and quality of the person who administers them. Other aspects of employee lifestyles – dramatic changes in financial worth, changes in spending habits, aberrant sexual practices, etc. – are also observed independently and may provide questions for future polygraph sessions as well as act as warning signs to counterintelligence officers.

When in-service monitoring is not successful, national security is weakened. A discussion of failures to detect treason while it was being committed should not detract from the many cases where it was detected and stopped. Open source information does not always reveal the extent to which professional counterintelligence techniques and hard work resulted in the capture of a traitor, often before the information was ever revealed.

A quarter of the 153 individuals in the PERSEREC data base were caught before information was transmitted and only 20 percent of them spied longer than five years. These facts attest to either successful counterintelligence or to poor tradecraft on the part of the traitors – probably a little of both. Taylor and Snow expressed amazement at "the poor level of tradecraft, even abject stupidity, displayed in many cases" of traitors appearing in their database.[6] Younger spies, enlisted military personnel, and others with no training in intelligence tradecraft were the most likely to make foolish mistakes that led to their capture.[7] But even those with intelligence tradecraft training (Walker, Ames, and Hanssen, for example) made serious errors while committing treason, often brought on by overconfidence after long years of successful betrayal.

Nevertheless, the record of practicing traitors being overlooked during in-service monitoring is one of the most discouraging aspects of counterintelligence. The failure of in-service monitoring can be illustrated in any of a number of cases, but nowhere more dramatically than in the case of one of the most famous and most damaging spies in American history – Aldrich Ames. Because of his father's long employment with the CIA, Ames began working as a document clerk for the agency while still a college student in Washington, DC in 1967. He continued with the agency through different positions and began his nine-year career of spying for the Soviet Union in 1985 and continued working for Russia after the Soviet regime collapsed.

Ames's behavior over those years should have alerted the CIA's counterintelligence officers and his colleagues to his treason. He openly violated agency rules many times. While stationed in Rome he either failed to report his meetings with Soviet intelligence officers or reported them but claimed he was trying to recruit them. Once back in the US, he openly displayed his new wealth by paying cash for a $540,000 home, flaunting his new red Jaguar automobile in the CIA parking area, and receiving expensive cosmetic surgery for his deteriorating teeth – all on a $64,000 annual salary. He offered no better explanation for this than that his foreign-born wife had inherited a lot of money. He apparently had few anxieties about his treason since he passed at least two polygraph tests while an active traitor.[8]

In-service vetting has not proven as effective as one would expect it to be. Perhaps when more sophisticated lie detection devices are available, it will be more successful.[9] Herbig and Wiskoff point out that at least "six Americans were screened [that is they received in-service vetting] and then maintained their security clearances during periods when they were also committing espionage."[10]

Maintaining employee job satisfaction

Many US intelligence officers, particularly over the last 30 years, have taken a first step towards treason when they have become dissatisfied or disgruntled because of career developments. Proactive counterintelligence must examine how various intelligence agencies are treating their employees. The secretive nature of intelligence work prevents many new employees from gaining a full understanding of their future careers before they actually get on the job. Surely it cannot be expected that every person hired will be successful in intelligence work. For a variety of reasons, attrition occurs throughout the employment period in every line of work. But when intelligence officers begin to find out they are neither "Q" nor Jack Ryan nor most certainly James Bond, or when poor performance evaluations start to roll in, when advancement slows down, or even when employees sense that neither they nor their work is fully appreciated, job dissatisfaction begins. Intelligence officers who are unhappy in their careers may turn to treason for revenge or excitement. Or they may become prime targets for foreign recruitment. But whether the record shows that they betrayed their country for money, for ideological reasons, or for any of the other usually listed reasons, the earliest thoughts of treason are often justified by job dissatisfaction.

When employees with access to national security secrets become disgruntled with their work, they start to search for ways to "get even" with their employers. Over the years, treason has been built on the twin foundations of ideology and money with money gradually, but clearly, becoming the most prevalent motive.[11] But people who are satisfied with their careers tend to be loyal to their employers and loyal people do not commit treason. And when one "considers those who, though not completely disgruntled, were not entirely 'gruntled' (to borrow from Oscar Wilde), then disgruntlement becomes a more prevalent motive" for treason.[12] Neither sympathy for a foreign cause nor a desire for more money will cause satisfied employees to betray a trust. Even dissatisfied employees will not commit treason as long as they believe they can resolve problems through a fair and open personnel system.

In fact, maintaining satisfied employees may become one of the better defenses against treason. In the future, the most significant counterintelligence efforts may well be made, not by the counterintelligence icons of fact or fiction (James Jesus Angleton or George Smiley, for example), but by the human resource staffs in each intelligence agency. Perhaps Andrew Roberts saw only the tip of the iceberg when he wrote in 1997, "Tomorrow's traitors are more likely to be driven to betray not from ideological convictions but from whining complaints about poor pension provisions or underfunded performance-related pay."[13] When those who handle secrets grudgingly plod through their daily tasks, they not only become targets for foreign recruitment, but they often see treason as a source of revenge against their employers. It is often only then that excitement, greater appreciation, and money become secondary motives.

Interviews with scores of former IC employees suggest that enlightened and responsive leadership and management practices, collegial work conditions, the absence of "cronyism" in salary and advancement decisions, fair rewards for quality service, work equality, and getting employees to "buy" into the mission of the agency for whom they work may be the best and most enduring counterintelligence practices. Some who have left intelligence work have reported that even an occasional verbal expression of appreciation would have made a difference in their feelings about their careers.[14]

Stella Rimington, a former director of MI5, the British internal security agency, appears to appreciate the importance of making employees feel wanted. In her novel about a fictional MI5 employee, she has the woman's supervisor say to her, "Liz, your work is highly valued" and "You've done exceedingly well."[15] Few intelligence officers can claim to have heard these words. A former Director of the CIA's Counterintelligence Center states this need very succinctly: "Honor Thy Professionals."[16]

Human resource personnel may also be able to ease employees through personal life crises that are related to stressful work conditions. As Herbig and Wiskoff have noted, "one-quarter of known American spies experienced a personal life crisis in the months before they attempted to commit espionage."[17] Many crises occur quite independent of work – parents, spouses, and children die, illness strikes, and so on. But one wonders how many of those crises were either work-related (divorce, illness, and psychological problems) or, though unrelated to work, nevertheless spilled over into the work environment.

William Kampiles is an example of an employee whose treason might have been prevented by more effective personnel practices. Kampiles joined the CIA's Directorate of Operations in 1977 and was assigned as a Watch Officer in the cable room. With his childhood dream of wanting to work for the CIA now fulfilled, he looked forward to an exciting career. But after failing to become a case officer, he resigned from the agency and concocted a plan to demonstrate to his superiors that he had what it took to become a spy. Taking a technical manual he had stolen from the Watch Room, Kampiles fled to Greece and sold the document to the Soviet intelligence officers for $3,000. It happened to be a manual for the highly classified and latest real-time overhead satellite – code-named KH-11. Kampiles was obviously unaware of the value of the document since the Soviets would undoubtedly have paid ten times that amount for it.

On his return to the US, Kampiles contacted someone at CIA by letter and told them he had conned the Russians out of some money and placed himself in a position to become a double agent for the CIA. Whether his treason could have been prevented through better personnel practices will never be known, but after failing to become a case officer, Kampiles would have been a perfect candidate for some sort of career counseling by a human resource office. Since he sold the manual, Kampiles is usually classified as having committed treason for financial gain. But disgruntlement over his failure to get into the clandestine service was his first step and it is a step that better career counseling might have prevented.

Kampiles also illustrates the effect of fantasy in some espionage. In fact, the number of traitors who wanted to play out a fantasy with espionage is surprising. PERSEREC lists 18 of their 153 traitors who were fulfilling some sort of fantasy. Taylor and Snow call this motive the "James Mitty" syndrome because it "combines the allure of a James Bond life style with a Walter Mitty sense of fantasy."[18]

Brian Patrick Regan's treason also illustrates the impact of disgruntlement. He worked for both the US Air Force and the National Reconnaissance Office (NRO) for 20 years, yet was arrested for attempting to sell national security secrets to China and Iraq in 2003. Regan complained to fellow workers many times that his small pension was an insufficient reward for his efforts. He complained about his job and about his treatment but was given no career counseling.

Herbig and Wiskoff point out that disgruntlement was a motive in 41 of their 153 cases and then write that "among individuals with access to highly classified information in a workplace, realizing that volunteering to spy is a potential outlet for people who are demoralized or resentful, management should redouble efforts to maintain a cohesive work environment."[19] This is especially the case for the 38 spies in the PERSEREC data base who were not recruited by a foreign intelligence service but who sought out foreign governments to whom they could sell their secrets. Disgruntlement and its closely related sentiment, revenge, are also the primary motives for the unauthorized disclosure of classified information – usually referred to as leaking – that will be discussed below.[20]

Facility security

Successful counterintelligence is impossible if facilities where secrets are produced and stored are not secure. Every IC agency as well as every government office, institute, business, or contractor that deals with classified information is responsible for its own facility security. Thus, facility security varies widely from location to location with some of America's worst security breaches occurring at defense contractor facilities. It is the responsibility of IC counter-intelligence officers to monitor security at all of these sites and to take actions when that security is lax.

Some of the most sensitive defense and intelligence information within the US government is actually in the hands of private contractors. Fourteen of the 153 traitors in the PERSEREC data base were affiliated with these kinds of contractors. Others had limited experiences with defense or intelligence contractors. Failure to maintain careful security at these facilities has resulted in very damaging security leaks.

Perhaps the most illustrative case is the one of Christopher J. Boyce who was a young employee at TRW, a major California defense contractor. He worked as a communication specialist in a vault used to secure highly classified information but where security practices were very lax. Along with his friend from high school days, Andrew D. Lee, Boyce stole or photocopied classified information that they sold to Soviet intelligence officers at the Soviet Embassy in Mexico City. The information compromised the Rhyolite intelligence satellite, one of America's most sophisticated satellite systems. Reportedly, it was the Rhyolite satellite that, among other things, was picking up Soviet Politburo communications from car phones until the system was compromised by Boyce and Lee.

A second example of this kind of failure is the case of Randy M. Jeffries who was a messenger for a private Washington, DC firm that recorded and made transcripts of classified hearings before the House Armed Services Committee. He was observed entering the Soviet Military Office in Washington, DC and later arrested as he attempted to sell documents to an FBI agent posing as a Soviet official. Jeffries had a checkered employment record. He worked as a support employee of the FBI for two years and, after losing that job, was arrested for heroin possession.

243

Nevertheless, he obtained work at a company that dealt with a broad range of highly classified military information. When pre-employment vetting failed to alert the company to his background, sound security practices on the part of the contractor should have prevented this treason. The judge before whom this case was tried even commented during the trial that poor security practices in the contracting firm contributed to the problem.

Communications security

The NSA is responsible for overall communications security. They provide, maintain, and verify secure communications equipment at most IC agencies and other offices that handle classified information. However, each agency also carries out some communications security functions within its own facilities.

How much information has been lost through a failure to communicate over secure lines or a failure to use sophisticated encryption equipment is not known. Obviously, foreign agencies are not in the habit of issuing reports on how much information they obtained through overheard conversations. Nevertheless, it is a counterintelligence failure when it occurs if only because it is an intelligence success to the foreign service that collects it.

But few areas of training for those who work with classified information are more important than communication security. All too often individuals who are likely targets for foreign surveillance will discuss classified information on open communication lines or in public settings merely with the false reassurance created by circumlocution rather than from secure communication practices. The security awareness posters used during World War II pictured employees who had access to classified information having a casual conversation outside of the office with a Nazi spy discreetly straining to overhear. The message printed on the poster was "Loose lips sink ships." With the spread of cell phones, text messaging, and other forms of wireless communication, the problem goes beyond "loose lips" today.

Classification and compartmentation

Information that might reveal sensitive national security secrets is classified by the government. This process is meant to prevent the information from falling into the wrong hands. Information may be classified both vertically and horizontally. There are three horizontal levels of classified information – CONFIDENTIAL (used with decreasing frequency), SECRET, and TOP SECRET. TOP SECRET information may be divided into vertical divisions called codeword compartments. The information in each compartment usually comes from a unique and specific intelligence collection source. That is, information derived from a particular human source or through a secret technical process will be classified as TOP SECRET and given a unique codeword. For example, intelligence derived from intercepted and decoded communications between Soviet military and diplomatic offices in the US and Moscow in the 1940s and 1950s was classified as TOP SECRET/VENONA.

Issues of classification and compartmentation are continual thorns in the side of democratic governments. Virtually no one believes they protect classified information as they should, but virtually everyone agrees that governments have a legitimate right to keep sensitive national security information secret and that a failure to do so can put security at risk.

The damage created when classified information falls into foreign hands may range from slight to very serious. However, those who steal and reveal that information usually do not know into which category it falls. They usually believe the seemingly insignificant bit of information they reveal is of little or no value to anyone. Or they may believe that it should not have been classified in the first place. But even though a single piece of a large puzzle may appear to be of little significance to the person who reveals it, it may be the last piece needed by the person who receives it in order to gain a clearer picture of some major plan, policy, or equipment of critical importance to the government. Some traitors sought and revealed information they knew to be of great significance, but others claimed their information was not particularly helpful to the foreign state, even though it may have compromised a significant human or technical source. Neither William Kampiles nor Christopher Boyce was aware of the damage done by their treason. The treason of Ames and Hanssen even resulted in the deaths of many individuals.

The same is usually true of those who leak classified information. A leak is an unauthorized disclosure of classified information and those who leak information may not be aware of its significance. The journalist, for example, who published a story in 1958 that US intelligence was able to monitor Soviet missile tests had no idea of the consequences of his revelation. American monitoring was possible because of the eight-hour advance warning the Soviets gave for their tests. This gave American intelligence time to place monitoring platforms in place. When the Soviets learned the Americans were monitoring their tests, they cut the advance warning time in half – an action that forced major changes in US monitoring practices and ultimately cost millions of taxpayer dollars.[21] The information may have been an insignificant piece of a puzzle to the reporter, but it revealed a clear picture to the Soviets.

In 1970, the US began a satellite surveillance program that allowed American intelligence to listen in on car telephone conversations of Soviet Politiburo members. Much of this information was extremely valuable but it was also compromised when an American reporter revealed US capabilities in a newspaper column.[22]

Many similar stories could be told, but one of particular interest since 9/11 is the story first related in 2002 by US presidential spokesperson, Ari Fleischer, that

> as a result of an inappropriate leak of NSA information, it was revealed about [sic] NSA being able to listen to Osama Bin Ladin on his satellite phone. As a result of the disclosure, he stopped using it. As a result of the public disclosure, the United States was denied the opportunity to monitor and gain information that could have been very valuable for protecting our country.[23]

The problem has been around for a long time. A 1985 law review article argued that lax enforcement of ambiguous laws has created a climate in which "persons who leak [classified] information . . . may do so with impunity."[24] It is obviously not an easy problem to solve for at least three reasons. To begin with, the First Amendment to the US Constitution protects freedom of speech. On more than one occasion, the publication of classified information focused public attention on dubious, or even illegal, government activities and the leakers were seen as heros. But at other times, this practice has compromised important government programs and weakened national security. Freedom of speech has never been interpreted as without limits. A citizen does not have the right to falsely shout "fire" in a crowded venue, is the oft-cited example of one limitation. But whether or not leaking classified information is akin to shouting "fire" depends on many things which need greater legislative clarification.

Second, the First Amendment also protects freedom of the press which has been interpreted to mean that journalists cannot be forced to reveal their sources. So leakers cannot be prosecuted because journalists do not have to reveal their names. America recently went through an agonizingly slow, and (as of this writing) unsettled, episode trying to determine who leaked the name of an undercover CIA case officer to a reporter. This case has called attention to this problem, but has not resolved it. This case also illustrates a fundamental axiom in dealing with leaks – the difficulty of prosecution rises with the political level of the leaker.

Third, the problem of leaks is complicated by the ubiquity and utility of them. Most leaking is done to either favor or hinder legislation or competing policies. The White House leaks the most, the Defense Department ranks next, and Congress trails in third place. As long as leaking appears to have no consequences and is seen as a useful policy tool, it will continue.

Intercepting and decoding foreign communications

For counterintelligence purposes, foreign communications must first be intercepted and then, if it is a coded communication, it must be decoded. If this can be done successfully, then foreign intelligence agents, or Americans reporting to them, can be identified and stopped or used as a source for disinformation. For example, what was given the codename VENONA (mentioned above) in the 1960s began in 1941 as a communications interception program run by the Army Security Agency and taken over by the NSA when it was created in 1952. The names of many well-known American and British traitors – Klaus Fuchs, Kim Philby, Alger Hiss, the Rosenbergs, just to name a few – were confirmed through VENONA, even though it took until several years after the treason was committed for all messages to be decoded.

Because of its extremely sensitive nature, very little is known about the government's contemporary codebreaking capabilities. Such information is, obviously, very highly classified and protected. Historically, however, we know that intercepted and decoded communications have made significant contributions to national security. The true intentions about German ambitions in 1917 were revealed in the famous Zimmerman telegraph – a codebreaking success of the British, not the Americans. The role of codebreaking in World War II is also well known. The ability to decipher intercepted German Enigma codes played a significant role in defeating German forces and in deceiving Germany as to the true location of the D-Day invasion in 1944.[25] Successful codebreaking contributed to several major victories in the Pacific theater as well.[26] Also, the American ability to read Soviet diplomatic and military communications emanating from the US (the VENONA effort) ultimately revealed the extent of Soviet penetration into the highest policy-making corridors of Washington, DC during the last years of World War II and into the Cold War.

However, today, freely available and sophisticated software programs can be downloaded from the internet that can make anyone's communications very secure. These programs turn plain text into code and are of great concern to counterintelligence officers. These encryption devices were formerly available only to NSA but now are available to all. The computer of more than one captured terrorist has contained coded communications, and such material now requires extensive time and effort to decode. Ramzi Yousef, often identified as the mastermind of the 1993 World Trade Center bombing, stored information about his terrorist activities on a personal laptop computer. He felt secure in doing so because he encrypted his information using encryption freeware. While living in Manila in order to conduct bombings against the Philippine government, Yousef had to rush out of his apartment when chemicals with which he was working caught fire. The encrypted information on the laptop he left behind was of great value to counterintelligence officers from many countries. Unfortunately, not all of the files could be decrypted.

While little is known about the government's ability to *decode* foreign communications, quite a bit is known about the scope of its ability to *collect* vast amounts of foreign communications.[27] The NSA collects foreign communications in its attempt to enhance American security, but is forbidden by law to collect communication involving US persons without a "warrant-like" document from the FISA Court, a special court created by the Foreign Intelligence Surveillance Act (FISA) of 1978. According to classified information leaked to the press in late 2005, the NSA may have violated these rules by intercepting the conversations of some Americans.

It appears that in late 2001, as part of the post-9/11 war on terrorism, the Bush Administration authorized NSA to eavesdrop on communications between identified terrorists and their contacts in the US. It did this without permission from the FISA Court. In late 2005, the program was leaked to the media and the administration became involved in a national furor over the legality of the operation. The Bush Administration claimed that the urgency of the war on terrorism justified by-passing the FISA Court but civil libertarians claimed that the government was violating the fundamental right to privacy guaranteed by the Constitution. As of this writing, neither the scope of the program nor the value of any information received through it is known for certain; however, it became a highly politicized matter and illustrates well the delicate balance between security and privacy.

Prosecuting traitors

Anti-espionage laws are not effective unless penalties exist for revealing or stealing secret information. Foreign agents in the US who are caught stealing secrets or receiving classified information will be expelled from the country if they are under official cover – that is, if they are employees of a foreign government. If they are not under an official passport, if they are ostensible employees of private businesses or in the country illegally, they may be arrested, prosecuted, and jailed. US citizens or US persons who are caught revealing classified information are subject to federal prosecution under a variety of anti-espionage Acts of Congress.

As with all crimes, some potential traitors may be deterred by fear of punishment and if there is no public perception of successful prosecution, the deterrent effect is vitiated. From 1945 to 1978, the prosecution of traitors (as opposed to leakers, who form a separate category) was complicated by the unwillingness of federal courts to accept presidential authorization for electronic surveillance as meeting constitutional standards. Similar surveillance for domestic crimes was carried out under court-issued warrants which met the "probable cause" and reasonable "search and seizure" requirements of the Fourth Amendment. In the absence of legislative authorization to conduct similar electronic surveillance for national security purposes, however, evidence presented to courts gathered under warrantless presidential authorization was usually not accepted. This made prosecution almost impossible.

Counterintelligence officers also were reluctant to take traitors to court for two reasons. First, to do so might confirm to a foreign state that the information it had received was, indeed, important and accurate. Secret information is always viewed suspiciously by the purchasing party for fear it might be phony information made up by the seller just to earn some money. Or, even worse, it might be disinformation designed to deceive the receiving state. Second, to reveal enough information to obtain a regular criminal warrant might compromise the sources and methods by which that information was obtained.

FISA changed all of that. It created a special court (usually called the "FISA Court") with unique procedures that are "consistent with the 'reasonable search' requirement of the Fourth Amendment."[28] While releasing the Department of Justice from the traditional Fourth Amendment "probable cause" requirement, FISA still required specified procedures that protected civil liberties and banned electronic surveillance of Americans merely on the order of a government official under vague "national security" justifications. FISA was supported by the IC and by various civil libertarian organizations and has been upheld in series of court cases since 1978.[29]

247

At least until the furor created by the Bush administration's use of surveillance without FISA Court orders beginning in 2002, the FISA court and its procedures have been quite widely supported and the more frequent and successful prosecution of traitors is usually attributed to them (see Table 18.1).

Table 18.1 Foreign Intelligence Surveillance Act Court Surveillance Orders issued annually

Year	Orders issued
1979 (partial year)	207
1980	319
1981	431
1982	475
1983	583
1984	635
1985	587
1986	573
1987	512
1988	534
1989	546
1990	598
1991	593
1992	484
1993	511
1994	575
1995	697
1996	839
1997	748
1998	796
1999	886
2000	1,012
2001	934
2002	1,228
2003	1,721 (4 rejected)
2004	1,758

Sources: US Senate, Select Committee on Intelligence and the Administrative Office of the US Court System.

Counterintelligence cooperation

While catching foreign agents or their American assets is a complicated task, primarily under the direction of the FBI, successful counterintelligence efforts require thorough cooperation between every intelligence agency. This is particularly true of the FBI and the CIA, but it is also true of the entire IC. But the success of counterintelligence in America rises or falls with the level of cooperation between the FBI and the CIA. The story of their competition and lack of cooperation is well known and of legendary proportions.

Community-wide cooperation is necessary, but the absence of cooperation between the CIA and the FBI, particularly, is a serious problem. The 9/11 Commission reported that it was a significant factor in the IC's failure to prevent the terrorist attacks in 2001. Since 9/11, both legislation and executive directives have mandated greater cooperation and collaboration. However, senior IC officials, intelligence scholars, and journalists have questioned whether an adequate level has been achieved.

Whether this competitive relationship results from some sort of a culture clash or is merely a good old-fashioned turf war is unclear. One of the lasting legacies of long-time FBI director, J. Edgar Hoover, was an unwillingness to cooperate with other IC agencies. And that attitude is not unique to the FBI. It is not uncommon in Washington, DC for agencies to compete for scarce resources by withholding information from other agencies in order to get more credit and, hopefully, more money in their budgets. In most cases, this may be unseemly, but it may not harm national security interests. However, when this kind of competition occurs within the IC, it is more than unseemly and can seriously weaken counterintelligence efforts.

This lack of cooperation goes back much earlier than 2001. Even before the CIA was created, its predecessor, the Office of Strategic Services (OSS) was prevented from placing personnel in Latin America because Hoover convinced President Franklin D. Roosevelt that the FBI could take care of that geographic area. After World War II, the FBI was limited to domestic jurisdiction and the CIA was limited to foreign jurisdiction. But even that fundamental distinction between the two agencies has gradually eroded with the CIA's domestic operations gradually growing and the FBI's international operations growing like Topsy. The FBI, which only a few years ago would station a few FBI "legal attachés" (legats) in a few critical US embassies around the world, now have a very large presence in embassies all over the world. Originally, legats were used to liaise with foreign police groups and extra-national groups like Interpol. The war on terrorism is now used to justify their presence in many more embassies where they are even allowed to recruit and run their own agents.

Some have argued that the problem between the CIA and the FBI is some sort of culture clash or a result of different operational codes. Siobhan Gorman has even argued that the FBI "is from Mars" and the CIA "from Venus," drawing on a popular book from several years ago.[30] It is true that the FBI measures success by its number of arrests and successful prosecutions while the CIA does so by the value of the information it provides to decision-makers. This has obviously and understandably created two different operational codes, but it should be used as an excuse for competitive behavior that damages counterintelligence. It was this very type of competition between these two agencies that delayed the detection and capture of Aldrich Ames for several months.

The absence of adequate cooperation within the IC led to the creation of the Director of National Intelligence (DNI) office in 2004. The DNI was supposed to be given the necessary personnel and budget authority to enforce greater cooperation. While cooperation is greater in some areas of the IC than it was earlier, the failure to include many of the Department of Defense (DoD) intelligence operations under the authority of the new DNI is widely seen as a weakness of the 2004 reorganization. Intelligence scholar Loch Johnson uses the metaphor of an "800-pound gorilla" – that is, a muscular secretary of defense unwilling to and strong enough to resist, ceding his authority over military intelligence – to highlight the absence of a motive for the DoD to cooperate as much as it should in the IC.[31] The intelligence activities of the DoD have grown dramatically since 2001, most recently by its placement of Military Liaison Elements (a euphemism for military special forces teams) in more than a dozen embassies around the world.

One of the ironies of the lack of cooperation within the IC is that efforts to fix the problem often make it worse. Virtually every time an "intelligence failure" occurs, a new agency is created to prevent a future failure. The new agency, however, often merely stakes out its own turf and the problem created by the proliferation of too many intelligence agencies is compounded by the new agency. The OSS and its successor, the CIA, were created to fix the problem created by the lack of cooperation between various military intelligence units prior to the Pearl Harbor attack in 1941. And literally scores of agencies and sub-agencies created since then have been justified as a way to fix subsequent failures but have, in effect merely added to the problem.[32]

Conclusion

The counterintelligence techniques and practices listed above constitute an arsenal of no small significance. Nevertheless, the record of treason in the United States suggests it could be much better. Every task or procedure must be performed exactly. Many American traitors have been detected, not through the CI techniques listed above, but through self-confessions, from captured foreign intelligence service records, by foreign intelligence offices who have defected, or through willing or unwilling partners in treason who have contacted US counterintelligence officers. As William Webster, former director of both the FBI and the CIA, stated before US Senate Hearings in 2002, "Almost every spy that we have found both in the CIA and the FBI, has been found with the aid of recruited sources of our own in other hostile intelligence agencies."[33] Surely the very existence of these sources within a foreign intelligence should be counted as a counterintelligence success. However, nearly all of them volunteered and were not recruited by US agencies.

In spite of having the most expensive and extensive intelligence services in the world, the US has suffered from many counterintelligence failures. The tools and techniques are all in place, but various weaknesses; negligence, gaps, failures to cooperate, the need to protect civil liberties, poor personnel management, and other factors discussed above have diminished America's counterintelligence shield.

Some developments are favorable, however. FISA procedures, when followed, have made the detection and prosecution of traitors easier. Clearly, the 1978 Act was not meant to stand as drafted forever. Although FISA originally allowed only electronic surveillance, it has subsequently been amended to allow physical searches and the post-9/11 USA PATRIOT Act made additional and controversial changes to the Act as well. As the techniques to elude detection improve, techniques to facilitate detection must also be reviewed and, if found to meet constitutional standards, adopted.

And, with the exception of DoD participation, intelligence cooperation between IC agencies has increased marginally. Nevertheless, to bring about greater cooperation in the two agencies that have resisted it for many years has not been an easy task. And the "go it alone" attitude of DoD remains a major problem.

In response to terrorist attacks in the 1980s, then Director of Central Intelligence (DCI) William Casey, under the direction of President George H. W. Bush created a CIA Counterintelligence Center (CIC) involving both FBI and CIA officers. (Moreover, NCIX, without much operational authority, is making progress in promoting counterintelligence awareness and cross-agency needs.) But, in response to the Ames case, President Clinton reorganized the National Counterintelligence Center in 1994 through Presidential Decision Directive (PDD) 24. It was now called the National Counterintelligence Center (NACIC). The Center was to be directed by a senior FBI official but was to be staffed by senior counterintelligence officials from both the FBI and the CIA. President Clinton's Decision Directive required an "exchange of senior managers between the CIA and the FBI to ensure timely and close coordination between the intelligence and law enforcement communities."[34] This "interagency forum" was meant to bring about the cooperation and collaboration needed in counterintelligence work and included representatives from virtually every agency in the IC.

Subsequent "intelligence failures," particularly 9/11, have suggested that the earlier re-organizations were not effective and on 21 March 2005, President George W. Bush announced a new reorganization for US counterintelligence capabilities. His new strategy called for a more pro-active effort, particularly in the area of recruiting assets from terrorist groups. Even that reorganization did not seem to have the desired effect and on 27 January 2006 President Bush appointed one of the Deputy Directors of the Office of the Director of National Intelligence to also act as the Acting National Counterintelligence Executive. Few intelligence functions have been reorganized as many times as the counterintelligence function. The latest plan should make budget and personnel easier to manage.

But a new strategy and a new Office of Counterintelligence Excutive (ONCIX) alone will not do the job unless budget and personnel authorities are really exercised by the DNI. The disjointed and fragmented counterintelligence effort of the US has seldom had more important tasks to accomplish. The giant poisonous snake America faced during the Cold War has disappeared, but in its place are hundreds of smaller poisonous snakes more difficult both to detect and deter. Every counterintelligence function has become even more critical. As former DCI Richard Helms wrote in his autobiography, "No intelligence service can be more effective than its counterintelligence component for very long."[35]

Notes

1 The number of agencies making up the US Intelligence Community varies, depending on what is counted. The official web page for the Director of National Intelligence contains the emblems of sixteen agencies. See <http.www//dni.gov>.

2 The best available list of all counterintelligence techniques is found in Frederick L. Wettering, "Counterintelligence: The Broken Triad," *Intelligence and National Security* 13 (2000): 265–300.

3 Stan A. Taylor and Daniel Snow, "Cold War Spies: Why They Spied and How They Got Caught," *Intelligence and National Security* 12 (1997).

4 Katherine L. Herbig and Martin Wiskoff, *Espionage Against the United States by American Citizens 1947–2001* (Monterey, CA: Defense Personnel Security Research Center, 2002), 78.

5 Robin Marantz Henig, "Looking for the Lie," *New York Times Magazine*, February 5, 2006, 47. Henig reviews much of the latest scientific research about lie detection.

6 Taylor and Snow, "Cold War Spies," 118.

7 One can only view with astonishment the would-be traitor who while drinking at a bar confided in the man on the adjacent stool that he wanted to sell secrets. The unknown drinking buddy was an off-duty undercover police officer who contacted Naval Intelligence Service officers. Nor should we forget another would-be traitor who, after failing to gain entrance to the Soviet embassy in Washington, DC, wrapped his secrets in a bundle with his name and phone number inside and threw them over the embassy wall. Embassy guards, suspecting it was a bomb, called local fire officials who retrieved the classified information and turned it over to the FBI. See Taylor and Snow, "Cold War Spies," 118.

8 The entire Senate Select Committee on Intelligence report on the Ames case can be found at <http:// www.loyola.edu/dept/politics/intel/sab4.html>.

9 See Henig, "Looking for the Lie," 47.

10 Herbig and Wiskoff, *Espionage Against the United States*, xiii.

11 See Taylor and Snow, "Cold War Spies," 103. The best open-source work on treason is done by PERSEREC in Monterey, California. See, for example, Susan Wood and Martin F. Wiskoff, *Americans Who Spied Against their Country Since World War II* (Monterey, CA: Defense Personnel Security Research Center, 1994), Herbig and Wiskoff, *Espionage Against the United States*, and Lynn F. Fischer, "Espionage: Why Does It Happen," at <http://www.hanford.gov/oci/maindocs/ci_r_docs/whyhappens.pdf>, accessed 20 December 2005. See also Theodore R. Sabin and others, *Citizen Espionage: Studies in Trust and Betrayal* (Westport, CT: Praeger, 1994).

12 Taylor and Snow, "Cold War Spies," 110.

13 The *Sunday Times* (London), May 25, 1997, as cited in Lathrop, *The Literary Spy* (New Haven, CT: Yale University Press, 2004), 398.

14 As a professor of national security affairs for over 40 years, I have had literally hundred of students gain employment with intelligence agencies. Many of the comments in this section stem from discussions with them. A minority of them have become dissatisfied and left those careers, but even the majority who have been satisfied in their work and remained have called my attention to personnel practices that cry out for change.

15 Stella Rimington, *At Risk* (London: Hutchinson, 2004), 52 and 172.

16 James M. Olson, "The Ten Commandments of Counterintelligence," *Studies in Intelligence* (unclassified edition), Fall–Winter, No. 11, 2001.

17 Herbig and Wiskoff, *Espionage Against the United States*, 55.

18 Taylor and Snow, "Cold War Spies," 118.

19 Herbig and Wiskoff, *Espionage Against the United States*, B12.

20 See Martin Linsky, *How the Press Affects Federal Policymaking: Six Case Studies* (New York: W.W. Norton, 1988).

21 Christopher Andrew, *For the President's Eyes Only* (New York: Harper Perennial Library, 1995) 359.

22 See Loch Johnson. America's Secret Power: The CIA in a Democratic Scoeity (New York: Oxford University Press, 1989), 201.

23 White House Press Conference, 20 June 2002.

24 Eric E. Ballou and Kyle E. McSlarrow, "Plugging the Leak: A Case for Legislative Resolution of the Conflict between Demands of Secrecy and the Need for an Open Government," *Virginia Law Review*, June 1985, 5.

25 Lest one assume that was an easy task, three messages sent on the German Enigma machine in 1942 have remained "uncracked" for over 60 years. These messages were sent using the four-rotor Enigma and were thought to be unbreakable. However, using what is called distributed open source computing, that is inviting anyone to have a go at the code, one of these messages was broken in mid-February 2006 using what is called a brute force attack. That is, every possible version of the message for each of the rotor settings was tried. Three remain enciphered. See Graeme Wearden, "Distributed Computing Cracks Enigma Code," *New York Times*, 6 February 2006.

26 The most enthusiastic review of the contribution of cryptography in World War II is found in Hervie Hauffler, *Codebreakers' Victory: How Cryptographers Won World War II* (New York: New American Library, 2002). A more conservative estimate of the impact of intelligence on war is found in John Keegan, *Intelligence in War: Knowledge of the Enemy from Napoleon to Al-Qaeda* (London: Hutchinson, 2003).

27 According to a former director of NSA, just one major listening post maintained by NSA can collect 2 million pieces of information each hour. See the PBS news broadcast of 20 December 2005 at <http://www.pbs.org/newshour/bb/terrorism/july-dec05/nsa_12–20.html>, accessed on 16 March 2006.

28 The quotation is from United States, Senate, *Foreign Intelligence Surveillance of 1978*, Report No. 95–701, 95th Cong., 2d sess. (Washington, DC), 9. The material is this section is drawn from Taylor and Snow, *Cold War Spies*.

29 The US Senate Select Committee on Intelligence reviewed many of these cases in its *Foreign Intelligence Surveillance Act of 1978: The First Five Years*, Report 98–660, 98th Cong., 2d sess. (Washington, DC, 1984), 1.

30 "FBI, CIA Remain Worlds Apart, *National Journal*, 1 August 2003, accessed at <http://www.govexec-.com/dailyfed/0803/080103nj1.htm> on 14 March 2006.

31 See Johnson, "The Aspin-Brown Intelligence Inquiry: Behind the Closed Doors of a Blue Ribbon Commission," *Studies in Intelligence*, Vol. 48, No. 3 (2004).

32 See Stan A. Taylor and Daniel Goldman, "Intelligence Reform: Will More Agencies, Money, and Personnel Help?" *Intelligence and National Security*, Vol. 19, No. 3 (Autumn 2004).

33 Cited in Lathrop, *The Literary Spy*, 58.

34 White House, Office of Press Secretary, 4 May 1994.

35 Richard Helms (with William Hood), *A Look Over My Shoulder: A Life in the Central Intelligence Agency* (New York: Random House, 2003), 34 and 35.

19

Émigré intelligence reporting

Sifting fact from fiction

Mark Stout

The book *Countdown to Terror* by Congressman Curt Weldon describes an Iranian expatriate referred to only as "Ali" who offered the Congressman, and through him the CIA, information about the situation inside the closed regime in Iran.[1] "Ali" lived in Paris and reportedly was a former high-ranking official in the Shah's government whose information derived from unspecified sub-sources. His information portrayed an Iran preparing to launch terrorist attacks against the continental United States, operating in cooperation with al Qaida, and on the verge of having a nuclear weapon.[2] However, his intelligence was not all doom and gloom. The secret apparatus of which "Ali" was a part was, he said, in contact with key clerics who were prepared to move against the government and establish a liberal democratic regime.[3]

"Ali" did not shy away from putting the hard sell on the United States. In June 2004 he told Congressman Weldon that Iran was preparing terrorist attacks against oil infrastructure. "If we get financial assistance," Ali wrote, "we could give exact *locations* and *means* for the attack."[4] By September 2004, "Ali," apparently discouraged that he was not getting through to the US Intelligence Community, had started to scale back his reporting. Of this time Weldon wrote, "Ali reminded me . . . that the information he is providing is merely a sample of much better, more significant, and detailed, intelligence that could be obtained. His sources expected him to use their secrets to buy a working relationship with the CIA which has the resources to pay them 'real money'."[5]

For indeed, the CIA did not bite. Aside from matters of interpretation, Weldon's account of the CIA's handling of the "Ali" case is quite similar to that of the former CIA chief in Paris who later discussed the case in an on-the-record interview with *The American Prospect*. According to the Congressman, the CIA dragged its feet before finally meeting with "Ali" and then dismissed his information as recycled from open press reporting, a claim that Weldon disputes. The CIA complained that "Ali" would not name his sub-sources. "Ali's" objections to this were that he did not wish to be subservient to the agency nor did he trust it to protect those sources, but in fact, he "refused to give me any information that would indicate he actually had access to people in Iran who had access to that information," the CIA officer said. Moreover, "this man never said a single thing that you could look back later and he said it would happen and it did happen." Perhaps the greatest concern that the CIA had about "Ali" was his quite open relationship with Manucher Ghorbanifar, an infamous figure from Iran-Contra days who had been the subject of a CIA "burn notice" alerting the Community to the agency's judgment that he was a fabricator. "Many information [sic] that I have given . . . is coming from Ghorbanifar," "Ali" told *The American Prospect*. "Ghorbanifar used me, in fact, to pass that stuff because I know he has problems in Washington."[6]

It is impossible to know for sure whether "Ali" is a charlatan, a sincere source who is unknowingly conveying bad information, or a sincere source reporting solid intelligence. The case illustrates, however, a number of tools and procedures which American intelligence collectors use to help judge whether they should accept proffered intelligence and to limit the damage done when fabricators are identified. These include efforts to ascertain the identity of sub-sources and preferably to get direct access to them and the use of "burn notices" or "fabrication notices" to alert all concerned intelligence personnel across the Community that fabrication has been detected. Finally, it is important to notice that though the public record is vague on this point, it appears that the CIA made its call not to trust "Ali" based on operational considerations, not on the judgment of analysts assessing the substantive "Ali's" information itself.

Intelligence collectors also employed these tools while collecting intelligence on Iraq before the war. However, there were added complications: some sources were controlled by foreign intelligence services, not by American services. Moreover, the burn notice mechanism turned out to be flawed and analysts came to play a role in the debate over the validity of human sources.

An Iraqi codenamed Curveball is probably the most infamous fabricator in American intelligence history. He was the major source for the allegation that Saddam's Iraq had mobile biological weapons laboratories. In purveying this story, however, he was merely telling his debriefers, officers of the German BND, what he thought they wanted to hear. Curveball's motives are, of course, difficult to determine for certain, and his behavior was rather erratic, but the desire to obtain a visa to enter Germany seems to have played a role.[7] Because Curveball was controlled by the Germans and moreover said that he did not like Americans, the Defense Intelligence Agency, which reportedly was the German point of entrée into the US Intelligence Community for this case, did not have access to the source and did not investigate his background and *bona fides*, though according to Deputy Director of Central Intelligence John McLaughlin the CIA made "strenuous and ultimately successful efforts to gain direct access to Curveball in order to settle the issue."[8]

At one point during the run-up to the Iraq war, CIA operators, who presumably knew the most about the source's operational background, and analysts who were subject-matter experts, reportedly differed about the value of Curveball's reporting. One analyst defended the information by noting that she had been able to confirm on the Internet much of the information he had provided. "Exactly! It's on the Internet! That's where he got it too," the cognizant operator answered in exasperation.[9]

Many problematic human sources also came to the attention of the US government (and US journalists) thanks to the Iraqi National Congress (INC). Between March 2000 and September 2003 the US State Department funded the Iraqi National Congress Support Foundation (INCSF) to the tune of nearly $33 million, with much of the money going to the INCSF's euphemistically titled "Information Collection Program" (ICP), though the INC's newspaper and television station broadcasting into Iraq also received funding.[10] The ICP's mission was to maintain contact with dissidents inside Iraq and use them to collect intelligence on the Saddam regime's political, economic, and military activities, including its alleged weapons of mass destruction program and its links with terrorist groups. The INC apparently accomplished this through field offices in Syria and Iran.[11]

The INCSF valued the ICP because it believed that the intelligence gathered could be used to provide content for its television broadcasts and its newspaper. Probably more importantly, however, in the words of a study by the General Accounting Office, the "INCSF believed that elements of that data could be used in its diplomatic activities to reinforce views of the international community that the [Saddam] Hussein government represented a danger to its neighbors." In February 2002, just a few months after the United States and its coalition partners had successfully overthrown the Taliban regime in Afghanistan, the INC seemed to realize that their hour had come; the INCSF sought an expansion of the ICP.[12]

The INCSF's relationship with the State Department soured during the summer of 2002, however, over allegations of sloppy bookkeeping at best and impropriety at worst. During this time the INC put together a memorandum outlining the purpose of the program: to "collect, analyze, and disseminate" intelligence from Iraq. More specifically, according to the memorandum, "defectors, reports, and raw intelligence are cultivated and analyzed and the results are reported through the INC newspaper, the Arabic and Western media, and to appropriate government, non-governmental, and international agencies." Among the officials to whom the INC claimed to be passing its material was a Deputy Assistant Secretary of Defense and the Vice President's special assistant for national security. The memorandum also listed 108 English-language news stories run in many of the most influential media outlets that included material collected through the ICP. One news reporter observed that Ahmed Chalabi had an "endless stable" of defectors available to substantiate any story that reflected poorly on the Saddam regime. In mid-2004, anonymous sources in the Intelligence Community told a *Los Angeles Times* reporter that they now suspected that the INC had channeled information to at least eight foreign intelligence services in an apparent effort to get these agencies to confirm each others' reporting and analyses.[13] Clearly, the ICP thought it was profoundly influencing the security debate in the United States and elsewhere, though the CIA later concluded that those INC sources with which it dealt directly had little or no impact on pre-war analyses.[14] Wherever the truth of that assertion, the Defense Intelligence Agency concluded in late 2003 that virtually all the intelligence received through the ICP before the war was useless.[15]

Congressman Weldon, in a letter to the editor of the *Washington Post* (a letter that the paper did not publish) implied that the CIA promulgated the view that they "can be trusted because of their superior intuition." For better or worse, however, the agency was not relying on intuition in rejecting the information from Weldon's source, "Ali," or in the way that it tried to deal with Curveball and the INC. Rather, the CIA relied on long-standing procedures that date back to the first decade of the Cold War.[16]

Cold War fabricators and paper mills

The same drivers that operated in the cases above – desire for visas, greed, the hope that they could maneuver the United States into carrying out otherwise impossible regime changes, possibly even self-delusion – existed in some émigrés from Eastern Europe during the early Cold War era. Moreover, fabricators today use the same techniques that the US became familiar with 50 years ago: selling slanted information to any US agency that will buy it (and to allied countries as well), and co-opting the media, the Congress and anyone else who can help them. During the late 1940s and early 1950s, however, it was even more difficult for the US Intelligence Community to tell the authentic and sincere intelligence sources from the fabricators than it is today because, at least initially, there were no agreed techniques for managing the problem.

The case of Bohumil Svoboda illustrates how bad the problem got. Svoboda was a Czech mining engineer who escaped from Czechoslovakia in 1948 and became an intelligence source, reporting some dramatic information. First, in August 1950 he had provided the text of a treaty between the USSR and Czechoslovakia giving the former the rights to the latter's uranium deposits for 15 years. Over the next two months a flurry of 76 reports had followed, each more tantalizing than the last. Svoboda claimed sources in the Czechoslovak Ministries of Internal Affairs and Industry, the Central Planning Institute in Moscow, the Soviet Atomic Institute, Marshal Zhukov's staff, the Soviet Ministry of Internal Affairs, and the Hungarian, Romanian, and Bulgarian armies. After a time, he was even providing information from China, which now apparently planned an invasion of Formosa.

Perhaps it was this last report that finally sparked some skepticism, but for whatever reason, the authorities were soon grilling Svoboda and in September 1952 the FBI reported that the Czech had admitted to fabricating these reports. The names in the reports were the names of people he knew in Czechoslovakia or that he read in the newspaper. He perpetrated this fraud in order to gain the money that could get him out of a crowded and unpleasant displaced persons camp.[17]

This was an all too common story during the early Cold War. In the late 1950s, an article appeared in *Studies in Intelligence*, the agency's classified in-house journal, written under the name of Arness, saying that "more than half of all the material received on several countries of greatest intelligence interest" was the product of fabricators or, worse yet in many cases, their bigger cousins the "paper mills."[18] Arness defined "fabricators" as "individuals or groups who, without genuine agent resources, invent their information or inflate it on the basis of overt news for personal gain or a political purpose."[19]

Individual fabricators and papers mills differed in scale and sometimes also in their purpose. The article defined paper mills as

> intelligence sources whose chief aim is the maximum dissemination of their product. Their purpose is usually to promote special émigré-political causes while incidentally financing émigré-political organizations. The information thus conveyed consists of a mixture of valid information, overt material, propaganda, and fabrication. Its bulk, form, and obscure origin frequently preclude successful analysis and evaluation.

The genesis of the problem

After World War II the United States faced an enormous intelligence challenge. It had to switch its primary intelligence focus from Germany and Japan to the USSR and its satellite states in Eastern Europe. Unfortunately America's clandestine services were mostly new and still in the steep part of their learning curves. Worse yet, the Soviet Union and its satellites were denied areas, extremely difficult targets for even the best espionage agencies. Though the security services in the Eastern European satellites states were new, the Soviet services had been in the business since the founding of the Bolshevik state decades before. They were long on experience and ruthlessly effective at counterintelligence.

Fortunately, or so it seemed, World War II and the subsequent communist takeovers in Eastern Europe had caused many people to flee westward. Some of these people came out with useful intelligence information in their head. Others said they were in contact with friends and associates still behind the Iron Curtain who themselves had access to sensitive information. Finally, former senior intelligence officers from the fascist regimes that had been Hitler's minor allies or from the short-lived post-war democratic regimes came West and offered their services and their existing agent networks, much as the German Reinhard Gehlen had done. For the entrepreneurs' contacts behind the Iron Curtain, working for Western intelligence seemed a moral imperative. Paul v. Gorka, a minor player in a British-run network in Hungary who served a prison term for his ultimately inconsequential intelligence efforts, was probably typical in this regard. "In contrast to the activities of the moles in the West," he wrote years later after escaping to the United Kingdom, "the people who risked their lives and their freedom behind the Iron Curtain were motivated by a deep sense of patriotism and a desire for national freedom and human liberties."[20]

Western intelligence agencies swarmed all over these émigrés, seeing in them opportunities to rapidly establish a flow of intelligence from behind the Iron Curtain that was otherwise impossible to obtain. Many of the émigrés, like Bohumil Svoboda, were fabricators from the very beginning, seeing this business as their ticket out of the desperate conditions that prevailed in post-war Europe. Some émigré or exile groups, however, had real assets behind the Iron Curtain. Unfortunately, because these groups lacked the technical infrastructure and know-how to run such operations, the communist security services were able to make short work of them. As Arness put it:

> [H]asty, uncoordinated, and totally insecure operational use of these assets by both émigré groups and Free World intelligence agencies permitted the Communist security services to identify and destroy or to use them. Initial failure in the West to recognize the ruthlessness and efficacy of the Soviet-type police state contributed to this process which, generally speaking, was completed by 1950.[21]

Such catastrophes notwithstanding, these émigré organizations generally stayed in business. In some cases, the émigré groups themselves may not have known the true state of their networks in the home country and that their assets had been turned or were being used to direct disinformation back to the West. Certainly, post-war intelligence history is replete with examples of apparently trustworthy individuals having been turned by the communist security services.[22]

Whether or not they really knew what was going on back home, the exile groups still had mouths to feed and, in some cases, leaders who had grown accustomed to a certain lifestyle. These factors alone served as a strong motive to fabricate juicy intelligence and sell it to whoever was willing to buy, long after effective contact had been lost with agents in the East. Their customers kept buying their reports at generous prices. The Americans were ignoring the fact that the needs of their intelligence services for accurate information were secondary, in the minds of the émigré leaders, to political considerations.[23]

For indeed, the motives of the émigrés often were not merely economic. The intelligence production of the émigré was, it seemed to Arness, a "weapon" which was "inevitably used to influence US policy in the direction of hostility to the Soviet Bloc and to satisfy the ambitions of political pressure groups," the leaders of which "knew that they could not return to power in their homelands except in the wake of war and Western victory."[24]

Not only did these groups endeavor to embroil the United States and the Western allies in a new war, but simply chasing these phantoms in the field and processing the haul from the paper mills and individual fabricators was a serious resource sink. According to Richard Helms, later head of the CIA's Clandestine Service and Director of Central Intelligence, as late as 1951 a third of the CIA's operational effort in Austria went to dealing with fabricators. This, of course, was in addition to the time devoted to the problem by the other US intelligence services, and in addition to the effort devoted by the British and French services (possibly among others). Helms judged that all this furious activity "took our attention away from developing the techniques that in the future were to produce significant results."[25]

Moreover, disagreements over paper mills sometimes led to nasty interagency disputes. Peter Sichel, the agency's Chief of Base in Berlin at the time, recalls a major battle with the US Army in the late 1940s or early 1950s. The CIA became aware that the Army was purchasing bogus intelligence from a "fabrication network" and forced the Army to shut it down. The Army intelligence chief in Berlin was so incensed that he went to the FBI and reported his suspicions that Sichel was a Soviet agent. A fruitless investigation ensued but "they never did find my Soviet handler," Sichel recalls, laughing ironically.[26]

The Association of Hungarian Veterans

No group better exemplifies the paper mill problem than the MHBK (*Magyar Harcosok Bajtársi Közössége*) or Association of Hungarian Veterans. The MHBK had its genesis in the last months of World War II in Europe when General András Zákó, the last wartime head of Hungarian military intelligence, and his assistant, Captain Miklos Korponay, formed an organization of members of the Arrow Cross party and paratroopers called Kopjas (Pikemen). Kopjas numbered about 1,500–2,000 officers and warrant officers pledged to resist the Soviet invaders by conducting sabotage and collecting intelligence. However, the war came to such a quick end that the group quickly became a stay-behind network.[27]

Accounts vary as to what happened to Zákó and Korponay after the war. According to one, Zákó went straight to Tyrol in Soviet-occupied Austria. There he met up with Korponay, gathered Hungarian soldiers about himself and planned for the future. Soon deciding that he needed further information about the situation in Hungary he went back into his home country disguised as a priest, probably in late 1946. Perhaps because Hungary was not yet fully under communist control, he was able to spend 15 months there laying the groundwork for resistance and intelligence work and reactivating Kopjas.[28]

Another version of the story is that Zákó was interned by the US Army and later extradited to Hungary as a war criminal. As he was being transported to Hungary, he escaped and went to the Soviet zone of Austria where he worked under an assumed name as an agricultural worker until 1947 when he went to Innsbruck.[29] According to that same story, Korponay during this time was the head of a group of about 25 Hungarians which remained inactive until the spring of 1946 when Sandor Lang, a naturalized British citizen from a Hungarian family, approached them. Lang was associated with British intelligence and seeking men to go back into Hungary and report from there. Korponay put a man who had connections to Kopjas at Lang's disposal and they set to work creating an intelligence network in Hungary.[30] Korponay was pleased with this connection with the British and was soon inspired to approach the French service, as well. The French were amenable to working with him and placed three men at his disposal, including the talented Attila Kovacs.[31]

In any event, Zákó came to Innsbruck in 1947 and linked up with Korponay. Soon thereafter they approached the US Army's Counterintelligence Corps (CIC) office in Hallein to offer their services. They neglected to mention that they were already providing intelligence to the British and French. Ignorant of this fact, the CIC accepted their offer. Zákó and Korponay appointed Lieutenant Colonel Georgy Kollenyi, a former Hungarian army intelligence officer, as their liaison to the Americans and soon intelligence started flowing to the CIC.[32]

Unfortunately for Zákó and Korponay, CIC personnel frequently talked with their British colleagues. It soon became clear that the two services were buying the same material. After a little inquiry, it was found that the French were also buying the same product. An investigation ensued and CIC and the British soon dropped Kollenyi. (Some time later he started working for the Gehlen Organization, forerunner of Germany's BND, in Pullach, near Munich where his work consisted primarily of passing reports from refugees).[33] Korponay protested to the CIC that his highest goal was defeating the communists and that it should not matter to which free powers he sold intelligence.[34]

In 1948 the MHBK, with its only serious customer now the French, approached a Baron Waldorf who, it was whispered, was the intelligence representative in Innsbruck of the Polish government in exile in London and who also, purportedly, worked for MI6. Waldorf soon was paying $1,000 a month in exchange for military intelligence from Hungary. The MHBK also approached an "American intelligence agency in Frankfurt, Germany," possibly the CIA. It is not clear what the response of the "American agency" was on this occasion. However, as Helms's memoirs make clear, at some time in the late 1940s the MHBK did establish a relationship with the CIA.[35] The nascent military émigré organization helped identify communist infiltrators in the Western zones of Germany and in France, at one point complaining to the French that their group had not received the public credit it was due for two recent arrests.[36]

Zákó was not only making connections with Western intelligence agencies, but also trying to draw as much of the exiled Hungarian military community to himself as possible. He successfully struck an agreement with Lieutenant General József v. Vasváry who had connections to the French government and with Gendarmerie General Pál Hódosy living in Munich.[37] In the spring of 1948, General Antal Radnóczy and General Staff Captain György v. Hegedüs urged the Hungarian officer community to formally accept Zákó as their leader. Radnóczy recalled that "from three countries, 100 general staff officers agreed to the plan, with only two who abstained." With these results in hand from the lower-ranking officers, Zákó sought the support of all the Hungarian generals he could find and they too accepted his leadership. Field Marshal Archduke Joseph, Hungary's most revered Habsburg, agreed that Zákó would be a good leader.[38] Zákó also met with Archduke Otto von Habsburg, the Habsburg pretender in Paris in August 1948 and according to one account gained his support, as well.[39] (Two years later Otto would arrange with Francisco Franco that in case of war in Europe the members of MHBK could take refuge in Spain.[40]) On 18 June 1948 Zákó even sought the support of Admiral Horthy, the wartime Regent of Hungary. Horthy, by now an old man of 80, wanted nothing to do with politics, but he, too, offered his tacit support.[41]

Seeking to create a political arm for Kopjas, Zákó merged his group with the Anti-Bolshevik Hungarian Liberation Movement (AHLM) headed by General Ferenc Farkas. The AHLM was an attractive partner because it had contacts with the French military and with Ukrainian, Croatian, Bulgarian, and Slovak officers.[42] On the other hand, Zákó tried to portray himself as distant from Farkas himself who was controversial because of his fascist background. Certainly the French pressured him to do this. In September 1948 a "Colonel Mondaine" told Zákó that previously agreed cooperation with the MHBK "could be realized more rapidly" if "General Farkas would in the future not occupy himself with politics, only with military affairs." Farkas was willing to agree and so too, of course, was Zákó.[43]

Nonetheless, Zákó's ecumenical approach to membership in the MHBK soon generated concern in the CIA. "General Zákó is somewhat less implicated as a former fascist than others of his staff," the CIA reported to the FBI in June 1950, "but is still so far to the right politically that none of the recognized and responsible Hungarian groups or politicians have supported or encouraged him or the MHBK."[44] Some Hungarian émigrés were also concerned about the political flavor of the MHBK. One émigré who was asked to join and declined told the FBI that "when the names of the [MHBK's] leaders began to appear, many people were filled with mixed emotions because these leaders were not the ones who had been trustworthy in the past." The FBI source particularly singled out Miklos Korponay for scorn saying that in 1945 Korponay "exchanged his Hungarian uniform for a German SS uniform."[45]

MHBK's activities

Aside from providing social support to its members, the MHBK's most important work, of course, was the sale of intelligence from inside Hungary. The headquarters for these activities was in Innsbruck under General Zákó, who sometimes went by the alias of "István Kovacs," as generic a Hungarian name as exists.[46] After a restructuring approved at a "mass meeting" attended by about 60 people in July 1950, the MHBK was organized with a Presidium presiding over four main sections. These were the "Strategic Section" which did operational planning and registered refugees; a "Press and Propaganda Section" under Miklos Korponay, who also posed as head of the MHBK intelligence sections to divert hostile attention from the real leaders of those sections; the "Offensive Intelligence Service," which collected intelligence and recruited and trained resistance units and radio operators should they be needed in wartime; and the "Defensive Intelligence Service."[47]

The MHBK claimed some intelligence successes. For example, Imre Horvath, a former Hungarian army officer who serving as a courier between the MHBK in the West and supposed resistance cells in Hungary claimed to have recruited two generals in the military police.[48] Beyond such penetrations as they thought they had in the Hungarian government, the MHBK also debriefed émigrés and refugees and hunted communists in émigré communities.[49]

The MHBK also included a small signals intelligence (SIGINT) effort in Graz in the British zone of Austria. Little information is available about this operation but it included former Hungarian army Sigint personnel and reported on deportations and political trials. One officer recalled of this group,

> their work was world class, and we were more informed than some of the leading communist organizations which were engaged in power struggles at the time. We had a clear view about the conditions at home, and the communist agents were hunting for the decipherers for years, but could never find them.

Ironically, while this may have been among the most reliable information that the MHBK passed on to its customers, it was hardly top-flight intelligence; the techniques of communist oppression were well known and sadly unstoppable.[50]

It is hard to know for certain the nature of the intelligence that the MHBK sold to its patrons. However, copies of the English-language *Hungarian Veteran*, a supplement to the group's flagship Hungarian-language newspaper *Hadak Utján*, may provide a clue. Three issues of this newspaper from early 1953 portray a Hungary ruthlessly oppressed by the secret police and being driven into economic ruin by the communists. They also contain tantalizing bits of military information, such as the article entitled "More subterranean armaments faktories [sic]" which reported that one factory was slated to produce "light military vehicles, hand grenades, and tommy guns," and another was known for cover purposes as the "chocolate factory."

Throughout, the paper also portrays a Hungary that is ripe for the retaking, if only the western powers would invade. Some members of the AVH (Hungarian security), it reported, "have become so corrupted by the unrestrained exercise of power that they are now ready to serve anybody who is willing to pay them. If the rule of the Muscovite satellites is only slightly endangered, these creatures would be the first to turn their weapons against their former masters." Similarly, "The Hungarian Communists place little confidence in the so-called 'People's Army,' . . . They realize that the majority of the soldiers would desert to the Western camp in case of war." A Hungarian officer was suspected of writing graffiti reading "Aj lájk Ajk!" ("I like Ike!").[51]

The paper also maintained the melancholy delusion that the MHBK could play a military role in the liberation of the homeland. The February 1953 issue of *Hungarian Veteran* contained an announcement from Zákó that 250 young émigrés in Bavaria had recently signed statements indicating their readiness to serve in "a Hungarian anti-bolshevik volunteer army, should such be established."[52]

Similar delusions led to a remarkable proposal to the Spanish military sometime before the 1956 Hungarian uprising. Zákó suggested the creation of an Eastern European force including 5,000-each Hungarians, Slovaks, Czechs, Sudeten Germans, Romanians and Bulgarians. This force would enter Eastern Europe in the wake of a US-financed uprising in Bohemia. Zákó even held open the possibility that the ensuing war would include a nuclear attack on the Soviet Union. The Spanish military showed some preliminary interest, but, unsurprisingly, nothing ever came of the project.[53]

By October 1950 CIA, already concerned about the MHBK's politics, was unenthused about the quality of the MHBK's reporting and its far-flung relationships with European intelligence services. "The MHBK maintains liaison with and disseminates reports to most of the Allied intelligence services in Western Europe," the agency reported. "A number of reports on Hungarian matters received from these services have been traced to the MHBK and, on occasion, have been duplicated by reports disseminated to this Agency by other services. Evaluations of this material, based on content rather than on source, have been uniformly low."[54]

The CIA's information about the MHBK's widespread clientele appears to have been true. Available – and probably incomplete – information indicates that at one time or another the MHBK provided its product to the CIA, the US Army's CIC, the US Air Force, the French, the Austrian police, the British, the Polish government in exile, Spain (though the scant available evidence indicates the MHBK never had a formal relationship with the Spanish) and probably the Gehlen Organization.[55]

The MHBK's closest relationship remained with the French. It gave intelligence to the French and organized border crossings into Hungary for unilateral French assets. In return, the French provided means of communication, false documents, deconfliction with other allied intelligence operations, name traces, and financial support.[56] In November 1949, for example, Zákó brought back from Paris 3 million francs (approximately $6–7 million in 2003 dollars) for intelligence operations.[57]

MHBK's security problem

Though the MHBK had no hesitation selling intelligence, from its earliest days it had severe difficulties actually acquiring this intelligence. In October 1947 Korponay admitted to the CIC that he had lost contact with the members of Kopjas or the "K Organization," as it was also known, but he felt sure that with proper funding, contact could be re-established.[58] A year later Zákó wrote to a French officer:

> Permit me, *Monsieur le Colonel*, to draw your attention to the circumstance that work against the east becomes more difficult each day, because the [communist security regime] strengthens itself in such a fashion that if we do not complete certain works one can foresee a time when all contacts will be impossible with the territories behind the Iron Curtain.[59]

In 1949 there came tangible evidence that these concerns were well-founded and that the heyday of MHBK's intelligence collection was rapidly coming to a close: Imre Horvath, the MHBK courier and case officer, was arrested along with the two generals he had recruited in the military police. The two generals were executed and Horvath got life in prison.[60] Also in 1949 several MHBK intelligence personnel and staff members in Austria and Germany were found to be working for the Hungarian communist regime.[61]

The Hungarian services were not above strong-arm tactics. In January 1950 Attila Kovacs, the head of the MHBK spy network, who apparently ran the entire network out of his head without writing anything down, was murdered by agents of the Hungarian government. Kovacs's murder, combined with the disasters of 1949, dealt a severe blow to MHBK's collection of intelligence in Hungary. In fact, as of October 1950 the CIA had information that

> until the past few months the "Kopjas"/MHBK maintained channels of communications to resistance groups within Hungary but it is believed that, by early 1950, the mother groups were virtually extinct due to the compromise, arrest or escape into exile of its members . . . and [due] to the scarcity of funds which were necessary to keep alive its channels with the West.[62]

The French were particularly annoyed about the Kovacs murder. One of his murderers was a man named Miklos Bognar about whom French intelligence had issued a warning just a few days before. Though informed that Bognar was a communist penetration agent, the MHBK did not act and Kovacs died as a result. The French were disgusted and scaled back their relations with the MHBK.[63]

The Hungarian secret police – essentially an arm of the experienced Soviet security services – was certainly ruthlessly effective, but poor tradecraft by the MHBK probably contributed to the problem. Michael Gaydacs, the FBI source who had declined an invitation to join the MHBK, remembered telling his would-be recruiter during a meeting in a cafe:

> If you want to bring into being an underground anti-Communist military organization, then you must really go underground and work in secret, but if you place your printed plans on the café tables then the Communist and Bolshevik agents will know of your activities, and consequently your organization will not be an underground movement, but one of treason instead. Betrayal of those here and those at home . . . It seems you are not aware of the past underhand activities of the Bolsheviks.[64]

The Hungarian service continued to find many people willing to double-cross the MHBK in one way or another. A set of documents on the MHBK obtained by the British in 1951 and shared with the Americans provides a long list of such people. One Jeges Kornel, a former Hungarian policeman who organized border crossing point "103" for the MHBK, had been in contact with the AVH. The French had told the MHBK that one Vilmos Kratky was a "driver for Americans" and also passed information to a man thought to be "in contact with eastern organizations." Laszlo Ivanyi who "was in touch with MHBK until summer 1950," was discovered "to have been engaged in document falsification and spying for two sides." A courier known as "S-31" who also "answers to the name Dodo" had disappeared from Vienna in the spring of 1950 and his fate was unknown, but he had often been seen in the company of a man thought to be in the employ of the Hungarian secret police.[65]

Then there was the case of Aladar Dajka who was involved in smuggling people out of Hungary and who also had a relationship with French intelligence and some knowledge of the MHBK. Arrested by the Hungarian police for his smuggling activities, he told them what he knew of an MHBK official based in Vienna known as "06" who was planning to enter Hungary soon in order to bring out his wife. Dajka reportedly also betrayed at least two other men, one of whom was working for the French and became the target of a heavy-handed approach from Soviet intelligence.[66]

In August 1951, Hungarian security arrested the wife of an MHBK official named Laszlo Sarvary who was in Vienna. (It is not clear where his wife was.) The AVH then approached Sarvary and attempted to blackmail him into spying for them. Sarvary played along before reporting the incident to his MHBK superiors. The MHBK leadership in Innsbruck decided not to tell their French sponsors, but also to play along, feeding the communists harmless or false information until Sarvary's wife was free.[67]

The French did find out, however, and recriminations ensued between them and the MHBK. Investigation of the whole muddle revealed the fact that an MHBK courier had recently gone over to the AVH and that the MHBK had potentially serious security problems, caused in part by sloppiness such as the fact that couriers always used the same routes and the same recognition signs. The fate of Sarvary's wife is not recorded, but Sarvary himself was later the target of an unsuccessful kidnapping attempt in October 1951.[68]

As if this were not enough, in 1951 sixteen members of the MHBK were arrested in Hungary. All were convicted, of course. One of them was executed and the other fifteen were sentenced to a total of 241 years in prison.[69]

The US Intelligence Community responds

By 1951 the MHBK was operationally gutted. During the same period, the CIA was wising up to the problem of paper mills. In the late 1940s, a CIA officer named Walter Jessel had begun to track the problem. He found that some émigré groups were selling slightly different versions of the same report to multiple different American intelligence services, each of which used it to maximum effect with their respective policy customers. "Given the proprietary interests of some of the American agencies involved, this was a sensitive bit of business," Richard Helms remembered later. "The impressive political backgrounds of some of the leading exile political figures gave them access to – and a measure of influence on – prominent businessmen, members of Congress, and others with ties to ethnic communities in the United States."[70]

Having laid the groundwork, Jessel now did a study focusing specifically on the MHBK. This was difficult to do because some senior US intelligence officials were heavily invested in the group and its product and when the study was finally completed the results were ugly. Jessel concluded that much of the MHBK's product was fabricated. He and Helms brought these results to the attention of DCI Walter Bedell Smith who directed that the study be briefed to the United States Intelligence Board, composed of the intelligence chiefs of the various service and agencies. The briefing, which took place on August 1951, was an eye-opener. "Who in the Air Force could be buying this crap?" the Air Force intelligence chief asked. Jessel noted that

263

the Air Force was far from alone in being clients of Zákó's MHBK. The MHBK would not be selling any more intelligence to the United States.[71]

However, the covert operators at Frank Wisner's Office of Policy Coordination (OPC, initially a *de facto* later a *de jure* component of CIA, charged with covert action rather than espionage) had its own relationship with the group. In 1950 and 1951 the OPC formed a Free Hungary Committee, essentially a government in exile, and the OPC's Carmel Offie named Zákó its "Defense Minister." During the Hungarian crisis of 1956, Zákó still apparently held that position. He and his staff in Vienna busily composed bulletins that Radio Liberty broadcast, telling the hapless Hungarian people that "the Western world's material aid is on its way to you."[72] (They also provided information at least to the Spanish government, and probably others, about the course of the uprising.[73])

After the disaster of 1956, Zákó hoped that another uprising could be engineered for the following spring and to that end tried to keep contact with the surviving insurrectionists, but his hopes were in vain.[74] One tantalizing FBI memorandum suggests that Zákó's contacts with French intelligence may have continued into the late 1950s. In early 1959, a recent Hungarian immigrant to the United States told the FBI that in the spring of 1958 a group of French generals approached Zákó, urging him to mount another uprising in Hungary. They offered him financial support, weapons, and even hinted at the possibility of help from a few French officers. Zákó's response is not known but the FBI source reported having heard from Zákó associates that the US government had gotten wind of the plan and told Zákó that he could not expect any support from them if he were to do such a foolhardy thing.[75]

After absorbing Jessel's bombshell study on the MHBK, the CIA started looking at other paper mills. A study presented to the Intelligence Advisory Committee in February 1952 looked at 18 cases with such names as "Orekhov," "London Polish," "Croat-Slovene," and "Scattolini."[76] These included six paper mills, six cases of fabricators, and five hybrid cases. It also considered an additional case that appeared to "involve planned Soviet provocation." The study found that despite the fact that only one case of Soviet deception was under consideration, the lack of coordination among the intelligence collection agencies gave the Soviets tremendous opportunities for "planting deception and provocation material in US intelligence channels at the moment of its choice." Moreover, the poor security of many of the paper mills meant that the Soviets probably had access to the same information that was being passed to US intelligence. This, of course, might allow them to design deception operations that would play to American preconceived notions. Finally, and perhaps most importantly, the study bore out "the total experience of [the CIA] that the only method by which fabrication and multiple false confirmation can be detected is . . . operational investigation of the source and transmission channels, combined with reports analysis."[77]

The study recommended a whole series of measures for dealing with the problem. Many of them related to controlling and limiting the payments made to intelligence sources. Others involved laying down the law to those who sold intelligence to American intelligence agencies, letting them know that they would no longer be allowed to keep secret the identities of their sources no matter what the reason. Furthermore, the report said that the feeling, common among American intelligence agencies, that fellow American intelligence agencies could not be trusted with the identities of clandestine sources must be eradicated. Such concerns

> bred a jealousy among intelligence officers of various government agencies which has prevented a long overdue exchange of information . . . As a result, an excessive amount of professional manpower had to be devoted to costly overseas investigation where simple headquarters co-ordination . . . would have revealed duplication or fraud.[78]

This led to the most important recommendation, that efforts be made to establish "source control."[79] There were two elements to this. The first was undertaken by CIA operators in the field. (It is not clear whether the humint collectors of the armed services and FBI undertook analogous measures.) They would buy a few reports from a suspected fabricator or paper mill. If the information seemed promising the agency would try to establish the bona fides of the middleman. This would entail the full range of investigative techniques, name traces, telephone taps, surveillance, and "an unconscionable amount of time," Richard Helms wrote.[80] But the technique was effective. As Peter Sichel put it, "the more you get into that, the more you find out what exists and what doesn't exist."[81]

The second component of source control was undertaken in Washington where a comprehensive registry of sources was to be created. The Community promptly approved a general plan for doing this, but it took them five years to agree on the details of how the new procedures would actually work. Finally, on May 14, 1957 the Community finally approved and established the "Interagency Source Register" or ISR in order to "provide a centralized file of clandestine sources in order to preclude multiple recruitment of sources and to facilitate the elimination of Paper Mills and Fabricators." Apparently the FBI had balked because though "all . . . agencies may avail themselves of ISR facilities," the formal participants in the ISR were the CIA and the intelligence components of the Army, Navy, Air Force, and State Department. The CIA was responsible for the running the ISR and agencies were to provide data on their clandestine sources to it. Agencies would also inform the ISR when they dropped a source for whatever reason. The reasons for dropping a source included "Paper Mill and Fabricator," "Security," "Compromise," "Ineptitude," "Blackmarketing, smuggling, or other violation of law," "Without prejudice," and "Deceased." When a source was found to be a fabricator or a paper mill this would be noted in the ISR and if the source seemed likely to continue selling his "spurious product," the CIA would in coordination with other agencies "disseminate a report 'burning' (denouncing) the source to United States Government agencies and to friendly foreign intelligence services as a given case may require."[82]

Lessons (re) learned?

The same motives for fabricating intelligence and selling it to American and allied intelligence agencies that once existed among émigrés from countries oppressed by communism may now exist among émigrés from other areas denied to US intelligence. Fortunately, the prophylactic measures and remedies that worked adequately during the 1950s remain in place. In the "Ali" case it appears, though it is always impossible to tell for certain, that they saved the CIA from potential future embarrassment.

In the cases of the Iraqi sources and the INC, these measures were not enough to prevent an intelligence and policy debacle. There are many reasons for this failure. Certainly, the Bush administration was leaning toward war with Iraq anyway (unlike the Truman and Eisenhower administration's policies toward Eastern Europe) and a forward-leaning policy line means that even small intelligence errors are likely to have big implications in terms of policy outputs. Moreover, in the particular case of Curveball careful examination was made difficult because the BND jealously guarded its access to the source, as intelligence agencies all over the world are wont to do. With regard to the INC sources, even when "burn notices" were issued, they were not clearly linked to the reporting that had already been disseminated from the source. Unfortunately, the analysts who helped Secretary of State Powell prepare his famous speech to the United States did not know that key pieces of

265

information that the Secretary intended to highlight were known by other components of the Community to be bad.[83]

The WMD Commission reported in early 2005 that the Director of the CIA was working on a system that would link "original [human intelligence] reports, fabrication notices, and any subsequent recalls and corrections." DIA has already taken similar steps for the reporting which it originates.[84] These are, indeed, important developments for it seems certain that as long as there are émigrés from closed regimes the major intelligence agencies of the free world will face the problem of fabricators and paper mills.

Notes

I would like to thank David Alvarez, Karl Lowe, Tom Quiggin, John Schindler, Peter Sichel, Pamela Stout, Michael Warner, and Harry Yeide for their assistance.

1 Curt Weldon, *Countdown to Terror* (Washington, DC: Regnery 2005).
2 Weldon, pp. 4–6.
3 Weldon, pp. 31–35, 41.
4 Weldon, p. 147.
5 Weldon, p. 151.
6 Weldon, pp. 8–12. Laura Rozen, "Curt Weldon's Deep Throat," *The American Prospect*, June 10, 2005, online edition, www.prospect.org.
7 Bob Drogin and John Goetz, "How U.S. Fell Under the Spell of 'Curveball'," *Los Angeles Times*, November 20, 2005, p. 1.
8 Drogin and Goetz, "Statement of John E. McLaughlin, Former Deputy Director of Central Intelligence, April 1, 2005," shttp://www.fas.org/irp/offdocs/wmd_mclaughlin.html.
9 Drogin and Goetz.
10 United States General Accounting Office (GAO), *State Department: Issues Affecting Funding of Iraqi National Congress Support Foundation* (Washington: General Accounting Office April 2004), summary (np).
11 GAO, pp. 3–4.
12 GAO, pp. 1, 3, 10, 11.
13 Douglas McCollam, "How Chalabi Played the Press," *Columbia Journalism Review*, July/August 2004, online edition, http://www.cjr.org/issues/2004/4/mccollam-list.asp.
14 The Commission on the Intelligence Capabilities of the United States Regarding Weapons of Mass Destruction (WMD Commission), *Report to the President of the United States, March 31 2005* (Washington, DC: GPO, 2005), pp. 108 and 225fn.
15 McCollam.
16 Accuracy in Media, "AIM Report: Media Attack Whistleblower Weldon," August 4, 2005, http://www.aim.org/aim_report/3913_0_4_0_C/.
17 FBI Memo, Los Angeles Field Office, "Bohumil V. Svoboda," 4 September 1952, National Archives and Records Administration (NARA), RG 319, Entry 47, Box 15, Folder "201 Choinski, Walter F. (Col.) 201 Svoboda, Bohumil V. 1952."
18 Stephen M. Arness, "Paper Mills and Fabrication", *Studies in Intelligence*, Vol. 2 (Winter 1958), p. 95, NARA, RG 263, Entry 27, Box 15, Folder 2.
19 Arness, p. 95.
20 Paul v. Gorka, *Budapest Betrayed* (Wembley, UK: Oak-Tree Books 1986), p. 150.
21 Arness, pp. 96–97.
22 See Igor Lukes, "The Rudolf Slansky Affair: New Evidence", *Slavic Review*, Vol. 58, No. 1, (Spring, 1999), pp. 160–187, for an interesting example from a Czechoslovak émigré intelligence service and a high-stakes operation that it mounted but which was betrayed from within.
23 Richard Helms, with William Hood, *A Look Over My Shoulder* (New York: Random House 2003) H, 97. Arness, pp. 96–97.
24 Arness, pp. 96–97.
25 Helms, p. 97.

26 Author's telephone interview with Peter M. F. Sichel, 14 February, 2005.
27 General Antal Radnócy (Magda Sasvári, trans.), "The Hungarian Veterans' Association," www.members.shaw.ca/czink/mhbk/mhbk.htm. Memo HQ US Forces in Austria (Rear), G-2 to G-2, General Staff, US Army Washington, DC, Subject "Collegial Society of Hungarian War Veterans," 11 October 1950, NARA, RG 65, Entry A1–136X, Box 1, File 97–2994. Unless otherwise noted, all material from NARA pertaining to the MHBK is from this FBI file. CIA Information Report, "Magyar Harcosok Bajtarai Kozosege (League of Hungarian Veterans)," 11 October 1950, NARA. Memo CIA to FBI, "League of Hungarian Veterans," 21 June 1950, NARA.
28 Radnócy. CIA Information Report, "Magyar Harcosok Bajtarai Kozosege (League of Hungarian Veterans)," 11 October 1950, NARA.
29 Memo HQ US Forces in Austria (Rear), G-2 to G-2, General Staff, US Army Washington, DC, "Collegial Society of Hungarian War Veterans," 11 October 1950, NARA.
30 Ibid.
31 Ibid.
32 Ibid.
33 Ibid. Heinz Hohne and Hermann Zolling, *The General Was a Spy* (New York: Bantam 1972), p. 170. The US forces in Austria (USFA) memo says merely that Kollenyi later went to work for a "US intelligence organization in Germany." Hohne and Zolling specify that this was the Gehlen Organization. Hohne and Zolling cite *Die graue Hand*, by "Julius Mader," a pseudonym used by East German intelligence in certain propaganda operations. "Mader," of course, is a somewhat problematic source, but he and the USFA source agree on Kollenyi's name and rank and, of course, the Gehlen Organization was, formally speaking, a US intelligence organization until the establishment of the BND several years later.
34 HQ US Forces in Austria (Rear), G-2 to G-2, General Staff, US Army Washington, DC, "Collegial Society of Hungarian War Veterans," 11 October 1950, NARA.
35 Ibid.
36 Radnócy. "Aide Memoire," 1947 or 1948?, Library and Archives Canada, (LAC), Ottawa Rakoczi Foundation Papers, MG 28, V162, Vol. 19, File 6. The Rakoczi Foundation papers include several thick folders of papers relating to the MHBK's intelligence activities. Almost all of this material is in Hungarian. This article exploits the small amounts of relevant French and German language materials in the collection. A scholar of intelligence history who reads Hungarian could certainly write a fascinating and much more insightful article on the MHBK.
37 Radnócy.
38 Radnócy.
39 Zákó to "Monsieur le Colonel," Innsbruck, 11 August, 1948, LAC, Rakoczi Foundation Papers, MG 28, V162, Vol. 18, File 6. Also "Pages 'A' to 'E' " (part of an 18-page report, most probably written by N. Korponay in the early 1950s, in German, LAC, Rakoczi Foundation Papers, MG 28, V162, Vol. 8, File 21).
40 CIA Information Report, "Magyar Harcosok Bajtarai Kozosege (League of Hungarian Veterans)," 11 October 1950, NARA.
41 Radnócy.
42 CIA Information Report, "Magyar Harcosok Bajtarai Kozosege (League of Hungarian Veterans)," 11 October 1950, FBI File 97–2994.
43 Zákó to "Monsieur le Colonel," 2 November 1948. LAC, Rakoczi Foundation Papers, MG 28, V162, Vol. 19, File 6.
44 Memo CIA to FBI, "League of Hungarian Veterans," 21 June 1950, NARA.
45 Memorandum Michael Gaydacs to Federal Bureau of Investigation, 24 September 1951, NARA.
46 FBI New York Field Office, "Collegial Society of Hungary Veterans," June 22 1950, NARA.
47 CIA Information Report, "Magyar Harcosok Bajtarai Kozosege (League of Hungarian Veterans)," 11 October 1950, NARA. Memo HQ US Forces in Austria (Rear), G-2 to G-2, General Staff, US Army Washington, DC, "Collegial Society of Hungarian War Veterans," 11 October 1950, NARA, RG 65.
48 Gorka, p. 136.
49 CIA Information Report, "Magyar Harcosok Bajtarai Kozosege (League of Hungarian Veterans)," 11 October 1950, NARA.
50 "Pages 'A' to 'E' . . .," Rakoczi Foundation Papers. Radnócy.
51 January, February, and March 1953 issues of *Hungarian Veteran*, NARA.

52 February 1953 issue of *Hungarian Veteran*, NARA.
53 Maria Dolores Ferrero Blanco, "Franco y la Revolución Húngara de 1956: La Contribución de España en la Resistencia Frente a la URSS," *Papeles del Este*, No. 7 (2003), pp. 28–29.
54 CIA Information Report, "Magyar Harcosok Bajtarai Kozosege (League of Hungarian Veterans)," NARA.
55 CIA and USFA: Helms, pp. 98–99. CIC: Memo CIA to FBI, "League of Hungarian Veterans," 21 June 1950, NARA. Austrian Police: CIA Information Report, "Magyar Harcosok Bajtarai Kozosege (League of Hungarian Veterans)," 11 October 1950, NARA. Spain: Ferrero Blanco, p. 25.
56 Memo FBI Salzburg Austria Liaison Office to Director FBI, "Hungarian Warriors Comradeship Society," 20 August 1953, NARA.
57 Memo HQ US Forces in Austria (Rear), G-2 to G-2, General Staff, US Army Washington, DC, "Collegial Society of Hungarian War Veterans," 11 October 1950, NARA.
58 Ibid. "Aide Memoire," 1947 or 1948?, LAC, Rakoczi Foundation Papers.
59 Zákó to "Monsieur le Colonel," 2 November 1948, LAC, Rakoczi Foundation Papers.
60 Gorka, p. 137.
61 CIA Information Report, "Magyar Harcosok Bajtarai Kozosege (League of Hungarian Veterans)," 11 October 1950, NARA.
62 Ibid. Memo CIA to FBI, "League of Hungarian Veterans," 21 June 1950, NARA, also mentions the murder of Kovacs.
63 Memo HQ US Forces in Austria (Rear), G-2 to G-2, General Staff, US Army Washington, DC, "Collegial Society of Hungarian War Veterans," 11 October 1950, NARA.
64 Memorandum Michael Gaydacs to Federal Bureau of Investigation, 24 September 1951, NARA.
65 Memo FBI Salzburg Austria Liaison Office to Director FBI, 20 August 20 1953, "Hungarian Warriors Comradeship Society," NARA.
66 Ibid.
67 Ibid.
68 Ibid.
69 Gorka, p. 152.
70 Helms, p. 98.
71 Helms, pp. 98–99. Central Intelligence Agency, "Paper Mills and Fabrication," IA–6, February 1952, obtained from the CIA through the Freedom of Information Act.
72 Burton Hersh, *The Old Boys*, (St Petersburg, FL: Tree Farm Books 1992), pp. 360–361. Bill Lomax, *Hungary 1956* (New York: St Martin's Press, 1976), p. 128.
73 Ferrero Blanco, p. 25.
74 Ferrero Blanco, p. 28.
75 FBI New York Field Office memo, "Josef Patakfalvi-Pinke," 15 January 1959, NARA.
76 "Scattolini" is presumably Virgilio Scattolini who from 1944 to August 1945 sold bogus information allegedly from inside the Vatican – a rather different government from those in Eastern Europe, but arguably a closed regime nonetheless – through middlemen to two different components of the OSS. Much of this information went straight to the President. See Timothy Naftali, "ARTIFICE: James Angleton and X–2 Operations in Italy," in George C. Chalou (ed.), *The Secrets War: The Office of Strategic Services in World War II* (Washington: NARA, 1992), pp. 230–233.
77 Central Intelligence Agency, "Paper Mills and Fabrication."
78 Ibid.
79 Ibid.
80 Helms, p. 97.
81 Sichel interview.
82 Intelligence Advisory Committee document IAC-D–54/3, 30 April 1957, found in the "CIA Records Search Tool," NARA under the serial number "CIA-RDP85S00362R000400090001-7".
83 WMD Commission report, pp. 108–110.
84 WMD Commission report, p. 109.

20

Linus Pauling

A case study in counterintelligence run amok

Kathryn S. Olmsted

During the Cold War, the United States fought a political, cultural, and technological struggle with the Soviet Union to prove its superiority and win the allegiance of citizens in non-aligned nations. The US government touted America's abundance of consumer goods, its artistic achievements, its democratic freedoms, and its scientific discoveries.

Yet at the height of this global competition, the Federal Bureau of Investigation attempted to impede the research of one of America's most distinguished scientists, Linus Pauling. The FBI and other government agencies tried to prevent the world-renowned chemist from speaking out publicly, traveling, and even conducting research that could advance the frontiers of American science. His crime? FBI chief J. Edgar Hoover suspected that Pauling had once been a supporter of the Communist Party.

Counterintelligence is an essential function of the US government, but security officials can sometimes overstep their bounds and abuse their authority. Instead of protecting national security, overzealous officials can waste valuable resources, endanger some of the nation's most cherished values, and harm its international image. Moreover, officials' use of intrusive, abusive counterintelligence methods against loyal dissidents like Pauling can erode public trust in government and cause some citizens to believe that secret government agents are guilty of conspiring against the republic. The FBI's surveillance and harassment of Pauling provides a case study in counterintelligence out of control.

The FBI first gained authorization to spy on "subversive" Americans during the New Deal. On August 24, 1936, as war clouds gathered in Europe and Asia, FBI chief J. Edgar Hoover and President Franklin Roosevelt met privately to discuss the Communist and fascist threats to American internal security. Hoover quickly briefed the president on native fascists, but American Communism was his main concern. On orders from Moscow, he said, the Communists might try to paralyze the nation's industry, communications, and transportation through their control of powerful unions. The Reds were also boring within the government by placing comrades in key agencies. According to Hoover, Roosevelt responded with a strong – and highly confidential – order to dramatically expand FBI surveillance of subversives in the United States. The president made this decision unilaterally and secretly. Indeed, as Hoover explained in a memo two years later, it was "imperative" to keep the program secret – not to thwart foreign spies, who undoubtedly knew they were being followed, but "to avoid criticism or objections which might be raised to such an expansion by either ill-informed persons or individuals having some ulterior motive."[1] In other words, he wanted to keep it secret from the democratically elected representatives in Congress.

Roosevelt had good reasons for authorizing the creation and expansion of American internal security services. The world was a dangerous place in the 1930s, and fascists and Communists *were* trying to undermine the American government. But his decision to avoid messy democratic discussion of the expansion meant that Hoover was able to create his surveillance state in total secrecy. Moreover, Roosevelt's failure to define "subversive" laid the groundwork, as a US Senate committee later noted, for "excessive intelligence gathering about Americans."[2]

Once the Second World War began in Europe in 1939, Roosevelt and Hoover shared an obsession with identifying potential enemies in America. "It is known," Hoover told Congress five days after the war started, "that many foreign agents roam at will in a nation which loves peace and hates war. At this moment lecherous enemies of American society are seeking to pollute our atmosphere of freedom and liberty."[3] He asked for, and received, more money from Congress to fight these enemies.

The president saw many potential benefits in increasing Hoover's budget and authority. In 1940, as the war raged in Europe and the "Great Debate" over intervention raged at home, Roosevelt expanded the definition of "subversive activities" to include Americans who sent him hostile telegrams after one of his fireside chats. "As the telegrams all were more or less in opposition to national defense," his press secretary, Steve Early, wrote to Hoover, "the President thought you might like to look them over, noting the names and addresses of the senders."[4] Hoover obliged, and Roosevelt thanked him for the "interesting and valuable" reports.[5] The president also ordered the FBI to tap the phones of people who might later engage in subversive activities.[6] Congress had explicitly prohibited wiretapping, but Roosevelt's attorney general at the time nevertheless approved the FBI's wiretap program. The law, he said, made it illegal to "intercept and divulge" communications, but the government had no intention of *divulging* the information – except, of course, to other parts of the government.[7]

Roosevelt ordered Hoover to wiretap, bug, and physically spy on his anti-interventionist opponents during the Lend–Lease debate of early 1941.[8] He suspected that his political enemies were getting money from the nation's enemies. Hoover complied with reports on leadings isolationists such as Senator Gerald Nye, Senator Burton Wheeler, aviator Charles Lindbergh, and the anti-interventionist America First Committee, among others.[9] The FBI's reports on the anti-interventionists were filled with gossip about the president's political opponents, but contained no evidence of crimes or foreign connections.

During the war, FBI agents also opened mail, planted bugs, and conducted break-ins. Sometimes the president or attorney general authorized these intrusive surveillance techniques; sometimes the bureau had no authorization; and sometimes Hoover directly disobeyed the orders of his superiors. For example, in 1943, Attorney General Francis Biddle told Hoover to abolish his Custodial Detention List – a list of Americans to be detained in case of a national emergency – because it was "impractical, unwise, and dangerous."[10] But Hoover did not abolish the list. He simply renamed it the Security Index and directed his field agents to keep the list "strictly confidential" from officials at the Justice Department.[11]

During the Cold War, the FBI expanded its surveillance operations and even began to conduct covert action programs against American dissidents. The FBI established its first COINTELPRO, or counterintelligence program, in 1956. Initially, COINTELPRO targeted the Communist Party, which Hoover viewed as a foreign-directed organization filled with "masters of deceit," as he called American Communists.[12] But soon COINTELPRO expanded to include infiltration and monitoring of the civil rights movement, the Ku Klux Klan, Black

Nationalist organizations, and New Left groups. FBI informants would infiltrate these organizations, report on their movements, disrupt their plans, and often attempt to discredit the groups' members – even, in some cases, to the point of encouraging them to kill one another or leave their spouses.[13]

The most egregious example of the FBI's abuse of its counterintelligence authority was its harassment of Martin Luther King, Jr. Not only did the bureau bug and wiretap the civil rights leader, it also tried to take him "off his pedestal and to reduce him completely in influence."[14] The FBI warned congressmen, university officials, and even the pope, of King's allegedly dangerous and immoral tendencies. The low point of the bureau's harassment program came thirty-four days before King was to accept the Nobel Peace Prize in 1964. King received an anonymous audiotape in the mail that purportedly recorded his extramarital affairs. The letter that accompanied the tape – written by assistant FBI director William Sullivan himself, it was later revealed – concluded with this suggestion: "King, there is only one thing left for you to do. You know what it is. You have just 34 days in which to do it."[15] King took this to be a suggestion to commit suicide.

In addition to infiltrating and disrupting dissident groups with the COINTELPROs, the FBI also spied on hundreds of thousands of individual Americans in the early Cold War who were suspected of subversive activity. By 1960, the bureau maintained 432,000 files at its headquarters on "subversive" groups and individuals, and FBI field offices around the country collected an even larger number.[16] The agents moved far beyond Communist Party members to monitor law-abiding citizens who espoused – in the view of the FBI – vaguely defined Communist sympathies. Even manifestly non-revolutionary groups like the National Association for the Advancement of Colored People (NAACP) were included in this category.[17]

To be sure, the US government needed a rigorous loyalty-security program for government workers during the early Cold War. Recent research has proved that some Americans did spy for the Soviet Union, and a handful of these spies even attained important positions in the federal government, especially during the US–Soviet wartime alliance. But the FBI's counterintelligence programs went beyond security checks on government workers to the surveillance and harassment of non-Communist dissidents with no access to sensitive documents. Moreover, many of these FBI counterintelligence operations were based on information from dubious sources, carried out with excessive zeal, and subject to little or no oversight by Congress or the Justice Department.

The counterintelligence programs of Hoover's FBI targeted thousands of law-abiding Americans, including teachers, actors, housewives, and ministers. As a Senate inquiry later concluded, many of these investigations used "dangerous and degrading tactics which are abhorrent in a free and decent society."[18] There were many individual victims of these abuses: the priest whose bishop received an anonymous letter after he allowed the Black Panthers to use his church for free breakfasts, or the teacher who lost his job for Communist "associations." But in Linus Pauling's case, the FBI did more than disrupt an innocent individual's life and undermine the First Amendment. By impeding a great American scientist's research, it also arguably harmed the national security it professed to protect.

Pauling's early life contained few clues that he would later become a controversial political figure. The son of a druggist, Pauling showed signs of brilliance as soon as he arrived at Oregon Agricultural College (now Oregon State University) in 1917 at age sixteen. He started teaching chemistry at the college while he was still an undergraduate there. He married one of his students, Ava Helen Miller, an idealistic young woman with a strong sense of social justice. The Paulings would go on to have four children and enjoy a long and happy partnership together.[19]

271

The "boy professor" attended graduate school at the California Institute of Technology, where he joined the faculty in 1927. Using the relatively new technology of X-ray crystallography, he studied photographic images of molecules and analyzed their structure and the ways that they bonded with one another. After publishing numerous groundbreaking articles on atomic structure, his interests turned from physics to living systems and biochemistry. He quickly established a reputation as one of the most innovative minds in American science, prompting revolutions in quantum chemistry and molecular biology. His seminal work, *The Nature of the Chemical Bond* (1939), transformed the field of chemistry. Its clear prose, detailed illustrations, and accessible analysis helped to make it one of the most widely cited scientific works of the century. During the Second World War, he put his research talents at the service of the US government. He invented an oxygen meter that tested the air in submarines, and for this achievement he earned the Presidential Medal of Merit, the highest award given to US civilians. After the war, Pauling, now at the peak of his productive career, published *General Chemistry*, a hugely popular undergraduate text that made him famous with generations of students and also helped him to become independently wealthy.[20]

In the early years of his career, Pauling devoted all of his time and energy to his research and his family. He had no time for politics. "Until I was forty," he later said, "I didn't take much interest in social concerns. I swallowed the argument that people in power use to suppress scientists – a scientist knows a great deal about his field but nothing whatsoever about war and peace."[21]

By the mid-1940s, though, he had established his reputation as the one of the world's most respected scientists. Once he was secure in his income and his academic achievements, Ava Helen urged him to read widely and speak out on politics. Beginning in 1946, he began to associate himself "in a smaller or larger way with every peace movement that has come to my attention," he later admitted proudly.[22] He condemned American racism, joined numerous progressive groups, and defended the Hollywood Ten. As Senator Joe McCarthy denounced "Commiecrats" and parlor pinks, Pauling continued his work with leftist groups, including the campaign to free the Rosenbergs, the National Committee to Repeal the McCarran Acts, and "Everybody's Committee to Outlaw War." He not only defended Communists, he also refused to say initially whether he had been a Communist himself.[23] Denying Party membership, he believed, just played into the hands of the witch hunters.

The FBI saw Pauling's vocal progressivism as potential evidence of subversive tendencies, and started keeping a file on him in 1947. Three years later, it received "proof" of Pauling's disloyalty from a professional ex-Communist named Louis Budenz. Budenz, who made his living by writing books about the evils of American Communism, named Pauling as one of the 400 "men without faces" who were secretly under Party discipline and preparing the country for a Communist takeover.[24] The "Budenz 400" included prominent artists, intellectuals, and scientists like Pauling who had denounced the Red Scare. Scholars have thoroughly discredited Budenz's list.[25] A charitable interpretation would be that his memory had faded during the five years since his defection from the Party leadership. A less charitable interpretation would be that he made up the list to sell more books, and then justified his lies out of a deep belief that liberals were as treasonous as Communists.

The FBI was never able to find another witness to confirm Budenz's secondhand accusations. Pauling's colleagues at the California Institute of Technology insisted that he was simply an "exhibitionist" rather than a Communist, and years of FBI interviews of Southern California Communists and informants never produced a single person who could remember seeing Pauling or his wife at a Party meeting.[26] The evidence for Budenz's identification of

Pauling as a secret Red remained so flimsy after two years of investigation that the special agent in charge of the Los Angeles FBI office suggested closing the case.[27]

Yet J. Edgar Hoover sternly insisted that the LA agents must pursue their man. When Pauling ultimately denied Party membership under oath, Hoover responded by suggesting that the Justice Department prosecute him for perjury.[28] Because of his leftist politics, the US State Department's passport division prohibited him from attending a scientific meeting held in his honor in England in 1952.[29] Pauling was sure that the government was not really worried about his loyalty, but "instead the denial of a passport to me is an effort by the Government to force me to change my political ideas or give up my activities."[30] He refused to pull back, and some scholars have speculated that he suffered his greatest scientific disappointment as a result. At the time he was at the forefront of a group of scientists racing to describe the structure of DNA. Had he been allowed to attend the conference, he might have seen the X-ray images of DNA taken by British scientists, and he, rather than James Watson and Francis Crick, might have solved the riddle of the double helix.[31]

Pauling did win a Nobel Prize in 1954 for his numerous contributions to chemistry. But several government officials opposed allowing him to travel to Sweden to accept the prize.[32] Secretary of State John Foster Dulles overruled them and gave Pauling his passport. Pauling's receipt of the Prize only convinced the FBI chief to work harder to prove his subversive tendencies. "You should continue to remain alert for any additional subversive information concerning Pauling and forward this to the Bureau by the most expeditious means," he wrote to his agents soon after the announcement of the Prize.[33] Not all American government officials shared Hoover's belief that Pauling was a danger to his country. An embassy official in Stockholm wrote that the peace activist was "definitely the most popular of the American Nobel Prize winners" in 1954 and that "far from injuring American interests or prestige, his visit substantially enhanced them."[34]

But such voices of reason were rare in the US government in the 1950s. The most famous American chemist of the century, Pauling was denied a grant from the US Public Health Service because he was "suspected of disloyalty to the country."[35] An FBI agent noted laconically that the health service "also turned down Pauling's request for forty thousand dollars to finance two investigations of blood and protein chemistry, a field in which he is world famous."[36] The US government, in short, did its best to ruin his career because of its conspiracy theory of his role as a Communist subversive. At a time when the US was engaged in a bitter political and scientific competition with a Communist country, government officials obstructed the work of an American scientist who could help to showcase the superiority of capitalism.

Pauling's career suffered in other ways as well. Disturbed by controversy over his alleged Red links, American universities rescinded invitations to have him speak at their campuses, the California Institute of Technology launched an internal investigation of his politics, and private corporations pulled their funding from Pauling's lab. Meanwhile, Pauling's alleged Communist sympathies did not win him fans in the Soviet Union. The Soviets considered Pauling's work on chemical bonds to be "un-Marxian," bourgeois, and anti-materialistic, and Soviets chemists denounced his research.[37]

But Pauling refused to end his peace campaigns. He knew that he could lose his job, he later explained, but "I kept on in order to retain the respect of my wife."[38] By the late 1950s, he had become a leader in the anti-nuclear movement. In 1958, he published *No More War*, an early jeremiad on the catastrophic consequences of nuclear war. "I believe," he wrote, "that the development of these terrible weapons forces us to move into a new period in the history of the world, a period of peace and reason, when world problems are not solved by war or by force, but are solved by the application of man's power of reason."[39] He and thirteen other scientists sued the Defense Department to stop nuclear tests, and he spearheaded a drive by 11,000 scientists to ask the United Nations to stop the tests in all nations. He was particularly worried that fallout from nuclear tests would lead to millions of miscarriages and birth defects around the world. The statements of a respected member of the US Atomic Energy Commission, chemist Willard Libby, especially outraged Pauling. Libby insisted that fallout was relatively harmless, which Pauling believed was a lie. "This is premeditated murder of millions of people," Pauling said after the Soviets ended a series of 50 tests. "It compares with the consignment of Jews to the gas chambers."[40]

As Pauling intensified his anti-nuclear activism, the FBI continued its fruitless investigation. "We have contacted every source we could find who might have useful information," one FBI official explained in 1958. "None has identified Pauling as a Communist Party member."[41] Still, the bureau continued to monitor Pauling's mail and track his movements.[42]

Pauling despised the FBI and the presidents who controlled it throughout the 1950s. When a new generation took charge of the White House in 1961, Pauling did not initially see much of a difference between the Eisenhower and Kennedy administrations. Like his predecessor, John Kennedy failed to understand the dangers of nuclear testing and nuclear war, Pauling believed. As he clipped and filed accounts of Kennedy's speeches, he annotated them with angry comments about the disastrous consequences of his policies. Next to a newspaper article quoting Kennedy's determination to prepare "in the final extreme to fight for our country and to mean it," Pauling wrote: "SUCH A POLICY WILL MEAN THE END OF CIVILIZATION."[43]

In 1962, Pauling briefly panicked the Secret Service when he and Ava Helen picketed the White House on the day before they were scheduled to attend a presidential dinner for Nobel laureates.[44] Kennedy's staff decided to allow the Paulings to attend the dinner anyway, and the two peace activists had their first personal encounter with the young president and his glamorous wife. Pauling could not help being charmed by the Kennedys. "I'm pleased to see you," the president said to the man who had picketed his residence. "I understand you've been around the White House a couple of days already." Jackie Kennedy said that Caroline Kennedy was perplexed by the picketing. "[S]he asked, 'Mummy, what has Daddy done now?' "[45] Pauling and his wife joined in the laughter and went on to enjoy a glittering evening with more than a hundred of the nation's top intellectuals.

Pauling was reluctant to associate this witty, urbane chief executive with the oppressive government that had set out to ruin him. After the Cuban missile crisis in October 1962, Pauling wondered angrily why Kennedy had undertaken "this *immoral* act of risking our lives." He concluded that the president was manipulated by powers beyond his control. The president was not forced to blockade the island by the Soviets, Pauling noted; instead, he "*was* forced by the militarists, the military–industrial complex."[46]

The next year, Kennedy redeemed himself in Pauling's view when he signed the Nuclear Test Ban Treaty with the Soviet Union and Great Britain, which ended the above-ground tests that had poisoned the atmosphere. The agreement, Pauling wrote to the president, "will go down in history as one of the greatest events in the history of the world."[47] Pauling also admired Kennedy's American University address in June 1963. In that speech, which some historians see as a sign of Kennedy's intention to ease the tensions of the Cold War, the president urged accommodation with the Soviet Union. "For, in the final analysis, our most basic common link is that we all inhabit this small planet. We all breathe the same air. We all cherish our children's future. And we are all mortal." Pauling clipped and filed the text of the American University speech.[48] The president, he believed, seemed to be freeing himself from the control of the military–industrial complex.

274

Pauling's work for nuclear disarmament was vindicated in October 1963, when the Nobel committee awarded him his second Prize, this time for Peace. He was recognized for his role in bringing about the Test Ban Treaty. Pauling valued the Peace Prize even more than his earlier Prize for chemistry. "[T]he Nobel Prize in Chemistry pleased me immensely," he said later, "but . . . it was given to me for enjoying myself – for carrying out researches in chemistry that I enjoyed carrying out. On the other hand, I felt that the Nobel Peace Prize was an indication to me that I had done my duty as a human being."[49] This time, the US government did not attempt to stop him from traveling to accept his prize.

Still, Pauling's FBI file continued to grow. He attracted bureau attention again in 1962 when he publicly supported the Fair Play for Cuba Committee, a group opposing US efforts to overthrow Cuban leader Fidel Castro. Hoover had denounced the organization as a threat to US security and a vehicle for Communist propaganda.[50]

Pauling did not cross paths with many of the six thousand national members of Fair Play for Cuba. He did not know, for example, the founder of the one-man chapter in New Orleans, an American Communist named Lee Harvey Oswald. Along with the rest of the nation, he would learn of Oswald on November 22, 1963. And like many Americans whose views had been labeled "subversive" in the McCarthy era, Pauling would soon become very suspicious of the government's official explanation of the events of that day.

Pauling immediately questioned the conclusion of the Warren Commission – the group appointed by President Lyndon Johnson to investigate the Kennedy assassination – that a Communist had killed the president on his own. Like several other early Warren Report critics, Pauling was skeptical of the government's attempt to blame a Communist. He knew from experience that the government had a habit of demonizing leftists.

Given his hatred for the FBI and his growing admiration for the president he saw as a force for peace, Pauling soon formed dark suspicions about the role of the "military-industrial complex" in the Kennedy assassination. He corresponded with prominent conspiracy theorists; he subscribed to conspiracy newsletters; he studied photographs of the assassination and tried to identify shadowy figures in the bushes.[51] In 1975, after more than a decade of reading books, articles, and newsletters on the assassination, he joined Mark Lane's Citizens' Commission of Inquiry, which demanded a congressional investigation of the US government's potential complicity in the murder.[52] The government's conspiracy theories about him prompted Pauling to develop conspiracy theories about the government.

Throughout his career, Pauling was an intuitive, innovative, and daring thinker. He found the answers to some of the twentieth century's most vexing scientific questions by glimpsing connections that previous investigators had missed. At the end of his career, he was vilified for his advocacy of massive doses of vitamin C to prevent and fight cancer, but by the 1990s the medical establishment had accepted his underlying assumption that antioxidants were important cancer fighters. He was always ready to disregard what other people told him he should think. His willingness to leap from the proven to the theoretical made him a brilliant scientist. It also made him a natural conspiracy theorist.

His experiences as a victim of FBI repression also made him a natural critic of the US government's official version of Kennedy's assassination. Pauling was the prototypical innocent victim of McCarthyism – an activist who had never joined the Communist Party, yet who was harassed and spied upon by his government because of his public denunciations of the Red Scare. He knew the FBI to be a vengeful, vindictive agency; the extreme anti-Communists, he said repeatedly, were the real un-Americans.[53]

Like Pauling, other individuals who suffered from the repressive effects of McCarthyism in the 1950s began to develop conspiracy theories about the real "masters of deceit" within the

American government in the 1960s. Pauling corresponded extensively with Sylvia Meagher, a researcher for the World Health Organization (WHO), who helped to organize the first group of Kennedy "assassination researchers," as they called themselves, and who published the first subject index of the Warren Report. Meagher had almost lost her job at the WHO during a long loyalty investigation in 1953.[54] Harold Weisberg, one of Meagher's close friends and a fellow assassination researcher, had been dismissed from the State Department for suspected Communist sympathies in 1947.[55] Weisberg self-published the first critical book on the Warren Report, and went on to publish a total of nine Kennedy assassination conspiracy books.[56]

For his part, Pauling could not understand why the US government had pursued the self-defeating policy of trying to destroy him, despite his stature as one of America's greatest scientists. The answer, he decided, was that the anti-Communist conspiracy theorists were themselves part of a great American conspiracy. J. Edgar Hoover, the FBI, and the "military-industrial complex" were conspiring to silence progressive voices in America. They would stop at nothing – even a coup – to attain their reactionary goals. Some progressives, including former Vice President Henry Wallace and former ambassador Joseph Davies, feared in the 1950s that the Reds-in-government conspiracists were dangerous extremists who were plotting an anti-government coup.[57] In the 1960s, Pauling came to believe that those extremists had succeeded in their coup.

In the 1970s, the US Senate investigated the scandalous practices of the FBI and CIA. A committee headed by Frank Church of Idaho recommended several reforms to ensure democratic oversight of intelligence agencies and prevent such abuses from occurring again. The most important law to come out of the Church investigation was the Foreign Intelligence Surveillance Act (FISA) of 1978, which required the National Security Agency to obtain warrants before it eavesdropped on the conversations of American citizens. FISA set up a special, top-secret court with responsibility for reviewing and approving warrant requests. In addition, Congress ultimately reorganized intelligence oversight and formed two permanent committees – the Intelligence Committees of the House and the Senate – with responsibility for looking over the shoulders of intelligence and counterintelligence agencies. With these reforms, Congress hoped to avoid the abuses of J. Edgar Hoover's reign at the FBI and similar abuses at the CIA. Future Hoovers would need to justify surveillance of loyal dissenters like Pauling.

Yet there are signs that the administration of George W. Bush has not learned the lessons of the past. After the terrorist attacks of September 11, 2001, President Bush ordered the National Security Agency to disregard FISA and to monitor Americans' international phone calls, emails, faxes, and instant messages without obtaining warrants.[58] According to James Bamford, the number of Americans monitored by the NSA has grown from about a dozen each year to as many as five thousand since 2002.[59] Once again, as at the peak of the Cold War, no overseers watch government counterintelligence agents; these agents need not show probable cause before they spy on American citizens. This total secrecy could allow abuses like the Pauling case to happen again. As Senator Church said in the midst of his famous investigation, "We've learned enough, I should think, to at least rephrase Lord Acton's famous admonition. I think that it could be said that 'All secrecy corrupts. Absolute secrecy corrupts absolutely.' "[60]

Notes

1 Senate Select Committee to Study Governmental Operations with Respect to Intelligence Activities (hereafter Church Committee), *Final Report* (94th Cong., 2nd sess., 1976), Book II, 25, 28.

Athan G. Theoharis argues that Roosevelt gave Hoover a somewhat narrow and vague directive, which the FBI chief then misrepresented and expanded. See Theoharis, "The FBI's Stretching of Presidential Directives, 1936–1953," *Political Science Quarterly* 91:4 (Winter, 1976–1977): 652–55.

2 Church Committee Report, Book II, 24. See also Church Committee Report, Book III, 393–97. For a detailed analysis of Roosevelt's expansion of the FBI, see Kenneth O'Reilly, "A New Deal for the FBI: The Roosevelt Administration, Crime Control, and National Security," *Journal of American History* 69:3 (December 1982): 638–58.

3 Quoted in Frank Donner, "Hoover's Legacy," *Nation*, June 1, 1974, 679.

4 Church Committee Report, Book II, 33.

5 Quoted in Curt Gentry, *J. Edgar Hoover: The Man and the Secrets* (New York: Plume, 1992), 226.

6 See Richard W. Steele, "Franklin D. Roosevelt and His Foreign Policy Critics," *Political Science Quarterly* 94:1 (Spring 1979): 15–32. For other discussions of the Roosevelt administration's attempts to monitor and discredit its enemies, see Leo P. Ribuffo, *The Old Christian Right: The Protestant Far Right from the Great Depression to the Cold War* (Philadelphia, PA: Temple, 1983), chapter 5; Geoffrey S. Smith, *To Save a Nation: American "Extremism," the New Deal, and the Coming of World War II* (Chicago, IL: Ivan R. Dee, 1973, rev. ed. 1992), epilogue; and Douglas M. Charles, "Informing FDR: FBI Political Surveillance and the Isolationist-Interventionist Foreign Policy Debate," *Diplomatic History* 24:2 (Spring 2000): 211–32.

7 Church Committee Report, Book II, 36.

8 O'Reilly, "New Deal for the FBI," 648.

9 Wayne S. Cole, *Roosevelt and the Isolationists: 1932–1945* (Lincoln, NE: University of Nebraska Press, 1983), 531–33.

10 Church Committee Report, Book II, 35.

11 Ibid., 36.

12 J. Edgar Hoover, *Masters of Deceit: The Story of Communism in America and How to Fight It* (New York: Holt, 1958).

13 See, for example, Church Committee hearings, *Federal Bureau of Investigation* (Volume 6), November 18, 1975, 26.

14 Ibid., 31.

15 Ibid., 33. For the most complete examination of the FBI's harassment of King, see David Garrow, *The FBI and Martin Luther King, Jr.* (New York: Penguin Books, 1981).

16 Church Committee Report, Book II, 47.

17 Ibid., 46–47.

18 Ibid., 211.

19 On Pauling, see Thomas Hager, *Force of Nature: The Life of Linus Pauling* (New York: Simon and Schuster, 1995); Thomas Hager and Clifford Mead, eds., *Linus Pauling: Scientist and Peacemaker* (Corvallis, OR: Oregon State University Press, 2001), David E. Newton, *Linus Pauling: Scientist and Advocate* (New York: Instructional Horizons, 1994); and Ted Goertzel and Ben Goertzel, *Linus Pauling: A Life in Science and Politics* (New York: Basic Books, 1995).

20 Hager, *Force of Nature*, 217–18, 249–52, 290–91.

21 Quoted in Newton, *Linus Pauling*, 56.

22 Quoted in report, "Linus Carl Pauling," October 21, 1952, FBI file 100–353404–27, box 2.025, folder 25.1, Pauling papers, Oregon State University.

23 See memo, SAC Los Angeles to director, November 21, 1950, FBI file 100–353404–10, box 2.025, folder 25.1, Pauling papers.

24 Memo, SAC New York to director, August 8, 1950, FBI file 100–353404–7, box 2.025, folder 25.1, Pauling papers. See also Budenz, *Men without Faces: The Communist Conspiracy in the U.S.A.* (New York: Harper, 1950). Budenz did not name the four hundred individuals in his book, but he named them later to the FBI.

25 See Robert M. Lichtman, "Louis Budenz, the FBI, and the 'List of 400 Concealed Communists': An Extended Tale of McCarthy-Era Informing," in *American Communist History* 3:1 (June 2004): 25–54. For an early, critical assessment of Budenz's truthfulness, see Herbert Packer, *Ex-Communist Witnesses: Four Studies in Fact Finding* (Stanford, CA: Stanford University Press, 1962), chapter 4.

26 Report, "Linus Carl Pauling," October 21, 1952, 100–353404–27, box 2.025, folder 25.1, Pauling papers.

27 Memo, SAC Los Angeles to director, October 21, 1952, FBI file 100–353404–27, box 2.025, folder 25.1, Pauling papers.

28 Memo, FBI director to attorney general, December 9, 1953, FBI file 100–353404–37, box 2.025, folder 25.1, Pauling papers.

29 Report, "Linus Carl Pauling," October 21,1952.

30 Quoted in Jessica Wang, *American Science in an Age of Anxiety: Scientists, Anticommunism, and the Cold War* (Chapel Hill, NC: University of North Carolina Press, 1999), 275.

31 Stanley Kutler, *The American Inquisition: Justice and Injustice in the Cold War* (New York: Hill and Wang, 1982), 90–91; Hager, *Force of Nature*, 414; Horace Freeland Judson, *The Eighth Day of Creation: The Makers of the Revolution in Biology* (New York: Simon and Schuster, 1979), 132.

32 Hager, *Force of Nature*, 454.

33 Director to SAC Los Angeles, November 29, 1954, FBI file 100–353404–54, box 2.025, folder 25.2, Pauling papers.

34 Foreign Service Despatch, American Embassy, Stockholm, to Department of State, Washington, 26 March 1956, 32685-D, box 2.030, folder 30.2, Pauling papers.

35 "Disloyal Scientists?" *Newsweek*, May 10, 1954, 57.

36 Report, "Linus Carl Pauling," December 2, 1954, FBI file 100–353404–162, box 2.025, folder 25.2, Pauling papers.

37 "Statement by Linus Pauling," April 22, 1951, box 2.025, folder 25.1, Pauling papers. See also Hager, *Force of Nature*, 383.

38 Lee Dye, "The Deeply Personal War of Linus Pauling," *Los Angeles Times*, June 2, 1985, section VI, p. 1. Quoted in Hager, *Force of Nature*, 360.

39 Linus Pauling, *No More War* (New York: Dodd, Mead & Company, 1983, first published 1958), 3.

40 Quoted in Hager, *Force of Nature*, 532.

41 Memo, A.H. Belmont to L.V. Boardman, April 10, 1958, FBI file 100–353404–148, box 2.026, folder 26.1, Pauling papers.

42 The FBI was still investigating Pauling in the Nixon administration. See summary, April 25, 1973, FBI file 100–353404–424, box 2.029, folder 29.2, Pauling papers.

43 See "The President's Address at Arlington," in box 198, folder 198.3, Pauling papers.

44 C.L. McGowan to Mr Rosen, April 28, 1962, FBI file 100–353404–295, box 2.027, folder 27.2, Pauling papers.

45 Quoted in Hager, *Force of Nature*, 537–38.

46 See the handwritten notes, undated, in box 198, folder 198.3, Pauling papers.

47 Pauling to Kennedy, August 1, 1963, box 198, folder 198.3, Pauling papers.

48 See box 198, folder 198.3, Pauling papers.

49 Quoted in Mead and Hager, eds., *Linus Pauling: Scientist and Peacemaker*, 194.

50 "Caribbean Export," *Newsweek*, 23 October 1961, 22–23.

51 See sketch and letters in box 198, folder 198.4, in the Pauling papers.

52 Letter, Kathy Kinsella to Linus Pauling, May 8, 1975, box 198, folder 198.4, Pauling papers.

53 Hager, *Force of Nature*, 524.

54 See the documents in "Loyalty Case (1953–54)," box 10, Sylvia Meagher papers, Hood College, Frederick, Maryland.

55 Report to director, November 8, 1966, FBI file 62–109060–4250, JFK collection, National Archives and Records Administration, College Park, Maryland.

56 Harold Weisberg, *Whitewash: The Report on the Warren Report* (Hyattstown, MD: 1965).

57 Richard M. Fried, "The Idea of 'Conspiracy' in McCarthy-Era Politics," *Prologue* 34:1 (2002), 43–44.

58 James Risen and Eric Lichtblau, "Bush Lets US Spy on Callers Without Courts," *New York Times*, December 16, 2005.

59 James Bamford, "Big Brother Is Listening," *Atlantic Monthly*, April 2006, 66.

60 Frank Church speech, July 8, 1975, in series 7.9, box 4, folder 1, Frank Church Collection, Boise State University Library.

21

The role of covert action

William J. Daugherty

Overview

Covert action operations, essentially absent from public view since the large operations of the 1980s in Afghanistan and Central America, again began generating news early in the twenty-first century as the Central Intelligence Agency quickly assumed a major responsibility for prosecuting America's war against terrorism. By the end of 2005 news media were reporting on numerous CIA activities, including identifying, capturing, and interrogating (or sometimes killing) members of Al-Qaeda and other terrorist elements threatening US interests worldwide. Once again, an American president had turned to covert action to further American national security objectives through programs intended to remain hidden from public view. In doing so, President George W. Bush followed precedents set by chief executives going back to George Washington and the origins of our nation. Yet, as always, legitimate disputes over the appropriateness and legality of covert action programs are complicated by a lack of knowledge about covert action in general and its role in supporting American foreign policy.

Perhaps the most important point to understand about covert action is that is it *not* a routine mission of the CIA, such as foreign intelligence collection or counterintelligence operations. Rather, covert action is very much an element of American presidential statecraft, joining the more familiar components of American foreign policy such as diplomacy, military force, economic assistance or sanctions, trade enhancements or restrictions, foreign aid, military training and assistance, financial credits or loans, government-sponsored information activities (e.g. Voice of America), and agricultural aid. But there are several crucial aspects that separate covert action from these other foreign policy tools.

Of primary import, covert action is a capability that, by the nature of the work and by presidential Executive Order (indirectly bolstered by the Intelligence Oversight Act of 1991), is provided solely by the CIA but employed *only* at the explicit direction of the President of the United States. Indeed, since 1974 federal law requires the president to notify the Congress that he has authorized these programs and that he "finds" the programs to be necessary for the national security of the United States. (The document the president signs is known, not surprisingly, as a "Finding"; there are now so many laws and rules governing the initiation and

279

conduct of covert action programs that all elements of every Finding are routinely scrutinized by lawyers in the CIA, the Congress, and at the National Security Council.) Also, unlike overt, or visible, foreign policy measures, covert action operations are conducted by the CIA utilizing clandestine methodologies for most or all phases of an operation save the final results, which may be highly visible. There is a two-fold purpose in this.

First, the purpose of any covert action program – that is, what the president and the CIA intend to accomplish – is generally to influence a foreign audience to do something, or refrain from doing something, in furtherance of US policy goals. That "audience" might be a nation's government or senior leadership, a nation's population, a segment of that population, or supranational groups such as a terrorist organization or a drug cartel. Programs directed against governments might be focused on influencing that government to change its policies on an issue or towards a geographic region in a manner that will parallel, *vice* oppose, American policies. Covert action operations against a population might be intended to generate pro-American support and, subsequently, to bring pressure on their government for a corresponding change. Programs to counter supranational organizations might seek to undermine their operations, capture members, induce defections, or disrupt their financial networks.

The results of covert action – i.e. influence – operations must be visible, at least to a part of the target population, since the idea is to create a change of behavior; and it is manifestly impossible for actions that are completely hidden from view to have that effect. While the recruitment and direction ("handling") of foreign citizens as agents to participate in these programs is done clandestinely, as in intelligence collection operations, for the security purposes, what those agents ultimately "produce" will be usually be readily apparent. For example, a labor leader in a foreign country might be recruited secretly to push his organization to support trade policies that favor United States interests but which his government opposes. This laborite might, at some point, be tasked to organize a nation-wide strike as a way to pressure his government to change direction, at least partially. Obviously, this labor action would not only be readily apparent to the government and citizens, but might also receive media coverage regionally or even internationally. While one event alone is rarely sufficient to being about the desired result, that labor leader might, over time and when aggregated with other covert action programs targeted against that government, achieve some positive effect in line with overall US policy objectives.

The second purpose behind employing covert action programs to achieve selected goals, *vice* reliance on traditional overt measures such as diplomacy, trade and military force, is that for the activities undertaken by the recruited agents to be viewed as "legitimate" by the intended audience, the sponsorship of the United States government must remain hidden. An editorial placed in the newspaper of a foreign capital that is openly written by the American ambassador to that country will have little-to-no effect (i.e. influence) if that population or government is anti-American, at least on that particular issue. However, if a highly respected public figure who is a citizen of that nation writes, or putatively writes, that same editorial, it may carry much more weight with the readership. Especially if the newspaper is regularly perused by that country's policy elites.

This "secret but not secret" characteristic of covert action is attractive and extremely advantageous to presidents in that it yields them a policy option situated between purely overt diplomatic and/or economic measures (which against certain regimes or organizations may be of limited use) and resort to open employment of military force (which might redound to the detriment of the US). Covert action allows the president to execute measures of varying and increasing pressure on regimes but without that regime realizing that the source of those pressures is the United States government. Or, if the hostile regime or entity does believe or conclude that the US government is behind damaging actions, it will be unable to prove it to the world, thus limiting its ability (and, perhaps, willingness) to respond. Covert action was relied upon by all Cold War presidents as a means by which the United States could create difficulties for the Soviet Union by applying pressure incrementally, thereby reducing the risk of war that an overt use of military force would have entailed.

Understanding now that covert action programs are authorized by the president for the purpose of influencing some foreign audience, the obvious question is, What exactly *are* these influence operations? Covert action is an "intelligence discipline," just as intelligence collection/analysis and counterintelligence are disciplines, within the overall responsibilities of the CIA or any other large intelligence agency. (The former Soviet intelligence service, the KGB, utilized covert action extensively, calling it "Active Measures.") Covert action is characterized by four "sub-disciplines": propaganda, political action, paramilitary, and information warfare operations. The individual influence operations subtended by these categories range across the spectrum from the nearly invisible to the spectacularly public; from the almost benign to the highly provocative; from a subtle appeal to the intellect to the violent taking of lives; from the amazingly cheap to the enormously expensive; from an event lasting but a few minutes to a years–long campaign.

A covert action operation may be as simple as a college boy's practical joke (printing fake and misleading campaign posters) or highly technical and deadly. Many activities are almost routine "tools–of–the–trade" and employed by authorities since biblical times, while others involve applications of emerging futuristic technologies limited only by human ingenuity. The ultimate value of covert action, perhaps, is that it yields to the president a vast array of means to aid in the achievement of his policy objectives. *ultimate value*

Covert action sub-disciplines

Propaganda — most often used

Propaganda – which we may define as merely the dissemination of information by various media for the purpose of influencing opinions – is perhaps the methodology most frequently relied upon by the president and the CIA, for it is frequently subtle, disarming, flexible, and low in cost. In any case, it is rare for propaganda programs to attain desired results in the near or even intermediate term, much less overnight. The intent of propaganda is to influence – to bolster or to change – what a person or group believes. Individuals who believe strongly in one point of view simply do not change their minds on the basis of one article, one editorial, one poster, or one pamphlet. While one item may impel an audience to begin thinking about alternative perspectives, the fact of the matter is that it takes time for people, individually or collectively, to absorb a new concept and still longer to adopt it in place of a previous position.

Similarly, it is difficult for the managing case officers to evaluate the results of a propaganda operation, at least not until the justification for it has long vanished, because (as a former senior CIA officer with responsibility for a large number of these programs would say) it is impossible to measure the effect of ideas on a person's mind. Hence, for those executing many propaganda programs, it is necessary to them to have faith that they are making a difference, even though they might never receive positive confirmation of those results.

Propaganda may be employed alone but is likewise a facile and effective tool to buttress overt policy measures, such as diplomacy and economic assistance. The best use of propaganda is simply to tell the truth. During the Cold War, the United States didn't need to lionize the

America ideal or the values of democracy to the citizens of the Soviet Union, nor did it need to tell the oppressed how awful and repressive their own government was, for they knew all of this. As such, many of the US propaganda efforts against the USSR (both covert measures from the CIA and overt measures originating in the State Department's United States Information Service) merely involved airing truthful accounts of events to counter the falsehoods about international and internal actions the Soviet government fed its own citizenry, to help keep alive the histories of the ethnic minorities persecuted by the Communist system, and to provide the population with desirable materials banned by Moscow (e.g. Bibles and other religious items, and Russian literary works such as those of Pasternak and Solzhenitsyn).

Propaganda that is truthful in nature and for which the source is accurately identified, such as a government agency's public information service, like USIS or Voice of America, whether objective or slanted (subtly or otherwise), is referred to as "white" propaganda. Similar propaganda disseminated with the source of that information disguised is "gray" propaganda. For example, an article published by a foreign scholar, under his real name in an academic journal read by his country's policy elites, that advocated a pro-American perspective, but done so at the secret behest of the CIA, would be gray propaganda. Gray propaganda can be as effective as white, in the right circumstances. In the 1960s the Soviet intelligence service, the KGB, had an agent who was a reporter write a story that appeared in an Italian newspaper claiming that the CIA was behind John F. Kennedy's assassination. Nearly fifty years later, there are still many people (even in the United States) who believe this.

Finally, there's "black" propaganda, which in plain terms is forgery, something created out of whole cloth to influence individuals or affect an event, but which is totally false. The Soviet Union also attempted to use black propaganda during the Cold War, primarily to generate negative feelings against the United States among Third World inhabitants. An allegedly official document under State Department letterhead "acknowledging" that the AIDS virus was produced American labs for the deliberation introduction into African societies turned up in a number of foreign countries and, like the Kennedy story, is still given credence by millions today despite the blatant crudeness of the forgery.

Political action

The second sub-discipline of covert action is political action, a broad term covering operations that are not only political in nature but may or may not have an economic component. Funds given secretly to aid a preferred political candidate or party to win an election in a foreign country is a simple, basic form of political action. A labor strike that brings a nation's workforce to a halt is both political and economic, creating or exacerbating economic stress among the population that possesses in turn the ability to generate political heat on the government leadership. A more serious operation might be the introduction of counterfeit currency into a country's money supply, wreaking severe economic damage to the country and undermining the legitimacy of that country's leadership. In the 1990s, highly accurate counterfeit US$50 bills – a favorite source of payment utilized throughout the Middle East – were printed in that region, to the great consternation of the American government and Department of the Treasury for most of a decade. Planting the fake currency of a nation already in serious economic straits could be nothing less than ruinous for that country's leadership. Obviously, political action is more provocative than propaganda because it is more visible and requires actual physical activity, as opposed to merely impacting ideas or attitudes.

Paramilitary activities

The third sub-discipline of covert action is the application of paramilitary operations, which are usually (but not always) found only in long-running programs with or against a hostile entity. They are, of course, the most provocative of all covert action operations because they may include acts involving destruction and even death. For this reason, paramilitary operations may also be the hardest programs to justify to the American public. In the 1980s, much of the world was at least aware of, if not following, America's "covert" wars being waged in Central America and Afghanistan; post-2001, activities of the CIA in the war against terrorism are routinely reported (accurately or not) in our major newspapers. While CIA elements may be involved in actual combat operations in these large paramilitary programs, they are more likely to be supporting and training indigenous forces (government or insurgents) than they are in fighting. In view of the openness of these "covert" programs, the question often raised is whether its appropriate for an espionage agency like the CIA to be the responsible organization or whether it would be better to give the Department of Defense (using American military personnel) the responsibility. This somewhat perennial issue was addressed in 2004 by a joint CIA–DoD panel and again it was determined that not only was the CIA paramilitary capability essential, but that the CIA's and DoD's special operations missions were both compatible and complementary.

But wartime isn't the only time CIA paramilitary units are employed. The training of friendly foreign militaries and other entities of allied governments, such as VIP protection services, are part and parcel of missions for the CIA's paramilitary personnel. And at times resources normally devoted to paramilitary operations might be used for other missions, such as the clandestine exfiltration of an agent from hostile territory. While some of the missions carried out by the CIA's paramilitary units are classic covert action operations, others are not. But all are denominated as "special activities" (*vice* routine intelligence measures) and so most require the president to sign a Finding and notify Congress, just as he does for the more standard covert action programs.

Information warfare

The last sub-discipline is a fairly new addition to the covert action inventory, and that is information warfare. In general, an intelligence program aimed at surreptitiously invading, either remotely or on-site, a computer or data banks with the intent of altering or destroying the hardware, software, or information in the computer, is considered to be covert action. (Secret intrusions into computer data banks simply to learn what that information is, without altering or damaging that data, is manifestly an intelligence collection operation and, while highly sensitive, does not require the special presidential Finding that must accompany all covert action activities.)

As the proliferation of computers grows around the globe, with governments, military forces, government-connected business enterprises, and even terrorist and narcotics organizations relying more and more on computers, the opportunity to exploit computer systems and data banks increases as well. What twenty years ago was a fledgling off-shoot of the intelligence collection business is now realizing its enormous potential as a component of covert action programs.

Policy considerations and consequences

The inclusion of covert action programs with other overt policy measures does not by any means guarantee the success either of that specific program or of the president's overall foreign policy objectives. Moreover, covert action is not itself a substitute in the absence of a coherent national policy. Covert action works only if it is a component subordinated to and coordinated with the overt activities of the other policy-implementing agencies, and employed in a unified campaign to achieve a broad, openly acknowledged United States policy. Ultimately, whether or not covert action should be added to a foreign policy scheme is up to the president and his national security advisors. This means that evaluating the utility and risk of a covert action element is a matter of judgment on their part.

While it is the president's ultimate decision whether to conduct a covert action program, it would seem reasonable to assume that the White House officials base their opinions to some degree upon the assessments of the operational professionals at the CIA. However, this is not always the case, and has resulted in fiascos. The CIA strongly advised President Richard M. Nixon three times not to run a program in the early 1970s involving Iraq, Iran, and the Kurds, a program that led to the deaths of thousands of Kurds at which point President Gerald R. Ford and Secretary of State Henry Kissinger abruptly cancelled the program. Also in the Nixon years, the CIA was adamantly against a covert action program to depose Chilean president Salvador Allende, which Nixon demanded be conducted regardless. And in a genuine aberration, Director of Central Intelligence (DCI) Casey knew full well that the great majority of agency officers would neither participate in nor support the activities that became known as the Iran–Contra disgrace. And so realizing that the disaffected would be tempted to leak the operations either to Congress or the media, Casey deliberately excluded the agency as in institution from involvement in that affair.

While a number of factors must be thoughtfully considered in deciding to include a covert action component in a particular foreign policy scheme, perhaps the most significant is deciding on the objectives to be achieved and then carefully balancing those goals against the attendant costs and risks. Expensive, high-risk program proposals that are apt to achieve little should, as a matter of course, be avoided. As the balance shifts to the less costly, less risky, and more effective, the greater the odds that a president and his advisors will accept it. Obviously, the ideal programs are low risk, low cost, and highly effective. As improbable as it may seem, during the forty years of the Cold War the CIA in fact ran hundreds, if not thousands, of individual covert action operations within dozens of umbrella programs of this nature – programs that never came to the public's attention, yet over time contributed much to a peaceful end to that struggle.

Some covert action programs fail simply because they are, by their very nature, intelligence operations, endeavors fraught with perils and conducted with absolutely no guarantee of ultimate success irrespective of the assessed risk level (Murphy's Law – anything that can go wrong will go wrong, and do so at the worst possible time – applies perfectly to covert action.) And some programs will collapse or be found wanting either because mistakes are made on the part of CIA personnel or its recruited foreign assets, and/or because the operation is discovered by foreign security services. When a covert action program or operation does prematurely become public, there will almost always be meaningful negative consequences, the extent of which depends on the target and objectives of the program, whether it was run unilaterally by the CIA or done with allies, and the cause of the exposure.

Domestically, a compromised covert action program will, if nothing else, embarrass the president, who is likely to have previously denied rumors that such a program existed or ascribed earlier visible results of the operation to the actions of elements unassociated with the US government. The embarrassment will be more acute if the surfacing of the program is, or is perceived by the American people to be, the result of ineptness. This circumstance may lower a president's standings in political polls assessing his general popularity or, more specifically, how well he is doing his job – potentially disastrous to a first-term president facing re-election. If the compromised covert action program is one that most Americans believe necessary or justifiable, the fallout might be neither intense nor long lasting. However, when the operations are contrary to goals acceptable to American public values or opinions, or are conducted in such a way that the public is angered or disgusted, then the repercussions to a president and his historical legacy may be permanently harmed.

Beyond the public's reaction, and potentially more harmful to a president's agenda, is the effect a compromised program will have on a president's relations with Congress. The opposing political party on the Hill is not likely to resist, in today's highly partisan atmosphere, figuratively taking the president to the woodshed over what they will portray, fairly or unfairly, as a "débâcle." And if the situation is bad enough, the president may even be deserted by members of his own party – particularly if his popularity polls are down.

America's allies overseas may also have unfavorable reactions to a compromised program, affecting their embrace of a particular foreign policy. Likewise, a president's relationship with individual foreign leaders suffer serious and lasting harm. The crux of this issue is that historically the great majority of the CIA's covert action programs have been instigated in times of peace, and so the essential determinant if often whether the targeted nation/government is an ally, a neutral, or a hostile. A secondary element is whether the participation of the intelligence or military services of allied countries was involved and/or whether an allied government suffered embarrassment. *failure = big consequences sometimes*

The exposure of a covert action program against the Soviet Union during the Cold War might have angered the Soviet leaders, but it would usually result only in a temporary set back to overall US–USSR relations. This was so if for no other reason than that the Soviets were doing much the same, if not more, against the West, and such was expected by both governments. In this instance, America's allies would perhaps be disappointed, but not necessarily irate, to learn that a CIA operation against the common enemy had become open knowledge. However, it would certainly be a different case if an ally's participation, or alleged participation, was part of that exposure. In that case, the repercussions to the United States' bilateral relations with that ally could be severe.

The implementation of a covert action program is most critical when it is conducted against an allied country and intended to influence secretly the policies of that country's government (which might well be a democracy). While this is rarely done, should such a program come to light it inevitably generates anger against the United States within that nation's leadership as well as among the citizenry. The trust that exists between the two democracies might be temporarily breached, to the detriment of the United States and the president's policy objectives. The British dared to run a covert action program against the United States government in 1939–1940, aimed at influencing the American public and isolationist government officials to support it with war materials, and to enter voluntarily the war on the side of the British. Had the program been exposed in 1940 or 1941, potentially negative American public opinion could have forced President Franklin D. Roosevelt to withdraw or withhold the assistance he had already been giving the British (e.g. naval escorts to convoys headed to Britain and the "sale" of 50 obsolete destroyers to the Royal Navy), or, worse, give priority to the war in the Pacific. Either way, it is probable that America's strategy for prosecuting the war would have been altered and history changed for all time.

Finally, whether deserved or not, a covert action that prematurely becomes public knowledge might, at least temporarily, sour relations between the CIA, on the one hand, and sister agencies in the US national security community on the other hand. Such a dispute might also become personalized between the Director of the CIA and a particular cabinet secretary, with harmful consequences. Director of Central Intelligence (as the post was known until the reforms of 2005) William J. Casey's actions and decisions in the Central American programs of the 1980s and in the Iran-Contra scandal so angered Secretary of State George P. Schultz that by the time Casey died, the two were barely speaking, to the detriment of cordial and cooperative relations in the lower ranks.

But a covert action program that somehow becomes public knowledge (whether through failure or other causes) doesn't necessarily have to be harmful to the president or to the CIA. A reader scanning media headlines from the mid-1990s would have found prominent play given, at least initially, to a covert action program conducted against the Iraqi regime, with the objective of eventually leading to an overthrow of Saddam Hussein's regime. The program collapsed amid a plethora of newspaper and television stories, with serious repercussions for many of the participating Iraqis. Contrary to past program failures that had been seized on by Congress for use as a political bludgeon on the CIA or the president, this program did not meet that fate.

One very significant reason that the Iraqi program did not suffer the same general condemnation as, for example, the overthrow of Iranian government in 1953 or the Central American programs of the 1980s, is that the risks attendant in the Iraqi effort were neither hid nor discounted. The president and his advisors, in considering the program's potential, were made thoroughly and continually aware of the program's elevated perils, which were substantial and unable to be ameliorated operationally. The CIA, as well, insured that the congressional intelligence committees were fully and frequently briefed on the program.

After extensive debate, the president and his national security team believed that the opportunity, however limited, for program success outweighed the risks and costs, and the president signed a Finding authorizing it. When the bottom dropped out, few in Washington could or did say that they were either surprised or that the end result was because of operational ineptitude. (The corollary lesson here is that the better Congress is informed, the more apt it will be to understand and accept problems that develop in covert action programs.) Today's war against international terrorism may also be viewed as a case in which at least some of the individual subordinate operations of what is said to be a massive covert program (in addition, of course, to the military occupation of Iraq and Afghanistan) might be high risk. But, when reviewing the very real dangers that Al-Qaeda and its brethren pose to American citizens and interests worldwide, these endeavors (should or when they become public) are very likely to be supported by a majority of American citizens.

Whether a covert action program ultimately succeeds, fails, or lands somewhere, in between, is often rooted in the degree to which a president and his advisor understand the limits and capabilities of what a covert action program might be able to attain. These sorts of operations have the ability to be highly effective in supporting an established United States foreign policy, *if* it is applied against the right target and with the appropriate methodologies. But no matter how effective a program's potential might be assessed, it is absolutely imperative that it must be within the confines of the United States Constitution, federal statutes passed by Congress, executive orders issued by the president, and the CIA's internal regulations. Yoked to these legal requirements is the need for Congress to be fully informed of each operation, including an honest evaluation of the risks and costs.

There are, additionally, what might be called "political" or "managerial" imperatives that the professional intelligence officer and the knowledgeable policy advisor should consider in deciding whether or how to employ covert action. The first has already been noted: covert action is not a substitute for an established national policy. When a president and his advisors either cannot agree on an overall policy, or simply have no idea how to solve a foreign policy issue, tasking the CIA to produce a "Chinese restaurant menu" of possible operational capabilities from which they will then pick and choose, almost randomly, those that appear the most promising, the president is simultaneously asking to waste money, assume unnecessary risks, accomplish little, and all at significant risk.

And needless to say, covert action is likewise unsuitable for use as a "last resort" option, turned to simply because there seem to be no viable overt policy. Still more important, covert action is not a solution to rescue other policy programs that are failing or have so done, particularly if it's a policy that the White House should never have attempted in the first place. *some bias here*

Second, given that the whole concept of covert action is to affect people's minds (either change them or reinforce currently held positions), it should not be surprising that the great majority of covert action programs will require time to evince results. Thus, covert action is not *impt!* and should not be employed for the resolution of crises, in which time is of the essence. There are also specific operational reasons why a covert action program cannot be hastily thrown together with the expectation of producing swift results: requisite detailed planning, developing *LBJ + Nixon chile* the necessary support infrastructure, recruiting and vetting the foreign nationals who will execute the program operations, and even working out budget priorities, may take months or years. This is especially so when there is not a "stable" of agents already recruited for other purposes who could be redirected to the new program.

Third, as implied above, not only for success but also for productive harmony with cooperating agencies, covert action programs must be fully coordinated with the other participating members of national security community, and seamlessly integrated into the larger policy schematic. *CIA + policy in CA ... inherently against CIA*

It should go without saying that the objectives for which a covert action program is implemented must be clearly stated and attendant risks understood. But, surprisingly, this is not always the case, especially with policymakers who lack a comprehension of covert action's limits and hazards.

Finally, but certainly not least in importance, it is highly desirable that the objectives sought by the president in approving any covert action program be compatible with American values and with openly stated policies. Should the program be compromised, the public (and Congress) will be much more understanding – and much more prone to forgive – if, upon examination of the program details and goals, Americans are able to say, "We're sorry (or angered, or disappointed) that the program failed, but we can see that the goals were worthy and that the president was trying to do the right thing." In 1986 President Reagan was in serious difficulty *vis-à-vis* the public's reaction after the Iran-Contra disgrace broke in the media, *also impt!* particularly in light of the revelation that the activities involved were in complete contradiction to the long-established United States policy of not negotiating with terrorists or trading goods for hostages.

But when the president held a press conference at which he acknowledged that "mistakes were made," and explained the motivations and thought processes that underlay his decisions, the public forgave him. (It also helped that he fired those on the White House staff who were responsible and constituted a special team of respected figures to investigate the causes and recommend remedial actions.) Similarly, President John F. Kennedy enjoyed augmented popularity polls after publicly assuming responsibility for the Bay of Pigs fiasco and providing an overview of the reasons behind it.

In summation, then, covert action is but one tool of presidential statecraft, albeit a very sensitive tool requiring great care in its implementation and equally meticulous heed for the legalities surrounding these operations. George Washington employed covert action while commander-in-chief during the Revolution, Thomas Jefferson used covert action, in the nature of bribery through a third party, to gain access to Indian tribal lands for government purposes and to aid in the prosecution of the war against the Barbary pirates. James Madison used measures that we would today label covert action to acquire West Florida from the Spanish. Chester A. Arthur, Teddy Roosevelt, and Dwight Eisenhower used covert action to overthrow hostile or potentially hostile regimes. And in 2001, President George W. Bush made covert action a staple of his war on terrorism and the war against Iraqi insurgents. President always have, and always will, turn to covert action when it suits their policy purposes. But whether they do it successfully is another matter entirely.

22

The future of covert action

John Prados

There are observers who think the post-9/11 era offers the possibility for a new golden age of covert operations. With the Bush administration having unleashed an open-ended war on terrorism and the clear need to meet Al Qaeda and affiliated groups on their own level, the potential for covert action seems clear, its utility obvious. The steady buildup of military special operations forces and reinvigoration of the CIA's Special Activities Division have provided fresh capability in this field. There are many possible locales for action. Certainly the Department of Defense under Secretary Donald H. Rumsfeld has been pressing at the bit for the role, while the CIA declared war on terror as long ago as 1998 when George J. Tenet still headed the agency. So it seems foreordained that we can expect a vigorous covert campaign and the further expansion of the envelope.

But it would be premature to conclude that these will be halcyon days for secret warriors. There are reasons to suspect not only that covert operations will be less effective than advertised, but that the technique may come under the kinds of attack that beset the Central Intelligence Agency during its darkest season of inquiry of the 1970s. This is so due to the match between United States capabilities and goals given existing international relations, structural weaknesses, and persistent management problems. Any one of these factors taken by itself might potentially derail the United States covert action agenda. In combination the totality of difficulties poses a substantial obstacle to the Director of National Intelligence (DNI) in leading the effort and the US intelligence community in executing it. The following analysis seeks to identify some of these difficulties and reflect upon their tractability.

The world and the secret warriors

The time has come for a serious assessment of the degree of permissiveness for covert action in the international environment. This is a very different question from the willingness of US leaders to approve and make use of the method. During the years of the Cold War – and certainly in World War II – when covert action techniques were perfected and first widely employed, operational necessity predominated. In addition, the Manichean struggle against totalitarianism and then between the West and communism provided relatively easy criteria for choice. One could enlist to fight a well-defined enemy, and local groups could allow themselves to be recruited for solid patriotic ends. Private agendas always lurked below the surface but the target remained state power. Moreover, the world held a generally favorable position toward the United States, and American democracy was an admired political form to be emulated.

This can be categorized as a permissive environment. Even under those relatively favorable conditions the United States encountered considerable international criticism when covert action went bad. The disaster at the Bay of Pigs and the political black eye that resulted from the Nicaraguan operation are but two examples among many.[1] But America had political capital to squander, as it were, making covert action embarrassments survivable even if painful.

The climate of international relations is different in the post-Cold War, post-Iraq invasion world. Now there is much less tolerance for American activity, covert or otherwise. In Chitral, Pakistan, for example, Americans said to be on the hunt for terrorist ringleader Osama bin Laden rented a house in the fall of 2005 but made no attempt to occupy it until May 2006. The mere appearance of the first American at the house triggered a street protest led by a local politician.[2] Pakistan is an American ally. Similarly, CIA relations with Italy have been soured by the fallout over an agency kidnapping of a Muslim cleric on the streets of Milan, several Western European countries have shown concern regarding overflights by CIA aircraft engaged in rendition operations, and Canada and Germany are embroiled over specific rendition cases involving their citizens who were sequestered by American authorities directly or reportedly at the hands of the CIA. These are other allies, indeed America's closest, whose cooperation in the war against terror has been the most fruitful. Indeed, public opinion in the United States is itself already shaky on the subject of erosions of civil liberties in the terror war, and if leaders in the US cannot marshal their own people in support of covert action, there is little reason to suspect that foreign politicians can do any better.

It is not sufficient to argue that friendly relations with other intelligence services make public opinion in those countries irrelevant, or that the irritating cases are passing issues. Intelligence services are creatures of their societies and political systems, and pressures on those systems will at some point affect links between them and the CIA or DNI. In Germany a parliamentary investigation of the *Bundesnachrichtendienst* (BND) is already underway that will in part focus on the degree of BND collaboration with the CIA in the rendition case and other matters. In Italy, similarly, the Italian military intelligence service SISMI is vulnerable to a parallel inquiry by a new parliamentary government due to claims that it cooperated in the Milan incident. There is also little hope in the idea that the cases will disappear. No doubt they will – but today's crop of irritants will be succeeded by fresh controversies because it is in the nature of the present secret war on terror. This proceeds by means of large numbers of operations at the margins of legality directed at individuals or small groups of persons throughout the world.

It is also the case that opinion is generally more brittle today than in the past. Consider the recent riots in more than a dozen countries after a Danish newspaper published cartoons held to ridicule the Prophet Mohammed. Or – in Pakistan again – the rioting that took place in early 2006 following a strike on a remote village by missiles from Predator drones seeking to kill Al Qaeda commanders. It is precisely in Pakistan and countries like it that secret warriors most need to operate, but their work balances on a knife edge of public volatility. *That* is what it means to have an environment not permissive toward covert action.

This point is sharper because – again in contrast to the Cold War era – a wide array of the publics in many lands now hold a negative view of the United States. In some places the percentages who admire America are tiny compared to those who consider the United States the greatest threat to world peace. And this is not just true for Middle Eastern or Muslim states. Australians, long our allies, do not put America even within their top *ten* favorite foreign countries.[3] At some level the poor image of the United States must contribute to the volatility of the public in the lands where secret warriors ply their trade.

To the judgment that the international environment is less permissive for covert action must be added the realization that US capabilities are also less well-adapted to the mission than *limitatio* they were during earlier periods. The CIA is far from the supple "Cold War agency" it was in those days. Langley's assets today are concentrated in a Special Activities Division within the Directorate of Operations (DO). Capabilities were reduced during the 1990s in the immediate aftermath of the disintegration of the Soviet Union, when the DO as a whole was significantly cut back. Undoubtedly, the clandestine service chose to limit losses to its espionage assets by cutting deeper among the secret warriors. Late in the decade DCI George J. Tenet began to resuscitate the Special Activities Division (SAD), but at today's prices and resource levels, the CIA is no longer a full-spectrum covert operations agency. *lim.*

In addition the rise of new entities, especially the DCI Counterterrorism Center (CTC), drew off additional experienced officers. Available accounts show that significant covert actions of the 1990s, including those in Iraq against Saddam Hussein and in Afghanistan against Al Qaeda, were undertaken by CTC, with SAD assistance, not by a DO area division or other entity.[4]

There has also been a major shift in CIA covert action tactics. Where during the Cold War the agency frequently created paramilitary armies and supported them with maritime and air assets to attain specified goals, the more recent pattern has been for agency officers to use CIA cash to buy the services of existing armed tribal groups or other factions. This was the case, for example, in the US invasions of both Afghanistan in 2001 and Iraq in 2003. Indeed in the Iraqi case when the agency attempted to create a unit along more traditional lines it called the "Scorpions," assorted difficulties in implementation yielded a smaller-then-planned force that was not available for action until the invasion was over.[5] The CIA role as comprador is clearly dependent upon the environment of permissibility for covert operations.

An additional dimension of CIA field experience is the increased centrality of "support to military operations" (SMO), which have absorbed an increasing proportion of such CIA capabilities as do exist, at least since the Gulf War of 1991. In Somalia, in Bosnia, in Afghanistan, and now in Iraq, the SMO function has tended to monopolize covert capabilities. Agency team leader Gary Berntsen's experience in Afghanistan is representative of this kind of activity.[6] The CIA in Afghanistan worked in conjunction with military special operations forces, sometimes in the leading role, sometimes subordinate. There is as yet no coherent account of CIA covert operations in the Iraq occupation, but the work of journalist James Risen suggests a similar pattern.[7] At his May 2006 confirmation hearing for director of the CIA, General Michael V. Hayden remarked that CIA officers now find themselves increasingly preoccupied by SMO activities, especially for tactical intelligence in Iraq, and offered this observation in support of military forces expansion of their own espionage activities, which could relieve some of the burden on the CIA.[8]

In the war against terrorism more generally there is a requirement for small-scale, highly targeted operations aimed at individuals and small groups. These depend on CIA alliances with friendly security services, further extending a pattern of growing dependence on intelligence liaison relationships that has characterized agency operations since at least the 1980s. Again the environment for covert action can be expected to assume key importance.

On the military side there exists a different set of constraints that yield similar results. Under the United States Special Operations Command (USSOC), the commander-in-chief for these forces, and the Joint Special Operations Command (JSOC), the headquarters that leads in counterterror operations, special forces have exercised a growing role in covert operations.

Directives from Bush administration secretary of defense Donald H. Rumsfeld have sought to widen that role even further. For example, the fiscal 2005 Intelligence Appropriation Act contained authorization for special forces to spend money to hire local groups for covert operations in the same fashion as the CIA, taking away another of Langley's few areas of exclusivity. These roles and missions remain in contention between Rumsfeld and John Negroponte, the Director of National Intelligence, who exercises theoretical control over all US intelligence operations, but at this writing Rumsfeld seems to have the upper hand.

In contrast to the CIA the military special forces do offer a full spectrum of capability. They are also available in unprecedented numbers: at 26,000 today, Army Special Forces are more than twice as numerous as at their Vietnam war peak, and form only one element of an all-service force that currently totals 44,000 men and women.[9] The Defense Department's most recent posture review nevertheless mandates a further increase of 15 percent in these forces along with new technology and additional spending. The Rumsfeld operational scheme would allow these forces to work covertly in espionage missions as well as to undertake a wider array of counterterror activities.

Though the special forces have substantial capability they have never carried out a full-scale secret war. Laos and Afghanistan (both wars there) were CIA enterprises in which detached military officers served (the first case), or Special Forces detachments worked in tandem with the agency (in the second Afghan war) with shared operational control. In Bosnia and the occupation of Iraq the special forces have worked as elite strike teams, and in Afghanistan's occupation in that role as well as in Vietnam-style pacification missions.[10] There are training missions underway as well in Colombia, Africa, and the Philippines. The court is out on how USSOC might perform in a full scale paramilitary operation.

Beyond the strike team role, special operations forces and CIA covert operators have exhibited a marked predilection for stand-off operations. These have featured use of the Predator unmanned aerial vehicle (UAV) armed with precision guided missiles. First introduced as a surveillance system over Bosnia in the 1990s, a version of this UAV armed with the Hellfire missile was developed by the CIA and the Air Force in 2000–01.[11] The first armed Predator mission took place on October 7, 2001. It has since been used in its combat role, as far as is known at this writing, in Afghanistan, Iraq, Pakistan, and Yemen. At present the Air Force is creating a dedicated UAV special operations squadron. Stand-off operations obviously reduce the vulnerability of US personnel but they have important rigidities, not being in actual physical proximity to targets, not being recallable, not being deniable (and thus not truly covert) since only the United States possesses this capability, and eroding the distinction between covert and conventional military operations. In at least one case so far a Predator strike has triggered large anti-US demonstrations in the target country.

In summary, the international environment is presently increasingly hostile to continued covert operations. For different reasons the CIA and military special operations forces have covert capabilities that are limited and in some respects mismatched to operational needs, while stand-off strike systems, presently being touted as a panacea, have their own rigidities. These are cautionary elements when considering the future of covert operations.

Classic conundrums of covert action

The covert operations most often cited as successes are the political action in Italy (1948), the CIA coups in Iran (1953) and Guatemala (1954), and the paramilitary action in Afghanistan (1979–1989). In terms of number, these amount to only a tiny fraction of the inventory of covert operations carried out since World War II. Further analysis shows that each of these operations was not exactly as advertised. Political action in Italy trapped the United States into open-ended intervention in Italian politics which Washington had a difficult time halting and which endured at least into the late 1960s, with a further burst in 1972. Charges of American meddling had a cost to US foreign policy globally which equaled if they did not surpass those benefits of the Italian operation itself. The coups the CIA carried out in Iran and Guatemala, far from being unalloyed successes, both skirted failure before reaching a tipping point, and both resulted in only short-term benefits. The Iranian operation contributed to the rise of an Islamic fundamentalism that has been a headache for every US president since Jimmy Carter, and that brought Ronald Reagan close to impeachment. Guatemala extinguished a democracy and empowered oligarchic and military rulers who eventually made war on their own people. The Afghan operation introduced into hostile hands US military technology that was highly threatening to American security interests and played a direct role in mobilizing the cadres of terrorism who threaten the United States today. Had the Afghan action not occurred there is a fair argument that the rise of fundamentalism would have been slowed, at least sufficiently to come to grips with the problem before the travesty of the 9/11 attack. The resulting subterranean terror war is now being fought out in ways with which the US is far less well-equipped to deal, a strategic equivalent of electing to fight on ground of the enemy's choosing.[12]

Beyond the "successes" are a wide array of failures. These are not worth substantive treatment here, except to say that the record shows successes to be few, failures far more numerous, and wartime-type actions to have been the most successful. The entire body of experience contributes to the taxonomy of problems mentioned below. First, covert operations, *especially* when successful, usually lead to long-term United States economic and military assistance to governments that, absent such aid, would not endure. But decisions on covert operations are uniformly based upon short-term cost/benefit analysis rather than expenditures over the long haul. The real costs of these activities often dwarf those of the covert operations themselves. Even on the short-term costs, in addition, real expenses are typically underestimated. This is true for *every* covert operation for which we have actual cost data, including Iran, Guatemala, the Bay of Pigs, Operation Mongoose, Laos, Vietnam, Nicaragua, Afghanistan, and Iraq. This is an endemic problem.

Second is the question of political allies. The United States has usually sought "third force" movements. In Cold War days those were non-communist, or preferably anti-communist ones. Today they would be Muslim democratic forces. In European countries these tended to be politically moderate or center-left, causing a certain discomfort for more conservative American secret warriors. In Third World lands, however, such movements have been associated with established oligarchies or tribes, usually disadvantaged minorities. Using such groups often does little to satisfy societal aspirations and frequently leads only to further upheavals, as in the Guatemalan case. Where organized political movements exist the choice is frequently limited. Too often Washington lands on the wrong side of these choices. Where there is no third force the standard practice is to resort to political action to create one. Such artificial groupings have limited popular appeal and are locally perceived as agents of US power, as was the case in Laos, Nicaragua, and the Congo. While Washington assumes that using third force tactics will generate wide support, such artificial movements sow few grass roots – *because* they know the US cannot back away short of abandoning its covert action goals.

One special problem of acting through local proxies – today the preferred form of CIA covert action – is exposure to political liability as a remit of acts by the local allies. Drug-dealing, "disappearances," and dastardly deeds have to be swallowed in service of the covert action goals, and the United States is tarred as a result. In debates over CIA regulations in the 1990s much was made of the necessity to be able to recruit the bad guys because they were the ones who had the assented information, or the capability to act on US instructions. But there is no avoiding private agendas. In an international environment that is not permissive for covert operations this problem is even sharper because that will restrict the available local allies to even more marginal groups.

In Tibet, Afghanistan, and the Indochinese war a proportion of CIA assistance was soaked up by its own allies while still in the pipeline. Such problems not only reduce effectiveness, they are unavoidable given the requirement for local proxies, often in countries whose own intelligence services are allied with the United States. The phenomenon has become characteristic of secret wars, even more so today when Langley's role has become that of banker, traveling the world handing out cash. A concomitant difficulty is the worry that local proxies – or allied services – will stay "bought." The most obvious recent example is the careenings of the Iraqi National Congress organization run since the 1990s by Ahmad Chalabi, which seems to have been on several sides of events in Iraq.

A hidden cost is the long-term US liability to the people who enlist in its covert legions. Today's partisan fighter can become tomorrow's litigant for veteran's benefits or other recognition. Bay of Pigs fighters and South Vietnamese commandos in the pay of the CIA or US Special Forces have conducted such suits. Laotian tribesmen have sued for citizenship. Not only is there "flap potential" in such suits, there is real money at stake, win or lose.

Political, as opposed to paramilitary, action represents a wild card. Operators purchase victory for local leaders who may not be the people Washington thinks they are – Chalabi again comes to mind. Activities begun for stipulated purposes can stimulate quite unanticipated events. The Hungarian Uprising of 1956 is a clear example from the old days. Today we have the menu of covert political actions undoubtedly going on to promote Muslim democracy and staunch the rise of Jihad. Washington has already been disturbed when elections in Palestine brought to power the most extreme group, Hamas. What if the push for Muslim democracy was completely successful, but resulted in a Middle East wholly dominated by fundamentalist governments?

Failed political action contains an inherent temptation to escalate, as tragically shown in Chile during the Nixon years. In many crisis situations, presidents can choose to intervene or resist doing so. But in a failed political action the threshold of intervention has already been passed, at a clandestine and relatively cheap level that obscures the gravity of the decisions made. With the United States already committed, going to the next rung of the ladder can seem preferable to accepting the humiliation of defeat. Political action should be viewed not as the simple act of seeking influence often portrayed, but as conveying escalatory danger. It should be placed in an overall perspective that frames decisions in terms of suitability at successive levels of involvement, not merely at the entry point.

These kinds of actions exist within a shifting local and global context, yet they are conceived for a specific purpose at a given moment in time. Evolving difficulties demand corresponding countermeasures, making the political action a tar baby from which it is hard to escape. In addition, positive control is almost always vitiated since CIA (or US) tactics must respond to the changing situation, not work from a simple menu of options. Thus Italy from 1949 to 1968 – or Chile from 1962 to 1973. Given a non-permissive international environment, problems of this sort can be expected to become more numerous.

Political action is also irretrievable. Presidents who approve a commando mission or a paramilitary operation can conceivably recall the operators up to the point of contact with no one the wiser. In political action the first bag of cash handed to a foreign national, the first article planted in a newspaper – the first act, in other words – contains the seeds of compromise. Even if the action is called off the evidence of US intervention remains, and is immersed in a foreign society not subject to American control. Since successful political action requires sustained activity with a broad range of foreign institutions, the evidence multiplies and deepens in a way that increases the likelihood of eventual revelation. In addition the pattern of widely dispersed evidence makes it highly likely that surfacing one piece, with attendant controversy, will lead to wider exposure.

Even if a covert action – political or paramilitary – is executed completely successfully, with no leaks to the world at large, it is not a secret to victims. Even successful actions can become embarrassments in retrospect owing to changing international relations, as with the relative success of CIA paramilitary endeavors in Tibet in the 1950s and 1960s in the context of the Nixon opening to the People's Republic of China. The covert actions suddenly become obstacles to better relations or to peoples' friendship – and thus the international environment.

Finally, the United States itself has not emerged unscathed. The term "blowback" has been coined to refer to the potential for actions to recoil upon the instigator. Beyond possible international and diplomatic consequences, covert actions have had a significant impact on American politics. The controversy over the Bay of Pigs forced John Kennedy into official acknowledgement and investigation, as that over CIA funding of the National Student Association did for Lyndon Johnson. Revelations of meddling in Chile significantly increased Richard Nixon's political difficulties during the Watergate affair. The linkage of the Iran coup with the Hostage Crisis contributed to Jimmy Carter's defeat in the election of 1980. The Iran–Contra Affair effectively drained Ronald Reagan's political capital. These were real costs, not to be pretended away. Blowback in turn has forced secret warriors to terminate operations to the peril of their assets in the field. In sum there are a variety of structural and inherent problems with the conduct of covert operations.

Problems of management and control

The system for proposing, coordinating, and approval of covert action remains largely identical to the Clinton era. The ultimate authority is still the Deputies Committee of the National Security Council. But the ongoing transformation of the US intelligence community is creating pressures that may be expected to generate cross-cutting interests and fresh demands for change. One source of the new dynamic is the existence of the Office of the Director of National Intelligence (ODNI) and the director himself. The other is the continuing growth of the Pentagon's role in intelligence activity in general and covert action in particular.

Under existing protocols the Director of the Central Intelligence Agency (DCIA), long known as the Director of Central Intelligence, had the primary responsibility for proposing and developing covert actions. Suggestions could come from sources throughout government, including the Pentagon, but also the State Department, the NSC staff, or working levels at the CIA. The Directorate of Operations would flesh out suggestions and give project proposals a first scrubbing. These would then be forwarded to the director, whose own staff subjected them to more intensive review. Only projects which pass the director's muster reach the Deputies Committee, which may then return them for revision, reject them, or approve them and order implementation. With occasional tweaks and cosmetic changes this set of management arrangements has been in place since at least the time of the Carter administration.

But today the DCIA occupies an anomalous position within the reformed US intelligence community. The Director of Central Intelligence, his predecessor, held formal control over the entire community where the DCIA is responsible only for the Central Intelligence Agency. The official with global authority is now the Director of National Intelligence (DNI), currently Ambassador John Negroponte. As a result of changes made by the 2004 reforms in the US, the DNI now exercises control over community-wide activity on key intelligence questions through a series of single-issue managers who are supposed to direct all aspects of work on those matters.

This system does not apply to covert action, though it could. The DCIA no longer occupies the central position of the DNI. One can anticipate a point when the Director of National Intelligence asks himself why covert action decisions are being made below his level, particularly since the CIA director at Langley cannot any longer automatically summon the services of other units – especially the Pentagon – in pursuit of the covert action goal. It is also not practical over the long run to make the CIA director the issue manager for covert action because other officials (like the secretary of defense) may object to not being given equivalent authorities. Such a solution might work for a certain combination of individuals with the right body chemistry, but not forever, and particularly not as the Pentagon's inventory of covert action resources eclipses that of the CIA. The most recent Pentagon policy review appears to have recommended not attempting to supplant the CIA in the covert action milieu, but does not track with the department's continued force-building measures.[13]

Meanwhile there are indications elsewhere that the DNI is already asserting his primacy over the CIA director. Agency station chiefs around the world have been told to install dual-channel reporting, going to Langley on strictly CIA matters and to the ODNI for community ones. This awkward arrangement cannot endure. Consider a hypothetical covert action: is the addition of an asset judged necessary to tip the balance a CIA matter or one for the DNI? Failure would certainly affect the entire US intelligence community. What if the asset were "owned" by Langley? Conversely, on the CIA channel, what if the asset belongs to the Department of Defense, how is it to be mobilized except through the DNI?

The specific subject of the Department of Defense requires separate comment. During 2005 the DCIA and secretary of defense negotiated a working agreement covering their relationship in our reformed intelligence world. This memorandum of understanding is classified but provides for a committee dominated by the CIA to approve Pentagon espionage or other covert activities, with the agency director as the final court of appeal, as a means of "deconflicting" military and CIA activities. According to General Hayden at his nomination hearing, the agreement has so far worked well. On the other hand, so far there has not been a whole lot to regulate. Pentagon clandestine activities to this point have been closely tied to ongoing military operations. There have not been autonomous Department of Defense covert actions that we know of, and if General Hayden's view is any guide, the CIA appreciates the Pentagon moving into the field of tactical military espionage and freeing up its own resources.

There are also legal complications. As came up at least twice during the Hayden confirmation hearing, Department of Defense activities are governed by Title 10 of the US. Code and CIA ones by Title 50. The Pentagon has legal requirements to follow US and international law, the CIA does not. Covert actions frequently involve violations of both international law – Nicaragua in the 1980s is a good example – and of domestic laws in the nations where they are carried out. Shifting the locus of covert action capability into the Pentagon not only creates a necessity for new statutory changes but it may threaten the legal status of US conventional military forces. In an international environment not permissive for covert action this problem acquires even greater importance.[14]

A different but also important set of points needs to be made regarding congressional oversight of covert action activities. First, the CIA and the US military report to different sets of congressional committees. This not only complicates effective oversight but opens up possibilities for disguising activities by juggling roles and missions between the civilian agency and the military forces. Further, the changing distribution of covert action resources between the CIA and the military will complicate this problem, as well as blur reporting requirements attached to covert action, which are located within statutes that apply to the intelligence agencies. Second, given the propensity of the current administration to avoid such requirements by invoking ultra-high levels of secrecy and restricting knowledge to a very small circle of legislators, the ability of Congress to play a role as a check and balance against overambitious operational schemes will be greatly reduced.

No one – not Michael Hayden, not John Negroponte or Donald H. Rumsfeld, not Stephen Cambone or Stephen Hadley; certainly not George W. Bush or his successor – has ever lived in an era of full-spectrum Pentagon covert action capability where the CIA is the relatively disadvantaged agency. When the United States Special Operations Command attains the size of a full army corps, and Langley's Special Activities Division is a fraction of that, it may be the CIA furnishing technical services to the military's covert operators and not the other way around. Secretary Rumsfeld expects to reach that level of force within the current defense budget plan. Under those conditions a working agreement that ensures CIA primacy in covert action may not be acceptable to the military. This viewpoint is already in evidence – officers arguing on the basis of experience in the 2001–2002 Afghan opening campaign and sequel maintain that CIA officers fighting alongside the military should be under Pentagon control.[15]

Apart from anything else the US intelligence reforms have created a new set of lacunae for covert operations, issues that will have to be worked through even while the war on terror is going on. It is probably right to say there is never a "good time" for reform, but George W. Bush seems to have chosen an especially awkward moment.

This brings the discussion full circle. Driven by the war on terror there will be new covert actions, managed by a system with its kinks yet to be fully worked out. Langley's secret warriors, hampered by a non-permissive international environment, will have trouble recruiting third force groups, and they will need help from military operators who may be doing this stuff for the first time. Alternatively, the military will engage in a covert action that goes beyond its traditional commando raids, say a "Bay of Goats," as the pundits styled one scheme to oust Saddam Hussein, triggering an uprising against him by means of landing a force of dissidents in Iraq. Again, such a large-scale covert action will be a first-time experience for the US military. Due to a variety of structural weaknesses in the nature of covert action the odds will be against success, odds further diminished by management problems and operational inadequacies. The hand of the United States will almost inevitably be revealed. Further negative impact on the international environment is predictable.

These methods have been oversold. Covert action is also under-engineered in the sense that problems inherent in the use of the technique have never been solved. The result is a set of policymakers seduced by visions of golden bullet solutions who are likely to face significant disasters instead. The consequences of those are indeterminate but problematical. The future for American covert action is cloudy, not bright.

Notes

1 For a detailed history of CIA covert operations see John Prados, *Safe for Democracy: The Secret Wars of the CIA*. Chicago, IL: Ivan R. Dee, 2006.

2 Carlotta Gall, "Remote Pakistan Town Believes Rumors of Bin Laden's Arrival Are Greatly Exaggerated," *New York Times*, May 16, 2006, p. A6.

3 Raymond Bonner, "US Image Sags in Australian Poll," *New York Times*, March 29, 2005, p. A8.

4 See Robert Baer, *See No Evil: The True Story of a Ground Soldier in the CIA's War on Terrorism*. New York: Crown Publishers, 2002; and also National Commission on Terrorist Attacks Upon the United States, *The 9/11 Commission Report*. New York: W. W. Norton, no date [2004].

5 On Afghanistan see Gary Schoen, *First In: An Insider's Account of How the CIA Spearheaded the War on Terror in Afghanistan*. New York: Ballantine Books, 2005; and Gary Berntsen's *Jawbreaker: The Attack on Bin Laden and Al Qaeda: A Personal Account by the CIA's Key Field Commander*. New York: Crown Publishers, 2005. For Iraq see Bob Woodward, *Plan of Attack*. New York: Simon & Schuster, 2004.

6 Gary Berntsen, *Jawbreaker*, op. cit.

7 James Risen, *State of War: The Secret History of the CIA and the Bush Administration*. New York: Free Press, 2006.

8 Senate Select Committee on Intelligence, *Hearing: Nomination of General Michael V. Hayden as Director of the Central Intelligence Agency*, May 18, 2006. Transcript.

9 Andrew Feickert, "US Special Operations Forces (SOF): Background and Issues for Congress," Congressional Research Service Report RS21048, April 17, 2006.

10 For a good analysis of Special Operations Forces in these conflicts see Armando J. Ramirez, *From Bosnia to Baghdad: The Evolution of US Army Special Forces From 1995–2004*. Thesis, Naval Postgraduate School, Monterey, California, September 2004.

11 George J. Tenet, "Written Statement for the Record of the Director of Central Intelligence Before the National Commission on Terrorist Attacks Upon the United States," March 24, 2004, pp. 11–12.

12 This section draws from my work in *Safe for Democracy*, which exhaustively re-examines the whole range of US covert operations, including the four mentioned here. The analysis follows the book's penultimate chapter.

13 Ann Scott Tyson, "Study Urges CIA Not to Cede Paramilitary Functions to Pentagon," *Washington Post*, February 5, 2005, p. A8.

14 Colonel Kathryn Stone, " 'All Necessary Means': Employing CIA Operatives in a Warfighting Role Alongside Special Operations Forces," US. Army War College Strategy Research Paper, April 7, 2003, pp. 8–10, 14–18.

15 Colonel Kathryn Stone, " 'All Necessary Means,' " pp. 18–21.

Part 6

Intelligence accountability

23

Intelligence oversight in the UK

The case of Iraq

Mark Phythian

Oversight of intelligence in the UK has developed considerably since the late 1980s. Indeed, the government did not even admit to the peacetime existence of its principal internal security and external intelligence organisations – the Security Service (MI5) and the Secret Intelligence Service (MI6) – until 1989 and 1992 respectively, even though both could trace their origins back to 1909. While select committees of the House of Commons secured only very limited co-operation from the executive branch in attempting to oversee the intelligence and security agencies, in 1994 the government established the Intelligence and Security Committee (ISC), a committee of parliamentarians but not of Parliament, specifically to undertake this task.

However, the ISC's performance has raised a number of questions about the nature and effectiveness of intelligence oversight in the UK, particularly in respect of its 2003 inquiry into pre-war intelligence on Iraqi Weapons of Mass Destruction (WMD). Indeed, investigations relating to Iraq in the period since 1992 provide a useful prism through which to assess the state of intelligence oversight in the UK, and the relative effectiveness of the various bodies that have attempted to undertake it – in this case a range of select committees, ISC, judicial and other inquiries beginning with the Trade and Industry Select Committee's (TISC) 1992 investigation of the supergun affair and concluding with the 2003–04 post-mortems conducted by the Foreign Affairs Committee (FAC), ISC, and Hutton and Butler Inquiries into the Blair government's case for war in Iraq and role of intelligence in this.

Oversight of the supergun affair

The first time that controversy over intelligence relating to Iraq formed a back-drop to an official inquiry was during the TISC's 1991–1992 investigation into the supergun affair. This was an inquiry into government policy on exports to Iraq in the context of the Iran–Iraq war, post-war tension with Iraq, the seemingly fortuitous dockside seizure of the last batch of supergun parts in April 1990, and the Iraqi invasion of Kuwait just over three months later. While the investigation secured a high degree of co-operation from businessmen and engineers involved in the often quite subterranean defence-related trade with Iraq, it failed to secure the co-operation of three key players. First of these was a backbench Conservative MP, Sir

Hal Miller, who had contacted the Ministry of Defence and what he termed "another agency" after being alerted by the managing director of a company in his constituency to the fact that it was fulfilling an unusual export order for Iraq – in fact, a prototype supergun subsequently assembled and tested in Iraq. He repeatedly declined to appear before the Committee and give evidence on this. Secondly, witnesses from Customs and Excise and the Department of Trade and Industry (DTI) consistently refused to provide information that might relate to the intelligence services. For example, when asked by a Committee member whether the DTI had known about the supergun contract and been requested by the intelligence services to allow it to proceed until the last minute "for the sake of surveillance", a DTI official replied that: "It is not the place of a government department to discuss matters of the intelligence service in public."[1] While a Customs official confirmed that Customs became aware of the supergun project just a week prior to its seizure as a result of a tip-off from within the "inter-departmental machinery", he declined to locate the source of the tip-off any more precisely, explaining that he was, "constrained in going any further in identifying certain parts of government".[2] As the Committee explained in its report, Customs' limited co-operation had a significant impact on their ability to investigate the issue: "As a consequence of Customs' unwillingness to reveal the circumstances in which they first commenced and then later dropped criminal proceedings, the Committee has no means of deciding whether either decision was justified."[3]

The role of intelligence was writ large in this case, and governmental unwillingness to provide evidence relating to it was a final insurmountable barrier to the TISC's attempts to fully investigate the affair. Those businessmen and engineers who gave evidence presented a picture of close intelligence – defence industry liaison on Iraq and Iran, both during and after the war between them in the 1980s. However, their evidence was not always consistent and raised a series of questions that the TISC could not answer without input from the agencies. It observed that: "The Committee has not had access to intelligence sources and several witnesses have made it clear that such access cannot be permitted. We believe the long range gun affair raises serious and important questions about the accountability of the intelligence services both to Ministers and to Parliament."[4]

Pressure for parliamentary oversight

The experience of the supergun inquiry was to be one of several sources of pressure for government to act to introduce a degree of intelligence accountability. By this time there was also an increasing momentum for greater accountability resulting from a series of scandals and exposés during the 1970s and 1980s. The November 1979 exposure of Sir Anthony Blunt, Surveyor of the Queen's Pictures and pillar of the establishment, as a former Soviet spy, had been quickly followed by the Prime and Bettaney spy cases, which provided fertile ground for Peter Wright's 1987 *Spycatcher* claim that former MI5 Director-General Sir Roger Hollis had also been a Soviet spy. Moreover, Wright alleged that elements in MI5 had conspired to undermine the Labour government of Harold Wilson, seemingly confirming fears on the Labour Left that MI5 saw itself as operating beyond the law and viewed its primary allegiance as being to the Crown rather than the government of the day. By the time of Paul Foot's 1989 book, *Who Framed Colin Wallace?* – an account of the "cowboy" era of military intelligence in Northern Ireland in the early 1970s – it seemed as if there was a reservoir of security and intelligence intrigue and scandal in little danger of running dry.

While such scandals created considerable *public* momentum for greater accountability, the most pressing impetus from the perspective of the British government (although it did not concede this at the time) arose from the impact of European law on the British polity, in particular the European Convention on Human Rights. The government had already fallen foul of this in the 1984 *Malone* v. *UK* case, leading it to enact the Interception of Communications Act the following year. Then, former MI5 officer Cathy Massiter revealed that two officials of the National Council for Civil Liberties, at the time classed as a subversive organisation by MI5, had been placed under MI5 surveillance. The two – both future Labour government ministers – prepared to take their case to Europe and the clear prospect of further adverse rulings led directly to the 1989 Security Service Act.

This put MI5 on a statutory footing and confirmed its function: the protection of national security, in particular "against threats from espionage, terrorism and sabotage, from the activities of agents of foreign powers and from actions intended to overthrow or undermine parliamentary democracy by political, industrial or violent means", together with safeguarding the economic well-being of the UK from foreign threats. It also created a situation which could not be sustained indefinitely, whereby the existence of MI5 was avowed but that of MI6 was not. Hence, in mid-1992 Prime Minister John Major admitted to the existence of MI6 and undertook to put it on a statutory footing. While briefings to journalists suggested that parliamentary scrutiny of the agencies was unlikely to be a feature of this opening, when the Intelligence Services Bill was finally introduced in 1993 it included provision for a form of intelligence oversight by parliamentarians.

It is worth considering why the Major government moved to introduce this degree of oversight at this time. Clearly, the end of the Cold War created a political space that made this possible. It also affected the agencies' own views as to the desirability of a degree of accountability. In part this was a response to the likely budgetary pressures the agencies could expect to face in a post-Cold War environment – their share of the "peace dividend". In this context, there was a sense that agreement to some form of scrutiny was essential to retaining public confidence, limiting the impact of any post-Cold War downsizing and protecting an intelligence budget worth £185 million in 1992. In this context, the more perceptive managers may have appreciated that overseers could also become advocates. There was also the prospect of a future Labour government seeking to introduce the more far-reaching reforms outlined in the party's 1983 election manifesto, which had spoken in terms of the "now widespread concern about our security services" and committed a future Labour government to introducing legislation to provide for oversight by a select committee.

Moreover, in searching for a post-Cold War *raison d'être*, MI5 had assumed the lead role in combating terrorism in Northern Ireland, a role previously occupied by the Metropolitan Police Special Branch, and as such were under some pressure to make themselves accountable for their part in this just as the police had been. Finally, in the post-Cold War context, with both agencies keen to justify their roles, allegations continued to emerge that strengthened the case for oversight – for example, those emanating from the Scott Inquiry into the arms-to-Iraq affair (discussed below) and concerning the alleged role of MI5 during the 1984–85 miners' strike. It should also be noted that MI6 reportedly took a more relaxed view of the prospect of oversight than MI5, on the basis that its operations abroad were less likely to be of concern to MPs than those of MI5 domestically, which carried greater implications for civil liberties. Nevertheless, legislating from a position of relative strength, rather than being driven by some scandal, allowed the government and agencies to control the agenda. A key dimension of this was the idea, to quote Foreign Secretary Douglas Hurd, that "the past is another country".[5]

This was also a time of greater select committee assertiveness – or, at least, restiveness – in respect to intelligence matters. The TISC's supergun report had outlined the need for improved oversight and its chairman had written to the Prime Minister to complain at the failure of the intelligence services to give evidence, thereby limiting the Committee's investigation. The Home Affairs Select Committee (HAC), which considered MI5 to fall under its remit given that its director-general reported to the Home Secretary, was also increasingly vocal in its discontent with existing arrangements. It had been rebuffed in its request that MI5 Director-General Stella Rimington – by this time named, photographed, and heading an organisation that operated on a statutory basis – give evidence before it. Home Secretary Kenneth Clarke told the Committee that Mrs Rimington was not accountable to Parliament. When it was pointed out that this was unreasonable given Mrs Rimington's willingness to take lunch with national newspaper editors, Clarke agreed that the Committee could also take lunch with her. In 1993 the HAC came out firmly in favour of parliamentary scrutiny, which it offered to perform, arguing that this would "meet an important public interest and help to protect against any possible abuse of power". With reference to MI5's assumption of new post-Cold War roles, it argued that "vital areas" should not be removed from parliamentary scrutiny, "simply as a result of administrative decisions that former policing matters should become matters for the security service".[6] While Clarke's argument that parliamentary convention dictated that MPs did not ask questions relating to MI5 had previously been a standard line of defence in deflecting calls for oversight, it was unsustainable in the more open environment of the 1990s.

While the government rejected the HAC's offer to provide oversight, its report, coming in the wake of the supergun affair and during the early stages of the Scott Inquiry, was a further milestone in moving towards some form of parliamentary oversight. The next significant step came in November 1993, when the Intelligence Services Bill was included in the Queen's Speech. As well as placing MI6 and Government Communications Headquarters (GCHQ) on a comparable statutory basis to MI5, this proposed the creation of a committee of six parliamentarians (but not of Parliament) – the ISC. Its members would be appointed by the Prime Minister, would meet in closed session and produce reports for the Prime Minister, who would lay them before Parliament after removing material considered prejudicial to the activities of the agencies. By the time the Act was passed in 1994, the only change to the draft Bill had been to extend the Committee's membership from six to nine.

The Scott Inquiry and BMARC investigation

The Scott Inquiry had been established towards the end of this period, and its proceedings added to the growing pressure for intelligence oversight. The issues at its core were, in a number of respects, an extension of those considered by the TISC supergun inquiry. Scott examined export policy towards Iraq during its war with Iran and after, and, in particular, the decision to prosecute three executives of machine tool manufacturer Matrix Churchill despite the fact that its managing director and export sales manager had supplied intelligence to MI6 and MI5 on Iraqi procurement and weapons development, something they were only able to do as a consequence of the access their trade allowed.

Scott provided a rare window on the intelligence services, especially in light of the very limited state of openness at the time. His inquiry heard evidence from 13 members of the intelligence and security services in closed session, and received or heard evidence which referred to even more. The role of intelligence emerged as key and led Scott to make a number of intelligence-related observations in his 1996 report that suggested areas of intelligence failure, one of which remained secret "in the national interest". He highlighted areas where intelligence reports did not get to all appropriate readers, recommended that systems should be put in place that would enable access to relevant historical intelligence information so as to avoid relying on memory and thereby ensure the adequacy of hand-over briefings, that each departmental customer should regularly review its declared intelligence requirements and question whether it was receiving all relevant reports, and that it should not be possible for submissions to ministers to attribute to an intelligence agency views or opinions which that agency did not hold and might repudiate.[7] In its 1996 annual report, the ISC would report that the agencies and their Whitehall customers had accepted the shortcomings identified by Scott and had outlined the steps they had taken to rectify them.

Hence, by 1995 the situation regarding intelligence accountability had advanced somewhat from that which existed just three years earlier. The Scott Inquiry had taken oral evidence from agency personnel and had been granted access to intelligence material, the ISC existed and had produced its first report, and even the HAC had been allowed to meet with the director-general of MI5, although low executive trust in members of Parliament remained a barrier to select committees being granted greater access to intelligence personnel or papers. This was the context in which, in 1995, the TISC returned, albeit reluctantly, to the theme of defence exports to Iraq and Iran, essentially two sides of the same coin during the period of the 1980–88 Iran–Iraq war. In that year the President of the Board of Trade, Michael Heseltine, revealed his concern that naval cannon notionally intended for Singapore, a well-known conduit, might well have actually been destined for Iran, just as the chairman of the exporting company, Gerald James of BMARC, had consistently claimed. Heseltine invited the TISC to investigate the matter. However, the TISC was reluctant to do so in light of its supergun experience. Hence, it sought assurances about access to information before agreeing to take on the inquiry. On receiving these, it accepted the government's invitation. As it noted in its report:

> We have not had difficulty in obtaining from the Government the witnesses or documents we wanted, with the exception of intelligence material. We received a summary of the intelligence reports, but requests that we be allowed to inspect the intelligence reports, in the form circulated to the Department, under the "Crown jewels procedure", and subsequently that one member of the Committee (a Privy Councillor and former Foreign Office Minister) be allowed to inspect that material, were turned down. While we regret this, we do not believe that it significantly hindered our inquiry, except in several specific areas . . .[8]

It argued that the "Crown jewels" procedure should be employed more widely where intelligence material was directly relevant to select committee investigations. This procedure related to the FAC's 1984–85 inquiry into the sinking of the *General Belgrano* during the 1982 Falklands war. Here committee members and staff were allowed to consult intelligence material (the "Crown jewels"), but not permitted to take away any notes. However, the government subsequently argued that this was "always seen as a one-off exception", because "the intelligence was at the heart of the matter . . . It was all about the precise intelligence available at that moment."[9] However, this was also the case here, just as it had been with the earlier supergun inquiry. The Report recorded the Committee's "regret that the Government was not willing to allow the Committee, or even a single member of the Committee . . . to inspect the original intelligence reports".[10]

Foreign Affairs Committee: the decision to go to war in Iraq, July 2003

Iraq would again provide the context for debate about the adequacy of intelligence oversight in the period following the 2003 war. By this time the ISC had matured as an oversight body over a decade, and undertook an inquiry into pre-war intelligence on Iraqi WMD and its presentation by the government, alongside the FAC's inquiry into the decision to go to war, a judicial inquiry resulting from the suicide of an eminent government scientist, and an inquiry by a group of Privy Counsellors into WMD intelligence led by former Cabinet Secretary Lord Butler.

The FAC inquiry into the decision to go to war in Iraq represented another textbook illustration of the weaknesses inherent in parliamentary efforts to call the executive to account in relation to intelligence matters. Following the March 2003 invasion of Iraq and the rapid advance on Baghdad, concern arose over the failure to uncover the stocks of WMD whose existence had constituted the official rationale for the war. Controversy grew throughout May and then erupted into the war between Downing Street and the BBC over Andrew Gilligan's radio broadcast alleging that the government had exaggerated claims relating to Iraqi WMD in a September 2002 dossier published by Downing Street and containing intelligence material approved by the Joint Intelligence Committee (JIC). Within a few days, the FAC announced that it would examine whether the government had "presented accurate and complete information to Parliament in the period leading up to military action in Iraq, particularly in respect of weapons of mass destruction".[11]

One problem facing the FAC was the familiar one that it could gain access only to those people and papers that the government allowed. While it did interview the Foreign Secretary in closed session it was denied access to the agency heads and John Scarlett, the Chair of the JIC. Its investigation was conducted rapidly, in not much more than a month, and concluded while that ministers had not misled Parliament, there were a number of concerns over its presentation of the case for war, including: the certainty of the assertion that Iraq had sought uranium from Niger; that the "45 minute" claim – that Iraq could deliver WMD within 45 minutes of an order to do so – did not warrant the prominence given to it in the dossier; and that the language used in the dossier was more assertive than traditionally used in intelligence documents.

In this case the FAC's task was particularly difficult for several reasons. Firstly, the case related to a divisive war. Secondly, the government enjoyed a large parliamentary majority. Thirdly, the main Opposition party had supported the case for war. Fourthly, in relation to such a potentially damaging inquiry, the government declined to offer the same degree of support it had offered earlier FAC inquiries into similarly grave and controversial questions. Denial of access to intelligence material and personnel meant that the FAC was potentially easy to mislead, its report could never be regarded as definitive, and its conclusions were therefore easier to dismiss. Finally, the existence of the ISC provided the government with cover for this course of action by allowing it to claim that oversight of the intelligence agencies was now being provided elsewhere, a situation of considerable constitutional significance and a source of considerable irritation to the FAC. When the ISC was created in 1994, Foreign Secretary Douglas Hurd had assured the House that it would not "truncate in any way the existing responsibilities of existing committees".[12] In practice, however, governments had repeatedly refused to allow select committees access to intelligence material or personnel, thereby eliminating any associated risk of political embarrassment or damage, on the grounds that parliamentary scrutiny of these was now the job of the ISC. The FAC lamented how:

> We have attempted, so far in vain, to explain to Ministers that for the FAC to discharge effectively its role of scrutinising the policies of the [Foreign Office], it will on occasion require access to intelligence material and, on rare occasions, to the agencies themselves. The present inquiry is a case in point. Ministers base their refusal to grant such access on the existence of the ISC, suggesting – in our view wholly wrongly – that Lord Hurd's undertaking has been honoured, because there was no such access before 1994.[13]

One particular grievance was the lack of "symmetry". For example, the ISC was able to undertake an investigation into intelligence and warnings relating to the October 2002 Bali bombings, a substantial part of which commented on matters relating to the Foreign Office and was based on evidence taken from it. However, following the government's own logic, it should have applied its policy of avoiding "competing jurisdictions" and denied the ISC such access, as this involved trespassing on FAC territory. The FAC regarded the government's "refusal to grant us access to evidence essential to our inquiries as a failure of accountability to Parliament, the more so as it does not accord entirely with precedent".[14]

Indeed, this refusal could be interpreted as a retrograde step given that the FAC had been granted access to the "Crown Jewels" papers after the Falklands War, and enjoyed some limited success in obtaining copies of classified telegrams in the course of its inquiry into Sierra Leone. Moreover, in both cases, parallel inquiries were under way (the Franks and Legg inquiries respectively).[15] At the same time, however, during its Sierra Leone inquiry the FAC had asked to interview the head of MI6 only for the Foreign Secretary to refuse on the grounds that the ISC was the appropriate committee to conduct such an interview. Similarly, when the FAC came to conduct its inquiry into the Kosovo campaign it was not allowed access to the JIC or the Chief of Defence Intelligence, being informed once more that the ISC was the appropriate vehicle. However, the ISC's coverage of Kosovo was so heavily redacted as to render it meaningless to the reader, raising questions about the impact of the ISC on Parliament's ability to police the executive in any area with an intelligence dimension, extending to fundamental issues of war and peace.

Partly as a consequence of this state of affairs, the FAC recommended that the ISC be recast as a select committee. In this it was effectively joining forces with the HAC, a long-time proponent of such a shift. This option would, it argued, offer a number of advantages, including the possibility of joint hearings, inquiries and reports, established structures for the management of overlap, and a more open way of working. Another key advantage of such a shift was held to be that select committees had the power to send for persons, papers and records to assist them in their work. While they could not summon members of either House (Commons or Lords) to appear before them, officials had a duty to attend when requested.[16] A significant minority of ISC members themselves favoured such a shift. In the first parliamentary debate on the ISC's annual reports, ISC member Allan Rogers had referred to the Committee's "strong debates on the possible adoption of a Select Committee style for our proceedings". Fellow member Dale Campbell-Savours was clearer still:

> I do not believe that oversight is fully credible while the Committee remains a creature of the Executive – and that is what it is. The problem at the moment is that the Committee considers its relationship with the Prime Minister more important to its operation than its relationship with Parliament. I strongly dissent from that view and find the arguments in favour of Select Committee status utterly overwhelming.[17]

In 1999 the HAC added its voice to this call. While recognising the "significant step forward over previous arrangments" that the ISC represented, it restated its 1993 view that oversight should be undertaken by a select committee, although not now by an existing departmental committee:

> In our view, it is inevitable that the intelligence services will one day become accountable to Parliament. That is the logical outcome of the process of reform embarked upon by the previous Government . . . the accountability of the security and intelligence services to Parliament ought to be a fundamental principle in a modern democracy.[18]

Not surprisingly, the government rejected this conclusion.[19] However, and significantly for some, in doing so it said that it was, "not convinced that there is a strong case for change in the fundamental structure of these arrangements *now*", opening up the possibility of a future progression.[20]

The FAC concluded its report into the decision to go to war in Iraq by stating that, the "continued refusal by Ministers to allow this committee access to intelligence papers and personnel, on this inquiry and more generally, is hampering it in the work which Parliament has asked it to carry out", and recommended that:

> the Government accept the principle that it should be prepared to accede to requests from the Foreign Affairs Committee for access to intelligence, when the Committee can demonstrate that it is of key importance to a specific inquiry it is conducting and unless there are genuine concerns for national security. We further recommend that, in cases where access is refused, full reasons should be given.[21]

The ISC Report: Iraqi WMD – intelligence and assessments

Given that the government had been able to justify the limited nature of its co-operation with the FAC by reference to the fact that the ISC was to investigate the issue, there was an additional weight of expectation on the ISC. This also represented the kind of controversial issue that for some observers would represent a litmus test of the ISC's ability to hold the agencies to account and demonstrate its independence from the executive that appointed it and to which it reported.

The ISC sought "to examine whether the available intelligence, which informed the decision to invade Iraq, was adequate and properly assessed and whether it was accurately reflected in Government publications".[22] It did not consider the decision to go to war *per se*. It reported four months later that, based on the intelligence it had seen, "there was convincing intelligence that Iraq had active chemical, biological and nuclear programmes and the capability to produce chemical and biological weapons."[23] As noted earlier, at the heart of the controversy over pre-war intelligence on Iraq was the September 2002 Downing Street dossier. In its 2002–03 annual report, the ISC had commented on this, saying that it supported the "responsible use of intelligence and material collected by the Agencies to inform the public on matters such as these".[24] The question here was how far this represented a responsible use of intelligence material. However, the ISC did not rise to the challenge, failing to probe, offering no commentary on evidence that the political case was in advance of the intelligence case for war, and exposing its highly limited investigatory capacity.

For example, in a draft version of Tony Blair's Foreword to the dossier, it was acknowledged that there was no threat of nuclear attack on the UK, but this fact was cut from the published version. This denied the public available reassurance and passed up an opportunity to bring some context to bear. In a tame criticism the ISC contented itself with observing that: "It was unfortunate that this point was removed from the published version of the foreword and not highlighted elsewhere."[25] While clearly recognising that the presentation of the case was misleading, the ISC's criticisms were mildly expressed, as with regard to the emphasis given to the "45 minute" claim. Here, the ISC concluded:

> The dossier was for public consumption and not for experienced readers of intelligence material. The 45 minutes claim, included four times, was always likely to attract attention because it was arresting detail that the public had not seen before. As the 45 minutes claim was new to its readers, the context of the intelligence and any assessment needed to be explained. The fact that it was assessed to refer to battlefield chemical and biological munitions and their movement on the battlefield, not to any other form of chemical or biological attack, should have been highlighted in the dossier. The omission of the context and assessment allowed speculation as to its exact meaning. This was unhelpful to an understanding of this issue.[26]

It was more than just "unhelpful". It was misleading, but the ISC was not prepared to say so unequivocally, instead taking refuge in a form of language that blunted the impact of any criticism. It was the language of mild reproach over minor misdemeanour.

The ISC also reported that the JIC had not been subjected to political pressures, its independence and impartiality uncompromised. It was assured by the Ministry of Defence and the Defence Secretary that no one in the Defence Intelligence Staff (DIS) had expressed serious concerns about the drafting of the dossier, only to find out subsequently that two members of DIS had written to their line managers to express their concern at the language being used in the dossier, "which was not in their view supported by the intelligence available to them".[27] The ISC called this failure of disclosure "unhelpful and potentially misleading".[28]

The government's response to the ISC's report represented a further stage in the presentational game that had begun in earnest with the September 2002 dossier. It emphasised those aspects of the ISC report that appeared to support its conduct over the production of the dossier, and rejected its criticisms. With regard to the charge that the dossier was 'unbalanced', its response was that:

> [T]he dossier did present a balanced view of Iraq's CBW capability based on the intelligence available. The dossier made clear (paragraph 14, page 16) that the withdrawal of the United Nations Special Commission (UNSCOM) had greatly diminished the ability of the international community to monitor and assess Iraq's continued efforts to reconstitute its programmes. It also noted (paragraph 13, page 16) that UNSCOM was unable to account for significant quantities of agents, precursors and munitions.[29]

But the government cannot have it both ways. Either – as this and the objective record both suggest – the intelligence picture on Iraq in 2002 was characterised by a significant degree of uncertainty, or, as Tony Blair wrote in his Foreword to the dossier, it was known that Iraq represented a "current and serious threat to the UK national interest".

The ISC was itself dissatisfied with the government's response which, "emphasised only four key conclusions while either rejecting or failing to address fully many of our other conclusions and recommendations. We regard this as extremely unsatisfactory . . . Our dissatisfaction was increased by the Government's decision to allow such little time for parliamentary debate" on its Iraq and annual reports.[30] While the government response to the ISC's 2003–04 annual report began a practice of responding to each ISC conclusion individually it never directly addressed the core issues raised here, simply stating that it regretted that the Committee found its response unsatisfactory. This did not amount to effective oversight. Key questions had gone unanswered and the ISC had effectively run out of the options in the face of the government's refusal to engage with it. The government's response suggested a high degree of discomfort with the ISC and affected parliamentary perceptions of its effectiveness.

Moreover, it emerged that, although the ISC thought it had seen all JIC assessments on Iraq produced between August 1990 and September 2002, and the eight produced in the period October 2002 to March 2003, in fact eight had been withheld – five from the former period, three from the latter. While the Committee was "satisfied that knowledge of them would not have led us to change the conclusions, including those that were critical, in our Report",[31] earlier access would have allowed it to include further material, and its conclusions would have been more securely rooted in a fuller picture.

The subsequent withdrawal of intelligence that had underpinned key claims made in the September dossier led the ISC to become "concerned at the amount of intelligence on Iraqi WMD that has now had to be withdrawn by the SIS".[32] It should have been, because it undermined certain of the conclusions the ISC reached in its report and suggested grounds for re-visiting the question of whether political pressure had been applied. Following the Iraq Survey Group report, it was clear that the July 2002 JIC conclusion that "Iraq is pursuing a nuclear weapons programme" was wrong. The 2002 JIC judgement that Iraq "retains up to 20 missiles over 1000 km" was wrong. The judgement that "Iraq could produce significant quantities of mustard [gas] within weeks, significant quantities of Sarin and VX within months and in the case of VX may already have done so" was speculative and not supported by post-war investigation. The 2002 JIC judgement that "Iraq currently has available, either from pre-Gulf War, or more recent production, a number of biological agents . . . Iraq could produce more of these biological agents within days", overstated the case. Essentially, in each area of CBW concern – nuclear, chemical, biological and missile development – intelligence was wide of the mark. While the ISC adopted a defensive position on behalf of the agencies, citing Saddam's intention to resume production in a post-sanctions environment, it was clear that the intelligence base had been flawed. Whether this base had been crucial to the case for war was a different question, and one which the Butler Inquiry was able to illuminate to a far greater degree than the ISC.

The Hutton and Butler inquiries

The Butler Report was not the first inquiry the government had been itself obliged to set up into matters relating to the case for war in Iraq. Following the suicide of Ministry of Defence biological weapons specialist Dr David Kelly (revealed as the source of Andrew Gilligan's May 2003 story that the government had exaggerated claims about Iraqi WMD in its September 2002 dossier) shortly after giving evidence to the FAC, Blair had felt obliged to set up an inquiry headed by Lord Hutton into the circumstances surrounding his death. The public hearings conducted by the Hutton Inquiry and evidence available to it (notably internal Downing Street email traffic concerning the production of the dossier, about which the ISC had seemed unaware) suggested a critical outcome. However, when the report finally appeared in January 2004, it exonerated the government of any bad faith in relation to the creation of the dossier and focused its criticisms instead on the collective failures of BBC management that had allowed the allegations to be broadcast in the first place.

However, on the same day that the Hutton Report was published, arms expert David Kay, charged with leading the post-war hunt for Iraq's WMD, was admitting to the Senate Armed

Services Committee that "we were all wrong" and that Saddam had destroyed such weapons, possibly as early as 1991. The intelligence that Blair had consistently cited was thus called into question. Pressure quickly built for a further inquiry, which Blair felt obliged to announce, to be chaired by former Cabinet Secretary Sir Robin Butler. Any assessment of the effectiveness of the ISC has to take account of the fact that, had it not been for Kelly's suicide and Kay's Senate testimony, the ISC report would have marked the end of UK inquiries into pre-war intelligence. Given the information that the Hutton and Butler inquiries revealed to the public, would such a situation have represented effective or adequate oversight?

In giving evidence to the earlier Hutton Inquiry, Blair had explained the case for war in terms of the strength of intelligence on Iraqi WMD:

> What changed was really two things which came together. First of all, there was a tremendous amount of information and evidence coming across my desk as to the weapons of mass destruction and the programmes associated with it that Saddam had . . . There was also a renewed sense of urgency, again, in the way that this was being publicly debated . . . Why did we say it was a big problem? Because of the intelligence . . . We were saying this issue had to be returned to by the international community and dealt with. Why were we saying this? Because of the intelligence.[33]

The Butler Inquiry had access to all of the intelligence reports Blair alluded to when giving evidence to the Hutton Inquiry. Its report, published in July 2004, concluded that: "The Government's conclusion in the spring of 2002 that stronger action (although not necessarily military action) needed to be taken to enforce Iraqi disarmament was not based on any new development in the current intelligence picture on Iraq." In his evidence to the Butler Inquiry, Blair endorsed the view that "what had changed was not the pace of Iraq's prohibited weapons programmes . . . but tolerance of them following the attacks of 11 September 2001". This was not entirely consistent with his answers to the Hutton Inquiry. However, the Butler Inquiry's access to intelligence documents meant that Blair had little option but to retreat from his earlier emphasis on the intelligence picture. The Butler Inquiry concluded that "there was no recent intelligence that would itself have given rise to a conclusion that Iraq was of more immediate concern than the activities of some other countries".[34] However, both in the Foreword to the September 2002 dossier and in presentations to Parliament as Blair moved the country closer to war, the intelligence, which his audience could not access for themselves, was used to justify the urgency of the case for war. As former Foreign Secretary Robin Cook argued, "Downing Street did not worry that the intelligence was thin and inferential or that the sources were second-hand and unreliable, because intelligence did not play a big part in the real reason why we went to war."[35]

The Butler Report suggested the possibility that one failure in the lead-up to war was that the "ultimate users of intelligence" – by virtue of his *modus operandi* essentially the Prime Minister and a small group of Downing Street advisers – did not fully understand some of the limitations inherent in intelligence. This may not be a far-fetched idea in relation to a Prime Minister who had not previously held an office where he would come into contact with it and was said to be somewhat in thrall to the world of espionage and intelligence. On the other hand, the need for an informed customer for intelligence would be of less importance if intelligence was not driving policy, but seized upon to provide a publicly defensible *raison d'être*.

As late as the eve of the Butler Report's publication, Blair was unwilling to publicly accept that the intelligence was flawed. However, he and his Cabinet colleagues were ultimately content to let the intelligence "failure" take the blame. When, under pressure to make some form of apology for his depiction of a case for war that the September 2004 publication of the

Iraq Survey Group Report confirmed to have no grounding in reality, Blair told the Labour Party Conference: "the problem is, I can apologise for the information that turned out to be wrong, but I can't, sincerely at least, apologise for removing Saddam." Trade and Industry Secretary Patricia Hewitt repeated this formula, telling a television audience: "All of us who were involved in making an incredibly difficult decision are very sorry and do apologise for the fact that that information was wrong."[36]

The conclusion that the decision to go to war was not driven by the intelligence picture gained further credence through the leaking of governmental documents from early-mid 2002 which indicated that Tony Blair had already committed the UK to support the Bush Administration's policy of regime change in Iraq by that summer. One of these was a summary of a meeting with Condoleezza Rice from David Manning, Blair's foreign policy adviser, which reported back that: "Bush is grateful for your support and has registered that you are getting flak. I said that you would not budge in your support for regime change but you had to manage a press, a parliament and a public opinion that was very different from anything in the States." The clearest evidence of all is contained in a minute of a meeting of Blair's inner circle held in July 2002. Here, the Head of MI6 reported on his recent visit to Washington, where "military action was now seen as inevitable. Bush wanted to remove Saddam, through military action, justified by the conjunction of terrorism and WMD. *But the intelligence and facts were being fixed around the policy.*"[37]

Conclusions

The case of Iraq, then, both allows us to monitor the progress made in intelligence oversight over the last decade or so, and alerts us to the limitations of the current arrangements and the ease with which they allow the executive branch to control the process, the more so in the absence of a sufficiently assertive ISC. As we have seen, the FAC was unable to hold the executive to account in this case. Judicial and other enquiries have represented a valuable means by which information can be placed on the public record, but these have not been without their problems and can only ever represent a "firefighting" rather than "police-patrolling" model of oversight. One of the reasons for the FAC's limited effectiveness was the government's use of the ISC's existence as an argument to deny it access to intelligence that would have informed and perhaps even shaped its conclusions. As we have also seen, the ISC's performance over Iraq raises a number of questions and has brought back into sharp focus a question that has been keenly debated ever since its creation – namely, whether the ISC should be reconstituted as a select committee. An implicit related question is whether the obvious limitations of the ISC are a consequence of its structures or personnel.

Ironically, perhaps, the conduct of the FAC in relation to Iraq has greatly reduced the likelihood of this happening in the foreseeable future. The treatment of Dr David Kelly at the hands of the FAC horrified and angered staff in the agencies in equal measure. Kelly liaised closely with both DIS and MI6 over Iraqi WMD, and his questioning and subsequent suicide represented a cautionary tale as to what could happen to any of them if exposed to parliamentary questioning on a controversial topic (as questions of intelligence almost invariably are), with the protective arm of the executive removed. Any agency enthusiasm for a select committee approach to oversight was extinguished at this point.

The key question is whether the efforts to oversee the behaviour of the executive in making the case for war in Iraq, and its use of intelligence in this, have been adequate. The conclusion would have to be that they have not. The most thorough appraisal was provided by the Butler

Inquiry, which might never have existed but for particular circumstances. Since the ISC considered the intelligence base, significant pieces of intelligence have been withdrawn. Its remit did not extend to considering the political aspects of the case for war, more properly the business of the FAC. However, the FAC was denied access to intelligence because of the existence of the ISC. The leaking of memoranda of meetings from 2002 expose both as being inadequate. In light of this fresh evidence, should the ISC now re-investigate the extent to which intelligence was "fixed" around a policy and the obvious corollary of this – that Parliament and public were misled? Is it capable of identifying policy as well as intelligence failure? Does it have the political will to do so?

Arguably, the only prospect of Parliament holding the executive to account in this case would have been via the co-operation of the FAC and ISC as select committees, undertaking joint or overlapping inquiries. This is especially so given that the failure over Iraq was clearly one involving mutually reinforcing intelligence *and* policy failure. In this case, the very existence of the ISC in its current form may have aided the executive in limiting the impact of legislative oversight. In short, the British public discovered more about the reality of the case for war in Iraq from leaked documents than from official oversight bodies, despite over a decade of dedicated parliamentary oversight. This must be a cause for concern.

Notes

1 Mark Phythian, "Britain and the Supergun", *Crime, Law and Social Change*, Vol. 19 1993, p. 368.
2 Ibid.
3 Trade and Industry Select Committee, *Exports to Iraq: Project Babylon and Long Range Guns*, Cm. 86, London, HMSO, 1992.
4 Ibid., para. 149.
5 As in Christopher Marlowe's *The Jew of Malta* (Act IV Scene i):

> Barnadine: Thou hast committed –
> Barabus: Fornication? But that was in another country, and besides, the wench is dead.

6 Home Affairs Committee, *Accountability of the Security Service*, HC 265, London, HMSO, 1993.
7 Sir Richard Scott: *Report of the Inquiry into the Export of Defence Equipment and Dual-Use Goods to Iraq and Related Prosecutions*, HC-115, London, HMSO, 1996, K7.7.
8 Trade and Industry Select Committee, *Export Licensing and BMARC*, HC 87-I, London, HMSO, 1996, para. 6.
9 Ibid., para. 168.
10 Ibid.
11 Foreign Affairs Committee, *The Decision to go to War in Iraq*, HC813-I, London, The Stationery Office, 2003, para. 4.
12 Hansard, 22 Feb. 1994, col. 164.
13 FAC, *The Decision to go to War*, para. 161.
14 Ibid., para. 163.
15 Foreign Affairs Committee, *Events Surrounding the Weekend of 1–2 May 1982*, HC 11, London, HMSO, 1985; Foreign Affairs Committee, *Sierra Leone*, HC 116-I, London, HMSO, 1999.
16 This was confirmed by Sir Robin Butler in 1990. See, Treasury and Civil Service Committee, *Civil Service Pay and Conditions*, HC 260, London, HMSO, 1990, Q.75–76
17 Hansard, 2 Nov. 1998. cols. 596, 618.
18 Home Affairs Committee, *Accountability of the Security Service*, HC 291, London, HMSO, 1999, para. 48.
19 Government Reply to the Third Report from the Home Affairs Committee, *Accountability of the Security Service*, Cm. 4588, London, HMSO, 2000.
20 Ibid., my emphasis. ISC member Dale Campbell-Savours subsequently revealed that, "the word 'now' in the Government's response was fought over and it indicates the way in which we are going." Hansard, 22 June 2000, col. 512.

21 FAC, *The Decision to go to War*, paras. 168–9.
22 Intelligence and Security Committee, *Iraqi Weapons of Mass Destruction – Intelligence and Assessments*, Cm. 5972, London, HMSO, 2003, para. 11.
23 Ibid., para. 66.
24 Intelligence and Security Committee, *Annual Report 2002–03*, Cm. 5837, London, HMSO, 2003, para. 81.
25 ISC, *Iraqi Weapons of Mass Destruction*, para. 83.
26 Ibid., para. 86.
27 Ibid., para. 101.
28 Ibid., para. 104.
29 *Government Response to the Intelligence and Security Committee Report on Iraqi Weapons of Mass Destruction – Intelligence and Assessments*, Cm. 6118, London, HMSO, 2004, para. 13.
30 ISC *Annual Report 2003–04*, Cm. 6240, London, HMSO, 2004, para. 87.
31 Ibid., para. 146.
32 ISC, *Annual Report 2004–05*, Cm. 6510, London, HMSO, 2005, para. 63.
33 See Mark Phythian, "Hutton and Scott: A Tale of Two Inquiries", *Parliamentary Affairs*, Vol. 58 No. 1 Jan. 2005, pp. 128–9.
34 *Review of Intelligence on Weapons of Mass Destruction*, HC 898, London, The Stationery Office, 2004, para. 427.
35 Robin Cook, "The Die Was Cast: The Dossiers Were Irrelevant", *The Independent on Sunday*, 18 July 2004.
36 Alan Doig and Mark Phythian, "The National Interest and Politics of Threat Exaggeration: The Blair Government's Case for War against Iraq", *The Political Quarterly*, Vol. 76 No. 3 2005, pp. 374–5.
37 My emphasis. The documents are available at www.downingstreetmemo.com/

24

Intelligence accountability

Challenges for parliaments and intelligence services

Hans Born and Thorsten Wetzling

Today's western derivates of the world's second oldest profession[1] share the paradoxical task of operating in secret in order to defend an open society. Recent intelligence scandals have illustrated that democracies are not immune from the politicization of intelligence services by members of the executive or from illegal practices by members of the intelligence services. One can point to the British and US governments' selective usage of intelligence assessments in the months before the Iraq war in 2003. The infamous "dodgy dossier" springs to mind, a UK government publication that inserted plagiarized excerpts from an academic source in an attempt to make the case for an imminent threat to international peace and security posed by Baghdad. The British intelligence community, the UK government claimed on numerous occasions, had fully endorsed the estimation that "Iraqi military are able to deploy chemical and biological weapons within 45 minutes of an order to do so".[2] In a similar fashion, Colin Powell, former US Secretary of State, addressed the UN Security Council in March 2003 by saying: "[T]hese are not assertions. What we are giving you are facts and conclusions based on solid intelligence". It was noted that, "at the very least, the case for the continued and threatening existence of WMD in Iraq was presented at a level of certainty quite unheard of in intelligence assessment".[3]

Surely, instances of abuse of intelligence services by the executives are not limited to cases when intelligence is being "processed" so as to fit a government's political agenda[4] but include also instances when politicians use the intelligence services for domestic political purposes, for instance by spying on political opponents[5] or when the intelligence services' assets have been used by the executive for commercial interests.[6] As for the illicit practices by the intelligence community, one can allude to the recent example of rendition practices of CIA agents in the US-led war against terrorism.

In the wake of 9/11, various countries have started special or parliamentary inquiries into the functioning of intelligence services. Examples are the Hutton Inquiry in the United Kingdom and the congressionally appointed Kean Commission in the United States. In Canada one can point to the Arar Commission. Also, the German Bundestag decided in March 2006 to establish a parliamentary investigation mandated to shed light on the amount of German involvement/cognizance of illicit CIA rendition and detention practices in Europe.[7] Moreover, the heightened public attention on questions concerning the control over intelligence cooperation practices is not only confined to national settings as both the Parliamentary Assembly of the Council of Europe (PACE) and the European Parliament are currently pursuing independent investigations on these matters, too.[8]

Against the backdrop of these latest and ongoing judicial and parliamentary investigations on national intelligence services and the way political leaders have handled intelligence, this chapter is based on the premise that contemporary governance and control of intelligence services in liberal democracies is confronted with a range of specific challenges. We confined ourselves to shedding light on three specific challenges that relate to the satisfactory pursuit of parliamentary intelligence oversight and the internal direction and control of intelligence agencies.[9] These are (a) to maintain *parliamentary ownership over intelligence oversight procedures* (b) to establish *"embedded" human rights in intelligence affairs*; (c) to safeguard *the political neutrality of intelligence services*.

We then conducted a comparative research of national intelligence legislation in democratic countries with a view to find good examples of how national intelligence control systems can master these challenges. While the text also discusses poor examples, i.e. national regulations that do not bode well for success in mastering the challenge, we have concentrated on examples than can be used as reference material for students of intelligence legislation and law-makers alike. These good examples are then listed in the three tables.

We used the following criteria for selecting national intelligence legislation and national intelligence oversight legislation into our sample: First, we considered only legislation from democratic countries. Second, we aimed at including a representative sample which embraces different constitutional models (presidential, parliamentary and Westminster-style democracies), different regions, and examples from "old" and "new" democracies. Third, we only considered those countries whose national intelligence laws are available in English.[10]

Intelligence accountability – why bother?

Before discussing the more detailed findings of our study, a few words seem in order to introduce the notion of democratic intelligence control. Most western democracies proclaim that their intelligence services are being held accountable.[11] But what level of scrutiny suffices for the *democratic* control of intelligence, who should be involved, and why bother?

Surely, the stakes are very high when politicians rely on intelligence service information: misuse of intelligence can lead to foreign and domestic policy decisions that can harm the security and the general social fabric of societies. The general danger exists that a nation is not confronted with a fine balance between security and civil liberties but enjoys less of each.[12] To prevent this, the control of intelligence services becomes an absolute necessity: if done in adherence with standard principles of democratic rule, it further assures the legitimacy, legality and even the efficiency of intelligence agencies. More concretely, it can prevent *ex ante* the occurrence of human rights abuses, the infringement of civil liberties, the mismanagement or inadequate approbation of public funds, the exercise of plausible deniability and other forms of ministerial abuse that have traditionally beset the governance of intelligence affairs.

While some concerns about intelligence services are ill-founded,[13] it is worth pointing out that intelligence and security services can hardly be described as ordinary government institutions either. "In most nations, intelligence agencies are treated as exceptions from the rest of government."[14] Yet such exceptional treatment, however motivated, is oblivious to the fact that intelligence agencies are nothing but government institutions. If government derives its power from the people, all government institutions ought to act on behalf of the people, too. Furthermore, in a democracy, no single area of government activity can be a "no-go" zone for parliamentarians, including the intelligence and security services. If this appears as a rather solid rationale for the necessity of parliamentary intelligence oversight, how can one then account for Johnson's observation on intelligence agencies' practice in most countries: "They are cloaked in secrecy, allowed privileged access to policy-makers, and given leeway to get the job done – even if that means breaking laws overseas and engaging in unsavoury activities that would be deemed inappropriate for other government agencies."[15] If an agency is cloaked in secrecy, this means that either virtually no independent overseers are being admitted to the "ring of secrecy" or that those overseers admitted are kept on a very tight leash by the government. Either way, the result is that the public has little say on what information is being held or circulated among the agencies and the executive.

Obviously, the importance of intelligence on national security issues raises difficult questions, such as how much knowledge (operational and non-operational) should be disclosed so as to inform the interested public whilst not simultaneously jeopardizing national security. The pursuit of a just and practicable balance between civil liberties and security is very difficult to achieve and has long occupied the minds of both practitioners and scholars alike. As with most complex balancing dilemmas, there exists no single blueprint adopted by all democracies for achieving this end. National intelligence laws, i.e. the embodiments of different national democratic wills, have proffered different ways to attain such a balance. Irrespective of the legitimate variety of such balancing efforts, all measures ought to be predetermined by the principles of democratic rule. Amongst these principles, the doctrine of the separation of powers and the rule of law are pertinent. The application of these doctrines to the governance of intelligence challenges any forms by which parliament would be excluded or insufficiently involved in intelligence affairs and requires that intelligence services are bound by fundamental human rights standards.

Comprehensive intelligence accountability

In line with these principles, the exercise of democratic intelligence control may be said to rest on five layers of accountability. These are: internal intelligence control by the services, strong executive control, parliamentary oversight, judicial review and external review by independent civil society organizations.[16] Each layer has a central task in the overall aim to avoid intelligence abuse. The intelligence services restrain themselves by means of internal control (whistleblower regulations, training of employees in accordance with a legislated code of conduct), the executive performs executive control, i.e. giving direction to intelligence services, including tasking, prioritizing and making resources available. The parliament oversees the services by passing intelligence laws (that define and regulate the services and their control), by adopting the corresponding budgetary appropriations and by questioning decision-makers in special hearings. In addition, the judiciary is tasked to monitor the use of the agencies' special powers (such as surveillance and interrogation practices) and to adjudicate wrong-doings. Last but not least, civil society organizations may curtail the functioning of intelligence services by giving an alternative view (think tanks), disclosing scandals and crises (media), or by raising complaints concerning wrong-doing (citizens).

The path towards the successful implementation of the general objective behind each of the five layers remains beset by complex organizational and legal challenges. To illustrate this, consider the summary of what the "Making Intelligence Accountable" research project's country studies have revealed vis-à-vis the implementation of parliamentary intelligence oversight: Oversight was hindered by a mixture of the following factors: (1) insufficient co-operation from the executive and the intelligence agencies; (2) scant and vague mandates of oversight committees; (3) lack of resources; (4) insufficient motivation of parliamentarians to engage in pro-active oversight; (5) lack of access to classified information by overseers in parliament.

These factors can be illustrated by material we have found in various countries. For example, the analysis of Poland's intelligence oversight practices revealed that the parliamentarians' access to classified information remains very much dependent on the discretion of the services.[17] The Canadian case study exposed that

> in every instance their [the intelligence overseers'] purview is limited to a single intelligence organization, a significant weakness given the cross-departmental nature of security and intelligence. [The Canadian parliamentary oversight body] has a pro-active capacity to conduct routine checks on the efficacy and propriety of CSIS, but no mandate to go further afield.[18]

The Norwegian case concluded that "the limited staff resources clearly restrict the committee's ability to conduct more extensive inquiries and investigations as well as its ability to be pro-active".[19] Lastly, while Loch Johnson acknowledges the robust nature of the US intelligence oversight system, he still deplores the insufficient motivation of parliamentarians to engage in pro-active oversight.[20]

Ownership over parliamentary intelligence oversight procedures

If spying is the second oldest profession in the world, democratic intelligence oversight is one of the more recent political phenomenon, starting only in the mid 1970s; it should, moreover, be pointed out while acknowledging that it took the next three decades to be incorporated by most western liberal democracies.[21] Similarly, while the belief that the security sector cannot remain the preserve of the executive alone without inviting potential abuse has been widely respected as intelligence oversight's rationale for the last four decades, the assertion that it takes an *active* participation by the people's elected representatives took longer to take root.[22] Even today, one must, of course, caution that intelligence oversight laws can only "go so far" to ensure the democratic control of intelligence services. Adopting comprehensive intelligence laws does, in other words, not resolve the many practical challenges that intelligence overseers are confronted with.

This said, the comparative review of intelligence oversight legislation can produce meaningful insight with respect to the democratic legitimacy of intelligence oversight. We turn to the notion of *parliamentary ownership* to illustrate this further. This notion emerged in our project as a decisive condition for the overall success of intelligence control. Ownership denotes the independence of parliamentary intelligence oversight committees from the executive and the services in all aspects related to the pursuit of their mandates. It enhances their position vis-à-vis the other institutions involved in intelligence governance. By studying the mandate and the composition of parliamentary oversight bodies, the vetting and clearance procedures, the parliamentary powers to obtain information, the reporting to parliament and budget control provisions, we have identified accountability mechanisms and related practices which contribute to parliament having full power over the way it wants to oversee the intelligence community, including the role and policy of the executive (see Figure 24.1).

318

1 Parliament is responsible for appointing and, where necessary, removing members of a body exercising the oversight function in its name (Germany, Act governing the Parliamentary Control of Intelligence Activities (PKGrG of 1978))[23]

2 Committee members have security of tenure at the pleasure of parliament itself, rather than the head of government (Australia, Intelligence Services Act 2001)[24]

3 Government ministers are debarred from membership (and parliamentarians are required to step down if they are appointed as ministers) as this compromises the independence of the committee. The same applies to former members of agencies overseen (Australia, Intelligence Services Act 2001)[25]

4 The chairman is chosen by the parliament or by the committee itself, rather than appointed by the government (Argentina, 2001 National Intelligence Law 25520)[26]

5 If members of parliament undergo a clearing or vetting procedure and where clearance is consequently denied to Members of Parliament by the security and intelligence services, procedures are established to deal with disputes authoritatively, giving the final decision to the parliament or its presidium (Bosnia and Herzegovina, Law on Intelligence and Security Agencies 2004)[27]

6 Disputes concerning access to information and monitoring: The decisions of the [parliamentary intelligence oversight] Committee concerning what information it shall apply for access to and concerning the scope and extent of the monitoring shall be binding on the administration; Norway, Instructions issued pursuant to Act No. 7 on Monitoring of Intelligence, Surveillance and Security Services (1997)[28]

7 The [parliamentary intelligence oversight] committee makes annual reports to the Storting [parliament] about its activities. Such report may also be made available if factors are revealed that should be made known to the Storting immediately. Such reports and annexes shall be unclassified (Norway, Act No. 7 on Monitoring of Intelligence, Surveillance and Security Services 1997)[29]

8 The committee decides what information is made public concerning matters on which the committee has commented (Norway, Instructions issued pursuant to Act No. 7 on Monitoring of Intelligence, Surveillance and Security Services 1997)[30]

9 The oversight body has access to all relevant budget documents, provided that safeguards are in place to avoid leaking of classified information (Germany, Act governing the Parliamentary Control of Intelligence Activities 1978)[31]

10 The US Congress designates the financial maximum limit for the intelligence agencies' budgets as well as the ceiling for the maximum amount of staff to be hired by the agencies in the upcoming fiscal year (United States, Intelligence Authorization Act for the Fiscal Year 2004)[32]

Figure 24.1 Best practice to ensure ownership over parliamentary intelligence oversight procedures.

Source: Born and Leigh 2005.

Figure 24.1 gives an overview of some of the accountability mechanisms which can lead to independent and effective oversight by parliament. The mechanisms 1 to 4 guarantee ownership by parliament over the appointment of the members and the chair of the parliamentary intelligence oversight committee. It is a safeguard against executive interference with the oversight process. That this is not self-evident illustrates the practice in the United Kingdom, where all members of the Intelligence and Security Committee, including the chair, are appointed by the Prime Minister rather than by members of parliament. The accountability mechanisms 5 and 6 of Figure 24.1 give parliament access to classified information and seem to be adequate procedures to keep classified information secret. Mechanism 7 and 8 contribute to the owner-ship of the parliamentary intelligence oversight committee over its reports to parliament and the wider public. It signifies that parliament is sovereign in how it wants to render account to the public. Mechanisms 9 and 10 give parliament a substantive role in overseeing and approving the intelligence budget. It is precisely because taxpayers' money is involved that budget control over government spending is at the heart of parliamentary control in general, and intelligence agencies are not exempt from this.

If it is not to be merely a veneer of democratic legitimacy, and to be effective truly, parlia-mentary intelligence oversight stands and falls with the pro-active, non-glamorous routine work that its members must engage in. Yet the parliamentarians' devotion to oversight tasks is often difficult to maintain – parliamentarians cannot speak openly to their constituencies on these matters, yet openness is important to attract people's votes so as to stay in office. A related danger shall be briefly alluded to, i.e. the danger that the intelligence services are drawn into political controversy. This can be the result of an immature approach by parliamentarians that allows unsubstantiated accusations and conspiracy theories being introduced into the public realm.[33] Should an intelligence oversight committee take on a sensationalist approach, this general public is likely to form an inaccurate picture and may discourage intelligence officials and executives from being benign supporters of the parliament's important oversight task. This can be avoided by introducing precautionary measures such as promoting only experienced parliamentarians to intelligence oversight committees and by extending regulations for the handling of documents to the committees' secretariat.[34]

Embedded human rights in intelligence affairs

Some activities that intelligence services engage in can be gravely at odds with fundamental human rights. Depending on whether the remit of intelligence agencies includes the direct countering or disruption of threats to security, some activities risk the violation of non-derogable human rights[35] whilst others risk the violation of human rights permissible only in exceptional circumstances.[36]

In this section, we refer to *embedded human rights* in respect of the internal organization of national intelligence structures. Ideally, it ought to be designed in such a way as to function as the first firewall against potential human rights abuses. To implement such a firewall requires adequate whistleblower protection, ample internal complaints mechanisms as well as the regular training of intelligence staffers to a codified code of intelligence ethics.[37]

Such purposeful design of internal intelligence control relates to the entire forum of intelligence activity – yet for the purposes of this chapter we focus on two hard cases: the authorization of special powers and the international cooperation of national intelligence services.

With regard to the former, special powers come into play with direct surveillance missions, body and house searches, the monitoring of conversations and the use of special interrogation techniques. To ensure human rights protection it is vitally important that the use of special powers is based on the law and in proportion to the security threat. Specific legal authority is necessary and for this the pertinent legislation should be clear as to the grounds for using special powers, the persons who may be targeted, the exact means that may be employed, and the period for which they may be used. Hence, if the law covers only some of the available techniques of information-gathering there will be an in-built temptation for an agency to resort to less regulated methods. The regulatory system that foresees the granting of special powers must also provide for the possibility of challenging the use of special powers before a court. The accountability mechanisms in Figure 24.2 (points 1 to 3) refer to the legal basis and the supervision as well as the proportionate use of the special powers, based on examples from the Netherlands, the UK and Germany. Concerning supervision of the use of special powers, in many countries this is done by a person outside the agency, e.g. a judge (in Bosnia and Herzegovina and Canada), a court (in the Netherlands and the US) or a minister (in the UK). In Germany, a minister approves the use of special powers, who reports them to the parliamentary intelligence oversight committee.[38] To provide an additional safeguard against abuse, the person who supervises the use of special powers must not be part of the same branch of government that prioritizes the services. This is in keeping with the balance of powers doctrine, whereby each of the three functions of government (legislation, execution and adjudication) is entrusted to a separate branch of government (legislature, executive and the judiciary, respectively). Its purpose is to fragment power in such a way as to defend liberty and keep tyranny at bay. Therefore, the first two examples are preferable to the later two examples.

Given the growth international cooperation among national intelligence services, one needs to caution against the risks that such activities may entail for basic human rights protection. How can the danger be averted that national intelligence policy-makers utilize cooperative arrangements to circumvent national human rights standards, for instance, those that govern the legality of practices applied to obtain information on suspected terrorists? Tentative solutions to this problem can be offered by extending the provisions that regulate the domestic conduct of intelligence services to the countries with which national intelligence services cooperate. For instance, the direct or indirect usage of information obtained as a result of torture ought to be outlawed and adherence to this principle regularly monitored. Thus, to install a system of embedded human rights protection that extends to such practices, cooperation with foreign agencies should only take place in accordance with arrangements approved by democratically accountable politicians. What is more, when information is received from a foreign or international agency, it should be held subject both to the controls applicable in the country of origin and those standards which apply under domestic law. Hence, information should only be disclosed to foreign security and intelligence agencies or to an international agency if they undertake to hold and use it subject to the same controls that apply in domestic law to the agency which is disclosing it (e.g. in Germany, see Figure 24.2, point 4). Furthermore, international cooperation could also place a duty on national intelligence services to cooperate with an international tribunal (e.g. Bosnia Herzegovina, see Figure 24.2, point five).

Admittedly, these and other requirements are demanding obligations for the services to fulfill without hampering their important contributions to a nation's security. Yet "embedded human rights" protection is also advantageous for the services as it avoids rendering the intelligence services toothless in the face of overwhelming international human rights obligations. This is because obligations arising from human rights standards can be said to have a much less distracting effect on the work of the services if they have been integrated into the design of an intelligence system. In this way the individual intelligence agent is much more familiar with the range of permissible action and can therefore make more efficient use of resources and tools available to him or her. Having said this, the adherence to a specific catalogue of intelligence norms also increases the professionalism and integrity of the services as well as its reputation among the general populace. A noteworthy initiative has been launched by the Council of Europe (CoE) which has adopted a European Code of Police Ethics based on the conviction that "public confidence in the police is closely related to their attitude and behavior towards the public, in particular their respect for human dignity and fundamental rights and freedoms of the individual".[39] Similar to this initiative, some countries have devised a professional code of intelligence ethics and have written this into their national intelligence laws (e.g. in South Africa, see Figure 24.2, point 8).

It is common practice for many professional groups where high risks and interests are at stake to turn to the creation of behavioral rules deemed necessary to perform the respective jobs in a just and morally satisfactory manner. Once such a code of intelligence ethics has been devised, it is equally important to offer regular training courses on intelligence ethics for intelligence staffers (e.g. in the US, see Figure 24.2, point 9). This is a useful way of setting, communicating

---

1 Special powers that the security or intelligence services possess are grounded in legislation (The Netherlands, Intelligence and Security Services Act 2002)[40]

2 In order to safeguard against arbitrary use of special powers and violations of human rights, the agency's actions are subject to appropriate supervision and review (Germany, Federal Constitution Protection Law 1990)[41]

3 International cooperation is authorized by ministers and subjected to safeguards to ensure compliance with domestic law and international legal obligations (Germany, Federal Constitution Protection Law 1990)[42]

4 The [Bosnian Intelligence] Agency shall cooperate with the International Criminal Court for the Former Yugoslavia, inter alia, by providing information to the Tribunal concerning persons responsible for serious violations of international humanitarian law in the territory of the former Yugoslavia since 1991 (Bosnia and Herzegovina, Law on the Intelligence and Security Agency, 2004)[43]

5 Professional staff should refuse compliance with orders which would imply committing a criminal offence. Any criminal offence shall be reported to the Director General, who will forward the report immediately to the Minister and the [Parliamentary National Security] Committee (Hungary, Act CXXV on the National Security Services 1995)[44]

6 In deciding whether the public interest in the disclosure outweighs the public interest in non-disclosure, a judge or court must consider: (a) whether the extent of the disclosure is no more than is reasonably necessary to disclose the alleged offence or prevent the commission or continuation of the alleged offence, as the case may be; (b) the seriousness of the alleged offence; (c) whether the person resorted to other reasonably accessible alternatives before making the disclosure and, in doing so, whether the person complied with any relevant guidelines, policies or laws that applied to the person; (d) whether the person had reasonable grounds to believe that the disclosure would be in the public interest; (e) the public interest intended to be served by the disclosure; (f) the extent of the harm or risk of harm created by disclosure; and (g) the existence of exigent circumstances justifying the disclosure (Canada, Security of Information Act 1985)[45]

7 It is the responsibility of the Director-General to issue a code of ethics which includes the consideration of the ethical boundaries to intelligence work (Bosnia and Herzegovina, Law on the Intelligence and Security Agency 2004)[46]

8 Intelligence Services staff are trained to a code of conduct which includes consideration of the ethical boundaries to their work. This training is kept up to date and available to staff throughout their tenure (South Africa, White Paper on Intelligence)[47]

9 Internal administrative policies are formalized with a clear legal status (Bosnia and Herzegovina, Law on the Intelligence and Security Agency (2004)[48]

Figure 24.2 Best practice aimed at creating "embedded human rights."
Source: Based on Born and Leigh 2005.

and maintaining a minimum level of shared practices among intelligence employees. The adherence to a professional ethos makes a valuable contribution to the internal administration of intelligence services. It ensures that discretionary decisions are taken in a structured and consistent fashion across the intelligence agency.

The political neutrality of intelligence services

The involvement, if not the outright politicization, of intelligence services before and during the war in Iraq in 2003 has rightly received much critical attention. In order to protect the services from being politically manipulated on the one hand, and in order to render the work of intelligence services more acceptable to national citizens on the other hand, some national intelligence systems have made very significant efforts to promote the professionalism and the political neutrality of the intelligence services. Indeed, this requires the acknowledgment of the inherent right of the services to fully brief government ministers on matters of extreme sensitivity. It is important that ministers have an open-door policy towards the agencies. In the same vein, the minister directing the intelligence services should be legally responsible for the formulation of a coherent policy on security and intelligence matters and the services have the corresponding duty to implement governmental policy. This entails a duty by the services to report to the ministers at regular intervals as well as to seek approval of sensitive matters (e.g. in Canada, see Figure 24.3, points 1 and 2).

To safeguard the political neutrality of the national intelligence services in various countries, their mandate is limited to such national security threats as are specifically accounted for in detail in the respective laws. Bosnia and Herzegovina's Law on the Intelligence and Security Agency provides a clear and comprehensive account of national security and threats to it (see Figure 24.3, point 3). A useful tool to ensure the political neutrality of the services is to include in the respective intelligence law institutional and legal safeguards to prevent the use of services by government officials against political opponents as well as to prevent them from exerting influence on the political institutions and media (e.g. in Argentina, see Figure 24.3, point 4).

Another means to ensure greater political neutrality of the services is the opening up to scrutiny of the process of appointing the agency head. Within the executive it would be preferable to have more than one cabinet member involved in the appointment process (e.g. in Hungary, see Figure 24.3, point 8). Outside the executive, legislation should regulate how to seek parliamentary approval for appointment proposals or how parliament can block the appointment by a formal vote. Of course constitutional traditions and political cultures have produced different practices in this regard, yet the underlying objective ought to be attainable in all intelligence systems. Additional measures such as the requirement that opposition in parliament should be involved in appointing the director of intelligence services and that the relevant legislation should contain safeguards against improper pressure being applied on the director can further ensure the political neutrality of the services (e.g. in Australia, see Figure 24.2, point 7). We have also found practices that were detrimental to the political neutrality of the services. For example, in the US, President Bush appointed in 2004 Porter Goss, member of Congress of his own Republican party, as Director of the CIA. In France the prime minister allegedly politicized the military intelligence service in the so-called "Clearstream" corruption affair.[49]

In addition, many countries have established safeguards against ministerial abuse of the intelligence services. One example is Hungary's and Australia's intelligence legislation

1 Intelligence legislation contains two distinct rights of access: the right of the executive to relevant information in the hands of the agency and the right of the agency heads to have access to the respective minister (Canada, Security Intelligence Service Act 1984)[50]

2 The Minister is legally responsible for the formulation of policy on security and intelligence matters. He is also legally entitled to receive agency reports at regular intervals as well as being legally responsible for the approval of matters of political sensitivity (Canada, Security Intelligence Service Act 1984)[51]

3 Threats to security of Bosnia and Herzegovina include terrorism, espionage, sabotage, organised crime, drugs, arms and human trafficking, illegal proliferation of weapons of mass destruction, illegal trafficking of internationally controlled products and technologies as well as acts punishable under international humanitarian law and acts of violence or intimidation against ethnic or religious groups in Bosnia Herzegovina (Bosnia and Herzegovina, Law on Intelligence and Security Agency 2004)[52]

4 No agency shall perform repressive activities, collect information on individuals because of their race, religion or due to their membership in partisan social, union, community or cooperative organisations; no intelligence agency shall exert influence over the institutional, political, military, police, social and economic situation of the country and the existence of legally formed political parties (Argentina, National Intelligence Law 2001)[53]

5 Legislation establishes the process for the appointment of the Director of a security or intelligence agency and any minimum qualifications or any factors which are disqualifications from office (Poland, Internal Security Agency and Foreign Policy Act 2002)[54]

6 The appointment is open to scrutiny outside the executive, e.g. in parliament (Australia, Intelligence Service Act 2001)[55]

7 The opposition in parliament is involved in appointing the Director of a security and intelligence agency (Australia, Intelligence Service Act 2001)[56]

8 More than one cabinet member is involved in the process of appointing a Director, e.g. the head of state/prime minister and the relevant cabinet minister (Hungary, Act on the National Security Services 1995)[57]

9 The minister shall determine in writing the topical tasks of the services for directors general semi-annually; [the minister] shall give orders in writing for meeting the information received from the members of the Government (Hungary, Act on the National Security Services 1995)[58]

10 As soon as practicable after the commencing day, the Minister must give to the Inspector-General a single copy of each direction or Guideline (Australia, Inspector-General of Intelligence and Security Act 1986)[59]

Figure 24.3 Best practice to ensure the political neutrality of the services.
Source: Born and Leigh 2005.

inasmuch as it stipulates that all directions and guidelines by the ministers to the agency should be in writing (see Figure 24.3, point 9), and copied to the Inspector-General (see Figure 24.3, point 10). Moreover, members of the executive should be required to brief the leader of the opposition, as a bipartisan approach to security and intelligence is more likely to be maintained if leading politicians of the opposition do not feel that they have been wholly excluded from the "ring of secrecy" (see Figure 24.3, point 7).

Conclusion

The development of national intelligence control systems is a relatively recent phenomenon. In many democracies intelligence control has long been considered an executive prerogative, as demonstrated by the fact that early intelligence control mechanisms were based on decrees instead of laws enacted by parliament. In the United Kingdom, intelligence services operated on executive decrees until the end of the 1980s, whereas French intelligence services are to this day not based on an act of parliament. Although the deepening and widening of democratic oversight of intelligence services has generally much progressed in recent decades, one can also point to new challenges and different levels of precision and aptitude in national oversight laws.

There could scarcely be a more appropriate time to address new challenges to the oversight of intelligence services. In the wake of 9/11 and the now re-named "long war" against terror, national parliaments, governments (*inter alia* in the US, the UK, Germany, the Netherlands, and Canada) as well as the parliamentary assemblies of regional international organizations (e.g. the European Parliament and the Council of Europe) have started to investigate the functioning of intelligence services and the use of intelligence by national governments. Other countries, such as France, have launched legislative initiatives to strengthen parliament's role in national intelligence control.

Drawing on research into national oversight legislation in liberal democracies, this chapter highlights intelligence accountability mechanisms that address well the challenges for the contemporary control of intelligence. We have confined our analysis to aspects that touch on (1) parliamentary ownership, (2) embedded human rights protection, and (3) political neutrality of the services.

Bearing in mind that most intelligence oversight systems are relatively young, the underlying question is to what extent they are strong enough to confront the new challenges in the current war against terror. Among the most prominent challenges are the higher level of international intelligence cooperation and the danger of politicization of the services. Concerning the former, the increase in bilateral and multilateral cooperation between the services begs the question whether national oversight systems have sufficient statutory powers and the capacity to oversee international cooperation activities. A second challenge is the danger of politicization of the services, i.e. the use of intelligence services for personal or political party purposes, something that is common in both new and old democracies. Interestingly, the danger of politicization of the intelligence services can be regarded as a downside of the increasing democratization of intelligence oversight. On the one hand, introduction of more transparency and public accountability leads to a better system of checks and balances on the services. On the other hand, the services and their activities are becoming part of the normal political debate, which leads to the danger that the actors in that political debate will use the services and their work for their own benefit.

Notes

1 Philip Knightley, *The Second Oldest Profession: Spies and Spying in the 20th Century* (New York: W.W. Norton, 1988).
2 Peter Gill, "The Politicization of Intelligence: Lessons from the Invasion of Iraq", in: Hans Born, Loch K. Johnson and Ian Leigh (eds), *Who's Watching the Spies? Establishing Intelligence Service Accountability* (Washington, DC: Potomac Books, 2005).
3 Peter Gill, op. cit., p. 20. L. Britt Snider puts it somewhat more mildly: "The intelligence judgments that had ostensibly prompted President Bush to wage war on Iraq . . . which Bush in turn had used to

persuade Congress and the American public to support the war, turned out to be wrong." L. Britt Snider, "Congressional Oversight of Intelligence after September 11", in: Jennifer E. Sims and Burton Gerber (eds.), *Transforming U.S. Intelligence* (Washington, DC: Georgetown University Press, 2005), p. 242.

4 For further insights into the aspect of intelligence politicization, see: Joseph Cirincione et al., *WMD in Iraq: Evidence and Implications* (Washington, DC: Carnegie Endowment for International Peace, 2004); Seymour M. Hersh, "The Stovepipe: How Conflicts between the Bush Administration and the Intelligence Community Marred the Reporting on Iraq's weapons", *The New Yorker*, 27 October 2003; Harry Howe Ransom, "The Politicization of Intelligence", in: Stephen J. Cimbala (ed.), *Intelligence and Intelligence Policy in a Democratic Society* (Dobbs Ferry, NY: Transnational Press, 1987).

5 *Le Monde*, "L'Elysée accuse les services secrets d'avoir enquêté sur M. Chirac sous le gouvernement de M. Jospin", 22 June 2002.

6 Hans Born and Ian Leigh, *Making Intelligence Accountable: Legal Standards and Best Practices for Oversight of Intelligence Services* (Oslo: Publishing House of the Norwegian Parliament, 2005), p. 68.

7 Bundestag, Drucksache 16/990.

8 "Secretary General's report under Article 52 ECHR on the question of secret detention and transport of detainees suspected of terrorist acts, notably by or at the instigation of foreign agencies", Council of Europe, SG/Inf (2006) 5, Strasbourg, 28 February 2006, point 101. Available at <http://www.coe.int/T/E/Com/Files/Events/2006-cia/>. The European Parliament has established a temporary committee on the alleged use of European countries by the CIA for the transport and illegal detention of prisoners. The committee's first draft interim report was released on 24 April 2006 and is available online at: <http://www.europarl.eu.int/comparl/tempcom/tdip/interim_report_en.pdf>.

9 In a previous publication we accounted in greater detail for challenges with respect to the internal control at the level of the agency, executive control, parliamentary oversight and oversight by independent oversight bodies. See Hans Born and Ian Leigh, op. cit.

10 We mention recommended accountability mechanisms from intelligence legislation in North and South America, Europe, Africa and Asia and Oceania. Our sample includes "new" (Poland, Hungary) and "old" (United Kingdom, The Netherlands) as well as examples from different constitutional models (US, Germany, the United Kingdom, respectively).

11 With the notable exception of France and Turkey, which have yet to fully incorporate parliamentary intelligence oversight into domestic practice. On the French experience with intelligence governance, see Hans Born and Thorsten Wetzling "Checks and Imbalances? Intelligence Governance in contemporary France" in: Hans Born and Marina Caparini (eds), *Democratic Control of Intelligence Services* (London: Ashgate Publishing, forthcoming). At last (in 2006), France seems ready to remedy this democratic deficit: Prime Minister de Villepin has introduced a "projet de loi" to the National Assembly which pertains to creating the country's first parliamentary intelligence oversight committee. Assemblée Nationale, Projet de loi No. 2941, 08 March 2006.

12 Ben Hayes, "There is no Balance between Security and Civil Liberties – Just Less of Both", *Essays for Civil Liberties and Democracy in Europe*, Number 12. Available online at: http://www.statewatch.org/news/2005/oct/ecln/essay-12.pdf.

13 Modern intelligence agencies serving democratic nations are providing an important service to their people by identifying and assessing new security threats. What is more, they are not comparable – neither with respect to the means nor with respect to the command structure – to the likes of the Gestapo or the KPG.

14 Loch K. Johnson "Governing in the Absence of Angels: On the Practice of Intelligence Accountability in the United States", in Hans Born, Ian Leigh and Loch K. Johnson (eds), op. cit., p. 102.

15 Ibid.

16 In this regard, one can also point to the connections between different layers: deficiencies at one level can affect other levels. For instance, parliamentarians can effectively scrutinize the performance of ministers only if the parliament possesses sufficient powers to control the executive, including spending and investigative authorities.

17 Andrzej Zybertowicz, "An Unresolved Game. The Role of the Intelligence Services in the Nascent Polish Democracy", in: Hans Born, Loch K. Johnson and Ian Leigh (eds), A similar observation with respect to German practice in intelligence oversight is documented in a recent article in the German weekly, *Die Zeit*. The author cites insufficient cooperation from the Bundesnachrichtendienst as the main cause of a series of resignations of parliamentary overseers from office. Martin Klingst, "*Der Frust der Kontrolleure*", in: Die Zeit, Nr. 4/2006, p. 3.

18 Stuart Farson, "Canada's Long Road from Model Law to Effective Oversight", in: Hans Born, Loch K. Johnson and Ian Leigh (eds), op. cit., p. 115.

19 Fredrik Sejersted "Intelligence and Accountability in a State without Enemies: The Case of Norway", in: Hans Born, Loch K. Johnson and Ian Leigh (eds), op. cit., p. 127.

20 Loch K. Johnson, op. cit., pp. 57–78. L. Britt Snider further criticizes the fact that bipartisanship in congressional intelligence oversight in the US has strongly increased in the aftermath of September 11. "One could only marvel at the degree to which partisanship had come to infect the work of the two committees. Once held up as models of how congressional committees should work, they now seemed no different from the rest", L. Britt Snider, op. cit., p. 245.

21 Though The Netherlands and Germany started earlier with parliamentary oversight of the services, i.e. 1953 and 1956 respectively.

22 A comprehensive overview of the reluctance of American legislators to adopt a pro-active stance towards the pursuit of intelligence oversight mandates is *inter alia* provided by Loch Johnson (Johnson 2005, 2005a).

23 See § 4 PKGrG.

24 See Section 15(1).

25 See Section 14(6).

26 See Title VIII and the Committees Internal Rules of Procedure.

27 See Art. 18.

28 Section 6.

29 Section 8.2.

30 Section 12.

31 See Section 2e (2).

32 See Section 102.

33 In this regard, one can point to L. Britt Snider's convincing account of the increasing partisanship between members of the two US oversight committees and its impact on the quality of intelligence control in the aftermath of 9/11. Brit L. Snider, op. cit.

34 See Section 9 of the Norwegian Act relating to the Monitoring of Intelligence, Surveillance and Security Services of 1995.

35 Recent allegations on secret detention, unlawful interrogation practices and rendition of suspected terrorists raise numerous questions on their compatibility with the right to life and the right not to be subjected to torture or to cruel, inhuman or degrading treatment or punishment. These basic entitlements amount to fundamental human rights established *inter alia* by the International Covenant on Civil and Political Rights (ICCPR), adopted by the UN General Assembly in 1966 and which entered into force in 1976.

36 For our purposes, the focus turns to surveillance and data-filing practices which are often incompatible with the right to private and family life (Art. 8.1, European Convention on Human Rights (ECHR)). Public authorities may in exceptional circumstances interfere with this right providing such intervention is "in accordance with the law and is necessary in a democratic society in the interests of national security" (Art. 8.2 ECHR). For a comprehensive analysis, see Iain Cameron, *National Security and the European Convention on Human Rights* (Uppsala/Dordrecht: Iustus/Kluwer, 2000).

37 An example would be the UN Code of Conduct on Law Enforcement, UN General Assembly Resolution 34/169.

38 Born and Leigh, *Making Intelligence Accountable*, op. cit., p. 42.

39 The Council of Europe, 2001, *The European Code of Police Ethics*, Recommendation (2001) 10.

40 See Arts 47 and 51.

41 See § 9(3)2.

42 See Art. 19(3).

43 See Art. 6.

44 See Section 27.

45 See Section 15(4).

46 See Art. 27(a).

47 See Annex A.

48 See Art. 27.

49 "France speculates on PM's future", *BBC News*, 30 April 2006.

50 See Section 6.

51 Ibid.

52 See Art. 5.
53 See Art. 4.
54 See Art. 16.
55 See Part 3, Section 17(3).
56 See ibid.
57 See Section 11.2.
58 See Section 11.
59 See Section 32B(2).

25

Intelligence and the rise of judicial intervention

Fred F. Manget

Perhaps the best way to give you a conception of our power and emplacement here is to note the state and national laws that we are ready to bend, break, violate, and/or ignore. False information is given out routinely on Florida papers of incorporation; tax returns fudge the real source of invest-ment in our proprietaries; false flight plans are filed daily with the FAA; and we truck weapons and explosives over Florida highways, thereby violating the Munitions Act and the Firearms Act, not to speak of what we do to our friends Customs, Immigration, Treasury, and the Neutrality Act . . . As I write, I can feel your outrage. It is not that they are doing all that – perhaps it is necessary, you will say – but why . . . are you all this excited about it?

(Norman Mailer, *Harlot's Ghost*)

Introduction

If only it were such an exercise in glorious outlawry as all that! It is widely believed that the intelligence agencies of the US government are not subject to laws and the authority of judges to apply them. No television cop show, adventure movie, or conspiracy book in two decades has left out characters that are sinister intelligence officials beyond the reach of the law.

The reality, however, is that the federal judiciary now examines a wide range of intelligence activities under a number of laws, including the Constitution. In order to decide particular issues under the law, federal judges and their cleared clerks and other staff are shown material classified at the highest levels. There is no requirement that federal judges be granted security clearances – their access to classified information is an automatic aspect of their status. Their supporting staffs must be vetted, but court employees are usually granted all clearances necessary for them to effectively assist the judiciary in resolving legal issues before the courts.

Judges currently interpret the laws that affect national security to reach compromises necessary to reconcile the open world of American jurisprudence and the closed world of intelligence operations. They have now been doing it long enough to enable practitioners in the field to reach a number of conclusions. This chapter proposes that judicial review of issues touching on intelligence matters has developed into a system of oversight.

The term "oversight" describes a system of accountability in which those vested with the executive authority in an organization have their actions reviewed, sometimes in advance, by an independent group that has the power to check those actions. In corporations, the board of directors exercises oversight. In democratic governments, the classic model of oversight is that of the legislative branches, conducted through the use of committee subpoena powers and the authority to appropriate funds for the executive branches. Legislative oversight has very few limits, by contrast with the model of judicial oversight described here, which is significantly limited. Legislative oversight is policy-related, as opposed to judicial oversight, which is concerned with legal questions. Legislative oversight tends toward micromanagement of executive decisions, where judicial oversight is more deferential. But a rule of thumb for a simple country lawyer is that when you have to go and explain to someone important what you have been doing and why, that is oversight, regardless of its source. Today intelligence community lawyers often do just that. But it has not always been that way.

Until the mid-1970s, judges had very little to say about intelligence.[1] Since intelligence activities are almost always related to foreign affairs, skittish judges avoided jurisdiction over most intelligence controversies under the political question doctrine, which allocates the resolution of national security disputes to the two political branches of the government, not the judiciary.[2] This doctrine was buttressed by the need to have a concrete case or controversy before judges, rather than an abstract foreign policy debate, because of the limited jurisdiction of federal courts.[3] Justice Scalia (as a federal appellate court judge) further developed the doctrine, opining that courts should exercise considerable restraint in granting any petitions for equitable relief in foreign affairs controversies.[4]

In addition, American intelligence organizations historically have had limited internal security functions, if any. Prior to the creation of the CIA, the military departments conducted most intelligence activities.[5] In 1947, the National Security Act expressly declined to give the CIA any law enforcement authority: ". . . the Agency shall have no police, subpoena, or law enforcement powers or internal security functions;" a prohibition that exists in the same form today.[6] Without the immediate and direct impact that police activity has on citizens, there were few instances where intelligence activities became issues in federal cases.

There is even an argument that to the extent that intelligence activities are concerned with the security of the state, they are inherent to any sovereign's authority under a higher law of self-preservation and not subject to normal judicial review. Justice Sutherland found powers inherent in sovereignty to be extra-constitutional in the 1936 *Curtiss-Wright* case.[7] Even that good democrat Thomas Jefferson wrote:

> A strict observance of the written laws is doubtless *one* of the high duties of a good citizen, but it is not *the highest* [emphasis in original]. The laws of necessity, of self-preservation, of saving our country, by a scrupulous adherence to written law, would be to lose the law itself, with life, liberty, property and all those who are enjoying them with us: thus absurdly sacrificing the end to the means. . . .[8]

The debate continues today over the President's constitutional ability to authorize the National Security Agency to intercept international communications into and out of the US of persons linked to certain terrorist organizations without using procedures established by the Foreign Intelligence Surveillance Act (FISA).[9]

This sense that somehow secret intelligence activities were governed by a higher law of self-preservation no doubt added to the federal judiciary's reluctance to exert its limited jurisdiction in such areas.

In the 1970s this reluctance began to dwindle, driven by a number of causes. After the Watergate Affair, the activities of the executive branch came under a growing and skeptical

above the law

scrutiny by the press, the public, and Congress. This scrutiny blossomed into the Church and Pike Committee investigations of the CIA, as well as the Rockefeller Commission report on CIA activities.[10] The federal judiciary was following right behind, in part due to a natural extension of the judicial activism that began in the 1960s. The expansion of due process rights of criminal defendants meant that judges would examine in ever-increasing detail the actions of the government in prosecutions.[11] The American tendency to treat international problems as subject to cure by legal process became even more pronounced, and the intelligence community found itself increasingly involved in the counterterrorism, counternarcotics, and non-proliferation activities of the law enforcement agencies of the US government.[12]

The other cause was simply the increasing number of statutes that Congress passed dealing with the Agency and the intelligence community. The more statutes there are on a particular subject, the more judicial review of the subject there will be. For example, in the late 1970s, Congress began to pass annual authorization bills for the intelligence community that generally contained permanent statutory provisions, a practice that continues today.[13]

Congressional inroads on all types of executive branch foreign affairs powers also increased in the 1970s. The constitutional foreign affairs powers shared by the executive and legislative branches wax and wane, but it seems clear that Congress began to reassert its role in international relations at that time. The War Powers Resolution and the series of Boland Amendments restricting aid to the Nicaraguan Contras in the 1980s were statutory attempts by Congress to force policy positions on a reluctant executive branch. The Hughes-Ryan Amendment required notification of oversight committees about covert actions.[14] When Congress passes laws to prevail in disagreements in foreign affairs, more judicial review will occur. De Tocqueville was right — all disputes in the US inevitably end up in court.

The result is the current system of judicial oversight of intelligence. By 1980, then-Attorney General Benjamin Civiletti could write that, "Although there may continue to be some confusion about how the law applies to a particular matter, there is no longer any doubt that intelligence activities are subject to definable legal standards."[16] It is not nearly so comprehensive as legislative oversight, because federal courts still have jurisdiction limited by statute and the Constitution. But it does exist in effective and powerful ways that go far beyond the conventional wisdom that national security is a cloak hiding intelligence activities from the federal judiciary.

Criminal law

Federal judges are required to examine the conduct of the government when it becomes a litigated issue in a criminal prosecution, and almost every case involves at least one such issue. Intelligence activities are no exception. What makes those activities so different is that they almost always require secrecy to be effective and to maintain their value to US policy-makers. The need for secrecy clashes directly with conventional trial procedures in which most of the efforts on both sides of a case go into developing the pre-trial phase called "discovery." As a result, federal judges review and decide a number of issues that regularly arise in areas where democratic societies would instinctively say that governmental secrecy creates problems. The pattern has developed that judges review intelligence information when protection of its secrecy could affect traditional notions of a fair trial.

For example, it would be manifestly unfair if the government could, without sanctions, withhold secret intelligence information from defendants that would otherwise be disclosed under rules of criminal procedure. In fact, under both Federal Rule of Criminal Procedure 16 relating to discovery and the decisions in the *Brady* and *Giglio* cases, federal prosecutors are required to turn over certain materials to the defense regardless of their secrecy.[17] For a number of years, judges fashioned their own procedures to balance competing interests. In the *Kampiles* case, the defendant was charged with selling to the Russians a manual about the operation of the KH-11 spy satellite. The trial court did not allow classified information to be introduced at trial. The court issued a protective order after closed proceedings in which the government presented evidence of the sensitive document that was passed to the Soviet Union, and of the FBI's counterintelligence investigation into the document's disappearance. The court of appeals upheld the espionage conviction based upon the defendant's confession that he had met with and sold a classified document to a Soviet intelligence officer and upon sufficient other evidence to corroborate the reliability of the defendant's confession.[18]

Classified Information Procedures Act

The Classified Information Procedures Act (CIPA) was passed in 1980 to avoid *ad hoc* treatment of the issues and to establish detailed procedures for handling such classified information in criminal trials.[19] It was a response to the problem of "greymail," in which defendants threatened to reveal classified information unless prosecutions were dropped or curtailed. Prior to passage of CIPA, the government had to guess the extent of possible damage from such disclosures, because there were no methods by which classified information could be evaluated in advance of public discovery and evidentiary rulings by the courts. Under CIPA, classified information can be reviewed under the regular criminal procedures for discovery and admissibility of evidence before the information is publicly disclosed. Judges are allowed to determine issues presented to them both *in camera* (meaning non-publicly, in chambers) and *ex parte* (meaning presented by one side alone without the presence of the other party).[20]

Under CIPA, the defendant is allowed to discover classified information and to offer it in evidence to the extent it is necessary to a fair trial and allowed by normal criminal procedures. The government is allowed to minimize the classified information at risk of public disclosure by offering unclassified summaries or substitutions for the sensitive materials. Judges are called upon to balance the need of the government to protect intelligence information and the rights of a defendant to a fair trial.[21] This is an area in which democratic societies would want judicial scrutiny of governmental assertions of national security equities, in order to preserve constitutional due process guarantees. Prosecutions are in fact dropped or severely curtailed after judicial review of information under CIPA because the defendant cannot get a fair trial without publicly revealing information damaging to US intelligence efforts.[22]

Surveillance

Judges also scrutinize intelligence activities involving surveillance. Because of the Fourth Amendment guarantee against unreasonable searches and seizures, intelligence collection is also reviewed under standards applied to search warrants. The federal judiciary has been reviewing surveillance in the context of suppression of evidence hearings for many years. For example, the issue of electronic surveillance was considered in 1928 in the Supreme Court case of *Olmstead*, which held that the government could conduct such surveillance without a criminal search warrant.[23] In 1967 the Supreme Court overturned *Olmstead*,[24] and the government began to follow specially tailored search warrant procedures for electronic procedures.[25]

FISA

In 1978, the Foreign Intelligence Surveillance Act (FISA) was passed to establish a secure forum in which the government could obtain what is essentially a search warrant to conduct electronic surveillance within the United States of persons who are agents of foreign powers. The FISA requires that applications for such orders approving electronic surveillance include detailed information about the targets, and the means of conducting the surveillance. Applications are heard and either denied or granted by a special court composed of federal district court judges designated by the Chief Justice of the United States. There is a three-member court of review to hear appeals of denials of applications.[26]

Thus judges conduct extensive review of foreign intelligence-related electronic surveillance operations prior to their inception. Intrusive collection techniques make this area especially sensitive, and their review by federal judges is very important in reconciling them with Fourth Amendment protections against unreasonable searches. For example, in the espionage prosecution of Aldrich and Rosario Ames, published accounts of the investigation revealed that a search of Ames's house was made by FBI agents without a search warrant, based upon the authority of the Attorney General to approve physical searches in foreign counterintelligence investigations.[27] If Ames and his wife had not pled guilty, it is highly likely that the search would have been fully litigated in light of *United States v. Truong*, an espionage prosecution brought in the same federal district some twenty years earlier. In *Truong*, the FBI had tapped conversations of a State Department employee who was furnishing classified information to the North Vietnamese. The trial court heard arguments from both sides and held that when an investigation's primary purpose becomes prosecution (rather than counterintelligence), a criminal search warrant then becomes required for further intrusive electronic surveillance.[28]

This primary purpose test was used for a number of years by the Department of Justice in reviewing FISA surveillance and maintaining a so-called "wall" between national security and counterintelligence activities and law enforcement activities. In May of 2002, the FISA Court issued an opinion imposing certain requirements and limitations accompanying an order authorizing electronic surveillance of a particular "agent of a foreign power" as defined in FISA. Those restrictions imposed a level of separation between intelligence and law enforcement activities that was unacceptable to the US government, which appealed the order to the Foreign Intelligence Surveillance Court of Review for the first time since passage of FISA. The Court of Review extensively examined the law and practice of FISA surveillance, and issued a detailed opinion dismantling the wall as something not required by FISA or the Constitution.[29] The Court of Review heard from the American Civil Liberties Union, the Center for Democracy and Technology, and the National Association of Criminal Defense Lawyers, among others, who all filed friend-of-the-court briefs. The opinion (which included some deleted pages containing classified information) demonstrated without any doubt that a significant number of government attorneys did a large amount of explaining to federal judges what their clients were doing. That is full-fledged judicial review of the government's actions under federal statutes and the Fourth Amendment.

Explaining continues. In January 2006, the Department of Justice held a classified briefing for a number of FISA Court judges in response to concerns about the President's authorization for the National Security Agency to conduct electronic surveillance in certain counterterrorism operations without FISA Court approval. The *New York Times* noted with probable understatement that, "At Monday's briefing, judges were expected to question Justice Department officials intensely about the legal underpinnings of the program, . . .".[30]

Armed conflict

After the 9/11 attacks on the United States, the ensuing global war on terrorism became a fertile ground for legal issues. On the one hand, unfettered and rapid action by the executive branch became essential to prevention of further terrorist attacks. On the other hand, the federal judiciary was asked to decide what are the legal boundaries to such executive action. As terrorists were captured on battlefields and in foreign venues around the world, federal courts stepped into the fray. Interrogation of captured combatants is a highly important intelligence method, especially when directed towards future threats of armed attack. The treatment of individuals incarcerated by the US government is a highly important aspect of constitutional due process rights. Federal courts are in the middle of addressing the issues that occur when these two principles meet.

In the *Hamdi* case,[31] the Supreme Court was asked to consider the legality of the government's detention of an American citizen on American soil as an enemy combatant and to address the process that the Constitution requires for challenging that status. The federal Appeals Court held that Hamdi's detention was legally authorized and that he was entitled to no further opportunity to challenge his enemy-combatant classification. The Supreme Court vacated the appeals decision and remanded the case, holding that while Hamdi could be detained, due process requires that a US citizen held in the United States as an enemy combatant be given a meaningful opportunity to contest the factual basis for that detention before a neutral decision-maker. That neutral decision maker would be a federal judge.

In a second case, *United States v. Moussaoui*, the defendant was charged with conspiracy related to the 9/11 attacks. The prosecutors and defense counsel fought a running discovery battle that resulted in the District Court issuing a series of rulings granting Moussaoui access to certain enemy combatant witnesses in US custody for the purpose of deposing them. When the rulings were challenged by the government on appeal, the Court of Appeals issued an opinion that stated, "We are presented with questions of grave significance – questions that test the commitment of this nation to an independent judiciary, to the constitutional guarantee of a fair trial even to one accused of the most heinous of crimes, and to the protection of our citizens against additional terrorist attacks. These questions do not admit of easy answers."[32] The appellate opinion went on to hold that enemy combatant witnesses who were foreign nationals in military custody outside the boundaries of the United States were not beyond the process power of federal district courts. It also held that ordering production of enemy combatant witnesses did not infringe on the Executive Branch's warmaking authority, in violation of separation of powers principles.

A third case involved Jose Padilla, an American citizen who was arrested as an enemy combatant upon returning to the United States from Pakistan and Afghanistan, where he allegedly was "recruited, trained, funded, and equipped by al Qaeda leaders to continue prosecution of the war in the United States by blowing up apartment buildings in this country."[33] The issue before the Appeals Court was whether the President possesses the authority to detain militarily an American citizen who was closely associated with a hostile terrorist group engaged in armed attacks against the United States and who traveled to the United States to further prosecute the armed conflict against American citizens and targets. The District Court said no, but the Appeals Court reversed and said yes, based upon information collected and provided by the government.

These and other terrorism cases continue to create issues that are currently being litigated.[34] One matter that seems to have been firmly decided, however, is that attorneys for the United

States will continue to explain to federal judges significant clandestine activities of the US intelligence and national security communities for many years to come.

Government authorization

In yet another area, judges review secret intelligence activities in the context of whether defendants were authorized by an intelligence agency to do the very actions on which the criminal charges are based. Under the rules of criminal procedure, defendants are required to notify the government if they intend to raise a defense of government authorization.[35] The government is required to respond to such assertions, either admitting or denying them. Should there be any merit to the defense, the defendant is allowed to put on evidence and to have the judge decide issues that arise in litigating the defense. This satisfies the notion that it would be unfair to defendants who could have been authorized to carry out some clandestine activity if they could not bring such secret information before the court.

For example, in the case of *United States v. Rewald*, the defendant was convicted of numerous counts of bilking investors in a Ponzi scheme. Rewald vociferously maintained that the CIA had told him to extravagantly spend the money of investors in order to cultivate relationships with foreign potentates and wealthy businessmen who would be useful intelligence sources. The opinion of the Ninth Circuit Court of Appeals panel that reviewed the convictions characterized Rewald's argument as his principal defense in the case, and in fact Rewald did have some minor contact with local CIA personnel, volunteering information from his international business travels and providing light backstopping cover for a few CIA employees. Rewald sought the production of hundreds of classified CIA documents and propounded over 1,700 interrogatories, but after reviewing responsive records and answers the trial court excluded most of the classified information as simply not relevant under evidentiary standards.[36] The Ninth Circuit panel noted that, "This court has examined each and every classified document filed by Rewald in this appeal."[37] It subsequently upheld the District Court's exclusion of the classified information at issue.

The significance is not that the defendants lost their arguments, but that they had the opportunity to fully litigate them before a federal judge. The Department of Justice does not prosecute defendants while the intelligence community denies them the information they need to have a fair trial. Who decides what a fair trial requires? An independent federal judge, appointed for life, who reviews the secrets. Judges generally defer to intelligence experts on intelligence judgments – e.g. whether information is classified. But the question of what a fair trial may require belongs to the judge alone.

Civil law

Although criminal law has the most direct and dramatic impact on individual citizens, civil law also requires judicial intervention in numerous cases where intelligence activities, and the secrecy surrounding them, become issues. Private civil litigants may demand that the government produce intelligence information under the laws requiring disclosure of Agency records unless they are specifically exempted. Individual civil plaintiffs may bring tort actions against the government under the Federal Tort Claims Act based on allegations that secret intelligence activities caused compensable damages. Private litigants may sue each other for any of the myriad civil causes of action that exist in litigious America, and demand from the government information relating to intelligence activities in order to support their cases. In all those instances, federal judges act as the arbiters of government assertions of special equities relating to intelligence that affect the litigation. Private civil litigants may not win their arguments that such equities should be discounted in their favor, but they can make their arguments to a federal judge.

FOIA

For example, under the Freedom of Information Act (FOIA)[38] and the Privacy Act,[39] there are exceptions to the mandatory disclosure provisions that allow classified information and intelligence sources and methods to be kept secret. Courts defer extensively to the executive branch on what information falls within those exceptions,[40] but there is still a rigorous review of such material. The CIA prepares public indexes (called "*Vaughn* indexes" after the case endorsing them[41]) describing records withheld under the sensitive information exceptions that are reviewed by the courts. If those public indexes are not sufficient for a judge to decide whether an exception applies, classified *Vaughn* indexes are shown to the judge *ex parte* and *in camera*. If a classified index is still not sufficient, then the withheld materials themselves can be shown to the judge.[42]

The *Knight* case illustrates this extensive process.[43] The plaintiff filed a Freedom of Information Act request for all information in CIA's possession relating to the 1980s sinking of the Greenpeace ship *Rainbow Warrior* in the harbor in Auckland, New Zealand, by the French external intelligence service. The CIA declined to produce any such records, and plaintiff filed a suit to force disclosure. Both public and classified indexes were prepared by the Agency, and when they were deemed by the court to be insufficient for a decision in the case, all responsive documents were shown in unredacted form to the trial judge in her chambers. Her decision was in favor of the government, and it was affirmed on appeal.

Historian Alan Fitzgibbon litigated another FOIA request to the CIA and the FBI for materials on the disappearance of Jesus de Galindez, a Basque exile, from outside a New York City subway station in 1956. The case was litigated from 1979 to 1990, and during the process the District Court conducted extensive *in camera* reviews of the material at issue.[44] That pattern has been repeated in numerous other cases.[45] Thus in areas where federal laws mandate disclosure of US government information, federal judges review claims of exemptions based on sensitive intelligence equities.

State secrets privilege

Federal courts also have jurisdiction over civil cases ranging from negligence claims against the government to disputes between persons domiciled in different states. In such cases, litigants often subpoena or otherwise demand discovery of sensitive intelligence-related information. The government resists such demands by asserting the state secrets privilege under the authority of *United States v. Reynolds*, a Supreme Court case that allowed the government to deny disclosure of national security secrets.[46] Other statutory privileges also protect intelligence sources and methods.[47] Judicial review of US government affidavits that assert the state secrets privilege is regularly used to resolve disputed issues of privilege.[48]

In *Halkin v. Helms*, former Vietnam War protestors sued officials of various federal intelligence agencies alleging violation of constitutional and statutory rights. Specifically, the plaintiffs alleged that the National Security Agency (NSA) conducted warrantless interceptions of their international wire, cable, and telephone communications at the request of other federal defendants. The government asserted the state secrets privilege to prevent disclosure of whether the international communications of the plaintiffs were in fact acquired by NSA and disseminated to other federal agencies.[49] The trial court considered three *in camera* affidavits and the *in camera* testimony of the Deputy Director of NSA, and the case was ultimately dismissed at the appellate level based on the assertion of the privilege. The plaintiffs lost the case, but they had the full attention of both trial and appellate federal court judges on the assertion of governmental secrecy.[50]

Allegations of abuse

Federal courts also adjudicate the substance of legal claims brought by private citizens alleging abusive governmental actions. For example, in *Birnbaum v. United States*, a suit was brought under the Federal Tort Claims Act by individuals whose letters to and from the Soviet Union were opened and photocopied by the CIA in the HTLINGUAL mail-opening program that operated between 1953 and 1973. Plaintiffs were awarded $1000 each in damages, and the award was upheld on appeal.[51]

Even suits against intelligence agencies by their own employees have given aggrieved individuals at least a half-day in court. In *Doe v. Gates* a CIA employee litigated the issue of alleged discrimination against him based on his homosexuality. Doe raised two constitutional claims – whether his firing violated the Fifth Amendment equal protection or deprivation of property without compensation clauses. He was heard at every federal court level, including the US Supreme Court. The judicial review even included limited evidentiary review pursuant to cross-motions for summary judgment.[52] The Supreme Court noted that section 102(c) of the National Security Act of 1947 could not be read to exclude judicial review of Doe's constitutional claims. The court went on to note that a serious constitutional question would arise if a federal statute were construed to deny any judicial forum for a colorable constitutional claim.[53]

It is a rare event when the Supreme Court scrutinizes intelligence activities. Nevertheless, that does occur in precisely the areas in which a wary citizenry would want it. For example, two recent cases explored the boundaries of claims against the United States government for wrongful actions against individuals.

In one case, a husband and wife filed suit against the United States and CIA, asserting estoppel and due process claims for CIA's alleged failure to provide them with the assistance it had promised in return for their espionage services.[54] Using the pseudonyms "John and Jane Doe", they claimed to be former citizens of a "foreign country" that at the time was considered to be an enemy of the United States, and John Doe was a diplomat for the country. After they expressed interest in defecting to the United States, CIA officers allegedly persuaded them to remain at their posts and conduct espionage for the United States for a specified period of time, promising in return that the United States would provide them financial and personal security for life. The Does alleged that after a number of years working in the United States, John Doe was laid off in a corporate merger and contacted CIA for a renewal of financial assistance. The request was denied, and the Does then sued, alleging CIA violated their procedural and substantive due process rights by denying them support and refusing to provide them with a fair internal process for reviewing their claims for assistance.

The government moved to dismiss the Does' complaint based upon a Civil War-era case, *Totten v. United States*.[55] In that case, the administrator of the estate of William A. Lloyd sued the United States for compensation for services that Lloyd allegedly conducted as a spy during the Civil War. Lloyd's administrator claimed that Lloyd had entered into a contract with President Lincoln in 1861 to spy behind Confederate lines, for which he was to receive $200 a month. The Supreme Court dismissed the claim and stated that the very essence of the alleged contract between Lloyd and the United States was that it was secret and had to remain secret. Since the nature of the contract was secrecy, it was incompatible for the courts to allow a former spy to sue to enforce it.

This defense finally prevailed when the Does' case reached the Supreme Court (in a unanimous decision). But the Does achieved an extensive review of their claims in three separate federal courts. Both the District Court and the Court of Appeals for the Ninth Circuit accepted the Does' argument that *Totten* did not bar some of their claims, including those related to the government's failure to allow them due process (a constitutional claim).[56] Both of those courts allowed the case to proceed.

The Supreme Court also heard the case of a widow of a Guatemalan rebel leader who vanished in his country in 1992.[57] She alleged that US government officials intentionally deceived her by concealing information that he had been detained, tortured, and executed by Guatemalan army officers paid by CIA, and that this deception denied her access to the courts by leaving her without information with which she could have brought a lawsuit that might have saved her husband's life. She sued a number of US government officials and departments, alleging common law and international law tort claims and constitutional tort claims.[58] The legal theories she advanced to support her claims were unusual (the District Court described her various requests for relief as "nearly unintelligible"[59]). Yet she was able to convince the District Court and the Court of Appeals that at least some of her claims should survive the government's challenge. She did not prevail in the end, but there is no question that the federal judiciary gave her every chance to bring a legal claim against the government for what were allegedly covert intelligence activities conducted in a foreign country.

The same can be said of the case brought in federal court by survivors of General Rene Schneider, the Commander-in-Chief of the Chilean Army, who died of wounds suffered in a failed kidnapping attempt in 1970.[60] The plaintiffs brought suit against the United States and former Secretary of State Henry Kissinger, alleging that General Schneider died as a result of covert actions directed by high-level United States officials and CIA in connection with an attempted coup in Chile. The United States moved to dismiss the case for failure to state a legal claim. In such cases, the court is required to accept as true all of a plaintiff's factual allegations and draw all reasonable inferences in favor of the plaintiff. In spite of that, the court held that the political question doctrine rendered the claim non-justiciable. The political question doctrine is a powerful defense against claims relating to sovereign actions of United States overseas, but at least a federal judge examined the plaintiffs' claims, assumed the facts pled by the plaintiffs were true, and measured them against the doctrine. A federal judge – not the Executive or Legislative Branches – made that call.

First Amendment

Federal judges also look at First Amendment protections of freedom of speech and the press as they relate to intelligence. One context is the contract for non-disclosure of classified information that employees, contractors, and others sign when they are granted access to sensitive information by agencies of the intelligence community. The contract requires pre-publication review of non-official writings by the government in order to protect sensitive information. Two separate lawsuits by former CIA employees Victor Marchetti and Frank Snepp challenged the contract as a forbidden prior restraint on publication. After extensive appellate review, the contract restrictions on freedom of speech were held reasonable and constitutional.[61] It is clear that federal courts will entertain claims of First Amendment violations from intelligence community employees, and will examine the claims closely.

For example, in 1981 a former CIA officer named Ralph McGehee submitted an article to CIA for pre-publication review pursuant to a secrecy agreement he had signed in 1952 when he joined the Agency. The article asserted that the CIA had mounted a campaign of deceit to convince the world that the "revolt of the poor natives against a ruthless US-backed oligarchy" in El Salvador was really "a Soviet/Cuban/Bulgarian/Vietnamese/PLO/Ethiopian/ Nicaraguan/International Terrorism challenge to the United States."[62] McGehee offered a few examples of CIA operations to support his assertion, and some were deemed classified by the Agency and permission to publish those portions of the article were denied.

McGehee sued, seeking a declaratory judgment that the CIA pre-publication and classification procedures violated the First Amendment. He lost, but the federal Appeals Court stated:

> We must accordingly establish a standard for judicial review of the CIA classification decision that affords proper respect to the individual rights at stake while recognizing the CIA's technical expertise and practical familiarity with the ramifications of sensitive information. We conclude that reviewing courts should conduct a *de novo* review of the classification decision, while giving deference to reasoned and detailed CIA explanations of that classification decision.[63]

When individual rights are affected, federal courts have not been reluctant to assert oversight and require intelligence community agencies to visit the courthouse and explain what they are doing.

The second context involving the First Amendment is government attempts to restrain publication of intelligence information by the press. When the Pentagon Papers were leaked to the news media in 1971, the attempt to enjoin publication resulted in the Supreme Court case of *New York Times v. US*[64] Because of the number of individual opinions in the case, the holding is somewhat confusing. Nonetheless, it seems clear that an injunction against press publication of intelligence information will not only be very difficult to obtain but will subject any petition for such relief to very strict scrutiny by the federal courts.

Conclusions

The exposure of federal judges to intelligence activities leads to number of conclusions. One is that judicial oversight operates to an extent overlooked in the debate over who is watching the intelligence community. Judicial oversight is limited, in contrast to expansive Congressional oversight. Judicial oversight deals with legal issues, as opposed to policy issues. Judges are deferential to the executive branch in intelligence matters, something not often true of Congress. But judges do act as arbiters of governmental society in a powerful way.

The basic conundrum for intelligence is that is requires secrecy to be effective, but widespread government secrecy in a western liberal democracy is generally undesirable. Government secrecy can destroy the legitimacy of government institutions. It can cripple accountability of public servants and politicians. It can hide abuses of fundamental rights of citizens. Excessive government secrecy can make excessive government activities more likely, because it hides them from the usual checks and balances.[65]

In the United States, federal judges dampen the tendency toward excess in secret government. They counterbalance the swing in that direction. In those areas most important to particular rights of citizens, they act as arbiters of governmental secrecy. The federal judiciary ameliorates the problems of government secrecy by providing a secure forum for review of intelligence activities under a number of laws, as surrogates for the public.

The developing history of judicial review of intelligence activities shows that it occurs in those areas where government secrecy and the need for swift executive action conflict with well–established legal principles of individual rights: an accused's right to a fair criminal trial; freedom from unreasonable searches and seizures; rights of privacy; freedom of speech and the press. Judges thus get involved where an informed citizenry would instinctively want judicial review of secret intelligence activities. The involvement of the federal judiciary is limited but salutary in its effect on executive branch actions. Nothing concentrates the mind and dampens excess so wonderfully as the imminent prospect of explaining one's actions to a federal judge.

The Constitution's great genius in this area is that it provides a system of government that reconciles the nation's needs for order and defense from foreign aggression with fundamental individual rights that are directly affected by intelligence activities. Nations devising statutory charters and legislative oversight of their foreign intelligence services might well include an independent judiciary in their blueprints. Federal judges are the essential third part of the oversight system in the United States, matching requirements of the laws to intelligence activities and watching the watchers.

All statements of fact, opinion, or analysis expressed are those of the author and do not reflect the official positions or views of the CIA or any other US Government agency. Nothing in the contents should be construed as asserting or implying US Government authentication of information or Agency endorsement of the author's views. This material has been reviewed by the CIA to prevent the disclosure of classified information.

Notes

1 For example, Loch Johnson characterizes the first phase of modern intelligence in the US (1947–74) as "the Era of Trust . . . a time when the intelligence agencies were permitted almost complete discretion to chart their own courses". Loch K. Johnson, *America's Secret Power: The CIA in a Democratic Society* (New York: Oxford University Press, 1989), p. 9.
2 *Chicago & Southern Air Lines, Inc. v. Waterman Steamship Corp.*, 333 U.S. 103 (1848); *U.S. v. Curtiss-Wright Export Corp.*, 299 U.S. 304 (1936).
3 *Japan Whaling Assn v. American Cetacean Soc'y*, 478 U.S. 221, 230 (1986).
4 *Sanchez-Espinosa v. Reagan*, 770 F.2d 202 (D.C. Cir. 1985)
5 John Ranelagh, *The Agency: The Rise and Decline of the CIA* (New York: Simon & Schuster, 1987), pp. 29, 110; Anne Karalekas, "History of the Central Intelligence Agency," in William M. Leary ed., *The Central Intelligence Agency: History and Documents* (Tuscaloosa, AL: University of Alabama Press, 1984), p. 13.
6 50 U.S.C.A. Section 403–4a(d)(1) (Westlaw 2006).
7 *U.S. v. Curtiss-Wright*, at note 3. Justice Sutherland's observations were *dicta*, not essential to the majority's holding in the case, and his theory has not been accepted by most legal authorities as a basis for wide executive discretion in foreign affairs. See also *The Chinese Exclusion Case*, 130 U.S. 581, 603–04 (1889), in which the Supreme Court held that Congress could legislate to exclude aliens because jurisdiction over its own territory is an incident of every independent nation.
8 Letter to J.B. Colvin, 20 September 1810, cited in *The Life and Selected Writings of Thomas Jefferson* (New York: Random House, 1944), pp. 606–7. Lincoln had similar musings: "Was it possible to lose the nation and yet preserve the Constitution?," quoted in Johnson, *America's Secret Power*, p. 252, n. 4.
9 See *Legal Authorities Supporting the Activities of the National Security Agency Described by the President*, U.S. Dept. of Justice White Paper (January 19, 2006); Loch Johnson, "Spy Law Works; Don't Bypass It," *Atlanta Journal-Constitution*, January 30, 2006, at A14.
10 See Loch K. Johnson, *A Season of Inquiry: The Senate Intelligence Investigation* (Lexington, KY: University of Kentucky Press, 1985).
11 See, for example, *Miranda v. Arizona*, 384 U.S. 436 (1966); *Escobedo v. Illinois*, 378 U.S. 478 (1964).

12 See *United States v. Yunis*, 859 F.2d 953 (D.C. Cir. 1988); G. Gregory Schuetz, "Apprehending Terrorists Overseas Under United States and International Law: A Case Study of the Fawaz Yunis Arrest," *Harvard International Law Journal*, 29, no. 2 (Spring 1988), pp. 499–531. In the late 1980s and early 1990s, CIA created the Counterterrorist Center, the Nonproliferation Center, and the Counternarcotics (now Crime and Narcotics) Center in order to centralize the efforts of the intelligence community and enhance its support to law enforcement in those areas of "thugs, bugs, and drugs."

13 See, e.g., Intelligence Authorization Act for Fiscal Year 1990, which established the position of the CIA inspector General as a presidential appointee (codified at 50 U.S.C.A. Section 403q (Westlaw 2006)).

14 The Hughes-Ryan Amendment (Section 662 of the Foreign Assistance Act of 1961, 22 U.S.C. Section 2422) was repealed when the National Security Act was amended by the Intelligence Authorization Act for Fiscal Year 1991 to codify and consolidate oversight provisions in Title V of the National Security Act.

15 The Office of General Counsel at CIA has grown from a handful of attorneys in the early 1970s to more than one hundred, an increase far above the proportional growth of CIA personnel or activity.

16 Benjamin Civiletti, "Intelligence Gathering and the Law," *Studies In Intelligence*, 27 (Summer 1983), pp.13, 15. This article was adapted from the Tenth Annual John F. Sonnett Memorial Lecture delivered by Mr Civiletti at the Fordham University School of Law on January 15, 1980. *Studies In Intelligence* is an official publication of the Central Intelligence Agency. Civiletti's article can also be found in the *Fordham Law Review*, 48, no. 6 (May 1980), pp. 883–906.

17 *Brady v. Maryland*, 373 U.S. 83 (1963); *Giglio v. United States*, 405 U.S. 150 (1974). Under these cases, the government has a constitutional responsibility to search for and produce to a criminal defendant admissible exculpatory and impeachment material.

18 *United States v. Kampiles*, 609 F.2d 1233 (7th Cir. 1979).

19 18 U.S.CA. App. III Section 1 et seq. (Westlaw 2006).

20 See Jonathan Fredman, "Intelligence Agencies, Law Enforcement, and the Prosecution Team," 16 *Yale L. & Pol'y Rev.* 331 (1998), for a thorough treatment of CIPA.

21 See, for example, *United States v. Smith*, 780 F.2d 1102 (4th Cir. 1985).

22 The Iran-Contra cases are examples. See especially *United States v. Fernandez*, No. CR89–0150–A (E.D. Va. April 24, 1988); *Final Report of the Independent Counsel for Iran/Contra Matters*, vol. 1, pp. 283–93.

23 *Olmstead v. United States*, 277 U.S. 438 (1928).

24 *Katz v. United States*, 389 U.S. 347 (1967).

25 Title III of the Omnibus Crime Control and Safe Streets Act, 18 U.S.C. Sections 2510, 2521 (Westlaw 2006).

26 FISA is codified in 50 U.S.C.A. ch. 36 (Westlaw 2006).

27 James Adams, *Sellout: Aldrich Ames and the Corruption of the CIA* (New York: Viking, 1995), ch. 15. In the Intelligence Authorization Act for Fiscal Year 1995, the issue of Attorney General physical search authority was overtaken by events when Congress extended the FISA process to include not only electronic surveillance but physical searches as well. The FISA Court will now provide judicial review in advance for searches such as that done in the Ames's house. 50 U.S.C.A. Sections 1821–1829 (Westlaw 2006).

28 629 F.2d 908, 915–16 (4th Cir. 1980).

29 *In re Sealed Case No. 02–001*, 310 F.3d 717 (Foreign Int. Surv. Ct. Rev. 2002)

30 Eric Lichtblau, "Judges and Justice Dept. Meet Over Eavesdropping Program," *The New York Times*, January 10, 2006, at A14.

31 *Hamdi v. Rumsfeld*, 542 U.S. 507 (2004).

32 *United States v. Moussaoui*, 382 F.3d 453, 456 (4th Cir. 2004), cert. den., 125 S. Ct. 1670 (Mar. 21, 2005).

33 *Padilla v. Hanft*, Case No. 05–6396 (4th Cir. Sept. 9, 2005), at 3.

34 See Jerry Markon, "*Terror Defendant Seeks Hearing To Find Whether He Was Spied On*," *The Washington Post*, January 10, 2006, at B1. (The story relates to a filing in federal District Court by a US citizen, Ali Al-Timimi, previously convicted on terrorism charges based upon his inciting his Northern Virginia followers to train for violent jihad against the United States; he claims that he was the target of a warrantless electronic surveillance program authorized by the President.)

35 Fed. R. Crim. Proc. 12.3.

36 *United States v. Rewald*, 889 F.2d 836, 838–9 (9th Cir. 1989). Rewald was convicted on 94 (out of 100) counts of various mail, securities, and tax fraud crimes, as well as perjury.

37 Ibid., at 852.
38 5 U.S.C. Section 552 (Westlaw 2006).
39 5 U.S.C. Section 552a (Westlaw 2006).
40 *CIA v. Sims*, 471 U.S. 159 (1985).
41 *Vaughn v. Rosen*, 484 F.2d 820 (D.C. Cir. 1973), *cert. denied*, 415 U.S. 977 (1974).
42 See, for example, *Knight v. CIA*, 872 F.2d 660 (5th Cir. 1989), *cert. denied*, 494 U.S. 1004 (1990); *Phillippi v. CIA*, 546 F.2d 1009 (D.C. Cir. 1976); *Miller v. Casey*, 730 F.2d 773, (D.C. Cir. 1984). The executive branch has taken the position that *de novo* review of the classification decision of the executive branch raises serious constitutional separation of powers issues. This position was strengthened by the case of *Dept. of the Navy v. Egan*, 484 U.S. 518, 527 (1988), in which the Supreme Court said that "[The President's] authority to classify and control access to information bearing on the national security . . . flows primarily from this constitutional investment of power in the President and exists quite apart from any explicit congressional grant." Nevertheless, executive branch affidavits asserting classification are still required and reviewed by judges.
43 *Knight v. CIA*, at note 36.
44 *Fitzgibbon v. CIA*, 911 F.2d 755, 757 (D.C. Cir. 1990). The CIA and FBI prevailed in withholding the information under FOIA exemptions after extensive District Court review of the records at issue, which related to intelligence sources and methods.
45 See, for example, *Patterson v. FBI*, 893 F.2d 595, 599–600 (3d Cir. 1990); *Hayden v. NSA/Cent. Sec. Serv.*, 608 F.2d 1381, 1385 (D.C. Cir. 1979); *Phillippi v. CIA*, 546 F.2d 1009, 1013 (D.C. Cir. 1976).
46 345 U.S. 1 (1953).
47 For example, the National Security Act of 1947, as amended, 50 U.S.C.A. Section 403–1(i) (Westlaw 2006), states that the Director of National Intelligence shall "protect intelligence sources and methods from unauthorized disclosure" (previously a duty imposed on the Director of Central Intelligence prior to the creation of the position of the Director of National Intelligence). See also Section 6 of the Central Intelligence Agency Act of 1949, as amended, 50 U.S.C. Section. 403g (Westlaw 2006).
48 *Kerr v. United States District Court*, 426 U.S. 394, 405–06 (1976); *United States v. Nixon*, 418 U.S. 683, 714–15 (1974); *Farnsworth-Cannon, Inc. v. Grimes*, 635 F.2d 268, 269 (4th Cir. 1980).
49 *Halkin v. Helms*, 598 F.2d 1, 5 (D.C. Cir. 1978).
50 Ibid., pp. 5–7.
51 *Birnbaum v. United States*, 588 U.S. 319 (2d Cir. 1978).
52 981 F.2d 1316 (D.C. Cir. 1993). The petitions of the plaintiff for a rehearing by the full Court of Appeals and for a writ of *certiorari* from the Supreme Court were denied.
53 *Webster v. Doe*, 486 U.S. 592, 603 (1988).
54 *Tenet v. Doe*, 544 U.S. 1 (2005).
55 *Totten v. United States*, 92 U.S. 105 (1876).
56 99 F. Supp. 2d 1284, 1289–1294 (W.D. Wash. 2000), and 329 F. 3d 1135 (9th Cir. 2003), respectively.
57 *Christopher v. Harbury*, 536 U.S. 403 (2002).
58 Constitutional torts are called "Bivens" actions, after the Supreme Court case of *Bivens v. Six Unknown Fed. Narcotics Agents*, 403 U.S. 388 (1971). Such actions are based upon the theory that under the Constitution itself, without further statutory waiver of sovereign immunity, courts may impose tort-like liability upon individual US government employees when they egregiously violate protections guaranteed to individuals by the Constitution. Such actions are rarely successful.
59 *Supra*, note 4, at 418.
60 *Schneider v. Kissinger*, 310 F. Supp. 2d 251 (D.D.C. 2004), aff'd, 412 F.3d 190 (D.C.Cir. 2005).
61 *U.S. v. Snepp*, 444 U.S. 507 (1980); *U.S. v. Marchetti*, 466 F.2d 1309 (4th Cir. 1972), *cert. denied*, 93 S.Ct. 553 (1972).
62 *McGehee v. Casey*, 718 F.2d 1137, 1139 (D.C. Cir. 1983).
63 Ibid., at 1148.
64 403 U.S. 713 (1971).
65 See William R. Corson and Robert T. Crowley, *The New KGB: Engine of Soviet Power* (New York: William Morrow, 1985) pp. 21–6, 129–30, 174–5; Harry Rositzke, *The KGB: The Eyes of Russia* (New York: Doubleday, 1981) pp. 79–81, 94–5.

26

A shock theory of congressional accountability for intelligence

*Loch K. Johnson**

Introduction

Scholars who have focused on intelligence accountability by lawmakers have found a system far less effective than reformers had hoped for when, in the aftermath of a domestic spy scandal, Congress tried to institute major improvements in 1974–76.[1] Similarly, a national panel of inquiry, the Kean Commission, concluded in 2004 that "congressional oversight for intelligence – and for counterterrorism – is now dysfunctional."[2]

Prominent members of Congress have conceded current inadequacies in their monitoring of government's hidden side. "We really don't have, still don't have, meaningful congressional oversight [of the intelligence agencies]," observed Senator John McCain (R–Arizona) in 2004.[3] Frustrated by yet another intelligence controversy that took Congress by surprise – this time, warrantless wiretaps by the National Security Agency (NSA), disclosed in December of 2005 – the leading Democrat in the House of Representatives, Nancy Pelosi (California), proposed that the House create a bipartisan, bicameral working group to recommend improvements to the oversight process.[4] Breaking ranks with her Intelligence Committee chairman (Representative Peter Hoekstra, R–Michigan), Representative Heather A. Wilson (R–New Mexico) urged a "painstaking" review of the controversial NSA eavesdropping program. This chapter examines attempts by lawmakers since 1974 to conduct intelligence oversight, and probes the questions of why reforms have fallen short and what might be done to strengthen intelligence accountability in the United States.

Shock as a stimulus for intelligence accountability, 1974–2006

On the general subject of oversight, political scientists McCubbins and Schwartz have offered a vivid metaphor contrasting "police patrolling" with "firefighting."[5] As patrollers, lawmakers *qua* overseers regularly review executive branch programs, just as a police officer might walk the streets, check the locks on doors, and shine a flashlight into dark corners – all in order to maintain a vigilance against potential criminal acts. In contrast, firefighters classically respond to alarms after a fire has broken out. In a similar fashion, lawmakers can carry out routine but careful reviews ("patrols") of executive branch programs; or they can wait, then rush to the scene after an alarm sounds that a program has run afoul of the law or other societal expectations.

The research on intelligence oversight on Capitol Hill indicates that efforts of lawmakers to patrol the secret agencies have been "sporadic, spotty, and essentially uncritical."[6] The chief cause of this inattentiveness derives from the nature of Congress: lawmakers seek re-election and they usually conclude that passing bills and raising campaign funds is a better use of their time than the often tedious review of executive programs. This is especially true of intelligence review. The examination of America's secret operations must take place, for the most part, in closed committee sanctuaries, outside of public view. Absent public awareness, credit-claiming – vital to re-election prospects – becomes difficult.[7]

An analysis of intelligence accountability indicates a pattern in recent decades: a major intelligence scandal or failure – a shock – converts perfunctory patrolling into a burst of intense firefighting, which is then followed by a period of dedicated patrolling that yields remedial legislation or other reforms designed to curb inappropriate intelligence activities in the future. Sometimes the high-intensity patrolling can last for months and, if the original shock was particularly strong, producing a media tsunami, even years. Once the firestorm has subsided and reforms are in place, however, lawmakers return to a state of relative inattention to intelligence issues.[8] This pattern is depicted schematically in Figure 26.1:

The pattern:

sporadic patrolling* > intelligence shock > intense firefighting > intense > sporadic patrolling
            (scandal/failure)   patrolling
                                                      and
                                                  reform

In "EKG" Form:

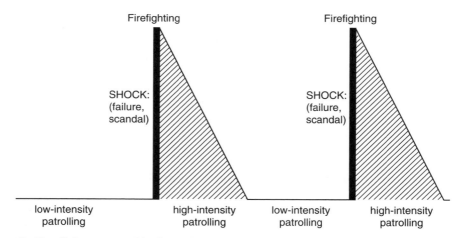

* A result of insufficient opportunities for credit-claiming and the enhancement of re-election prospects, which in turn produce an inattentiveness to oversight duties and a concomitant ripening of conditions for scandal or failure.

Figure 26.1 The dominant pattern of intelligence oversight by lawmakers, 1975–2006.

To reach an alarm or shock level, an allegation of intelligence wrongdoing or failure would have to have sustained coverage in leading newspapers, say, several weeks running with at least a few front-page stories. In 1974, the *New York Times* had an unusually high run of stories on the Central Intelligence Agency (CIA) from June through December: 200. In December, an unprecedented (at the time) nine stories on the CIA made the front page of the *Times*. Here was a steady drumbeat of mainly negative reports about the Agency, setting the stage for a strong public (and therefore congressional and presidential reaction) to the most explosive news item: the CIA's alleged involvement in domestic spying. On the eve of the next major intelligence scandal and investigation, the Iran-Contra affair, the *Times* carried eleven front-page stories about possible intelligence abuses related to the covert war in Nicaragua in both October and November 1986, jumping to eighteen front-page stories in December and setting the stage for joint congressional hearings into the scandal in 1987.[9]

Further research will be necessary to determine the more precise relationship between newspaper coverage and the onset of major scandal on intelligence failure. One thing is clear, though: as Ransom has put it, "the press, with all of its problems, remains the chief accountability enforcer."[10] Congress has more authority to investigate intelligence operations, including the power of the subpoena – unique among parliaments around the world when it comes to intelligence oversight[11] – but evidently the media has more will.

Intense media coverage may not be enough in itself to sound a major fire alarm. Such considerations as the personalities of congressional overseers, especially committee chairs, and the existence of divided government play a role, too.[12] In early 2006, the media coverage of possible presidential abuse of the Foreign Intelligence Surveillance Act was extensive (though less than for the 1974 spy domestic spy scandal or the 1987 Iran–Contra scandal). The Republicans controlled the White House and the two Houses of Congress, however, and GOP lawmakers resisted Democratic calls for a major investigation into the allegations.[13]

The shocks and alarms

Thirty-one years have passed since Congress began to take intelligence accountability more seriously in December of 1974, following charges in the *New York Times* that the CIA had spied illegally on American citizens.[14] Since then, lawmakers have devoted about six years of attention to intensive, retrospective investigations (firefighting) into intelligence controversies. The remaining twenty-five years, a little over 80 percent of the total, consisted of periods of patrolling. The patrolling was characterized by varying degrees of intensity among overseers, some of it vigorous in the immediate aftermath of "fires"; but mostly the patrolling was of a perfunctory nature. The period from 1974 to 2006 began with a domestic spy scandal that, since the creation of the CIA in 1947, was the first intelligence alarm of sufficient shrillness to bring about a major congressional response. Several more alarms would sound during the coming decades, as outlined below.

Alarm No. 1, 1974: A Domestic Spy Scandal. The Senate and House investigative committees (the Church and Pike panels), established by Congress in the wake of the *New York Times* exposés in 1974, discovered extensive spying at home not only by the CIA, but also by the NSA, the Federal Bureau of Investigation (FBI), and various military intelligence units. The findings of the committees not only confirmed but went far beyond the allegations leveled by the *Times*. The Church Committee issued a voluminous set of reports critical of CIA assassination plots and a wide range of domestic intelligence operations. At the center of its reform proposals, the panel recommended the creation of a permanent oversight committee in the Senate. On the House side, the Pike Committee blasted the poor quality of intelligence assessments ("analysis") of worldwide threats over the years.[15]

Alarm No. 2, 1986: The Iran–Contra Scandal. Congress established a combined Senate–House investigating panel (the Inouye-Hamilton Committee) that revealed unlawful intelligence activities by the staff of the National Security Council (NSC) and a few officials of the CIA. The scandal had two interconnected parts: a secret sale of arms to Iran in hopes of influencing the release of US hostages in nearby Lebanon; and covert support by the Reagan administration for the Contras in Nicaragua, in defiance of Congress. The Contras sought regime change in Nicaragua, to regain power themselves and oust a left-leaning government. The Joint Committee issued a detailed report on improprieties committed by the intelligence agencies during the five-year period in which the scandal unfolded (1982–1986).[16]

Alarm No. 3, 1994: The Ames Counterintelligence Failure. Congress insisted on joining an executive probe (the Aspin-Brown Commission) into intelligence shortcomings. Lawmakers were especially concerned about a spy case that revealed how the Soviet Union had been able to recruit an American agent (Aldrich Hazen Ames) high within the echelons of the CIA's headquarters in Langley, Virginia. This national commission published a report calling not just for improvements in counterintelligence, but for reforms across the board of intelligence activities.[17]

Alarm No. 4, 2001: The 9/11 Attacks. The failure of the intelligence agencies to warn the nation about the catastrophic terrorist attacks against the American homeland led Congress to form another joint committee of inquiry (the Graham-Goss Committee) and, subsequently, to urge the creation of a presidential investigative panel (the Kean Commission) to further examine the issue.[18] The House Permanent Select Committee on Intelligence, which had been set up in 1977 (a year after its Senate counterpart), also conducted a special probe into the CIA human intelligence or "humint," especially in the Middle East and Southwest Asia, producing a critical internal report on worldwide humint inadequacies.[19]

Alarm No. 5, 2003: Weapons of Mass Destruction in Iraq. In light of an erroneous intelligence prediction about the likely presence of weapons of mass destruction (WMDs) in Iraq – a National Intelligence Estimate (NIE) published in October 2002 – Congress supported the creation of another presidential commission on intelligence, the Silberman-Robb panel, to investigate the analytic failure.[20] Moreover, the Senate intelligence oversight committee undertook an inquiry of its own into the faulty WMD estimate.[21]

As indicated by the findings in Table 26.1, Congress produced several key legislative proposals related to intelligence during the time span from 1974 to 2006.[22] Of the twelve major initiatives displayed in the figure, only one occurred outside the context of a major fire alarm response. That single exception, the Intelligence Identities Act of 1982, was the result of a conclusion reached by lawmakers (at the urging of the CIA and other US intelligence agencies) that a law was necessary to provide stiff penalties against anyone who revealed, without proper authorization, the name of a US intelligence officer or asset.[23] The rest of the oversight initiatives were the result of shocks and resultant alarms going off, followed by subsequent inquiries and a stint of aggressive patrolling.

Some of the initiatives took a considerable amount of time for the Congress to craft, such as the Intelligence Accountability Act of 1980 that required four years to enact. In this example, some lawmakers originally hoped to pass an "Intelligence Charter" – an omnibus statute over 270 pages long – to provide a broad legal framework for the secret agencies. Their intention was to write a law that would replace the dated language of the 1947 National Security Act. This sweeping measure attracted many dissenters, however, especially inside the intelligence agencies, and the bold charter proposal ultimately collapsed under the weight of effective

Table 26.1 Type of stimulus and intelligence oversight response by US lawmakers, 1975–2006

Year	Stimulus	Oversight response	Purpose of response
1974	FA (#1)	Hughes-Ryan Act	Controls over covert action
1976–77	FA (#1)	Est. oversight committees; critical reports[1]	More robust oversight
1978	FA (#1)	FISA	Warrants for electronic surveillance
1980	FA (#1)	Intel. Oversight Act	Tighten oversight rules
1982	P	Intel. Identities Act	Protect intel. officers/agents
1987	FA (#2)	Critical report[2]	Improve intelligence oversight
1989	FA (#2)	Inspector General Act	Improve internal CIA oversight
1991	FA (#2)	Intel. Oversight Act	Further tighten oversight rules
1996	FA (#3)	Est. DCI assistants; critical reports[3]	IC management improvements; strengthening CI
2001	FA (#4)	Patriot Act; authorization of war against Al Qaeda and Taliban regime; increases in counterterrorism funding	Surveillance of suspected terrorists; paramilitary counterattacks against Al Qaeda and Taliban
2004	FA (#4)	Critical reports[4]	Improve humint and analysis
2004	FA (#4, #5)	Intel. Reform & Terrorism Prevention Act	Strengthening CT, IC coordination

Abbreviations:

    FA = fire alarm (#1 = domestic spying; #2 = Iran-Contra; #3 = Ames; #4 = 9/11; #5 = WMDs in Iraq)
     P = patrolling
humint = human intelligence
     IC = intelligence community
  FISA = Foreign Intelligence Surveillance Act [P.L. 95–511; 92 Stat. 1783 (Oct. 25, 1978)]
   DCI = Director of Central Intelligence
CI, CT = counterintelligence, counterterrorism

Notes

[1] The Church Committee Report [Select Committee to Study Governmental Operations with Respect to Intelligence Activities, *Final Report*, 94th Cong., 2nd Sess., Sen. Rept. No. 94–755, 6 vols. (Washington, DC: Government Printing Office, 1976)]; Rockefeller Commission Report [Commission on CIA Activities within the United States, *Report to the President* (Washington, DC: Government Printing Office, June 1975)]; and Pike Committee Report ("The Report the President Doesn't Want You to Read: The Pike Papers," *Village Voice*, February 16 and 23, 1976).

[2] The Inouye-Hamilton Report [*Report of the Congressional Committees Investigating the Iran-Contra Affair*, S. Rept. No. 100–216 and H. Rept. No. 100–433, 100th Cong., 1st Sess., US Senate Select Committee on Secret Military Assistance to Iran and the Nicaraguan Opposition and US House of Representatives Select Committee to Investigate Covert Arms Transactions with Iran (Washington, DC: Government Printing Office, November 1987)].

[3] Aspin-Brown Commission Report [*Preparing for the 21st Century: An Appraisal of US Intelligence*, Report of the Commission on the Roles and Capabilities of the United States Intelligence Community (Washington, DC: Government Printing Office, March 1, 1996)]; and Staff Study, *IC21: Intelligence Community in the 21st Century*, Permanent Select Committee on Intelligence, House of Representatives, 104th Cong., 2nd Sess. (Washington, DC: Government Printing Office, March 1, 1996)].

[4] The Graham-Goss Committees Report [*Joint Inquiry into Intelligence Community Activities before and after the Terrorist Attacks of September 11, 2001*, House Permanent Select Committee on Intelligence and Senate Select Committee on Intelligence, S. Rept. 107–351, 107th Cong., 2nd Sess. (2002)]; the Goss Committee Report [*Intelligence Authorization Act for Fiscal Year 2005*, House Permanent Select Committee on Intelligence, H. Rept. 108th Cong., 2nd Sess. (2004)]; and the Roberts Committee Report [*US Intelligence Community's Prewar Intelligence Assessments on Iraq*, Senate Select Committee on Intelligence, S. Rept. 108–301, 108th Cong., 2nd. Sess. (2004)].

lobbying by the senior managers of intelligence. In its place sprouted a two-and-a-half-page bill. This short law was much stronger, though, than its length would suggest. Among other provisions, it required the Director of Central Intelligence (DCI) reports to the Congress *in advance* on *all* important intelligence activities. The president could delay contacting lawmakers only in "extraordinary circumstances," and even then was expected to report in a timely manner.[24]

The frequency of intense intelligence accountability

The most important intelligence "wake-up call" for congressional overseers in the period before the formal creation of the CIA and America's modern intelligence community in 1947 was the Japanese attack against Pearl Harbor on December 7, 1941. The intelligence portions of the National Security Act of 1947 were a delayed response to that intelligence failure, coupled with a growing concern about a new threat to the United States: the rise of the Soviet Union as a global rival guided by a Marxist philosophy that was anathema to America's espousal of market-based liberal democracies.[25]

Following the establishment of the modern intelligence community in 1947, several low-threshold fire alarms sounded during the early years of the Cold War. Among the most notable were a result of the CIA's failure to predict the outbreak of war on the Korean peninsula (1950), the CIA's Bay of Pigs disaster (1961), the controversy over CIA ties to the National Student Association and other domestic groups (1966), and an alleged CIA connection to the Watergate burglars (1973).[26] None of these alarms was as shattering as the subsequent high-threshold shocks delivered by the domestic spy scandal, the Iran–Contra affair, the Ames case, the 9/11 attacks, or the mistaken WMD report that helped fuel an American war in Iraq in 2003. With the possible exception of the Ames case, these latter fire alarms caught the attention of Americans across the nation, which in turn led lawmakers to focus on the events that caused the alarms to sound. Whether or not the Ames case attracted broad citizen attention, this act of treason certainly set off an alarm among national security officials and lawmakers inside the DC Beltway.

Members of Congress may well have reacted sharply to the Iran-Contra scandal even if the public had not taken an interest, since it amounted to a provocative disregard for the congressional appropriations process. Prior to the scandal, a Democratic-led Congress rebuffed the efforts of the Reagan administration to fund covert action in Nicaragua; as a result, the NSC staff resorted to the secret raising of private funds as a means of carrying out these secret operations in Nicaragua, in defiance of laws passed by Congress (the Boland Amendments[27]) that strictly prohibited such activities against the incumbent Sandinista regime. Lawmakers reacted strongly as well to the Ames counterintelligence case, since a Soviet penetration at the highest levels of the CIA – the worst counterintelligence failure in American history – was difficult to ignore, striking as it did at the heart of the Agency's mandate in the 1947 National Security Act to protect "sources and methods."

In contrast to these high-threshold alarms, Korea in 1950 and the Bay of Pigs in 1961 – while obviously disconcerting – dealt with situations that had occurred outside the United States. The flaps over the CIA's relationships with students and with the Watergate caper both took place at home, but the former came across as a fairly narrow issue (chiefly involving CIA support for US students attending international conferences) and the latter proved to have little substance. One of the men implicated in the Watergate burglary was a former CIA officer (E. Howard Hunt) who had requested a wig and other disguise paraphernalia from the Agency's Directorate of Science and Technology for use in the infamous break-in; but investigations disclosed that the CIA had not realized the purpose of Hunt's request and had no prior knowledge of the plot. Indeed, the CIA's efforts to steer clear of Nixon administration efforts to draw it into the Watergate conspiracy stand as a high-water mark in the Agency's history.

An examination of the frequency of alarms, both low- and high-threshold (see Table 26.2), discloses the periodicity of intelligence scandals and failures in the modern era.[28] Eliminating the CIA–Watergate "scandal," since it was in reality an insignificant intelligence matter (however important Watergate was as a political and historical event in the United States), an

Table 26.2 The frequency of low- and high-threshold intelligence alarms, 1941–2006 (with high-threshold in bold)

Year	**1941**	1950	1961	1966	1973	**1974**	**1987**	**1994**	**2001**	**2003**	
Alarm	F	F	F	S	S	S	S	F	F	F	
Interval (Yrs)	9	11	5	7	1	13	7	7	2		Av.: 7.6*

The events: Thresholds:

1941	Pearl Harbor attack	High
1950	Outbreak of war on Korean Peninsula	Low
1961	Bay of Pigs	Low
1966	CIA–National Student Association scandal	Low
1973	CIA–Watergate "scandal"	Low
1974	Domestic spying scandal	High
1987	Iran–Contra scandal	High
1994	Ames counterintelligence failure	High
2001	9/11 attacks	High
2003	Faulty WMD analysis (Iraq)	High

* excluding the CIA-Watergate case (see text)

Abbreviations:
    F = failure of collection and/or analysis
    S = scandal or impropriety
WMD = weapons of mass destruction

intelligence alarm sounded roughly every seven-and-a-half years, on average. The longest gap – twice the average – occurred between the domestic spying scandal exposed in 1974 and the Iran–Contra affair that came to light in 1987, a total of thirteen years. The domestic spying scandal and the ensuing investigations were deeply traumatic to the intelligence agencies; officers at the CIA still remember 1975 as the "Year of the Intelligence Wars" – *annus horribilis*. The investigations established a new standard of ethics and accountability for the intelligence agencies that may have significantly contributed to the reduced incidence of improper behavior by intelligence officers over the next decade. This clean record came to an end as the Reagan administration's obsession with Nicaragua led NSC staffers to misuse the government's intelligence agencies, and even develop their own new secret organization ("The Enterprise") in an attempt to eliminate the Sandinista regime.

The briefest interlude between alarms occurred from 2001 to 2003, with the Iraqi WMD ill-judgment coming quickly on the heels of the 9/11 failure – a double blow to the reputation of the CIA and a primary reason for its dramatic decline in 2004–5 as America's premier intelligence agency. Now the CIA is just one of sixteen agencies in the intelligence community, no longer "central" – an assignment given by the Intelligence Reform and Terrorism Prevention Act of 2004 to a new Director of National Intelligence or DNI. In June 2005, the White House informed the Director of the Central Intelligence Agency (D/CIA) that he would no longer be a regular attendee at NSC meetings or the lead person to conduct the daily intelligence briefs for the president.[29]

The conclusions presented here about the periodic inattentiveness of lawmakers as patrollers should not overshadow the fact that intelligence oversight since 1975 has been vastly more robust than "in the good old days," as some mossback intelligence professionals recall the years from 1947 to 1974 when Congress left the secret agencies largely to their own devices.[30] Intelligence overseers since 1976–1977 have benefitted greatly from the existence of the two standing intelligence oversight committees, formerly known as the Senate Select Committee on Intelligence (SSCI) and the House Permanent Select Committee on Intelligence (HPSCI), each armed with budget and subpoena powers and staffed by many intelligence experts. The authority of these panels extends far beyond that enjoyed by any other legislative chamber in the world, today or in the past. Moreover, while lawmakers have been less than fully engaged in patrolling, in the extraordinary circumstances of major scandals or intelligence failures they have been dedicated – even zealous – firefighters.

Even during the more quotidian years since 1976, the staffs of the intelligence committees (some 50–70 individuals, well educated and experienced) have regularly queried intelligence professionals about their activities, pored over annual budget requests line-by-line, visited intelligence installations at home and abroad, and prepared detailed briefing books for the use of committee members during hearings. Very little of this kind of persistent staff work was carried out before 1975, underscoring the deep structural changes wrought by the domestic spying scandal of 1974 and the sixteen-month-long Church and Pike Committee investigations – the most extensive probes into the operations of the intelligence agencies ever, surpassing even the Aspin-Brown and the Kean inquiries in 1995 and 2004.

Intelligence failures and scandals

An important feature of the findings presented here is the contrast between intelligence failures and scandals. Intelligence failures are frequently inadvertent, resulting from the lack of a well-placed agent, a surveillance satellite in a helpful orbit, the rapid translation of an intercepted telephone conversation in Farsi, or an experienced analyst. Of course, less excusably, a CIA officer might also be lazy, an agent might be double, or an analyst poorly trained. Whatever the case, often as not failures are a result of human fallibility and, in that sense, are inevitable.[31] This condition can be mitigated to some degree by improving a nation's capacity to gather reliable information from around the globe, say, by building more sophisticated spy satellites or reconnaissance airplanes, or by establishing capable spy rings in "hot spots" overseas; but, the probability of failure can never be eliminated. The future is an unknown place, shrouded in fog.

Through the expenditure of some $44 billion a year on intelligence, the United States attempts to pierce as much of the fog as possible; nevertheless, the world will never be fully transparent. The planet is too large and adversaries are too clever at hiding their activities, whether planning attacks against the United States from remote caves in Afghanistan or constructing atomic bombs in deep underground caverns in North Korea or Iran. Further, some things are simply unknowable in advance – "mysteries," as opposed to "secrets" that might be stolen from a safe. An example of a mystery is the question of who will follow Vladimir Putin as the next Russian president. No one can know, until it happens. When intelligence failures occur, as with the outbreak of war in Korea in 1950 and the absence of WMDs in Iraq in 2003, the United States takes measures to improve its collection and analysis; still, new and unexpected threats are bound to rise somewhere in the world.

In contrast to failures, scandals and improprieties are usually intentional. Someone breaks a law, a regulation, or a standard operating procedure in order to achieve a goal. The violator hopes to avoid discovery, and may be convinced anyway that the importance of the goal trumps all other considerations. When called upon to explain why they had broken the law during the Iran-Contra affair, NSC staffers from the Reagan administration said they were responding to a "higher law" that required them to fight communism in Central America, even if Congress had foolishly passed the Boland Amendments and made that objective more difficult.[32]

In theory at least, intelligence scandals could be eliminated by recruiting only virtuous people for high office: men and women who would never succumb to illegal spying on US citizens, flaunt laws like the Boland Amendments, infiltrate and subsidize student groups and other organizations in American society, provide disguises to former intelligence officers without checking on the purpose, or lie to congressional overseers as happened during the Iran–Contra affair.[33] Yet, intelligence scandals are as inevitable as collection and analytic failures. Indeed, the entire rationale for accountability presented by James Madison in *Federalist Paper* No. 51 rests on the supposition – confirmed every day – that human beings are not angels. They will make mistakes and they will sin. So, with respect to failures and scandals within the intelligence domain (or within any other organization, public or private), one can anticipate more of both.

At the same time, however, a nation can take steps to decrease the odds of mistakes and wrongdoing by improving its intelligence collection-and-analysis capabilities, carefully recruiting men and women of high integrity, and steadfastly patrolling the secret agencies in search of incipient gaps in performance and signs of flaws in the human character (such as Ames's abuse of alcohol and luxury spending beyond a CIA officer's government salary). That is why oversight patrolling is so important: ideally, one would like to find and correct conditions that might lead to a fire (whether a failure or a scandal) before the flames ignite. Implicit in the notion of accountability is the hope that a few more eyes of elected officials available to examine policy initiatives – from the vantage point of Capitol Hill, not just from the White House – might help discover problems before they lead to catastrophes.

Taking the shock out of the shock theory

After the 9/11 terrorist attacks, lawmakers lamented their inattention to intelligence oversight duties. "We didn't understand. . . . the need for human intelligence," admitted SSCI overseer Mike DeWine (R-Ohio), "we simply did not provide the resources."[34] Bob Graham, the SSCI chairman who co-chaired the Joint Committee investigation into the 9/11 intelligence failure, has said, "We probably didn't shake the [intelligence] agencies hard enough after the end of the Berlin Wall to say: 'Hey, look, the world is changing and you need to change the way in which you operate . . . new strategies, new personnel, new culture.' We should have been more demanding of these intelligence agencies."[35] The HPSCI chair at the time, Porter J. Goss, who served as the other co-chair of the Joint Committee inquiry, issued a separate report prepared by HPSCI in 2004 that was scathing in its criticism of CIA human intelligence.[36]

What if these lawmakers and their colleagues had been sufficiently exercised about such intelligence deficiencies in the years preceding September 11, 2001? The planned attacks might have been uncovered in advance with better humint, faster translation of communications intercepts from Al Qaeda plotters, and sharper analysis. Would it have been possible to avoid, or at least lessen the effects of, the five major intelligence shocks if lawmakers had been more dedicated to their patrolling duties in the lead-up to catastrophe? It is worthwhile examining each of the alarms from this vantage point, although what follows is an impressionist first-look and warrants a closer research effort. The impressions are mindful of how Monday morning quarterbacks always play better than their real weekend counterparts; still, one remains hopeful that an examination of past events can yield useful insights for the future.

The 1974 Domestic Spy Scandal. Soon after James R. Schlesinger was appointed DCI in 1973, he requested from officials in the CIA a listing of any improprieties of which the Agency might be guilty. The new DCI wanted to clean house, as well as avoid culpability himself for old sins.

To his surprise, the list (known by insiders as the "family jewels") proved to be quite extensive, indeed, 693 pages long.[37] Some of the items on this list leaked to *New York Times* reporter Seymour Hersh, whose investigative reporting in turn spawned the "Year of Intelligence" in 1974.

From the point of view of intelligence accountability, one would like to know why law-makers had to rely on this stunning leak to realize that many things were awry at the CIA, and not just Operation Chaos (the CIA's domestic spying program at the heart of Hersh's reporting). Thorough, day-to-day oversight might well have caught wind of at least some of these "jewels." The answer, probably, is that the small intelligence oversight subcommittees that existed on Capitol Hill before 1975 were operating in an era when Congress had a "hands-off" attitude toward intelligence activities. Further, with small staffs on the subcommittees, lawmakers were poorly equipped for serious and continuous intelligence program review, even though these staff personnel were well regarded and did engage in some degree of budget and program review.[38] Poring over budget figures, though important, is unlikely to lead to infor-mation about a program like Operation Chaos, which was buried and disguised in the funding for the Office of Security and the Counterintelligence Staff at the CIA. That kind of discovery would have taken a larger staff and a focus beyond financial spreadsheets.

Even with a larger staff, though, the hands-off philosophy that dominated the thinking at the time among lawmakers with intelligence oversight duties would have proscribed intense day-to-day patrolling. For the Congress rather than DCI Schlesinger to have uncovered the family jewels, lawmakers would have had to be fully engaged in continual hearings and asked serious questions about ongoing intelligence agencies; paid visits to the intelligence agencies; had informal conversations with intelligence officers at various levels of government; and carried out all the other approaches used by overseers possessed of serious intent.[39] Little of this focused review occurred.

The 1987 Iran–Contra Scandal. This scandal occurred well after Congress had set up its "New Intelligence Oversight" procedures in 1976–80, yet the safeguards failed to prevent or even reveal the affair. (A Mideast newspaper disclosed the operations in 1986.) Rumors to the effect that the Reagan administration remained involved in covert actions in Nicaragua, despite the Boland Amendments, circulated throughout Washington, DC in 1984–6. Finally, SSCI and HPSCI leaders decided to meet with two key NSC staff members, the national security adviser Robert C. MacFarlane and staffer Lt. Col. Oliver L. North, to probe the validity of the rumors. The lawmakers sat across the table from the NSC officials at the White House and asked them point-blank whether the Council staff had secretly raised funds to pursue further covert action in Nicaragua. MacFarlane and North lied, denying any NSC staff involvement.[40] Almost as bad, the lawmakers took their disclaimers at face value and dropped the topic. The accountability lesson: when the charges are particularly grave, overseers must question suspects under oath on Capitol Hill. They still may lie, but the odds are reduced; penalties rise sharply when one has committed perjury, perhaps enough to make would-be dissimulators think twice before misleading Congress.

The 1994 Ames Counterintelligence Failure. Most of the time, counterintelligence (CI) is a neglected stepchild on the congressional oversight agenda. It is an arcane topic, requiring the kind of patience that George Smiley exhibited in early Le Carré novels. James J. Angleton, the legendary CIA Chief of Counterintelligence for twenty years (1954–74), did not refer to his discipline as a "wilderness of mirrors" for nothing.[41] Tracking down defectors, false defectors, dangles, and double-agents requires an intense devotion to archival research and persistent cross-checking of bona fides that is unlikely to appeal to members of Congress. Yet surely SSCI and HPSCI have an important obligation to maintain a close watch over how well the intelligence agencies are protecting their own facilities, operations, and documents – the essence of counterintelligence.

By showing more interest in the topic and holding more closed hearings than they did, lawmakers on the Intelligence Committees might have prodded security and counterintelligence officials toward a keener attention to the matter of whether or not hostile intelligence services had managed to penetrate America's secret services. With Congress constantly asking pointed questions about the state of counterintelligence, perhaps the CIA and the FBI would have been more sensitive to the lavish lifestyle of Ames and the erratic behavior of FBI traitor Robert Hanssen. When DCI William E. Colby fired Angleton in 1974, counterintelligence plunged as a priority interest at the CIA, as Colby shifted responsibility for this mission to decentralized elements throughout the Agency.[42] With no one at a high level guiding the CIA's counterintelligence defenses, the Agency became more vulnerable to successful penetrations by America's adversaries. During the 1980s and 1990s, the nation experienced its worst CI setbacks – Ames, Hanssen, and many more.

The 2001 Terrorist Attacks. In 1995, a top secret memo (now partially declassified) came from the CIA's Counterterrorism Center (CTC) to the Aspin-Brown Commission. It warned that "aerial terrorism seems likely at some point – filling an airplane with explosives and dive-bombing a target."[43] This warning appeared in the *President's Daily Brief*, delivered by the CIA to President Bill Clinton and his top national security advisers; and, as well, the Agency briefed members of SSCI and HPSCI about this hair-raising possibility.[44] Yet, six years before the prediction became a reality, none of these policymakers took significant steps to alert US commercial pilots to the danger, urge the FBI to watch flight training schools, or tighten airport security.[45]

When George W. Bush replaced Clinton as president, both the White House counterterrorism expert Richard A. Clarke and the CTC provided fresh warnings to the new national security adviser, Condoleezza Rice (as well as, again, to members of SSCI and HPSCI), that Al Qaeda might resort to aerial terrorism and other methods of attacking the United States. The Bush administration temporized from January to September of 2001; and the congressional oversight committees also did little to improve America's defenses against airplane attacks by terrorists.[46] The 9/11 tragedy was an intelligence failure, certainly; but it was a policy failure, too, in the White House during both Democratic and Republican administrations. Further, it was a failure of accountability on Capitol Hill. What if SSCI and HPSCI had held extensive, executive session hearings on the CTC warning, then followed through to see if commercial pilots, the FBI, and airport security understood the danger and were taking steps to protect the public?

Moreover, government inquiries have discovered that the intelligence agencies failed to coordinate and act on the few shards of specific information they did have regarding the September 11 terrorists.[47] For instance, the agencies proved unable to track two of the nineteen terrorists, despite warnings from the CIA to the FBI about their arrival in San Diego, California. Moreover, the FBI failed to respond to warnings from its own agents in Phoenix and Minneapolis about suspicious flight training undertaken by foreigners in those cities; and the Department of Defense appears to have smothered warnings from the "Able Danger" group of military intelligence officers, whose research had apparently come across the presence of sixty suspected foreign terrorists in the United States almost two years before the 9/11 attacks.[48] On the list were four of the September 11 hijackers, including their Egyptian-born leader, Mohamed Atta. While it would have been difficult – but not impossible – for SSCI and HPSCI to have known about the specific CIA–FBI liaison snafu in 2001 or the internal Bureau memos from Phoenix and Minneapolis, the Committees did know about the Able Danger allegations. What if the Committees had taken them more seriously? And to what extent were lawmakers and their staffs keeping up with the always important question of CIA–FBI relationships, especially with respect to the sharing of intelligence on high-level threats to the United States?

At a deeper level, September 11 was an intelligence failure because the CIA had no assets within Al Qaeda; because the NSA fell far behind on translating relevant signals intelligence ("sigint") intercepts involving suspected terrorists; and because all of America's intelligence agencies lacked sufficient language skills and understanding about nations in the Middle East and South Asia, or even about the objectives and likely motivations of Saddam Hussein or the Al Qaeda leader Osama Bin Laden. To what extent were SSCI and HPSCI probing these questions and encouraging better humint recruitment and training?

The 2003 WMD Failure. The intelligence failures regarding Iraqi WMDs were, in some ways, even more troubling than those that preceded the September 11 attacks. A National Intelligence Estimate (NIE) of October 2002 concluded, as did most intelligence agencies and outside analysts, that unconventional weapons were likely to be present in Iraq. This assessment was based on several inaccurate sources of information. First, because the intelligence community had no significant human assets in Iraq during the interwar years (1992–2002), analysts in the United States extrapolated from what they knew when Americans had "boots on the ground" there as part of the war effort in 1991. During the first Iraqi war, the CIA learned that its prior estimates regarding WMDs were wrong; Saddam's weapons program had advanced far beyond what the CIA's analysts had anticipated. After America's troops departed Iraq in 1991, the CIA lacked reliable ground-based sources; thus, in the run-up to the second war in Iraq, its analysts compensated for their earlier underestimates by, this time, overestimating the probability of WMDs.

Reports from the German asset "Curveball," whose reliability was vouched for by the Germans, also factored into the CIA's calculations. Only recently have the Germans conceded that the Iraqi exile was in fact fabricating his reports. Moreover, the confessions of a captured Al Qaeda member, Ibn al-Shaykh al-Libi, interrogated by the Defense Intelligence Agency (DIA), proved to be further fabrications.[49] In addition, the Iraqi National Congress, led by another Iraqi exile, Ahmed Chalabi, claimed solid knowledge of Iraq's activities. The INC and Chalabi told US intelligence agencies and the second Bush administration that Saddam was indeed pursuing nuclear weapons. Chalabi's reliability has since been called into question. Critics maintain that his purpose may have been chiefly to push for a US invasion, so that he might advance his personal political agenda: the toppling of Saddam, followed by his own rise to power in Iraq (where he is currently positioned high in the provisional government).

Analysts in the Intelligence and Research (INR) arm of the State Department and in the Department of Energy pointed out that controversial aluminum tubes purchased by the Hussein regime were probably combustion chambers for conventional rockets, not meant for use in uranium enrichment chambers. They were also skeptical about Curveball's reports on Iraqi mobile biological weapons labs. Further, US Air Force Intelligence disputed the administration's assertion that Iraq's unmanned aerial vehicles (UAVs) had a long-range capability. For the most part, though, these were internal government disputes that took place outside the hearing of the American public; the dissenting views of the smaller agencies were largely dismissed by the larger and more powerful agencies.

Had SSCI and HPSCI examined these issues more closely, they would have understood that the 2002 NIE was anything but a definitive report on Iraqi WMDs. In reality, the estimate was a rush job prepared in days, rather than the usual time of several months for an NIE, resulting in what has been called "one of the most flawed documents in the history of American intelligence."[50] Lawmakers would have learned that additional on-the-ground fact-finding was sorely needed; and that many intelligence analysts felt uneasy about the humint reporting provided by Curveball, al-Libi, and Chalibi. Armed with this understanding, the Congress could then have contributed significantly to the debate on whether war against Iraq was justified immediately in March of 2003, or should await further information on the WMD hypothesis. Instead, lawmakers (as well as *New York Times* reporters) swallowed whole the arguments of the White House for war, without any countervailing evidence they might have developed themselves had they probed into the NIE process and the other sources of intelligence (INR, the Energy Department, US Air Force Intelligence) that questioned the White House and Defense Department intelligence arguments for war.

Continuing barriers to effective intelligence oversight

Success in improving intelligence oversight on Capitol Hill will require above all a stronger motivation among the members and staff of the SSCI and HPSCI. Since the creation of these committees, their members have already outperformed their marginally engaged predecessors from 1947 to 1974. And their staffs are considerably larger and better prepared. Even so, the efforts of the two panels fall short of full engagement at the member level, and even the best of staffs cannot compensate for lawmakers who treat their oversight responsibilities as a secondary concern (although a few lawmakers over the years have been deeply committed to their oversight responsibilities[51]). Worse still, since the early 1990s the two Intelligence Committees have been beset with partisan bickering, overturning the tradition since 1975 on Capitol Hill of keeping sensitive intelligence issues apart from interparty rivalries.[52]

Neither SSCI nor HPSCI managed to sniff out the Iran–Contra operation; the weakened counterintelligence posture that allowed the acts of treason by Ames, Hanssen, and others; the poor humint prior to the 9/11 attacks; or the misleading WMD analysis that provided a rationale for the war against Iraq in 2003. The venerable saying, "Eternal vigilance is the price of liberty," is wise counsel. This is the price, cheap in return for the benefits of freedom, that SSCI and HPSCI members must pay – or they should be replaced by the congressional leadership or the voters in their constituencies.

Lawmakers must really want to be effective overseers, or else the constitutional safeguards extolled by the founders are doomed to failure. Nurturing of this motivation depends upon building into the congressional culture better incentives to encourage attention to the duties of intelligence accountability. Incentives could include prestigious awards presented by the congressional leadership and civic groups to dedicated and accomplished overseers, Capitol Hill perks dispensed by the leadership based on the devotion of lawmakers to accountability, and publicity in national and hometown newspapers underscoring admirable oversight achievements by individual members. Voters must also become more aware of the importance of accountability, rewarding those lawmakers at the polls who work industriously in order to make existing laws work better and improve the performance of the federal bureaucracy. Journalists and educators can contribute much to this task of civic awareness.

Membership motivation is, however, only half of the equation for success. The other half has to do with executive branch cooperation in the quest for improved intelligence accountability. A common term of derision among intelligence professionals and White House officials toward SSCI and HPSCI members is that they are "micro-managers" – an accusation suggesting that lawmakers and their staffs are meddlers apt to harm sensitive intelligence operations.

Former President George H.W. Bush, who served as DCI near the end of the investigations carried out by the Church and Pike Committees, referred recently to the members and staff of those panels as "untutored little jerks."[53] A spate of *Wall Street Journal* op-ed pieces in 2003 placed the blame for the 9/11 and WMD intelligence failures on legislative overseers and the damage they had caused by their probes into the operations of the intelligence agencies. In 2006, the chairman of the Republican National Committee pointed to the reforms of the Church and Pike Committees as a primary source of America's intelligence weaknesses on the eve of the 9/11 attacks.[54] These critics evidently wish to turn the clock back to the pre-1975 era, when oversight was weak and the intelligence agencies slipped into domestic spying and other questionable activities.

If the executive branch insists on viewing lawmakers as "an outside interference," as the nation's national security adviser, Vice Admiral John M. Poindexter, referred to Congress during the planning of the Iran–Contra operations and as the second Bush administration has treated lawmakers in the controversy over NSA's bypassing of the Foreign Intelligence Surveillance Act or FISA Court,[55] then overseers will be cut off from the information they need to properly evaluate intelligence programs. The end result will be an intelligence community more and more isolated from any semblance of checks-and-balances and increasingly likely to present the nation with its next major intelligence scandal or failure. When Congress attempted to investigate the 9/11 failure, the White House, the DCI, and various intelligence officers delayed and obstructed the work of the Joint Committee.[56] Stonewalling and slow-rolling are prime enemies of accountability and the form of government envisioned by Madison and other founders. The essence of genuine oversight is an attitude of comity between the branches, as executive officials and lawmakers join together to stamp out inept and improper intelligence activities.

The Congress must also put its own house in order, designing a more sensible division of labor for intelligence oversight. Presently, the tangled jurisdictional lines for accountability over the secret agencies make the Gordian knot seem like a simple bowline. In addition to SSCI and HPSCI, the Committees on Armed Services, Judiciary, and Appropriations also presently have a claim on intelligence review. In all but the most extraordinary circumstances, this list needs to be reduced to SSCI, HPSCI, and the Appropriations Committees. Further, the Appropriations Committees must closely adhere to the budget ceilings and priorities of the authorizing committees, rather than ignoring the work of SSCI and HPSCI as is frequently the case today.[57] Only when the Armed Services and Judiciary Committees have an overwhelming case for involvement in intelligence hearings – as in the case of the Senate Judiciary Committee's long interest in the proper functioning of the Foreign Intelligence Surveillance Act of 1978 – should intelligence jurisdiction be temporarily widened to accommodate their concerns. Along with the creation of attractive oversight incentives for lawmakers, nothing is more vital for improved intelligence accountability on Capital Hill than the correction of this current jurisdictional confusion.

Conclusion

Intelligence accountability since 1975 has been infinitely more serious than before that watershed year; still, it is nowhere near as effective as it can and should be if the United States hopes to reduce the odds of another major intelligence failure or scandal in the future. In place of the sporadic patrolling and ad hoc responses to fire alarms, lawmakers and their staffs will need to redouble their commitment to a continuous, day-in-day-out scrutiny of intelligence activities, praising meritorious operations, suggesting ways to improve new or faltering programs, and rooting out improper initiatives and miscreant officials before they lead to full-blown disasters that harm the nation's security and good reputation. For this to work, the public will need to acquire a better understanding and appreciation of accountability. Scholars, journalists, and public officials must engage in more effective "public diplomacy" at home to educate Americans about the value of accountability as carried out by members of Congress. None of this will be easy. Yet, as America's founders understood, the virtue of democracy lies not in its ease, but in its promise to protect the people from the abuse of power – perhaps most especially secret power.

Notes

*This chapter is an amalgamation, revision, and extension of a series of papers presented by the author during 2005 and 2006, at conferences held by the University of Nebraska in Lincoln; the Canadian Centre of International and Security Studies, Carleton University in Ottawa; the RAND Corporation in Washington, DC; and the International Studies Association in San Diego. The author is grateful for the helpful suggestions of colleagues who commented on these earlier drafts.

1 See Hans Born, Loch K. Johnson and Ian Leigh, eds., *Who's Watching the Spies? Establishing Intelligence Service Accountability* (Washington, DC: Potomac Books, 2005); Loch K. Johnson, "Accountability and America's Secret Foreign Policy: Keeping a Legislative Eye on the CIA," *Foreign Policy Analysis* 1 (Spring 2005), pp. 99–120; "Presidents, Lawmakers, and Spies: Intelligence Accountability in the United States," *Presidential Studies Quarterly* 34 (December 2004), pp. 828–37; and "Supervising America's Secret Foreign Policy: A Shock Theory of Congressional Oversight for Intelligence," in David P. Forsythe, Patrice C. McMahon, and Andrew Wedeman, eds., *American Foreign Policy in a Globalized World* (New York: Routledge, 2006), pp. 173–92. On the domestic spy scandal and the ensuing investigations that led to a new and much more serious era of intelligence oversight, see Loch K. Johnson, *Season of Inquiry: The Senate Intelligence Investigation* (Lexington, KY: University Press of Kentucky, 1985); and Frank Smist, *Congress Oversees the Intelligence Community, 1947–1989* (Knoxville, TN: University of Tennessee Press, 1990).
2 The Kean Commission (led by former Governor Thomas H. Kean, R–New Jersey), *The 9/11 Commission Report: Final Report of the National Commission on Terrorist Attacks Upon the United States* (New York: Norton, 2004), p. 420.
3 Sen. John McCain, remarks, "Meet the Press," NBC Television (November 21, 2004).
4 Rep. Nancy Pelosi, "The Gap in Intelligence Oversight," *Washington Post* (January 15, 2006), p. B7. For the breaking story on NSA warrantless wiretapping, see James Risen and Eric Lichtblau, *New York Times* (December 16, 2005), p. A1.
5 M.D. McCubbins and T. Schwartz, "Congressional Oversight Overlooked: Police Patrols and Fire Alarms," *American Journal of Political Science* 28 (1984), pp. 165–79.
6 Harry H. Ransom, "Secret Intelligence Agencies and Congress," *Society* 123 (1975), pp. 33–8. This description of intelligence oversight seems to fit congressional approaches to accountability across the policy board, based on the author's observations as a Hill staffer for six years and, more importantly, the broad scholarly literature. See, for example, Joel D. Aberbach, *Keeping a Watchful Eye: The Politics of Congressional Oversight* (Washington, DC: The Brookings Institution, 1990); and Christopher J. Deering, "Alarms and Patrols: Legislative Oversight in Foreign and Defense Policy," in C.C. Campbell, N.C. Rae, and J.F. Stack, Jr., *Congress and the Politics of Foreign Policy* (Upper Saddle River, NJ: Prentice-Hall, 2003), pp. 112–38.
7 David Mayhew, *The Electoral Connection* (New Haven, CT: Yale University Press, 1974).
8 Johnson, "Accountability and America's Secret Foreign Policy," op. cit.
9 I am grateful to my research assistant, Rachael Lee Stewart, for providing these data.
10 Harry Howe Ransom, e-mail communication to the author, February 7, 2006.
11 See Born, Johnson, and Leigh, op. cit.
12 See Loch K. Johnson, John C. Kuzenski, and Erna Gellner, "The Study of Congressional Investigations: Research Strategies," *Congress & the Presidency* 19 (Autumn 1992), pp. 138–56.

13 See, for example, Scott Shane, "Senate Panel's Partisanship Troubles Former Members," *New York Times* (March 12, 2006), p. A18.

14 Almost every day from December 22 through 31,1974, *Times* reporter Seymour Hersh wrote articles that charged the CIA with malfeasance at home and abroad. For example: "Huge C.I.A. Operation Reported in U.S. Against Antiwar Forces, Other Dissidents in Nixon Years," *New York Times* (December 22, 2006), p. A1; and "Underground for the C.I.A. in New York: An Ex-Agent Tells of Spying on Students," *New York Times* (December 29, 1974), p. A1. The immediate response by Congress was to enact the Hughes-Ryan Amendment on December 31, 1974, which put into place closer legislative supervision of covert actions (special intelligence operations designed to manipulate events overseas). The new law, the first ever to place controls on the CIA since its founding legislation in 1947–49, was a reaction to Hersh's claim that the CIA had acted improperly against the democratically elected regime of Salvador Allende in Chile. In January 1975, lawmakers then established major panels of inquiry in the Senate and House to investigate all of the allegations advanced by the *Times* and other media sources: the Church Committee in the Senate (led by Frank Church, D-Idaho) and what would become the Pike Committee in the House (led by Otis Pike, D-New York). Of greatest concern to most members of Congress were the stories of illegal domestic spying by the CIA. The author served as special assistant to Senator Church throughout the sixteen-month inquiry. For a recollection of these days, see Loch K. Johnson, "Congressional Supervision of America's Secret Agencies: The Experience and Legacy of the Church Committee," *Public Administration Review* 64 (January 2004), pp. 3–14.

15 For the main Church Committee reports, see Select Committee to Study Governmental Operations with Respect to Intelligence Activities, *Final Report*, 94th Cong., 2nd Sess., Sen. Rept. No. 94–755, 6 vols (Washington, DC: Government Printing Office, March 1976). The Pike Committee report was leaked and published as "The CIA Report the President Doesn't Want You to Read: The Pike Papers," *Village Voice* (February 16 and 23, 1976).

16 US Congress, *Report on the Iran-Contra Affair*, Senate Select Committee on Secret Military Assistance to Iran and the Nicaraguan Opposition and House Select Committee to Investigate Covert Arms Transactions with Iran, S. Rept. 100–216 and House Rept. 100–433 (November 1987). The chairs of the combined committees were Daniel K. Inouye (D-Hawaii) and Representative Lee H. Hamilton (D-Indiana). For an account by two senators involved in the investigation, see William S. Cohen and George J. Mitchell, *Men of Zeal: A Candid Inside Story of the Iran-Contra Hearings* (New York: Viking, 1988).

17 This investigation was led by former Secretaries of Defense Les Aspin and, upon his death in the middle of the inquiry, Harold Brown. See Loch K. Johnson, "The Aspin-Brown Intelligence Inquiry: Behind the Closed Doors of a Blue Ribbon Commission," *Studies in Intelligence* 48 (Winter 2004), pp. 1–20. On the specifics of the Ames case, see David Wise, *Nightmover* (New York: Harper Collins, 1995); and "An Assessment of the Aldrich H. Ames Espionage Case and its Implications for U.S. Intelligence," *Staff Report*, S. Prt. 103–90, Select Committee on Intelligence, US Senate, 103rd Cong., 2nd Sess. (November 1, 1994).

18 See Joint Inquiry into Intelligence Community Activities Before and After the Terrorist Attacks of September 11, 2001, *Final Report*, US Senate Select Committee on Intelligence and US House Permanent Select Committee on Intelligence (led respectively by Senator Bob Graham, D-Florida, and Representative Porter J. Goss, R-Florida), Washington, DC: December 2002; Kean Commission, op. cit.

19 "Intelligence Authorization Act for Fiscal Year 2005," *Report 108–558*, Permanent Select Committee on Intelligence (the Goss Committee), US House of Representatives, 108th Cong., 2nd Sess. (June 21, 2004), pp. 23–7.

20 The Commission on the Intelligence Capabilities of the United States Regarding Weapons of Mass Destruction was led by former Senator Charles S. Robb (D-Virginia) and Judge Laurence H. Silberman.

21 *Report on the US Intelligence Community's Prewar Intelligence Assessments on Iraq* (the Roberts Report), Senate Select Committee on Intelligence (the Roberts Committee), US Senate, 108th Cong., 2nd Sess. (July 7, 2004). For the British counterpart investigation, see "Review of Intelligence on Weapons of Mass Destruction," *Report of a Committee of Privy Counsellors*, Chairman, Lord Butler (July 14, 2004).

22 In December 2005, the *New York Times* charged the Bush administration with illegal domestic spying by the NSA. Whether this allegation would rise to the level of an alarm remained unclear, but unlikely, by mid-2006.

23 This law (Public Law 97–200, Title VI, Sec. 601, 50 U.S.C. 421) would become front page news in 2004 when administration officials leaked the name of a CIA operative, some claimed as revenge for her husband's criticism of the second President Bush's rush to war in Iraq. See Douglas Jehl, "Through an Indictment, A Glimpse Into a Secretive and Influential White House Office," *New York Times* (October 30, 2005), p. A28.

24 94 Stat. 1981, Title IV, Sec. 501, 50 U.S.C. 413. See Loch K. Johnson, "Legislative Reform of Intelligence Policy," *Polity* 17 (Spring 1985), pp. 549–73.

25 Rhodri Jeffreys-Jones, "Why Was the CIA Established in 1947?" in Rhodri Jeffreys-Jones and Christopher Andrew, eds., *Eternal Vigilance? 50 Years of the CIA* (London: Cass, 1997), pp. 20–41; and Loch K. Johnson, "A Central Intelligence System: Truman's Dream Deferred," *American Journal of Intelligence* 21 (February 2006), pp. 16–36.

26 See Loch K. Johnson, *America's Secret Power: The CIA in a Democratic Society* (New York: Oxford University Press, 1989), and *Secret Agencies: US Intelligence in a Hostile World* (New Haven, CT: Yale University Press, 1996).

27 Sections 106 and 107 of Public Law 99–569 (Intelligence Authorization Act for Fiscal year 1987); see Permanent Select Committee on Intelligence, *Compilation of Intelligence Laws and Related Laws and Executive Orders of Interest to the National Intelligence Community*, US House of Representatives, 104th Cong., 1st Sess. (July 1995), pp. 739–41.

28 This analysis does not attempt to include every intelligence scandal or failure; that list is much longer (see, for example, Johnson, *Secret Agencies*, op. cit.). But, in the author's opinion, it does include the most significant. Not everyone will agree with the choices. For instance, some think that the CIA's failure to predict the fall of the Soviet Union is one of its most significant analytic errors (see, for example, Daniel P. Moynihan, "Do We Still Need the C.I.A.? The State Department Can Do the Job," *New York Times* (May 19, 1991), p. E17). The author believes that this sets the bar too high; no one could, or did, predict that epic event with any accuracy. The CIA's Soviet analysts (SOVA), however, performed remarkably well in tracking the decline of the Soviet economy during the 1980s and suggesting that this could lead to a profound political upheaval in Russia and beyond (Johnson, *Secret Agencies*, op. cit.). The excellence of this tracking is why the surprise of the Soviet fall is not included here as a major failure.

29 Timothy J. Burger, "A New White House Memo Excludes CIA Director," *Time* (June 5, 2005), p. 21.

30 David M. Barrett notes, however, in his *The CIA and Congress: The Untold Story from Truman to Kennedy* (Lawrence, KS: University Press of Kansas, 2005), that lawmakers did not ignore their oversight duties completely and sometimes behaved as aggressive patrollers. For the most part, though, Barrett concedes that the state of intelligence accountability before 1974 paled in comparison to the supervision that occurred after the Congress established the two Intelligence Committees as permanent and well-staffed organizations on Capitol Hill.

31 See Richard K. Betts, "Analysis, War and Decision: Why Intelligence Failures Are Inevitable," *World Politics* 31 (October 1978), pp. 61–89.

32 The Inouye-Hamilton Report, op. cit.; and Cohen and Mitchell, op.cit.

33 Ibid.

34 Remarks, CNN (October 14, 2002); see, also, Kevin Whitelaw and David E. Kaplan, "Don't Ask, Don't Tell," 137 *U.S. News & World Report* (September 13, 2004), p. 36.

35 Remarks, "The Lehrer News Hour," PBS Television (October 17, 2002). See, also, Senator Bob Graham with Jeff Nussbaum, *Intelligence Matters: The CIA, the FBI, Saudi Arabia, and the Failure of America's War on Terror* (New York: Random House, 2004).

36 House Permanent Select Committee on Intelligence, *Report 108–588* (2004), op. cit.

37 See William E. Colby and Peter Forbath, *Honorable Men: My Life in the CIA* (New York: Simon & Schuster, 1978), pp. 340ff.

38 See Barrett, op. cit.

39 See Aberbach, op. cit.; and *Workshop on Congressional Oversight and Investigations*, U.S. House of Representatives, 96th Cong., 1st Sess. (October 22, 1979).

40 The Inouye-Hamilton Report, op. cit.; and Cohen Mitchell, op. cit.

41 See David C. Martin, *Wilderness of Mirrors* (New York: Harper and Row, 1980). Angleton drew the metaphor from a T.S. Eliot poem, "Gerontion."

42 See John F. Elliff and Loch K. Johnson, "Counterintelligence," *Foreign and Military Intelligence, Final Report*, The Church Committee, op. cit.

43 Johnson, "The Aspin-Brown Intelligence Inquiry," op. cit., p. 12.

44 Author's interviews with officials in the Clinton administration and members of SSCI and HPSCI, Washington, DC (March and July, 1995).

45 Kean Commission 9/11 Report, *Final Report of the National Commission on Terrorist Attacks upon the United States* (New York: W.W. Norton, 2004).

46 Richard A. Clark, *Against All Enemies* (New York: Free Press, 2004).

47 Kean Commission, op.cit.; Loch K. Johnson, "A Framework for Strengthening U.S. Intelligence," *Yale Journal of International Affairs* 2 (February 2006), pp. 116–131.

48 Louis Freeh (the former FBI Director), "Why Did the 9/11 Commission Ignore 'Able Danger'?" *Wall Street Journal* (November 17, 2005), p. A16.

49 Douglas Jehl, "Report Warned Bush Team About Intelligence Doubts," *New York Times* (November 6, 2005), p. A14. The report in the title is a DIA analysis prepared and circulated to government officials in February 2002.

50 David Barstow, William J. Broad, and Jeff Gerth, "How the White House Used Disputed Arms Intelligence," *New York Times* (October 3, 2004), p. A18.

51 See, for example, Loch K. Johnson, "Congress and the CIA: Monitoring the Dark Side of Government," *Legislative Studies Quarterly* 5 (November 1980), pp. 477–99.

52 See Johnson, "Accountability and America's Secret Foreign Policy," op.cit.; and L. Britt Snider, "Congressional Oversight of Intelligence after September 11," in Jennifer E. Sims and Burton Gerber, eds., *Transforming U.S. Intelligence* (Washington, DC: Georgetown University Press, 2006), pp. 239–58. The exception was the partisan wrangling over covert action in Nicaragua during the 1980s.

53 Quoted in Bob Drogin, "Spy Agencies Fear Some Applicants Are Terrorists," *Los Angeles Times* (March 8, 2005), p. A1.

54 Ken Mehlman, remarks, ABC News, "This Week with George Stephanopoulos," February 5, 2006. The actual reasons for the intelligence weaknesses are much more complex and have nothing to do with the Church or Pike Committee inquiries, which were designed to weed out wrongdoing by the intelligence agencies and focus their energies on more effective collection and analysis; see Johnson, *Season of Inquiry*, op.cit., note 1, and "A Framework for Strengthening U.S. Intelligence," op.cit.

55 For the Poindexter quote, see US Congress, the Inouye–Hamilton Report, vol. 8, op.cit., p. 159; on the resistance of the Bush administration to keeping the intelligence oversight committees fully informed on NSA wiretapping, see Scott Shane and Eric Lichtblau, "Full Committee Gets Briefing on Eavesdropping," *New York Times* (February 9, 2006), p. A20.

56 Joint Inquiry, *Final Report,* op.cit.

57 Whitelaw and Kaplan, op.cit., p. 36.

Appendices

Appendix A

The US Intelligence Community (IC), 2006*

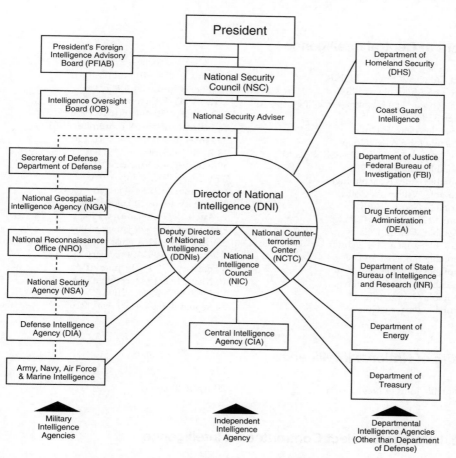

* From 1947 to 2004, a Director of Central Intelligence (DCI) led the Intelligence Community, rather than a Director of National Intelligence. The Department of Homeland Security and the Coast Guard did not become part of the IC until 2003, and the Drug Enforcement Administration, in 2006.

Appendix B

Leadership of the US Intelligence Community (IC), 1947–2006

Directors of Central Intelligence

Rear Adm. Sidney W. Souers, USNR	23 January 1946–10 June 1946
Lt. Gen. Hoyt S. Vandenberg, USA	10 June 1946–1 May 1947
Rear Adm. Roscoe H. Hillenkoetter, USN	1 May 1947–7 October 1950
Gen. Walter Bedell Smith, USA	7 October 1950–9 February 1953
The Honorable Allen W. Dulles	26 February 1953–29 November 1961
The Honorable John A. McCone	29 November 1961–28 April 1965
Vice Adm. William F. Raborn, Jr., USN (Ret.)	28 April 1965–30 June 1966
The Honorable Richard Helms	30 June 1966–2 February 1973
The Honorable James R. Schlesinger	2 February 1973–2 July 1973
The Honorable William E. Colby	4 September 1973–30 January 1976
The Honorable George Bush	30 January 1976–20 January 1977
Adm. Stanfield Turner, USN (Ret.)	9 March 1977–20 January 1980
The Honorable William J. Casey	28 January 1981–29 January 1987
The Honorable William H. Webster	26 May 1987–31 August 1991
The Honorable Robert M. Gates	6 November 1991–20 January 1993
The Honorable R. James Woolsey	5 February 1993–10 January 1995
The Honorable John M. Deutch	10 May 1995–15 December 1996
The Honorable George J. Tenet	11 July 1997–11 July 2004
The Honorable Porter J. Goss	24 September 2004–20 April 2005

Directors of National Intelligence

The Honorable John D. Negroponte	20 April 2005–

Chairs, US Senate Select Committee on Intelligence

1976–77	Daniel K. Inouye, Democrat, Hawaii
1977–81	Birch Bayh, Democrat, Indiana
1981–85	Barry Goldwater, Republican, Arizona

1985–87	David Durenberger, Republican, Minnesota
1987–93	David L. Boren, Democrat, Oklahoma
1993–95	Dennis DeConcini, Democrat, Arizona
1995–97	Arlan Specter, Republican, Pennsylvania
1997–01	Richard C. Shelby, Republican, Alabama
2001–02	Bob Graham, Democrat, Florida
2002–	Pat Roberts, Republican, Kansas

Chairs, House Permanent Select Committee on Intelligence

1977–85	Edward P. Boland, Democrat, Massachussetts
1985–87	Lee H. Hamilton, Democrat, Indiana
1987–89	Louis Stokes, Democrat, Ohio
1989–91	Anthony C. Beilenson, Democrat, California
1991–93	Dave McCurdy, Democrat, Oklahoma
1993–95	Dan Glickman, Democrat, Kansas
1995–97	Larry Combest, Republican, Texas
1997–2004	Porter Goss, Republican, Florida
2004–	Peter Hoekstra, Republican, Michigan

Membership, Senate Select Committee on Intelligence, 2006

Republicans	*Democrats*
Pat Roberts, Kansas, Chair	John D. Rockfeller, IV, West Virginia, Vice Chair
Orrin G. Hatch, Utah	Carl Levin, Michigan
Mike DeWine, Ohio	Dianne Feinstein, California
Christopher S. Bond, Missouri	Ron Wyden, Oregon
Trent Lottt, Mississippi	Evan Bayh, Indiana
Olympia J. Snowne, Maine	Barbara A. Mikulski, Maryland
Chuck Hagel, Nebraska	Russell D. Feingold, Wisconsin
Saxby Chambliss, Georgia	

Membership, House Permanent Select Committee on Intelligence, 2006

Republicans	*Democrats*
Peter Hoekstra, Michigan, Chair	Jane Harman, California, Vice Chair
Ray LaHood, Illinois	Alcee L. Hastings, Florida
Terry Everett, Alabama	Silvestre Reyes, Texas
Elton Gallegly, California	Leonard L. Boswell, Iowa
Heather Wilson, New Mexico	Robert E. (Bud) Cramer, Jr., Alabama
Jo Ann Davis, Virginia	Anna G. Eshoo, California
Mac Thornberry, Texas	Rush D. Holt, New Jersey
John McHugh, New York	C.A. Dutch Ruppersberger, Maryland
Todd Tiahrt, Kansas	John Tierney, Massachussetts
Mike Rogers, Michigan	
Rick Renzi, Arizona	
Darrell Issa, California	

Appendix C

The intelligence cycle

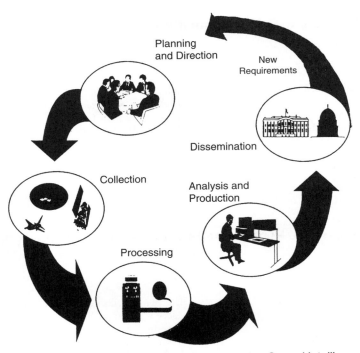

Planning and Direction

New Requirements

Dissemination

Collection

Analysis and Production

Processing

Adapted from *Factbook on Intelligence*, Office of Public Affairs, Central Intelligence Agency (October 1993), p. 14.

Select Bibliography*

Aldrich, Richard J. 2002. *The Hidden Hand: Britain, America, and Cold War Secret Intelligence.* Woodstock, NY: Overlook Press.

Andrew, Christopher. 1995. *For the President's Eyes Only: Secret Intelligence and the American Presidency from Washington to Bush.* New York: Harper Collins.

Aspin-Brown Commission. 1996. *Preparing for the 21st Century: An Appraisal of U.S. Intelligence,* Report of the Commission on the Roles and Capabilities of the United States Intelligence Community. Washington, DC: Government Printing Office: March 1.

Bamford, James. 1984. *The Puzzle Palace.* Boston: Houghton Mifflin.

Berkowitz, Bruce, and Allen Goodman. 2000. *Best Truth: Intelligence in the Information Age.* New Haven, CT: Yale University Press.

Betts, Richard K. 2002. "Fixing Intelligence," *Foreign Affairs* 81 (January–February): 43–59.

Bissell, Richard M., Jr., with Jonathan E. Lewis and Frances T. Rudlo. 1998. *Reflections of a Cold War.* New Haven, CT: Yale University Press.

Born, Hans, Loch K. Johnson, and Ian Leigh. 2005. *Who's Watching the Spies? Establishing Intelligence Service Accountability.* Washington, DC: Potomac Books.

Brugioni, Dino A. 1969. "The Unidentifieds," *Studies in Intelligence* (Summer): 1–20.

Burrows, William E. 1986. *Deep Black: Space Espionage and National Security.* New York: Random House.

Campbell, Duncan. 2003. "Afghan Prisoners Beaten to Death," *The Guardian* (March 7): 1.

Central Intelligence Agency. 1983. *Fact Book on Intelligence.*

Church Committee (Select Committee to Study Governmental Operations with Respect to Intelligence Activities). 1975a. Declassified CIA memorandum, Committee files, U.S. Senate, 94th Cong., 2d Sess.

———. 1975b. "Alleged Assassination Plots Involving Foreign Leaders," *Interim Report. S. Rept. No. 94–465.* Washington, DC: U.S. Government Printing Office, November 20.

———. 1976. *Final Report, Sen. Rept. No. 94–755,* vol. 1. Washington, DC: U.S. Government Printing Office.

Cirincione, Joseph. 2000. "Assessing the Assessment: The 1999 National Intelligence Estimate of the Ballistic Missile Threat," *Nonproliferation Review* (Spring): 125–37.

Cohen, William S., and George J. Mitchell. 1988. *Men of Zeal: A Candid Inside Story of the Iran-Contra Hearings.* New York: Viking.

Colby, William E., and Peter Forbath. 1978. *Honorable Men: My Life in the CIA.* New York: Simon & Schuster.

Cradock, Percy. 2002. *Know Your Enemy: How the Joint Intelligence Committee Saw the World.* London: John Murray.

Currie, James. 1998. "Iran-Contra and Congressional Oversight of the CIA," *International Journal of Intelligence and Counterintelligence* 11 (Summer): 185–210.

Daugherty, William J. 2004. *Executive Secrets: Covert Action and the Presidency.* Lexington, KY: University Press of Kentucky.

Davis, Jack. 1995. "A Policymaker's Perspective on Intelligence Analysis," *Studies in Intelligence* 38: 7–15.

Gates, Robert M. 1996. *From the Shadows.* New York: Simon & Schuster.

Gill, Peter, and Mark Phythian. 2006. *Intelligence in an Insecure World.* Cambridge: Polity Press.

Godson, Roy S. 1996. *Dirty Tricks or Trump Cards: U.S. Covert Action and Counter-intelligence.* Washington, DC: Brassey's.

Graham, Senator Bob, with Jeff Nussbaum. 2004. *Intelligence Matters.* New York: Random House.

Halpern, Samuel, and Hayden B. Peake. 1989. "Did Angleton Jail Nosenko?" *International Journal of Intelligence and Counterintelligence* 3 (Winter): 451–64.

Harden, Toby. 2003. "CIA 'Pressure' on Al Qaeda Chief," *Washington Post* (March 6): A1.

Hastedt, Glenn. 1986. "The Constitutional Control of Intelligence," *Intelligence and National Security* 1 (May): 255–71.

Hennessy, Peter. 2003. *The Secret State: Whitehall and the Cold War.* London: Penguin.

Herman, Michael. 1996. *Intelligence Power in Peace and War.* New York: Cambridge University Press.

Heuer, Richards J., Jr. 1981. "Strategic Deception and Counterdeception," *International Studies Quarterly* 25 (June): 294–327.

Hitz, Frederick P. 2004. *The Great Game: The Myth and Reality of Espionage.* New York: Knopf.

Hulnick, Arthur S. 1986. "The Intelligence Producer-Policy Consumer Linkage: A Theoretical Approach," *Intelligence and National Security* 1 (May): 212–33.

——. 1999. *Fixing the Spy Machine: Preparing American Intelligence for the Twenty-First Century.* Westport, CT: Praeger.

Jackson, William R. 1990. "Congressional Oversight of Intelligence: Search for a Framework," *Intelligence and National Security* 5 (July): 113–37.

Jeffreys-Jones, Rhodri. 1989. *The CIA and American Democracy.* New Haven, CT: Yale University Press.

Jervis, Robert. 1986–87. "Intelligence and Foreign Policy," *International Security* 11 (Winter): 141–61.

Johnson, Loch K. 1980. "The U.S. Congress and the CIA: Monitoring the Dark Side of Government," *Legislative Studies Quarterly* 5 (November): 477–99.

——. 1985. *A Season Inquiry: The Senate Intelligence Investigation.* Lexington, KY: University Press of Kentucky, 1985.

——. 1989. *America's Secret Power: The CIA in a Democratic Society.* New York: Oxford University Press.

——. 1996. *Secret Agencies: U.S. Intelligence in a Hostile World.* New Haven, CT: Yale University Press.

——. 2001. "The CIA's Weakest Link," *Washington Monthly* 33 (July/August): 9–14.

——. 2002. *Bombs, Bugs, Drugs, and Thugs: Intelligence and America's Quest for Security.* New York: New York University Press.

——. 2004. "The Aspin-Brown Intelligence Inquiry: Behind the Closed Doors of a Blue Ribbon Commission," *Studies in Intelligence* 48 (Winter): 1–20.

——. 2006. "A Framework for Strengthening U.S. Intelligence," *Yale Journal of International Affairs* 1 (Winter/Spring): 116–31.

—— and James J. Wirtz, eds. 2004. *Strategic Intelligence: Windows Into a Secret World.* Los Angeles, CA: Roxbury.

Johnson, Paul. 1997. "No Cloak and Dagger Required: Intelligence Support to UN Peacekeeping," *Intelligence and National Security* 12 (October): 102–12.

Johnson, William R. 1987. *Thwarting Enemies at Home and Abroad: How to Be a Counter-intelligence Office.* Bethesda, MD: Stone Trail Press.

Kaiser, Frederick M. 1992. "Congress and the Intelligence Community: Taking the Road Less Traveled," in Roger H. Davidson, ed., *The Postreform Congress.* New York: St Martin's Press: 279–300.

Knott, Stephen F. 1996. *Secret and Sanctioned: Covert Operations and the American Presidency.* New York: Oxford University Press.

Krieger, Wolfgang. "German Intelligence History: A Field in Search of Scholars," *Intelligence and National Security* 19 (Summer 2004): 185–98.

Lowenthal, Mark M. 2005. *U.S. Intelligence: Evolution and Anatomy,* 3rd ed. Westport, CT: Praeger.

——. 2006. *Intelligence: From Secrets to Policy,* 3rd ed. Washington, DC: CQ Press.

Manget, Fred F. 2006. "Intelligence and the Criminal Law System," *Stanford Law and Policy Review* 17: 415–436.

Masterman, Sir John. 1972. *Double Cross System of the War of 1939–45.* New Haven, CT: Yale University Press.

May, Ernest R. 1992. "Intelligence: Backing into the Future," *Foreign Affairs* 71 (Summer): 63–72.

Millis, John. 1998. Speech, Central Intelligence Retiree's Association, Langley, Virginia.

368

Naylor, Sean. 2003. "The Lessons of Anaconda," *New York Times* (March 2): A13.

9/11 Commission. 2004. *Report* (New York: Norton).

Olmsted, Kathryn S. 1996. *Challenging the Secret Government: The Post-Watergate Investigations of the CIA and FBI.* Chapel Hill, NC: University of North Carolina Press.

——. 2002. *Red Spy Queen: A Biography of Elizabeth Bentley.* Chapel Hill, NC: University of North Carolina Press.

Pelosi, Nancy (D, California). 2002. Remarks to Loch K. Johnson, Athens, Georgia (November 26).

Pillar, Paul R. 2006. "Intelligence, Policy, and the War in Iraq," *Foreign Affairs* 85: 15–27.

Powers, Thomas. 1979. *The Man Who Kept the Secrets: Richard Helms and the CIA.* New York: Knopf.

Prados, John. 1986. *Presidents' Secret Wars: CIA and Pentagon Covert Operations Since World War II.* New York: Dial.

Ransom, Harry Howe. 1970. *The Intelligence Establishment.* Cambridge, MA: Harvard University Press.

Richelson, Jeffrey T. 1999. *The U.S. Intelligence Community*, 4th ed. Cambridge, MA: Ballinger.

——. 2005. *The Wizards of Langley.* Boulder, CO: Westview Press.

Rockefeller Commission. 1975. *Report.* Washington, DC: Government Printing Office.

Russell, Richard L. 2005. *Weapons Proliferation and War in the Greater Middle East.* London: Routledge.

Schelling, Thomas C. 1962. "Preface" to Roberta Wohlstetter, *Pearl Harbor: Warning and Decision.* Stanford, CA: Stanford University Press.

Schwarz, Frederick A.O., Jr., 1987. "Recalling Major Lessons of the Church Committee," *New York Times* (July 20): A25.

Scoville, Herbert. 1976. "Is Espionage Necessary for Our Security?" *Foreign Affairs* 54 (April): 482–95.

Shulsky, Abram N., and Gary J. Schmitt. 1993. *Silent Warfare: Understanding the World of Intelligence*, 2nd rev. ed. Washington, DC: Brassey's.

Sims, Jennifer E., and Burton Gerber, eds. 2005. *Transforming U.S. Intelligence.* Washington, DC: Georgetown University Press.

Smist, Frank J., Jr. 1994. *Congress Oversees the United States Intelligence Community*, 2nd ed. Knoxville, TN: University of Tennessee Press.

Snider, L. Britt. 1997. *Sharing Secrets with Lawmakers: Congress as a User of Intelligence.* Washington, DC: Central Intelligence Agency, Center for the Study of Intelligence.

Steele, Robert D. 1999. "Relevant Information and All-Source Analysis: The Emerging Revolution," *American Intelligence Journal* 19: 23–30.

——. 2006. *Information Operations.* Oakton, VA: OSS International Press.

Taylor, Stan A., and Daniel Snow. 1997. "Cold War Spies: Why They Spied and How They Got Caught," *Intelligence and National Security* 12 (April): 101–25.

Theoharis, Athan G. 1978. *Spying on Americans: Political Surveillance from Hoover to the Huston Plan.* Philadelphia, PA: Temple University Press.

——, ed. 2006. *The Central Intelligence Agency: Security Under Scrutiny* Westport, CT: Greenwood Press.

Treverton, Gregory F. 1987. *Covert Action: The Limits of Intervention in the Postwar World.* New York: Basic Books.

——. 2001. *Reshaping National Intelligence for an Age of Information.* New York: Cambridge University Press.

Troy, Thomas F. 1991–92. "The 'Correct' Definition of Intelligence," *International Journal of Intelligence and Counterintelligence* 5 (Winter): 433–54.

Turner, Michael A. *Why Secret Intelligence Fails.* Washington, DC: Potomac Books, 2005.

Turner, Stansfield. 1985. *Secrecy and Democracy: The CIA in Transition.* Boston, MA: Houghton Mifflin.

——. 2005. *Burn Before Reading.* New York: Hyperion.

US Congress. 1987. Senate Select Committee on Secret Military Assistance to Iran and the Nicaraguan Opposition and House Select Committee to Investigate Covert Arms Transactions with Iran, *Hearings and Final Report.* Washington, DC: Government Printing Office.

Warner, Michael, ed. 1994. *The CIA under Harry Truman.* CIA Cold War Records. Washington, DC: History Staff, Center for the Study of Intelligence, Central Intelligence Agency.

——. 2006. "The Divine Skein: Sun Tzu on Intelligence," *Intelligence and National Security* 21 (August): 483–92.

West, Nigel. 2005. *The Guy Liddell Diaries.* London: Cass.

Westerfield, H. Bradford. 1995. *Inside CIA's Private World: Declassified Articles from the Agency's Internal Journal, 1995–1992.* New Haven, CT: Yale University Press.

Wicker, Tom, et al. 1966. "CIA Operations: A Plot Scuttled," *New York Times*, April 25: A1.

Wirtz, James J. 1991. *Intelligence Failure in War: The American Military and the Tet Offensive*. Ithaca, NY: Cornell University Press.

Wise, David. 1976. *The American Police State: The Government Against the People*. New York: Random House.

Woolsey, R. James. 1993. Testimony, *Hearings*, US Senate Select Committee on Intelligence, 103d Cong., 2d Sess.: March 6.

Zuehlke, Arthur A. 1980. "Counterintelligence," in *Intelligence Requirements for the 1980s: Counterintelligence*, Roy S. Godson, ed. Washington, DC: National Strategy Information Center.

* In addition to the books in this brief bibliography, the reader is encouraged to examine the endnotes in each of the articles in this volume as a further guide to studies on intelligence. See, also, "An Introduction to the Intelligence Studies Literature," in Loch K. Johnson, ed., *Strategic Intelligence: Vol. 1, Understanding the Hidden Side of Government* (Westport, CT: Praeger, 2007).

Index

Directorate of Intelligence (DI) (CIA) 149, 155, 161, 179, 180, 181, 183, 192
Directorate of Operations (DO) (CIA) 192, 291
Doe v. *Gates* 337
Domestic Spy Scandal (1974) 351–2
Donner, Frank 40, 46
Donovan, William J. 43, 48, 119
Dorn, Edwin 30
drones (pilotless aircraft) 108
Drug Enforcement Administration (DEA) 4
DSP satellite 113
Department of Trade and Industry (DTI) (UK) 302
Dulles, Allen W. 119, 120
Dulles, John Foster 273
Dunning School of Reconstruction 49
Dydayev, Dzokhar 61

ECHELON system 59, 110, 164
École de Guerre Économique (EGE) 164
economic espionage 163, 165–8
Economic Espionage Act (EEA) (USA) (1996) 168
economic intelligence 163–9; collection methods 166–7; counterintelligence challenge 168; global challenge 167–8; national competitiveness 164; types of industries targeted 166
Eisenhower, General Dwight D. 119, 120, 150, 274, 288
electronics intelligence (ELINT) 109, 110, 114
Elliff, John T. 45, 46
Ellsberg, Daniel 135
e-mail 20–1, 194
embedded human rights 318–23
émigré intelligence reporting 253–66
Enigma codes 114, 246
Enterprise, The 349
Environmental Protection Agency (EPA) 134
estimates 2
estimative intelligence 214
ethics, intelligence 52–63
ethnocentrism 221
European Code of Police Ethics 321
European Convention on Human Rights (ECHR) 75, 77, 303
European Court of Human Rights 75, 76
European Parliament 316, 324
Executive Orders 61; 12333 151
Expeditionary Factors Analysis Model 141
expert networks 141

fabrication notices 254
Fair Play for Cuba Committee 275
Falklands War 307
Farkas, General Ferenc 259
Feder, Stanley 203

Federal Aviation Administration 154
Federal Bureau of Investigation (FBI) 1, 4, 6, 10, 12, 31, 118, 122, 238–9, 248–50, 265, 331, 345; historiography 39–49; office code 62; origin of 42–3
Federal Tort Claims Act 335, 337
film-return satellite 106
Fitzgibbon, Alan 336
flap potential 294
Fleischer, Ari 245
Floyd, 'Pretty Boy' 44
Folker, Robert 204
Foner, Eric 49
Foot, Paul 302
Ford, Gerald R. 61, 122, 284
Foreign Affairs Committee (FAC) (UK) 301, 306–8, 312–13
Foreign Broadcast Information Service (FBIS) 196
foreign instrumentation signals intelligence (FISINT) 109
Foreign Intelligence Surveillance Act (FISA) (USA) (1978) 76, 247, 250, 276, 330, 332–3, 345, 356
Foreign Intelligence Surveillance Court 126, 247, 248, 333, 356
formal citation analysis 141
Forrestal, James 118
Fouché, Joseph 44
Franco, Francisco 259
Frank, Leo 42
Free Hungary Committee 264
Freedom of Information Act (FOIA) 335–6
Freeh, Louis J. 40, 47
Fremde Heere Ost (FHO) 92, 93, 95
Fuchs, Klaus 246
fusion of intelligence with policy makers 194–5

Gaddis, John Lewis 205–6
Galindez, Jesus 336
Galloway, Donald 98
Gannon, Dr John 133
Gaps in Information Analysis 181
Garrow, David J. 39, 45, 46
Gates, Robert M. 34, 175, 195
Gaydacs, Michael 262
Gehlen, Reinhard 91, 92, 93–4, 95, 96, 97, 98, 99, 257
Gehlen Organization 99–100, 259, 261
General Accountability Office (GAO) 204, 205
General Belgrano, sinking of 305
George, Alexander 32
geosynchronous satellites 109
Ghorbanifar, Manucher 253, 254
Giglio case 331
Gilligan, Andrew 306, 310
Global Hawk UAV 108